THE COLLECTED WORKS OF

CHARLES
SWINDOLL

THE COLLECTED WORKS OF

*C*HARLES *S*WINDOLL

Living on the Ragged Edge

Living Above the Level of Mediocrity

TWO BESTSELLING WORKS COMPLETE IN ONE VOLUME

Inspirational Press

CONTENTS

LIVING ON THE RAGGED EDGE

This volume is dedicated to two couples whose leadership and loyalty have meant more to the Swindolls than words can possibly express, our unfailing friends

BILLY AND BETTY HAUGHTON

and

LAWSON AND FRAN RIDGEWAY

For more than two decades of genuine friendship, they have remained strong in their commitment to each other and consistent through times of relentless testing, proving themselves models of maturity in the midst of ragged-edge reality.

CONTENTS

INTRODUCTION

"The ragged edge." I don't know of a better way to describe the lives of people living in the last quarter of the twentieth century.

Maybe I should qualify that—not *all* people. Some have tuned out. For whatever reason, a few have decided that it isn't worth the hassle of being involved . . . of staying in step with the times . . . of staring reality in the face and refusing to back down. And so, for them, life has become an irresponsible shrug of the shoulder, a bland existence between easy come, easy go and who-really-gives-a-rip? Periodically, I bump into these individuals and find myself surprised that people like that really do exist, and even more surprised that such an out-of-touch lifestyle is what they really want. Let me say up front, this is not a book for that small minority of folks who have opted for a warm, lazy snooze in the sunshine. Come to think of it, I wouldn't know how to address them even if I tried!

No, this is a book for folks in the trenches—down there in the dirt of responsibility, where the grit of reality and the grind of accountability hold their feet to the fire. It's for people who can't free themselves from the demands of competition or escape the pressure of deadlines. It's a series of chapters offering plain, straight talk on coping with life *as it is* . . . not as we wish it were or as it used to be back in the horse-'n-buggy days when things were simple and time was ample. If it is dreamy devotionals and syrupy verse you're looking for, better pass this one up. This is ragged-edge reality, I remind you, not misty-eyed nostalgia.

My world is like that. As a resident in the Los Angeles area since 1971, I have discovered that survival is directly linked to living in the ever present, fast-moving realm of reality. Out here in the West, we think fast, talk fast, drive fast, read fast, and usually eat fast. I don't always like that—it gets a little testy at times—but most of us have learned how to live with it. Some, however, get weary of this rat-race pace. They decide that happiness is California in a rear-

9

view mirror, so they move to Oregon—which thrills Oregonians to death! I heard recently that there is a sign at the Oregon state line on one of the roads leading out of California that warns:

YOU ARE NOW LEAVING CALIFORNIA
PLEASE RESUME NORMAL BEHAVIOR

But no matter where you live, in fast-moving Smogsville or easygoing Dreamsville, it isn't long before you realize that you're back on the ragged edge of reality . . . especially if you're the type who wants to make a contribution to this old world before you're six feet under.

As a husband (for thirty years) and a father of four, I find myself unable to drift into mystical musings, even if I try. Because of the way my wife Cynthia and I have reared our children, there are no secrets in the family. No one gets preferential, kid-glove treatment. It's "honesty city" among the Swindoll tribe, but certainly not to the exclusion of an abundance of love and affirmation. What I mean is this: Communication is open, everyone is respected and therefore free to state his or her mind, and nobody lets a problem stew very long without getting it said. And when it gets said, everybody listens. Even if it hurts. Once again, I guess some would call the way we relate around the house "ragged-edge reality." There's not much room to hide from the truth.

As a minister, my context is again anything but sheltered. I pastor a pacesetting, enthusiastic congregation made up of you-name-it—a true cross section of humanity. We have multiple services each Sunday and activities too numerous to mention throughout the week. Since I happen to believe that the Bible is uniquely inspired of God, absolutely trustworthy, and incredibly relevant, everything I have to say finds its source in the pages of this Book. And that never fails to grab the attention of our first-time guests (I sometimes think of them as "tire-kickers") who drop in to see what all the excitement is about. Once folks get beyond our formal name, the "First Evangelical Free Church of Fullerton," and our frightening size, they usually find themselves helplessly hooked. This place is downright contagious! Our worship services are full of tasteful variety and spontaneity. The message we proclaim is one of authenticity and relevance . . . and (may I brag?) our music ministry is second to none. The place throbs with infectious enthusiasm, yet the worship is quiet, deep, meaningful, and often profound, thanks to the balance we attempt to maintain.

But that's only a tip of the iceberg. The "real" ministry—the part that touches people by bringing the gospel up close—occurs behind the scene, on the ragged-edge of people's needs. We have support groups for virtually every need a person wrestles with: single parents, the handicapped, the unemployed, those struggling with alcoholism and drugs, incest victims, the aged (to name only a few)—*plus* opportunities for folks to meet in smaller groups during the week for mutual encouragement and prayer. And I haven't even mentioned the splendid staff of men and women who surround me, working with me as a leadership team. They are among my dearest friends, my most trusted confidants, my source of direct affirmation and, when necessary, personal reproof. It is wonderful! I cannot imagine being so fulfilled elsewhere.

As if that were not enough, back in the late 1970s, I began a thirty-minute-a-day, five-day-a-week radio ministry independent of the church where I serve and apart from my church-related activities. "Insight for Living" is now aired hundreds of times each day. Our staff of more than one hundred employees (which my wife so efficiently directs) helps me minister to millions around the world, thousands of whom write in for counseling. This continual stream of mail is more than sufficient to keep my head objectively riveted to planet Earth rather than subjectively soaring in the heavens. Any time I am tempted to step away from reality's ragged edge and drift into the fog of theory, all I have to do is work my way through a stack of "Insight for Living" mail. Believe me, it's enough to break the hardest heart!

But how does all this relate to the writing of this book? Directly. Back in the summer of 1983, I began preaching a series of messages each Sunday from the Old Testament book of *Ecclesiastes*. Because Solomon wrote it, I knew it would contain wise counsel. And because it dealt with some bottom-line issues of life, I felt it would have a great deal to say to us out here who live in this fast-moving California scene. But I had no idea how far-reaching or how pertinent its message would be to our whole world at large. The response in Fullerton was remarkable. Then, Cynthia chose to air the taped messages over the radio in the fall of 1984 . . . and the help this series provided was so overwhelming that we lost count of those who urged me to put this information into a book to help people deal with life as it is. At long last, the request has been fulfilled.

It is now in your hands . . . a book about our times that tells the truth about our lives. As you will soon discover, the scenes aren't always pleasant, but they are realistic. I have the people at Word Books to thank for seeing the project to completion, especially my longtime friend, Ernie Owen, who never fails to affirm my ideas, appreciate my work, and stretch my vision. I am also grateful to Michael Standlee, my artistic friend, for the cover design and creative layout . . . plus Carla Randolph for her beautiful calligraphy woven through the pages of the book, adding that personal touch. My gratitude also includes, of course, Beverly Phillips and Sheri Livingston, who edited the manuscript with such incessant and careful attention to detail.

And to my secretary, Helen Peters, I openly declare my amazement along with my appreciation. How does she do it? All day long this efficient and patient woman handles my calls, types my correspondence, hears my gripes, laughs at my jokes, takes my guff, files my stuff, adjusts to my schedule, keeps my calendar, and "covers" for me when I would otherwise look foolish and inept. Then, on top of all that—in her own "spare time"—she has typed, retyped, and final-typed every manuscript to every book and every booklet I have ever done, including this one. Color her amazing and mark me grateful.

Certainly, I want to state my deepest thanks to my wife Cynthia and our two teenagers still living at home—Colleen and Chuck—understanding people, all three! While I have been submerged beneath the pile, preoccupied with the project, and, more often than I like, physically absent from their presence, not once have I sensed irritation or misunderstanding. Thank you. Hopefully, some of that patience will rub off on me.

Finally, to you, the reader, I want to express my gratitude. This is my tenth year as a writer. During the decade many of you have established a relationship with me, even though we have never met. Your prayers, your reassuring letters, your continual support, and your confidence—demonstrated by the way you have read and responded to the things I have written—have provided much of the impetus I needed to stay at the task. So, let me thank *you* for keeping me at it.

Who knows? Without you I might have slacked off, tuned out, and moved to some sleepy spot far removed from reality. Thanks to you, *Living on the Ragged Edge* is not only a book I have finally completed, it's a lifestyle I am learning to handle.

CHARLES R. SWINDOLL
Fullerton, California

1

JOURNAL OF A DESPERATE JOURNEY

Journal Entry

In my opinion, nothing is worthwhile; everything is futile. . . .

So I turned in despair from hard work as the answer to my search for satisfaction. For though I spend my life searching for wisdom, knowledge, and skill, I must leave all of it to someone who hasn't done a day's work in his life; he inherits all my efforts, free of charge. This is not only foolish, but unfair. So what does a man get for all his hard work? Days full of sorrow and grief, and restless, bitter nights.

There is another serious problem I have seen everywhere—savings are put into risky investments that turn sour, and soon there is nothing left to pass on to one's son. The man who speculates is soon back to where he began—with nothing.

*C*ountry-western singer Glen Campbell cut a hit record several years ago entitled "Gentle on My Mind." Like all ballads it tells a story. This one is about a man who longs to be free. He wants a life that's uncluttered with irritating things like binding contracts and lifelong commitments. He's satisfied to stop off for a night or two, but he doesn't want anyone to hassle him with talk of a permanent relationship. As in another popular song, he's "gotta be free"; it's enough for him just knowing that the "door is always open" and the "path is free to walk." That's sufficient.

Woven through the lyrics of that same piece is an interesting expression most of us can remember. He mentions again and again "the back roads of my memory" that keep things "gentle on my mind." Looking back over his shoulder with a superficial shrug, the playboy-cowboy refuses all attempts others make to tie him down. Not even a wife and a houseful of kids—*his* kids—can anchor him down . . . that wouldn't be "gentle." He's on a search for another path, another pleasure . . . another back road that will somehow satisfy. You get the distinct impression he will never find what he's looking for.

I thought about those lyrics recently as I worked my way through another man's story about another kind of journey. William Least Heat Moon is his name, and his gentle journey is recorded in his book *Blue Highways*. What the cowboy sang about, the author did. He struck out in his half-ton van to explore the unsung flip side of America, those tiny towns and backroad villages strung together on the map by threadlike lines colored blue. For example, Dime Box, Texas; Scratch-Ankle, Alabama; Remote, Oregon; Nameless, Tennessee; Whynot, Mississippi; Igo, California (just down the road a piece from Ono), and hundreds of other holes in the road.

By his own admission, Moon states that he left "an age that carries its own madness and futility" as he set out "to the open road in search of places where change did not mean ruin and where time and men and deeds connected."[1]

Whether it's in a song we like to sing or in a book we like to read, most of us have entertained thoughts of pursuing a few of those back roads. For the most part those thoughts remain in "the rivers of our memories," but for a few they have literally passed by in front of our windshields. Such journeys (like most vacations) usually seem better in a dream than they ever would be in reality. Nevertheless, deep in the back roads of our minds, we think a fantasy journey like that would somehow satisfy. For many, *anything* would be an improvement on the current pain of reality.

A Man and His Perspective

There once lived a man who had the time, the money, and the energy to take such a journey. Not just a mind trip, but in actuality. Not across the imaginary back roads of his memory by simply following the blue lines on a map, but into life itself. Because he was "free to walk" and because no one was able to restrain him, he held nothing back. Thankfully, he kept an accurate journal of his journey, which is available for all to read.

The man's name was Solomon. The journal he kept is a book in the Bible named *Ecclesiastes*. Sounds like a strange name for the book, doesn't it? It means "preacher," or "one who addresses an assembly." If you prefer, "speaker of the house"—and the house is symbolic of life itself. In the book, Solomon speaks to all of us about all of life.

I should tell you ahead of time that the journey this man took, while mind-boggling, left him deflated, depressed, and disillusioned. The best word is *empty* . . . his favorite and most often repeated description of how he felt. In fact, Solomon's motto appears on the frontispiece of his journal:

> Vanity of vanities . . .
> Vanity of vanities! All is vanity (1:2).

Being interpreted in today's terms, it is "a wisp of a vapor . . . a puff of wind . . . a hollow, empty ring . . . zero . . . ZILCH!" That is the way Solomon described how he felt *before* he took his journey, *while* he endured his journey, and *after* the journey was over. Nothing satisfied. There was nothing that he saw, discovered, attempted, produced, initiated, or concluded as a result of his lengthy search that resulted in lasting significance or personal satisfaction.

But wait. Before we allow ourselves to accept his desperate, sweeping admission, we must ask why. Why was it such a pointless, empty treadmill? Why wouldn't the man who was king, who had such an endless supply of financial resources, find something—*anything*—that would have purpose?

This is a good time to clarify Solomon's perspective, especially since it's the same perspective most people operate from today. To quote from his own testimony, it is an "under-the-sun" perspective. Time after time, Solomon mentions his horizontal, strictly human viewpoint. In virtually every major section of his journal he uses the words "under the sun" and "under heaven," which I shall repeatedly call to your attention throughout this book. Because he seldom looks "above the sun" to find reassurance, life seems drab and depressing, hopelessly meaningless. In spite of the extent to which he went to find happiness, because he left God out of the picture, nothing satisfied. It never will. Satisfaction in life under the sun will never occur until there is a meaningful connection with the living Lord above the sun. Nevertheless, we, like Solomon, continue to try to find meaning in life, only to wind up on a dead-end road called Emptiness.

Talk about a relevant book! Ecclesiastes has today's world woven through the fabric of every page. Whether or not we are willing to admit it, deep within most of us there is this restless, irresponsible, adventuresome itch. Deadlines and responsibility grate at us. We find ourselves ready to run—to escape into the back roads of our memories, to travel down the blue highways of life under the sun. "Surely, there I will find what it takes to fill the void." Before we are able to crank up the car, Solomon's advice brings us back to reality: "Don't bother, it's a pipe dream, empty as a puff of smoke, lacking in substance. It may look like it's worth the effort, but don't bother . . . life without God under the sun is despair personified."

Frankly, I am pleased that we have this ancient book available today to set the record straight. All around us are people who are buying into this empty, horizontal, who-needs-God perspective. Their world is strictly visible, their whole frame of reference is humanistic. We see it lived out in soap operas every afternoon and on prime time every night. We hear it in political speeches. We learn it in the halls of academia, on the streets of any city.

GOING ALONG WITH THE FLOW

Allow me a few minutes to set the stage by offering a bird's-eye view of Solomon's journal. A quick survey will reveal how hard the man tried to find meaning and satisfaction in life.

Pursuing and Exploring

In the first half of his journal, the monarch recorded much of what he encountered during his mid-life crisis. He really went for it! With unrestrained determination he set out on a pursuit to find a purpose in existence. With painful honesty he recorded how boring and how monotonous his search became. Right out of the chute, he said, "There's no advantage . . . there will be no remembrance."

> No one remembers what has happened in the past, and no one in days to come will remember what happens between now and then (1:11, TEV).

Yet, in spite of this up-front admission, he was off on a search . . . determined to find *something* under the sun that would satisfy. What did he try? Hedonism—pleasure at all cost—was his first stop off. Laughter, comedy routines, booze, sex, entertainment, ego-building projects, art collections, fun trips, serious work, singing troupes, and a half dozen other attempts at happiness blew up in his face. Everything he tried, everywhere he turned . . . zero. Read it for yourself.

> Then I thought about all that I had done and how hard I had worked doing it, and I realized that it didn't mean a thing. It was like chasing the wind—of no use at all.
>
> So life came to mean nothing to me, because everything in it had brought me nothing but trouble. It had all been useless; I had been chasing the wind. Nothing that I had worked for and earned meant a thing to me, because I knew that I would have to leave it to my successor (2:11, 17–18, TEV).

Next, he tried a couple of philosophical trips, fatalism and humanism. Those mind trips looked and sounded impressive on the surface, but in the end, once again, nothingness. In fact, he wound up muttering heresy!

> I decided that God is testing us, to show us that we are no better than animals. After all, the same fate awaits man and animal alike. One dies just like the other. They are the same kind of creature. A human being is no better off than an animal, because life has no meaning for either. They are both going to the same place—the dust. They

> both came from it; they will both go back to it. How can anyone be
> sure that a man's spirit goes upward while an animal's spirit goes down
> into the ground? (3:18–21, TEV).

It shouldn't surprise us to read that kind of thinking from the
pen of a man whose perspective was one hundred percent horizontal.
Humanistic philosophy never has led mankind anywhere but into
further confusion.

Since none of that worked, maybe the answer rested in social action,
reaching out to those who hurt. Or, on the other hand, since the
pathetic and the poor are always with us, perhaps it's wealth that
will satisfy. But, again, neither brought him any lasting pleasure.

> In addition, I have also noticed that in this world you find wickedness
> where justice and right ought to be. . . .
> If you love money, you will never be satisfied; if you long to be
> rich, you will never get all you want. It is useless. The richer you are,
> the more mouths you have to feed. All you gain is the knowledge
> that you are rich. . . . It isn't right! We go just as we came. We
> labor, trying to catch the wind, and what do we get? (3:16; 5:10–11,
> 16, TEV).

There it is again—toiling for the wind! And he repeats it in the
following chapter.

> A man may have a hundred children and live a long time, but no
> matter how long he lives, if he does not get his share of happiness
> and does not receive a decent burial, then I say that a baby born
> dead is better off. It does that baby no good to be born; it disappears
> into darkness, where it is forgotten. It never sees the light of day or
> knows what life is like, but at least it has found rest—more so than
> the man who never enjoys life, though he may live two thousand years.
> After all, both of them are going to the same place.
> A man does all his work just to get something to eat, but he never
> has enough. . . . How can anyone know what is best for a man in
> this short, useless life of his—a life that passes like a shadow? How
> can anyone know what will happen in the world after he dies? (6:3–
> 7, 12, TEV).

What an apt description of many who are grinding out an existence
today. Did you catch that? "The few years of a futile life!" There
aren't enough uppers or downers to keep life right side up. The

desperate stories of so many film-star celebrities, entertainers, professional athletes, and top o' the world entrepreneurs tell their own tales of woe. Whether it's Johnny Cash or John Belushi, Elvis Presley or Howard Hughes, Mercury Morris, Bob Hayes, or "Hollywood" Henderson, the desperation is inescapable. Nothing ultimately brings satisfaction if it is limited to "life under the sun."

When will we ever learn? Not even "the straight life" ultimately pays off! And what is that? One writer colors it relentlessly drab:

> The straight life for a homemaker is washing dishes three hours a day; it is cleaning sinks and scouring toilets and waxing floors; it is chasing toddlers and mediating fights between preschool siblings. (One mother said she had raised three "tricycle motors," and they had worn her out.) The straight life is driving your station wagon to school and back twenty-three times per week; it is grocery shopping and baking cupcakes for the class Halloween party. The straight life eventually means becoming the parent of an ungrateful teenager, which I assure you is no job for sissies. (It's difficult to let your adolescent find himself— especially when you know he isn't even looking!) Certainly, the straight life for the homemaker can be an exhausting experience, at times.
>
> The straight life for a working man is not much simpler. It is pulling your tired frame out of bed, five days a week, fifty weeks out of the year. It is earning a two-week vacation in August, and choosing a trip that will please the kids. The straight life is spending your money wisely when you'd rather indulge in a new whatever; it is taking your son bike riding on Saturday when you want so badly to watch the baseball game; it is cleaning out the garage on your day off after working sixty hours the prior week. The straight life is coping with head colds and engine tune-ups and crab grass and income-tax forms; it is taking your family to church on Sunday when you've heard every idea the minister has to offer; it is giving a portion of your income to God's work when you already wonder how ends will meet. The straight life for the ordinary, garden-variety husband and father is everything I have listed and more . . . much more.[2]

So? So the guy decides to break away. Angered by the endless, pointless, unsatisfying monotony and feeling like a vending machine dispensing products, the man endures the tension just so long. So, he's off to the Porsche showroom floor. Next, it's a new wardrobe . . . his shirt opened down to his belly button . . . a big gold chain or medallion dangling loose . . . tight britches . . . sun shades . . . a chic chick on his arm and he's off to the disco for a little fun and frolic. He tried the straight life—it didn't satisfy. It's time to shift gears and go with the flow. Only one problem, it won't satisfy either! Horizontal happiness won't last.

That's the whole point of Solomon's journal—and that's what makes his words so relevant. Change the names, the geography, the year, the culture, and you've got today's scene portrayed in living color. It only intensifies the further you go into his journal. Read on and you can take your choice—the mid-section of his journal is a veritable smorgasbord of dissatisfaction, discouragement, and despair. Not until we arrive at the end of his pursuit does Solomon finally turn the corner.

COMING TO A WISE CONCLUSION

The brakes on the sports car suddenly screech to a halt. The fast-lane, fast-living escape artist gets out, slams the door, and looks the reader right in the eye. In a thundering voice, like a mixture of Orson Wells and John Wayne, he shouts, "Now you listen to me!" Then, as he thinks through his journey and sums up his thoughts, he continues.

"Do you want meaning? Are you looking for purpose? An investment that will yield lasting dividends? Something to fill the void . . . something that will give real satisfaction? Then wake up and wise up! I can tell you before you go one step further—in order for your horizontal life to make up its mind, it is absolutely essential that you get your vertical life in place. Not until then will you *really* begin to enjoy this thing called living."

He urges the reader not to waste a lot of time on a futile search (as he had done) . . . but rather, while in the prime of life, to secure a relationship with the living Lord once and for all. Here is his advice.

> Be grateful for every year you live. No matter how long you live, remember that you will be dead much longer. There is nothing at all to look forward to.
>
> Young people, enjoy your youth. Be happy while you are still young. Do what you want to do, and follow your heart's desire. But remember that God is going to judge you for whatever you do.
>
> Don't let anything worry you or cause you pain. You aren't going to be young very long. . . .

After all this, there is only one thing to say: Have reverence for God, and obey his commands, because this is all that man was created for. God is going to judge everything we do, whether good or bad, even things done in secret (11:8–10; 12:13–14, TEV).

His journal ends with such wise counsel. If I had my wish, it would be that every person on a quest for happiness would only heed his advice! But they won't. Many will still take that painful path that's "free to walk," where an irresponsible don't-fence-me-in philosophy stays "gentle on my mind." They will still have to learn for themselves that those blue highways may bring adventure and new vistas of experience . . . but no lasting hope, no permanent satisfaction. Escaping reality always leaves us shortchanged. Always.

Before we travel with Solomon through his journal account, allow me to state in three simple comments how directly his observations and experiences, though ancient, tie in with our journey today.

1.   The sensual lure of something better tomorrow robs us of the joys offered today.

2.   The personal temptation to escape is always stronger than the realization of its consequences.

3.   The final destination, if God is absent from the scene, *will not satisfy.*

itch + lust

The good life—the one that truly satisfies—exists only when we stop wanting a better one. It is the condition of savoring what *is* rather than longing for what *might be.* The itch for things, the lust for more—so brilliantly injected by those who peddle them—is a virus draining our souls of happy contentment. Have you noticed? A man never earns enough. A woman is never beautiful enough. Clothes are never fashionable enough. Cars are never nice enough. Gadgets are never modern enough. Houses are never furnished enough. Food is never fancy enough. Relationships are never romantic enough. Life is never full enough.

Satisfaction comes when we step off the escalator of desire and say, "This is enough. What I have will do. What I make of it is up to me and my vital union with the living Lord."

That, in essence, is the message Solomon announces in his journal and I affirm in this book. Honestly now, do you believe it?

2

CHASING THE WIND

Journal Entry

In my opinion, nothing is worthwhile;
everything is futile. For what does a man
get for all his hard work?

Generations come and go but it makes no
difference. The sun rises and sets and
hurries around to rise again. The wind
blows south and north, here and there,
twisting back and forth, getting nowhere.
The rivers run into the sea, but the sea is
never full, and the water returns again
to the rivers, and flows again to the sea . . .
everything is unutterably weary and
tiresome. No matter how much we see, we
are never satisfied; no matter how much
we hear, we are never content. History
merely repeats itself. . . .

And I applied myself to search for
understanding about everything . . . I
discovered that the lot of man, which God
has dealt to him, is not a happy one.

*I*n bold, sprawling letters, two words of graffiti appeared on the walls of a university library.

APATHY RULES

Perhaps they were written by a disillusioned student who had spent endless hours in the pursuit of some intellectual study, only to realize how futile the whole project was.

If he had had more time, he might have written what Malcolm *lies of* Muggeridge wrote about the futility of education. *Education*

> Education—the great mumbo jumbo and fraud of the ages—purports to equip us to live and is prescribed as a universal remedy for everything from juvenile delinquency to premature senility.
> For the most part it serves to enlarge stupidity, inflate conceit, enhance credulity, and put those subjected to it at the mercy of brainwashers with printing presses, radio, and television at their disposal.[1]

I can hear weary students applauding all across America. How bitter is the disillusionment of those who come to the end of their academic pursuit and make that discovery!

Apathy rules. Every time I hear that word *apathy*, I remember the words of a friend of mine who taught high school just long enough to realize he shouldn't have been teaching high school. It took him several years to come to that realization.

He was assigned to teach a course filled to the brim with students who did not want to learn. In fact, it was one of those classes where you had to arrive very early to get a back seat. A couple of the fellas got there so late, they were stuck on the front row. There they sat in their cutoffs and sneakers without socks. They couldn't care less what the subject was.

The teacher finally got fed up with their apathy. He grabbed a piece of chalk, whirled around to the chalkboard and began to slash away in big, foot-high letters, "A-P-A-T-H-Y!" He underlined it twice, then slammed an exclamation point on it that broke the chalk as he hammered it against the board.

One of the dull students up front frowned as he struggled to read the word. Unable to pronounce it, he tilted his head to one side as he started spelling it aloud, "A–P–A–T–H–Y." He mispronounced it, "Aa—*payth*—ee." Then he leaned over and muttered to his buddy, "What in the world is 'a-paythee'?" His friend yawned back with a sigh, "Who cares?"

Apathy rules and nobody seems to care. Life isn't simply tragic. Life is dull. H. L. Mencken said it well, "The basic fact about human experience is not that it is a tragedy, but that it is a bore. It is not that it is predominantly painful, but that it is lacking in any sense."

No one ever said it better than Thoreau: "Most men lead lives of quiet desperation." We don't want to believe that. Motivational speakers who cheerlead seminars all across America hope that we won't believe that. It would blow a hole in their business. The last thing we're supposed to realize is that we have been lied to most of our lives.

✓ EXPOSING FOUR LIES ABOUT LIFE

I can think of at least four falsehoods many still call the truth.

1. "Laugh and the world laughs with you. Cry and you cry alone." I've found quite the opposite is true. "Laugh and you laugh alone. Cry and you get a crowd. The whole world will cry with you."

2. "Every day in every way our world is getting better, better, better." I'd like to meet the guy who first wrote those words, wouldn't you? I'd string him up before sundown. What a tragic, disillusioning dream!

3. "There's a light at the end of every tunnel." Keep hoping . . . keep looking for it. Murphy was right when he said that the light at the end of the tunnel was really "the headlamp of an oncoming train."

4. This fourth one comes from the pop music world of yesteryear: "Things never are as bad as they seem. So dream, dream, dream." Want to sing it with me? No, probably not. Things are not really as bad as they seem. They're often *worse*, and dreaming won't make them better!

I heard recently of a man who looked like he lived every day of his life on top of all circumstances . . . never had a down day . . . came to work happy . . . went home cheery. The people around him couldn't stand the fact that he had some secret in life. They kept wondering if that was the real truth.

At the coffee break one morning, a man said to this happy guy, "Say, friend, now I know why you're always so cheery. You have really got it made! Just yesterday afternoon I was driving along in a taxi, and I passed you. You were sitting there with this beautiful young woman whose back was to the street at this romantic 'sidewalk cafe.' You and she were sitting close and you were listening intently."

The guy leaned over and whispered, "Let me tell you the truth. That lovely young woman is really my wife who was telling me she was leaving me, and what looked like a 'sidewalk cafe' was really our *furniture* out on the street!"

Things aren't as bad as they seem; they're worse.

Why do they tell us those lies? Why do they keep telling us to look for the light at the end of the tunnel? Why do people conduct great seminars all around the world and tell people to smile more, to believe "there's a bright, beautiful tomorrow . . . just grab for it . . . go for the gusto . . . hitch your wagon to a star . . . you'll make it someday"?

You know why they tell us those things? There's one simple answer: to make us believe there's purpose and happiness if we simply *keep on hoping*.

But hope cannot exist in a vacuum where facts are ignored. The fact is that the world is not wonderful. The world is wicked, corrupt, and depraved. And work isn't enriching and fulfilling; it's tiring and it's futile and it blows up in your face. People aren't kind and generous; people are selfish and cruel.

Life on planet Earth isn't a great big bowl of cherries; it's the pits. It is boring. It is empty. It is a grind. It is "chasing the wind." And to make matters worse, apathy rules!

That's true if you're educated or untaught. That's true if you're young or old. It's true if you're a professional person or a blue-collar worker. It's true if you live in a penthouse or a little second-story flat. And it won't be different if your circumstances change. Don't believe me . . . believe God. And instead of blaming Him, realize He had a reason for our horizontal lives being so void of purpose.

TELLING THE TRUTH ABOUT EXISTENCE

As we learned in the previous chapter, many years ago there lived a king who decided he would write in a journal what he had discovered about life. His father, David, had left a rather large estate in his care. His father had fought the battles and now the son Solomon enjoyed peace—forty years of it. Imagine! He ruled four decades over a nation free of war.

Instead of money being poured into the war machine, peacetime money was available . . . and Solomon used it to finance his pursuits to discover life. One day, after the pursuit was over and done with, he sat down with a pen in hand and wrote in his journal the truth about all that he had discovered. There's not one lie in his book. I should warn you, however, it is not your basic *Here's How to Be Rich and Famous* volume. But it *is* trustworthy information all the world needs to read.

The king's journal, as we have seen, has one basic premise . . . he doesn't make us wait until the end of the book to read it. He says it right at the beginning.

A Basic Premise

"Vanity of vanities," says the speaker. "Vanity of vanities! All is vanity."

In Hebrew literature, when the same word is repeated even once, it is for the purpose of emphasis. It is like our exclamation point. It is as though Solomon wants to declare the superlative, "Super vain! Completely empty! Nothing to it!" Or, if you please, "*Apathy rules!*"

Life appears to have substance, yet when you dig into it, there's nothing there. It holds out hope that it is a bright, warm dream; but when you go for it, you stumble into a cold, dark nightmare. Remember this is under-the-sun counsel. It won't satisfy. It won't work.

Solomon even asks: "What advantage does man have in all his work [good question!] . . . which he does under the sun?" (Eccles. 1:3).

The key word is *advantage*, which comes from the original Hebrew word, meaning "that which is left over when the transaction is complete."

We would say, "When it is all said and done, when you turn the light out at the end of life, when you finally close the door to your business and retire, when you walk away from the fresh grave of someone you loved, when it's 'curtains,' the final advantage is reduced to *zero* satisfaction." David Allan Hubbard, president of Fuller Theological Seminary, writes:

> Futile days we can expect from time to time. Some of what we plan will miscarry. Paths that look promising will peter out and force us to backtrack. Pillars that we lean on will collapse and send our hopes tumbling down on us.
>
> When sickness strikes or financial reverses hit, futile days stretch into empty weeks or months. There have been times when we heaved huge sighs as we ripped December's page from the calendar and welcomed a new year that offered better days than the old.
>
> This futility is akin to irony, because it is full of surprises. We find it where we least expect it. Values that we treasure prove false; efforts that should succeed come to failure; pleasures that should satisfy increase our thirst. Ironic futility, futile irony—that is the color of life. . . .[2]

Are you willing to believe that? Will you accept that, not as some other man's journal, but as the truth concerning your life? If you're married and your only focus is horizontal—that is, you're not living "above the sun"—chances are good that your marriage is on its way to failure. The tragedy is that you don't realize it. If you're operating your business with human strength in your own wisdom and might (and God is conspicuous by His absence), you can forget lasting satisfaction. You certainly will not know permanent fulfillment.

If you're pursuing an education and you've gotten this degree and you're going for another one and you have all these people around you telling you, "It's worth it; you can do it!" and it's all being pursued for selfish purposes and strictly with your goals in mind, I've got disappointing news for you. You're going to wind up bored and frustrated.

Hugh Prather writes in his book *Notes to Myself:*

> If I had only forgotten future greatness and looked at the green things and reached out to those around me and smelled the air and ignored the forms and the self-styled obligations and heard the rain on my roof and put my arms around my wife. . . . Perhaps it's not too late.[3]

We who worship our work and play at our worship have gotten things all fouled up. The journal writer tells us before we even begin that, it's "nothingness under the sun."

Take an honest look at your labor. If your office is like most, the in-box looks like The Leaning Tower of Pisa. Right? You never finish. On top of that, plans for the sale collapse right in front of your eyes. To make matters worse, the partnership you began so happily ends in a premature and offensive manner. What a drag!

Your financial savings decrease in value, rather than increase. You toil for a raise and the guy next to you gets the promotion. Promises for relief from the government fail. Your ship didn't come in . . . it sank! There's nothing left. There's no advantage.

Are you getting the depressed picture? Are you getting weary of the same old line? Good! That's exactly what the writer wanted. The sparkling jewel of hope (which he waits a long time to display) needs a somber, black backdrop of utter futility. Things will get much darker before there's any glimpse of dawn, I warn you.

Examples of Futility

Do you want some examples? Do you want to hear some specifics about life under the sun? Look at this statement: "A generation goes and a generation comes . . ." (1:4). There's futility even in the cycle. There is a group of people born this day and another group of people who will die this same day. There will be beautiful and winsome people like Princess Grace and Dag Hammarskjöld who will die. Tough and determined people like Jack Dempsey and Winston Churchill will die. Gifted, talented, and entertaining people like Natalie Wood and James Dean will die. People who make us laugh, who make us think, who make us gain courage to go on will die. And some of those bright, beautiful, fun-loving, capable people will die just as empty as those who grieve at their funerals. The cycle is terribly futile.

> A generation goes and a generation comes, but the earth remains forever.

When God arranged the solar system and flung it into space, He put purpose and meaning on the earth. Originally, that is; but now it is "subjected to futility" (according to Romans 8:20).

Consider some illustrations. Look at the sun.

> Also, the sun rises and the sun sets; and hastening to its place it rises there again (Eccles. 1:5).

I feel monotony written in Solomon's words, don't you?

There is considerable difference between the words of Solomon the king and Jeremiah the prophet. Jeremiah says that even the rising of the sun reminds him of his Lord, "great is Thy faithfulness." But Solomon says, "The rising of the sun, . . . [Yuck!]" (Swindoll paraphrase).

Why? Because Solomon is seeing only as far as the sun, not beyond it. Remember, his earthly pursuit is *under* the sun. I refuse to let you forget his theme: There is no meaning to this crummy existence called "life on planet Earth." If you live only beneath the perspective of the sun, it is an endless, wearisome, nagging cycle.

Well, how about the wind?

> Blowing toward the south, then turning toward the north, the wind continues swirling along; and on its circular courses the wind returns (1:6).

In the news report every evening, there is this great satellite picture. We see the earth and the movement of the wind. Its bright white swirls stand against the stark blue of the sea and brown of this earth. You see the wind in its currents, and you'll look at it again tomorrow. It'll still be there, still swirling, still moving in its currents; its course is a monotonous, repetitive thing.

And the rivers?

> All the rivers flow into the sea, yet the sea is not full (v. 7).

Do you know why? The sun evaporates enormous quantities of water. As the moist air cools, the vapor condenses and forms clouds, and clouds in turn drop water from the skies onto this earth in the form of rain, sleet, and snow. Our friends in the Midwest suffer from terrible floods or tornadoes and other natural disasters; the rains fall and the rivers swell and flow into the sea.

The old songwriter was right, "Old Man River just keeps on rollin' along." Maybe Kristofferson had Ecclesiastes 1:7 in mind when he wrote: "I'm just a river that rolled forever and never got to the sea. . . ."

Do you ever feel like that—like your life is as monotonous as the swirling wind or the rolling river? Have you ever felt like your life is on a boring cycle like the sun? Do you know why you feel like that? Because it *is!* If it's under the sun, it's running around in circles.

I think Solomon wrote verse 8 with a deep, long sigh: "All things are wearisome; man is not able to tell it. . . ."

As little children, we were told to keep looking and keep discovering, because there are things out there we have never seen before. There is beauty to be found, there's wonder out there. And it's true—to a point. But as we get older, we get more sophisticated and start wanting telescopes and microscopes so we can look into the depths of our natural world. Yet we cannot seem to get telescopes large enough or microscopes with lenses thick enough to see completely enough. Our curiosity is aroused . . . but frustrated.

And have you noticed this? What we find is not satisfaction, but another question mark. So we pursue another degree to answer that question mark, and when we get *that* question mark removed, there's *another* degree we've got to have, and still more questions fail to be answered because another dimension opens up to us, another world of endlessness. And either we become jaded in our sophistication or disillusioned in our futility. It is maddening! So? So we decide to become philosophers . . . people who talk about stuff they don't understand, but make it sound like it's everyone else's fault!

Remember, none of this is new. This is no great, modern discovery. "Not even the *ear* is filled with hearing." If you doubt that, you haven't looked for an audio sound system lately. You go to one place and they'll say, "This is fine, it will cost you a thousand bucks." Then they'll say, "But you know, there is something much better." Naturally, you ask, "What is it?"

"Well, if you want to go twenty-five hundred dollars, we'll include two huge speakers and we'll put two of 'em in your room and you'll have stereophonic sound. But if you really want the big-time tingles, you'll need to get *quadraphonic.*" Four speakers . . . plus soundproofing for the walls, so your neighbor's ears won't bleed!

I saw a guy in his car last week who had four speakers. They were so big you couldn't see around them in his little Volkswagen. We're talking wall-to-wall speakers. You could just see the windows vibrate— Boom! Boom! Boom! Boom! (like a drum) Boom! Boom! I got out of his way fast! The guy is a rolling sound system, and I'll guarantee you one thing: He's *not satisfied with it.* Why? Because there's always a better sound. It is unbelievable! I can hear some salesperson say, "You think this sounds good in a VW bug? Man, you put this in a Mercedes and double the size of the speakers and it'll blow you away!"

The ear isn't satisfied with the hearing. Is this new? No way. Look at verse 9:

That which has been is that which will be, and that which has been done is that which will be. So, there is nothing new under the sun.

Rudyard Kipling expressed the same thought on one occasion when he wrote:

> The craft that we call modern;
> The crimes that we call new;
> John Bunyan had them typed and filed
> In 1682.

I've got news: Nothing is new out there, friends and neighbors. And if you find something that is—something you didn't know before—I've got other news; it still won't satisfy.
Solomon in effect even says, "I'd like to forget it."

> There is no remembrance of earlier things; and also of the later things which will occur . . . (v. 11).

Have you ever felt like that at the end of the day? "I'd like to forget this day." How about at the end of a pursuit of some academic achievement? "I'd like to forget that school. All that stuff that I studied and all those hours I spent and all that work I put in, I'd just like to forget it." Do you know why? "Apathy rules!" Furthermore, "Who cares?"

The Searcher and His Pursuits

In verse 12, Solomon suddenly introduces himself to us. He says: "I, the Preacher, have been king over Israel in Jerusalem." Then in his next statement we see the same kind of resolve you and I might feel when we take off on a backpacking trip. It is as if he were saying, "I've decided I will take that climb." He has set his sights and is ready to push forward on his journey to seek and explore everything under the sun.

> And I set my mind to seek and explore by wisdom [that's human wisdom] concerning all that has been done under heaven (v. 13).

Let me give you a little bit of insight into those two words *seek* and *explore*. They describe his mission. In Hebrew, the word translated *seek* means "to investigate the roots of a matter." It's what you would do as a doctoral candidate writing your dissertation.

Any person who claims to be academically respected must pay the price and do research. So you roll up your sleeves and dig into the libraries. You pursue every possible angle so that your research is thorough. Perhaps you travel and spend two, three, or more years working toward the completion of that dissertation. You are (in terms of this Hebrew word) "seeking" in your research.

Likewise Solomon said, "I decided I would research the *Roots* roots of those things." So he began to pursue the origin of them. He began to reason out the outworking of each pursuit, and he made notes on the results of them as he pursued this study. He stayed at it. He shoved aside all of the affairs of state. He apparently ignored the needs of his home. He set aside all his religious moorings as he dug into each subject. Whether it was passion or pleasure or philosophy or sex or money or some creative project—whatever—he went after each subject, every objective, to find out all he could about them, how they got started, and what were the final results. His research was thorough.   *Explore*

But that's not all. This man is a unique kind of intellectual. He also *explored*. This second term means "to examine all sides." It's a practical word for experimentation. In other words, Solomon is saying, "Not only did I seek to study the gardens and the lakes and rivers and reservoirs and streams, I did experiments with them. I pursued those things to the point of getting involved. I got wet in the streams. I participated in the sex orgies. I investigated the whole world of pleasure. I went after it (as they say in the South) 'whole hog!'

"I got into it and I felt the burn of the booze as it went down my throat, and I felt the heavy feeling in my head when I gave myself to it. I experienced all angles of the full-orbed world of pleasure."

This is the journal of a man who stopped at nothing when he sought to explore, by human wisdom, all things under the heavens. Remember, there was no limit to his brains and no limit in his bucks. No limitations . . . no reservations . . . just thorough research . . . *full* investigation! And what does he say? In the final analysis, what was his opinion?

> ✓   It is a grievous task which God has given to the sons of men to be
> afflicted with (v. 13).

And what is this grievous task? Living life under the sun.

I've taken a moment to mark some things in my Bible that describe his initial findings. In verse 13 I marked "grievous task" and "affliction." That saves me a lot of searching. If I want to read truth from a man inspired of God—who was not only researching it, but experiencing it—and save myself the headache, time, scandal, and hassle of it all, I just need to remember his honest appraisal: "It's a grievous task; it's an affliction."

I notice in verse 14 he says that life under the sun is "striving after wind." Actually, the words mean "chasing the wind." He says it again only a few lines later—it is "striving after wind." And he says it more strongly than ever by the end of this journal entry:

> Because in much wisdom there is much grief, and increasing knowledge results in increasing pain (v. 18).

I think if my two teenagers were reading that, they would be tempted to write in the margin of the king's journal: "Homework." What's the use? To go back to familiar words, apathy rules!

> And I set my mind to know wisdom and to know madness and folly; I realized that this also is striving after wind (v. 17).

Here the writer is saying, "I've been there." You know, there's nothing quite like talking to a person who has been there.

I was running on a local college track a number of months ago when I looked up and noticed in the distance a man named Fred Dixon, who was training for the decathlon. Soon I was running next to my friend, this awesome athlete. Remember now, I'm running for survival. He's running for fun. If you've ever run alongside a decathlete, you fight that urge to run off the track very quietly and hide in the closest house you can find.

As he came up alongside me, I immediately felt intimidated. I didn't tell Fred that. He knew when I started to cry that I had trouble running alongside him. Of course, I joked about it. I said, "I don't want to slow your pace down, Fred." He responded, "I saw you runnin' over here, so I thought I'd run along with ya."

We talked for a few minutes after the run. He described the whole Olympic event. It was helpful. Believe me, there's nothing like talking to somebody who has actually participated in the decathlon to know what it's about. He's been there twice. He is a seasoned athlete. He is also very handsome and in great shape, which is great. It's not fair . . . but it is great. Amen

Talking to him is better than trying to discover in a history book all the theoretical things about the decathlon. Just talk to Fred Dixon, then listen and learn.

What Fred Dixon is to the decathlon, King Solomon is to the pursuits in life "under the sun." If you want to save yourself all the headache of the pain connected to involving yourself in the consequences of wrongdoing, just listen to Solomon. In fact, we would be foolish not to listen to Solomon.

We don't have his money and we don't have his brains, so we couldn't go to the depths he went to even if we tried. That's all the more reason to listen to the man who's been there. He's even thoughtful enough to say, "I'm anxious to tell you what I experienced." He's going to say, in effect, "It's not worth it to go into drugs." He's going to say, "You're a fool if you give yourself to booze." He's going to tell us, "If you think that an affair is going to satisfy, I've had every possible affair you can have, and I can tell you before you get involved, it won't make you happy. Furthermore, if you think the answer is some high-powered business or money or a great athletic achievement, you'll one day wonder why you thought it was such a big deal. If your life is being lived strictly on the horizontal plane . . . it won't bring you lasting happiness!"

That's Solomon's advice. He's been there. Let's listen. Let's learn.

I really must add one more comment about the emptiness of sheer intellectualism. If intellectualism were the major key to purpose and fulfillment, our campuses would be "Camelots" of peace. People would gravitate to those campuses, finding there the fulfillment of their dreams.

But what do you find on the campuses around the country? Boiling pots of controversy . . . political activism, try-harder humanism and no-God communism at work, all kinds of weird ideas, dissatisfied and disillusioned faculty members, along with a pile of "professional students" who do not find lasting satisfaction under the sun. There are exceptions, I realize, but they are rather rare. Instead of feeling enlightened, most find themselves increasingly more confused in the morass of endless, pointless philosophies.

The answer isn't just studying more. Can you name one secular scientist who is genuinely happy with life? I can't. Can you think of one authority who lives in this heady, high-minded world of intellectualism-without-God who finds himself (or herself) fully satisfied, rather than in a maddening pursuit for something else? I can't think of one.

When we remove Jesus Christ from the center of an intellectual pursuit we're headed for ultimate disaster. As we are going to learn from Solomon, the only way to find satisfaction and relief from boredom is through a relationship with the living God. Apart from Him, we're back to the graffiti, "Apathy rules!"

Solomon writes:

> I said to myself, "Behold, I have magnified and increased wisdom more than all who were over Jerusalem before me; and my mind has observed a wealth of wisdom and knowledge." And I set my mind to know wisdom and to know madness and folly; I realized that this also is striving after wind (vv. 16–17).

Look at that! He's saying, "I stopped at nothing. I have pored over it. I have been there. I gave it my best shot! I set my mind to know wisdom, madness, folly. I finally realized I was merely chasing the wind."

On Sunday, June 5, 1983, in the *Los Angeles Times*, Richard Eder wrote a review of a secular book by Walker Percy called *Lost in the Cosmos: The Last Self-Help Book*. This reviewer said the author was "thinking about who we are and how we got into this mess."

> What mess? Basically, the fact that everything we engage in—science, art, pleasure, wealth, politics, war—is conducted without any real knowledge of what or whom we are doing it for. We have lost sight of ourselves. . . .
>
> When we are children we see things more or less as follows: Cows are to give milk. Mountains are to climb. Cars are to ride in. Germs are to be sick with. Children draw houses with a face at every window. (How could there not be a face?—windows are to look out of.) And people? Policemen are for helping us cross streets, farmers are for growing food, fathers are for making a noise in the shower and going to work, mothers are for smelling nice and maybe going to work.
>
> As we grow older, our perception of the physical world becomes more complex. . . .
>
> Man, lacking a sense of himself, lacks any sense of relation to the cosmos, Percy suggests, and is therefore capable of perpetrating almost

any foolishness or horror upon both. Artists and scientists are OK as long as they are out exercising their transcendence; when they come home at night they are as screwed-up as anyone else. The beauty or knowledge that they are quarrying for does not enlighten them much. It is a familiar enough notion, back through Socrates and Ecclesiastes; . . . He [Percy] does not actually suggest that man can know himself only through some kind of religious faith, but he does not leave much of any other possibility either.[4]

That's why Percy called his book *Lost in the Cosmos*. When will we ever learn?

I'm not saying you shouldn't pursue an education. You know better than that. Nor am I saying that ignorance is what reigns supreme, of course not. The answer is not ignorance. The answer is a life that is lived in connection with the living Lord. Only through Him can there be meaning.

Thinking Through the Practical Ramifications

A couple of ideas emerge from between the lines of Solomon's journal:

1. *If there is nothing but nothing under the sun, our only hope must be above it.* Are you willing to go that far with me? If there's nothing but nothing under the sun, then our source of hope must be *beyond* it.

As a minister I often find myself in a position of communicating this information to others. It has been my observation that most folks have their heads so firmly riveted to the here and now that they virtually ignore any other dimension in life. It's not that they consciously intend to block God out of their lives (most people would be shocked to think of themselves as atheists), it's just that they seldom mentally catapult themselves "above the sun." But it is there that hope shines eternal.

2. *If a man who had everything, investigated everything visible, . . . then the one thing needed must be invisible.* Can you agree with that? Solomon had everything. He explored every visible realm of stimulation, yet found no satisfaction. It seems only logical that the satisfaction he searched for will come only from that which is invisible.

Do you realize how few people really *hear* the inaudible? How few really *see* the invisible?

An Indian was walking in downtown New York City alongside a friend who was a resident of the city. Right in the center of Manhattan, the Indian seized his friend's arm and whispered, "Wait. I hear a cricket."

His friend said, "Come on! Cricket? Man, this is downtown New York."

He persisted, "No, seriously, I really do."

"It's impossible!" was the response. "You can't hear a cricket! Taxis going by. Horns honkin'. People screamin' at each other. Brakes screeching. Both sides of the street filled with people. Cash registers clanging away. Subways roaring beneath us. You can't possibly hear a cricket!"

The Indian insisted, "Wait a minute!" He led his friend along, slowly. They stopped, and the Indian walked down to the end of the block, went across the street, looked around, cocked his head to one side, but couldn't find it. He went across another street, and there in a large cement planter where a tree was growing, he dug into the mulch and found the cricket. "See!" he yelled, as he held the insect high above his head.

His friend walked across the street, marveling, "How in the world could it be that you heard a cricket in the middle of downtown, busy Manhattan?"

The Indian said, "Well, my ears are different from yours. It simply depends on what you're listening to. Here let me show you." And he reached in his pocket and pulled out a handful of change—a couple of quarters, three or four nickels, and some dimes and pennies. Then he said, "Now watch." He held the coins waist high and dropped them to the sidewalk. Every head within a block turned around and looked in the direction of the Indian.

It all depends on what you're listening for. We don't have enough crickets in our heads. We don't listen for them. Perhaps you have spent all your life searching for a handful of change and you've missed the real sound of life.

I think I may be writing to a few people who are really pursuing excellence. In fact, you're probably some of the "beautiful people" in the world's terms. You look good. You may be bright, with great potential. You're well-educated. You carry on a decent life. You even dress well . . . and mind your own business . . . and pay your bills.

You are still dreaming. You keep hoping that there is a real light at the end of that tunnel. You keep telling yourself that it is life and happiness you're listening for, the real life. But I want to warn you; it is nothing more than a handful of change. There's no life in one of those coins. The only way you will find satisfaction is in believing the invisible. It's in trusting the inaudible. His name is Jesus Christ. He wants to rule your life. Why should apathy rule if He is available?

3

EAT, DRINK, . . . AND BE *WHAT?*

Journal Entry

I said to myself, "Come now, be merry;
enjoy yourself to the full." But I found
that this, too, was futile. For it is silly to
be laughing all the time; what good does
it do! So after a lot of thinking, I
decided to try the road of drink, while
still holding steadily to my course of seeking
wisdom. Next I changed my course again
and followed the path of folly, so that I
could experience the only happiness most
men have throughout their lives. Then I
tried to find fulfillment by inaugurating
a great public works program . . . Next I
bought slaves, both men and women . . .
I collected silver and gold as taxes from
many kings and provinces.

And then there were my many
beautiful concubines. . . . But as I
looked at everything I had tried, it
was all so useless . . .

The slogan of today's lifestyle can be reduced to six single-syllable words: "If it feels good, do it."

These words may not appear in bold, bronze letters, but they are nevertheless sandwiched between the lines of our advertisements and hidden within the script of our commercials. Sometimes they are openly stated, but more often than not they are subliminal, placed there by those who author our books, compose our music, design our clothing, publish our magazines, direct our films, and write our plays . . . "If it feels good, do it."

You've heard it, haven't you? The motto emerges on T-shirts and bumper stickers, car license frames, and handcrafted signs in spiffy little boutique shops. Not always in those explicit words, but the idea is there, nevertheless. Even the titles of best-selling books like *Looking Out for #1* and *Pulling Your Own String* boldly encourage us to give less attention to others and more to ourselves, and they tell us we deserve it.

All this may sound ultra modern, but the tentacles go back into ancient days when the Greeks coined and modeled the term *eros*. The Epicureans lived and died by it. Put in the language of their fast lane philosophy, "Eat, drink, and be merry . . . for tomorrow we die!" And the implication goes even further, "Since we die like dogs, never to live again, we might as well give it all we've got while we're alive." Or, in the words of that once-famous television commercial, "You only go around once."

Years ago, John Steinbeck wrote a letter to Adlai Stevenson. In it he said, "There is a creeping all-pervading gas of immorality which starts in the nursery and does not stop until it reaches the highest offices both corporate and governmental."[1] The famous author was referring to that which is sensual—having to do with the senses—that which we can taste, smell, see, hear, and touch. In the broadest sense of the term, it would include the feelings that attach themselves to the creature comforts, the bodily cravings, the good as well as the evil. Though each one of the senses is not wrong in itself (obviously not, since God gave us our senses), any of us could be pushed to such an extreme that we would traffic in the realms of heresy or perversion. And that brings us to this section of Solomon's journal . . . another up-to-date analysis of horizontal living.

A Quick Review

You will recall it is written by a man who had the highest office in the nation. He was the king. His nation enjoyed peace and prosperity. His very name, taken from the Hebrew word *shalom*, means "peace." And in a nation that had enjoyed decades of peace on the heels of four decades of war under David's leadership, there was sort of a yawning, aching desire to lie back, relax, and enjoy life for a while.

Remember also, the theme of the book is life "under the sun" or "under heaven." We have already noted how often those words appear in Solomon's journal, almost as if they formed the slogan of *his* day, "enjoy life under the sun!"

In other words, this king was looking under the heavens to find happiness *without God.* In the first chapter of his journal, we have seen that he tried educational stimulation and a measure of scientific exploration, and both left him empty. Surely there's got to be more in life than *this!* So he decided to pursue another course, to scratch some itches that have been there all his life, deep down in the *eros* zone. He begins, "I said to myself. . . ."

An Open Invitation

I thought it interesting, when I first read these opening lines, that the man began this new course in his journey by talking to himself. He didn't tap a seasoned counselor on the shoulder and say, "Come here, my friend. You're older than I. Talk to me about what this might mean. Give me some advance warning of the dangers." Rather than seeking the counsel of another wiser or more experienced than he, he plunged in with both feet.

Nor did he check into the historical record of how his father, David, endured the consequences of sensuality. He didn't even look up to God in prayer and ask for divine counsel. He talked to himself. In fact, literally, it reads, "I said in my heart. . . ."

It might be paraphrased: "I resolved." Perhaps that's a little bit strong. It began as a fantasy, but he decided to shift his mental excursion into reality. And so he says, "Come now. I will test you with pleasure." In other words, "Eros, here I come!" or "Come along,

Pleasure; get on board. Join me in the mainstream of where this sensual life is, and help me see what it's all about."

By the way, Hugh Hefner holds no original claim on erotic pleasure. His "playboy philosophy" is nothing more than an old tune with new lyrics. The hedonism of our times is as old as Solomon; in fact, much older than that—in both its ecstatic delights and its tragic consequences.

Solomon decides, nevertheless, he will pursue it. And so he says to himself what the waitress says when she serves you that delicious meal—"Enjoy."

> I said to myself, "Come now, I will test you with pleasure. So enjoy yourself." And behold, it too was futility (2:1).

He didn't beat around the bush when it came time to express his evaluation of it, did he? It was just another empty experience!

Let's consider for a moment the directness of Solomon's writing style. Hebrew scholar H. C. Leupold states:

> It is a style of writing that is frequently employed by Hebrew authors that, even before a matter is given in a more detailed description, the outcome of it all is indicated. . . . We could paraphrase this typical sentence: "I found no lasting values in this attempt."[2]

Now that's not the American style. Those who write and photograph pornography don't tell us beforehand that it is empty, it is futile, it is dissatisfying, it is lacking in fulfillment. We're left to discover that on our own. But Solomon tells us to begin with that it isn't all it was cracked up to be.

Frankly, I appreciate such honesty. Erotic sensuality has deceived us long enough!

Dr. Pitirim Sorokin, a former professor of sociology at Harvard University, wrote a book back in the mid 1950s entitled *The American Sex Revolution*. Even then he wrote:

> The sex drive is now declared to be the most vital mainspring of human behavior. In the name of science, its fullest satisfaction is urged as a necessary condition of man's health and happiness. Sex inhibitions are viewed as the main source of frustrations, mental and physical illness and criminality. Sexual chastity is ridiculed as a prudish superstition. Nuptial loyalty is stigmatized as an antiquated hypocrisy. Father is

painted as a jealous tyrant desirous of castrating his sons to prevent incest with their mother. Motherhood is interpreted as a "mommism," wrecking the lives of children. Sons and daughters are depicted as filled with the "complexes" of seduction of their mother and father, respectively. Sexual profligacy and prowess are proudly glamorized. . . . The traditional "child of God" created in God's image is turned into a sexual apparatus powered by sex instinct, preoccupied with sex matters, aspiring for, and dreaming and thinking mainly of, sex relations. Sexualization of human beings has about reached its saturation point. . . . Our civilization has become so preoccupied with sex that it now oozes from all pores of American life.[3]

Our friend Solomon, with a limitless supply of money and without any sense of accountability to others, took that trail as far as one could take it. And when it was all said and done, he said, "What an empty, futile trip!"

Will every young person hearing these words please listen to Solomon rather than the hype from our times? Will the novice, the inexperienced, the virgin, the person who has not yet been scarred by that journey . . . will you hear, *ahead of time*, the truth rather than a lie? Equally important, will you be mature enough to heed it?

Solomon, who trafficked in it and lived to tell us about it, is going to save us months, even years of heartache if we will only heed what he says. Not some present-day, wild-eyed, prophet of doom, but the wisest and richest man who ever lived is telling us the truth about illicit sex, about alcohol, about drugs, about the occult, and all the things that appeal to our erotic desires. Common sense says we'd be wise to listen.

Wild 'n' Crazy Fun 'n' Games

Now . . . he's off on another tangent! Right out of the chute, like a racehorse. Solomon decides to laugh his way through life: "Laughter, I'll try that! Bring on the jesters, show me the clowns, the comedians! Let's hear those funny one-liners . . . let's laugh at those comedy acts, those wild 'n' crazy little sitcoms!" And out they came with their silly burlesque skits, their slapstick routines, their funny-face masks, their jokes, and their endless stream of zany humor. Solomon paid good money, and plenty of it, to get ultimate pleasure: "Bring on the fun 'n' games—let's live it up! After all, it feels good

to laugh and have a great time in life. Surely, that's going to bring
me the satisfaction I long for. Maybe *that* holds the secret."

But it didn't. His admission is as honest as it is blunt:

> I said of laughter, "It is madness," and of pleasure, "What does it
> accomplish?" (2:2).

Let's understand that the man is not attacking a healthy and necessary sense of humor or periodic times of enjoyable, God-honoring
pleasure. We know better than that. The point is: There is no lasting
satisfaction if your only reason for living is to make people smile, to
leave them laughing.

Who knows how many comedians there are in this world who,
upon turning in at night, sigh with those same feelings, "Madness.
What does it accomplish?" I think of the Rodney Dangerfields and
Bill Cosbys and Steve Martins . . . the Joan Rivers and the Don
Rickles and the Bob Newharts and Phyllis Dillers and so many more,
and I wonder how many of them are sincerely satisfied in life . . .
how many are truly fulfilled.

I understand there's a motto that Jerry Lewis hangs in his dressing
room that reads:

> There are three things that are real: God, human folly, and laughter.
> Since the first two are beyond our comprehension, we must do what
> we can with the third.

A disturbed and deeply troubled individual went to a psychiatrist
to relieve his anxiety. He awoke melancholy every morning, and he
went to bed in the evening deeply depressed. His day was marked
by darkness and clouds. He couldn't find relief for this anxiety. In
his desperate condition, he decided to seek the counsel of a medical
doctor. The psychiatrist listened to him for almost an hour. Finally,
he leaned toward his patient and said to him, "You know, there's a
local show at a theater. I understand a new Italian clown has come
into our city, and he's leaving 'em in the aisles. He's getting rave
reviews from the critics. Maybe he is the one that will bring back
your happiness. Why don't you go see this professional clown and
laugh your troubles away?"

With a hangdog expression, the patient muttered, "Doctor, I *am*
that clown."

As Solomon says, "It is madness. . . . What does it accomplish?" I can hear him now, "Well, if it isn't laughter . . . if it's not amusement, maybe there's something in the world of liquid spirits. Perhaps the satisfaction I'm looking for is in a bottle."

> I explored with my mind how to stimulate my body with wine while my mind was guiding me wisely, and how to take hold of folly, . . . (v. 3).

It is easy to read these words and form a false impression. You probably imagine a debauched, seedy-looking gutter drunk. You envision a person who is at the end of the row, in the dregs, a pathetic victim of alcohol who stumbles through the rear door of a rescue mission. But that is not the picture Solomon is painting.

This is a very sophisticated, wealthy man. This is a brilliant individual who decides that he will let his mind guide him into all realms of alcoholic beverages. He plans to become a connoisseur of that whole world of liquid, sensual delights.

Back to H. C. Leupold, the Hebrew scholar:

> "To nourish my flesh with wine" should be taken as a reference to a consumption of wine which enables a man to get the highest possible enjoyment by a careful use of it, so that appetite is sharpened, enjoyment enhanced, and the finest bouquets sampled and enjoyed. Approximating or falling into drunkenness is plainly not under consideration. The very thought of such crude extravagance is barred by the expression, "my mind was still keeping control by means of wisdom." In other words, here was a carefully controlled experiment.[4]

Solomon is not saying, as one might say in a fit of anger or exasperation, "I think I'll go out and get bombed." No, it's like he's saying, "Maybe there is more than I realized to this fantastic world of the spirits—the kind they bottle. I think I'll try that." But, again, it fails miserably to satisfy.

Now, terribly disillusioned that several of his fantasies have been nothing more than bad dreams, he decides to roll up his sleeves and really go to work. Maybe *that* is the answer . . . not projects that the nation requires of him, but personal projects. Notice how many times he refers to "I" and "my" in this section of his journal. It's intensely personal:

I enlarged my works: I built houses for myself, I planted vineyards for myself; I made gardens and parks for myself, and I planted in them all kinds of fruit trees; I made ponds of water for myself from which to irrigate a forest of growing trees. I bought male and female slaves, and I had homeborn slaves. Also I possessed flocks and herds larger than all who preceded me in Jerusalem. Also, I collected for myself silver and gold, and the treasure of kings and provinces. I provided for myself male and female singers and the pleasures of men—many concubines. Then I became great and increased more than all who preceded me in Jerusalem. My wisdom also stood by me. And all that my eyes desired I did not refuse them. I did not withhold my heart from any pleasure, for my heart was pleased because of all my labor and this was my reward for all my labor (2:4–10).

So he tried architecture. Decided he would design beautiful structures. Indeed he did! What a place he built for himself—one of the famed seven wonders of the world! But this journal entry includes more than that one structure. It's plural. He built houses—a number of houses.

When that didn't satisfy, he decided to take on horticulture and agriculture. So he planted vineyards for himself and then lovely gardens . . . then sprawling parks. He planted trees in that park, fruit-bearing trees which would yield those lovely, scented blossoms every spring. The landscape must have been breathtaking . . . elegance in full bloom.

He needed ponds of water to keep the place green, so he dug reservoirs and had irrigation canals carved along the terrain. This man stopped at nothing. He decided he would irrigate this forest of growing things . . . yet he remained lonely, always restless, never fulfilled. Tragic scene. The place was quiet—too quiet!

Then Solomon decided what he needed could be provided by other people only, and so he bought them, too. Don't miss his comment:

I bought male and female slaves, and I had homeborn slaves.

He filled the place with slaves. He had them reproduce, and they had their own harems. Still he wasn't satisfied.

. . . Also I possessed flocks and herds larger than all who preceded me in Jerusalem (v. 7).

He decided he would have more than anyone else around. There would be no limit.

He then moved into collecting precious gems and articles of silver and gold, ". . . the treasure of kings and provinces." He even brought in male and female singers. They must have been something! He wrote over a thousand songs and perhaps he put some of his compositions in front of the singers and they sight-read his work. He sat back and listened. Here he was, surrounded by his own forest and personally designed gardens and vineyards and trees and the smell of the blossoms and the sound of fresh, flowing water in the background, plus numerous soft-footed slaves to wait upon his every whim. His own music filled the chambers of his houses and echoed through the forest, yet he *still* failed to find inner peace.

What do you do for an encore? Well, you keep hoping . . . you keep lying to yourself . . . like the person who wrote the following statement, the source of which I've been unable to trace:

✱ Excellent

. . . my journey through the darkness has only accelerated. I have become adept at inventing counterfeit lights—bright-colored, flashing lights. Pseudo rainbows; artificial sunsets; celluloid stars.

More recently I discovered that God is dead, anyway. I am a product of organic evolution. A cosmic accident. A unique moment in a mysterious 30-billion-year process. It is an adventure filled with suspense—and cruelty and meaninglessness. And though I do not know what is ahead, never fear, I am on my way!

Even today, after reading the morning news and the latest issue of *Time* magazine, and even though I acknowledge countless gallons of human tears, the endless cycle of agonizing tragedy, I, along with the world's majority, maintain that Adam made the right decision. Even as I swallow my tranquilizers, rush to my psychiatrist, take that extra drink, endure my third divorce, and watch my children reject all the ideals I have tried to pass on—I still say there is hope!

I have a simple, straightforward question: What hope? He's come to the place where he says, "I've run completely out of stuff. I don't know who to turn to next, but I still say there is hope." Do you have any idea how many today are hanging onto such a ragged edge by their fingernails?

Are you ready for more? Next Solomon chose to turn to "the pleasures of men—many concubines." Elsewhere in Scripture, we read of the extent to which he went with this:

And he had seven hundred wives, princesses, and three hundred concubines; and his wives turned his heart away [from the Lord] (1 Kings 11:3).

One thousand women—absolutely unbelievable! They were available to him any time of the day or night, any number at a time, to fulfill whatever sensual desire he had. Yet his boredom could not be described. He ran out of words to say it. It just simply came back to "futility." All the erotic pleasure they could provide left him empty, bored, more frustrated than ever in his hell-on-earth existence.

E. Stanley Jones, in his book *Growing Spiritually*, talks about a fictional person who lived out a fantasy life. All he had to do was think of it and (poof!) it happened. So this man, in a moment of time, sticks his hands in his pocket and leans back and imagines a mansion and (poof!) he has a fifteen-bedroom mansion, three stories with servants instantly available to wait upon his every need.

Why, a place like that needs several fine cars. So he again closes his eyes and imagines the driveway full of the finest wheels money can buy. And (poof!) there are several of the best vehicles instantly brought before his mind's eye. He is free to drive them himself, or sit way back in the limousine with that mafia glass wrapped around the rear, and have the chauffeur drive him wherever he wishes.

There's no other place to travel so he comes back home and wishes for a sumptuous meal and (poof!) there's the meal in front of him with all of its mouth-watering aromas and beauty—which he eats alone. And yet . . . there was something more he needed to find happiness.

Finally, he grows so terribly bored and unchallenged that he whispers to one of the attendants, "I want to get out of this. I want to create some things again. I'd rather be in *hell* than be here." To which one of the servants replies quietly, "Where do you think you are?"

But you see, the attitude of "if it feels good, do it" has done such a number on us that such a lifestyle seems the *last* thing compared to hell. We live in the dream, on the brink of some great hope that's just beyond the chasm. "If I could just earn that amount, I could buy that dream and *that* thing would do it." Solomon says, "Don't go to the trouble!"

Is there an aggressive businessman reading these words who doesn't understand? Is there a career-minded woman who is gifted in business (entrepreneur type) who has any trouble grasping the point? Certainly not! You fully understand.

The Good Life

You wake up with a dream. Your mind moves in the realm of dreams. You think of how you can organize and orchestrate and finance this dream. Your idea is born and your company grows. It enlarges. It emerges into something of a giant over one part of our country and you're invited to join a conglomerate. You become part of that broad picture and now you have a larger office with deeper pile carpet and *more* to wait on you, and a larger salary. You become great! Yet your dreams don't stop. There is a hunger for more, more, more. But more never seems to satisfy.

The problem is that you've got to live with *yourself*. And unless you are most unusual, in the process of time you lose the eternal things that once were around you—close friends, family relationship, your marriage, an unselfish generosity, a heart for God . . . those things that make life worth living.

You become great and you don't become insane. Solomon talks about that—you still have wisdom that stays with you. You still have ideas. He says, "My wisdom stood by me" (meaning *human* wisdom). Why, he's got the good life. He's got it by the tail!

> And all that my eyes desired I did not refuse them. I did not withhold my heart from any pleasure, for my heart was pleased because of all my labor and this was my reward for all my labor (2:10).

What was his reward? Feeling good. Now let's not kid ourselves. The momentary feeling *is* good. There's a lot of pleasure in it. It is fleeting, but no one can deny the feel-good part of sensuality. As one man puts it:

> Pleasure offers to lift us above the routine. So much of our living seems bound to the ordinary. It is hobbled by the patterns we learned in childhood; it is grooved by the habits we developed as teenagers; it is fettered by the cords of conformity our culture puts upon us. . . . Often we long to kick over the traces and bolt off on our own free course. Pleasure lets us do that. Temporarily, we can hang our inhibitions in the hallway and go to the party without them. . . .[5]

I was listening to a radio talk show recently. Several well-known professional athletes were talking about drug abuse and the struggle they have had with it. One said, "What kept me going back to it was that warm feeling down the back of my neck that helped me go to sleep every night. Frankly, it felt marvelous!"

Another one admitted, "When you do drugs, you open doors inside you that nothing else can open. It's spectacular. It's indescribable! Ah! With the pressure I'm under and the money I'm making and the public that's after me and the job I've got to keep up—I got to have a little coke. I got to have a few drugs. It helps me get goin'. It helps slow me down. It'll put me into the right frame of mind so I can do my thing, 'cause I'm great."

It sounds so appealing, so tantalizing. Yet, in reality, when the fun 'n' games are over, it's the *pits*. I know. It's my job to work with those folks *after* the party is over. The pleasure came, but it didn't last.

It's Time to Face the Truth

Solomon's wrap-up counsel deserves prime-time exposure. It belongs on the marquee of every X-rated theater. Like a note, it could be inserted inside every bottle of drugs. It would be a great neon sign in front of every tavern.

> I considered all my activities which my hands had done and the labor which I had exerted, and behold all was vanity and striving after wind and there was no profit under the sun (v. 11).

A few lines later Solomon adds:

> There is nothing better for a man than to eat and drink and tell himself that his labor is good (v. 24).

Or, said another way, "Eat, drink, and be *what?*" You won't find that on the mirrors in Vegas. You won't find that in the packet you get as you attempt to escape your sorrows on a cruise around the world. You won't find it on the label of the Seagram's bottle. Those things don't sell the product, but this is the truth. Solomon says it straight. He's been there, he ought to know. If you asked me to paraphrase his comments, I'd be able to do so in three truthful sentences. I will state them if you will face them.

1. *Sensual pleasures hold out promises that lack staying power.* The little line of white powder that invites you to snort it up into your system holds out a feeling. It holds out a promise that says, "That'll do it, man! That'll do it for you. It feels so good—do it!"

And it does. It does feel good at first. It keeps its promise temporarily . . . but it doesn't have staying power, so it takes more of the same. And so it gets more expensive. By and by you start caring less and less about the game you're playing, or the job you're doing, or the home you're trying to run, or the business, or the practice. The feel-good promise lacks staying power. As one user admitted to me, "I could never get a feeling as good as the first time, but I kept trying."

2. *Sensual pleasures offer to open our eyes, but in reality they blind us.* They say, "If you do this, your eyes will be open. You'll see a world . . . a panoramic, psychedelic world that you've never even known existed." But, in fact, that world blinds you of all the things that are important and real.

I think the greatest tragedy connected to illicit sensuality is hypocrisy, which introduces my third sentence.

3. *Sensual pleasures disillusion us, making us cover-up artists.* We leave the impression that we've got life wired (a cover-up because we refuse to tell ourselves and others the truth about our emptiness. What a hypocritical illusion! And how easy it is to forget that. "If it feels good, do it" has a flip side, which is neither attractive nor satisfying.

How else can you explain the ugly side of so-called beautiful people? People like Richard Cory, for example.

> Whenever Richard Cory went down town,
>   We people on the pavement looked at him:
> He was a gentleman from sole to crown,
>   Clean favored, and imperially slim.
>
> And he was always quietly arrayed,
>   And he was always human when he talked;
> But still he fluttered pulses when he said,
>   "Good-morning," and he glittered when he walked.
>
> And he was rich—yes, richer than a king,
>   And admirably schooled in every grace:
> In fine, we thought that he was everything
>   To make us wish that we were in his place.
>
> So on we worked, and waited for the light,
>   And went without the meat, and cursed the bread;
> And Richard Cory, one calm summer night,
>   Went home and put a bullet through his head.[6]

4

MORE MILES OF BAD ROAD

Journal Entry

Now I began a study of the comparative
virtues of wisdom and folly, and . . . wisdom
is of more value than foolishness, just as
light is better than darkness; for the wise
man sees, while the fool is blind. And yet I
noticed that there was one thing that
happened to wise and foolish alike—just as
the fool will die, so will I. So of what value
is all my wisdom? . . . So now I hate life
because it is all so irrational; all is
foolishness, chasing the wind. . . .

So I turned in despair from hard work
. . . For though I spend my life searching
for wisdom, knowledge, and skill, I must
leave all of it to someone who hasn't done
a day's work in his life . . . So what
does a man get for all his hard work?
Days full of sorrow and grief, and restless,
bitter nights. It is all utterly ridiculous.

Most of us have better sight than insight. There's nothing wrong with our vision; it's perspective that throws us the curve. And that is especially true when it comes to people. We tend to see only the obvious, but we overlook the significant. We focus on the surface while we fail to sense what is deep down inside.

It is at this point that we humans are so unlike God. An old Israeli judge once recorded this fact in a book that bears his name. Here's the way he described it as he quoted what God had revealed to Him:

> But the Lord said . . . , "Do not look at his appearance or at the height of his stature, because I have rejected him; for God sees not as man sees, for man looks at the outward appearance, but the Lord looks at the heart" (1 Sam. 16:7).

Realizing the truth of this human trait, many become fairly good at acting. Because we know no one can actually see us down inside, we give a false image on the outside . . . leaving others with an impression of ourselves that is quite different from actuality. It is this very fact that prompted Mark Twain's appraisal: "Everyone is a moon, and has a dark side which he never shows to anybody."

Guillermo Vilas—a superb Argentinean tennis pro whose name is a synonym for confidence, strength, and inner security—once dropped his guard in a *Sports Illustrated* interview:

> Fervently, I think that many times one feels oneself to be secure and, suddenly, one's world falls down like a pack of cards in a matter of seconds.

Respected, healthy athletes leave fans screaming words of praise, yet down inside those same men and women often struggle with great personal insecurities and low self-esteem. Even some who are paid to make us smile sustain a dark side when you get below the surface. Take for example cartoonist Ralph Barton. He wrote:

> I have had few difficulties, many friends, great successes. I have gone from wife to wife, from house to house, and have visited great countries of the world. But I am fed up with devices to fill up twenty-four hours of the day.[1]

Who would've ever guessed that he would have taken his own life? On the surface he seemed so happy. Amazing . . . the same one many envied for his clever humor was actually full of despair.

How very many there are who *appear* to be suave, stable, and successful but who, down inside, are dreadfully frustrated! The term "frustrated" comes from a Latin term *frustra*, which means "in vain." In other words, one who is "frustrated" feels that all he does is void of purpose. In spite of great effort and constant pursuit, the frustrated individual fails to realize his dreams. A sense of helplessness evolves into hopelessness . . . even though great pains are taken to hide the awful truth. Few are those who peel off their masks and admit how greatly they struggle. When they do, however, our admiration for them is enhanced. Vulnerability is a rare but much-respected trait.

A Glance Back

It is this quality, perhaps more than any other, that causes us to appreciate Solomon. We don't have to possess great insight. We aren't forced to guess what is rumbling around inside his head. He tells us. He is *absolutely* transparent. Without hesitation he has admitted his frustration.

- He was unable to find satisfaction in intellectual pursuits.

- He found laughter and pleasure nothing short of maddening.

- He turned to wine, women, and song, only to enter into greater boredom.

- He tried personal projects, pools, and well-scented parks . . . again, no satisfaction!

- He attempted to be fulfilled with harems of beautiful concubines, hundreds of wives, and fine singers—*zero*.

- He then began to collect exquisite gems and priceless pieces of jewelry and art, but nothing satisfied. Nothing!

Like cartoonist Barton, King Solomon was fed up with devices to fill up his day. But, *unlike* the cartoonist, he didn't take his life. He just kept driving. And what did he find? More miles of bad road. New pursuits, same conclusion. And best of all, he doesn't hide the truth. Solomon may be frustrated and bored, but he's no hypocrite.

The Search Continues

Since Solomon was still in possession of his mental faculties, he decided to put his mind to work. If all the sensual delights and practical projects wouldn't produce lasting happiness, maybe a change in direction would.

"So I turned . . ." (Eccles. 2:12); in other words, "I decided to turn in another direction . . . to pursue several things I'd not yet explored." The new direction led him into three comparisons. He would compare wisdom with foolishness (2:13–17), the immediate with the ultimate (2:18–21), and daily work with evening relief (2:22–23). Want a hint? These things didn't satisfy any more than his previous pursuits.

Wisdom Compared to Foolishness

> So I turned to consider wisdom, madness and folly, for what will the man do who will come after the king except what has already been done? And I saw that wisdom excels folly as light excels darkness. The wise man's eyes are in his head, but the fool walks in darkness. And yet I know that one fate befalls them both. Then I said to myself, "As is the fate of the fool, it will also befall me. Why then have I been extremely wise?" So I said to myself, "This too is vanity." For there is no lasting remembrance of the wise man as with the fool, inasmuch as in the coming days all will be forgotten. And how the wise man and the fool alike die! (2:12–16).

His goal is to determine whether he would adopt a lifestyle marked by wisdom or by folly. Should he be a serious thinker, a man who uses his head, or should he blow the lid off life and let it all hang out? He was the king, so nobody could dictate his destiny. It was up to him. Whatever turned him on, he could choose.

Initially, he realized wisdom had it all over folly. As he states it, a wise person walks through life with eyes wide open . . . lots of clear-thinking vision. But the fool operates as if in a dark room . . . not knowing what's up next. He gropes and wanders all around. Some of today's kids would say of the fool that Solomon describes, "He's not wrapped tight." Between the two, obviously wisdom wins hands down. But in the final analysis, both wise and foolish are impacted by the same fate—death. So what if I get a fine education? So what if I pursue a responsible job? So what if I order my private world on the basis of good, common sense? So what if I decide to practice a profession or learn a trade? I may live with my eyes wide open . . . raise a fine family and plan wisely for retirement. But the fact is: The axe falls on my neck just like it does on the neck of a fool. I, like the fool, am going to die.

This is the kind of thought that dawns on a person who has recently graduated with high honors from a great university and cannot find a job. He's highly qualified, yet feels completely useless. It's a terrible feeling. He has a degree, or maybe multiple degrees, and he cannot find work. He looks out on the world of fools and sees most of them employed, and he says, "What use is all this wisdom? What use are all these degrees? What's the meaning of it all? Why have I been extremely wise?" So I said to myself, "This too is vanity. It's an empty dream, this expensive, exhaustive pursuit of knowledge."

> There is no lasting remembrance of the wise man as [is true] with the fool, inasmuch as in the coming days all will be forgotten. . . . (v. 16).

How hard we try to keep that from happening! We don't build our tombstones out of cardboard. We build them out of *granite*. We don't paste names on the stones with masking tape. We etch the names into solid stone and we hope the sands of time and the winds of weather won't wear those words away. Why? Because these graves represent our loved ones and we never want them forgotten. But all tombstones eventually do wear down and the names grow faint. Memories do finally fade.

If you want an impressive example of how humanity is committed to preserving the memory of the dead, look at the Egyptian pyramids.

> They were a wonder of the ancient world, and forty-five centuries after they were built we sons and daughters of a modern era still gaze at them in awe. The pyramids of Egypt, especially those at Giza, just outside of Cairo, are massive monuments to ancient technology. They demonstrate what can happen when a great civilization bends its back to achieve its purposes.
>
> The Great Pyramid of the Pharaoh Khufu is staggering in size. Nearly 500 feet tall, it contains about 2,300,000 blocks of stone, each of which weighs at least two tons. Many comparisons have been used to try to convey an accurate impression of its vastness. One scholar has suggested

that within its base there would be room for the great Italian cathedrals of Florence, Milan, and St. Peter's in the Vatican, as well as St. Paul's Cathedral and Westminster Abbey in London. One of the most striking comparisons comes from Napoleon's time. While some of his generals climbed to the top of the Great Pyramid, the Emperor waited below calculating the mass of stone in the three pyramids that jut up from the Giza plateau. When his generals descended Napoleon is said to have greeted them with this startling announcement: If all the ston in the three pyramids could be exported to France it would serve to build a wall ten feet high and one foot thick around the entire realm of France.[2]

Don't tell me that when one dies he is quickly forgotten! Indeed not! Rather, it is announced: "Let's build a pyramid. Let's build several of them so that those who achieved greatness on earth can somehow ascend to the skies and find their way into heaven and be remembered forever." But wait. We need to ask ourselves, who in the world are we kidding?

Solomon would suggest, "Don't waste your time on pyramids; they'll soon be forgotten." Isn't it true? Only a few ancient history buffs would even be able to name the pharaohs today, much less tell where their tombs are located. Most of them are forgotten. The wise, like the foolish, die. "It's vanity." Meaning? Nothing is worth that kind of effort! So? So the man finds himself at the same dreadful dead-end street.

> So I hated life, for the work which had been done under the sun was grievous to me; because everything is futility and striving after wind (v. 17).

Have you ever felt like that? Sure you have! It is the ultimate expression of disgust. "I *hated* life! I looked at all the labor, all the projects, all the little hobbies, all the plans, all the hours, all the years of education, all the investment of time and energy, and I saw it accomplishing little more than stirring up the dust of tomorrow and finally being forgotten. I *hated* it?" Why? ". . . because everything is futility and striving after wind."

The journey continues, but the scenery hasn't changed. Maybe Solomon's perspective could be enhanced if he would consider the possibility of building an enterprise from scratch, then leaving his fortune to his children. Maybe *that's* what will give satisfaction.

The Immediate Compared to the Ultimate

> Thus I hated all the fruit of my labor for which I had labored under the sun, for I must leave it to the man who will come after me. And who knows whether he will be a wise man or a fool? Yet he will have control over all the fruit of my labor for which I have labored by acting wisely under the sun. This too is vanity. Therefore I completely despaired of all the fruit of my labor for which I had labored under the sun. When there is a man who has labored with wisdom, knowledge and skill, then he gives his legacy to one who has not labored with them. This too is vanity and a great evil (2:18–21).

Get the picture? How can anyone miss it? Work, work, work. Think. Compete. Strategize. Plan. Sacrifice. Travel. Worry. Skip vacations. Add hours. Increase responsibility. Scratch the right back. Invest. Save. Risk. Work, work, work! Then, when everything is in place, when all the ducks are in a row, wham!

Dennis Barnhart was president of an aggressive, rapidly growing company, Eagle Computer Incorporated. His life is a study in tragedy. From a small beginning, his firm grew incredibly fast. He finally decided they should go public. The forty-four-year-old man, as a result of this first public stock offering, became a multimillionaire virtually overnight. Then, for some strange reason, while he was in his red Ferrari only blocks from the company headquarters, he drove his car through twenty feet of guard rail into a ravine and died.

A *Los Angeles Times* account read:

> Until the accident at 4:30 Wednesday afternoon, it had been the best days for Barnhart and the thriving young company, which makes small-business and personal computers. Eagle netted $37 million from the initial offering of 2.75 million shares. The stock which hit the market at $13 a share quickly rose as high as $27 before closing at a bid price of $15.50.[3]

After describing the stock, the article added: "That made Barnhart's ownership of 592,000 shares worth more than $9 million." And that same afternoon he died in an auto accident.

What of your kingdom? What of your plans for the future? What are you hanging onto? Dreams, of course. That's what keeps you going, right? Hope. Exciting plans. You're working on them now. You work on them on your "vacation." And you think about them in your "spare time."

But you know, all of that will seem terribly irrelevant when you face the fact that you'll be reduced to death in only a brief span of time. For some it could be less than a decade; for others, less than a year. For Barnhart, it was that same afternoon.

Derek Kidner in *The Message of Ecclesiastes* asks incisively, "If . . . every card in our hand will be trumped, does it really matter how we play?"[4]

Euripides, the poet, called death, "the debt we all must pay." And rich and poor, young and old, king and pauper alike are either in the grave or on the way. And so it will continue to be.

If I read Solomon's words correctly, he decides to address not only death, but also the ultimate legacy of one who has been successful. One day all the estate will fall into the hands of the person's sons and daughters. Is that going to work?

Let me get painfully personal. I do not care how capable, how competent, how perfectly suited your children may be to continue your dream, there's something in *you* they don't possess and never will possess . . . your indomitable, innovative spirit. You were the original dreamer, the tough-minded pioneer. You hammered that dream out on the anvil of time. Though you had nothing, you came to something. And no matter how closely you've had your children work alongside you, there's something you've got that they lack. And that's what worries you, right?

Part of what they get, they get *free*. And when you get something for nothing, it breeds irresponsibility, if not in their generation, certainly in the next—your grandchildren. Greed will replace dedication.

Several years ago, *Newsweek* magazine included a story of a West German industrialist whose life portrayed this very point.

> When West German industrialist Freidrich Flick died, he left a personal fortune estimated at 1.5 billion dollars [if you can imagine], a business empire that embraced all or part of some 300 firms, and a reputation as perhaps the crustiest and craftiest magnate ever to operate on the German business scene.
>
> Flick was dedicated wholly to his work (he buried his wife at 3 P.M. one day in 1966 and was back at his desk two hours later). . . .
>
> At his death, the Flick empire generated annual sales in excess of $3 billion [that's every year in West Germany]. But for all his enormous power and wealth, the old man had one very human shortcoming: he could not control his family. By last week a Flick family fight over *der alter Herr's* empire had employees, bankers and politicians alike

shuddering over the eventual impact it might have on the West German economy.[5]

As one man put it: "Flick scored at the office, but struck out at home."

There is a price to be paid for building an empire, isn't there? If we are willing to face the ultimate, the scene will be anything but ideal. The empire must be turned over to the very ones you haven't prepared for such requirements and assignments.

> Therefore I completely despaired of all the fruit of my labor for which I had labored under the sun. When there is a man who has labored with wisdom, knowledge and skill, then he gives his legacy to one who has not labored with them. This too is vanity and a great evil (vv. 20–21).

Solomon throws his hands high in the air and shouts, "It isn't worth it!" And he finds himself back at square one in the futility game.

Daily Work Compared to Evening Relief

So he thinks, "Well, maybe the answer is getting relief in the evening. If I work very hard in the day, and take time off in the evening to do the things that will prepare my family to handle the empire, maybe that will satisfy." Look at his remarks about this . . . and hang on!

> For what does a man get in all his labor and in his striving with which he labors under the sun? (v. 22).

An evening's rest? Hardly.

> Because all his days his task is painful and grievous; even at night his mind does not rest. This too is vanity (v. 23).

Isn't that the truth? How many entrepreneurs do you know who really kick back in the evening? Can you honestly name a half dozen really success-driven people who leave all their work at the office? There is a reason that Valium is still the number one prescription drug in America. Most people who are at the top or climbing to the top bring home all kinds of work from the office. Not even at night do we put our minds into neutral.

Perhaps Solomon's mind was on his son, Rehoboam. What a tragic story! After four decades of peace, Solomon handed over this kingdom to his son. Rehoboam took the kingdom from his father and had available to him either wise counselors or foolish ones. He could choose to listen to the seasoned men of God who would warn him, or listen to the young, self-serving upstarts who cared nothing about God. You guessed it, he chose the latter.

Within a brief span of time, hardly a year, the country was in civil war. Then Egypt came marching in and Rehoboam went to the temple—Solomon's temple and took the solid shields of gold and handed them over to the Egyptians to keep them from invading. By filling their coffers with Israeli gold (the gold his dad had put in the temple), Rehoboam hoped to calm the Egyptians' aggression. What a joke. As expected, they kept wanting more.

According to 1 Chronicles, chapter 12, Rehoboam substituted shields of brass for shields of gold. And I'm sure he shined them brightly to make them look just like gold, but they were nevertheless brass. Perhaps Solomon foresaw tragedy in the life of his unprepared, impulsive son and was saying, "Not even when I spend an evening at rest do I see the possibility of hope in my boy."

A FLASH OF INSIGHT

So what do I do? How can I make it, since it's all so empty? Solomon gets a rare flash of insight that suddenly grabs his attention. And it comes, ironically, on the heels of this bleak series of frustrating scenes. Translated literally from the Hebrew, Solomon's next statement reads:

> There is nothing in a man to eat and drink and tell himself that his labor is good (v. 24).

Here is his first flash of insight: *There is nothing inherent in humanity that makes it possible for us to extract enjoyment and purpose from the things we do.* Go back and read that again.

Solomon said, "I've seen this, because it comes from the hand of God. God has revealed this piece of information to me, and I'm ready to announce to all who will listen: 'This is true; there is nothing within you (or your children) that will automatically give you happiness or keep them at peace and bring them joy.'" Riches will not result in the satisfied life. Happiness cannot be purchased.

In his book, *The Rockefeller Billions*, Jules Abels says that John D. Rockefeller had an income of approximately a million dollars a week toward the end of his life. Yet his doctors allowed him to eat only a bare minimum. One of his biographers said he lived on a diet a pauper would have hated. "Now, less than 100 pounds in weight, he sampled everything (at breakfast): a drop of coffee, a spoonful of cereal, a forkful of egg, and a bit of chop the size of a pea." Rockefeller was the richest man in the world, but he didn't have the ability to enjoy even his food.

About now you're probably asking, "How can I ever enjoy life? What will it take for me to get purpose and meaning back into life?" Well, the next line in Solomon's journal offers a second flash of insight: *Enjoyment is God's personal gift.*

> For who can eat and who can have enjoyment without Him? (v. 25).

Isn't that the truth! Unless God is in the middle of it, lasting enjoyment is impossible. Is there any place better to be than with a group of Christians who get together to have fun? It's incredible how hilarious our times can be when, as believers, we get together and enjoy what we commonly call "fellowship"!

When I was growing up, my family lived next door to a family that had many of the world's goods we didn't have, but they didn't have the joys Christ can bring—which we had in abundance. I remember one Christmas when we were singing together as a family. My dad was playing his harmonica; my brother was playing the piano; and my sister, mother, brother, and I were singing some of the old carols and some of the folk songs of the Christmas season. We were laughing like crazy, singing to the top of our voices.

Suddenly, my mom said, "We're making so much noise, we better close the windows or we'll disturb all the neighbors." So we closed the windows.

Within minutes our phone rang. It was a girl who lived next door. She asked, "Why'd you close the windows?"

"Well, we didn't want to disturb you," was Mom's answer.

The girl blurted out, "Disturb us? That's the most laughter we've heard the entire Christmas season! Please open your windows . . . that's beautiful music!"

We have the idea that the world is the one that gives enjoyment and God's the One who clubs us when we have fun. But the fact is, it's the other way around. If you really want to have fun—I mean the kind of fun that is really enjoyment (without a hangover)—then you need only one ingredient in your midst; you need a relationship with the living God. According to Solomon, "Who can have enjoyment without Him?" As God's people, we're the ones who ought to be having the time of our lives! But it's been my observation that far too many Christians look like they've been baptized in lemon juice!

Now comes Solomon's third flash of insight: *Those who are right with God derive the benefit of everyone's labor.* The world thinks it's building its fortune for itself, yet, ultimately, the Christian benefits from most of it. Look at verse 26.

> For to a person who is good in His sight He has given wisdom and knowledge and joy, while to the sinner He has given the task of gathering and collecting so that he may give to one who is good in God's sight. This too is vanity and striving after wind.

Think of the man who strives and labors and tries extra hard to satisfy his family with an enormous, beautiful mansion—and his wife doesn't even want to live there. So he winds up with a big pile of wood and stone, cabinets and carpet, elegant rooms lavishly furnished, but his wife won't even live there. He ends up having to sell it to a little Christian organization that turns right around and fills it and uses it.

Such was the case of Glen Erie in Colorado Springs, Colorado, headquarters of The Navigators. That beautiful English-style mansion was built by a man who had hoped to please his wife. But after being there only a few days, she sighed, "Who needs this?" (What was she going to do with thirty-five rooms anyway?) But what about The Navigators? They bought it and filled it! The irony of it all is that those who are right with God ultimately derive benefit from everyone's labor.

So guess what? If you don't have the living Lord in the right perspective, if you don't have Jesus Christ in the nucleus of your plans, you are facing endless miles of bad road. If you remove God, then you remove enjoyment, purpose, direction, meaning, and anything eternal connected with life. And you're left with twenty, thirty, forty years of sleepless nights and nothing to show for it when they put you in the box.

I could easily leave the impression, and maybe I have, that once you become a Christian it is a downhill slide. You move into mansions on easy street. You enjoy great food all of the time. Life's a great big bowl of cherries. You laugh, laugh, laugh . . . eat pie and ice cream and never get fat (we wish!).

No. Remember? Back to our problem of perspective. Even a Christian can get strangely mixed up in his perspective. And if one is not careful, life can still seem very, very empty.

I received a heartbreaking letter from a Christian friend of mine. He was going through an extremely difficult time. Things have now turned the corner for him, and his life is back on target. But when he wrote me he was . . . well, just read his candid remarks and imagine.

> I've been asking myself some of these kinds of questions, and now I'm beginning to answer myself. I want to make some things clear up front. I may not be very old, but I figured out a long time ago that pursuing the world's pleasures wouldn't satisfy. I know running away is no answer either. But don't you dare think that these feelings are confined to those who choose these roads. Don't you dare think that only middle-aged, money-grubbing entrepreneurs face this crisis. I'm not yet 28 years old, I talk heart to heart with God every day, and I live a life within the confines of a sensitive conscience. I have a beautiful wife and daughter.
>
> But I'm empty. I've come to the conclusion that living is a waste of time. All is vanity, striving after wind. There is not one thing on this earth to make it worth staying. I used to think that ministering to others was reason enough to live. It isn't. Neither is raising a family.
>
> Yet, far be it from me to sin against God by taking my own life. I have no intention of doing anything like that. I've just realized that this life has nothing to offer. It does not mean I am without hope. I'm gambling on eternity's being worth it. . . . I have to take that gamble. It's my only choice. I've run out of other choices. Responsibilities make me feel like I should stay, but only the hope of God's smile makes me willing to stay.
>
> Chuck, don't forget that this book [meaning Solomon's journal] applies even to growing Christians. Many of us wonder daily if it's worthwhile to go on.[6]

If you're a Christian perhaps this letter sounds like something you could have written. If so, please understand that I am not leaving you out. Bad roads and futile dead-end streets aren't limited to non-Christians, I can assure you. But the difference comes in being able to persevere in spite of the difficulty. Without Christ, there is no way through. With Him, more miles of bad road only mean you're closer than ever to God's ultimate destination for you—His greater glory! That kind of insight will improve your vision.

5

DO YOU KNOW WHAT TIME IT IS?

Journal Entry

There is a right time for everything:
A time to be born; a time to die;
A time to plant; a time to harvest;
A time to kill; a time to heal;
A time to destroy; a time to rebuild;
A time to cry; a time to laugh;
A time to grieve; a time to dance;
A time for scattering stones; a time
    for gathering stones;
A time to hug; a time not to hug;
A time to find; a time to lose;
A time for keeping; a time for
    throwing away;
A time to tear; a time to repair;
A time to be quiet; a time to speak up;
A time for loving; a time for hating;
A time for war; a time for peace.
What does one really get from hard
work? I have thought about this. . . .
Everything is appropriate in its own time.

*L*et's play "Let's Pretend."

Let's pretend that your banker phoned you late last Friday and said he had some very good news. He told you that an anonymous donor who loves you very much has decided to deposit 86,400 pennies into your account each morning, starting the following Monday morning. That's $864 a day, seven days a week, fifty-two weeks a year.

He adds, "But there's one stipulation . . . you must spend all the money *that same day*. No balance will be carried over to the next day. Each evening the bank must cancel whatever sum you failed to use."

With a big smile, you thank your banker and hang up. Over that weekend you have time to plan. You grab a pencil and start figuring: $864 times seven equals over $6,000 a week . . . times fifty-two. That's almost $315,000 a year that you have available to you *if* you're diligent to spend it all each day. Remember, whatever you don't spend is forfeited.

So much for "Let's Pretend."

Now let's play "Let's Get Serious." Every morning Someone who loves you very much deposits into your bank of time 86,400 seconds of time—which represent 1,440 minutes—which, of course, equal twenty-four hours each day.

Now you've got to remember the same stipulation applies, because God gives you this amount of time for you to use each day. Nothing is ever carried over on credit to the next day. There is no such thing as a twenty-six-hour day (though some of us wish there were). From today's dawn until tomorrow's dawn, you have a precisely determined amount of time. As someone has put it, "Life is like a coin. You can spend it any way you want to, but you can spend it only once."

One of the most fascinating (and, I might add, *frustrating*) of all subjects is this four-letter word *time*. It's amazing. We all have the same amount of time. Whether we are penniless or whether we happen to be the richest person on earth, whether we are young or old, single or married, employed or without a job, an adolescent in school or the President of the United States of America—we have exactly the same amount of time.

Think of how much "time" is woven into the fabric of our conversation every day. Here is a list of some familiar lines.

- "What time does the meeting start?"
- "I don't have time."
- "How much time will it take?"
- "Don't waste your time on that."
- "It's time to go."
- "Time out."
- "It's time we had a long talk."
- "What time is supper?"
- "Take out a clean sheet of paper. It's time for a quiz."

Time: A Few Pertinent Questions

What about this thing called "time"? First of all, what is it? Even though we talk about it every day, even though every one of us checks the time throughout the day, it's an elusive, slippery subject.

What Is Time?

I think the best definition I have read is "a stretch of duration in which things happen." Whether we are awake or asleep, whether we are conscious or unconscious, whether we are serving it well or wasting it, time is a duration, a measurable period, in which things happen. Lots of things happen. Isaac Watts' words often come to my mind: "Time, like an ever-rolling stream, bears all its sons away."[1] Without question, time is important.

Why Is Time So Important?

Time is significant because it is so rare. It is completely irretrievable. You can never repeat it or relive it. There is no such thing as a literal instant replay. That appears only on film. It travels alongside us every day, yet it has eternity wrapped up in it. Although this is true, time often seems relative, doesn't it? For example, two weeks on a vacation is not at all like two weeks on a diet. Also, some people can stay longer in an hour than others can in a week! Ben Franklin said of time, ". . . that is the stuff life is made of." Time forms life's building blocks. The philosopher William James once said, "The great use of life is to spend it for something that will outlast it."[2]

When Will Time End?

Will time be here forever or will it come to an end? Since man is the one who invented the clock, then obviously that device will not be with us throughout eternity. The planets that were arranged in space by almighty God continue to be the most perfect chronometer that has ever been created, but when those planets stop, time stops. So time is temporary. And that means we need to invest it wisely and find ways to enjoy it while it is ours to claim.

I think it's this dimension of life that causes Solomon to pull over from his journey into philosophy and stop long enough to write a practical analysis of time in his journal. He seems to have been prompted to do that toward the end of the chapter we just concluded. Remember his closing comment?

> There is nothing better for a man than to eat and drink and tell himself that his labor is good. This also I have seen, that it is from the hand of God. For who can eat and who can have enjoyment without Him? (2:24–25).

What is from the hand of God? Well, the ability to work, the ability to eat, the ability to drink, the ability to tell one's self that life is good—all of it comes from the hand of God. And without Him, none of these things can be enjoyed. Apart from Him and the perspective that He alone can give, what is there to laugh about? Or who is there to laugh with? You can't even have enjoyment or an appetite without God. And then toward the end, Solomon seems to throw his hands up in the air and say, "All is vanity; it's like playing tag with the wind." But he doesn't leave the subject. He ponders it.

LIFE: MEASURED ACCORDING TO ITS EVENTS

After pondering the whole idea of not being able to enjoy life apart from God, the writer breaks life down into measurable chunks which he calls "events."

> There is an appointed time for everything. And there is a time for every event under heaven . . . (3:1).

Following that opening line, he names no less than fourteen contrasts in life, all of them familiar scenes . . . almost like a cross section of life.

All-Pervading Opposites

Of course, not everything could be included in these contrasts, but it's remarkable how pervasive these opposites are.

1. *A time to give birth, and a time to die.* You cannot hasten either, have you noticed? You haven't the control over those things. Those are given to you by God; you are the recipient of birth and you are the recipient of death.

Depressed people have a tendency to ask: *Why was I born? Why can't I die?* It seems as though when life boils itself down to the basics, we go back to birth and death. Life carries with it a lot of those symbols, doesn't it? "A time to be born, and a time to die." Job asked those two questions: "Why was I born, and [having been born] why didn't I die?"

2. *A time to plant, and a time to uproot what is planted.* Most of us are not farmers; we've never worked the field or harvested crops. But even though that is true, we're smart enough to know that there is a time for planting and there is a time for uprooting. You don't mess around with Mother Nature. You cooperate with the seasons. It's the only way to get a crop. You don't plant when it's harvest time. You don't harvest at the wrong time either. You don't even prune a tree whenever you feel like it. Whether it's a little fruit tree in your yard or a vast, commercial orchard, you must prune at precisely the right time. And when the fruit is ripe, you must see that it's picked promptly. Timing is everything when it comes to the field.

By the way, it's also true on a personal level, have you noticed? There are times when you feel you should move on, and you try to uproot yourself; but you can't because things don't fall into place. And there are other times when you are convinced that you'll be there forever and, lo and behold, two months later (or less!) you are hundreds of miles away. God has a way of uprooting us and planting us, and He does it in His time.

3. *A time to kill, and a time to heal.* We don't like this part. Life seems somewhere strangely fixed between a battlefield and a first-aid station, between murder and medicine.

There is the Mafia in one part of our world and a Mother Teresa in another. Sometimes they appear in adjacent columns in our newspaper, and we are forced to deal with those opposites, killing and healing, at the same point in time. One article tells about a murderer who took someone's life in savage, cold blood, and there's another article that tells about a miracle drug that will help you live much longer. There's a time to kill, and a time to heal. *my life*

4. *A time to tear down, and a time to build up.* A perfect illustration is urban renewal. We see it all around us in metropolitan cities. If you live back East, you will see it even more often than we do out here in the West. Demolition crews are followed by construction crews; first there is blasting and then comes building. We see it in the restoration of old homes. We see it in the familiar scenes of life. There is a tearing-down time, and there is a building-up time. Sometimes what we witness prompts this next contrast.

5. *A time to weep, and a time to laugh.* C. S. Lewis probably said it best when he said, "Pain is God's megaphone. He whispers to us in our pleasure [when we laugh], but He shouts to us in our pain [when we weep]."[3] Along the same lines, Malcolm Muggeridge wrote about affliction in his book *A Twentieth Century Testimony*.

> Contrary to what might be expected, I look back on experiences that at the time seemed especially desolating and painful with particular satisfaction. Indeed, I can say with complete truthfulness that everything I have learned in my seventy-five years in this world, everything that has truly enhanced and enlightened my existence, has been through affliction and not through happiness, whether pursued or attained. In other words, if it ever were to be possible to eliminate affliction from our earthly existence by means of some drug or other medical mumbo jumbo, as Aldous Huxley envisaged in *Brave New World*, the result would not be to make life delectable, but to make it too banal and trivial to be endurable. This, of course, is what the Cross signifies. And it is the Cross, more than anything else, that has called me inexorably to Christ.[4]

Are you weeping these days? If you've been weeping for an extended period of time, you may be beginning to doubt. Low tides are hard times. You feel unfruitful. You feel scarred by doubt and you have reservations concerning a loving heavenly Father with a "wonderful plan for your life." Those words may cause you to sneer as a cynic. And you long for times to laugh, because they're much more enjoyable. Though I am convinced laughter does not teach us as much as tears, I love to laugh. I desire to cultivate a good sense of humor. I especially appreciate it in preachers. Unfortunately, it is all too rare among the clergy. I have people who listen to our radio broadcasts and write me things like, "You can stop preaching, but don't stop *laughing!*" Some have even said, "The only laughter heard in our homes comes through your voice. We're not a laughing family." How tragic!

Charles Haddon Spurgeon, a man I admire, faced a grim-faced crowd of proper Englishmen and said:

> There are things in these sermons that may produce smiles, but what of them? The preacher is not quite sure about a smile being a sin, and at any rate he thinks it less a crime to cause a momentary laughter than a half-hour of profound slumber.[5]

So many of us ministers spend our time trying to set people straight (which, being translated, means "make 'em agree with us").

I heard about a pastor who left the pastorate after twenty years. He decided to become a funeral director. Somebody asked, "Why did you do that?"

He answered: "Well, I spent about twelve years trying to straighten out John. He never did get straightened out. I spent fourteen months trying to straighten out the marriage of the Smith's, and it never did get straightened out. I spent three years trying to straighten out Susan, and she never did get straightened out. *Now* when I straighten them out, they stay straight."

Not only a time to weep, but also a time to smile, a time to laugh—how we need those times! I am not too concerned that my family remember me as a profound person, but rather as a husband and father who was fun to live with. I really do not care if they're able to repeat rules and regulations that came from my lips, but I hope they never forget the sound of my laughter. I hope it is absorbed in the walls of my home. That's one particular contribution I desire very much to make permanent.

6. *A time to mourn, and a time to dance.* I think of a few families I know quite well who have mourned together. As a pastor over the past twenty-five years, I've seen families in a dark funeral parlor leaning hard on one another, enduring the loss of a family member. I've also seen children in fractured families mourn the divorce of parents and try to put life back together in the weeks and months that followed.

Sometimes I think a death would have been less painful than the divorce. What mourning!

Then I've seen that same family, less than a year later, dance at the reception of a daughter who got married. How quickly the scene of mourning can change to dancing. As the song from the Jewish musical says, "Sunrise, sunset, swiftly fly the years. One season following another. Laden with happiness and tears."[6] *man carrying bag of*

I think the next two opposites fit together. *rocks, gets in cart +*

7. *A time to throw stones, and a time to gather stones.* *Still hold over*

8. *A time to embrace, and a time to shun embracing.* *his head— let go—all rocks +*

I link together the throwing stones with the shunning of embraces *let* and the gathering of stones with the times to embrace. And I take *God be* this to mean times of affirmation pushed up next to times of confronta-*resp— where* tion. *"don't want rock to kill someone"* *order not chaos —I'm not resp. fly.*

There are occasions when we need the embrace of a friend who pulls our head close and whispers in our ear words of understanding, encouraging us not to quit, reminding us that life will go on . . . we will make it. Such embraces put steel into our bones. They help us make it through the night.

And then there are times when that same person may take us by the shoulders, hold us at arm's length, and confront us with the hard truth, "Now listen to this, I can't agree with you. I must be honest with you . . . I think what you are doing is wrong." That is not a time for embracing. As Solomon puts it, that's a time stones are thrown. For a life to stay balanced, both affirmation and accountability are needed.

Verse 6 introduces an interesting opposite: *desertion* DC. 3-19-06 •

 "gave over to Satan"

9. *A time to search, and a time to give up as lost.* Rescue squads continually face this dilemma. They search and search through days and nights, sometimes the search wears on for *weeks.* There was recently a human drama which occurred not too many miles from where I live. Little three-year-old Laura Bradbury somehow was separated from her parents at Joshua Tree National Monument. The search continued for twenty anguishing days. But then authorities decided the search should be stopped. The homecoming of Laura's anxious parents, Mike and Patty Bradbury, was "a devastating experience," according to the *Los Angeles Times.*[7] Why? Because they felt like they were deserting their daughter. What a painful yet inescapable feeling! But in the opinion of the experts, it was time to "give up as lost." Solomon saw it in his day just as we do in ours.

10. *A time to keep, and a time to throw away.* I think of my

closet when I read that line, don't you? There's a time when you can no longer cram one more garment in that closet, unless you remodel the house. So it's time to take some of the stuff out and give it to a friend or haul a pile down to Goodwill Industries.

There's a time to clean out the garage and get rid of that stuff. There's a time to rid yourself of excess baggage and get a fresh start on life. And there's a time to keep. Some things you never throw away. Some things you would rather die than part with, like those things that find their way into the trunk in your attic or basement.

11. *A time to tear apart, and a time to sew together.* That seems to go with the previous phrase. The next one—oh, how I wish I knew this ahead of time! *like a garment*

12. *A time to be silent, and a time to speak.* Don't you wish someone invisible could be dispatched to stay near you to say, "Psst, speak up," when you should. And when you shouldn't be talking, that same wise counselor could say, "Psst, be quiet; don't talk." More often than not we're wiser to say less. I heard someone admit, "I never felt sorry for the things I did *not* say." (However, there are times when we need to say it and to say it well—times in which, though it is a struggle, we ought to stand and speak, even when others might think we look foolish.)

The longer I live, the more I want to listen to wise people. Not so much intelligent people as wise people. A person who is wise not only has intelligence, but understands life and can help put it all together. I suppose this accounts for my appreciation and admiration for Aleksandr Solzhenitsyn. I don't believe he walks on water and I certainly realize he is far from perfect, as we all are; but I do think you would agree that he's a wise and seasoned man.

A couple of years ago in an interview for *The Wall Street Journal* Solzhenitsyn was asked, "What hope is there for the West?" His answer must have caused some to suck in their breath.

The time when the West could save itself by its own exertions may already have passed. To save itself would require a complete change in its attitudes when in fact these attitudes are still going the wrong way. Instead of girding one's self for struggle, the West is still hoping for outside forces to save it, through some kind of miracle . . . perhaps a miracle in the Kremlin. Solidarity was hailed as such a miracle, but the only miracle that the people of the West can pray for is a profound change in their own hearts.[8]

Another question followed: "What about our young people and their concern for disarmament?" Solzhenitsyn answered wisely:

> It is normal to be afraid of nuclear weapons. I would condemn no one for that. But the generation now coming out of Western schools is unable to distinguish good from bad—even those words are unacceptable. This results in impaired thinking ability. Isaac Newton, for example, would never have been taken in by communism. These young people will soon look back on photographs of their own demonstrations and cry. But it will be too late. I say to them: "You're protesting nuclear arms. But are you prepared to try to defend your homeland with nonnuclear arms?" No! These young people are unprepared for any kind of struggle.[9]

In yet another question Solzhenitsyn was asked: "Do we have a single main underlying moral ill that one can identify?" The answer:

> Besides cowardice, selfishness. We hear a constant clamor for rights, rights, always rights, but so very little about responsibility. And we have forgotten God.[10]

Solzhenitsyn showed wisdom, yes. But he also showed courage . . . strong, unbending, straight-talking courage. In Solomon's words, as there are times to be silent, so there are also times when it's appropriate to speak. The man ought to speak. And when we can make a contribution, we should do so.

You are responsible to declare your convictions, to be true to your character, and to be true to your heritage. You are to speak the truth as you understand it. There's a time to be silent, but we're not to live our lives as mystical stoics, as though perpetually mute and neutral when faced with issues that will affect our tomorrow. Solomon was, again, correct: There's a time to be silent, and a time to speak.

13. *A time to love, and a time to hate.* Here is another contrast that makes us uncomfortable. We are from a generation that has talked about love, love, love until most of us are practically nauseated over the word. We seem to be in love with love . . . a love that's almost unthinking, nondiscerning, gullible—loving anything!

But the statement from Solomon (actually, from God!) puts it into perspective. There is a time to demonstrate love, but there is also a time to hate. Acts of injustice, acts of prejudice, and inequities ought to be hated and ought to be withstood. I remember reading a biography of the young Abraham Lincoln. The first time he saw a living slave offered in New Orleans on a slave block, he recoiled within. He said, "There was a rising hatred inside of me against slavery, and I swore if someday I could do something about it, I *would* do something about it." With all his heart he hated slavery. There's a time to hate, and there's a time to love.

Finally, the ancient king mentions a contrast that applies most directly to us as a nation.

14.   *A time for war, and a time for peace.* When tyranny runs roughshod over the rights of mankind, war is necessary. We often sit in a quiet place as we worship. We worship without the fear of infringement from law because someone has fought for the right to be heard and to speak freely, to stand and (if necessary) die for what one believes to be the truth. There is a time for war.

I realize, as I write those words, that we live in a volatile era where people will sue for the slightest provocation. We continually hear: "It's my right. I've got my rights. Rights to privacy. Rights to what I want. Rights to my will. Rights to do as I please. You'd better give me my rights." Perhaps in that extreme sense Solomon adds: "And there must be a time for peace."

Are you a peacemaker? Do you keep the peace? Are you a peacemaker in your neighborhood? Are you a peacemaker in the church where you worship? Are you aware that that's a basic requirement? We are to "keep the unity of the Spirit in the bond of peace." In the groups that you socialize with, do you keep peace? Or do you stir up conflict? Do you silence rumor, or do you pass rumor on? Are you a peacemaker and a peacekeeper, or do you make war? There's a time for war, and a time for peace.

When you look back over this lengthy list of opposites, perhaps you begin to feel a tension that can't be overlooked. Sometimes you and I don't know which is the appropriate reaction. Other times we know which we should do, yet the timing is not right. To do the right thing at the wrong time can be almost as inappropriate as failing to do the right thing at all. It's hard to know what "time" it is, isn't it? Frequently, our questions leave us with further questions.

Two All-Encompassing Questions

Two questions seem to leap from the page of Solomon's journal when we come to the end of this list. One is stated; the other, implied.

The first one is: What's the profit? When you look at life and you slice it down to the essentials, what's the profit? What is the gain? What is the reason?

To amplify that question and to tie it into the issue of time, God gives me 86,400 seconds each morning. By the end of the day, what's left of it? I once saw in a photograph the familiar octagon-shaped, yellow sign on a street that read, "Dead End." And someone had spray-painted two more words on the sign: "What isn't?"

Solomon gave us a long list of opposites. Fourteen are positive; fourteen are negative. In some ways they seem to cancel out each other, so that the net result is zero. Many of these tensions leave me on a dead-end street. What's the profit?

That's not only the point of this section, that's the message of this entire journal. Under the sun, when you slice life across the middle and analyze all the strata . . . when you boil it down to its basics and put yourself into it at 86,400 seconds a day, there's zero in it for you! That is, if it's only a horizontal trip from birth to death. If you leave God out of the scene, 86 billion seconds a day wouldn't help. It would still be profitless.

Times to laugh are empty. Times that kill are frightening. Times to mourn seem forever as do times of throwing stones. The times to gather stones and the times to embrace one another seem merely futile activities without God. It's all so empty. It's as empty as war and peace following one another. What a miserable cycle! What's the profit?

The second question is: What's the purpose? Where's life going? You will not learn from the universities where life is going. You may get a graduate school degree; you may, in fact, earn several of them. But you *still* won't learn where life is going. Universities aren't designed to tell you where it's going. They're equipped to help you question life. You graduate having learned the questions . . . not the answers. And those questions will solve nothing! As a matter of fact, in many institutions of higher learning you are considered intellectually incompetent if you come to hard-and-fast conclusions. You ask questions, you don't answer them. You raise them, you don't solve them. And in our humanistic world, there is this sophisticated idea that such people are getting brighter and brighter when, in fact, they are becoming increasingly more confused. And Solomon asks, "Where is it going? What profit is there to the worker from that in which he toils?"

Now, let's not kid each other. This chapter has endured just long enough to get most of you bored. I can tell. It's by design! (Solomon planned it that way, not I.) It's to show you how futile and empty life is. We're just about convinced, aren't we?

All-Important Conclusions

What we need are some conclusions that take away the futility. I am pleased to announce that Solomon does that. He even brings the name of God into it . . . what a shocker for a man on a horizontal journey!

> I have seen the tasks which God has given the sons of men with which to occupy themselves. He has made everything appropriate in its time (3:10–11).

First, *God has made everything appropriate in His time.* That's such an important, never-to-be-forgotten statement! It's the first time in this skeleton of thought that the writer has given you something he can build on "*above* the heavens."

In the margin of my Bible, I find an alternate rendering of the word *appropriate.* Literally, the Hebrew word means "beautiful." God has made everything *beautiful* in its time. When He gives the perspective we need, our times become "sensible" and "meaningful." When all that falls together, when the pieces of the puzzle fit into one another, beauty emerges. Does that remind you of a chorus of worship? Christians love to sing it when they gather. It was born out of this statement in the book of Ecclesiastes.

> In His time, in His time
> He makes all things beautiful
> In His time.
>
> Lord, please show me everyday
> As You're teaching me Your way
> That You'll do just what You say
> In Your time.[11]

How much we fail to see when we miss God's timing! If I look at life strictly as it is laid out before me, if I fail to see it through the lens of faith, I curse and swear and fight. I shake my fist in

God's face. But when I see it through His eyes, in His time, the beautiful picture comes together; and as it does, I give Him praise.

I see purpose in tragedy. I see reason in calamity. I see His sovereign hand at work as He is reminding me He is still in charge. And I acknowledge my need for greater dependence. As I do that, I willingly relinquish the controls to Him. So easy to say. So hard to do.

Now for the second conclusion:

> . . . He has also set eternity in their heart, yet so that man will not find out the work which God has done from the beginning even to the end (v. 11).

What is it? *God has put eternity in our hearts.* What in the world does that mean? Well, let me help you with the key word—*eternity.* Let's expand it to mean "curiosity about our future."

God has not only put things into perspective by having a timetable in which events run their course, He has also put within every human being's heart a curiosity about tomorrow . . . an eternal capacity that prompts me to probe, to be intrigued, to search. That explains why your child—just about the time that little fella or gal starts to run around the house and talk—begins to ask questions about tomorrow, about life, and about life beyond. Children can ask the most profound questions. And when they grow up, they don't stop asking questions. It's the way God made human beings. God has not put eternity in the heart of animals, only into the hearts of men and women. And since that is true, since we will not find out about tomorrow without God, our pursuit must be of Him.

Meaning what? Meaning you and I are not really ready to handle life until we are ready to face death. When we get eternity securely in place, it's remarkable what it will do to time.

Let me go back to where we started. Have you answered that question? Do you know what time it is? It's time to come to terms with eternity!

At the beginning of this chapter, we played "Let's Pretend." Then we turned our attention to more serious considerations. Now I'd like to suggest that we turn our full attention to "Let's Plan Ahead." Since God has put eternity in our hearts and since He makes all things beautiful in their time, we've got to focus on planning ahead or we'll never put this into the right perspective. Rather than hammering away on the subject, allow me to approach it a little more creatively.

"God's Trombones" is a series of seven sermons in verse, written by James Johnson. It's a compilation of sermons from the black culture of the twenties. And if you have ever heard black preachers, you have heard vivid terms about whatever the subject may be—creation, life, death, and in this case, the judgment day. Take special note of how this preacher describes the after-life when "time shall be no more. . . ."

> In that great day,
> People, in that great day,
> God's a-going to rain down fire.
> God's a-going to sit in the middle of the air
> To judge the quick and the dead.
>
> Early one of these mornings,
> God's a-going to call for Gabriel,
> That tall, bright angel, Gabriel;
> And God's a-going to say to him: "Gabriel,
> Blow your silver trumpet,
> And wake the living nations."
>
> And Gabriel's going to ask him: "Lord,
> How loud must I blow it?"
> And God's a-going to tell him: "Gabriel,
> Blow it calm and easy."
> Then putting one foot on the mountaintop,
> And the other in the middle of the sea,
> Gabriel's going to stand and blow his horn,
> To wake the living nations. . . .
>
> Oh-o-oh, sinner,
> Where will you stand,
> In that great day when God's a-going to rain down fire?
> Oh, you gambling man—where will you stand?
> You whore-mongering man—where will you stand?
> Liars and backsliders—where will you stand,
> In that great day when God's a-going to rain down fire?
>
> And God will divide the sheep from the goats,
> The one on the right, the other on the left.
> And to them on the right God's a-going to say:
> "Enter into My kingdom."
> And those who've come through great tribulations,
> And washed their robes in the blood of the Lamb,

They will enter in—
Clothed in spotless white, . . .

And to them on the left God's a-going to say:
"Depart from Me into everlasting darkness,
Down into the bottomless pit."
And the wicked like lumps of lead will start to fall,
Headlong for seven days and nights they'll fall,
Plumb into the big, black, red-hot mouth of hell, . . .

Too late, sinner! Too late!
Good-bye, sinner! Good-bye!
In hell, sinner! In hell!
Beyond the reach of the love of God.

And I hear a voice, crying, crying:
"Time shall be no more!
Time shall be no more!
Time shall be no more!"
And the sun will go out like a candle in the wind,
The moon will turn to dripping blood,
The stars will fall like cinders,
And the sea will burn like tar;
And the earth shall melt away and be dissolved,
And the sky will roll up like a scroll.
With a wave of his hand, God will blot out time,
And start the wheel of eternity.

Sinner, oh, sinner,
Where will you stand
In that great day when God's a-going to rain down fire?[12]

Time has begun for you and me, but it hasn't yet ended, by His grace. Are you ready for that moment when God will "blot out time and start the wheel of eternity"? What will be your hope, your secure confidence, when God steps on the scene and announces, "Time shall be no more"? If you're not absolutely sure that at the breathing of your last breath you have heaven as your destiny, you're not really even ready to live. I point you to Jesus Christ . . . Jesus Christ, who came to give men and women hope, forgiveness, and assurance, along with eternity in their hearts. Read this next sentence very carefully:

But as many as received Him [Christ], to them He gave the right to become children of God, even to those who believe in His name (John 1:12).

The gift of eternal life is there to be received. So take God's gift while you still have time. Along with Solomon's list of contrasts, there is still one more worth considering. There's a time to reject and a time to accept. Make this your time to accept.

6

INTERLUDE OF RARE INSIGHT

Journal Entry

But though God has planted eternity in the hearts of men, even so, man cannot see the whole scope of God's work from beginning to end. So I conclude that, first, there is nothing better for a man than to be happy and to enjoy himself as long as he can; and second, that he should eat and drink and enjoy the fruits of his labors, for these are gifts from God.

And I know this, that whatever God does is final—nothing can be added or taken from it; God's purpose in this is that man should fear the all-powerful God.

Whatever is, has been long ago; and whatever is going to be has been before; God seeks what has been driven away.

A long time ago in a galaxy far, far away . . ." So begin three of the most successful films that have ever emerged from the movie industry. Whether your favorite was *Star Wars* or *The Empire Strikes Back* or *Return of the Jedi*, the thing that held your attention during those hours of viewing was a world outside your own—a fantasy galaxy that existed long ago in a world originating in the mind of a creative genius named George Lucas. Some of the most talented minds in Hollywood teamed up to hold the public's attention in one film after another.

You see, being earthbound carries with it a number of limitations. For one thing, we are continually held by the force of gravity. Everything that goes up must come down, sometimes faster than we expect.

Furthermore, most of us are relatively unaware of the vast spaces and numerous galaxies outside our own solar system. The best we can do is imagine them. That's why we enjoy fantasizing our way through the experiences of imaginary characters like Luke Skywalker or Darth Vader or Jaba the Hut or R2D2 (and a bunch of others with weird names), but we have never actually been there. Chances are good that we'll never get much closer to it than in a film or maybe through descriptive stories told by one of those *true* space people, an astronaut.

I will never forget talking with one of the men who was on the crew that made the successful moon walk of yesteryear. I listened with great intensity as Colonel James B. Irwin told a few of us sitting around dinner one evening about life outside Earth's atmosphere. Most of what he shared transpired in a space capsule free of the clutches of gravity.

He talked about the time he and his companions floated over to the window and watched what he called "earthrise." That immediately caught my attention. I have seen sunrises all my life, but I doubt that I will ever live to see an earthrise. The best part of all was that it was not an unreal rising of an earth imagined by some creative thinker. It was a literal earthrise seen by human eyes from a vantage point different from those of us who are connected to this earth.

You see, the thing about being earthlings is that we are bound (whether we like it or not) to a dull, predictable, routine lifestyle . . . and often we *don't* like it. We would love to be able to change that, but God has designed it so that there is just so much to see within the sphere of our planet. Even though you and I may travel all the way around this world and see many interesting sights, not too much will be brand new.

None of the people on earth will ever be as different as those in the fantasy films. Compared to C3PO, Chewbacca, and Jaba, folks like Jane and Clyde or Ken and Barb are not that exciting. No offense . . . that's just the way it is being stuck on this old globe. And none of the places you visit will even come close to places you saw in *Star Wars*. Earthlings and earth places are pretty predictable. Compared to that "galaxy far, far away," we're in Dullsville! Welcome to life on the horizontal plane.

LIFE WITHOUT GOD

You will not find one imaginary character in the book of Ecclesiastes—not one. You will not really find much creativity as it relates to living on earth; nor will you find one word about a galaxy far, far away. But you *will* find inspired truth concerning life on this planet. And if you wonder what it's like, you don't have to look very far. In this ragged-edge reality called earthly existence, life is somewhere between sad and bad. All it takes is a quick look around to discover why we line up to watch fantasies that take us to galaxies far, far away. Who wouldn't want to escape from an existence as boring and painful as ours? For many, it's downright horrid. It's drug abuse. It's sleepless nights. It's headaches. It's heartaches. It's hate, rape, assault, jail sentences. It's sickness and sorrow. It's broken lives. It's distorted minds. Mainly, as Solomon discovered long ago, it's *empty*. There's nothing down here under the sun that will give you and me a sense of lasting satisfaction. It is planned that way! How else would we realize our need for the living God?

I don't care how good your professional practice is, much of it is boring. I don't care how big your house is or how exciting your future is. I don't care how hard you work or how large your paycheck or how sincere your efforts, when you boil life down to the nubbies . . . when the lights are turned off at night, you're back to reality— it is *boring* and horribly empty. To quote Solomon the realist, it is like chasing the wind.

You work so that you can make money, so that you can spend it, so that you can work and make more money, so that you can spend it, so that you can get more, which will mean you spend more, and you'll work harder to make more. So goes this endless cycle called "striving after wind."

That explains why people will line up by the millions to view a fantasy on film and sit in silent amazement at someone's imaginary world of imaginary characters who do imaginary things—because life under the sun is so dreadfully, unchangingly boring.

To put it bluntly, life on planet Earth *without* God is the pits. And if I may repeat my point (Solomon does numerous times), that's the way God designed it. He made it like that. He placed within us that God-shaped vacuum that only He can fill. Until He is there, nothing satisfies. There is no hell on earth like horizontal living without God.

Can you imagine being raised in a country that teaches everyone that "there is no God"? Perhaps you remember the Soviet athlete who in following his coach's instruction to do a three-and-a-half somersault, tucked position, cracked his head on the ten-meter platform. Today he's dead.

That tragedy made me stop and think how I'd feel if I were a parent in the Soviet Union, sitting in a hospital room with my boy dying on the bed in front of me. Think about it. There I sit, helpless to do one thing to revive him. I have no God to talk to. I find no comfort coming from the Supreme Being, because I do not think He exists. And there is no one to put his arm around me and tell me there's an eternal purpose in it all.

I need another dimension for the puzzle of life to fit together or I am stuck with a profitless, purposeless, boring, empty existence. The same is true of anyone living without God—your neighbor, the guy you work with, that lady at the next desk, the other students in the classroom, the professor or teacher, all the way up to the administration or the corporate president.

Ecclesiastes says it straight. Look at chapter 3, verse 9: "What profit is there to the worker from that in which he toils?" The answer? Zero. None whatsoever!

Now all of a sudden the writer pushes a door open. You can almost hear it squeak. In music, we call such a transition an interlude. Solomon inserts an unannounced yet much-needed change of pace.

Life with God

This interlude is full of insight. Like a hinge on the door, a transition provides a pivot point that takes us from one phase of his search to another. And right here, quietly yet sovereignly, enters the One non-earthling that George Lucas left out—*the living God*, the Creator of heaven and earth. The only One who can change my focus. The beautiful thing about His entrance is that when He steps onto the scene and gives me the lenses through which I am able to gain new perspective, life changes. It changes from boredom and emptiness, profitlessness and purposelessness, to meaning, direction, definition, hope, encouragement, and—best of all—deliverance from despair.

I want you to see in this section of Solomon's journal two or three things about God. We'll see first what God *makes;* next, what God *gives;* and last, what God *does.*

What God Makes

> He has made everything appropriate in its time. He has also set eternity in their heart, yet so that man will not find out the work which God has done from the beginning even to the end (3:11).

When God steps on the scene and we see life through His eyes, first we discover that *He makes everything appropriate.* Or, as I suggested earlier, He makes everything "beautiful in its time." When God takes charge, beauty emerges. We developed that idea in the previous chapter.

Among Christians a favorite verse of Scripture is Romans 8:28:

> And we know that God causes all things to work together for good to those who love God, to those who are called according to His purpose.

The key part of the verse is "work together." That verse does not say "all things are good"—just as Solomon's comment does not say "everything is beautiful." It says, "All things are good as they work together for His purpose." This says, "He makes everything beautiful *in its time.*" And I've got news for those who struggle with God's timing. You may not live to see God's time completely fulfilled. You may live to a ripe old age, carry out your reason for existence, and die before the full program of God has reached its ultimate and completed purpose. But His promise stands—He will make everything beautiful in its time.

Quite frankly, our problem is that we focus our attention on the wrong thing. We see the fuzzy, ugly cocoon; God plans and sets in motion the butterfly. We see the painful, awful process; He is producing the value of the product. We see today; He is working on forever. We get caught up in the wrapping; He focuses on the gift, the substance down inside. We look at the external; He emphasizes the internal. He makes everything beautiful in its time, including your loss, your hospital experience, your failures, your brokenness, your battles, your fragmented dreams, your lost romance, your heartache, your illness. Yes, even your terminal illness. And one more word on this, God wouldn't say "everything" if He didn't mean "everything." That includes whatever you're going through. He makes it beautiful in its time. Without Him, life is purposeless and profitless, miserable and meaningless. With Him, it will ultimately make sense.

There's something else God makes. "He has also set eternity in their hearts"—*He makes everybody curious.* When Solomon says, "He sets eternity in our hearts," he has in mind the idea of giving humanity the capacity to see beyond today.

God has given us that eternal itch for tomorrow. He makes us curious about what's coming around the corner. He gives us a hunger to know what's next. That's why we have to have hope to go on. Yet a brute beast in the field needs no hope at all. That old mule can plow the field continually without any hope of a different tomorrow, but you and I can't. We figure out the scene real fast. Once we've plowed it the first time, we know there's not a whole lot to get excited about the next time we have to plow.

God has given mankind the ability to see beyond the present. And he has not given that ability to any other creation. He has given us eternity in our hearts, without which "man will not find out the work which God has done from the beginning even to *the end.*"

I have italicized "the end" for the sake of emphasis. Let me tell you why. It doesn't take a lot of brains to realize that if there is a sunrise, there must also be a sunset. To borrow from the astronaut's word, if there is an "earthrise," there must also be an "earthset."

So let's take that one step further. If there is an earth beginning, there must also be an earth ending. And if I'm existing on this boring earth without God, then I'm certainly not ready for an earth ending when I must face the One who made me. That just adds to the misery of the whole package. Even with a master of arts degree, even with a doctorate, even with world travels behind me for fifty or sixty years, I have no hope that I can handle earth's ending. And He's *given* me that curiosity about the ending. Without that curiosity, I will never discover that there is a God.

Fantasy characters don't find God. Robots don't find God; they don't even seek after God. They have no such curiosity. Then why does mankind? Because God made us that way. And if it gets boring enough on this earth, chances are great that we will search for God.

What God Gives

Since God has made everything appropriate and beautiful and since He has made mankind curious about tomorrow, what's next? Well, let's take a look—God gives us four gifts.

> I know that there is nothing better for them than to rejoice and to do good in one's lifetime, moreover, that every man who eats and drinks sees good in all his labor—it is the gift of God (3:12–13).

First, *God gives us the ability to rejoice and enjoy life.*
There's nothing better for us than to rejoice. Have you ever seen a person who didn't have God really and truly enjoying life on a regular basis? How about the one who has no place in his or her life for God? Have you ever known one individual like that who was continually rejoicing? I haven't either.

The only one who enjoys and exudes the gift of rejoicing is the believer. Why? Because God alone can give the perspective and refreshing hope needed to sustain a life of joy, regardless. And I mean regardless.

I heard about a man who gave his business to God. He had hassled over it for years. He had wrestled with it and fought it for two decades. One day he decided, "I've had it; that's enough!" He had heard from his pastor that Sunday morning about the value of turning his entire business over to God. It was when he drove away from church that he decided he had worried enough. By the time he got home, he had totally and unequivocally committed his business to God.

That very night his place of business caught on fire. He got an emergency call. He rather calmly drove down to the commercial residence and was standing on the street, watching the place go up in flames. He was sort of smiling to himself. One of his colleagues raced to his side and questioned his relaxed attitude about what was happening. "Man! Don't you know what's happened to your . . . It's . . . it's burning up!"

He replied, "I know it. I know it. No problem, Fred. This morning I gave this company to God, and if He wants to burn it up, that's His business."

Not even a fire, not even a disaster like that is sufficient to take the gift of rejoicing from you when God gives it to you.

The second gift is that *God gives us the ability to do good in our lifetime.* That's exactly what this statement means:

> I know that there is nothing better for them than to rejoice and to do good in one's lifetime; . . .

So much today is a two-way exchange rather than a one-way expression. I do good because you're going to do good back to me. I treat you nice, and in return I expect you to treat me nice. Reciprocity brings us pleasure. But God says He gives us the ability to do good in our lifetime . . . whether or not others do us good in return. And let me urge you not to wait. *Now* is the time to do good.

You and I don't do anyone else a bit of good once we are six feet under. It's all over. Don't wait until then to make life happier for someone else, to give someone else some financial relief, to express your availability and to help them through a hard time, to baby-sit, to house-sit, to help them purchase a car, or help them get an education. Don't wait until later to invest in others' relief. God says He gives you the ability to do it *in your lifetime;* it's a gift from Him. Which means that no one can explain in human terms why you would do it. It doesn't come from any heart of love and compassion, because you and I don't have hearts like that. Face it, our natural heart is depraved and desperately wicked. That's the kind of human nature we have. Without help from "above the sun," we're sunk.

But when God, in the person of Jesus Christ, comes into a life, He gives that once-selfish individual the capacity to do good. And that means the ability to do good without being thanked, getting credit or receiving applause. You find yourself motivated to do good, because God's life is at work in you. This is not a *Star Wars* fantasy. I'm talking ragged-edge reality.

Now let's look at the third gift:

> . . . moreover, that every man who eats and drinks sees good in all his labor—it is the gift of God (v. 13).

God gives us an appetite to eat and to drink. This is the gift of appetite . . . the ability to enjoy our food. People who make a lot of money don't automatically have a good appetite. People who live in high-class places don't always have a great desire for good. That appetite comes from God, as does our entire internal mechanism.

It's just like a good night's sleep. You can't buy it. You can buy the drugs that'll knock you out and keep you drugged through the night, but you cannot buy the ability to fall asleep and rest peacefully through the night. That is a gift from God.

There's also a fourth gift. *God gives us the ability to see good in all our labor.* I call it "perspective." Under-the-sun perspective says, "I earn what I get." Above-the-sun perspective says, "You get what you will never deserve and can never earn"—forgiveness, eternal life, grace, hope, life beyond the grave, a reason to go on—regardless.

We've heard from Solomon's journal what God *makes.* He makes everything beautiful in its time. He makes us curious about our future. We have also discovered what God *gives*—the ability to rejoice, the capacity to do good, an appetite for food and drink, and also perspective in our labor.

What God Does

In this interlude of rare insight, the best is saved until the last. I'm referring to what God *does.*

> I know that everything God does will remain forever; there is nothing to add to it and there is nothing to take from it, for God has so worked that men should fear Him. That which is has been already, and that which will be has already been, for God seeks what has passed by (vv. 14–15).

The first two things Solomon mentions here emphasize the quality of God's actions—they are *permanent* and they are *complete.* God is thorough. The last two things mentioned emphasize the activity itself . . . *God performs things that cultivate respect for Him* and

God repeats things until they are learned and firmly etched into our lives. Let's take a moment to think about each of these.

First, look at the quality of God's work: *it's permanent.* Whatever God does is permanent. "It will remain forever." God does nothing with shallowness, nothing superficially. He doesn't glue on a thin layer of veneer. His work is solid. It's got substance. It's got staying power. It'll be there tomorrow and for an eternity of tomorrows. If God does it, you can mark it down—it's permanent.

Second, *it's thorough and complete.* Nothing can be added to it (so there's nothing missing when it comes) and nothing can be taken from it (so it's never excessive or superfluous). Isn't that great? Everything God does is thorough. It's never too little, never too late . . . it's never too much, never too early, and there's never anything missing.

Not long after my younger daughter, Colleen, got her first car, she had a little fender bender. As a result, she needed to purchase the lens on the right front parking light which had been broken. It was just an inexpensive lens that screws on, so I said, "Don't worry, honey; I'll take care of it."

I went down to the dealership where I had purchased the car and told the guy, "I want a right, front lens parking light for a 1983 Honda Prelude."

He said, "Okay. What's the number of the part?"

We looked in the catalog. He wrote the number down, checked his stock, came back and said, "We've got to order it."

"That's all right. We'll wait," I responded.

"It'll be a while," he warned me.

"That's okay," I assured him. "You can order it."

So he ordered it. I stood there and watched to make sure he wrote down the exact number. When it came in, it was the left, rear lens for another model. Different year too! I couldn't believe it.

So, we walked through it again. I looked on the chart and said, "This one right here; you know, the one we picked out five weeks ago." He yawned, stared at me rather blankly, and ordered the part once again. After the third visit, we finally got it all worked out. Something so simple, yet it became so complicated.

When *man* does something, he, almost without exception, leaves out something. Or there's something that will need to be added to make it right. We aren't thorough . . . nor do we do permanent work! We design things to become obsolete fast, to frustrate people, to make us scream and shout and run around in circles.

God doesn't do that. He does it thoroughly. He does it completely, permanently. And when you see the work of God, guess what! You stand in awe. ". . . for God has so worked that men should fear Him."

That's the third thing God does. He performs things that cultivate respect for Him. *God is awesome!* When was the last time you took a glance at a mountain? You don't glance at pictures of Mount Everest and say, "Hmm, nice hill. Maybe a little taller than some mountains." You don't witness the glaciers in Alaska and say, "Oh, yeah, that's a pretty nice glacier." You stand in silent awe.

I remember when my Marine battalion flew over Japan's Mount Fuji. Not one man on our plane, when they looked out and saw Fuji, said, "Sure, sure, that's nice." No, indeed! I mean, it was click, click, click . . . it was picture-taking time! *This* was picturesque, awesome Fuji!

Who made Fuji? God! And like that mountain, the rest of His creation is equally awesome. Consider the stars in space, for example. Though we were to study for a lifetime, we still could not fathom them. When God does it, it makes us stand back in respect. It puts all human achievements on the lowest level.

Now look again at the comment in verse 15.

> That which is has been already, and that which will be has already been, for God seeks what has passed by.

Herein lies an important principle: *God patiently repeats things until they are learned.* The last part of this journal entry might be rendered: "for God seeks what has been driven away."

We are the ones who pass it by. We are the ones who walk away, so God brings us back to the same lesson to learn it again. And He doesn't give up when we pass it by. He brings us back again and again to learn our lesson well. We get weary of learning the lesson and we run from it. We turn it off. Yet He repeats the same lesson. He repeats it and repeats it and repeats it until finally the light comes on and we learn it. Why? Because God seeks what you and I try to escape. God pursues what you and I turn off. God makes a permanent lesson out of what you think is a temporary and passing experience.

One thing I have discovered from life is that until we have learned the complete lesson from a crushing experience, we'll pass through it again at a different age and under different circumstances. For example, one marriage that doesn't work will reap another marriage that doesn't work until you learn that you, in fact, are the problem.

A special word to pastors: As you move from church to church to church, you'll learn more and more, but you'll keep shifting. You'll keep changing, keep uprooting, keep searching to find the ideal spot to serve. The problem is you've got to take yourself along every time you move! And it'll be imperfect as soon as you get there, until you learn that *you* are, more than likely, a major part of the problem. God comes back and seeks what has been driven away.

LIFE FROM GOD

There are two specific points I'd like to make in this chapter. First of all, *life from God comes from outside this galaxy—not from within it.* I come across Universalists rather often who believe that there's a little bit of God in everybody. That's simply not the truth.

They tell us there is human greatness. There's human goodness. There's positive thinking. There's self-help and self-effort. We can certainly appreciate those things. But the only place we can find life from God is at the source—Jesus Christ. Jesus says, "I am the way, and the truth, and the life; no one comes to the Father, but through Me" (John 14:6). God says, "I give eternal life to them, and they shall never perish; and no one shall snatch them out of My hand" (John 10:28).

God gives us "the real life" through His Son, Christ. And only through His Son. Please get that straight. That's the basis of the gospel. That's why Christ is the preeminent message—not good works, not positive thinking, not good books, not being widely traveled or earning a good education (as fine as all those things may be). Christ, and Christ alone, will give you the life of God, and He's from outside this galaxy. He's not within it.

The second thought is this: *Life from God is supernatural power now—not a vague force limited to a long time ago.* You know, the greatest evidence of power is change. Take a trip to Hoover Dam and look at that massive amount of water; it's really impressive. But you don't say, "My! Look at that power." What you see is not the greatest evidence of power. That's just water going over a dam. If you want to see the evidence of power at Hoover Dam, you need to drive to a residential section in a nearby city that draws its source of electricity from the dam . . . walk into a darkened room in the middle of the night and flip on the light. In one simple "click" you've got the greatest evidence of the power at that massive dam. It's able to change darkness into light. It's able to transform a cold house into a warm home.

Now, the wonderful news is that God dispenses His supernatural power to anyone who says, "I want it." It doesn't cost you a thing. You don't have to see a film. You don't have to visit a territory of the country. There are no Meccas. You don't have to read a series of books. You don't have to be on probation for a year and a half. You don't have to keep going to a church to earn your way in. You don't have to pray a whole lot. You don't even have to "give up your sins" (an impossibility). Whether you're the richest of the rich, the poorest of the poor, or anywhere between, all you have to do is take a gift. And the gift is the power of God, through faith in His Son.

Maybe it's time for you to pause and take care of that issue once and for all. Make this your interlude of rare insight, . . . and when you do, my friend, the Force will not only be *with* you, it will be *in* you.

7

CONFESSIONS OF A CYNIC

Journal Entry

Moreover, I noticed that throughout the earth justice is giving way to crime and even the police courts are corrupt. I said to myself, "In due season, God will judge everything man does, both good and bad."

And then I realized that God is letting the world go on its sinful way . . . so that men themselves will see that they are no better than beasts. For men and animals both breathe the same air, and both die. So mankind has no real advantage over the beasts; what an absurdity! All go to one place. . . For who can prove that the spirit of man goes upward and the spirit of animals goes downward into dust? So I saw that there is nothing better for men than that they should be happy in their work, for that is what they are here for. . . so let them enjoy it now.

*E*verybody loves a story. We especially like stories that have neat and tidy endings. We don't mind if there is sadness and hardship—just so there's justice in the end. We like for right to win and wrong to lose. We want the guys in the white hats to come out on top and the ones in the black hats to wind up in jail. Let me illustrate this from a few well-known fairy tales.

Humpty Dumpty

As children we were never bothered by the fact that even though all the king's horses and all the king's men worked feverishly to put Humpty Dumpty back together again, they were unable to do so. Part of the reason we could live with Humpty's situation was the realization that nobody pushed him off that wall. That would have been unfair and unjust treatment. Eggs have no way to defend themselves. Since nobody was to blame for his condition and since everybody from the king's horses to the king's men tried everything they could do to help him out, we can tolerate the sad ending. His story may be unhappy, but it is not unjust.

Cinderella

This lovely young woman was raised in a cruel home by a cruel stepmother. Her cruel stepsisters only added to her misery. As you recall, she went to the ball and had a great time, but at midnight the carriage she was traveling in turned into a pumpkin. But that was okay. We can live with that because she was warned about the possibility of that happening. And it's especially okay since, in the end, she got the glass slipper and lived happily ever after. Justice won out.

What we would not have been able to live with is that if somehow one of the cruel stepsisters would have gotten that slipper. That would not have been just. Cinderella's foot deserved the slipper. We smile at such poetic justice.

Robin Hood

As a little boy I thought a lot about the tales of Robin Hood. You remember Robin Hood. He was the one who took from those who had far too much to give to those who didn't have enough. We had to do a little ethical shuffle with the right and wrong of that when we read the stories, but in our child's mind, that was fair play. After all, the goods wound up in a better place than where they would have otherwise. The peasants certainly needed them more than the rich. So we applaud the adventurous intrigue in the stories of Robin Hood. Why? We know that ultimately fairness prevailed—at least it seemed that way in our young minds.

What we would not have tolerated was to discover later on that Robin Hood was really a con man with a bank in Switzerland and all that money wound up over there. We could not have handled his ripping off the peasants and building his own empire, then secretly living in a mansion he built from the bucks he siphoned off the rich, all the while playing the role of Mr. Nice Guy.

Sad endings we can handle, but not unjust ones. Suffering makes us sad, but injustice makes us mad. In our childlike minds we still long for fairness and equity. We still want stories to end well so that people can live happily ever after. But life is not that neat and tidy. Only in fairy tales does right always triumph. In life, the helpless are pushed around, cruel people often get the slipper, and some of those we thought were generous, unselfish givers were actually greedy, self-serving takers. And have you noticed? If a person lives with injustice long enough, especially if he or she lacks divine perspective, that person becomes disillusioned . . . ultimately, cynical. And that cynicism results in a twisted kind of injustice itself.

All that brings us back to this intriguing, up-to-date account Solomon recorded. Much of his journal could be described as the confessions of a cynic. Here's Solomon, wearing an invisible yet thick visor. He is unwilling to look up in dependence on God and too stubborn to bow his head in prayer. To quote another humanist, his "head is bloody but unbowed." He is only willing to look around. By the end of the third chapter, if I count correctly, no less than eleven times we read the words "under heaven" and "under the sun."

Remember the theme of the king's journal? Everything is barren, futile emptiness. The man who writes it is not sad, he's mad. The injustices in life have taken their toll. So it is with us. We can handle affliction and mistreatment so long as it passes. But if the pain persists and the hurt is not relieved, we become cynics. When we get near the edge of panic, we look up and cry out against God. And if we don't have the faith to get us through such horizontal injustices, we simply die a cynic.

Solomon is not near death, but he is fast approaching rank cynicism. And since his perspective is strictly horizontal, we are not surprised to find that his patience is running thin. All of his observations lack vertical perspective and all of his conclusions are humanistic. As we saw in the previous chapter, there are a few rare interludes of divine viewpoint, but, for the most part, it's page after page of human wisdom. For example, look at this next paragraph.

> Furthermore, I have seen under the sun that in the place of justice there is wickedness, and in the place of righteousness there is wickedness. I said to myself, "God will judge both the righteous man and the wicked man," for a time for every matter and for every deed is there. I said to myself concerning the sons of men, "God has surely tested them in order for them to see that they are but beasts." For the fate of the sons of men and the fate of beasts is the same. As one dies so dies the other; indeed, they all have the same breath and there is no advantage for man over beast, for all is vanity. All go to the same place. All came from the dust and all return to the dust. Who knows that the breath of man ascends upward and the breath of the beast descends downward to the earth? And I have seen that nothing is better than that man should be happy in his activities, for that is his lot. For who will bring him to see what will occur after him? (3: 16–22).

The phrases "I have seen" and "I said to myself" underscore a basic, philosophical commitment to human perspective. You will not find Solomon on his knees, but on his feet. You will not find Solomon looking up, but looking out. You won't find Solomon quietly seeking patience in prayer, but rather shouting back at God. As a man who was driven from the human point of view, looking strictly on this earth and not into the heavens, he sneers, "There is no advantage for man over beast."

The Problem That Creates Cynicism

Solomon's opening statement may give us some insight into the problem that caused him to fall into such a cynical slump.

> I have seen under the sun that in the place of justice there is wickedness, and in the place of righteousness there is wickedness (v. 16).

I've seen that too, haven't you? There is something amazingly relevant about this problem of wickedness winning over justice. Every generation repeats the same rotten story. As James Russell Lowell put it:

> Truth forever on the scaffold,
> Wrong forever on the throne.

People don't take their turn at the stop sign. Have you noticed that? They don't patiently wait their turn. Neither do they stay in line when they're buying tickets; they cut in line! When we were children, we naively believed that everyone would take turns, but we soon discovered they didn't.

I remember the very first time it ever dawned on me that someone was actually cutting in line. My first reaction was shock. Then I entertained thoughts of punching his lights out! The older I got, the more I wanted people like that to be punished. I wanted life to be fair. I was waiting my turn, so I wanted the other person to wait as I had been waiting. But people don't do that.

Why? "Because in the place of justice there is wickedness." In the very place where righteousness ought to appear, there is really corruption.

If life can't be comfortable, at least it can be fair! Solomon, too, felt life's injustice as he describes in the following observation:

> Then I looked again at all the acts of oppression which were being done under the sun. And behold I saw the tears of the oppressed and that they had no one to comfort them; and on the side of their oppressors was power, but they had no one to comfort them (4:1).

Can you feel the sigh in his words? There is something within humanity that longs for judicial justification. If one is oppressed, there at least ought to be someone there to comfort. Better than that, there ought to be someone there to relieve the oppression. When such support is absent, it isn't right. Something inside us recoils.

Even later, the same cynic complains about a scene all of us have wrestled with.

> Don't be surprised when you see that the government oppresses the poor and denies them justice and their rights. Every official is protected by the one over him, and both are protected by still higher officials (5:8, TEV).

Does that sound like city hall? You'd think the man had just visited one of our bureaucratic civil service offices. His words sound like he's describing some kind of red-tape "officious" group!

The scene is nauseatingly familiar. The longer you plead your case to officials, the more you realize all of their bases are covered by yet higher officials. And the higher they get, the more secret and untouchable they become . . . and the higher your blood pressure rises, because it isn't fair. It's enough to make cynics out of all of us!

Still later, Solomon observes:

> I saw all this when I thought about the things that are done in this world, a world where some men have power and others have to suffer under them (8:9, TEV).

There it is again. One person exercising authority at another person's expense. And it's as though Solomon's hands are tied behind his back. He's at a loss to reach out and take charge. And he knows it's neither right nor fair.

You feel it when your children are mistreated in their own neighborhood or when some bully pushes them around at school or on the bus and you're not there to help make things right. You don't like it when injustice occurs in the classroom or in your office. You don't like to know that the police department, for example, might harbor corruption. You realize it may be going on, but you despise the thought, because if there's any place where there ought to be justice, it's there. We especially don't like to see a courtroom marked by a lack of integrity.

I have an attorney friend who will no longer do court cases simply because of the corruption he is forced to wade through in the courtroom . . . the legal games courtroom attorneys are expected to play. It's no longer a question of whether one has a good case. It's more often a question of whether one has enough money to buy the right attorney, to pull the right strings, to play the right game. (I'm sounding like a cynic, right?) "I've seen it," says Solomon, "and it makes me mad."

Henry Wadsworth Longfellow put together a poem many years ago that describes these ambivalent feelings that we get when exposed to such injustice. His lines have found their way into our repertoire of Christmas carols. They appear in a piece entitled "I Heard the Bells on Christmas Day."

As the poet listens to the ringing of the yuletide bells, he remembers that it was promised by the angels that there would someday be peace on earth and good will to men. But then, wrestling with reality, he admits:

> And in despair I bowed my head:
> "There is no peace on earth," I said,
> "For hate is wrong, and mocks the song
> Of peace on earth, good-will to men."

Even a compassionate poet finds himself despairing over the lack of justice.

DOES CYNICISM HAVE A SOLUTION?

Let's get to the other side of all this. Let's see if we can find a way to cope with injustice. Read this next section very carefully. Even in his angry despair, Solomon seems to project a little hope coming first from God, then from our fellow human beings.

> I said to myself, "God will judge both the righteous man and the wicked man," for a time for every matter and for every deed is there. I said to myself concerning the sons of men, "God has surely tested them in order for them to see that they are but beasts." For the fate of the sons of men and the fate of beasts is the same. As one dies so dies the other; indeed, they all have the same breath and there is no advantage for man over beast, for all is vanity. All go to the same place. All came from the dust and all return to the dust. Who knows that the breath of man ascends upward and the breath of the beast descends downward to the earth? (3:17–21).

Solution One: Injustice Will Have Only a Temporary Reign

For a rare moment, Solomon actually looks above the sun. He seems to be saying, "For there is a time for every matter and every deed. Relief is coming. Wrong won't last forever. It's going to be judged under the sovereign hand of a just God. Injustice will have only a temporary reign. Rest easy."

Too bad Solomon couldn't stop there, but he goes on. I think he's fed up with injustice. And just like any other man or any other woman living today writing a journal based on humanistic observations, he lets his cynicism show through.

> I said to myself concerning the sons of men, "God has surely tested them in order for them to see that they are but beasts." For the fate of the sons of men and the fate of beasts is the same. As one dies so dies the other; indeed, they all have the same breath and there is no advantage for man over beast, for all is vanity. All go to the same place. All came from the dust and all return to the dust (vv. 18–20).

If you press gross injustice to the maximum, if you focus your attention on corruption and unfair oppression long enough, you will come to this exasperating and heretical conclusion.

Solution Two: Injustice Reveals Our Beastlike Behavior

Perhaps I should put quotation marks around the term *"solution,"* since this hardly seems like much help in dealing with the problem. An explanation, no doubt, is needed. In his cynical rage, the man exclaims that there is no advantage in being a human being. "We're all just like a bunch of beasts, a herd of animals . . . and since that is true, our destinations are the same!" His point is this: Injustice may be hard to bear, but at least it reveals the ragged-edge reality— we are animalistic to the core!

Most commentators will say, "Of course, we're all like beasts in that we all go to the dust; i.e., we all die." But what does that "advantage" comment mean? "We have no advantage over animals," he snarls. "We have the same breath, the same purpose, the same destiny!"

What does all this mean? Well, among other things, it means that by living in an unjust world without God, we become beastlike in nature, beastlike in action, beastlike in reaction, beastlike in destiny. Simply the realization and admission of this terrible fact will convince us that we need help outside ourselves . . . from *above* the sun. Why? Because apart from that, our depravity knows no bounds.

If you question that, take the time to look over the homicide files at any local police station. Or recall the attitude of your own heart when you have been dealt an unjust blow and you're operating from the flesh. If that's not enough, call to mind the bestial imagination that is yours when your smoldering lust bursts into a bonfire.

Consider the international scene. Think of the weapons that we as nations build—to destroy, to annihilate one another, and, yes, to protect. The nation that wins is the one with the biggest arsenal. So now that global warfare has come to such proportions (and I have no political axe to grind in all this), it's just a question of who pulls the trigger first and who lives long enough to answer back. National defense is one thing . . . but when was the last time you seriously imagined being involved in a nuclear attack?

Why has it come to such extremes? It's our beastlike nature . . . our beastlike style. Solomon is saying that since the fate of men is the same as the fate of beasts, we shouldn't be surprised that we take injustice to its farthest extreme.

If you press Solomon's cynical summation to the ultimate, do you know what he is saying? He's saying that the beast in the field today that dies and drops into a hole in the soil and turns back into dust has a future that is exactly like yours and mine. When you die, you're dropped into a hole. You turn to dust and that's it. No advantage. Notice the question he asks:

> For who can prove that the spirit of man goes upward and the spirit of animals goes downward into dust? (v. 21, TLB).

I hardly need to tell you that this section of Scripture has become a haven for biblical critics. They affirm, on the basis of this statement, that Scripture teaches there is no eternal distinction between the species, including *homo sapiens*. Since we live like beasts, we shall also die like beasts. They say, "You Christians base your beliefs on the inspired Bible? Take a close look at Ecclesiastes 3:19–21!" Allow me to address this issue.

Let's understand that the doctrine of biblical inspiration affirms the accuracy and inerrancy of the biblical text . . . nothing more. It assures us that what we find in Scripture is what was written by the original author. But in no way does it endorse the doctrinal certainty and practical application of every single comment found in the Bible. Discernment applied to the whole of Scripture guards us from embracing half truths or out-and-out heresy based on independent statements pulled from their contexts.

Here is a classic case in point. These are the musings of a miserable man, the confessions of a confused cynic named Solomon. These words represent precisely how he felt at the time of writing and exactly what he said ("I said to myself . . . I said to myself"), but they are no more representative of truth to live by than any other borderline heresy found in a random sampling of any other similar section of Scripture.

For example, there are blatant lies that men and women spoke which are recorded in the Bible. Their words are accurately recorded, but surely we are not to claim and apply those lies as truths today simply because they have been preserved in Scripture. There are disobedient, sinful acts people did which are carefully and correctly stated in the inspired record. Again, it is ridiculous to think that all who read of such deeds should duplicate them in order to prove their confidence in the Scriptures. No, we may hold to an inspired text without being obligated to emulate every word and deed.

Solomon has unwisely and rashly stated heresy. The inspiration of Scripture guarantees that that is indeed what he wrote. But discernment from the complete body of scriptural truth restrains us from blindly believing the same thing. You see, cynicism mentally confuses us. It angers us emotionally. It numbs us spiritually. It leaves us scarred, bitter, disillusioned, and, for sure, feeling distant from God. That aptly describes Solomon at this phase of his journey.

HOPE BEYOND CYNICISM . . . SOME CONCLUDING THOUGHTS

Read again Solomon's concluding comments in this section:

> And I have seen that nothing is better than that man should be happy in his activities, for that is his lot. For who will bring him to see what will occur after him? (3:22).

I believe we are given here a very godly philosophy to follow regarding disadvantages, unfair treatment, and injustice. I think that God's counsel, through Solomon, is remarkably on target . . . I say remarkably, because the man had just finished spouting heresy!

Leaving verse 21 as a question mark hanging in our minds, Solomon comes back with a solution as his conclusion.

Does he say, "Try to understand your circumstances"? No. Does he say, "Compare your lot with another person's and see how much better yours is than his"? Hardly. Does he say, "Retaliate, resent, become bitter; you didn't get a fair shake"? No way. Does he say,

"Move to some lonely spot and grind out your twilight years in resentful silence"? Absolutely not.

How about this one? Does he say, "Get into a fantasy world; build a dream. Live there. Work here, but live there and you can make it" (like some kind of positive air that you blow into a bubble of idealism)? No, a thousand times, no! This is ragged-edge reality, remember.

Then what *does* he say? Namely this: "Reject self-pity. Reject revenge. Reject resentment. Reject retaliation. Find ways to discover advantages to your disadvantages."

> And I have seen that nothing is better than that man should be happy in his activities, for that is his lot. . . .

We usually can do very little to change our lot. We can only change our reaction to our lot. We cannot change our past, for example. I don't care how brilliant we are, our past stands in concrete. We cannot erase it. But we can learn today to see our past from God's perspective, and use the disadvantages of yesterday in our life—today and forever.

In fact, Solomon's closing sentence in this chapter states that as a very real possibility. "For who will bring him to see what will occur after him?" I'd like to think he is asking, "Who knows the impact it will have on others? Who will bring us to see what will occur after such a positive attitude of response?"

You and I constantly bump up against people submerged in self-pity. They are hopelessly lost in the swamp of life. And all they can tell you is how wrong this was, or how unfair she was, or how someone's promise was broken, or how that man walked away and left "me and the kids," or that guy broke up a partnership and "took me to the cleaners," and on and on and on.

But Solomon says, in effect, "I suggest to you that there's nothing better than that you look for an advantage and then dwell on it. Make that your life's message. Who knows what impact it will have?"

Three Questions

To help you replace stale cynicism with fresh hope, I want to ask three questions. I'm learning in my later years in life that it is better to ask questions than to make a lot of dogmatic statements. So, I'd like to ask these three dogmatic questions:

First: *What is your unjust disadvantage?* Think about it. I don't mean little petty irritations that happened this past week. What is a major unjust disadvantage in your life? Try to name at least one example from your life.

Second: *When do you plan to replace passive self-pity with active courage?* What I'm asking is that you stop the "woe-is-me" whine and start thinking in terms of "Here's my message, world!"

Before I go on to the third question, let me develop this one. Some time ago I did something that I seldom do . . . very, very seldom. I listened to an entire cassette recording. It was the tape of a speech delivered by a man named Tom Sullivan. He was addressing five thousand men and women in Dallas, as he spoke to the prestigious Million Dollar Round Table of the insurance companies around the world. What a great talk he delivered!

You may have seen Sullivan on the "Good Morning, America" program; he's one of their frequent guests. He's also done guest television appearances on "M-A-S-H" and "Fame." He was in the film *Airport '77*. He's a world-class athlete—with two national championship records in wrestling. He was on the 1958 Olympic wrestling team. He earned a degree at Harvard in clinical psychology. He's a musician. He's an author. He's a sports enthusiast. He runs six miles a day on the beach. He swims. He skydives . . . and has thirty-seven jumps to his credit.

I should also tell you that Tom Sullivan is blind. His is the life that was portrayed so graphically in the film *If You Could See What I Hear*. Amazing man!

Five thousand successful insurance people were on the edge of their seats—applauding, enjoying, laughing, and learning—as they listened to a man who couldn't even see the podium in front of him, to say nothing of seeing the smiles on their faces.

He had one major point in his talk: "You've got a disadvantage? Take advantage of it! People don't buy similarity. They buy differences." (That's a great line!)

That disadvantage is what makes you distinct and different. The similarities are no big deal. They only mean you're like everybody else. He tells about the first time he realized he was blind. He was eight years old (that's what I call parents doing the right job).

He was in his backyard, and heard a baseball game going on next door. He heard the crack of the bat as it hit the ball. New sound. He then heard the thud of it as it hit the glove. Another new sound.

He listened and thought, "They're playing a game." He later learned it was called baseball.

So he got a rock and a stick and he taught himself how to bat a ball. He didn't know where to hit it, so he put a little transistor radio up on a tree stump. He walked several paces back and hit the rock toward the radio. He got to where he could knock that transistor radio off every time.

Shortly thereafter he told his dad, "I want to play baseball."

Dad said, "Oh, really? Well, uh, . . . which position would you like to play?"

"Oh, I want to be a pitcher."

"Uh, yeah . . . sure, Son. Right!"

So the dad talked to the guy who managed the Little League club in his neighborhood and got Tom on the team. The boy who could not see became the pitcher. He had a guy stand by him to catch the ball when the catcher threw it back.

Tom asked the crowd, "Can you picture this little, frightened nine-year-old boy at the plate, ready to have the ball thrown at him by a blind kid on the mound?" After he knocked out several boys, he decided to get out of baseball, which probably pleased his opponents greatly . . . and he took up wrestling.

He had the ability to pop his glass eyes out on occasion, so he claims he won a few of his wrestling records that way. What a sense of humor! It's an amazing story . . . the story of a man who replaced cynical self-pity with incredible courage. Let me ask you again—when do you plan to replace self-pity with that kind of courage?

"I've determined that my disadvantage in life is blindness," says Tom Sullivan. "I will therefore become, as a blind person, all that I can possibly be. That will become my distinctive message!"[1]

It's time for some of you to hear this. Cynicism is eating your lunch. You've been sinking in the quicksand of self-pity long enough. You're almost drowning and you're sucking other people under with you. If that's the case, you need to take this challenge personally.

Third: *Have you ever considered the impact your distinctive message would have on the world around you?* My friend, if you could ever get above your disadvantage long enough to see how God could use you to impact the lives of others who are victims of their disadvantage, it would blow your mind.

When I talk about the struggles I had with insecurity as a child, I'm amazed how many insecure people I minister to. When I talk about going beyond the difficulty of being the one of three children in a family who (at least in my estimation) did not have much loving encouragement to reach my full potential—that touches and encourages people who are going through the same experience.

When I talk about how I overcame my battle with stuttering and the fear of speaking in public, I find that really puts hope into others who struggle with stuttering. When I talk about a few of the minor injustices that have occurred in my life (minor by comparison to people like Tom Sullivan), it's remarkable how it opens doors of hope in people's lives.

You have been set on this earth as a unique jewel, as a gem that has certain sparkling possibilities when the light of the Son hits them. As you glisten and gleam, you encourage, enlighten, and strengthen those who are lost in the gloom of their personal swamp. Even though you may feel insignificant and not that gifted, God can use you!

During the fourth century there was an Asiatic monk who spent most of his life in a remote community of prayer, studying and raising vegetables for the cloister kitchen. When he was not tending his garden spot, he was happily fulfilling his vocation of study and prayer.

Then one day this monk, whose name was Telemachus, felt the Lord was leading him to go to Rome, the political center of the world—the busiest, wealthiest, biggest city in the world. Telemachus wondered why he was being drawn to Rome. He didn't fit Rome. He fit this little, quiet place, this cloistered community, this sheltered little garden where his convictions were deepening and his faith in God was strong. But he couldn't fight God's direction. So he left.

By and by, he found his way to the busy streets of Rome, and he was stunned by what he saw. The people were preoccupied. They were angry. They were violent, in fact. And on one occasion the bewildered little monk was swept up in the group, pushed along by the crowd. Finally he wound up in a place he didn't even know existed—the coliseum—where animalistic gladiators fought and killed one another for little reason other than the amusement of the thousands that gathered in Rome's public stadium.

He stared in disbelief as one gladiator after another stood before the emperor and said, "We who are about to die salute thee." He put his hands to his ears when he heard the clashing of swords and shields, as one man after another fought to his death.

He couldn't stand it any longer. But what in the world could he do? He was nothing! Still, he ran and jumped up on top of the perimeter wall and cried, "In the name of Christ, forbear!" He could not bear this senseless killing. "Stop this now!"

No one listened. They kept applauding the fight as it went on. Another man fell. Finally, unable to contain himself, he jumped down onto the sandy floor of the arena. What a comic figure he must have appeared to be—of slight build, a small man in a monk's habit, dashing back and forth between muscular, brutal fighters. Again, he shouted, "In the name of Christ, forbear!"

The crowd looked at him and sneered, and one of the gladiators, with his shield, bumped him aside and went after his opponent. Finally, he became an irritation to the crowd as well as the gladiators. Someone in the stands yelled, "Run him through! Kill him!"

The same gladiator that had pushed him aside with his shield came down against his chest and opened his stomach with one flash of the sword. As he slumped to his knees, the little monk gasped once more, "In the name of Christ . . . forbear!"

> Then a strange thing occurred. As the two gladiators and the crowd focused on the still form on the suddenly crimson sand, the arena grew deathly quiet. In the silence, someone in the top tier got up and walked out. Another followed. All over the arena, spectators began to leave, until the huge stadium was emptied.
>
> There were other forces at work, of course, but that innocent figure lying in the pool of blood crystalized the opposition, and that was the last gladiatorial contest in the Roman Coliseum. Never again did men kill each other for the crowd's entertainment in the Roman arena.[2]

Am I writing to a Telemachus today? Or maybe a Tom Sullivan? If so, I ask you again: Can you imagine the impact you could have on the world if you counteracted your cynicism and self-pity by the power of Jesus Christ? Can you imagine the lives you could reach and strengthen simply by being all you can be?

What is your story? Everybody has a story. Sure, it's got some injustice in it. You think it's the thing that has caused you to become a failure? No, that is not true. Your attitude, perhaps, but not your struggle. The message of this chapter is simply this: Disadvantages need not disqualify. You can become significantly used by God if you refuse to let your disadvantages turn you into a cynic.

Allow me to state my feeling in this prayer:

It's not often, Father, that we make such a statement, but today we thank You for the injustices that have crippled us and broken us and crushed us. We want to express our appreciation for the things that have brought us to the place of submission. The only way we can look is up.

We express our gratitude for the things You have taught us through blindness and loss and paralysis; for growth through broken dreams, dissolved partnerships, illness, and sadness; for the character development through insecurity, failure, and even divorce. We see the storm, but we are beginning to see You beyond the storm. How essential is our attitude!

Thank you especially for helping us conquer our cynicism.

I pray for those in these and a hundred other categories, that we may be able to go beyond them and find in Jesus Christ the strength to go on, especially for those who, only a few moments ago, had just about decided to give up. I pray that they will rather give it all to You in full surrender.

In the strong name of Jesus Christ, the Conqueror, I pray, Amen.

8

THE LONELY WHINE
OF THE TOP DOG

Journal Entry

*Next I observed all the oppression and
sadness throughout the earth—the tears of
the oppressed, and no one helping them,
while on the side of their oppressors were
powerful allies. So I felt that the dead
were better off than the living. And
most fortunate of all are those who
have never been born, and have never
seen all the evil and crime throughout
the earth.*

*Then I observed that the basic motive
for success is the driving force of envy and
jealousy! But this, too, is foolishness,
chasing the mind. . . .*

*I also observed the case of a man who
is quite alone, without a son or brother,
yet he works hard to keep gaining more
riches, and to whom will he leave it all?
And why is he giving up so much now?
It is all so pointless and depressing.*

*I*f I were to ask you to think of someone who is lonely, chances are good you would not choose someone who is busy. It is also doubtful that you'd select someone in a top-management position, the chief executive officer in a growing corporation, or the leading, well-paid salesperson in an aggressive, competitive organization. "Not them!" we think. "They're successful. They're fulfilled. They've made big bucks. They've got it made. Furthermore, with all those people around, they haven't the *time* to be lonely!"

Don't bet on it. More often than not, those who find themselves approaching the top of the steep ladder of financial success have few friends (if any). They struggle to keep peace at home. Furthermore, they often live on the precipice of disillusionment—sometimes despair.

Loneliness is the plague of the loner . . . and, by and large, "top dogs" are loners. Either by design or by default, most executives operate in a very private world where companionship and happiness elude them. Contentment and inner tranquility are seldom found in the penthouse. Instead, there is boredom and stark feelings of emptiness. As Thoreau states so well, these are people who "lead lives of quiet desperation."

Solomon's favorite term, which he constantly repeats as he admits his frustration, is *vanity*. Again and again he exclaims, "All is vanity!" Even though he, the king of the land, had all the money, brains, resources, and time to acquire or experience the zenith life could offer, he kept returning to that monotonous heavy sigh, "All is vanity." Although busy, rich, powerful, and famous, Solomon was the personification of boredom and loneliness. I remind you, the man pulls no punches.

In our examination of his writing, we have come to a journal entry that addresses the emptiness of those who make it to the top. If you are there, chances are good you'll find yourself nodding in agreement. If you are en route, take special notice that such a destination isn't all it's cracked up to be. Those who envy the ones who make it to the top don't stop to think of the price paid to get there. The top dog is usually a lonely, frustrated individual. If you listen closely, you can almost hear a whine from his lips.

> Then I looked again at all the injustice that goes on in this world. The oppressed were crying, and no one would help them. No one

would help them, because their oppressors had power on their side. I envy those who are dead and gone; they are better off than those who are still alive. But better off than either are those who have never been born, who have never seen the injustice that goes on in this world.

I have also learned why people work so hard to succeed: it is because they envy the things their neighbors have. But it is useless. It is like chasing the wind. They say that a man would be a fool to fold his hands and let himself starve to death. Maybe so, but it is better to have only a little, with peace of mind, than be busy all the time with both hands, trying to catch the wind.

I have noticed something else in life that is useless. Here is a man who lives alone. He has no son, no brother, yet he is always working, never satisfied with the wealth he has. For whom is he working so hard and denying himself any pleasure? This is useless, too—and a miserable way to live (4:1–8, TEV).

What Ought to Be Isn't What Is

Some things ought to be, but they never will be—like these words from Solomon's ancient journal, for example. These statements *ought* to be required reading at Harvard and Stanford business schools, but they never will be.

Peter Drucker's 839-page volume entitled *Management* ought to quote Solomon's words so every reader would have the benefit of hearing divine counsel alongside human advice regarding success, but that never will be.

I'd also like to see Ecclesiastes 4:1–8 printed just below the heading of every issue of *The Wall Street Journal*, right up there at the top, so that businessmen and career women around the world, upon picking up that newspaper, would read Solomon's wisdom first. But that never will be.

If I had my way, I would see to it that every young executive, every entrepreneur, every professional man or woman climbing the corporate ladder of success, hoping to fulfill life-long dreams, would receive a postcard immediately following New Year's Day with this passage of Scripture printed on it—just as a reminder. That *ought* to occur annually, but it won't.

Here's another idea—you know how every one of the cigarette ads includes a warning? It says, "The surgeon general has determined that cigarette smoking is dangerous to your health." I wish a similar warning could appear at the bottom of every diploma of every person who graduates with a degree in business or finance. I suggest that it read: "Warning! The God of heaven has determined that success can be lethal." That kind of warning *ought* to be standard procedure, but it never will be.

And since none of these things ever will occur, we're left to our own devices, assumptions, and observations. Our options are reduced to listening to the counsel of the world's system, watching our peers, observing our parents, taking note of those so-called "success models," and convincing ourselves that the dream is real. But it is not. Let me level with you, it is high-powered hype—a bold-faced lie!

IDENTIFYING THE VICTIM

Solomon doesn't have in mind the man who barely ekes out a living, who is satisfied with simplicity, and who is not too worried about going beyond where he is—just willing to get along. That's not the person in the focus of Solomon's sights. No, not on your life!

The words from this section of his journal are directed to the senior executives, the high rollers, the top ranking in the military, the shakers and the movers . . . or to use some of today's slang, the "big cheeses." I often refer to them as the "top dogs." Those are the ones who look successful and appear to have it made. But the truth is they don't, even though most of them hide the truth rather well. They may appear to be victors, but, more often than not, they are victims.

Keep in mind that Solomon is a king. He's not looking from the ground up. His vantage point is from the top. And he's looking around at others in those top positions. He certainly ought to know what it's like! His world is a world of elegance, opulence, and lavish affluence. We are beginning to realize that his inability to find satisfaction in that realm is the major subject of his journal.

So he replaces the rose-colored glasses of laid-back idealism with crystal-clear glasses of ragged-edge realism as he informs his readers of the truth. In today's world, he writes to physicians whose practice is growing and expanding. He writes to attorneys whose clients and personal finances are increasing. He is writing to salespeople who are cleaning up financially. He's talking to people who own their own prosperous businesses . . . to entrepreneurs . . . to presidents and would-be heads of corporations. He's saying, "Let me tell you how it *really* is. Let me urge you to face the truth regarding where all this is leading."

A Realistic Appraisal

In this realistic view—which, by the way, is a very empirical thing—all mysticism is removed. The New American Standard Version renders verse 1, "I looked again," and verse 4, "I have seen." *Solomon is looking around.* He's not dreaming up something from a classroom. This isn't theoretical academia. This isn't jargon from the ivy-covered halls of some university. This is real-life stuff, right from the office where you work, or from that privileged position where you sit—or hope to sit someday.

As he looks around, he observes several categories of life. Three, as a matter of fact—not one of which is satisfying. The first is enough to stop any of us in our tracks.

Oppressive Conditions

> Then I looked again at all the acts of oppression which were being done under the sun (4:1).

Here once again Solomon uses the phrase—"under the sun." It's a phrase that emphasizes the horizontal dimension of life . . . existence *under* the sun, not above it.

Solomon says, in effect, "I looked all around my world. I observed the way people were being treated in Jerusalem. I looked beyond the city and observed my whole nation as well. I saw in all those places many, many people who were being controlled by a dominant few. I witnessed many caught in the grip of oppression."

What he really sees is a body of people who have most of the money, the influence, the power . . . and therefore the control of others. And what Solomon saw was anything but pleasant. Look carefully at the rest of verse 1:

> And behold I saw the tears of the oppressed and that they had no one to comfort them; and on the side of their oppressors was power, but they had no one to comfort them.

It's a very vivid scene.

Remember the old Negro spiritual of yesteryear? It began, "Nobody knows de trouble I seen. Nobody knows but Jesus." When I hear those words, I can feel the tears, the pain, the inescapable sadness of the one who wrote them.

Likewise, Solomon says, "As I look around and see the tears and witness oppression, it's heartbreaking. I am caught up in despair." His reaction to what he observes is equally vivid:

> So I congratulated the dead who are already dead more than the living who are still living (v. 2).

As he looked upon those who had already died, he thought, "How fortunate you are to be gone from this earth, rather than to still be living under this oppression! In fact, better than both living and dead is the one who has never even been born!"

It's a strange moment in Scripture when the unborn are addressed.

> But better off than both of them is the one who has never existed, who has never seen the evil activity that is done under the sun (v. 3).

I'm sure you've thought about that at times: those of you who are married and have no children; those of you who have gone through the experience of losing your only child and now witness the difficult times in which we live. On occasion, I'm sure you must think that maybe it is better your offspring don't have to endure a society as insane as ours.

It suddenly occurs to me that suicide probably never came to Solomon's mind. It was then considered such a heinous sin (an alien concept in the mind of the Jews) that he wouldn't even offer it as a way out. But that's certainly not true in our day.

In my travels some time ago, I met a wonderful, well-educated Christian woman. She not only has her nursing degree, but has gone on to even higher academic achievements. She now has the vision to cultivate hospices in these United States to help those who are dying. She wants very much for us to be a model of hands-on compassion as a nation—even beyond what Europeans are doing—for those who are terminally ill and find themselves in need of a place where they can be cared for, yet, at the same time, be surrounded by family love.

She said, "You know, Chuck, while I was completing my research, I came across a group of people who approached terminal illness from a different slant. I attended one of their meetings, which happened to be held at a church in San Francisco. If you can believe it, it was a group that met to dialogue at length about ways to take one's own life. They discussed various methods of suicide, but especially the method of ingesting dosages of medication that affect your body so severely that you die suddenly and quietly."

She told me that they even have a book on the subject, and she let me borrow it. It's called *Let Me Die Before I Wake*. It is on what is called "self-deliverance" for the dying . . . over one hundred pages explaining how to take one's own life. I was jolted again with a reminder that in our times there is no longer a resistance against suicide. It is seriously considered an intelligent escape from our pain. Suicide, for many, is a real option.

Solomon says, "Those who have never been born are better off than those who are now living, as well as those who have gone on ahead." He then continues his appraisal of the world around him, turning from oppressive conditions to a second observation.

Competitive Determination

> And I have seen that every labor and every skill which is done is the result of rivalry between a man and his neighbor. This too is vanity and striving after wind (v. 4).

That's an interesting observation. This perceptive man is saying, "As I look at the act of business—buying and selling—as I watch people accomplishing their goals, as I look at the acceleration of success running its course from the bottom to the top, I observe a severe rivalry, a competitive determination, a 'dog-eat-dog' mentality."

He's not referring to healthy competition between independent corporations. He's not putting down a system of free enterprise that's necessary in business and helps keep a nation strong and great. He's talking about one-on-one rivalry—fighting and devouring, clawing and pushing at one another. He's describing the outworking of carnal, savage-level selfishness.

You see, he's got individuals in mind more than large businesses. In other words, he says, "I have seen such a determined and aggressive competition between individuals . . . they fight against one another and, if necessary, assault each other!" It's a maddening, vicious craze to outdo and outsell and outshine the other guy at any cost.

You may have little difficulty identifying with that. You may even see yourself portrayed in this scene. If so, then you're not the type that can easily take second place. You're not comfortable until you've captured that top position. You're making your moves and you're determined.

Several months ago I had occasion to look into the face of a frustrated, anxious forty-seven-year-old man. His past life was strewn with the litter of the consequences of high-pressured competition. In the process of becoming "successful," his relationship with his wife and children had completely eroded. They were like a group of strangers living under the same roof (his precise words), passing by each other like ships in the night. It must have been a hell-on-earth existence.

First, there was a son who would no longer speak to him. Next, a younger daughter had said to him rather bluntly, "I don't like being with you anymore, Dad." And his wife was afraid of him. Now keep in mind, he had made it to the top of his profession—six-figure salary, numerous perks, influential position, country-club membership, luxurious company car, private jet . . . the whole package. He had everything—or so it seemed. But he had recently been caught stealing from his company—*over $15,000*. The company chose not to indict him and take him to court on embezzlement charges. Instead, he promised to pay the money back, even though he was immediately dismissed from the organization. He had lost his job, lost his reputation, lost the one thing that gave him identity, the only thing he had been trained to do. And don't forget, his family was happier when he wasn't around.

He had been working half days on Sundays, so that by the time they caught up with him he was working six and a half days a week. He admitted to me, "Had I continued, it would have been a solid seven days a week with at least twelve to fourteen hours a day. I was on my way. Your classic, driven workaholic."

As he looked at me, tears were streaming down his face. He sobbed, "How do I build back a home? How do I relate to a son or daughter who doesn't respect me and won't talk to me anymore? How do I go back and do it over?" Mentally, he's a very sick man. I was watching his personality disintegrate before my very eyes. It was frightening. He paced back and forth as we talked. A rather steady stream of profanity flowed from his tongue. One time, he reached up and literally swung in the doorway and hung there, full of anxiety, crying like a baby. What a pathetic sight! He had served a cruel taskmaster—success at any price. Now he was like a leopard cornered in a cage . . . dangerously near a complete breakdown.

I thought to myself, *There stands a product of "the system."* He confessed, "I bought into it all the way down to the soles of my shoes, but I couldn't handle it."

Now some would swing the pendulum to the opposite extreme and suggest, "Well, the best answer to that is to drop out. Just give up. You know, drift. Become indifferent and complacent. Live off the land." Which is another way of saying, "Live off people who are working and let *them* pay your way through."

But according to Solomon, that's not the answer, either. He calls that person a fool.

> The fool folds his hands and consumes his own flesh (v. 5).

No, dropping out of responsible living isn't the solution. A balance is what Solomon is pushing for. See the healthy balance in the words that follow?

> One hand full of rest [that's beautiful in the Hebrew; it says "quiet-ness"—one hand full of quietness] is better than two fists full of labor . . . (v. 6).

That would be a pretty good thing to write on the visor of your car, where you could look at it every morning on the way to work or print on the mirror in your bathroom, where you get ready to face the day.

Did you hear his counsel? One hand full of contentment and respon-sible living is better than two fists clawing, scraping, striving, pushing, pulling their way to the top.

For a moment, let's go back to another book Solomon wrote, the Proverbs. Tucked away in chapter 15 is more counsel worth some serious thought. First, Proverbs 15:16:

> Better is a little with the fear of the Lord, than great treasure and turmoil with it.

Isn't that the truth! Now look at the next verse. These are compara-tive proverbs—"better than, better than."

Better is a dish of vegetables where love is, than a fattened ox and hatred with it (v. 17).

In other words, better is a little bowl of vegetable soup, served at a table where there's a lot of love, than a big, thick prime rib shoved in front of you by somebody who can't stand having you around!

Look next at chapter 16, verse 8, another comparative proverb.

Better is a little with righteousness than great income with injustice.

Read that again. Let it sink in! In our competitive world of more, more, more, we tend to forget the profound wisdom of these words. No amount of money is worth the consequences of injustice. As you recall, we dealt with that in chapter 7 of this book. No income—I don't care how lucrative—is sufficient to wash away a guilty conscience. On the other hand, a little when it is accompanied with righteousness is much better.

But the push for success, no matter the compromise, leads to a terrible crisis. Disillusionment follows. As competition intensifies, we push for more . . . we start burning the candle at both ends, and we finally run out of candle. And instead of stopping, instead of evaluating, we simply run faster and farther without facing the music. We refuse to ask where it's all heading . . . or what the ultimate result of this maddening pursuit will be. And our loneliness intensifies!

And then comes what our generation has termed the "mid-life crisis." This has been described as a time of intense personal evaluation, when frightening and disturbing thoughts surge through the mind. We start questioning who we are and why we're here and why everything matters so much. It is a period of self-doubt and disenchantment with everything . . . everything familiar and stable. The mind plays tricks on us. We entertain terrifying thoughts that can't be admitted or revealed even to those closest to us. And, I repeat, our loneliness borders the unbearable.

There are enemies that fight within us during such mid-life crises. One is the body. The guy they called "Joe College" just a few years ago is now growing older. Physical stamina decreases. And before long, words assume new meaning to "ol' Joe." As one comic puts it, he gets winded on escalators! The Rolling Stones are in ol' Joe's gallbladder. When he takes a business trip, the flight attendant now offers him coffee, tea, or Milk of Magnesia. Age begins to show on Joe.

Maybe you'll identify with the way one man described it: "The cells in his face then pack up and run south for the winter, leaving a shocked and depressed Joe standing two inches from the mirror in disbelief."

Another enemy is the man's work. It's no longer satisfying. It's now demanding. It's a slavery, in fact. It's disillusioning, and he hates it. But he can't get out of it because he's got to keep paying the freight. And so the home becomes a part of the rivalry. And finally the whole thing goes up in smoke. Why? Because enough is never enough.

That's why Solomon says, "Better is a little . . . better is a hand full of contentment, love, and tranquility than two fists that keep fighting."

Personal Disillusionment

There's a third scene that Solomon observes. Along with oppressive conditions and competitive determination, he also saw personal disillusionment. Like the other two, it's a scene that is characterized by awful emptiness. He says so in his next statement: "I looked again at vanity" (4:7).

He saw a personification of vanity in this "under the sun" observation. In modern terms, we would say that he saw emptiness in three-piece suits . . . he saw brokenness and disillusionment across the face of the assertive career woman . . . he saw professional people with that tired-blood look, even though they possessed a pile of dough . . . he saw "successful" men absolutely bored in their slavery to success.

Specifically, in this case, Solomon saw a "certain man."

> There was a certain man without a dependent, having neither a son nor a brother, yet there was no end to all his labor. Indeed, his eyes were not satisfied with riches and he never asked, "And for whom am I laboring and depriving myself of pleasure?" This too is vanity and it is a grievous task (v. 8).

Did you notice something? In the first view Solomon has of this old earth, there are *many* people—many oppressed and many doing the oppressing. In the second scene, there are *two* people—one against the other in competitive rivalry. But in this third scene, there's only *one*—"a certain man." How significant! You see, as you climb higher on this ladder of so-called "success," you get increasingly lonely . . . you have fewer friends . . . fewer and fewer personal contacts . . . less and less accountability. While in the process of acquiring more stuff, you become less involved with in-depth friendships. So it is with the lonely executive.

I had a colonel in the military stop me shortly after I shared some of these ideas in a talk several months ago. With great intensity he said, "The next time you talk about loneliness at the top, don't forget the military officer. You're describing my life as a full-bird colonel." Once again we hear the whine of a top dog crying for lasting satisfaction, for true companionship, because so little of that accompanies the leader the nearer he or she gets to the top.

Now let's take a closer look at that "certain man" Solomon tells us about. Here's a guy who is all alone "having neither a son nor a brother." One might assume that his thoughts would go something like this: "Since I don't have a lot of family to worry about, I'm going to enjoy myself. I've got this great position and I'm making more money than ever, so I'm going to lie back and take that hand full of quietness along with this fist full of work and balance the two. I'll say, 'Enough *is* enough.' " Does he say that? Not on your life! According to Solomon's observation "there was no end to all his labor." See, the tragic truth finally comes out; he doesn't know how to quit. He *can't* slow down.

> His eyes were not satisfied with riches and he never asked, "And for whom am I laboring and depriving myself of pleasure?" (v. 8).

Isn't that something! This executive-type is such a driver that he isn't stopping and asking the obvious, such as "Why isn't this satisfying?" and "What's the outcome?" and "Why am I knocking myself out and enjoying so few pleasures?" Solomon exclaims: "This too is meaningless—a miserable business" (v. 8, NIV).

A PENETRATING ANALYSIS

Face it—the dream of the great society is that we work, work, work; fight, fight, fight; earn, earn, earn; sell, sell, sell; labor, labor, labor to get more, more, more! So is life at the top. It's crazy, but there's something so ego-satisfying about being up there. It offers all of those perks that we didn't have down below. And by climbing into that cage at the top, we think we'll then personify our long-awaited dream: "I'm now in laid-back city . . . relax . . . rejoice. I have finally arrived!"

Stop and think about some of those super-duper perks: your own parking spot . . . your own bathroom attached to your office . . . a little thicker pad beneath your carpet . . . wood paneling around the room . . . a chair you can lean *way* back in . . . maybe a sofa (I mean, just think of a sofa in light of eternity!) . . . drapes—big window, a broad panoramic view of the landscape. Let's throw in your own personal valet . . . a company car . . . several credit cards . . . a boat to pilot around a harbor twice a year . . . tax write-offs . . . and that extra special ego satisfaction that sweeps over you when people call you "president" or "doctor" or "chairman."

Solomon says, "Face it, it won't satisfy." Will you hear him? Will you be honest enough to pause in the middle of the ladder and think about stuff others refuse to think about? Hang on right there. Hang onto that rung and ask, "What do I gain by fighting to the next one?" Don't resume climbing until you can answer this: "If I'm not satisfied *here*, why do I think I'll be satisfied *there?*"

AN ANCIENT YET RELEVANT STORY

Jesus had a certain special way of telling stories like no one else who has ever lived. One particular story, found in the twelfth chapter of Luke, revolves around an independent-thinking, very capable entre-preneur. Actually, the story unfolds as a dialogue between Jesus and a guy who feels he's getting ripped off.

> And someone in the crowd said to Him, "Teacher, tell my brother to divide the family inheritance with me" (v. 13).

Now how's that for a rather practical place to begin? "The folks have died. My brother is the executor of the estate and he's taken it all, or most of it. Tell him to divide it with me." Jesus responds, not to the actual statement, but to the motive behind it:

> "Man, who appointed Me a judge or arbiter over you?" And He said to them, "Beware, and be on your guard against every form of greed . . . ." (vv. 14–15).

Not a bad warning to appear on the bottom of a diploma. Not a bad piece to mail annually to success-driven people.

> "Beware, and be on your guard against every form of greed; for not even when one has an abundance does his life consist of his possessions" (v. 15).

And He then told a story, a parable, that began: "The land of a certain rich man was very productive" (v. 16). Now hold it! If you're a farmer, you'll understand and identify with the story. But you may be a white-collar professional. So let's paraphrase it this way: "The practice of a certain physician was increasing" or "The clients of a certain attorney were growing in number" or "The quota of a certain salesman was higher than ever before" or "The dreams of a certain entrepreneur were bigger, and more of his creative ideas were finding completion. The money was rolling in!" That's the scene.

Now the man in Jesus' story talks to himself. Nobody else is around. He's alone at the top, so the only guy to talk to is himself. The problem is, he doesn't give himself the right answers. He asks: "What shall I do, since I have no place to store my crops?" (v. 17). (We could add, "And the government is gonna eat my lunch!" to complete the idea.) He needs to do something with his profit.

"What am I gonna do about my taxes? What am I gonna do about my prosperity? What am I gonna do about my enlarged income? I've earned a bundle this year, and if I get more, I'll move into a higher percentage bracket. What am I gonna do?"

Now the answer:

> "This is what I will do: I will tear down my barns and build larger ones, and there I will store all my grain and my goods" (v. 18).

Sound familiar? "I'll just plow it back into the company!" I call that as familiar as the morning paper. "I'll just build it bigger. We'll add another building. We'll open another office in the suburbs. We'll go public. We'll make this thing one of the largest going." The implication is clear: " . . . because that's going to bring me the satisfaction I've been looking for."

It doesn't right now, you understand; but he keeps on hoping . . . he keeps enlarging . . . keeps feeding the ego. "Why, I've got a winner here! There's a market for it." Or the common rationalization,

"This'll meet needs. My family will be happier because they'll have more things to enjoy. So naturally, I'll tear down all those things and build more and more. I'll store more and more so I can enjoy(?) more and more." But then he takes one giant step too far . . . without asking, "May I?"

> "And I will say to my soul. 'Soul, you have many goods laid up for many years to come; take your ease, eat, drink, and be merry'" (v. 19).

"All these physical things will satisfy all my deep, soul-level needs, right?" *Wrong!* Nothing physical touches the soul. Nothing external satisfies our deepest inner needs. Remember that! The soul belongs to God. He alone can satisfy us in that realm.

The soul possesses an inescapable God-shaped vacuum. And not until He invades and fills it can we be at peace within—which is another way of saying, "If God isn't in first place, you can't handle success." If God fills your soul, if God fills your mind, if God satisfies your spirit, there is no problem whatsoever with prosperity. You've got it all put together. Your priorities will be right, and you will know how to handle your life so you can impact the maximum number of people. If He prospers you, if He entrusts you with material success and you continue walking with Him, God can use you mightily in His plan. Furthermore, if you lose it all, He can give you what it takes to handle the loss and start all over again.

This chapter isn't designed to be an attack on prosperity. It isn't saying, "Everyone take a vow of poverty. Stand with your arm raised and repeat after me: 'I swear to get out of this successful business' or 'I promise never to make a profit.'" It is, rather, a plea—a strong warning against losing a grip on right priorities.

Many of those who become successful, wealthy, and famous have a great struggle handling all that. Some are able to keep a clear perspective, but it's tough. It's like putting a camel through the eye of a needle. Remember Jesus' words? How seldom do we find the successful genuinely humble!

The man in this story told himself to "eat, drink, and be merry." He could eat and he could drink, but he couldn't be merry, because being truly happy is a gift from God. And all of a sudden an angel steps up beside this man—right into his office where he's talking to himself, leaning back in that leather chair. It is the death angel who appears with his lips pursed, saying:

"You fool! This very night your soul is required of you; and now who will own what you have prepared?" (v. 20).

Great question! Every person pursuing success owes it to himself to ask that question. Jesus adds:

"So is the man who lays up treasure for himself, and is not rich toward God" (v. 21).

Two Haunting Questions

When you boil all these words down to the bare essentials, two questions emerge: First, *are you telling yourself the truth about possessions?* Do you know what the truth will do? It will make you free. You can count on the truth to do that. So, are you telling yourself the truth about possessions?

Second, *are you hearing God's warning about priorities?* Just where is God in your business or your profession? As you climb that ladder, at which rung do you plan to meet Him and come to terms with eternal things? Are you hearing God's warning about priorities?

It might help to remember Yussif, the Terrible Turk! Yussif was the three-hundred-and-fifty-pound wrestling champion in Europe a little over two generations ago. After he won the European championship, he sailed to the United States to beat our champ, whose name was Strangler Lewis—a little guy,. by comparison, who weighed just a shade over two hundred pounds.

Although he wasn't huge, Strangler had a simple plan for defeating his opponents. It had never failed to work. He'd put that massive arm of his around the neck of his opponent. He'd pump up that bicep and cut the oxygen off, right up there near the Adam's apple. Many an opponent had passed out in the ring with Strangler Lewis.

The problem he had when it came to fighting the Turk was that the Europeon giant didn't have a neck! His body just went from his head to those massive shoulders. Lewis could never get the hold, so it wasn't long before Yussif flipped Lewis down on the mat and pinned him. After winning the championship, the Turk demanded all five thousand dollars in gold. After he wrapped the championship belt around his vast middle, he stuffed the gold into the belt and boarded the next ship back to Europe. He was now the possessor of

America's glory and gold. He had won it all . . . all except immortality.

He set sail on the *SS Bourgogne*. Halfway across the Atlantic, a storm struck and the ship began to sink. Yussif went over the side with his gold still strapped around his body. The added weight was too much for the Turk, and he sank like an iron anvil before they could get to him with the lifeboats. He was never seen again.

"What a fool!" you think. I mean, he should've had a lot more class than that! Successful people don't wear their gold! But you know where yours is, don't you? You've got it stashed away. Whenever you need it, you can cash it in. Right?

But the bottom line is this. Gold won't get you into glory! It isn't going to help you. The whole point of Jesus' parable can be stated in a few words: You're not really ready to live until you're ready to die. If you aren't absolutely certain that heaven is your ultimate destination, then it is very doubtful you'll be able to handle earth's pressures.

Remember, some things ought to be, but they never will be. I mentioned this at the beginning of the chapter. Let me mention a couple of other "ought tos" now that we've thought about the "top dog." Possessions *ought* to satisfy, but they never will. Priorities *ought* to come automatically to smart people, but they don't. That's why we need God's Book, the Bible. No other book except that one keeps bringing us back to the truth concerning possessions. No other book keeps bringing us back to the basics concerning priorities.

A FINAL WORD

You say your problem is not your income. Well, Solomon's words are addressed just as much to those who struggle to make ends meet as to those "top dogs" who have got it made financially. As a matter of fact, there are just as many envious people fighting their way up (maybe more!) as there are top dogs whining in the penthouse of success. You can be just as greedy and lonely on your way up as those already at the top.

I ask you again, are you telling yourself the truth about possessions? Are you hearing God's warning about priorities? If you haven't been doing that, do it now.

It's quite disillusioning to work your way up and become "king of the hill" or "top of the heap," the mogul of the residential district where you live or the pacesetter of your profession, . . . only to have it crumble before you—but it can happen. The good news is this: It doesn't have to!

Sure you're lonely! Chances are good you got yourself into your predicament. To put it simply, you forgot to bring God along with you. By His grace, He hasn't written you off. He hasn't let you die. But you will someday. No amount of money will allow you to escape that.

Jesus, the Authority on life—and life after death—once said, "But seek first His kingdom and His righteousness; and all these things shall be added to you" (Matt. 6:33). All those other "things" will fall into the right perspective if Christ has first place in your life.

Has there ever been a time in your life when you've said, "Jesus Christ, You be the King. You take first place. I invite You to take charge. You be the One who gives me counsel when I ask questions. Jesus Christ, You died for me. You have been raised from the dead. I lay my life before You—all the mess that I've made of it, all the oppression, all the competition, all the disillusionment of it. Take me. Save me. I come just as I am. As a sinner, I need Your forgiveness, Your life."

If not—if you've never prayed such a prayer—do so now. Take the gift of eternal life which He offers you. Turn to Him in faith. Don't wait! This decision, my "top dog" friend, deserves top priority. I know of nothing else that will silence a lonely whine.

9

ONE PLUS ONE EQUALS SURVIVAL

Journal Entry

Two can accomplish more than twice as much as one, for the results can be much better. If one falls, the other pulls him up; but if a man falls when he is alone, he's in trouble.

Also, on a cold night, two under the same blanket gain warmth from each other, but how can one be warm alone? And one standing alone can be attacked and defeated, but two can stand back-to-back and conquer; three is even better, for a triple-braided cord is not easily broken.

A bewildered foreign-exchange student once blurted out in my presence: "Americans are loners." I was, at first, defensive. His evaluation seemed unduly harsh. But since the time I heard the young man make that statement, I have come to the conclusion that he is correct. There are some wonderful exceptions, but they are only that—exceptions rather than the rule.

Ralph Keys, author of *We the Lonely People*, says that above all else we Americans value mobility, convenience, and privacy. "Of these," he adds, "privacy is our most cherished value." Think before you disagree.

It may surprise you to know that this cherished privacy which means so much to us here in America is relatively modern. Historian Jacob Burchhardt says that " . . . before the Renaissance, Western man was barely aware of himself as an individual. Mostly he drew his identity from membership in groups—family, tribe, church, guild." And according to Marshall McLuhan, "it took the invention of print to tear us from our tribes and plant the dream of isolation in our brains." Which, I suppose, is another way of saying that most of us would rather curl up all alone with a book than with another person.

Furthermore, our overemphasis on privacy has caused us to value technology far more than relationships. Two classic illustrations come to mind. . . . First, most of us can recall the first time our nation put a team of astronauts on the moon. It was 1969. What a magnificent event! When our president a few days later referred to that national dream come true, he stated it was "the greatest event in all of world history." As I heard that statement, I challenged it. "Really? The greatest event in the entire history of the world? Hardly!" After considering his remark I realized it was indicative of our ultra-high appraisal of technology. Technologically, it *was* a stupendous achievement . . . perhaps "the greatest" in that category. But the absolute, all-time highest peak in history? Hardly.

Second, I recall hearing a news broadcast in 1983 that included a brief wrap-up comment. The newscaster stated that divorce is on the rise in the Silicon Valley of Northern California. That wasn't surprising to me. What *was* surprising was what the commentator added. He said that many of the mates now alone were not that disturbed by their breakdown in domestic relationships. Why? Because "now they had more time to spend alone . . . *with their computers.*"

If ol' Rip Van Winkle stumbled onto the scene today after sleeping away the past twenty-five to thirty years, I think he might have a coronary to see how well we relate to green screens and clicking machines, yet how poorly we relate to flesh and blood. We're not only loners, we're also lonely.

COMMON CRIES OF THE LONELY

There are familiar cries that come from lonely lips. We've all heard them. The first cry I'll mention comes out of a heart of blame. It says, in effect, *"Why don't people love me and help me out of my problems?"* In answer to that I would say that friendships must be cultivated. They don't automatically occur when calamity strikes. And I have never heard of a rent-a-friend business either.

The second cry comes out: *"If only others realized how difficult things are!"* Without sounding callous, let me say that there are few things that weaken and ultimately ruin relationships like self-pity. It is the one attention-getter that soon wears out the other person's attention.

If you haven't drawn others into your life, don't blame them if they are not there when calamity strikes. Furthermore, feeling sorry for yourself won't get you out of it. It may be hard work to build and cultivate meaningful companionships, but what rich dividends it pays!

The third cry comes from feeling like a martyr. *"Nobody really cares! I am all alone in this!"* Anybody who doesn't know we're in pain can't be criticized for not responding. To put it positively, if we hope to survive the aching, heartbreaking times on this old lonely planet, being with others is essential. The equation isn't meant to sound clever—one plus one really does equal survival.

There's an old Swedish motto that hangs in many a kitchen in the Old Country. It says: "Shared joy is a double joy. Shared sorrow is half a sorrow." I have written an entire book that addresses the value of open relationships,[1] so I'll not repeat myself here. Suffice it to say, without others, life slows to a grind rather rapidly. As the little kitchen motto states, the secret of survival is not simply enjoying life's joys and enduring its sorrows, it is in sharing both with others.

SURVIVAL COUNSEL FOR THE LONELY

All this prepares us for more of Solomon's wise counsel. You may have sensed that he has been building to a climax. He's been talking about the oppressive, competitive, compulsive world of the one who works his or her way to the top of the ladder, becoming the "top dog." Having arrived, the successful entrepreneur discovers there aren't too many people around. Having climbed the pyramid, the leader usually finds that he has also become a loner.

Why of course! Don't you remember how a pyramid looks? There isn't room at the top for several. There's only a point. So this person who influences so many people is strangely bereft of friends. Often, as we have seen, not even family members are close.

Therefore, Solomon, with a great deal of honesty and insight, addresses loners. In fact, he speaks to all of us in this section of his journal:

> Two are better than one because they have a good return for their labor. For if either of them falls, the one will lift up his companion. But woe to the one who falls when there is not another to lift him up. Furthermore, if two lie down together they keep warm, but how can one be warm alone? And if one can overpower him who is alone, two can resist him. A cord of three strands is not quickly torn apart (Eccles. 4:9–12).

If you felt left out in the previous chapter, you have no reason to feel left out in this one. This is for those at the top, those in the middle, those on their way, those at the bottom, as well as those who don't even know which way they're going!

Statement of Fact

The opening line sets the stage with a statement of fact: "Two are better than one."

If you are married (especially if you are happily married) and read these words, you probably think that this means marriage. But this is for the married or the unmarried. Marriage is never once mentioned in this section. This is for people who are humans on this lonely earth wondering how to survive in our "dog-eat-dog" culture of ragged-edge reality. He says: "Two are better than one [and then he tells us why] because they have a good return for their labor" (v. 9). The Living Bible puts it even more simply, "The results can be much better."

We gain perspective by having somebody at our side. We gain objectivity. We gain courage in threatening situations. Having others near tempers our dogmatism and softens our intolerance. We gain another opinion. We gain what today, in our technical world, is called "input."

In other words, it is better not to work or live one's life all alone. It's better not to minister all alone. It's better to have someone alongside us in the battle. For that reason, during my days in the Marines, we were taught that if the command "dig in" were issued, we should dig a hole large enough for two.

I love the poem I recently happened upon:

> Oh, the comfort—the inexpressible comfort
>   of feeling safe with a person,
> Having neither to weigh thoughts,
> Nor measure words—but pouring them
> All right out—just as they are—
> Chaff and grain together—
> Certain that a faithful hand will
> Take and sift them—
> Keep what is worth keeping—
> And with the breath of kindness
> Blow the rest away.[2]

That's why "two are better than one."

Reasons Two Are Better Than One

After making the statement, Solomon takes the time to spell out why. He mentions three reasons: mutual encouragement when we are weak, mutual support when we are vulnerable, and mutual protection when we are attacked. Let's take them in that order.

1. *Mutual Encouragement When We Are Weak.*

> . . . if either of them falls, the one will lift up his companion.

In times of personal failure, in times when we would be ensnared, when we could easily stumble or become entrapped (not "if," but "when"), when we fall on our faces, when we have gotten into trouble, we need a companion to keep us from getting too bruised and bloody. And that companion will not walk away. If one of them falls down, the other can help him up. Isn't that great?

I'd like to address just the men for a few minutes. Many of you were raised, like I was, by well-meaning teachers, parents, and coaches in a masculine world that thought it was doing us a great service by underscoring that we're tough. We are rugged. We win. We can make it. We are pioneer types . . . survivors . . . winners . . . "always on top." We were given counsel from our coaches, like: "Tough it out." "Take it like a man." "Grit your teeth and bear it."

You want the straight scoop? A lot of us tough guys sound strong, but the truth is, we are weak. We sound like we've got it all together, but we don't. Take me. I sound independent, without much need for others, able to hang in there regardless . . . but that's not always true of me. I come across as a person who doesn't lean that much on someone else, but the lady I married knows how much I need her. Does she ever! And she and I have children who occasionally minister to our needs, as well. My best teachers on earth are five in number. I'm referring to those who bear my name. I also have a small group of men who know me very well. They are trustworthy and confidential guys I really need. Why? Because I am weak and I need their counsel. Furthermore, I occasionally blow it. If you doubt that, take it by faith! I need those men to encourage me and, when necessary, to reprove me.

The words of David W. Smith express the feelings many of us understand.

> Within each man there is a dark castle with a fierce dragon to guard the gate. The castle contains a lonely self, a self most men have suppressed, a self they are afraid to show. Instead they present an armored knight—no one is invited inside the castle. The dragon symbolizes the fears and fantasies of masculinity, the leftover stuff of childhood.
>
> When men take the risk and let down the barriers (or drawbridge . . .) people respond to one another as whole persons and try to communicate with openness and intimacy. Openness brings with it opportunity for a growing relationship, for a wider range of deeply felt experiences. This is the stuff from which friendships are formulated and sustained.[3]

Solomon put it this way: "If either of them falls, the one will lift up his companion. But woe to the one. . . ." Let's stop momentarily and consider the term *woe*. We could easily substitute the words *God help! Horrors! Peril! Danger!* Now continue with the rest of verse 10, ". . . woe to the one who falls when there is not [someone there to catch him]."

Who catches you when you fall? No one? Well, no wonder you're lonely! And the strange irony of it all is that getting married doesn't guarantee a solution to loneliness. I talk to people rather often who are married, but who are *still* lonely. Some marriage partners have a search-and-destroy-the-adversary relationship rather than a support-and-encourage, affirming relationship. It's tragic, yet true, that some are married to mates who do not lift up their companion. Few woes are more difficult to bear.

2. *Mutual Support When We Are Vulnerable.*

> Furthermore, if two lie down together they keep warm, but how can one be warm alone?

Isn't that a good statement? Now, here again, it's our tendency to take passages literally and miss the point of the whole idea.

It's true that married partners who slide in bed together on a cold, windy, wintry night find a great deal of warmth from one another. (Of course, some mates are so cold-natured that there's no way sufficient warmth can be generated without an electric blanket on level ten! Or, you may be married to a blanket hog that takes up all of your covers!)

But let's not limit this to bedtime warmth. We need someone when there are elements that we can't change—when we can't make it hot if it's cold. We can't get warm if everything around us is cold. That's the point. We're exposed. We are unguarded. We're vulnerable. And in this vulnerable state, we need somebody to warm us up. To put it another way, it's better to have two than one, because the other person will support us when we're in a vulnerable spot.

Let me mention some vulnerable times just in case you can't think of some. Let's start with the first day on a new job—isn't that the pits? First day on a new job you feel like all forty pairs of eyes in the office are looking right through you. It's good to have a friend at times like that.

First day in a new school—now there's another one. Chances are good (if you've just moved to the area where you live) you've heard one of your kids say something like, "But I don't know what I'm gonna do next week when I go to school with all those dragons, all those . . . all those animals, all those strangers." They feel exposed, unable to handle it.

How about if you're sitting in a courtroom, soon to take the witness stand? At such a threatening time, it's good to look out there and see a friendly face. How about waiting in a hospital room, or a dentist's office, or other threatening places like that? How about standing in line at the Department of Unemployment, waiting to pick up your check? Your dignity is lower than a whale's belly. In Solomon's words, you need someone to keep you warm. It's "cold" out there without a job. At times like that, it's great to have a friend.

Any time or place where you feel self-conscious and your major battle is "How am I going to make it through this right now?" be reminded of verse 11—you are cold and you need help in keeping warm. Two are better than one.

3. *Mutual Protection When We Are Attacked.*

> And if one can overpower him who is alone, two can resist him. A cord of three strands is not quickly torn apart.

All of us can identify with this. There is an adversary we all fight. He is relentless, determined, and clever. He's also invisible. He's called the devil. There is also an entire demonic force that would intimidate us even more if we could see them at work. But even though we cannot see them, we sense their presence and we are aware of their attack.

Sometimes a companion who is near us is able to say, "I think this is an enemy from Satan's domain. I think what you're wrestling with is a demonic attack." And the companion helps us through those times. I've had it happen in my life and many of you have also. Talk about valuable relationships!

Perhaps the adversary is some other person who has manufactured vicious rumors and is responsible for a pack of lies that is being spread against you. Or it may be that someone who is suspicious of your motive is out to get you for reasons you don't even understand. Maybe you have become the face on that person's mental dart board. And there is no way through it except enduring it. At such times companions are the next thing to essential. We're back to that all-important equation: One plus one equals survival.

Verse 12 concludes with "A cord of three strands is not quickly torn apart." This is not simply a reference to Christ, who certainly is our Companion—the best of all—it's a reference to more than just one companion. It may be several—two or three. But the thought here is that a cord of three strands is held with comforting words, or arms around the shoulder, or visible presence so that the waters of your soul are calm.

BIBLICAL EXAMPLES, PRACTICAL PRINCIPLES

If you are like I am, there are times you find it helpful to find in the Bible some flesh-and-blood examples, actual men and women who personify the truth. Such people never fail to provide hope as they incarnate the theory and demonstrate how it can be fleshed out. And with each of these examples I want to add a principle that I think will help make it real in your minds.

Elijah and Elisha

The first one I'm thinking of is a prophet who had a double problem. First, he was led by God to stand in front of intimidating rulers and make an unpopular prediction concerning a drought that was to come.

The second problem was to experience pain himself as a result of that drought—because the very prediction caused his own brook to dry up. His name was Elijah. He walked into the throne room of Ahab and Jezebel. Boldly and clearly, he announced God's message to these godless people. They listened and sneered and doubted. Nevertheless, the drought occurred just as he had predicted it would. No more rain.

By and by the bloated carcasses of animals could be seen all across that land as the lack of rain mixed with the searing rays of the sun caused the rivers and the brooks to dry up, including Elijah's own personal supply of water. He lost physical strength at that time.

But before long, he was back on the scene to face the prophets of Baal on Mount Carmel. What an emotional encounter! He fought fire with fire and he stood alone against their strong words as Jehovah-God made the prophet's words even stronger. The prophets of Baal were ultimately slain in front of him. It must have been an exceptionally draining experience.

Next came an incredible downpour of rain, followed by a threat on his life from Jezebel. While Elijah was physically weak, emotionally vulnerable, and spiritually depleted, Jezebel attacked and said, "You will die before twenty-four hours have passed." That did it!

Elijah ran to a wooded section. He left his servant and traveled alone deep into the wilderness. He finally slumped down under a tree and asked God to take his life. He was that low. The same strong man who stood alone in front of Ahab and Jezebel was now praying that God would take his life. He was falling—falling fast.

What did God do? Well, it's wonderful! He never said, "I'm ashamed of you, Elijah." God never comes on the scene and says, "Straighten up! You're a man!" He never once does that.

You know what He said to the prophet? "You rest for a while; I'm going to bring you a meal." So He catered this delicious meal, and Elijah went in the strength of it forty days and forty nights.

On top of that, following the long rest and the nourishment from this delicious meal, Elijah came to terms with himself and God. And in the very next scene, guess what happened. God gave Elijah a friend. His name was Elisha.

In fact, the last verse of 1 Kings 19 says Elisha followed Elijah and ministered to him. It's a great scene. Elijah sees him, realizes what a bond of kinship there was between them, and he throws his mantle around Elisha as if to say, "We're in this together, my friend. We're going together from now on." And there's renewed strength as Elijah survives, thanks to the presence of a companion. In fact, he steps into a whole new vision of God's directives for him. In the words of Solomon, "If one can overpower him who is alone, two can resist him."

Principle 1: Companions calm the troubled waters of our souls. There are times your soul will be troubled. There are times you will entertain thoughts that five years ago would have been heretical. You may even contemplate suicide—"God, take my life!" There are times that you will have to face the fact that you are in this terrible situation because of wrong actions or foolish things you have done. You are at fault, which damages your self-esteem even further. Your troubled soul won't calm down. You need help. And God graciously steps on the scene and provides you with a friend. Companions calm the troubled waters of our souls . . . as Elisha did for troubled Elijah.

Naomi and Ruth

There's another Old Testament scene that comes to my mind. It is a scene revolving around two women, Naomi and Ruth. Naomi was a godly woman, a wife and mother of two sons. By the time the print is dry in the book of Ruth, chapter 1, the sons are grown and married. And the biographer tells about these lovely daughters-in-law (one of whom is Ruth) who married Naomi's two sons.

Suddenly, for some unrevealed reason, a calamity struck the home of Naomi. She not only lost her husband—her two sons also died. Naomi was more than a grief-stricken widow. Adding to her pain was the tragic loss of her two grown sons.

In this vulnerable state, Naomi graciously said to her two daughters-in-law, "Why don't you go back to your homes and start over?" There was also this strong implication in Naomi's words that she planned to go back to her home. Broken, lonely, and fragmented in her spirit, she would attempt to put the pieces of her life together and simply die a quiet death.

But Ruth wouldn't let her do it. It's a great story! Ruth said to her mother-in-law/friend:

> "Don't urge me to leave you or to turn back from you. Where you go I will go, and where you stay I will stay. Your people will be my people and your God my God. Where you die I will die, and there I will be buried. May the Lord deal with me, be it ever so severely, if anything but death separates you and me" (Ruth 1:16, NIV).

It's a great speech! And Naomi's daughter-in-law put her arms around her dear mother-in-law and loved her back to dignity and life.

Principle 2: Companions build bridges of hope and reassurance when we are vulnerable, exposed, and self-conscious.

David and Jonathan

I can't omit two final examples—David and Jonathan. There once lived a king who began as a good man, humble and available, yet after a few years in public office, he lost this quality. His name was Saul. As he led Israel's army in battle, Saul and his troops faced Goliath, the Philistine giant. And Saul was intimidated. Even though he was strong and tall (though not nearly as tall as Goliath), Saul shrank in his tent and shook with fear.

Out of the hills of Judea there came a teen-aged boy who with only a sling and a stone, put the giant out of commission. Following that heroic act, the people began to sing, "Saul the king has slain his thousands and David his *ten* thousands."

Now Saul, insecure as he was, figured up the difference, and it was more than nine thousand in David's favor. He felt his position was threatened by young David. And he allowed himself to become a victim of all kinds of imaginations. How wicked imaginations can be when we're insecure and unstable! Instead of encouraging David as a fine young warrior—and asset to his army—he viewed him as an enemy.

He could have trained and tutored David and prepared him for the throne, but he wouldn't. He could have honored David and promoted him to a position of leadership, but he didn't. He made David the target of his hostilities. He hunted and haunted David. And David, the once-brave giant killer, came to the end of his emotional rope. He couldn't handle it, so he ran for his life, literally.

Meanwhile, along came Jonathan, Saul's son. The Scripture says, "Jonathan loved David as his own soul." One paraphrase adds, "He gave him dignity and reassurance." Again and again Jonathan strengthened his friend David.

Principle 3: Companions take our part when others take us apart. When we have nowhere else to turn, when the adversary is bearing down on us with verbal spears and swords of slander, there's nothing like a companion to get us through.

And that brings us back to Solomon's excellent counsel:

> Two are better off than one, because together they can work more effectively. If one of them falls down, the other can help him up. But if someone is alone and falls, it's just too bad, because there is no one to help him. If it is cold, two can sleep together and stay warm, but how can you keep warm by yourself? (Eccles. 4:9–12, TEV).

CONCLUSION: A SONG FOR THE LONELY TO SING

Back in the disillusioning days of the late 1960s and early 1970s, our country was ripped apart by factions and turmoil. The war in

Southeast Asia went on and on. Our governmental leaders were confused and our youth were rebellious. You and I may not have agreed, and even *now* may not agree with how they expressed their disillusionment; nevertheless, we all survived—we all made it through, though not without some scars.

These young men and women saw a lack of integrity in our government even before many adults did. We refused such a thought right to the last (by the mid seventies we finally admitted it). In the meantime they were rejected by the "establishment," rejected by up-and-coming entrepreneurs, career people, and often rejected by Mom and Dad. We despised their lifestyle and chose not to listen to their songs. Nevertheless, they continued to live their style and sing their songs. And many of them wound up on the streets of our cities. The "establishment" didn't know what to do with those who lived on the street and strummed their guitars through the night.

Paul Simon, you may remember, gave them a song to sing in 1969. The song reassured them, telling them that when everything else fails and falls, when there is nothing but trouble all around, there's one thing that will get them through—a friend. That friend will be "like a bridge over troubled waters." Look at the second verse of that song:

> When you're down and out, when you're on the street,
> When evening falls so hard, I will comfort you.
> I'll take your part.
>
> Oh! When darkness comes and pain is all around,
> Like a bridge over troubled waters, I will lay me down.[4]

Did you get that? Did you notice the writer's insightful words? He didn't say, "I'll give you a book to read." Neither did he say, "I'll tell you what to do," nor, "I'll give you a job." No. He said that when things get rough, "I'll lay *me* down. *I'll* comfort you. *I'll* be your bridge."

If you hope to make it through days of disillusionment and times of trouble, the secret is friendship. Or, to repeat the terms of an equation, "One plus one equals survival." There's no bridge quite like a friend, especially when you're forced to live on the ragged edge of troubled waters.

10

WHAT EVERY WORSHIPER SHOULD REMEMBER

Journal Entry

As you enter the Temple, keep your
ears open and your mouth shut! Don't
be a fool who doesn't even realize it is
sinful to make rash promises to God, for
he is in heaven and you are only here
on earth, so let your words be few. Just
as being too busy gives you nightmares,
so being a fool makes you a blabbermouth.
So when you talk to God and vow to
him that you will do something,
don't delay in doing it, for God has
no pleasure in fools. Keep your promise
to him. It is far better not to say you'll
do something than to say you will
and then not do it. In that case, your
mouth is making you sin. Don't try to
defend yourself . . . that would make
God very angry; and he might destroy
your prosperity. Dreaming instead of
doing is foolishness . . . fear God instead.

*S*o many of Solomon's ideas and observations are horizontal musings
. . . the bitter, barren, boring side of life seen through disillusioned
eyes. But on a few, rare occasions the man breaks out of his cynical
syndrome. At those times his comments contain a remarkable vertical
perspective that scrapes away the veneer of empty religion and takes
us back to the bedrock of a meaningful relationship with the living
Lord.

In this chapter we are going to examine one of those insightful
occasions. Like a cool, much-needed oasis in the middle of an arid
desert, these words refresh our spirits and restore our souls. They
allow us to take an unguarded look at those special times when we
step away from the press of our occupational and social involvements
and step into the awesome presence of our God to worship and focus
our full attention on Him . . . and Him alone.

To set the stage for our thinking, take time to read and think
through the following sections of Scripture. It is from a New Testament letter written originally to the Hebrews.

> For the word of God is living and active and sharper than any two-
> edged sword, and piercing as far as the division of soul and spirit, of
> both joints and marrow, and able to judge the thoughts and intentions
> of the heart. And there is no creature hidden from His sight, but all
> things are open and laid bare to the eyes of Him with whom we have
> to do (Heb. 4:12–13).

Basic Simplicity in a Complex World

In Search of Excellence is a book that became an overnight national
best seller in the secular marketplace. Its popularity was due, in part,
to the fact that it is not a theoretical volume based on untried ideas
and academic dreams. No, the coauthors, Thomas Peters and Robert
Waterman, wrote the book after researching several of the best-run
companies in America with a view to discovering the reasons behind
their success. But the book doesn't end there. It goes on to explain
how those same principles and techniques can be implemented in
any organization, large or small.

Men and women all over the country have appreciated the work of these two authors because the book presents in plain, everyday language how companies can be successful in the complicated marketplace of conglomerates and other complex circumstances. Just before listing the eight attributes that characterize those innovative, successful companies in America, the authors make this statement:

> The excellent companies were, above all, brilliant on the basics. Tools did not substitute for thinking. Intellect didn't overpower wisdom. Analysis didn't impede action. Rather, these companies worked hard to keep things simple in a complex world.[1]

Two phrases stand out in that statement. First, "brilliant on the basics," and second, "simple in a complex world." It's no surprise to any of us that the book became a best seller. In our fast-paced, complicated times, too little is being said about the basics and about simplicity.

People continue to be hungry for basic answers and simple solutions—not simplistic, you understand; but simple, easy to comprehend, free of mumbo-jumbo. People are hungry for answers they can grasp and put to use as they search for excellence in their lives—especially in a world that seems to focus our attention on the complex, the oblique, the fuzzy, the confusing.

THE WORD OF GOD: HOPE FOR OUR TIMES

It occurred to me after reading Peters and Waterman's book that what is true in our public world of work is all the more true in our private world of worship. Worship has been covered over long enough with the veneer of the ritualistic, complicated ways of reaching God. People today, as always, are looking for sensible basics and profound simplicity as they attempt to connect with the Lord God.

I think the best seller of all times, the Bible, remains in great demand for that very reason: It is both brilliant on the basics and simple in a complex world. For example, look again at Hebrews 4:12–13.

> For the word of God is living and active and sharper than any two-edged sword, and piercing as far as the division of soul and spirit, of both joints and marrow, and able to judge the thoughts and intentions

of the heart. And there is no creature hidden from His sight, but all
things are open and laid bare to the eyes of Him with whom we have
to do.

God's Book is not full of dead wood and dull thoughts. It's a Book
that is "living and active." Equally important, it is "sharper than
any two-edged sword." As a result, it does two remarkable things,
and it works for two clearly stated reasons.

What God's Word Does

If you'll look closely at verse 12, you'll see the things that it does.
And from verse 13 you'll see why it works. First, it "pierces." The
word *pierce* means "to cut through." God's Word cuts through the
"garbage" of our lives. It cuts through the phony fog. It cuts through
the lame excuses, the intricate rationalizations we manufacture, the
traditional walls we hide behind. It pierces every layer right down
to the heart that has become calloused in time. It cuts to the core
of the issue. It punctures and penetrates "as far as the division of
soul and spirit, of both joints and marrow."

The second thing that God's Word does is judge—it is "able to
judge" (v. 12). We get the word *critic* from the Greek term translated
"judge." Literally, it means "to sift." God's Word is a critic of the
thoughts and the intentions of our inner person. It reads and reveals
the truth, the whole truth, and nothing but the truth—like an all-
knowing judge. Unlike the surgeon's scalpel that can pierce only flesh,
God's Book cuts through, sifts out, then exposes to us the facts as
they are—even the motives that prompted our words and our actions.
No wonder His Word is said to be "living and active!"

Why It Works

What is it that makes these basic, profoundly simple truths (compared to the complex information in our high-tech age) so workable?
What is it about God's Word that, when its truths are declared
and believed, they work—regardless of culture, age, sex, maturity,
circumstance, era, or location? Verse 13 gives us a couple of reasons.

First, God's Word works when applied to our lives because it is
universal in scope. No one is hidden. In fact, the writer to the Hebrews
goes on to say "all things are open and laid bare." No creature can

hide from its truths. Furthermore, when an issue in our lives is addressed, nothing is left unexposed.

Second, it works because it is limitless in its exposure. The word *open* in verse 13 means "uncovered." The term *laid bare* comes from the Greek word from which we get our English word *trachea*.

What does a trachea have to do with something being "laid bare"? Well, if you were a sacrificial animal in the first century, you'd find out the hard way. When animals were sacrificed, the one who carried out the act of sacrifice would grab the animal beneath the chin and lift the head so as to "lay bare" the throat. The knife would then be plunged in deeply and the throat of the animal would be cut, from which the blood would be drawn for the sacrifice. So the meaning we have is exposed, laid bare—as if giving the throat to the knife. God's Word, if you please, "goes for the jugular."

Most of us have undergone a very intense physical examination at one time or another. We have stood before a physician who begins with our tongue and ends with our feet. He starts at the top and works all the way to the bottom. And this thorough physical examination, along with X-rays that are taken, questions that are asked, observations that are made, and tests that are given, gives the physician a fairly complete analysis of our anatomy.

Sometimes this leads the doctor to suggest that we need surgery. Sometimes he may suggest we need exercise or rest or a change in our diet. Occasionally, he may simply say, "You're doing great! Come back next year."

What is interesting is that, in all those sophisticated and brilliantly devised tests, there is no technique, no test or X-ray that can reveal the thoughts of your heart or the intentions of your actions. You see, only God's two-edged sword is able to pierce behind the action to the motive, deep into the thought life, so that He alone is able to expose the whole truth. Therefore we need to listen to His counsel as we open our eyes and ears to His truth. When we do this, we tap into the most phenomenal source of information available to mankind—and only then do we truly begin to worship.

THE WORSHIP OF GOD: TRUTH FOR OUR MINDS

A beautiful example of this search for excellence in our lives is Solomon's journal. As we continue our guided tour of his journey, we come to one of those scenic sections that make any trip more memorable. This particular view is especially scenic because it differs so drastically from the terrain we've been observing. The writer moves from the realm of the secular, where he seems to spend most of his time, to the world of the religious.

There's something about unrolling the scroll of Scripture and allowing its penetrating truths to speak for themselves—to get hold of us and, at times, to burn their way through the fog that often surrounds our worship. Sometimes we are shocked to find something we never expected.

I remember, as a little boy many years ago, going with my father during the fall of the year to open up my granddad's bay cottage down in South Texas. It was one of those unusual visits prior to a family reunion, as I recall. We couldn't get everyone's family together at the same time in the summer months, so we agreed to meet around Thanksgiving. My dad and I went early to prepare the place, and we encountered something that I shall never ever forget.

As he got out his key to open the door to the little cottage, we saw wasps between the shade that had been pulled and the glass on the door. My stomach churned a little, but the scene we were about to view was the real mega-shocker! We opened the door slowly and could not believe our eyes. Across the floor and on the walls and even up into naked light sockets and (if you could believe) *in between the mattresses* on the cots and the bunks were wasps. Hundreds of thousands of wasps! They crunched under our feet as we walked in our sneakers across the floor.

Interestingly, neither of us was stung because it was at that particular, strange time of their existence when stinging wasn't on their minds. They seemed to be in a dormant state. And we literally swept them out of the house by the thousands. We thought we got them all until my dad pulled down a shade at one of the windows and out came dozens more.

When I finally turned in for the night, I heard strange buzzings in my ear. My dad tried to convince me it was just my imagination. And I told him that one doesn't *feel* imaginations under one's head. When we turned the light on and lifted the mattress back, there was another layer of more wasps we had overlooked.

When I think of that incredible experience, I think of opening the door to God's Word. When we unfold its truths, when we get inside its pages, it's remarkable what surprising (and sometimes stinging) things come out. We often find ourselves shocked once we get inside. Take, for example, Solomon's first statement in chapter 5:

> Guard your steps as you go to the house of God, and draw near to listen rather than to offer the sacrifice of fools.

He begins with a strong, sentinel-like declaration. "Guard your steps as you go to the house of God." Picture an exclamation point at the end of that statement. "Guard your steps as you go to a worship service!"

Solomon is writing to people who are about to attend the place of worship. He warns, "As you are on your way to the place of worship, guard your steps. Walk gingerly. Stay alert!" It's the idea of not being dull or insensitive. Even though you may be very familiar with your surroundings, "stay alert!" In spite of the fact that you may have heard the things being said numerous times in your life, "guard your steps!" Fools are characterized by mental thickness. They hear words and turn them off.

This reminds me of a familiar scene at most busy airports. There are lots of different people moving all around, but one thing is monotonously the same—at least it is at the Los Angeles International Airport. It is a recording that comes over loud and clear as travelers stand at the curb waiting for their drivers to pick them up or the bus to come by. It says, "The white zone is for loading and unloading only. No parking." It is a recording that continues day and night. And guess what? The curb area is loaded with people who have parked their cars alongside "the white zone." Each white zone is crawling with policemen, and they are giving out tickets as fast as they can write them.

I wish there were some way to announce over a loudspeaker system outside every worship gathering, "The pew zone is for learning and listening and changing only. *No parking.*" God is saying. "Guard your steps! You're about to take a risk. Watch out! Be alert! Listen carefully. Truth will be deposited in your head that is designed to change your life." But chances are good that even though a loudspeaker made such an announcement, the same thing would occur—folks would still "park" and turn a deaf ear to the recording.

You see why that's important? Because our favorite place to park is in a pew. Just come, sit ("Whew! Finally got a seat!"), listen, and leave. This passage says, "Don't do that." It says, "As you go to the place of worship, be ready. Be alert. Sleep later. Pay attention now."

In the first seven verses Solomon unfolds no less than four commands—each of which has its own reason connected to it. Allow me to state all four of the commands and their respective reasons before we examine each one:

COMMANDS	REASONS
• Draw near and listen well!	Because God is communicating.
• Be quiet and stay calm!	Because God hears the inaudible, sees the invisible.
• Make a commitment and keep it!	Because God believes it and doesn't forget it.
• Don't decide now and deny later.	Because God doesn't ignore our decisions.

First: Draw Near and Listen Well (Because God is Communicating)

> Guard your steps as you go to the house of God, and draw near to listen rather than to offer the sacrifice of fools; for they do not know they are doing evil (Eccles. 5:1).

What great counsel Solomon offers! We know from another section of Scripture that "the sacrifice" quite likely is a reference to words, "the sacrifice of praise, the fruit of lips" (Heb. 13:15). For that reason, I suggest that Solomon's comment in verse 1 means "Don't offer up foolish words." Or, more forcefully, "Don't talk so much. Don't fill the air with noise from your throat. Be quiet. Listen well. Draw near!"

I have often thought about ways to make that happen. I've thought it might help to dim the lights—or maybe increase the volume on the organ, but it's impossible to outshout all those vocal cords working hard in a congregation.

I've even wondered about putting an enormous sign in the narthex that says, "Shhhhhh!" I've thought of playing music through the system, but that doesn't quieten the heart. There's nothing wrong with a gracious and calm greeting, a warm affectionate embrace, a "Hello, how are you?" "Nice to meet you," followed by "I'll talk with you later." But there is everything wrong if one's entire preparation for worship is filled with words, needless jabber with a great deal of volume. Perhaps that had begun to happen in the days of Solomon?

Apparently, worship had become trite. Religion had become stale. And people gathered just like they had gathered at other places, just to hear, to sit, to talk, to leave. This man says, "Don't do that."

So much of today's worship is dull-edge stuff—meaningless words, clichés that sit like tombstones over dead ideas. God is speaking. That's the reason for the command. The living God is communicating.

Henry David Thoreau once wrote: "It takes two to speak the truth. One to speak and another to listen." Walt Whitman confessed: "To have great poets there must be great audiences." I like that!—someone to write and someone to appreciate. To have great messages from God, there must be a well-prepared spokesman and there must be an equally well-prepared congregation. They work in tandem with each other.

Before we go any further in the unrolling of the shade, allow the truth of this to sting you. Come to terms with your lips, with your ears, as you envision yourself preparing for worship. Experiment with something different for a change. Be quiet. Try silence.

From the first strains of music to the last word of the benediction (except for times of response, of course, which is a most beautiful part of worship), learn to hitchhike on God's thoughts. Sometimes those thoughts come in the silence of the offertory. Sometimes they come as someone else is leading in prayer. Occasionally they come in the singing of a hymn. Draw near. Listen well, because God is communicating.

I strongly recommend the small but potent book *Up with Worship* written by my good friend, Anne Ortlund.[2] My copy is literally dog-eared and falling apart, due to repeated readings. In it she offers great insight on how to prepare for and participate in worship.

Second: Be Quiet and Stay Calm (Because God Hears the Inaudible and Sees the Invisible)

> Do not be hasty in word or impulsive in thought to bring up a matter in the presence of God. For God is in heaven and you are on the earth; therefore let your words be few. For the dream comes through much effort, and the voice of a fool through many words. . . . For in many dreams and in many words there is emptiness. Rather, fear God (Eccles. 5:2–3, 7).

Putting all that on the bottom shelf, "Don't daydream!"

I like the way Derek Kidner explains this command—"The dreams appear to be daydreams, reducing worship to verbal doodling."[3] Isn't that descriptive? It's easy for us to "doodle" our way through a worship service, as we let our dream world take us from one imaginary vista to another: yesterday's experience on the ocean, or tomorrow's experience in the office, or the needs of the kids, or the concern of this problem, or that decision we've got to make by Wednesday, or that stack of ironing, or the roast that's burning—whatever. God's counsel is, "Let it burn. Let it go. Be quiet. Stay calm." When you're churning like an angry ocean, God's truth doesn't drop anchor.

We are explicitly told to let our words be few . . . to reject being "hasty" as well as "impulsive." We are to allow ourselves to be calm and meditative. I think of the line from Charles Wesley's hymn *Love Divine, All Love Excelling*, as he writes of being "lost in wonder, love, and praise." That's a vivid description from a man who truly understood worship.

A statement from Psalm 46 also comes to mind. That great psalm of worship begins by portraying God as "our refuge and strength" and concludes with the reassurance that He is our stronghold. And in the central core of the psalm (v. 10) there is a command that is familiar to all of us. "Be still and know that I am God." Actually, it's a single word in the Hebrew text—"cease" or "stop." Some marginal references suggest "relax . . . let go." It's saying, "Stop striving!"

The verb stem in the original Hebrew text conveys the idea that we are to cause something to drop off, to abandon something. What is it we are to abandon? I think the editors are correct in adding words like "striving, anxiety, preoccupation with the cares of this age." Let all that go!

We can be so preoccupied that we simply go through empty, meaningless motions of worship without really hearing. We don't respond well because we're not taking it all in. The writer is saying, "Be still." Why? "So you'll know that I am God."

That brings us back to Solomon's words and the reason for this second command: "For God is in heaven and you are on the earth." What picture do you have in your mind when you read that God is in heaven and we are on the earth? I would hazard the guess that most of you would say, "He is way out there, or way up there in heaven, and we are way down here on earth. So we'd better listen well."

In actuality, this is a statement of perspective, not distance. God is in the realm of the infinite. He alone hears the inaudible. He alone sees the invisible. That's the reason we're to be calm and quiet. God penetrates deeply into that which is inaudible to human ears, and He peers intently into that which is invisible to human eyes. Knowing that is true, take a close look at Him and listen to what He's saying.

John White, in his book *The Fight*, offers this insight:

> It is God who wishes to establish communication. He is more anxious to speak to us than we are to hear Him. He is incredibly persistent in trying to get through. Our real problem is that we tend to avoid hearing Him. Truth liberates. It not only reveals a standard, but will set you free to keep it. This is what makes Scripture so different from other ethical systems which are powerless to help the struggler.[4]

We come as fellow strugglers to hear God's basic and simple answers to life in all of its complexity. But if we're not careful, we drag into the scene all the tumult and turmoil of our problems. And we are quick to dump them out, rather than to hear Him out. He says, "Be still."

Third: Make a Commitment and Keep It (Because God Believes It and Doesn't Forget It)

> When you make a vow to God, do not be late in paying it, for He takes no delight in fools. Pay what you vow! It is better that you should not vow than that you should vow and not pay (Eccles. 5:4–5).

These are some of the most overlooked words in all of Scripture—and especially so in a day of shallow roots and superficial commitments. We'd much rather bail out than follow through. As a result, a promise is little more than a casual hope. A vow is a nice idea, but a hard-and-fast covenant? A permanent commitment you can count on? Hardly. Whether it's a commitment to pay back fifty dollars or a commitment to stay faithful in marriage, the idea of sticking with a vow *regardless* is almost unheard of.

Not so in God's eyes! Again, His truth penetrates. He says, "You vowed it . . . you keep it." He's not asking, "*If* we make one, would we keep it?" But, as Solomon says in verse 4, *when* we make one. I personally believe in commitments. I believe they're biblical. And I believe vows become the seed plot for action.

Consider for a moment some vow or commitment you have made to God. No doubt some of you can say such things as "I made a commitment to meet with God every day of the week." Or, "I made a commitment to spend time with my family—to give that top-priority attention." Others may say, "Years ago I took a vow at an altar with the person I loved, where I promised to be faithful for the rest of my life." Or, "I made a vow before God's people with my baby in my arms to rear that child God's way." And still others can say, "When I heard God's Word address the subject of purity, I made a vow to remain morally pure for my marriage partner. I made that vow before God."

This command in verse 4 is simply a follow-up reminder: "Keep your word!" God believed you when you took that vow and He doesn't forget it.

We are living in troublesome times in which there are alleged authorities who feel it is their calling to relieve us from any and all guilt. Period. I am all for the relief of false guilt. It has no place in our lives. I think false guilt is a killer. It's destructive. It leads us to poor mental health and certainly gives us emotional turmoil.

But I think there is a place for authentic guilt. At such times it is healthy and essential for change. I think that's the work of the Spirit of God, His "convicting" work. It may be subtle or it may be bold and relentless, but it's there, nevertheless. There are many who would take away even the slightest turmoil and say, "You don't have to live under that load of guilt."

Wait a minute! Says who? What in the world is a vow if it isn't a commitment to accountability? What is a commitment if it isn't saying to our heavenly Father and to others, "I will carry this out, painful and difficult though it may be."

Be careful about relieving *all* commitments so that you can be "free." That's dangerous. It is also unbiblical.

There once lived a rebel who happened to be a prophet. A rather unusual combination—yet this rebel-prophet had taken a vow before God that as His spokesman he would say what God told him to say and go where God told him to go. That's standard operating procedure for prophets.

So God said to this rebel-prophet, "Go to Nineveh." And all of a sudden Jonah's political zeal outstripped his religious fervor as he took a ship to Tarshish instead.

He decided, "I will forget my commitment as God's prophet and split the scene." Bad decision. You know exactly what happened, don't you? Ultimately, he wound up in Nineveh by way of the first amphibious landing in history. God got His way. And when Jonah finally got there, he declared to these people of Nineveh what God told him to say—which resulted in the greatest revival in the history of mankind!

What made Jonah change his mind? We hear the story of Jonah and always smile. We always think about a big fish and this rebel prophet. But in doing so, we miss the real secret of the story. Tucked away in Jonah, chapter 2, we find that the prophet gives his testimony *while drowning in the Mediterranean Sea.*

He cries out to God in prayer. Talk about a beautiful illustration of keeping a vow!

> "I called out of my distress to the Lord, and He answered me. I cried for help from the depth of Sheol; Thou didst hear my voice. For Thou hadst cast me into the deep, into the heart of the seas, and the current engulfed me. All Thy breakers and billows passed over me. So I said, 'I have been expelled from Thy sight. Nevertheless I will look again toward Thy holy temple.' Water encompassed me to the point of death. The great deep engulfed me, weeds were wrapped around my head. I descended to the roots of the mountains. The earth with its bars was around me forever, but Thou hast brought up my life from the pit, O Lord my God. While I was fainting away, I remembered the Lord; and my prayer came to Thee, into Thy holy temple. Those who regard vain idols forsake their faithfulness, but I will sacrifice to Thee with the voice of thanksgiving. *That which I have vowed I will pay.* Salvation is from the Lord" [italics mine] (vv. 2–9).

The prophet's repentance was directly linked to his keeping the vow he had made earlier.

That's what Solomon's journal is teaching. Sometimes it takes a difficult, painful experience like being tossed overboard, like being fired from a job or being laid aside in illness, like being pushed in the corner through several painful relationship breakdowns to teach us the importance of a vow. And then we finally come to our senses and return to our vow. When we make a commitment, we must keep it because God believes it and doesn't forget it.

Fourth: Don't Decide Now and Deny Later (Because God Doesn't Ignore Decisions)

> Do not let your speech cause you to sin and do not say in the presence of the messenger of God that it was a mistake. Why should God be angry on account of your voice and destroy the work of your hands? (Eccles. 5:6).

The fourth command is saying, in effect: Don't allow yourself to worm out of something you once took seriously in the presence of God. You haven't the right to say:

—"You know what? Uh . . . that . . . that commitment back then was a mistake."

—"I made a mistake. I . . . I married the wrong person, you see."

—"Oops! I shouldn't have said that I'd rearrange my priorities and spend more time with such and such."

—"I . . . I didn't think that through. It was a mistake to commit myself to this project, especially since it's so time-consuming and exhausting."

—"I made a mistake in saying I'd stay morally pure. I mean, God knows I'm only human."

—"I was pretty young back then. I guess it's what you'd call a 'youthful mistake.' "

God puts no age limit on serious decisions. God says, in today's terms, "That doesn't wash." Even so, you'll still find a lot of "authorities" that will tell you, "Oh, that's the way you've got to live. I mean, after all, God understands!" The reason for this fourth command is that God does not ignore or overlook our decisions. I remember a little phrase from childhood that goes like this: "Cross my heart and hope to die. Stick a needle in my eye." Remember saying that? I never once saw anybody stick a needle in his eye, but I saw a lot of little kids break their "cross my heart and hope to die" promise.

There's no "King's X" in decisions we make. There's no "time out." Don't come back and say, "Aha! God, You've got to understand. I'm twenty years older and I've learned a lot since then." Keep short accounts. Keep your promise. Keep your vows.

THE WARNING OF GOD: STRENGTH FOR OUR LIVES

For in many dreams and in many words there is emptiness. Rather fear God (v. 7).

Look at those last two words in Solomon's warning—"fear God." In other words, *take Him seriously.*

I sometimes think about people that have been of great help to me in my spiritual life. I thank God for them. And I ask myself, "Why do they mean a lot to me? They each put another rung in my ladder as I was climbing toward maturity." They were people who convinced me that I was to take God seriously. They were the people who built the most into my life—and still do. It wasn't so much that they never had fun. A lot of these people had a well-exercised sense of humor. But when it came to God, they modeled the same message: "We don't play games here, Chuck! Get serious. If God says it, believe it! Do it!"

As one man put it:

> Babbling, rambling, wild words may be all right in dreams, but they do not belong in worship. Our relationship to God is one of sober, respectful, reverent awe. . . .
>
> . . . False worship is as much an affront to him as obscene insults are to a wife or husband. Better to bribe a judge than to ply God with hollow words; better to slap a policeman than to seek God's influence by meaningless gestures; better to perjure yourself in court than to harry God with promises you cannot keep. The full adorations of our spirit, the true obedience of our heart—these are his demands and his delights.[5]

In Search of Excellence is more than the title of a book. It's the pursuit of a life. People who take God seriously are on a constant search for excellence. In case you have begun to drift, I invite you to return. We need to form a united front in this all-important pursuit of excellence.

11

STRAIGHT TALK TO THE MONEY-MAD

Journal Entry

If you see some poor man being oppressed by the rich . . . don't be surprised! For every official is under orders from higher up, and the higher officials look up to their superiors. And so the matter is lost in red tape and bureaucracy. . . .

He who loves money shall never have enough. The foolishness of thinking that wealth brings happiness! The more you have, the more you spend, right up to the limits of your income, so what is the advantage of wealth—except perhaps to watch it as it runs through your fingers! . . . All the rest of his life he is under a cloud—gloomy, discouraged, frustrated and angry. . . .

To enjoy your work and to accept your lot in life—that is indeed a gift from God. The person who does that will not need to look back with sorrow on his past . . .

*T*here once lived a very famous queen who paid a visit to a very rich king. She had heard so much about the man's immense wealth and opulent lifestyle that she could restrain her curiosity no longer. In fact, the reports had been so excessive that the queen seriously questioned their validity. It was one of those tongue-in-cheek visits, where suspicion held her excitement in check.

She knew that some things she had heard were true. She knew of his architectural gifts, his astounding accomplishments as a builder, a poet, a musical composer, an authority on the life sciences, and his skill as a political diplomat—all that was internationally known. She expected to be impressed with his elegant surroundings and exquisite furnishings. She was certain that the king's brilliance would be equally impressive. But she still reserved a few doubts. "Surely nobody could be *that* wise," she mused en route from her palace in Ethiopia to his throne in Palestine. So the queen of Sheba paid a visit to the king of the Hebrews, whose name was Solomon.

She had a number of questions—tough, probing questions—to ask this imposing monarch. He listened and responded to every one. She toured his kingdom. She ate at his table. She spoke with his servants. She observed and absorbed the whole scene.

> When the queen of Sheba had seen all Solomon's wisdom and skill, the house he had built, the food of his table, the seating of his officials, the standing at attention of his servants, their apparel, his cupbearers, his ascent by which he went up to the house of the Lord [or the burnt offerings he sacrificed], she was breathless and overcome. She said to the king, "It was a true report I heard in my own land of your acts and sayings and wisdom. I did not believe it until I came and my eyes had seen. Behold, the half was not told me. You have added wisdom and goodness exceeding the fame I heard. Happy are your men! Happy are these your servants who stand continually before you, hearing your wisdom! (1 Kings 10:4–8, AMPLIFIED).

In today's slang, she was "blown away" . . . her mind was "boggled." Dumbfounded, the woman exclaimed, "I wasn't told the *half* of it!" Although she was acquainted with elegance and enjoyed enormous wealth herself, the queen was left speechless. The luxury, the beauty, not to mention the diplomacy, that dripped from Solomon's kingdom stunned the queen of Sheba. She knew no better way to express her commendation than to add to his wealth!

159

And she gave the king 120 talents of gold, and of spices a very great store, and precious stones. No more came such abundance of spices as these the queen of Sheba gave King Solomon (v. 10, AMPLIFIED).

We often hear of the wisdom of Solomon. The phrase is as familiar as "the patience of Job." But we do not as often hear of his wealth. Allow me a moment to inform you. His base annual income in gold alone was in the neighborhood of $20 million . . . not to mention his export-import trade lines and the limitless "perks" that came with being king. The throne upon which he sat was carved ivory overlaid with beaten gold, and his furnishings literally defy exaggeration. Picture this:

All Solomon's drinking vessels were of gold, and those of his house were of pure gold. The shields of his mighty men were made of beaten gold, and his great throne was made of ivory and overlaid with the finest gold. Silver in Jerusalem became as common as stones.

Solomon literally built himself *a paradise of pleasure.* One of his chief resorts was Etham where, when the mornings were beautiful, he often went in stately progress, "dressed in snow white raiment, riding in his chariot of state which was made of the finest cedar, decked with gold and silver and purple, and carpeted with the costliest tapestry worked by the daughters of Jerusalem; and attended by a bodyguard of sixty valiant men of the tallest and handsomest of the young men of Israel, arrayed in Tyrian purple, with their long black hair, freshly sprinkled with gold dust every day, glittering in the sun."[1]

We're talking "filthy rich." The man's spread—which included parks, a zoo, a wonder-of-the-world temple, his personal residence (which was more like a museum than a home), lavish resorts, and riding stables—would make the Taj Mahal look like a local bus depot by comparison. Affluence personified. You and I, honestly, cannot comprehend the immensity of his wealth.

Why have I taken the time to lay this on you? Because a person that rich knows what he is talking about when the subject of finances is brought up. When Solomon writes on money, it's time to take notes. The man knows whereof he speaks. And that is exactly what he does on this new page of his journal. Let's go to school on Solomon's counsel. Let's learn our lesson well. And if you happen to be the type who tends toward materialism and greed, I suggest you read his straight talk with an exceptional amount of concentration.

PROVERBIAL PRINCIPLES TO LEARN

> If you see oppression of the poor and denial of justice and righteousness in the province, do not be shocked at the sight, for one official watches over another official, and there are higher officials over them. After all, a king who cultivates the field is an advantage to the land. He who loves money will not be satisfied with money, nor he who loves abundance with its income. This too is vanity. When good things increase, those who consume them increase. So what is the advantage to their owners except to look on? The sleep of the working man is pleasant, whether he eats little or much. But the full stomach of the rich man does not allow him to sleep (Eccles. 5:8–12).

I find no less than three principles written between the lines of that journal entry. Each relates directly to money matters. The first has to do with *oppression,* the second relates to *dissatisfaction,* and the third addresses the struggle of *frustration.*

Oppression

> If you see oppression of the poor and denial of justice and righteousness in the province, do not be shocked at the sight, for one official watches over another official, and there are higher officials over them. After all, a king who cultivates the field is an advantage to the land (vv. 8–9).

The "proverb" I find written between the lines of these two verses goes like this:

> THE RICH TEND TO TAKE CHARGE AND THEIR
> POWER INTIMIDATES AND OFFENDS THE POOR.

This first proverb, or principle, has to do with the influence and control the rich have over the poor. The rich, simply because they have money, tend to take charge of territory, of a province, of a nation, even of a continent. The rich tend to be leaders. They are often the best educated, the most influential, and because they run with the rich, they gain control—control of the money, the land, the gross national product, the political arena. They usually become the lawmakers. They become the officials who run the government, both state and national. They become those who establish the "red tape" procedures, those who place in office more officials who "watch over another official," as Solomon puts it.

And by and by, the red tape gets so thick and complex that the poor can no longer gain entrance and be heard by the rich. Those with wealth tend to take charge and the poor become intimidated. One man drew a scene from the first century when he wrote:

> The glimpse of that vista of officials suggests possibilities of evasiveness to baffle the citizen who presses for his rights. He can be endlessly obstructed and deflected. As for moral responsibility, it can be sidestepped with equal facility. Every officer can blame the system, while the ultimate authorities hold sway at an infinite distance from the lives they affect.[2]

Those of us who have served our country in the military smile with understanding as we read those words. In my outfit we called it "the system." How often we agreed, "You can't beat the system." You can reach just so far, and you don't go any further because one officer watches over another officer. There's a name for a guy in the military who tries to beat the system—"victim." The major problem is that woven into the fabric of that tightly controlled system is unaccountability and insensitivity. I am certainly not advocating anarchy. Someone must be in charge. A certain amount of the "system" has to be in place. But my concern—Solomon's concern—is the untouchable and often corrupt power that occurs when those with money gain total control.

Does this mean that there is never a need for any kind of leadership? I repeat, leadership is essential, biblical, in fact. Remember how Solomon put it? "A king who cultivates the field is an advantage to the land" (v. 9). There still needs to be leadership. And some governments still advocate a monarchy. But wealthy kings must guard against being oppressive because money has a way of dulling the senses of a powerful leader.

Dissatisfaction

> He who loves money will not be satisfied with money, nor he who loves abundance with its income. This too is vanity.

Solomon knew this subject like few others. When he says it won't satisfy, he ought to know. As they say in the South, "We can put 'er down." The second proverb allows us a personal glimpse at those who become downright money-mad.

GREED AND MATERIALISM HAVE NO BUILT-IN
SAFEGUARDS OR SATISFYING LIMITS

Before I go any further, observe the word Solomon uses is *loves* — not *possesses.* This is not an attack, nor is there ever an attack in Scripture against those who possess riches. This is, however, a frontal assault on loving money. This is an attack on greed, an open assault on the materialist who must have more, more, more. Did you catch how the king described that grabbing, greedy individual? Empty. "This too is vanity."

To the money-hungry, there is never enough. He who loves money will never reach the level of personal satisfaction. He who loves the abundance that comes with that kind of income will never know the day when he will lean back, smile contentedly and sigh, "That's plenty. I have enough."

Isn't it amazing? Money can buy us tons of comfort, but not an ounce of contentment. Profits, dividends, investments, interest benefits, and capital gains only whet the appetite for more—like the pathetic person who stands at the slot machine and drops in one quarter after another. Even when the bells ring and the whistles scream and the gambler "strikes it rich" as four hundred dollars' worth of quarters plunge into his lap, that's never enough. Those coins wind up back in the machine to go through another time. Never enough. When we're financially strapped, we think otherwise. We tell ourselves that we'll be content, if only. . . . But we're not. Wise was the man who said, "How much does it take to satisfy us? A little bit more than we have!"

As the gambler, so the materialist. That's what verse 10 is saying. The one who has a love affair with money is addicted to it and will never ever have enough.

Frustration

> When good things increase, those who consume them increase. So what is the advantage to their owners except to look on? The sleep of the working man is pleasant, whether he eats little or much. But the full stomach of the rich man does not allow him to sleep (vv. 11–12).

Isn't that vivid? How often we have seen this occur! Especially when riches have come to one whose background was borderline poverty.

I'm thinking of some heavyweight boxer who emerges from a dirt-poor ghetto into the limelight. Able to punch some guy's lights out, the young man becomes "champion of the world." His big toothless grin is plastered across the front page of our magazines. And the next time you see this overnight success, he's got an entourage in front of him and behind him. He's driving a Rolls Royce. He's got four bodyguards (that always surprises me), plus a house full of people who hardly knew his name several months earlier are on his payroll. Everything is fine and dandy until *his* lights go out!

I think of Elvis Presley, just a dirt-poor kid out of Memphis, who, with the guitar slung over his shoulder, suddenly struck it rich. And it was only a matter of time before he had more people living off his income than he even knew by name. They were folks who, as Solomon writes, "consume the increase."

That brings us to the third proverb.

WITH INCREASED MONEY AND POSSESSIONS COMES AN
ACCELERATED NUMBER OF PEOPLE AND WORRIES.

Taken to its logical conclusion the proverb could be expressed in an axiom: More money, more people. More people, more worries. More worries, less sleep.

> The sleep of the working man is pleasant, whether he eats little or much. But the full stomach of the rich man does not allow him to sleep (v. 12).

Isn't that true? Take, for example, a guy who perhaps welds all day—punches in at seven in the morning and punches out at three-thirty in the afternoon—what a simple game plan! He drives his pickup home. He and his son drive over to the ball field and he shags flies with his boy. In fact, he's probably one of those guys who helps coach the Little League team in the neighborhood. He has a great time—just a hard-working, fun-loving, easy-going "working man." When the game ends, he drives home, eats a bowl of chili and a fist full of Fritos, watches TV until the late newscast is over, then drops into bed about ten-thirty. Within sixty seconds, you can hear him snoring!

There's little anxiety connected with that lifestyle. Not many folks to hassle over. Just flip the ol' mask down and weld eight hours a day, five, maybe six days a week. Freedom from all those high-pressure decisions that keep others awake. But the rich? We're back to that third proverb. They've got a lot of stuff on their minds. As that wise, rich king expressed it, "But the full stomach of the rich man does not allow him to sleep."

Tell me Solomon isn't practical. It certainly isn't a problem of not enough food. The rich man has *more than enough* food. What's missing? Peace of mind. A relaxed mentality. He hasn't people who love him just for who he is. And he is forever preoccupied with pursuits that have financial entanglements—problems that don't go away when he leaves the office long after dark or when he tries to drown them at the bar. And when he finally drops into bed by two in the morning, he tosses and turns as he wonders, "Is that deal gonna pay off? What if I get caught short? Is he gonna rip me off? Is it too big a risk? Will that sucker fly?" Around and around he turns . . . over and over he twists.

Solomon says it again a different way in Proverbs 19:

> Wealth adds many friends,
> But a poor man is separated from his friend.
>
> A false witness will not go unpunished,
> And he who tells lies will not escape.
>
> Many will entreat the favor of a generous man,
> And every man is a friend to him who gives gifts.
>
> All the brothers of a poor man hate him;
> How much more do his friends go far from him!
> He pursues them with words, but they are gone (vv. 4–7).

Why? Because they're looking for somebody with a pile of dough. People hang around those who have big bucks. Or, as one man describes it rather bluntly:

> When man's possessions increase, it seems there's a corresponding increase in the number of parasites who live off him: Management consultants, tax advisers, accountants, lawyers, household employees, and sponging relatives.[3]

Some time ago, I came across a very interesting statement written by the prophet Isaiah. I don't believe I had ever seen it before. The main character is a king named Eliakim, the son of Hilkiah. The Lord God has promoted him. And look at how vividly the prophet describes this king's promotion:

> "And I will drive him like a peg in a firm place, and he will become a throne of glory to his father's house" (Isa. 22:23).

The word picture of a peg driven firmly in place portrays Eliakim as firmly entrenched as the king. Now think for a minute of a peg on the kitchen wall.

> "So they will hang on him all the glory of his father's house, offspring and issue, all the least of vessels, from bowls to all the jars" (v. 24).

Isn't that vivid? All the stuff from the kitchen will wind up on the peg on the wall. Now look at the next verse.

> "In that day," declares the Lord of hosts, "the peg driven in a firm place will give way; it will even break off and fall, and the load hanging on it will be cut off, for the Lord has spoken" (v. 25).

What a pertinent warning to the money-mad! In effect, God says to the rich, "You're driven in the wall like a peg. You become significant to an entourage of people and before long they hang upon you, they pull at you, they weigh heavily upon you—and the meal you eat no longer satisfies as it once satisfied. The bed upon which you lie no longer gives sleep as it once gave sleep. The refreshment of a family that was once your delight is no longer within the realm of your interest. And finally, in that aching, awful moment—CRACK!—the peg snaps."

If I could draw from those words that the queen of Sheba uttered, I would say that the truth concerning the dark side of riches is "the half" that wasn't told her. From the outside looking in, we are so impressed with this wonder of Solomon's wealthy world. But that's only *half* the story. The other half is not usually seen by the public. It's the lack of contentment, the frustration, the awful lonely nightmare of a life that leaves the greedy clutching for more and more—but sooner or later the peg breaks.

Back to the journal, to this honest man's account of life on the ragged edge. Here is a man with increased money and increased possessions who has more anxieties than ever and more people living off his salary than he would ever have dreamed possible. He can't even enjoy a restful night of sleep.

Now wait a minute! These aren't the words of some young educator who is hoping to research and write a best-selling book. No. This is a middle-aged, brilliant, rich king who knows what he's talking about. And it's recorded right here in front of us in his journal. What no one was able to tell the queen of Sheba, he admits to us. This is the other half. In fact he calls the next series of things he endured "grievous evils."

"Grievous Evils" to Remember

The first "evil" that riches can bring is this: *Those who have clutched can quickly crash.*

> There is a grievous evil which I have seen under the sun: riches being hoarded by their owner to his hurt. When those riches were lost through a bad investment and he had fathered a son, then there was nothing to support him. As he had come naked from his mother's womb, so will he return as he came. He will take nothing from the fruit of his labor that he can carry in his hand (Eccles. 5:13–15).

Of the dozens upon dozens of funerals that I have conducted, I have never conducted one where the casket was occupied by anyone who had anything in his hand. And none of the suits wrapped around those bodies required pockets. "You can't take it with you."

Solomon forces us to face that moment we all tend to ignore—the moment of death. He backs up three spaces and looks at the crash and says, "This is the grievous evil: Those who have clutched can quickly crash." Put another way, "Those who grabbed and rose to the top will ultimately release and drop to the bottom."

Can you imagine the scene? I envision a man who hoarded what he had and then lost it through a bad investment. I can see another who fights and wins his way to the top, only to have the bottom drop out of his life as the stock market plunges. And how about the individual who spends himself in a maddening pursuit of some financial goal, who drops dead of a heart attack? It happens every day. In Solomon's words, he "toils for the wind." He departs exactly as he entered life . . . naked and without a thin dime to his name.

We sometimes have the opportunity to be in the presence of some opulent, elegant soul who does everything first class. And I do mean everything. Not a stone is left unturned. Not a detail is unaddressed. It is a place of beautiful appointments. Days later you will still recall the succulent aroma of the wonderful meal you are served. It is just an absolutely fantastic place. The carpet is deep and the furnishings are exquisite, and who knows how many cars are in the garage? It's gorgeous! It is, as we often say, "the last word."

Such a place is described in Proverbs 23. Solomon calls it the home of a king (he ought to know!). And he gives us some counsel when we slip our feet under the table of a king like that.

> When you sit down to dine with a ruler, consider carefully what is before you; and put a knife to your throat, if you are a man of great appetite (vv. 1–2).

Now that's a diet that will work. Absolutely guaranteed. You will not gain an ounce if you employ *that* method. But Solomon doesn't have in mind a literal knife or a literal throat. His is a symbolic statement. What he's saying is this: "Catch yourself before you fall into the trap of wanting all that you see. Do not desire his delicacies, for it is deceptive food. You don't know that there are entanglements that come with it. There are tentacles that are never on display."

Next he gives a warning:

> Do not weary yourself to gain wealth, cease from your consideration of it. When you set your eyes on it, it is gone. For wealth certainly makes itself wings, like an eagle that flies toward the heavens (vv. 4–5).

On the back of a dollar bill is a picture of an eagle with his wings stretched out. When I saw it recently I thought, "Now that's appropriate—absolutely perfect. In fact, it's *biblical.*" And that old dollar bill will just fly right out of my wallet and so will the next one and so will the next hundred and so will the next thousand. Solomon tells us why. They make themselves "wings." No person has ever bought security—ever! "Wealth certainly makes itself wings." This is precisely Solomon's point in his journal.

The man who had much made a bad investment. And even though

he had a family, there was nothing to support him or them. It is a grievous evil that those who clutch can quickly crash.

Solomon lists another "grievous evil" in Ecclesiastes 5:16: "And this also is a grievous evil—exactly as a man is born, thus will he die."

In other words: *Those who live high often die hard.* Solomon has a way of bringing us back to the grave again and again in his "under the sun" counsel. And he continues to show us just how brief life really is.

> Through his life he also eats in darkness with great vexation, sickness and anger (v. 17).

Sometimes I am given an eloquent reminder of just how close death really is. Early one foggy morning not long ago, I was on a predawn jogging trek up a hill alongside a local cemetery which is encircled by a chain-link fence. I've run by that graveyard scores of times. Therefore, my mind was a hundred miles away as my body was grinding its way up the hill.

The cemetery caretaker had apparently arrived early that morning and was watching my approach through the fence, hidden in the early-morning fog. Just when I was about to run past him, his voice boomed out of the fog: *"Well—good morning! How are you today?"*

Startled, I wound up halfway across the street, thinking the graves had opened up and God was greeting me! I thought later as I tried to swallow my heart back into my chest, "That's a good question when you run uphill by a cemetery: 'How are you today?' "

There are many who once ran fast, lived fast, made a pile of money and spent it fast, who also fell awfully fast and died hard. It's the picture of a person we've seen portrayed on page after page of Solomon's penetrating journal—the touch-me-not, I've-got-it-made, fast-lane materialist who lived in earthly opulence. All for what? Solomon tells us straight: an empty, unsatisfying, tragic dead-end street called the grave.

I am reminded of the following classic example:

> He was the world's ultimate mystery—so secretive, so reclusive, so enigmatic, that for more than 15 years no one could say for certain that he was alive, much less how he looked or behaved.
>
> Howard Hughes was one of the richest men in the world, with the destinies of thousands of people—perhaps even of governments—at

his disposal, yet he lived a sunless, joyless, half-lunatic life. In his later years he fled from one resort hotel to another—Las Vegas, Nicaragua, Acapulco—and his physical appearance became odder and odder. His straggly beard hung down to his waist and his hair reached to the middle of his back. His fingernails were two inches long, and his toenails hadn't been trimmed for so long they resembled corkscrews.

Hughes was married for 13 years to Jean Peters, one of the most beautiful women in the world. But never in that time were the two seen in public together, and there is no record of their ever having been photographed together. For a while they occupied separate bungalows at the Beverly Hills Hotel (at $175 per day each), and later she lived in an opulent and carefully guarded French Regency house atop a hill in Bel Air, making secretive and increasingly infrequent trips to be with Hughes in Las Vegas. They were divorced in 1970.

. . . Hughes often said, "Every man has his price or a guy like me couldn't exist," yet no amount of money bought the affection of his associates. Most of his employees who have broken the silence report their disgust for him.[4]

I ask you—is there a more vivid illustration of Solomon's words?

Good and Fitting Gifts to Claim

All is not darkness and gloom, I'm glad to say. Before he brings his thought to a close, the wealthy king smiles as he lists three priceless gifts, which he says are "good and fitting." We need some good news like that! And these gifts are so valuable, money cannot buy them.

Here is what I have seen to be good and fitting: to eat, to drink and enjoy oneself in all one's labor in which he toils under the sun during the few years of his life which God has given him; for this is his reward. Furthermore, as for every man to whom God has given riches and wealth, He has also empowered him to eat from them and to receive his reward and rejoice in his labor; this is the gift of God. For he will not often consider the years of his life, because God keeps him occupied with the gladness of his heart (vv. 18–20).

Claim the gift of enjoyment in your life. Joy is a gift from God. Solomon encourages us as we're eating and drinking—that is, living out our lives—to enjoy ourselves. In other words, refuse to allow yourself to get caught in the greed trap. Refuse to attach yourself to the dollar sign. Refuse to place top priority on making more, more, more just to make more.

He says, "This is good and fitting and God has given us this as a reward. Enjoy life! Laugh more. Find pleasure in the simple things. Go back to the things that brought you happiness as a child and capitalize on them once again." How desperately we need such reminders!

Claim the gift of fulfillment in your work—another of God's gifts. In your life and in your work, find fulfillment. It's not always true that there's a better job around the corner. The greener grass is indeed a myth. So find fulfillment in your work. Invest more in the vertical dimension of life, less in the horizontal. Invest your riches for God's work. Invest your time for His glory. Give generously. That way you'll find a rejoicing in your labor that gives a new dimension.

Claim the gift of contentment in your heart. Enjoyment in your life, fulfillment in your work, contentment in your heart—what an ideal mix!

You're single. You didn't plan to be. So? So, find ways to discover contentment. You're growing older and you're more alone than you ever thought you would be. So? So look for ways to discover contentment. God is there. God gives contentment to you as a gift. He has ways for you to discover contentment even in your sunset years.

You were once in the action. You're now sidelined. You're on a shelf, as it were. You never dreamed you would be. There's a place of contentment even there. You're in obscurity where you once were not. God will give you contentment there, as well.

Remember the words of the queen of Sheba? "The half was not told me!" This is the other half. Solomon told us what no one told the queen. I realize she meant the physical appearance of his kingdom when she said, "I hadn't heard the half of it!" But we know, philosophically, that Solomon saved the best half for us in his journal. The grievous evils, the warnings, the proverbial principles, and these beautiful conclusions—they have no price tag.

If Solomon were living today, I suspect he would admit, "I may look successful and secure, but the half hasn't been told you. I may appear to be fulfilled and happy, but the half hasn't been told you. My possessions would lead people to think that I've got it all together. Many may have the idea that I've got life wired, but those who think that don't know the other half."

This chapter began with the true account of a visit when a queen dropped in on a king. I'd like to end the chapter with an imaginary visit—with *you!*

From the looks of things, you're pretty impressive. You've got a nice place. And I suppose your neighbors would agree that you're a hard worker . . . climbing right on up that ladder toward success, right? I realize you're not into big bucks; but face it, nobody's going hungry. Far from it. Your job is fairly secure. Making more money than ever, you're on your way. But wait, I want to know about the "other half." These things I've mentioned are all external—physical and material stuff. What I want to know is how things are internally.

You look secure and successful, but the half has not been told, right? Part of you is insecure and fearful. Underneath, you're pretty weak. You appear to be happy, easy-going, and fulfilled; but the half has not been told, has it? You wonder about where all this is leading you. Your restless drive for more and your desire for calm, peaceful contentment seem poles apart . . . because they *are* poles apart. Deep down, nothing within you smiles.

Your salary is good and your material possessions are growing in number, but again, the half has not been told. The truth is that you are empty on the inside and you're faking it on the outside. Not one thing you own in all your "kingdom" has brought you the happiness you long for. So you're thinking, "Maybe if I could land that better job," or "get into that bigger house," or . . . or . . . .

But don't allow the smoke screen of more money to blind your eyes to the truth. There's a lot more to being rich than making more money. Seneca, the Roman, was right, "Money has never yet made anyone rich." Do you want riches? Then listen to Jesus:

> But seek first His kingdom and His righteousness; and all these things shall be added to you (Matt. 6:33).

For the *real* riches, try switching kingdoms.

12

THE FEW YEARS OF
A FUTILE LIFE

Journal Entry

There is a very serious evil which I have seen everywhere—God has given to some men very great wealth and honor . . . but he doesn't give them the health to enjoy it, and they die and others get it all! This is absurd . . .

Even if a man has a hundred sons and as many daughters and lives to be very old, but leaves so little money at his death that his children can't even give him a decent burial—I say that he would be better off born dead. For though his birth would then be futile and end in darkness, without even a name, never seeing the sun or even knowing its existence, yet that is better . . . though a man lives a thousand years twice over, but doesn't find contentment—well, what's the use? . . .

The more words you speak, the less they mean, so why bother to speak at all?

*D*imitri Vail is an artist, a portrait painter. If you like literalism, you would really enjoy Vail's work. It is so authentic-looking that at first glance you wonder if you are looking at a photograph instead of a painting.

For many years his paintings have hung in a gallery in Dallas, Texas. I have enjoyed strolling those halls and observing the colorful portraits on display. It is like visiting an all-star cast of the top entertainers and celebrities in the country. His paintings include the familiar faces of film stars, television personalities, outstanding athletes, influential politicians and statesmen, famous prize-winning authors, educators, scientists, astronauts, and other professionals in the fields of business, law, medicine, and the arts. It is no exaggeration to say that Dimitri Vail's artistry forms an impressive who's who on canvas.

While viewing his work several years ago, I stopped in front of an unusual painting. Not only was the face unfamiliar, there was no name on the small brass plate at the base of the frame as there was on each of the other paintings.

Intrigued, I asked the guide if she could identify the man on the canvas. She smiled, and in a soft Texas drawl, replied, "I'm often asked about this one. Folks are always surprised to know that this is a self-portrait of the artist, Mr. Vail himself." As we talked briefly, I told her that I, too, was surprised. Having never met the man, I suppose I expected him to be as colorful as his brush. Anyone *that* gifted, it seems, should be rather exciting in appearance, with perhaps even a touch of flair. "No, not at all," she responded, "the truth is he looks exactly like the painting . . . it's almost as if it were an enlarged photograph."

REVIEWING SOME FAMILIAR PORTRAITS

Solomon's journal is a lot like that gallery. Even though he uses pen and paper instead of a brush and canvas, Solomon paints realistic pictures which his readers can easily identify. As we've seen already, his pen portraits include:

- the serious philosopher who is bored and bewildered
- the funny-face clown who makes us laugh

- the hedonistic playboy who forgets all restraint
- the "good times Charlie" who is living it up
- the industrious worker who hopes to find satisfaction in his job
- the committed worshiper who tries to connect with God
- the blue-collar welder who labors without much anxiety, yet not without his own struggles
- the entrepreneur who loses it all in bad investments, who tosses and turns through the night
- the wealthy person, the "filthy rich," who seeks to find satisfaction in his possessions

What realistic portraits! With vivid, broad-brush strokes of his pen, Solomon has painted people in real life, none of whom lives free of frustration. The faces and frames may differ, but the bottom line is depressingly the same—"vanity". . ."futility". . ."chasing the wind."

An Enlargement of a Single Portrait

As we look at the next section of Solomon's journal, we come to a single portrait done in browns, grays, blues, and blacks. And the closer we study this one, the more apparent it becomes that we have arrived at a self-portrait of the troubled king. He doesn't actually put his name on it, but it's obvious that we are looking at the man himself.

The Situation

> There is an evil which I have seen under the sun and it is prevalent among men—a man to whom God has given riches and wealth and honor so that his soul lacks nothing of all that he desires, but God has not empowered him to eat from them, for a foreigner enjoys them. This is vanity and a sore affliction (Eccles. 6:1–2).

The paradoxical situation described here is commonly found among the affluent. In today's terms, we would say this individual has "got it made." God has given him riches and wealth, honor and influence, along with anything else his soul desires. Yet, in spite of the enviable delights, the man is blocked from enjoying these benefits. We're back to the overriding theme of the book: "This is vanity."

Interestingly, the very same "list" of benefits appears in the ancient book of 2 Chronicles, referring to Solomon.

> And God said to Solomon, "Because you had this in mind, and did not ask for riches, wealth, or honor, or the life of those who hate you, nor have you even asked for long life, but you have asked for yourself wisdom and knowledge, that you may rule My people, over whom I have made you king, wisdom and knowledge have been granted to you. And I will give you riches and wealth and honor, such as none of the kings who were before you has possessed, nor those who will come after you" (2 Chron. 1:11–12).

It is as if God said to His servant Solomon, "Besides granting this unselfish request, I will also add riches and wealth and honor. Whatever your soul desires, it's yours!"

That explains why the description in the opening lines of this section of the journal is probably a self-portrait of Solomon. Don't forget, however, the same God who gave him those things ". . . has not empowered him to eat from them." In other words, God did not give him satisfaction nor cause him to enjoy the benefits of riches and wealth and honor. Solomon had honorable and enviable privileges, yet he was not allowed to draw from them the pleasure that they can bring.

Now this is a tragic state of affairs. Today's cynic would call it a "cruel irony," an "unfair twist" that God would give someone these things yet remove from that person the joy those things could bring.

When such events occur, it causes us to evaluate God. See how the verse concludes? "For a foreigner enjoys them." The reason that man can't enjoy them is a foreigner has come and "ripped off" the enjoyment.

The foreigner is not identified. It could signify an *adversary*, some personal enemy who gave the king grief. Perhaps he was undermining Solomon's leadership. The king once had riches and wealth and honor. Now he knows nothing but hiding and other serious consequences.

It could be *sickness*. He once enjoyed good health, but now that "foreigner" has attacked his body and he can no longer enjoy the delights of riches and wealth and honor. We have all seen illustrations of that.

It could be *domestic conflicts*. There is nothing like trouble at home to take away the fun of life. When this "foreigner" enters, joy exits.

It could be a *natural calamity*. In Southern California, we occasionally have earthquakes or mud slides or fires that sweep across vast canyons. Other places struggle through floods, tornadoes, hurricanes, and blizzards. The "foreigner" may be a natural disaster, a calamity.

The presence of these "foreigners" often causes people to think, "What kind of God am I serving?" Some come to rather extreme conclusions. Rabbi Harold Kushner, in his popular book *When Bad Things Happen to Good People*, writes:

> Life is not fair. The wrong people get sick. And the wrong people get robbed. And the wrong people get killed in wars and in accidents. Some people see life's unfairness and decide "there is no God; the world is nothing but chaos."[1]

You see how the "foreigner" causes some people to evaluate God? The one who is impacted most severely may say, "There is no God. It's just chaos." Kushner comes to his own conclusion. He writes a little later, "Are you capable of forgiving and loving God even when you have found out that He is not perfect?"[2]

Well, I swallowed hard when I read that the first time, because I never imagined forgiving and loving a God who is not perfect. It's at this point I would disagree with the rabbi. This good man has addressed the subject of the living God through the eyes of a grieving father. It was the death of his own son that prompted Kushner to write his book. And it is from that perspective that he reaches certain conclusions about God and asks questions like:

> Even when He has let you down and disappointed you by permitting bad luck and sickness and cruelty in His world and permitting some of those things to happen to you, can you learn to love and forgive Him despite His limitations?[3]

But when we read words like that we cluck our tongues and say, "My! What a blasphemous statement! Those thoughts should never enter anyone's mind!" But they do.

"Foreigners" do a number on us, as do wars and concentration camps and terminal illnesses and tragic natural calamities. They take away our hopes and ruin our dreams. They even cause us to look into the face of heaven and rethink things, don't they?

That is Solomon's perspective, and he calls it "a sore affliction." In the writing of this ancient journal, he has been so frank, so painfully honest in his evaluation of life that some people question whether it even belongs in the Bible. This is a man with a cynical eye. He's painting himself, and the colors aren't attractive; they're drab—like the somber self-portrait of Dimitri Vail.

A Few Helpful Details

In order to make it palatable, in order to live through this unfair power play, Solomon suggests adding a few things to put some color or shading into this portrait. He begins by adding *many children*. Maybe having more children will make life more satisfying.

> If a man fathers a hundred children and lives many years, however many they be, but his soul is not satisfied with good things, and he does not even have a proper burial, then I say, "Better the miscarriage than he, . . ." (Eccles. 6:3).

The point is this: Having many, many children won't make a depressed life free from depression. On the contrary! There is something about having a whole family in front of you to care for and take care of and deal with and relate to and love and discipline and affirm and prepare for life and release that brings increased and often thankless responsibilities.

We don't live under the delusion that our problems are solved by having many, many children. Solomon would say, "On top of that, this man has life taken from him and he isn't even allowed a proper burial." He adds that a miscarriage is better than that.

> ". . . for it comes in futility and goes into obscurity; and its name is covered in obscurity. It never sees the sun and it never knows anything; it is better off than he" (vv. 4–5).

He has no history to live up to. The tiny baby, now dead, has no problems to endure. He doesn't even have a name to bear. This little life is no longer a life and it's placed into a tiny little casket, put into a grave, and is gone—"covered in obscurity."

Well, since having more children isn't the solution to frustration, some would say we need to add *more years*. Maybe what is needed is a longer life. He adds that detail in the next statement:

> "Even if the other man lives a thousand years twice and does not enjoy good things—do not all go to one place [wind up in the grave]?" (v. 6).

If your life is marked by pain and hardship and calamity and tragedy, what good is it to add to it a thousand more years? That only adds a thousand more sorrows. It's been my observation that those who live lives like that want to live shorter lives—not longer ones. They want out of this mess.

Well, maybe what we need to add is *hard work*. Perhaps the person's problem is just having too much time on his hands.

> All a man's labor is for his mouth and yet the appetite is not satisfied (v. 7).

The term translated "appetite" is the Hebrew word *nephesh*. It's the term often rendered "soul" in other Old Testament passages. The soul is not satisfied. Work doesn't bring satisfaction to an empty life. Hard work doesn't bring relief from depression if there are conflicts that feed the soul with discouragement.

Since none of those things help, maybe we should add a *bright mind, wisdom, a good education.*

> For what advantage does the wise man have over the fool? What advantage does the poor man have, knowing how to walk before the living? (v. 8).

This statement seems to suggest that even if a poor man's life is marked by charm or charisma, that man is no better off than one who is bright, wise, and well-educated but not satisfied with his existence. Solomon seems to shout at himself, "Stop dreaming! Stop thinking you can add a few details that will make you think you can put color into a life that is grim. Many children? Who are you kidding? Many wives? More years? Longer hours? Better education? Brighter mind? No . . . a thousand times, no—it won't work!"

Personally, I appreciate his candor when he says, "What the eyes see is better than what the soul desires" (v. 9). He's saying, "Come to terms with reality. What you're able to see—the real thing you see—is better than all of the dreams that you may hope for." He's saying, in effect, "Don't hitch your wagon to the stars of your imagination."

Robert Louis Stevenson once wrote, "To arrive is better than to travel hopefully."⁴ That's not bad! Or, as another often quoted phrase puts it, "A bird in the hand is worth two in the bush." And, in light of what Solomon said about eating, I offer words every American can understand: "A Big Mac in your mouth is better than pheasant under glass in your mind!" It's better to be full with a hamburger than to dream about eating a delicious meal at some ritzy place. Give me a hamburger, fries, and a cola rather than a dream about a steak. Dreams don't fill empty stomachs.

Let me hasten to add that we still need dreamers. While I would warn people against quickly marrying dreamers, we still need some dreamers around. I hum along with the country western tune, "Don't fall in love with a dreamer. They'll break you every time." There's something about dreamers that makes them keep saying, "It'll happen tomorrow." We do need dreams. They keep us hoping through the tough times. They restrain us from tossing in the towel.

I was reading a little book recently called *Blessed Is the Ordinary* and I found this great statement:

HEZEKIA 6:14

"The reason mountain climbers
are tied together
is to keep the sane ones from going home."

I don't know who said it,
or when, or where,
but I've chuckled over it,
thought about it, and quoted it, too.

With a mountain of mercy behind me
and a mountain of mission ahead,
I need you, my sister, my brother,
I need to be tied to you,
and you need me, too.

We need each other . . .
to keep from bolting,
fleeing in panic, and returning
to the "sanity" of unbelief.

Wise words, whoever said them;
I've placed them in my "bible";
they are my Hezekia 6:14.[5]

That is great counsel, isn't it? You know where the dreamers are when you climb the mountain? They're up front saying, "Come on, you guys!" Now some of those in the rear wouldn't come if they weren't tied on. They'd go home. So it takes a few dreamers out front to tell them what it's going to be like, to keep their hopes up. And so it is with life. But the problem comes when we live only in a dream world and refuse to face reality. That's what Solomon is talking about. He's saying, "Untie the knot. Stop attaching yourself to a dream. Don't think that by simply imagining amazing thoughts that suddenly your life will become all you imagine. Dreaming sets us on a collision course where fantasy hits reality broadside. Face the inescapable truth." In other words, *You need God!* So now Solomon comes back into the frame of his self-portrait and speaks from the heart of God as he makes three observations.

Solomon's Observations

To begin with he writes "Whatever exists has already been named . . ." (v. 10).

The first observation then is: *God is sovereign.* At the heart of life's major struggles is a theological issue. Putting it in the form of a question: Is God in charge or is He not?

If we could, by some wonderful force from heaven, be allowed to slip from this earth in our present state and into the glory of heaven, we would not find one shred of evidence that reveals panic. You would never once hear "Oops" from the lips of God, or "I wonder what we're going to do about that!" Never. Nor would we ever observe anxiety across the face of the living God. We would be stunned with amazement at how calm things are around His awesome throne. As a poet once put it:

> Not till the loom is silent and the shuttles cease to fly
> Will God unroll His canvas and explain the reason why. . . .
> The dark threads are as needful in the weaver's skillful hands
> As the threads of gold and scarlet in the pattern He has planned.

From this side of glory we see the tapestry from underneath, and it is full of knots and twisted threads and frayed ends that lack meaning and beauty. From God's perspective, it is all under control.

But I warn you, you will doubt that when the "foreigner" invades; even so, it is true. God is sovereign. That is of primary importance.

Solomon continues his journal entry: ". . . and it is known what man is; . . ." (v. 10). This second observation is: *Mankind is not sovereign.* Let's put it another way. God is the potter; we are the clay. God is infinite; we are finite. God is all-powerful; we are limited in strength and ability. God is faithful; we are unfaithful and inconsistent . . . irresponsible, fractured, and so often confused. The point is clear: We may be a lot of things, but sovereign is not one of them!

> . . . for he cannot dispute with him who is stronger than he is.
> For there are many words which increase futility. What then is the
> advantage to a man? (vv. 10–11).

The third observation is: *Disputing is a waste of time and effort.* C. S. Lewis said it well: "To argue with God is to argue with the very power that makes it possible to argue at all."[6]

These observations are also illustrated in other eloquent Old Testament scriptures:

> Does a clay pot dare argue with its maker, a pot that is like all the others? Does the clay ask the potter what he is doing? Does the pot complain that its maker has no skill? Does anyone dare say to his parents, "Why did you make me like this?" The Lord, the holy God of Israel, the one who shapes the future, says: "You have no right to question me about my children or to tell me what I ought to do! I am the one who made the earth and created mankind to live there. By my power I stretched out the heavens; I control the sun, the moon, and the stars (Isa. 45:9–12, TEV).

Clearly, God is sovereign. We are not. Quarreling with Him is a waste of time. He does precisely as He pleases.

Now look at Daniel 4:35.

"And all the inhabitants of the earth are accounted as nothing, but He does according to His will in the host of heaven and among the inhabitants of earth; and no one can ward off His hand or say to Him, 'What hast Thou done?' "

I first discovered this verse when I was completing my pastoral internship many, many years ago. It was the greatest truth God revealed to me that summer. When I finally put the issue of God's sovereignty to bed, I stopped the fight. It was great! I could not escape from this Old Testament statement.

I wonder how often words of argument have been uttered from the grieving at a graveside. How often they must have come from someone leaving the hospital room! How frequently on the way home from a physician's office! How often after birth defects are discovered! "God, what have You done?"

"I have done My will," is the answer. See how Solomon states it?

> Whatever exists has already been named, and it is known what man is, for he cannot dispute with him who is stronger than he is (Eccles. 6:10).

That's the whole point: Disputing is a waste of time and effort.

So long as I fight the hand of God, I do not learn the lessons He is attempting to place before me. Everything that touches me comes through the hand of my heavenly Father who continues to love me, who continues to maintain control of my life, who continues to be totally responsible for my life as He does with all His created things. That's why He's God!

I encourage you to put this issue to rest. Come to terms with it. Recognize and confess how futile it is to fight against the sovereign hand of God. That is one of the greatest things that has reduced my anxiety level in the ministry. When I find myself getting anxious again it is usually because the size of mankind has gotten greater than the size of my God. The horizontal has overshadowed the vertical . . . and I have momentarily lost sight of who is still on the throne. Even a capable, strong-willed king named Solomon had to admit his inability to fight a winning battle against the living God.

A Look at Our Own Portrait

Our great goal in this book is not simply to learn a lot of facts about Solomon. It's to enable us to see ourselves better through His counsel . . . to better understand life and how to deal with it . . . to help us come to terms with reality. With that in mind, let's ponder a couple of questions. One of them has to do with life today; the other with the future. Both are in this final statement:

> For who knows what is good for a man during his lifetime, during the few years of his futile life? He will spend them like a shadow. For who can tell a man what will be after him under the sun? (v. 12).

Look at that opening line: "Who knows what is good for a man during his lifetime?"

Question 1: *Does life seem futile?* We've all wrestled with this one. Perhaps you've even heard some young man say, "I prayed, 'Lord, if I could just go with that lovely woman, I'd be the happiest guy on earth. If I could *marry* her, I'd be twice as happy.'" They meet and later marry. But after a few years, the same man is praying, "Lord, if I could just get rid of that woman, I'd be the happiest man alive!"

We laugh at that, but underneath we have had similar statements flow from our lips. "I want this. If I could have that, that would really bring me contentment." But once we get it, we find it doesn't satisfy. It isn't best for us. Futility rears its head.

"If I could work for this company. If I could live there. If I could make that salary. If only I could own one of those. . . ." But the inescapable fact is this: None of those conditions give us what we are looking for, and we dispute with God. He graciously tolerates us in our circular journey and says, "I'm working on your life. Don't fight Me."

Question 2: *Are you fearful about the future?* Who knows what the future holds?

> For who knows what is good for a man during his lifetime, during the few years of his futile life? He will spend them like a shadow. . . .

Now that is quite a commentary!

Sometimes the rapid passing of time suddenly hits us in the face. We're living our lives in a pretty common and predictable manner, then all of a sudden, life rushes upon us.

I was fixing breakfast for my younger son Chuck one morning

while he was getting ready to go to school. I was somewhere between the bacon and the waffles and syrup as he yelled from across the family room, "Hey, Dad! I was just thinking, in eight years you're gonna be 58. I'm gonna marry some beauty, and you and Mom are gonna be all alone!" There had been no prior warning; it was just a comment straight out of the blue. But I found myself fighting the urge to dump all the waffles, the bacon, the syrup, and the milk into the blender and serving everything quickly—"There. You eat that! That'll give your mouth something to work on."

Eight years just passed in review, right up there in one little bundle. I pondered his remark half the morning. Maybe he is right. Or maybe life won't be like he said it would be. Who knows if I'll even *be* here in eight years? Who can say for sure that we'll even have *him* in eight years? Who knows if he will marry some beauty? (I mentioned that to him later.) I mean, who knows if any of the Swindolls will be living at my place? Who knows if I'll even have my wife in eight years—or if she'll have me? Death doesn't announce its arrival. Who knows what death will do to our family?

I was intrigued the other day as I sat reading the last part of the Sermon on the Mount. As you may recall, Jesus compares the people who were listening to Him to houses—some would build their lives on sand, some on rock (Matt. 7:24–27). He tells them that those who hear Him and *do not act* upon what they hear are like houses built on the sand. But those who hear Him and *act upon it* are like houses built on a rock.

Since they all hear the same thing, the difference is not in the hearing, but in the acting. Therefore, when the storm comes, one house falls and the other stands for one simple, specific reason: the response.

Does your life seem pretty futile? If so, it's really nothing to be ashamed of. God made us like that. Clay can't shape itself; it needs a potter. Colorful oils can't paint by themselves; they need an artist—an artist who is a literalist, who tells us the truth.

Is your house on the rock? Or is it on the sand? Well, depending on that answer, you'll have the answer for your future. Are you ready to face the living God? No matter how much time you have left—be it eight years or eight months—the foundation of your life must be solid rock, or life *will* be futile. I urge you not to close this chapter and hurry on your way, thinking that reading is the ultimate end of a book like this. It's not; it's following through on the truth you read. Remember what Jesus said about people who build rocklike lives? They *respond* correctly to truth—they act upon it.

Wherever you are, Jesus Christ (the Rock) is ready to take over the foundation of your house. He'll personally remove all the sand and replace it with Himself. He'll take you just as you are—finite, troubled, argumentative, broken, fragmented, disillusioned, confused, and sinful. And He'll make you like you ought to be.

Your years may be few, but they need not be futile.

13

WISE WORDS FOR BUSY PEOPLE

Journal Entry

A good reputation is more valuable than the most expensive perfume.

The day one dies is better than the day he is born! It is better to spend your time at funerals than at festivals. For you are going to die and it is a good thing to think about it while there is still time. Sorrow is better than laughter, for sadness has a refining influence on us. Yes, a wise man thinks much of death, while the fool thinks only of having a good time now. . . .

The wise man is turned into a fool by a bribe; it destroys his understanding.

Finishing is better than starting! Patience is better than pride! Don't be quick-tempered—that is being a fool.

Don't long for "the good old days," for you don't know whether they were any better than these!

We have reached the halfway point in Solomon's journal. By now we have a pretty good handle on the man's mental perspective as well as his method of pursuit. But something has been conspicuous by its absence: wisdom. That may surprise you, since the common opinion of Solomon is that he was a man of considerable wisdom. What patience was to Job, wisdom was to Solomon. That's true . . . except for a strange segment of time in his life when he tossed restraint to the winds and acted out a role altogether unusual for a man of his heritage, position, and stature.

Had he lived in our generation, I suppose we would have explained his escapades as being the result of a midlife crisis. Things that were once important and dear to him began to be viewed with cynicism, especially the simplicity and purity of the walk of faith. Wisdom took a back seat as rebellion took control, grabbed the wheel, and jammed the accelerator to the floor, screaming to every passion within, "Let 'er rip!" And even though lasting satisfaction eluded him, he kept taking every corner on two wheels. Funny thing about us humans, we tend to run faster when we have lost our way. And when we do, wisdom waits, refusing to keep pace with our frantic, maddening race to find happiness. The story is repeated a thousand different ways every year.

A Pilgrimage of Futility

I remember a special phone call I received a few years ago. It made me cry. But they were long-awaited tears of joy, not sorrow. The man didn't know it, but his call came on my birthday—and it was the finest gift I could possibly have received. "Hello, Charlie," came the husky voice which had been so familiar to me back in the early 1960s. "I just wanted you to know I've come back home." Words fail to describe my ecstasy. Dumbfounded, all I could do was utter his name and ask, "Where in the world have you been?" And I added, "How much I have missed you!" The tears flowed as we visited for almost an hour. As he unveiled the account of his fifteen-year downward spiral, my mind flashed back to a handsome young high-schooler who had become acquainted with Cynthia and me during our early days in seminary. What a bright, teachable, humble guy he was. And his hunger for spiritual truth seemed insatiable. My wife and I agreed that we'd never met anyone with more promise or greater potential.

By the time he was out of high school, he was convinced that the ministry was his ultimate destination, which only increased our interest in his training and further education. Academically capable, he really had his choice of where he preferred to study. And since he was so gifted in languages, he greatly desired to capitalize on this during his college years, which led him to complete his undergraduate studies abroad. And that's when things began to change.

The lack of regular contact and accountability with Christians who could have supported and stabilized him during those formative, tender years took its toll. He was surrounded by a lifestyle that was much more loose. His studies took him into philosophical realms he wasn't able to handle on his own with sufficient objectivity. His roots in the church were virtually severed. There was no consistent biblical intake. A romance with a young woman of another culture and with interests much different from his own blossomed and resulted in marriage. All this and more caused the young man's simple faith and humble spirit to erode. Back in the States, he entered his first year of seminary. And it soon became clear that his wife would rather have been anywhere but there. A collision was inevitable.

He became bored and disinterested. He felt his intelligence was being insulted as the studies continually required his poring over the basic truths of Scripture. Although he breezed through the languages and had little difficulty grasping the finer points of theology, his attitude became increasingly sour. His opinion of the faculty was that they were far too rigid and narrow. He had little in common with his classmates, and even Cynthia's and my interraction with him was seldom and strained.

A little over halfway through his graduate studies, he dropped out of the school, angry and disillusioned. He became all the more cynical. He took up habits to prove to others he was "free." His marriage weakened. Profanity replaced praise. A hard, glazed stare drilled its way through you from eyes that once revealed sensitivity and compassion. His education turned the corner and he opened himself to an entirely different theological perspective. He found himself despising his evangelical roots. By and by, he went to Europe to work on his doctorate, studying under one of the prominent scholars in the field of archaeology. He learned a new language and, in fact, became conversant in it. Years passed. The marriage ended in a divorce. He earned a graduate degree and involved himself in further research, teaching—all the things he thought he wanted.

But he was empty . . . horribly, desperately, tragically empty. He drank heavily. He became a chain smoker. Days ran together into weeks and meaningless months. Picture the scene. Sitting in a lonely, dark apartment halfway around the world was a brilliant man in his thirties, holding some of the most enviable academic credentials one could imagine, seriously considering suicide. I do not know anyone who better epitomizes Solomon in the midst of his miserable journey. My long-lost friend could have posed for the portrait Solomon paints in his journal.

During our telephone conversation, my friend verbally walked through his long journey back, periodically pausing and attempting to describe the emptiness and the futility he felt. I'll never forget one of his remarks.

"You remember telling me that I'd not find God in a seminary?"

"Yes, I remember."

"Well, you were right. There's nothing to be found simply in the academic truths of theology. If the heart isn't right, theology won't help."

"That's exactly what I was getting at."

He added, "Well, I've got another statement you can pass along— you won't find wisdom in the halls of intellectualism!"

After all he'd been through—after a decade and a half of running, fighting, struggling, wrestling, arguing, and, yes, absorbing everything the horizontal, humanistic plane had to offer—the man had returned to his senses. And wisdom came out of hiding. He was older, but so much wiser. His journey reminds me of the poet's words:

> When I have ceased to break my wings
> Against the faultiness of things,
> And learned that compromises wait
> Behind each hardly opened gate,
> When I can look Life in the eyes,
> Grown calm and very coldly wise,
> Life will have given me the Truth,
> And taken in exchange—my youth.*

*Reprinted with permission of Macmillan Publishing Company from "Wisdom," *Collected Poems* by Sara Teasdale. Copyright 1917 by Macmillan Publishing Company, renewed 1945 by Mamie T Wheless.

As I hung up the phone, I immediately thought of Solomon's admission:

> So I hated life, for the work which had been done under the sun was grievous to me; because everything is futility and striving after wind. Thus I hated all the fruit of my labor for which I had labored under the sun, for I must leave it to the man who will come after me (Eccles. 2:17–18).

A CHANGE IN SCENERY

The man is describing life *under* the sun—ragged-edge reality, without God. Thus far in his journey, that has been his mindset, and it continues to be. But from here on, something begins to come into focus—the wisdom that has been conspicuously absent. The terms *wise* and *wisdom* appear almost thirty-five times in the latter half of his journey. Why? Well, to quote my prodigal friend, Solomon is "coming back home." He still has quite a way to travel, but his pilgrimage now takes a turn in the right direction.

Perhaps that best explains the change in Solomon's writing style when we arrive at the midpoint in his journal. Instead of continuing the narrative style he has employed thus far, he turns to the proverbial style—brief, crisp, simple-sounding statements that offer insightful principles for handling life. Often, proverbs in Scripture come in the form of couplets. When they do, they appear in one of three ways:

- *Contrastive couplets*, connected by the terms *but* or *nevertheless.*

  A wise son accepts his father's discipline,
  But a scoffer does not listen to rebuke (Prov. 13:1).

  Through presumption comes nothing but strife,
  But with those who receive counsel is wisdom (Prov. 13:10).

- *Completive couplets*, connected by the terms *and* or *so.*

  The heart knows its own bitterness,
  And a stranger does not share its joy (Prov. 14:10).

> Even in laughter the heart may be in pain,
> And the end of joy may be grief (Prov. 14:13).

- *Comparative couplets*, connected by the terms *better/than* or *like/so.*

  > Better is a little with the fear of the Lord,
  > Than great treasure and turmoil with it.

  > Better is a dish of vegetables where love is,
  > Than a fattened ox and hatred with it (Prov. 15:16–17).

  > It is better to live in a corner of the roof
  > Than in a house shared with a contentious woman.

  > Like cold water to a weary soul,
  > So is good news from a distant land (Prov. 25:24–25).

As wisdom begins to return to Solomon, it reveals itself in a series of seven "comparative proverbs" as the man records seven specific things that are "better than" their counterparts. Read the list and count them for yourself.

A good name is *better than* a good ointment,
And the day of one's death is *better than* the day of one's birth.
It is *better* to go to a house of mourning
Than to go to a house of feasting,
Because that is the end of every man,
And the living takes it to heart.
Sorrow is *better than* laughter,
For when a face is sad a heart may be happy.
The mind of the wise is in the house of mourning.
While the mind of fools is in the house of pleasure.
It is *better* to listen to the rebuke of a wise man
Than for one to listen to the song of fools,
For as the crackling of thorn bushes under a pot,
So is the laughter of the fool,
And this too is futility.
For oppression makes a wise man mad,
And a bribe corrupts the heart.
The end of a matter is *better than* its beginning;
Patience of spirit is *better than* haughtiness of spirit.

Do not be eager in your heart to be angry,
For anger resides in the bosom of fools,
Do not say, "Why is it that the former days were better than these?"
For it is not from wisdom that you ask about this (Eccles. 7:1–10, italics
mine).

COUNSEL FOR THOSE IN THE CRUNCH

Let's take each comparison, one after another, and get a little wisdom. We may discover how and why Solomon began to find his
way back home.

1. *"A good name is better than a good ointment."* The word *ointment*
might better be rendered "a good perfume," "a good cologne," or
even "a good aftershave." To make it more relevant, a good name
is better than Polo or Pierre Cardin . . . a good name is better than
Cartier or Nina Ricci. Now what is this comparison supposed to teach
us? A good name is that which has influence and character . . .
that which changes lives . . . that which has a fine reputation. A
good name is certainly to be preferred to that which simply has a
pleasant aroma.

That's true not only of people, but it's true of restaurants as well.
All restaurants smell good. Well, most restaurants smell good. But
you seldom, if ever, go by the smell. You choose your restaurant by
the name—by its reputation. The same is true of most products we
purchase. When we choose what is referred to as a name-brand product, it's usually because the name has come to stand for quality. One
manufacturer says it this way: "The quality goes in before the name
goes on."

Likewise, as quality goes into a life, the good name goes on. And
that good name, based on internal quality, is always "better than"
external fragrances. For no matter how expensive the ointment, nothing is more valuable to an individual than the character behind his
or her name.

Look at the next proverb. It is not derived from our Western culture.

2. *"The day of one's death is better than the day of one's birth."*
That throws us a curve, doesn't it? We Westerners celebrate birthdays,
but we mourn deathdays. How could one's death be better than one's
birth? The best way to answer that is with a section of Scripture
from the New Testament—Philippians 1:23–24:

> But I am hard-pressed from both directions [like the old saying, "I'm between a rock and a hard place"], having the desire to depart and be with Christ, for that is very much better; yet to remain on in the flesh is more necessary for your sake.

Both Paul and Solomon are saying, "If I had my 'druthers,' I'd rather be out of this life and into eternity. I'd rather be with God than among humanity. I would much rather be beyond this veil of tears and at home in glory, enjoying the presence of the Lord. That's a lot better." So in that sense, the joyous days following our death are better than all of the painful and stressful days that follow our birth. Those who know the Lord in a personal and intimate manner (deep down, Solomon did) can make such a statement.

The next two comparative proverbs are interwoven with this one.

3. *"It is better to go to a house of mourning than to go to a house of feasting."* A blunt paraphrase of the comparison would read, "Visiting a funeral parlor is better than gorging oneself at a banquet" or "A thirty-minute stroll through a graveyard is better than an entire afternoon at a carnival, or spending a weekend in Vegas."

Why is this man saying such a thing? In our day of feasting and laughter, fun and games, what kind of counsel is that? Is he into some kind of depression syndrome? No, not at all. Remember the unspoken subject is wisdom. And when you get beneath the shallow surface of life, it's amazing how quickly you get rid of the superficial. It's amazing how empty most jokes are . . . how hollow the places of entertainment seem in comparison to that which is eternal.

See the next proverb? These two belong together.

4. *"Sorrow is better than laughter."* Our thought process is seldom more shallow than when we have some clown dump a joke into our ears. After a quick laugh it's amazing how quickly the joke is forgotten. But we seldom forget a stroll through a graveyard and what we learn there about the great men and women who have shaped lives. As a pastor, I've seldom had a wiser audience than in a funeral service. They really listen.

Sure it's frightening, but it's amazing how much perspective is gained when we get a glimpse of life from the back door. That's what Solomon means when he makes the next statement:

> The mind of the wise is in the house of mourning,
> While the mind of fools is in the house of pleasure (v. 4).

There's a true story that comes from the sinking of the *Titanic*. A frightened woman found her place in a lifeboat that was about to be lowered into the raging North Atlantic. She suddenly thought of something she needed, so she asked permission to return to her stateroom before they cast off. She was granted three minutes or they would have to leave without her.

She ran across the deck that was already slanted at a dangerous angle. She raced through the gambling room with all the money that had rolled to one side, ankle deep. She came to her stateroom and quickly pushed aside her diamond rings and expensive bracelets and necklaces as she reached to the shelf above her bed and grabbed three small oranges. She quickly found her way back to the lifeboat and got in.

Now that seems incredible because thirty minutes earlier she would not have chosen a crate of oranges over even the smallest diamond. But death had boarded the *Titanic*. One blast of its awful breath had transformed all values. Instantaneously, priceless things had become worthless. Worthless things had become priceless. And in that moment she preferred three small oranges to a *crate* of diamonds.

Death gives you that kind of wisdom. Those who live their lives suffering from a terminal disease usually demonstrate a remarkable degree of wisdom in the way they spend their time. It is amazing what happens even to one's conversation! Solomon seems to have lost interest in the silly side of life. He's beginning to come back home. Wisdom is beginning to pay its dividends.

5. *"It is better to listen to the rebuke of a wise man than for one to listen to the song of fools."* If you want to know what the fool's song sounds like, just read Solomon's next words:

> For as the crackling of thorn bushes under a pot,
> So is the [cackling, silly] laughter of the fool (v. 6).

It's empty. There's nothing to it. In his words, ". . . this too is futility."

Hearing a wise person's rebuke is far better than humming a fool's song. That's the idea. Most of us fail to hear the rebukes of the wise. Sometimes the wise person is a boss who attempts to evaluate our job. At other times it's a parent who pulls us up close, in one of those nose-to-nose encounters, and tells us some things we need to hear. But we find such occasions difficult to bear. There are times when the rebuke of the wise person comes through the lips of a coach who has an incredibly gifted athlete, though somewhat of a rebellious maverick, on his hands. And the reprimand coming from the wise coach is all-too-often tuned out.

The wise person who rebukes us is occasionally a judge in the courtroom. The law requires such officials to carry out a sentence against us when we have done wrong. The penalty may be difficult to bear, but if we are wise, we can not only learn from it, we will be grateful for it.

John Ehrlichman was one of the most powerful men in the United States during the Richard Nixon era. He's written his memoirs in a vulnerable volume entitled *Witness to Power.* I have chosen just a few excerpts from the last chapter because they illustrate so vividly the value of listening to the rebuke of the wise, painful though it may be.

> When I went to jail, nearly two years after the cover-up trial, I had a big self-esteem problem. I was a felon, shorn and scorned, clumping around in a ragged old army uniform, doing pick and shovel work out on the desert. I wondered if anyone thought I was worth anything. . . . For years I had been able to sweep most of my shortcomings and failures under the rug and not face them, but during the two long criminal trials, I spent my days listening to prosecutors tell juries what a bad fellow I was. Then at night I'd go back to a hotel room and sit alone thinking about what was happening to me. During that time I began to take stock. . . .
>
> I stayed about two weeks. Every day I read the Bible, walked on the beach and sat in front of my fireplace thinking and sketching, with no outline or agenda. I had no idea where all this was leading or what answers I'd find. Most of the time I didn't even know what the questions were. I just watched and listened. I was wiped out. I had nothing left that had been of value to me—honor, credibility, virtue, recognition, profession—nor did I have the allegiance of my family. I had managed to lose that too. . . .
>
> Since about 1975 I have begun to learn to see myself. I care what I perceive about my integrity, my capacity to love and be loved, and my essential worth. I don't miss Richard Nixon very much, and Richard Nixon probably doesn't miss me much either. I can understand that. I've made no effort to be in touch. We had a professional relationship that went as sour as a relationship can, and no one likes to be reminded of bad times. Those interludes, the Nixon episodes in my life, have ended. In a paradoxical way, I'm grateful for them. Somehow I had

to see all of that and grow to understand it in order to arrive at the place where I find myself now.[1]

Are we listening to the rebuke of the wise? Sometimes the wise rebuke comes from a former mate. Or the wise person could be a pastor, or a therapist, or a physician, or an attorney. We must be open and willing to learn from rebukes.

It isn't time to laugh at more jokes when life's crashing in around you. The crunch is on . . . and it's time to come home again. Enough of shallow entertainment! Wisdom can return, but often it takes time and pain and loss and brokenness before its counsel is heard. Coming to terms with reality includes our being open to the rebuke of the wise.

There are two remaining proverbs in this section worth our consideration.

6. *"The end of a matter is better than its beginning."* That makes sense in light of what we've just considered, doesn't it? You see, the end of a matter is maximum reality. Those little idealistic dreams have ended. The whole truth is on display. There are no more unrealistic expectations, no gaps of ignorance, no lack of awareness. The complete picture has developed. Once we reach the end, we know the whole story, and that is better than the beginning of a matter where desires lack substance.

How many times we have said, "Oh! If I could have just lived that over again." "Oh! If I could have just entered into my practice another way." "Oh! If I had just seen marriage then like I see it now." Or, "If only I could go back and raise my children again— how much better a parent I would be!" These thoughts come back to haunt me too.

Now that we have grandchildren, my wife and I have a fresh perspective on child-rearing. As much as we enjoyed our children, we find ourselves anticipating with even greater delight the pleasure of investing ourselves in these new additions to our family. While holding little Ryan recently (our older son's and daughter-in-law's firstborn), I thought about some of the wisdom that my wife and I might be able to pass along. I thought about the passing of time. The tune from *Fiddler on the Roof* is so true:

Sunrise, sunset . . . sunrise, sunset;
Swiftly fly the years. . . .[2]

I had a grandfather tell me recently that he plans to put a lot of his thoughts on a cassette tape because, he said, "I don't know how long I'm gonna live and I don't know how long I'll have my mind, so I'm gonna record some important counsel and let my grandchildren listen to it later on."

The most influential man in my life was my mother's father. I can still hear his wise counsel. Such counsel is better than most advice given to a child because it is end-of-the-matter information coming from one who has been seasoned with wisdom.

There's a seventh and final proverb that follows right on the heels of that one, and I will openly confess, it is the one that gives me a battle.

7. *"Patience of spirit is better than haughtiness of spirit."* Few things hit me harder than this one. How I struggle with patience! And the struggle has lasted a lifetime! As I look back, I think of how much better it would have been to wait, rather than to blow off steam . . . to allow God to intervene rather than to hurry things up and create such a man-made mess. I think of needless moments I have spent fuming at red lights, for example. Isn't that silly? Eventually, all red ones turn green, so why sweat it? Ridiculous. But Solomon's point goes much deeper than temporary hassles like minor irritations and red-light delays. Notice he mentions the contrast, "haughtiness of spirit."

How much better to be calm than angry, because with a patient spirit there emerges a groundswell of wisdom. On this pilgrimage from earth to heaven, one of God's great goals is the development of our inner character, which implies the replacement of a proud spirit with a patient spirit. As that transpires, wisdom has a platform upon which to work. Our haughty spirit pushes wisdom aside, and when it does, we play the fool. That explains why he writes what he does on the heels of this seventh proverb.

> Do not be eager in your heart to be angry,
> For anger resides in the bosom of fools (Eccles. 7:9).

And while we're at it, let's guard against languishing over yesteryear—another favorite indoor sport of many a soul. See how he counsels us?

> Do not say, "Why is it that the former days were better than these?"
> For it is not from wisdom that you ask about this (v.10).

Today is today. It will never be yesterday, nor should we try to make it so. Wisdom stays on the cutting edge. God is forever up-to-date, well able to sustain us through these tough and challenging times. And let us never think that His love is mere sentimentality, longing for an ideal context in which to express itself. We don't need "the good ol' days" in order to survive. Wisdom is quite capable of flourishing in the midst of gut-wrenching reality. I especially like the way C. S. Lewis brings us back to sound bottom-line basics.

> We want . . . not so much a Father in heaven as a grandfather in heaven . . . whose plan for the universe was simply that it might be truly said at the end of each day, "a good time was had by all". . . . I should very much like to live in a universe which was governed on such lines. But since it is abundantly clear that I don't, and since I have reason to believe, nevertheless, that God is love, I conclude that my conception of love needs correction.[3]

He then wraps up his thoughts with:

> The problem of reconciling human suffering with the existence of a God who loves is only insoluble so long as we attach a trivial meaning to the word "love," and look on things as if man were the centre of them. Man is not the centre. God does not exist for the sake of man. Man does not exist for his own sake. . . . We were made not primarily that we may love God (though we were made for that too) but that God may love us. . . .[4]

WISDOM: WHAT MAKES IT SO SPECIAL?

All these proverbs on wisdom prompt a pile of questions in our heads. What's so great about this wisdom? Why is it worth coming home to? Why shouldn't I live the balance of my life in the carnal corral? Why shouldn't I run wild and follow the urges of my emotions and give all of the surges of my passion a chance to be expressed? Why not "let it all hang out"? Why do I want to stop a self-satisfying ego trip and turn to wisdom? What's the big deal with wisdom?

Interestingly, Solomon doesn't abruptly stop this section of his journal before extolling two specific and all-important virtues of wisdom. It's almost as if he hopes to grab the attention of some (like my friend I mentioned earlier) who may be teetering on the fence of indecision. First, let's read what Solomon wrote, then let's discover why wisdom is vital to a victorious life.

> Wisdom along with an inheritance is good
> And an advantage to those who see the sun.
> For wisdom is protection just as money is protection.
> But the advantage of knowledge is that wisdom preserves
>   the lives of its possessors.
> Consider the work of God,
> For who is able to straighten what He has bent?
> In the day of prosperity be happy,
> But in the day of adversity consider—
> God has made the one as well as the other
> So that man may not discover anything that will be after
>   him (Eccles. 7:11–14).

Wisdom offers two major benefits:

1. *Wisdom preserves our lives from human pitfalls.* The pitfalls? Go back to what the man wrote. I can think of several examples:

- With an inheritance comes the pitfall of *pride.* Wisdom preserves us from that.

- With affliction comes the pitfall of *doubt and disillusionment.* Wisdom preserves us from that.

- With the anticipation of relief, vindication, even rewards for doing what is right comes the pitfall of *resentment and bitterness.* Wisdom preserves us from that.

Solomon is absolutely correct: "Wisdom is protection." But it is more than that.

2. *Wisdom provides our lives with divine perspective.* We are first invited to "consider the work of God," then we are given several occasions when that will provide us the perspective we need:

- "For who is able to straighten what He [God] has bent?"

The Lord our God is ultimately in control. Theologians call this *divine sovereignty.* Unfortunately, it has become a point of argumentation rather than our personal ally. God is in charge, meaning if He has "straightened" something, it's wasted effort to try to bend it. This divine perspective is designed to replace resistance with relief.

- "In the day of prosperity be happy!"

Times are good? Great! Or, in today's vernacular, "Enjoy!" There is no reason whatsoever to allow guilt to rob you of the joy that should accompany prosperous times. Divine perspective frees us to be happy.

- "But in the day of adversity consider—God has made the one as well as the other."

Again, this divine perspective wisdom brings reminds me that the Lord God is just as involved and caring during adversity as during prosperity.

The Hebrew term translated "consider" suggests the idea "to examine for the purpose of evaluating." In the hard times—when the bottom drops out, enduring days of financial reversal, or severe domestic conflicts—wisdom allows us to examine, to evaluate with incredible objectivity.

> In the day of prosperity be happy,
> But in the day of adversity consider—
> God has made the one as well as the other.

He wants us to walk by faith, not by sight. He won't reveal the future, which is why the next phrase reads, "So that man may not discover anything that will be after him."

God's ultimate design is nothing short of perfect. He's got a plan, but without operating on the basis of His wisdom, we'll panic and run or we'll stubbornly resist His way. This causes me to add these two concluding thoughts. The first has to do with the decisions we make; the second has to do with the vision we employ.

Regarding *decisions*—we dare not make a major decision without asking for the wisdom of God. Since wisdom is His specialty, His unique gift to us, it's imperative that we seek it prior to every major decision. Remember these great words?

> But if any of you lacks wisdom, let him ask of God, who gives to all men generously and without reproach, and it will be given to him (James 1:5).

Regarding *vision*—we cannot see the whole picture without drawing upon the wisdom of God. That was Solomon's primary blind spot. Like my friend who chunked it all and plunged into that fifteen-year drift, awash in a sea of confusion and carnality, the king failed to see God at work. The absence of wisdom ushered in the presence of misery. It always does.

GIVING BIRTH TO WISDOM

Most of us have traveled down a road of futility. But the good news is that the self-inflicted pain and heartache of those times provide us with the ideal background for the birth of wisdom into our lives. There is nothing like the labor pains brought on by misery and futility to help bring wisdom to term and turn our lives around.

A book that has really meant much to me in my own spiritual pilgrimage for the last several years is *Where Is God When It Hurts?* In the latter part of the book, author Philip Yancey offers some descriptive words that form an ideal conclusion to this chapter. See if you can find yourself in these words.

> Your world is dark, safe, secure. You are bathed in warm liquid, cushioned from shock. You do nothing for yourself; you are fed automatically, and a murmuring heartbeat assures you that someone larger than you fills all your needs. Your life consists of simple waiting—you're not sure what to wait for, but any change seems far away and scary. You meet no sharp objects, no pain, no threatening adventures. A fine existence.
>
> One day you feel a tug. The walls are falling in on you. Those soft cushions are now pulsing and beating against you, crushing you downwards. Your body is bent double, your limbs twisted and wrenched. You're falling, upside down. For the first time in your life, you feel pain. You're in a sea of roiling matter. There is more pressure, almost too intense to bear. Your head is squeezed flat, and you are pushed harder, harder into a dark tunnel. Oh, the pain. Noise. More pressure.
>
> You hurt all over. You hear a groaning sound and an awful, sudden fear rushes in on you. It is happening—your world is collapsing. You're sure it's the end. You see a piercing, blinding light. Cold, rough hands pull at you. A painful slap. Waaaahhhh!
>
> Congratulations! You've just been born.[5]

The thought of leaving the womb seems frightening, portentous, full of pain. We're afraid of the unknown. But when we emerge into that bright, fresh world of wisdom our tears and hurts from yesteryear will be mere memories.

We have not even begun to live if we lack the wisdom God wants to give to us. That wisdom is ours, simply for the asking, and it brings us into a whole new and exciting world! Like birth, it will take time and it may be a painful process. But when it comes, you'll be amazed how clearly things will come into focus. You'll begin to feel like a new creature.

No wonder Jesus referred to it as being "born again."

14

PUTTING WISDOM TO WORK

Journal Entry

In this silly life I have seen everything,
including the fact that some of the good
die young and some of the wicked live
on and on. So don't be too good or too
wise! Why destroy yourself? On the
other hand, don't be too wicked either—
don't be a fool! Why should you die
before your time?

Tackle every task that comes along,
and if you fear God you can expect his
blessing.

A wise man is stronger than the mayors
of ten big cities! And there is not a
single man in all the earth who is
always good and never sins. . . .

I have tried my best to be wise . . . but
it didn't work. Wisdom is far away, and
very difficult to find.... though God
has made men upright, each has turned
away to follow his own downward road.

*L*ife tends to move faster and become more complicated the older I get. But I find that I'm better able to deal with the fast pace of life when I return to the basics for extended periods of time. Sometimes I do that when I'm jogging—I blow the dust off a few fundamental facts and turn them over in my mind for forty-five minutes to an hour. Occasionally, when I get away for an entire day of sailing or fishing or a few nights of camping, I'll zoom in on a primary thought and meditate for several hours.

Here's one, for example: *God has the whole world in His hands.* Remember the old gospel song? He's got the wind, the rain, the tiny little baby, yes, even you and me in His hands. How easy it is to forget that! And it isn't limited to our geography or our culture, you know. He's got the Middle East in His hands (that's a relief, isn't it?), not to mention Central America and Red China, Ethiopia and India, Indonesia and Russia—all right there in the palms of His sovereign hands. And while we're at it, He's got our future, our children, our circumstances, our friends, and our foes in His hands . . . within His grasp . . . under His control. Even when imaginary fears slip in like the morning frost to blight our faith, He's there—in charge. What a grand comfort! That basic thought really helps to stabilize us.

I needed it several months ago. I was parasailing off the western coast of Mexico—I'd always wanted to try something as adventurous as that. So, along with a couple of "I-dare-you" buddies of mine, it was zip . . . up, up, and away! Suddenly, it occurred to me (after I reached maximum altitude) that maybe I should examine the contraption I was sitting in and see how carefully the thing was put together. With the wind whipping at me, almost tearing off my swimsuit, I made the frightful discovery that my entire life was dependent upon a granny knot tied by some ten-year-old Mexican kid. I immediately imagined him before dawn that morning giving the thin rope a quick yank as he made his way to the beach. There I was, a good fifteen to twenty stories up, high above the hotels and cruise ships (which resembled large paper clips in the harbor) wondering why.

Suddenly, I wanted to run . . . out of the question. I certainly didn't want to drop everything! In fact, by then I had a white-knuckle grip on my harness that made me wonder if I'd ever let go. I reviewed every Scripture verse I'd ever committed to memory, confessed every sin I'd ever done—commission and omission!—and I promised God if He would just get me back on that beach, I'd double my evangelistic fervor . . . I'd even sing in the choir and work in the nursery, if necessary!

Well, I made it back. What a wonderful feeling, warm sand between my toes! I tried to look cool and confident as I touched down, but it was tough masking my fear. It's a great illustration of operating by faith, but let me tell you, while I was up there I never once thought about how secure I was in God's hands. I *should* have, but I didn't. Looking back, I can laugh at the whole crazy episode, but I want to assure you, there were several minutes up in the wild blue yonder that had me gasping.

But then there are times that don't make us laugh. There are times when we find it really hard to believe that our circumstance is truly in His hands. Not only are the wind and the rain and the tiny little baby (plus those crazy, fanciful experiences called a dare) in His hands, but life's minor interruptions as well as major calamities are too. In fact, would you believe they never leave His attention?

Now we may doubt that. There will be times we will need the reminder of the wise prophet named Isaiah. In verses 14 through 16 of chapter 49 we find that the nation is speaking. And why shouldn't it? There's threat all around. There are impending signs of destruction. Clouds of an on-coming enemy can be seen on the horizon. It is inevitable that bondage is near, a similar kind of bondage the European Jews could sense at the outset of the Holocaust.

> But Zion said, "The Lord has forsaken me, and the Lord has forgotten me."

Perhaps you've said something similar such as, "I prayed for healing and healing hasn't come." Or, "I prayed for relief and relief hasn't come." Maybe, "I prayed for my wife and my wife hasn't returned." Or, "I prayed for my husband and my husband hasn't stopped and turned around." Or, "I prayed for my wayward and rebellious child, and God (for some reason) has forsaken me and forgotten me." Zion said, "Jehovah has forsaken and forgotten us." Then Isaiah asks a penetrating question:

> Can a woman forget her nursing child, and have no compassion on the son of her womb?

In other words: "Tell me. Is it possible for a nursing mother to place her baby in the crib and walk away?" Yes, it's possible—not only possible, it happens every day. "Tell me. Can a woman who has had compassion on the little boy who has come through her womb . . . can she ever desert that boy and leave him for someone else to find?" Look at God's answer: ". . . Even these may forget, but I will not forget you." I've circled that statement in my Bible. "I will not forget you." God is more faithful than a mother is to her child, more faithful than the president is to his country, more faithful than the king is to his domain. He is more faithful than a coach is to the team, more faithful than a devoted father is to his family. Why? Because He is God.

> Behold, I have inscribed you on the palms of My hands; your walls are continually before Me.

In other words, He sees us exactly as we are . . . walls and all, warts and all, needs and all. He sees everything. And how close does He view it? It's in the palms of His hands.

Look at your hands a few moments. Pick a line. You've got several to choose from. You know those lines better than anyone else on earth—better than your mate, better than your parent, better than your child, better than your closest friend. We know our hands better than anyone.

My dad used to say, "It's as plain as the back of my hand." But God says, "You are as clear to me as the palm of My hand." Just as you, friend, know the lines in your hand, God knows your ways . . . and He knows them *continually.* That includes your responses, your experiences, your reactions, what you call your calamities, your dead ends, your impossible situations.

See, not only does He have you and me, the wind and the rain, and the tiny little baby in His hands, He has yesterday's failures. He has today's challenges, He has tomorrow's surprises right there in His hands. And not one of them causes God to gasp. Not one causes Him to react with surprise, "Ah! I never knew that." Not one. He is unshockable, He is immutable. He's got the whole world in His hands. What's more, He has inscribed you and me on His palms.

I spoke on this great fact a number of years ago, and when a missionary in the Philippines heard the message via cassette tape, he sent me a carving. This very faithful missionary found a Filipino artist who took a chunk of mahogany and carved that solid piece of wood into the shape of a hand larger than life. He then carved a person alongside the open palm of the hand and had that person lean into it, almost like a child will lean on the breast of his mother, or like you'd lean on the shoulder of your friend when you're weary. Etched on a brass plate at the base of this hand-carved piece of art are the words: "Your ways are continually before Me. I have inscribed you on the palms of My hands." Every time I glance at the carving I am reminded that God is in control. My ways are as familiar to Him as the lines in the palms of my hands are to me.

Solomon said a similar thing in his journal:

> There is nothing better for a man than to eat and drink and tell himself that his labor is good. This also I have seen, that it is from the hand of God. For who can eat and who can have enjoyment without Him? (Eccles. 2:24–25).

Oh, we can put food in our mouth. We can swallow and even digest it, but there's something about the blessing, the presence, the joy of the Lord that gives us delight in the meal, joy in the experience, and, yes, even perception in the hurts we face. There's something about God's wisdom that enables us to take life from the palm of His hand and handle it.

> For to a person who is good in His sight He has given wisdom and knowledge and joy, while to the sinner He has given the task of gathering and collecting so that He may give to one who is good in God's sight. This too is vanity and striving after wind (v. 26).

We are in the palms of His hands. Isaiah says that He has inscribed us in the palms of His hands. Solomon adds, in effect, "Now that we are there, in the palms of His hands, God is giving to us wisdom, knowledge, and joy."

An Analysis of Wisdom

This above-the-sun wisdom equips us to see and to handle life under the sun as it really is. Since Solomon spends most of the latter half of his journal writing about wisdom, perhaps a definition is in order. I've thought about what the Scriptures are teaching on wisdom and I've come up with this: *Wisdom is the God-given ability to see life with rare objectivity and to handle life with rare stability.*

When we operate in the sphere of the wisdom of God, when it is at work in our mind and in our life, we look at life through lenses of perception, and we respond to it in calm confidence. There's a remarkable absence of fear. We are not seized with panic. We can either lose our jobs or we can be promoted in our work, and neither will derail us. Why? Because we see it with God-given objectivity. And we handle it in His wisdom.

We can dip into an unexpected valley or we can soar to the pinnacle of prosperity, and we can cope with both extremes. His wisdom provides us the necessary objectivity and stability. That's the way life is when it is lived in the palm of His hand. This is not some dreamland fantasy. It is reality. It is the ability to live above the drag of human opinion and horizontal perspective. It is what happens within us when wisdom goes to work.

THE OUTWORKING OF WISDOM

As I've mentioned before, wisdom is not something to be learned in a classroom; it is neither academic nor theoretical. It is practical. It is designed to be put to work. And this is Solomon's message in the seventh chapter of his journal.

Whether you're a business man or woman, a career person, single or married, young or old, you'll be pleased to know that this wisdom will work for you. In so many words God speaks from between these lines, saying, "Test Me. Put it to use. Give it a try. Trust Me. I'll give you perspective that is rare and rewarding. And I'll give you stability that is reliable and secure."

Let me show you how this section of Solomon's journal unfolds. He begins by saying, "I've seen it all!" He's not bragging, just stating facts.

> I have seen everything during my lifetime of futility; there is a righteous man who perishes in his righteousness, and there is a wicked man who prolongs his life in his wickedness (Eccles. 7:15).

We've all said much the same thing. A friend who happens to be an upright person of integrity and strong character suddenly dies.

Our response? "I've seen it all." Or someone else who has lived an irresponsible, ungodly life (who, to be blunt about it, doesn't deserve a long, easy life) lives on and on and on. And when that happens, we respond in the same way. "Now I have seen it all!"

That's what Solomon is saying here. Having "seen it all," the perceptive king realizes the value of wisdom. He mentions three great benefits wisdom affords us as it works its way out. First of all, wisdom gives us *balance*. Second, it gives us *strength*. And third, it gives us *insight*. None of these is a natural trait, each is a by-product of wisdom. We don't get these things just because we're human beings. They must come from God. Let's consider each one.

The Balance Wisdom Gives

> Do not be excessively righteous, and do not be overly wise. Why should you ruin yourself? Do not be excessively wicked, and do not be a fool. Why should you die before your time? It is good that you grasp one thing, and also not let go of the other; for the one who fears God comes forth with both of them (vv. 16–18).

The Amplified Bible renders verses 16–18 like this:

> Be not [morbidly exacting and externally] righteous overmuch, neither strive to make yourself [pretentiously appear] overwise; why should you [get puffed up and] destroy yourself [with presumptuous self-sufficiency]? [Although all have sinned] be not wicked overmuch or willfully, neither be foolish; why should you die before your time? It is good that you should take hold of this, and from that withdraw not your hand; for he who reverently fears and worships God will come forth from them all.

Can you detect the emphasis on balance? Solomon's words paint a picture of a superpious, overly zealous individual who finds it terribly important to impress others. This person is a master of external impressions and "presumptuous self-sufficiency"—those little innuendos regarding how much a person may pray and those unbelievably pious looks.

It's a good idea for us periodically to take a look at our "looks." It's all too easy to become foolishly fanatical and model an out-of-balance Christianity. When that happens, it's religion "gone to seed," and it is one of the most unpleasant things to be around.

It's helpful to realize that no one is very impressed with our overwise and superspiritual lifestyle. As a matter of fact, if we've got the authentic stuff, we don't have to say a word. People will notice and they will long to know the secret of our life. In fact, our humility (I mean *true* humility) will absolutely cut their feet out from under them.

If there is one virtue we can't have enough of, it is balance—balance to "grasp one thing, and also not let go of the other" (v. 18). As this wisdom works its way out, I believe God's counsel is: Really fall in love with the Lord, but don't lose touch with humanity, don't check out of reality. Get hold of the Scriptures and make a study of them for yourself, but don't get caught in bibliolatry (where you begin to worship the print on the page). We've all seen Christians like that. Be committed to witnessing—absolutely committed to making Christ known—but please, please give the non-Christian a break. Have a little wisdom and tact. Have a little understanding. In other words, have a heart! See how Solomon's statement ends? "One who fears God comes forth with both of them." There's balance there. We're to fear God, but we are not to lose our perspective.

The Strength Wisdom Produces

> Wisdom strengthens a wise man more than ten rulers who are in a city. Indeed, there is not a righteous man on earth who continually does good and who never sins. Also, do not take seriously all words which are spoken, lest you hear your servant cursing you. For you also have realized that you likewise have many times cursed others (vv. 19–22).

We need to be discerning and careful as we attempt to untie the knots of this section. Solomon begins by saying that the one who operates in the sphere of wisdom possesses an inner strength that cannot be matched by ten influential city officials. That's quite a statement! He goes on to say that those who are wise possess a strength to accept painful tensions in life.

There are some whose greatest struggle is accepting life's questions and living with life's tensions. God bless you if you're a perfectionist . . . and God help you! God especially help those who live with you! I read this humorous definition of a perfectionist recently:

> A perfectionist is one who takes great pains . . . and gives them to others!

Perfectionists want everything to fit into an exact four-by-four square. Things must be black or they must be white, right? Grays drive them wild.

But the more we glean God's wisdom, the more strength we gain to live with questions and tension. He doesn't issue rules and regulations for every moment. He provides some overall guidelines and principles, then He allows us to make the decisions. Why? By doing this the wisdom of God goes to work, and we begin to learn how to walk through life—which is often full of subtle and unseen "land mines." His wisdom provides the sixth sense we need. It matures us so that we can press on in spite of the unanswered questions.

When I was fresh out of seminary, there weren't many questions I couldn't answer. In fact, I occasionally answered questions no one was asking. But I've learned in the past couple of decades that I don't know all the answers. And furthermore, in many cases, it doesn't matter. Who *really* cares?

It takes *strength to handle the painful tensions* of unanswered questions, especially if you have a family. To maintain the respect of your children, you need the wisdom to handle those tensions. We've got to live with the fact that there are mysteries. Wisdom gives us the ability to accept that and to have an understanding of it. I often think of wisdom as a mental cushion—a buffer that handles the blows. We don't have to fill in all the blanks or sweep every theological corner absolutely clean. We are not doing sterile surgery; we're living a life. Wisdom gives us breathing and thinking space.

There's another strength that comes with wisdom—*the strength to avoid the pitfalls of gullibility*. Remember what Solomon wrote? "Do not take seriously all words which are spoken. . . ."

When admirers offer lavish praise we must not take them seriously. There are many young men who will say to young women, "Oh, honey, you are the woman of my dreams." Ladies, don't take them seriously *every* time. They may sincerely believe it and they may even feel the big-time tingles as they say how thrilled they are to be in your presence. But don't take those words too seriously.

Wisdom has a filtering system that rejects such verbiage and gives us the ability to keep from believing it. It keeps us in touch with reality and helps us avoid the pitfalls of gullibility.

Neither should you believe every word of criticism. That's Solomon's point here. Some people have the "gift of criticism." They are amazing! They can tell you three things wrong with your life each week. And they will faithfully carry out the exercise of their gift by mail, by phone, or face to face. And if they can't get to you directly, they will reach you indirectly.

3.   And so, there's a third strength wisdom gives. And that's *the strength to resist criticism*, or handle it well. Look at the way the ancient king put it:

> Also, do not take seriously all words which are spoken, lest you hear your servant cursing you.

Note that Solomon mentions the servant as the source of critical words. This person represents someone who knows you very well—someone with whom you work, perhaps . . . some employee, a "close friend," or a former boss.

Let's think about the problem of "the cursing servant." Some of you are living your life intimidated because of criticism. I understand. Few people understand that better than I. I may look tough and write with an air of confidence, but deep down underneath I can be too soft, too sensitive. Criticism hurts me, too. I may sound self-assured, but (believe me) if you want to hurt me, say enough bad things about me and I, too, begin to believe it. Why? Because I am my worst critic. Your criticism simply verifies what my conscience has been telling me all these days.

But I am learning that many of those things that once hurt me are better forgotten. My dad used to say, "Son, when a mule kicks you, just consider the source." Sometimes it's nothing more than a mule kicking. They're not much good for anything but plowing and kicking and they do a lot of both. But since when is a mule worth worrying over?

I do, however, want to hear valid criticism. I want to hear criticism from a person who knows me well and therefore loves me too much to let me traffic in wrong. We are wise to hear the reproofs of the wise. I really care about listening to that person, and, frankly, I don't care too much about listening to anybody else.

The words of J. Oswald Sanders in his book *Spiritual Leadership* are among the best and wisest that I've read regarding this issue of handling criticism. They have really helped me. Here is one of the passages I've underscored in that book.

> What leader or preacher does not desire to be popular with his constituency? Certainly there is no virtue in unpopularity, but popularity

can be purchased at too high a price. Jesus made this crystal-clear when He said, "Woe unto you when all men speak well of you." And He expressed the complementary truth when He said, "Blessed are ye when men revile you and persecute you, and utter all kinds of evil against you falsely for my sake."[1]

And then he quotes from Helmut Thielecke's book *Encounter with Spurgeon* regarding the famous British pulpiteer Charles Haddon Spurgeon, who, while he was still in his twenties, had hundreds of people lined up and waiting in the snow for the doors of the Tabernacle in London to open so they could hear him preach. They couldn't build a building big enough to house the people who wanted to hear Spurgeon. Even before he reached middle age, he was a highly visible and therefore greatly criticized preacher. Spurgeon said:

> Success exposes a man to the pressure of people and thus tempts him to hold on to his gains by means of fleshly methods and practices, and to let himself be ruled wholly by the dictatorial demands of incessant expansion. Success can go to my head, and will unless I remember that it is God who accomplishes the work, that He can continue to do so without my help, and that He will be able to make out with other means whenever He cuts me down to size.[2]

Spurgeon demonstrated wisdom as he maintained that realistic perspective.

Look again at Solomon's journal. He warns us to examine our own habits when criticism comes our way: ". . . lest you hear your servant cursing you. For you also have realized that you likewise have many times cursed others" (vv. 21–22). That's an eloquent twist of the sword, isn't it? It hurts, but it's true.

Please remember that the truth of the matter is that you know worse things about yourself than anyone will ever know. And aren't you glad they're known by no one else?

So when you get punched around by the blow of someone's verbal missile, when you are shot at and hit, just remember if the "cursing servant" knew how bad you *really* are, he or she would have much worse to say. So give God thanks that they are hitting just the visible—not the whole truth. That's been very helpful for me in my life.

Wisdom can help us rise above both giving and receiving false criticism. And it can also expose pride in our lives if we will let it.

✓   It is a good test to the rise and fall of egotism to notice how you
listen to the praises of other men of your own standing. Until you
can listen to the praises of a rival without any desire to indulge in
detraction, or any attempt to belittle his work, you may be sure there
is an unmortified prairie of egotistic impulse in your nature yet to be
brought under the grace of God.[3]

What we all need is the kind of wisdom Solomon and J. Oswald
Sanders write about, the kind Spurgeon modeled so well—a wisdom
we can only find in God. This wisdom gives us the ability to see
life with rare objectivity and to handle life with rare stability. It provides us with much-needed balance in a world of extremes; it gives
us inner strength in a world of weakness and uncertainty. And, as
we'll see in Solomon's next statements, it raises our level of discernment. Let's look now at three specific insights wisdom offers.

The Insight Wisdom Offers

The first insight is this: *We cannot understand ourselves, nor can
we make ourselves wise.* Both are implied in the following remarks:

> I tested all this with wisdom, and I said, "I will be wise," but it
> was far from me. What has been is remote and exceedingly mysterious.
> Who can discover it? (vv. 23–24).

Not even Solomon, on his own, could pull it off.

Many New Year's resolutions include, "This year I'm going to be
wise"—and by the second day of January the resolution is already
broken. We can't make ourselves wise. We can't grit our teeth or
grunt real hard or double up our fists tightly or read enough chapters
of the Bible to bring "instant wisdom" into our lives. When Solomon
tried to manufacture it, even he had to admit that it was far from
him. Wisdom is a gift handed to us directly from the hand of God.
And by the way, who knows why some are wiser than others? It's
all part of the mystery.

Not only can we not make ourselves wise, we can't even understand
ourselves! "What has been is remote and exceedingly mysterious. Who
can discover it?" Very often I hear folks say, "He just doesn't understand me. If he just understood me better, then he . . ." The truth
is *you* don't understand you either.

In a recent telephone conversation, a man said to me, "Chuck, you are an enigma to me." (I think he meant it in a negative sense, though he said it very nicely.) I swallowed hard after I hung up the phone. And I thought about his comment for several days before coming to the conclusion that I'm an enigma to *me*, too! I don't always know why I do what I do. Sometimes I don't even know how I do what I do. Many of the things that make me *me* are mysterious. And that's true with all of us. But that's what makes life so exciting, isn't it? In Solomon's words, we are "remote and exceedingly mysterious."

This leads me to my second insight. It's the toughest of the three: *Intimate relations are compelling, but often unsatisfying.* Take a look at how the writer expresses this insight:

> I directed my mind to know, to investigate, and to seek wisdom and an explanation, and to know the evil of folly and the foolishness of madness (v. 25).

Solomon sought the counsel of people. He talked to men and women. He held dialogues with scholars and people on the street. He pulled together all the information he could get. And what did he find? Look at his next statement.

> And I discovered more bitter than death the woman whose heart is snares and nets, whose hands are chains. One who is pleasing to God will escape from her, but the sinner will be captured by her (v. 26).

I think he's saying this: "I've probed this to the depths. While with the opposite sex I was seduced into a deep relationship that involved sex and all the other things that go with an intimate relationship and it was unfulfilling. It was just plain flat."

Solomon had a thousand women—seven hundred concubines, three hundred wives. He had plenty of experience. He was a sexual athlete, a sensual animal, if you please. And none of that caused him to gain any sense of wisdom.

Ray Stedman, a man I have long admired for his biblical perception, suggests that Solomon found:

> . . . that he was trapped by sexual seductions. He went looking for love. Many a man or woman . . . can echo what he is saying. He

went looking for love, and thought he would find it in a relationship with a woman. He went looking for that which would support him, strengthen him and make him feel life was worth the living, but what he found was nothing but a fleeting sexual thrill. He found himself involved with a woman who did not give him what he was looking for at all; he still felt the same empty loneliness as before.[4]

The "affair" is a myth—an empty mirage. Outside of marriage, intimacy arrests the mutual process of discovery. The beauty of marriage is that there is one man with one woman committed together so that there is mutual discovery of one another and of life. And the beautiful part of that is the intimate relations interwoven through the fabric of that marriage.

Let that be broken by an alien relationship and not only is there confusion on the part of those two outside the bonds, but a deep confusion is now added to those who are bound in a marriage. And the mutual discovery, which is such an integral part of the marriage, is lost.

The *second* thing that he discovered is that he was troubled by a recurring enigma.

> "Behold, I have discovered this," says the Preacher, "adding one thing to another to find an explanation, which I am still seeking but have not found. I have found one man among a thousand, but I have not found a woman among all these" (vv. 27–28).

Solomon was saying, "When I was with men and trying to work through some of these answers, I found one in a thousand." That's another way of saying, it was very, very rare. "But I found I couldn't discover it when I worked to perceive it with the women of my life." Could it be that his preoccupation with sexual seduction cancelled out the joy of that discovery? From a practical point of view, trying to juggle both a marriage and an extramarital affair leads to absolute and certain confusion.

What's true of sexual relationships, by the way, is sometimes true of close friends. Folks occasionally find that friendships fall flat. That which drew them close begins to erode, leaving them distant and dissatisfied, because they fail to discover the thing they thought the relationship would yield.

Notice that these "insights" deal with the relationships every person experiences. The first one involves the relationship with *self*. We can't know ourselves, we can't fully understand ourselves, and we can't give ourselves wisdom. The second insight has to do with *other people*—a whole spectrum of relationships. And the third is about our relationship with *God*.

> "Behold, I have found only this, that God made men upright, but they have sought out many devices" (v. 29).

When God first secured this planet in space and put man and woman on the earth and designed marriage, planned children, and arranged the original lifestyle, everything was right. Those original people were "upright." The original "beautiful" people, Adam and Eve. There was nothing wrong with the human race. Life itself was actually a paradise. Everything that originally flowed from God's hands was upright, perfect, wholesome, and good. Then tragedy struck as sin invaded the innocent domain, setting off a chain reaction of man-made attempts to fill the void. In Solomon's words, "they . . . sought out many devices." Many alternatives, many synthetics and substitutes were devised to replace the original order of things.

The third insight is clear: *Our basic problems are not above us; they're within us.* They're not around us; they're within us. They're not with God; they're with ourselves. The very ones God made upright have sought out many, many devices. We have become creative, but our creativity is misdirected and our devices are destructive. Sometimes those devices are alternate thoughts and words. Sometimes those devices reveal themselves in attitudes, sometimes in actions. We have replaced true peace with mere talk of peace. We have replaced genuine righteousness with a mask of righteousness. And none of our man-made "devices" brings us back to God. On the contrary, they push us further away from him.

WISDOM: THREE QUESTIONS

We have uncovered a lot of information about wisdom in this chapter. Wisdom is not simply a theoretical, sterile subject to be tossed around by philosophers and intellectuals. Neither is it merely a theological concept to be discussed along cloistered seminary hallways. It is practical. It's designed to work for us. Our definition makes that clear: *Wisdom is the God-given ability to see life with rare objectivity and to handle life with rare stability.*

The good news is that such wisdom is ours to claim through an intimate relationship with God's Son, Jesus. He is the channel through which wisdom comes to us. In coming by faith to the Lord Jesus Christ, we are given open access to the wisdom of God. With the Son of God comes the wisdom of God. It's all part of the package.

> But God has brought you into union with Christ Jesus, and God has made Christ to be our wisdom. By him we are put right with God; we become God's holy people and are set free (1 Cor. 1:30, TEV).

Finally, three quick questions, each one based on the subjects we've been thinking about.

- Regarding *balance:* Is wisdom guarding us from extremes? In our day of fanatical extremism, a wise balance will protect us from the lunatic fringe. When we put wisdom to work, we become easier to live with. As Will Rogers once put it, "We need to sit loose in the saddle." Wisdom helps make that happen as it keeps us balanced.

- Regarding *strength:* Is wisdom keeping us stable? Under the blast of criticism, as well as the subtle traps of pride, an inner strength is essential. When we put wisdom to work, we gain a "buffer" to cushion the harsh blows of life.

- Regarding *insight:* Is wisdom clearing our minds? Surrounded by any number of persuasive and appealing voices, we need the filtering system only wisdom can give. When we put wisdom to work, it is remarkable how it raises our level of discernment.

Yes, God has the whole world in His hands—the wind, the waves, the tiny baby, even you and me. Things aren't out of control. The ragged-edge question is not: Will His wisdom work? But rather: Are we putting His wisdom to work?

15

THE QUALITIES OF A
GOOD BOSS

Journal Entry

*How wonderful to be wise, to understand
things, to be able to analyze them and
interpret them. . . .*

*Obey the king as you have vowed to do.
Don't always be trying to get out of doing
your duty, even when it's unpleasant.
For the king punishes those who disobey.
The king's command is backed by great
power, and no one can withstand it or
question it. Those who obey him will not be
punished. The wise man will find a time
and a way to do what he says. Yes, there
is a time and a way for everything, though
man's trouble lies heavy upon him; for
how can he avoid what he doesn't know
is going to happen?*

*No one can hold back his spirit from
departing; no one has the power to prevent
his day of death . . . . Certainly a man's
wickedness is not going to help him then.*

*B*eing a good boss is neither accidental nor automatic. It isn't easy, either. Employers or supervisors who are a joy to follow are rare individuals. Clear-thinking, hard-working, fair-minded, honest-dealing leaders are the exception rather than the rule. That is most unfortunate since our productivity and creativity are directly linked to the relationship we sustain with those to whom we are accountable.

It has been my observation that bosses all too frequently fall into one of two extreme categories. First, there is the *incompetent* individual. Numerous people in positions of responsibility have been promoted to their level of incompetence. They are personifications of the "Peter principle." They are not qualified for the tasks they are expected to perform, but they have the ability to make failure look like it's someone else's fault! Such people are extremely difficult to work for since they are usually negative and discouraging rather than affirming and encouraging. Behind much of their leadership style is a hidden insecurity which only fuels the fire of their incompetence. That's one extreme.

Second, there is the *intolerant* individual. This person may be competent and knowledgeable, but no one can please him or her. Intolerant bosses are frequently workaholics, perfectionistic by nature, and superdemanding. The job means everything to this person. To such high-achieving, hard-charging, tough-minded skippers, enough is never enough. Unlike the incompetent leader, this person is often overqualified, demanding more than is reasonable of others. And when expectations are not met, it is the employee's fault.

I recently saw a cartoon that perfectly illustrates what I am trying to describe. The scene is a classroom. A fourth-grader is standing nose-to-nose with his teacher, both frowning. Behind them is a chalkboard full of unsolved mathematical problems. You can feel the frustration as the boy has worked, erased, struggled, and strained to perform before his class. Quite likely his teacher had just announced in front of everyone that he should have been able to solve the problems. Perhaps she labeled him an underachiever. With a fair measure of perception, the boy is answering back, "I'm not an underachiever— you're an overexpecter!"

Intolerant individuals are usually "overexpecters." They come in all different shapes and sizes, roles and responsibilities. Some of them are fathers and fathers-in-law, some of them are husbands. Occasionally, they are mothers or mothers-in-law or grandparents! Sometimes "overexpecters" are coaches. Sometimes they are teachers. And I can't ignore the fact that frequently they are preachers. Many a congregational flock today is not being led, it's being driven. Rather than being encouraged to model the life of Christ, it's being chided and whipped, put down and verbally battered by a well-meaning, but intolerant, grim-faced shepherd who simply cannot live with anything less than the ultimate. How easy it is for zealous and strongly committed spiritual leaders to become intolerant "overexpecters"! All who are in positions of authority need to take an honest look at their style of leadership.

This shoe fits everyone, not just some small segment of humanity. There isn't a person reading these words right now who is not affected by someone in authority. Whether it's in your home or at your school, where you work or in some organization that you are a part of, authority is on display. And either you are in authority over others or you are under the authority of someone—perhaps both.

Some of you are moving rapidly toward being in greater authority over many. And it is your attention I want the most, because you are on the verge of making an impact on others' lives—significant or slight. You're not there yet, but you are in that formative, moldable stage where you can be of tremendous help to others by being the kind of authority figure everyone loves to be around.

A Brief Review

Believe it or not, Solomon's memoirs include a brief section on being a good boss. I'm referring to the first nine verses of Ecclesiastes 8. In the previous chapter we discovered once again that wisdom is not academic. It is designed to go to work in our lives. It is practical, not theoretical. Solomon is careful to give the reader down-to-earth, easily grasped principles (proverbs) to live by. But his concern is that we not leave these truths alone. They are to be lived out!

For example, we learned in chapter 14 that wisdom provides us with needed balance and inner strength and rare insight in this business of handling life with stability. But it's still not fleshed out. Wisdom needs to be modeled, not simply discussed.

The thing I have always appreciated about the Bible is that when great truth is given, God frequently incarnates that truth in lives with whom we can identify. He doesn't stop at theory as He teaches us about the abstract importance of faith. He mentions Abraham as a model "who staggered not at the promise of God through unbelief."

He doesn't just talk about standing alone and being people of character and resiliency—He gives us Elijah. He shows us the prophets because we have much greater difficulty identifying with abstract truth. We can, however, identify with people.

Take forgiveness for example. God doesn't just say, "You ought to forgive." He gives us Joseph, who forgave his brothers for their mistreatment of him. God paints His heroes "warts and all." Since there are scars and a dark side to every life, we're not shielded from the Jonahs and the Samsons, from the pride of the King Sauls or the adultery of the King Davids. We see it in raw, living color.

As we deal with these things about wisdom, we also need to have a "for instance." So God prompts Solomon to provide us with that in this next journal entry. That's why I suggest that this section paints for us the portrait of a good and wise individual who is in a position of authority. Again I remind you, his words apply to all who are managers, CEOs (chief executive officers), entrepreneurs, industrial foremen, or medical supervisors—to anyone who is in authority over the lives of others.

> Who is like the wise man and who knows the interpretation of a matter? A man's wisdom illumines him and causes his stern face to beam.
>
> I say, "Keep the command of the king because of the oath before God. Do not be in a hurry to leave him. Do not join in an evil matter, for he will do whatever he pleases." Since the word of the king is authoritative, who will say to him, "What are you doing?"
>
> He who keeps a royal command experiences no trouble, for a wise heart knows the proper time and procedure. For there is a proper time and procedure for every delight, when a man's trouble is heavy upon him. If no one knows what will happen, who can tell him when it will happen? No man has authority to restrain the wind with the wind, or authority over the day of death; and there is no discharge in the time of war, and evil will not deliver those who practice it. All this I have seen and applied my mind to every deed that has been done under the sun wherein a man has exercised authority over another man to his hurt (Eccles. 8:1–9).

Look at his reference to "the command of the king." He's obviously a person of authority. And again, "the word of the king is authoritative"

. . . another reminder of a superior. Then he mentions "a royal command," and a little further on he speaks of "every deed wherein a man has exercised authority over another man." Clearly, this depicts those in authority. If you are exercising authority over other people, if your word is the command, if you are in charge, then I suggest that you take these words to heart.

CHARACTERISTICS OF A WISE LEADER

I find at least five qualities of a good boss in the counsel Solomon offers: a clear mind, a cheerful disposition, a discreet mouth, keen judgment, and a humble spirit.

A Clear Mind

> Who is like the wise man, and who knows the interpretation of a matter? (v. 1).

It's a rhetorical question. It is not meant to be answered verbally, but to be answered mentally. Actually, it is designed to make the reader think, rather than come up with "the" precise answer. Here's the thought: "There is no one to be compared to a wise leader. Such an individual possesses an understanding of the whole picture." The key term is *interpretation*. It is from the Aramaic word *pah-shaar*. It means "solution, someone who sees through the mystery of something." It suggests knowing how to explain difficult things, having the ability to unfold mysteries—in short, understanding how to go to the foundation of things. Solomon has in mind an individual who knows *why* things are as they are.

A qualified skipper is one who knows, philosophically, where the ship is going and *why*. He doesn't have to know all the "how-tos" of the ship, but he does need to know the whys. Someone stuck his head in my office several years ago and passed on a piece of advice regarding leadership I think I'll never forget. He suggested to me that "the person who knows *how* will usually have a job, but that individual will usually work for the one who knows *why*." Think about that. The follower needs to know how; the leader needs to know why. Solomon says it this way: "He knows the interpretation of a matter." A good boss knows *why* things are as they are. Above all, that calls for a clear mind.

A ministry, for example, must have men and women in leadership who know why. Why do we meet when we do? What's the purpose of the meeting? Why do we continue doing things the way we do? Why did we stop doing certain things? Why do we believe what we believe? Why is our youth ministry moving in a certain direction? Why do we minister to single adults as we do? Why do we feel like we do about families? Why do we set aside an important role for the senior adults of our church? Why do we care about these folks but not those? Why? Why? Why?

Obviously, it's not just related to ministry. The leader Solomon mentioned is a king. This represents a wise man in any field. You may be in sales. You may be an attorney, a physician. You may be a certified public accountant. Your role may be that of a homemaker and your leadership is over the most influential people of the future—little children today. Why do you raise them like you raise them? Why have you set that standard? What's the philosophy of your home? Leaders know those answers. That's "knowing the interpretation."

Some people will look at an organization and it may seem foggy and confusing. It better not be to the person at the top or the outfit is in bad trouble! The interpretation of a thing is the basic assignment of the leader. A clear mind is primary to commanding everyone's respect.

Let me mention one more thing. Frequently the one at the top is action-oriented and very energetic regarding a product. It's extremely important that the boss not let action outrun thinking. Those who are in positions of authority are, first and foremost, paid to think—to think through, to think about, to think of.

An executive friend of mine sets aside one full day a month to do nothing but think. He thinks about where his organization is going. He evaluates his leadership. He thinks about future staff. He receives consulting assistance about the strategy of his company. And, by the way, he has done a phenomenal job with his business. He's got a clear mind.

When there's confusion at the top, there is even greater confusion down the line. In the church scene we could say, "A mist in the pulpit puts a fog in the pew." Churches with senior pastors or elders who are uncertain of where they are going become churches that lose their way. It's nothing short of a tragedy on display. First and foremost, those in charge need clear minds.

A Cheerful Disposition

> . . . a man's wisdom illumines him [literally, a man's wisdom illumines *his face*] and causes his stern face to beam (v. 1).

Solomon makes an intriguing statement here. The most often-seen expression on the face of one who is intent on leading is a "stern face." A "stern" look is one that comes naturally. The root word is translated "fierce countenance" elsewhere in the Old Testament. It's translated in Daniel 8 "impudent" or "insolent." An appropriate paraphrase might read, "A man's wisdom lights his face up and causes his otherwise fierce countenance to beam."

The second quality of a good leader is a cheerful disposition. There are few things more contagious among leaders than cheerfulness. Unfortunately, a stern boss can also infect an organization. It's the all-too-common picture of being stiff, tough, unsmiling, and intense. I've heard it referred to as having "the eyes of a shark"—wearing a face that resembles severe determination. And this frequently telegraphs a negative mentality.

When I mention those descriptive terms, I think of a body of men in America that perfectly illustrates this appearance: the head coaches of most professional football teams. Haven't you seen television close-up shots of them on the sidelines? I suppose we shouldn't be too critical of those men. The pressure they live with is enough to give three or four people ulcers. But how much better to operate in the sphere of God's wisdom and have our dispositions "illumined."

And I must add another group that runs a close second to head coaches. That would be ministers. I have no desire to pick on my profession, but take a look at how grim we have become! If we are to represent an invitation to the kingdom of God, we would do well to develop a contagiously cheerful disposition.

Helmut Thielecke once wrote:

> Should we not see that lines of laughter about the eyes are just as much marks of faith as are the lines of care and seriousness? Is it only earnestness that is baptized? Is laughter pagan? We have already allowed too much that is good to be lost to the church and cast many pearls before swine. A church is in a bad way when it banishes laughter from the sanctuary and leaves it to the cabaret, the nightclub and the toastmasters.[1]

I agree with that and frankly I *preach* that. I even preach that in some very, very stern places where folks seem terribly uptight. You can almost hear the squeaks when they blink!

I was at a place like that several years ago and I was having the time of my life along with two other people in the crowd of thousands. Everybody else seemed sober as a judge. But one young fellow was really connecting with me. He was so young he hadn't learned the rules yet, so he was still having fun—really a great guy.

After I returned home, he sent me a note of thanks on the back of a frisbee. "Just want to thank you for your week of ministry. I dare you to sail this down the office hallway in the church where you work." What he didn't know was that we enjoy a very relaxed relationship among our staff. I'm not saying we toss frisbees to each other, but believe me, laughter is frequently heard in our hallway.

Some stern-faced souls are probably thinking, "What kind of place is that? All frivolity and fun?" No, as a matter of fact, in my opinion, it's *still* too serious. Everything we do in our work seems terribly serious. Think of the situations we must deal with—life, death, divorce, disease, pain, prayer. Everything is serious. It's enough to put all of us six feet under in an early grave. So a bit of laughter every now and then is a marvelous relief. A good, hearty, appropriate sense of humor is, in fact, essential in a balanced, effective ministry.

Some time after I entered the ministry I determined I wouldn't let it be the early death of me. In order to carry out such a goal, I have often had to remind myself that some things are God's responsibility. It is God's job to bear the burdens of ministry! If I attempt to do so, it isn't long before I start wearing that "stern face" Solomon writes about. I start looking like a preacher is expected to look!

Ministry is a joy. It's a pleasure. It's a delight. There are some burdensome people to hassle, but ministry is more than a *burden.*

Furthermore, I want my kids to remember me as being fun to live with. I want them to remember me as the guy who tossed their mother in the pool and lived to tell the story. I want them to remember the laughter in the walls of our home that came from the fun we had together because Dad was there. Hopefully, they will remember me as being easy to live with. "Preached with all of his heart, ministered with all of his soul, but had the time of his life, and lived a long, full, happy life." That's what I want them to remember. If they can never repeat a line out of one of my sermons, it won't bother me a bit, but I certainly hope they will remember me as somewhat of a model. In fact, I would be brokenhearted if they didn't remember a cheerful countenance on their dad's face. That's a major goal for my life in my home.

If your face is stern, chances are good you're not acting in wisdom. If you carry out your role with a stern face regularly and it no longer "beams," you're operating in your own wisdom. I believe Lincoln's words are true: "Every person over forty is responsible for his own face." If you wish to be a good boss, start with a clear mind. But don't omit a cheerful, charming disposition.

A Discreet Mouth

> I say, "Keep the command of the king because of the oath before God. Do not be in a hurry to leave him. Do not join in an evil matter, for he will do whatever he pleases." Since the word of the king is authoritative, who will say to him, "What are you doing?" (vv. 2–4).

If we apply this to a place of employment, these verses are addressed to employees—those being led by the king, or in our case, the boss. Twice the king's "command" or "word" is mentioned. Clearly, the major vehicle of communication from those who lead to those who follow is the *tongue*. Employees are urged to be loyal, to be faithful, to be fair and trustworthy. But behind the scene the boss's authoritative word is most prominent.

> Since the word of the king is authoritative, who says to him, "What are you doing?"

In other words, there are some things one just doesn't skip into the boss's office and say. But there is another side of the story. A wise boss takes a close look at his or her own tongue which is a tell-tale sign of leadership. In other words, what comes out of a boss's mouth sets the tone of the organization.

In many ways, both tone and tongue have a lot to do with employees remaining loyal and cooperative. That's what encourages them to stick with the company. That's what causes them, in turn, to be fair and supportive. They respect a discreet mouth. They know their boss cares about such things as tact and diplomacy, sensitivity and compassion. How? The tongue reveals it all.

Many good things have been written on tact. We leaders need

to read all we can on the subject. Tact is the ability to avoid needless offense. It includes having an awareness of and an appreciation for the other person's feelings in a situation. It is dexterity in managing affairs, reconciling opposing viewpoints without giving needless offense or compromising one's own principles. I have heard it said that tact is the ability to make someone feel at home when you wish they were. A discreet mouth is so important.

Supportive bosses enjoy the benefit of supportive employees. It's contagious. When workers know their boss believes in them and sees potential in them, they will be more cooperative and more productive. A discreet mouth works like glue in keeping relationships tight.

Keen Judgment

> He who keeps a royal command experiences no trouble, for a wise heart knows the proper time and procedure. For there is a proper time and procedure for every delight, when a man's trouble is heavy upon him. If no one knows what will happen, who can tell him when it will happen? (vv. 5–7).

As I began writing those words from Solomon's journal, it occurred to me that the opening sentence would make a great plaque on the wall of every chief executive officer. Look again at his opening remarks.

First of all, as leaders we have a royal command. Keen judgment fits such a God-given position. An authoritative position *is* God-given, you know. As the psalmist said:

> For not from the east, nor from the west, nor from the desert comes exaltation; but God is the Judge; He puts down one, and exalts another (Ps. 75:6–7).

We didn't manipulate, push for it, or play politics to get where we are. God has graciously given us the gifts that resulted in our being in high command.

Whether it's owning a business or running a shop or supervising an entire region or guiding a sales force, God graciously gave that "royal command." It is from *Him.* It is from His royal hand. And He asks, as a result, that we operate with keen judgment. That includes knowing the proper time to do what ought to be done and having a successful procedure thought through. "There is a proper time and procedure for every delight." It's the idea of a finished product. An accomplished task is a delight to the heart. Solomon says there's a time and procedure for it "when a man's trouble is heavy upon him." Such a leader remains stable under pressure.

No wonder Paul tells Timothy to pray for those who are in authority over us (1 Tim. 2:1–2). When I read those verses I always think of our nation's president and the pressure he lives with. But stability under pressure creates, on the part of an entire nation, a growing sense of respect. We don't panic because our leader doesn't panic. A good leader remains calm and steady when trouble is all around. He or she continues to think clearly and to make tough decisions that may or may not be popular at the time. And more often than not, no one else will know what advice to give.

By this I mean: *Leaders who are most effective have independent intuition.* We can't learn intuition from a book. We can't pick up intuition by simply watching it in someone. More often than not, either we have it or we don't. But it's an essential quality for successful leadership.

Good leaders have that extra "sense." They taste it. They feel it. It's all part of having a sensitive spirit. They know the attitude or the atmosphere in the company or in whatever scene they find themselves or in whatever ministry. They have a sensitive heart toward what's happening. I think of this as "internal, spontaneous savvy."

I can hardly overemphasize the value of keen judgment. In summary, Solomon has underscored four things such judgment includes:

- knowing the right time (sense of timing),

- mapping out the proper procedure (wise strategy),

- having stability under pressure (calm and decisive amidst trouble),

- possessing independent intuition (spontaneous "savvy").

There's one more quality worth our attention. No matter how influential the king, no matter how important the president or the CEO or the chairman of the board, this fifth and final quality is invaluable.

A Humble Spirit

> No man has authority to restrain the wind with the wind, or authority over the day of death; there's no discharge in the time of war, and evil will not deliver those who practice it (Eccles. 8:8).

There's no way to escape it; all of us have our limitations. We are impotent to change the wind when it's moving in a certain direction. We can't harness the forces of another wind current and send it in a contrary direction to restrain the wind and weather. All of us, bosses included, are only finite.

We cannot change or shape the day of impending death. We cannot discharge in the time of war. So? So there is a final bottom line from which all leaders must operate. This includes not only a clear mind, a cheerful disposition, a discreet mouth, and keen judgment, but perhaps most importantly, an awareness of one's own limitations—a humble spirit.

Interestingly, the term *wind* is translated from *ruach* as "spirit," on occasion. It's the Hebrew word that is used in Genesis for the spirit of man. God breathed into him the "*ruach* of life"—the breath of life.

It's also rendered "wind" in many places, so it can mean one or the other. Just as we cannot change the wind, neither can we change another person's spirit. Regardless of our influential role, we haven't the power to alter another's spirit. We're limited. No matter how much we may be respected, we are finite. No matter what authority God may have given us over hundreds—maybe thousands of people—there are still many things we cannot do. And good leaders never forget that. They demonstrate a humble spirit, a teachable spirit.

It was said of William Carey, the missionary to India:

> He has attained the happy art of ruling and overruling others without asserting his authority, or others feeling their subjection—all is done without the least appearance of design on his part.[2]

With some people we feel manipulated. We feel either used or abused—sometimes, both. When we struggle with that feeling, more often than not the one who is responsible lacks a humble spirit. How much better to have the attitude expressed by the man who wrote:

> If I appear great in their eyes, the Lord is most graciously helping me to see how absolutely nothing I am without Him, and helping me to keep little in my own eyes. He does use me. But I am so concerned that He uses me and that it is not of me the work is done. The axe cannot boast of the trees it has cut down. It could do nothing but for the woodsman. He made it, he sharpened it, and he used it. The

moment he throws it aside, it becomes only old iron. O that I may never lose sight of this.[3]

A wise leader will allow the Lord God to maintain control over his or her power. He will realize that he is gifted by the grace of God to do a job, and sometimes a vast and terrible job, a hard and demanding job. In humility he will enter the Lord into his decision-making process, problem-solving solutions, and future-planning strategy. But in all of the rigors and the disciplines of getting the job done, those who follow this leader will continue to feel dignity and importance. They will not feel like insignificant pawns on a chessboard of activity.

Two Warnings for Those in Authority

There are a couple of warnings that evolve out of Solomon's closing words. First, notice the words, "Evil will not deliver those who practice it." He's referring directly to war and indirectly to the whole scene of taking advantage of people.

So the first warning is this: *It is inexcusable to take unfair advantage of those under our charge.* Evil won't deliver us. We can rewrite the rules and call evil "good" and good "evil," but such rationalizations will not deliver us. It's inexcusable to oppress, to take unfair advantage—no matter how powerful we may be.

> All this I have seen and applied my mind to every deed that has been done under [heaven] wherein a man has exercised authority over another man to his hurt (v. 9).

It's this idea: "I have seen under the sun this kind of leadership, and it results in the person's own hurt. The leader himself gets hurt."

So the second warning is: *Whoever does take unfair advantage of others hurts himself more than others.* A boss who runs roughshod over others just *thinks* he gets away with it. In the long run, he will suffer the most.

I've thought long and hard about particular individuals who have held positions of authority in my life. And as I reflect on their influence, I can see that almost without exception, they have personified all or most of these same five qualities:

- a clear mind,
- a cheerful disposition,
- a discreet mouth,
- keen judgment,
- a humble spirit.

PERSONAL APPROPRIATION OF THESE QUALITIES

I began this chapter by saying that being a good boss is neither accidental nor automatic. It is a tough assignment to be a person in authority and at the same time to be both competent and fair. But for some of us, the ragged edge of life means we are to serve in leadership roles. It is our calling. As I think about making such a calling effective in my life, a couple of overriding and all-important thoughts are worth mentioning. The first is: *We must never forget the value of being a model.* High-achieving, hard-charging leaders often overemphasize the achievement itself—the product—getting the job done. Admittedly, a job must get done, but the leaders who forget that they are first models short-circuit the influence they can have. They build in the mind of those around them that the most important thing is things or activity, motion, movement, or objectives. "Get it done—regardless." They forget that the model is what will last and is going to be remembered. It is easy to forget that our example outlives our achievements. We have all had mentors. We can't remember all the things they said. We can't even remember many of the things they did—but we cannot forget their model.

That's why Christ Jesus continues to be that. In the history of time, no one has shaped the thinking of mankind like that Model. "We've never seen a man like this man!" said His peers. And Pilate, after examining Him, said, "I find no fault in the man." The perfect model. As He hung on the cross He said, "Father, forgive them. They know not what they do." He was a continuous living model of His message, right up to the very end.

Each of us exemplifies leadership, whether in the home or in the work place. Those under our influence cannot forget the person who is doing the leading, nor could they if they tried. Again, it's the value of being a model!

Another thought on leadership is this: *We must never lose the vision of seeing a cycle.* We are greatly tempted as leaders to see only the objective in front of us. We've got to get the job done. And that becomes the single drive of our lives, forgetting that around this objective and beyond it are people who will someday take our place in leadership.

We are actually cycling ourselves out of leadership each year and cycling new leaders into our places at the same time. It's called "discipleship" in the church. It's called "rearing a family" when it happens in the home. It's called "raising up a fresh crop" in other circles. We are cycling new leaders. We are cycling new parents. The vision of seeing a cycle will do great things to our leadership style. Sales managers are training up-and-coming sales managers. Pastors are training new pastors. Mothers are training future mothers—dads are training future dads. A fresh crop is in the making. How else do they learn the ropes unless we "cycle" them? Don't underestimate it. Even when we may not think it's that significant, our leadership is having an impact.

Boris Cornfeld needed that reminder. He was a Jew who lived in Russia. And for some reason, no one really knows why (maybe a slip of the tongue where he referred to Stalin as finite), but for some reason he was dumped in the Gulag and was to live there the rest of his life.

Since he was a medical doctor, he was to keep practicing medicine and keep the slaves alive so they could die with all the right things said on their records. Dr. Cornfeld was to rewrite the records and say, "This person is healthy," whether it was true or not. The slave was then put back into the slave block and expected to do the work. If slaves died of starvation out there, that was fine—but they were *not* to die in the hospital.

Slowly, the physician began to see through all of his misapplied politics and philosophy of life. He finally decided there must be another way. And through the influence of a fellow inmate, he heard of Jesus Christ and ultimately came to know the Messiah—Dr. Boris Cornfeld personally received Jesus Christ into his life.

The transformation was slow but steady. On one occasion he did surgery on the very guard who had beaten slaves. He had a chance to tie an artery loosely so the man could bleed to death and no one would know it. But now that Christ lived in his life he found himself unable to kill. He even mumbled to himself on occasions, "Forgive us our trespasses as we forgive those who trespass against us."

Strange words to come from the lips of a Jew in a Russian prison camp! I'm sure he didn't realize what a model he was and I'm sure he didn't think very much about the cycle. But on one occasion he was working with another inmate who had cancer of the intestines. The man looked like he wouldn't live.

Boris Cornfeld was so concerned for that man's faith that he leaned over and spoke quietly to him as the patient drifted in and out of the anesthesia. He told the man about Christ and explained God's love which was demonstrated in the Savior's death and resurrection. When the man would come to, he would tell him more. At one point, the patient awoke, and in his groggy state, he heard a noise down the hall. His surgeon, Dr. Cornfeld, was being brutally murdered.

When the patient finally did regain consciousness, he realized all that it meant for Dr. Cornfeld to have given his life for a cause, and the patient himself personally received Christ as well.

Because Boris Cornfeld had a vision of the cycle, he used his influence to shape a life that did not die, but lived on to challenge and exhort the thinking of prosperous and materialistic Western America. His patient's name: Aleksandr Solzhenitsyn.[4]

Having the right kind of influence is neither accidental nor automatic. It isn't easy, either. But those who model authenticity, dedication, and genuine love for others shape the future of our world— even when they are not aware of it.

16

MYSTERIES THAT DEFY EXPLANATION

Journal Entry

Because God does not punish sinners instantly, people feel it is safe to do wrong. But though a man sins a hundred times and still lives, I know very well that those who fear God will be better off, unlike the wicked, who will not live long, good lives— their days shall pass away as quickly as shadows because they don't fear God. . . .

Providence seems to treat some good men as though they were wicked, and some wicked men as though they were good. This is all very trying and troublesome!

Then I decided to spend my time having fun, because I felt that there was nothing better in all the earth than that a man should eat, drink, and be merry, with the hope that this happiness would stick with him in all the hard work which God gives to mankind everywhere.

Sir Winston Churchill was seldom at a loss for words. Whether he was making a brief comment to the press or delivering a lengthy address before Parliament, the late British statesman distinguished himself as a master of the English language. He seemed never at a loss for words—except when it came to an explanation of the actions of Russia.

Neither the French nor the Americans baffled him. Not even Nazi Germany left him bewildered. But Russia's unpredictable and illogical actions frequently threw him for a loop. On one occasion as he found himself once again confounded by the Soviets' surprising decision, he exclaimed in utter frustration, "It is a riddle, wrapped up in a mystery, inside an enigma." That's about as complicated as something can get!

Reading over Churchill's descriptive turn of a phrase, you may feel as I do that it's an apt description of many things in life. There are numerous riddles in life that remain wrapped in mystery and shrouded inside an enigma. The sea, for example, is an unexplainable phenomenon. Who can fathom its tide affected strangely by the moon, not to mention its enormous content of salt, or its incredible swells and currents that form those amazing yet mysterious paths from continent to continent?

And how about the immeasurable spaces above us? Who can unravel the mysterious yet vast movement of the perfectly synchronized planets and stars displaying the most accurate timepiece in existence? Even a hurried look through a telescope makes our mouths drop open.

On the other extreme, when is the last time you peered through a microscope? Talk about a riddle wrapped up in a mystery! Although invisible to the naked eye, there is a *world* of unseen action going on around us (and inside us) that boggles the mind. And it's all so unbelievably small. And while we're considering the microscopic world, we can't overlook just how tiny each individual cell really is. Did you realize that if an electron were increased in size until it became as large as an apple and a human being grew larger in the same proportion, that person could hold the entire solar system in the palm of his hand, and would need to use a magnifying glass in order to see it?

Not all mysteries are as profound as that. Some are somewhere between baffling and humorous. There's the mystery of a washing machine for example. Forgive me if this sounds a bit ridiculous, but I would imagine that my home is not that different from yours. We can put in twelve pairs of socks that perfectly match and in some phenomenal, mysterious manner thirty minutes later we remove eight socks, none of which match anything!

Then there's the mystery of traffic lanes. You've noticed this mystery often on the freeway, I realize. The mystery is that no matter which lane you get into, it slows down more than all the others. Who can ever explain it?

There is also the mystery of the open-faced peanut butter and jelly sandwich. It never falls in the kitchen on the linoleum floor. It always falls in the living room. One wag says that whether it falls face down or face up is in direct proportion to the cost of the carpet!

Another is the mystery of the auto repairman. Your car gives you trouble for three weeks. You finally squeeze in the time and one morning before work you hurriedly drive it to the auto shop. It runs perfectly as the mechanic looks it over. The repairman scratches his head, wondering why you even brought it by. Baffled, you drive away and head for work—and the car stalls halfway between his shop and your office.

There are dozens of other mysteries. There are murder mysteries still unsolved in police files. There are diseases that still remain a mystery—simple-sounding ailments like the common cold and a headache. Several years ago I had a competent physician tell me that the medical world still has no definitive diagnosis for eighty percent of the headaches suffered by people.

There is the Loch Ness monster and the Abominable Snowman and Big Foot and the Bermuda Triangle. And we can't forget the UFOs. Ripley's *Believe It or Not* will be in business forever. We manage to continue on, though brilliant scientists have been trying to solve and/or explain life's mysteries for years. And we seem to have little trouble going on through life with dozens of riddles still unanswered, hundreds of mysteries still unsolved.

But when God leaves us with a mystery that isn't solved in a week or two, most of us go through desperate struggles believing that He is good or fair. I mean, after all, if we're going to trust a good God, He should do only good things, right? No fair doing mysterious stuff!

The Bible that I read simply doesn't present that as the way life is. Yet the world I live in seems to expect that. And that's certainly the cynic's line: "You mean to tell me you are going to trust a God who treats you like that? And you're going to tell me He is fair and good and loving? I mean, how stupid can you get?" When will we ever learn that cynics have no capacity to understand the profound and unfathomable ways of God? To them, God's will is the classic "riddle, wrapped up in a mystery, inside an enigma."

Actually, the Bible is full of mystery talk. I find the mystery of the kingdom in the first chapter of the gospel of Mark. There is the mystery of Israel in Romans 11 and the mystery of resurrection in 1 Corinthians 15—"Behold, I tell you a mystery; we shall not all sleep, but we shall all be changed, in a moment, in the twinkling of an eye . . ." (vv. 51–52). The whole thing is a mystery! (It's always amazed me how some scholars can write massive, multiple volumes explaining in minute detail that which the Scripture simply calls "a mystery.") The little letter to the Ephesians mentions no less than four mysteries: the mystery of God's will (chapter 1); the mystery of the church (chapter 3); the mystery of marriage (chapter 5); and the mystery of the gospel (chapter 6). Second Thessalonians presents the mystery of lawlessness. And Paul mentions the mystery of godliness in 1 Timothy 3. God's Word, like God's will, is full of mysteries.

Why should we be surprised, then, when God steps in and does mysterious things? Why should that make us wonder if He is good—or wonder if we want to keep believing? Since when must everything be easily or logically explained?

A section in 1 Corinthians 2 has often brought me back to my senses. When I've been tempted to put God in human skin and think He should operate like earthlings, I have been reminded that there's a connection between His mysterious dealings and wisdom.

> Yet we do speak wisdom among those who are mature; a wisdom, however, not of this age, nor of the rulers of this age, who are passing away; but we speak God's wisdom in a mystery, the hidden wisdom, which God predestined before the ages to our glory; the wisdom which none of the rulers of this age has understood; for if they had understood it, they would not have crucified the Lord of glory (vv. 6–8).

Is that a phenomenal statement? God operates in the realm of a mysterious wisdom—a wisdom not based on human logic, a wisdom not based on human knowledge. When we forget that, we're headed for trouble.

As I mentioned in previous chapters, God's wisdom is not academic.

You cannot go to a school and get a degree in God's wisdom. Neither is there any such thing as being an authority on God's mysteries. Those who think they have most of those mysteries solved are the closest to insanity. You'll meet them sometime. Talk about scary! Their pockets are stuffed full of heavyweight materials. They start unfolding them—it looks like a world map by the time they finish. They claim to understand the pyramids in Egypt. The Sphinx gives them no trouble either. They understand the books of the Bible—totally, thoroughly. They're wild-eyed fanatics. They are intense, super-serious individuals living an unbalanced and extreme lifestyle. Quite frankly, I find such so-called experts an embarrassment to the cause of Christ. Where did we get the hair-brained idea that we must understand all the mysteries of our awesome heavenly Father?

Our God is profoundly wise—deep and mysterious. Consider this:

> The wisdom of any creature or of all creatures, when set against the boundless wisdom of God, is pathetically small. For this reason the apostle is accurate when he refers to God as "only wise." That is, God is wise in Himself, and all the shining wisdom of men or angels is but a reflection of that uncreated effulgence which streams from the throne of the Majesty in the heavens.
>
> The idea of God as infinitely wise is at the root of all truth. . . . Being what He is without regard to creatures, God is of course unaffected by our opinions of Him, . . .
>
> Wisdom, among other things, is the ability to devise perfect ends and to achieve those ends by the most perfect means. It sees the end from the beginning, so there can be no need to guess or conjecture. Wisdom sees everything in focus, each in proper relation to all, and is thus able to work toward predestined goals with flawless precision.
>
> All God's acts are done in perfect wisdom, first for His own glory, and then for the highest good of the greatest number for the longest time. And all His acts are as pure as they are wise, and as good as they are wise and pure. Not only could His acts not be better done: a better way to do them could not be imagined. An infinitely wise God must work in a manner not to be improved upon by finite creatures.[1]

Our God represents thoughts and ways that are far beyond our ability to grasp. Some of these things are known only by His Spirit, as Paul says in 1 Corinthians 2:

> For who among men knows the thoughts of a man except the spirit of the man, which is in him? Even so the thoughts of God no one knows except the Spirit of God (v. 11).

Every once in a while the Spirit of God will break in upon the mind of a seeking believer and open a mystery. When this happens, if you're like me, your mouth drops open and your eyes bug out and your heart beats a little faster. And you say, "Ahhh!" And that's about all you can say, because you can't pass it on to someone else— it's too profound and personal. To everyone else it remains a riddle, wrapped in a mystery, inside an enigma! But to you, it makes sense. It's one of those great moments that you simply cannot share with another soul. I know, I have had that happen to me.

SOLOMON'S ADDITIONAL MYSTERIES

With all of that as background information, we now come to a segment of Solomon's journal that talks about three rather familiar mysteries: the mystery of unjust triumph, of unfair consequences, and of untimely pleasure.

Before we get to the core of this chapter, I'd like to go to the last part of Ecclesiastes 8 (a little like going to the back of the book for the answers), then read that into the rest of what I want to share with you. Take a look at what the wise man concluded:

> When I gave my heart to know wisdom and to see the task which has been done on the earth (even though one should never sleep day or night), and I saw every work of God, I concluded that man cannot discover the work which has been done under the sun. Even though man should seek laboriously, he will not discover; and though the wise man should say, "I know," he cannot discover (vv. 16–17).

It is terribly important that we have the right perspective on God's mysteries which are connected to His wisdom.

God's mysteries defy human explanation. Even though we stay up night after night, even though we give ourselves laboriously to the task of searching out God's mind in all of God's plan, we are not equipped to explain God's mysteries. Most of His mysteries defy human explanation.

God's mysteries go beyond human intellect and wisdom. The wise man, even though he may say, "I know," cannot discover the full picture of what God is about.

All of us have had mysteries of some kind that have invaded our lives. No doubt you have had things happen that have shaken and stunned you. And perhaps you've decided to wait until He unfolds the meaning of the drama. And the longer you wait, the less you seem to grasp why. And the further you seek to understand why, the more oblique the mystery becomes. That's one of the illustrations that should prove to us we're on target with something terribly relevant. It's marvelous to all of us how amazingly relevant God's truth is. We don't have to *make* the Bible relevant, it *is* relevant.

Let's notice in this passage some of the mysteries that make us struggle.

The Mystery of Unjust Triumph

> So then, I have seen the wicked buried, those who used to go in and out from the holy place, and they are soon forgotten in the city where they did thus. This too is futility (Eccles. 8:10).

Remember, Solomon is coming to terms with reality and it's a painful journey. Here he refers to a common experience that we have all witnessed: A wicked individual is buried and is given such an impressive funeral that the wickedness of that person's life is glossed over. *The Living Bible* offers this helpful paraphrase of verse 10.

> I have seen the wicked buried, and as their friends returned from the cemetery, having forgotten all the dead man's evil deeds, those men were praised in the very city where they had committed their many crimes! How odd!

There's something amazing about a burial. It's remarkable what an honorable burial can do for a dishonorable life.

Shakespeare, borrowing from Euripides, wrote these familiar words in *Julius Caesar:* "The evil that men do lives after them; the good is often interred with their bones."

Solomon's point is quite the opposite—and far more realistic. The good that men do lives after them and the evil is often buried. And to make matters worse, the evil seems quickly forgotten. It bothered Solomon so much he called it "madness." We're calling it "mystery." "This is futility," says the king. And akin to this, we see in verse 11 that the unjust triumph:

> Because the sentence against an evil deed is not executed quickly, therefore the hearts of the sons of men among them are given fully to do evil.

Let me illustrate. Someone does something bad. You care enough to warn that individual of the consequences. Because he or she did something that was wicked you are convinced "judgment is going to fall." But it doesn't. And guess what—the person does something even worse later on, right? And *still* judgment doesn't fall. Because the consequences of evil don't happen right away, rather than turning away from wrong, the individual *intensifies* his wrong. Mysteriously, those who traffic in unjust actions often get away scot-free. And they even increase their evil deeds. That's the point of verse 11.

As James Russell Lowell wrote in his poem *The Present Crisis:* "Truth forever on the scaffold; wrong forever on the throne."

We don't like those rules. We like wrong falling off the scaffold and truth standing firm on the throne. Isn't it amazing how some individuals can get away with cheating and deception and dishonor and go right on into more extreme acts of disobedience and dishonor virtually untouched by the God of justice? The lack of immediate judgment prompts them to continue unjust actions.

Skipping ahead just a bit in Solomon's journal, let's look at a second mystery he uncovered.

The Mystery of Unfair Consequences

> There is futility which is done on the earth, that is, there are righteous men to whom it happens according to the deeds of the wicked. On the other hand, there are evil men to whom it happens according to the deeds of the righteous. I say that this too is futility (Eccles. 8:14).

The scene is so familiar and relevant you'd think Solomon lived in the final decades of the twentieth century. *The Living Bible* says, "Providence seems to treat some good men as though they were wicked, and some wicked men as though they were good." It's the age-old puzzle, another of those riddles, wrapped up in a mystery, inside an enigma. Why is it that courageous, godly missionaries are martyred rather than brutal murderers? Why is it that a sweet, loving Christian family traveling down a highway is hit head-on by an irresponsible drunk driver who walks away without a scratch, while the family members are all killed? That is precisely what occurred in my city shortly before the Christmas holidays in 1984. A mother and all her children were killed by a drunk who demolished their car when he lost control of his. Think of that dear husband and father of the family! Why is it that the Mafia gets rich on porno shops, mind-twisting drug abuse, prostitution, and illegal gambling, and you can barely make ends meet, even though you try to walk with God? It's another of those mysteries, isn't it?

You may not agree with all of the conclusions Rabbi Harold Kushner reaches in his book, *When Bad Things Happen to Good People.* I certainly don't. But some of his observations are issues most thinking people ponder.

> There is only one question which really matters: why do bad things happen to good people? All other theological conversation is intellectually diverting. . . . Virtually every meaningful conversation I have ever had with people on the subject of God and religion has either started with this question, or gotten around to it before long. . . .
>
> The misfortunes of good people are not only a problem to the people who suffer and to their families. They are a problem to everyone who wants to believe in a just and fair and livable world. They inevitably raise questions about the goodness, the kindness, even the existence of God. . . .
>
> Like every reader of this book, I pick up the daily paper and fresh challenges to the idea of the world's goodness assault my eyes: senseless murders, fatal practical jokes, young people killed in automobile accidents on the way to their wedding or coming home from their high school prom.

Further into the book he continues:

> Does God "temper the wind to the shorn lamb"? Does He never ask more of us than we can endure? My experience, alas, has been otherwise. I have seen people crack under the strain of unbearable tragedy. I have seen marriages break up after the death of a child, because parents blamed each other for not taking proper care or for carrying the defective gene, or simply because the memories they shared were unendurably painful. I have seen some people made noble and sensitive through suffering, but I have seen many more people grow cynical and bitter. I have seen people become jealous of those around them, unable to take part in the routines of normal living. I have seen cancers and automobile accidents take the life of one member of a family, and functionally end the lives of five others, who could never again be the normal, cheerful people they were before disaster struck.[2]

It's a mystery that defies explanation—the mystery of unfair consequences. Who hasn't wrestled with it?

There's a third mystery which Solomon mentions, although it seems to be out of place.

The Mystery of Untimely Pleasure

> So I commended pleasure, for there is nothing good for a man under the sun except to eat and to drink and to be merry . . . (v. 15).

One could say, "I read that in the playboy philosophy. Sounds hedonistic to me. Eat, drink, be merry! Live it up! Go for all the gusto you can get!" But wait—don't miss the rest of what he writes:

> . . . and this will stand by him in his toils throughout the days of his life which God has given him under the sun (v. 15).

In a world of unjust triumph and unfair consequences, I see an individual here who is a personification of the mystery of untimely pleasure. Well, why not? What's the alternative? The alternative is becoming bitter, cynical, questioning, never at peace, neurotic in one's pursuit of answers to why, why, why. Instead of going mad, attempting to solve all the mysteries of heaven and earth, which cannot be done, the writer suggests a simple plan: "Eat, drink, and happily trust God!" God gives us this alternative in order to endure life's circumstances. That's the space where we exist. Throughout the days of our lives God will give us the ability to accept and cope with reality even though we're at a loss to explain it.

If you're beginning to need an explanation, it's time to return to those words we omitted a little earlier:

> Although a sinner does evil a hundred times and may lengthen his life, still I know that it will be well for those who fear God, who fear Him openly (v. 12).

There is no way to find any merriment in life, any genuine relief apart from the truth of those words. Solomon isn't denying the reality of sin. Even though sin goes on a hundred times over, even though a life may be lengthened in spite of a sinful lifestyle, and even "though He slay me, I will hope in Him" (Job 13:15). Though I am without answers, yet will I believe in Him.

Check out the next statement:

But it will not be well for the evil man and he will not lengthen his days like a shadow, because he does not fear God (v. 13).

Let's put this into perspective. Let's be painfully realistic. Neither you nor I can grasp God's plan. We don't know when it will reach its goal. It's like we are looking through a thick fog and we can't see the sun, so we don't know how or when God's going to deal with wrong, but we do know this—we know God will keep His word. So until then we eat, we drink, we find happiness and contentment in this simple lifestyle. Though evil triumphs, though there are unfair consequences happening all around us, we trust our God to see us through. He is working it out.

Let's look once again at Solomon's words from an earlier section of his journal:

> I have seen the task which God has given the sons of men with which to occupy themselves. He has made everything appropriate in its time. He has also set eternity in their heart, yet so that man will not find out the work which God has done from the beginning even to the end (3:10–11).

Perhaps it would be better rendered: "God has made everything appropriate in its time. He has set eternity in their heart, without which we will not find out the work which God has done from the beginning even to the end." If we miss the eternal perspective, we will spend the rest of our lives wringing our hands and waving our fists heavenward asking, "Why?" and protesting "How dare You!"

Ruth Harms Calkin once wrote:

> Lord, I'm drowning
> In a sea of perplexity.
> Waves of confusion crash over me.
> I'm too weak to shout for help.
> Either quiet the waves
> Or lift me above them.
> It's too late to learn to swim.[3]

I've had days like that, haven't you?

Pastors often get caught in the crossfire between people and God. Many folks have the strange idea that because a person is a minister, a priest, a rabbi, or any other spiritual leader that somehow God has given that individual a fail-safe answer sheet. In other words, it's the popular idea that the shepherd has the ability to see through all of those mysteries and to dispense miracles whenever they are needed—almost like a divine slot machine. Just drop in your offering, learn how to manipulate the handles, and you'll be able to play that game. Out will come the satisfaction you need—an answer, a miracle, whatever.

Some time ago I read *Five Smooth Stones for Pastoral Work* by Eugene H. Peterson, a fellow minister. I quote from it because it helped me think through this whole issue of wrestling with miracles, answers from God that are tied into mysteries and wisdom.

> So pastoral work takes place in a context in which every kind of spiritual expectation is directed to the pastor (which is encouraging); it is also, though, a context in which other answers are being offered by better-budgeted competitors, skilled in the arts of bedazzlement, who elbow their way in and get a hearing (which is frustrating). In our privileged position of having people come to us with the most profound and intimate of needs we are jostled by fast-talking and big-promising others. We are not the only preachers on the block. If we cannot make good on what people want done for them spiritually, there are plenty around who will—or say they will.
>
> A cursory sorting out of people's expectations (at least the kind that get channeled through the conduit of the pastoral vocation) ends up with two piles, miracles and answers. The miracles are an expectation that God will do for us what we cannot do for ourselves; the answers are an expectation that God will tell us what we can't figure out for ourselves. Both expectations are plausible, having a certain commonsense reality to them. Since God is both omnipotent and omniscient it would seem to follow that if we get close to him some of what he is ought to rub off on us. It is not unreasonable to suppose that his power will rub off in the form of miracles and his wisdom in the form of answers. . . .
>
> At this point pastoral work encounters a complex difficulty, for the vocation of pastor does not permit trafficking in either miracles or answers. Pastors are in the awkward position of refusing to give what a great many people assume it is our assigned job to give. We are in the embarrassing position of disappointing people in what they think they have a perfect right to get from us. We are asked to pray for an appropriate miracle; we are called upon to declare an authoritative answer. But our calling equips us for neither. In fact, it forbids us to engage in either the miracle business or the answer business.[4]

It is not the pastor or the Bible study leader or the author who has the answers. We all seek the same answers; we all need the same miracles. So trying to put a spiritual leader in the place of God can only lead to disillusionment and disappointment. It is God alone who has the wisdom to give the answers; it is God alone who has the power to do the miracles.

A long time ago I ran out of excitement concerning cheerleading miracle-workers. We cannot depend on some person for the answer or the miracle to deliver us from our problems. Although some spiritual leaders are often tempted to try to provide that answer or that miracle, there is only one qualified for that job—God. In Him is the hope of the riddle wrapped in a mystery inside an enigma.

Ways to Handle the Mysteries

So how do we handle the mysteries? What do we do with those unsolved questions? What do we do with unjust triumphs and with unfair consequences? How do we live realistically in the realm of untimely pleasure?

I have come up with three suggestions that might answer those questions:

(1) We must each admit: "I am only human"—and admit it daily. We should say it to ourselves first thing in the morning, a couple of times a day, and just before we go to sleep every night. And we should do that week in, week out—until it sinks in! We must not become so impressed with our spiritual redemption that we forget that we are human, finite, and fallible.

(2) We must each admit: "I don't understand why—and I may *never* on this earth learn why." We must then try our best, by the power of God, not to let that affect our faith. In fact, we should ask God to use that lack of knowledge to *deepen* our faith. The fact that I may never understand "why" should cause me to be more like Abraham, who didn't stagger at the promises of God through unbelief, but was strong in faith. Every once in a while I remember that a ninety-year-old woman and a one hundred-year-old man had a little tiny baby and my faith is strengthened. That's a marvelous moment when we realize that God could do it and *nobody* can explain how He could pull it off. But God kept His word—that's wisdom. And God gave Abraham and Sarah a baby—that's a mystery alongside

a miracle. If He could do it then, He can do it now, and we'll wait patiently on Him. If He doesn't, He has a better plan in the long run for His whole will, so let's be quiet and let it happen.

(3) We must each admit: "I cannot bring about a change." We may have tried. We may have done everything we know to do— but we can't change this situation. It is another mystery, a riddle, an enigma. We can't explain it, so it is time to admit, "I have no power to change it . . . Lord, God, You know what is best for Your child. I wait. I will eat and drink, I will find my joy in You. This is what You have given me throughout the days of my life in the midst of all this toil. This is what You have given me under the sun. I will walk in it." And that explains how the Christian can have joy in the midst of wild and crazy, mysterious and strained circumstances.

When we respond to mysteries in this manner, we no longer struggle with unjust triumph and unfair consequences. And as a result, *we'll* become a mystery. Our untimely pleasure will create all kinds of interest in the phenomena of how we think. We will have doors opened to us. Sometimes, people who don't even know me will ask me, "Why are you so happy? Why do you seem to be enjoying life so much?" It has happened at places like the grocery store, the dry cleaners and the service station. Not long ago it happened on a bridle trail where I was running. The fellow who asked me had heard me humming a song and he wondered how that could be? He must have thought that people don't sing in a day and time like this! Well, with a God like ours, there's no way we can help enjoying life and its happiness!

Andrae Crouch, a contemporary composer, captures this truth in a song called "Through It All":

> I've had many tears and sorrow,
> I've had questions for tomorrow;
> There've been times I didn't know right from wrong
> But in ev'ry situation, God gave blessed consolation
> That my trials come to only make me strong.
> I've been to lots of places,
> And I've seen a lot of faces;
> There've been times I felt so all alone,
> But in my lonely hours,
> Yes, those precious, lonely hours
> Jesus let me know that I was His Own.

I thank God for the mountains and
I thank Him for the valleys,
I thank Him for the storms He brought me through,
For if I'd never had a problem
I wouldn't know that He could solve them,
I'd never know what faith in God could do.

Through it all, through it all,
Oh, I've learned to trust in Jesus,
I've learned to trust in God.
Through it all, through it all,
I've learned to depend upon His Word.[5]

That, dear friend, is the way to live. Through all the misery and the mysteries—to trust in Jesus, to trust in God, to depend upon His Word! And when we do that, we too become a mystery, personifying untimely pleasure in the midst of unjust triumph and unfair circumstances. What a challenge!

17

HAVE A BLAST WHILE
YOU LAST

Journal Entry

> This, too, I carefully explored—that godly
> and wise men are in God's will; no one
> knows whether he will favor them or not.
> All is chance! The same providence confronts
> everyone, whether good or bad, religious or
> irreligious, profane or godly. It seems so
> unfair, that one fate comes to all. . . .
> There is hope only for the living. . . . For
> the living at least know that they will die!
> . . . Whatever they did in their lifetimes—
> loving, hating, envying—is long gone,
> and they have no part in anything here
> on earth any more. So go ahead, eat,
> drink, and be merry, for it makes no
> difference to God! Wear fine clothes—
> with a dash of cologne! live happily
> with the woman you love through the
> fleeting days of life, for the wife God
> gives you is your best reward down
> here for all your earthly toil.

*I*t is often necessary for us to blast before we are able to build. This is not only true in construction work but also in life. Before something beautiful and new can become a reality, the old and the ugly must be destroyed. Blasting precedes building.

There once lived a young man named Jeremiah. Called by God to be a prophet, he faced a life of being misunderstood and maligned. Realizing that such a future would hardly be an encouraging one, the Lord God reassured him with words of affirmation and confidence-giving counsel early in his ministry.

> Now the word of the Lord came to me saying, "Before I formed you in the womb I knew you. And before you were born I consecrated you; I have appointed you a prophet to the nations." Then I said, "Alas, Lord God! Behold, I do not know how to speak, because I am a youth." But the Lord said to me, "Do not say, 'I am a youth,' because everywhere I send you, you shall go, and all that I command you, you shall speak. Do not be afraid of them, for I am with you to deliver you," declares the Lord. Then the Lord stretched out His hand and touched my mouth, and the Lord said to me, "Behold, I have put My words in your mouth. See, I have appointed you this day over the nations and over the kingdoms, to pluck up and to break down, to destroy and to overthrow, to build and to plant" (Jer. 1:4–10).

God told Jeremiah that his assignment was "to pluck up . . . break down . . . destroy and to overthrow" *before* he was expected "to build and to plant." Even ancient prophets followed the same game plan: Blasting precedes building.

I find it fascinating that what was true prophetically for Jeremiah was also true philosophically for Solomon. For nine chapters of his journal the man blasts away! Most of the under-the-sun lifestyles are blown out of the water by the man who gave them his best shot— only to find them nothing more than exercises in futility, or, as he usually put it, "Vanity of vanities, all is vanity." They looked and sounded so satisfying, but they were neither.

FAMILIAR PHILOSOPHIES OF LIFE THAT WON'T WORK

Let's dip back into four of Solomon's earlier empty pursuits—materialism, epicureanism, humanism, fatalism—and realize again how

relevant they are today. Before we can ever expect to build a meaningful life, all four need to be blasted into oblivion!

Materialism

Let's look first at materialism. In brief, this philosophy says, "Possessions satisfy—provide yourself!" When we buy into this system, we
accumulate things because we think objects will make us happy or
comfortable, somehow bringing us contentment. So off we go to cap-
ture the good life, believing that possessions will bring us satisfaction.

Not far from where I live are some of the most luxurious beach
communities in all the world. The finest in homes, furnishings, clothing, automobiles, restaurants, artworks, yachts, and craftsmanship can
be found in the Newport Beach-Balboa Island-Laguna Beach region.
If you ever want to witness materialism on parade, just visit that
elegant stretch of real estate.

While driving on the Balboa Peninsula to meet a man for lunch
one day, I found myself momentarily behind a bright red Porsche,
a beautiful little German-made sports car, meticulously cared for by
the owner, who was whipping in and out of traffic. Obviously, he
was familiar with the road. As I pulled up behind him to wait for a
traffic light, I noticed several appointments on him and his car that
revealed he was very much at home in the chic scene. As I smiled
at his clever license plate, personalized, of course, I caught a glimpse
of the lettered frame that bordered it—which told me volumes about
the man's lifestyle, had I had any doubt up to that point. It contained
eight words: *He who dies with the most toys wins!* That, friends
and neighbors, is "materialism to the max," as some teenagers would
say. Before we can ever expect to build a life that is meaningful
and fulfilling, we must see the futility of materialism.

Epicureanism

The equally popular epicurean philosophy says, "Life is a ball—
enjoy yourself!" Tell me now, doesn't that have a familiar ring to
it? Years ago hedonistic souls put it this way, "Eat, drink, and be
merry . . . for tomorrow we die." Today, it's "If it feels good, do
it!" It speaks of being completely free, unaccountable, available for
anything, just so it feels good. Epicureanism is lust on the prowl,

letting it all hang out, throwing moral restraint to the wind. It is best portrayed in today's *Playboy* philosophy.

It may sound like a fun way to live, unless you happen to be married to someone who has adopted this free-for-all philosophy. While you expect and long for the necessary checks and balances that make a marriage strong and give it stability, your partner doesn't want all that hassle. Instead of shared responsibility you encounter independence, passivity, irresponsibility, and a half dozen other domestic disappointments.

Songs often say it best. Back in the 1970s a song entitled "She's Got to Be a Saint" by Joe Paulini and Mike DiNapoli told a familiar story and displayed the very scenes I've been trying to describe.

> I'm out late ev'ry night, doin' things that ain't right,
> And she'll cry for me.
> When I'm down in the dumps and she nurses my lumps
> How she cries for me.
> And she'll never complain, she keeps hiding the pain
> But I know all the while:
> She's not feeling too well 'cause I've put her thru hell;
> Still she forces a smile.
> She's got to be a saint, Lord knows that I ain't.
> I finally realized right before my eyes,
> Here is a saint.
>
> There's a dress in the shop that'll make her eyes pop
> But she'll look away.
> She'd a gotten a lift if I bought her that gift
> For her birthday.
> But her birthday has come and I feel like a bum
> 'Cause I spent my last dime
> On a worthless old friend on a drunken weekend.
> I've done it time after time.
> She's got to be a saint, Lord knows that I ain't.
> I finally realized right before my eyes,
> Here is a saint.
>
> Should I stay, should I go? I really don't know,
> My mind's in a blur.
> Soon it's gonna be dawn and if she finds me gone
> Would it be best for her?
> I see her cry in her sleep so I kiss her wet cheek
> I kneel by her and pray.

And I'll turn off the light, step out in the night,
    and I'll go on my way.
She's got to be a saint, Lord knows that I ain't.
I finally realized right before my eyes,
    Here is a saint.[1]

Fun guy, huh? Really bright. And lots of character! If the truth could be told, he is the kind of jerk every father fears is going to marry his daughter. Don't kid yourself, epicureanism is nothing more than Greek for hell at home. Anyone who hopes to construct a satisfying life must blast away at that lie.

Humanism

Humanism is yet another philosophy that can eat your lunch. In few words, it says, "Humanity is glorious—exalt yourself!" I warn you, it's subtle. Very tricky. It's the age-old idea that there is no such thing as depravity. On the contrary, we humans possess great and grand potential. We can therefore do it on our own. We're good enough, strong enough, and certainly capable enough to pull it off, regardless. It was first on display at the Tower of Babel, and in every generation it gains fresh momentum.

No one ever wrote of it more eloquently than William Ernest Henley did in his famous poem, "Invictus."

Out of the night that covers me,
Black as the pit from pole to pole,
I thank whatever gods may be
For my unconquerable soul.

In the fell clutch of circumstance,
I have not winced nor cried aloud:
Under the bludgeonings of chance
My head is bloody, but unbowed.

It matters not how strait the gate,
How charged with punishments the scroll,
I am the master of my fate;
I am the captain of my soul.

Got the picture? Humanists teach we are masters of our own fate, captains of our own souls. We are indomitable, unconquerable, invincible. This is definitely a philosophy that needs to be blasted.

Fatalism

Fatalism is the philosophy that says, "The game is fixed—resign yourself!" Of the four, this philosophy makes us the most passive and tempts us to be uninvolved. Since events follow an irrational, blind process—regardless—then we might as well kick back and accept *whatever* comes. Obviously, if we track such a message far enough, we find ourselves neck deep in a doctrine of despair. And we ultimately shrug, "Aw, what's the use?"

Back in 1983 the television industry promoted and presented a film that had been made for TV. Because its story was so relevant, an unusually large number of viewers watched the film, entitled "The Day After." It was an imaginary albeit realistic portrayal of a nuclear attack on mid-America and the tragic, horrifying consequences that follow such a disaster. Those who watched the program witnessed fatalism personified in one of the characters who survived. While stumbling across the bleak landscape, she sighed, "If all this is going to occur—why go on living?"

Fatalism sucks the hope and motivation from life. It leaves us feeling like trapped robots, destined for misery. Life becomes depressing— an absolutely and unchangeably dreadful existence. Before we can ever hope to build a life of purpose and meaning, fatalism, like the other three philosophies of futility, must be blasted.

Not wanting his readers to get caught up in any of the man-made philosophies that distort our view "under the sun," Solomon has blasted until there is little more to blast. Now it's time to build, which should encourage all of us! Frankly, I'm glad to see him turn the corner. A body can take just so much negativism. Let's take a look at his more positive mindset.

For I have taken all this to my heart and explain it that righteous men, wise men, and their deeds are in the hand of God. Man does not know whether it will be love or hatred; anything awaits him. It is the same for all. There is one fate for the righteous and for the wicked; for the good, for the clean, and for the unclean; for the man who offers a sacrifice and for the one who does not sacrifice. As the good man is, so is the sinner; as the swearer is, so is the one who is afraid to swear. This is an evil in all that is done under the sun, that there is one fate for all men. Furthermore, the hearts of the sons of men are full of evil, and insanity is in their hearts throughout their lives. Afterwards they go to the dead. For whoever is joined with the living, there is hope; surely a live dog is better than a dead lion. For the living know they will die; but the dead do not know anything, nor have they any longer a reward, for their memory is forgotten. Indeed their love, their hate, and their zeal have already perished, and they will no longer have a share in all that is done under the sun. Go then, eat your bread in happiness, and drink your wine with a cheerful heart; for God has already approved your works. Let your clothes be white all the time, and let not oil be lacking on your head. Enjoy life with the woman whom you love all the days of your fleeting life which He has given to you under the sun; for this is your reward in life, and in your toil in which you have labored under the sun. Whatever your hand finds to do, verily, do it with all your might; for there is no activity or planning or wisdom in Sheol where you are going (Eccles. 9:1–10).

A BIBLICAL PHILOSOPHY ON LIVING THAT WILL WORK

The New International Version begins this section a little differently: "So I reflected on all this and concluded. . . ." The man is turning the corner in his journey. He's bringing everything to a climax. I suppose we could say he's coming to terms with reality. Thus far, chapter after monotonous chapter, his journal has been devoted to an exposé of emptiness. In effect he is saying, "I've tried all those things and they do not satisfy. Allow me to save you the trouble, my reader friend. Let me introduce to you that which has substance— the things you can count on. These things are reliable. I know, I've been there!" And then he presents to us the major realities that give life definition and meaning. There are four of them stated or implied here.

The Sovereign Hand of God

. . . righteous men, wise men, and their deeds are in the hand of God. Man does not know whether it will be love or hatred; anything awaits him (9:1).

Among the inescapable, inevitable realities, first and foremost there is the sovereign hand of God. Regardless of rank, status, color, creed, age, heritage, intelligence, or temperament, "the hand of God" is upon us. The late philosopher-theologian Francis Schaeffer was absolutely correct: "God is there and He is not silent." What reassurance this brings! It tells us, among other things, that nothing is out of control. Nor are we useless, despairing robots stumbling awkwardly through time and space, facing a bleak fate at the end. But neither does this mean we are given periodic briefings about His strategy. Did you miss the last three words? ". . . anything awaits him." And that means *anything*.

Being in the hand of God is not synonymous with or a guarantee for being economically prosperous, physically healthy, protected from pain, enjoying a trouble-free occupation, and having everyone smile and appreciate us. As Solomon wrote "Man does not know whether it will be love or hatred; anything awaits him." But what *does* help is the knowledge that behind whatever happens is a God who cares, who hasn't lost a handle on the controls.

The picture isn't complete yet. There's another inescapable factor that various human philosophies would try to diminish—the absolute certainty of death.

The Absolute Certainty of Death

> It is the same for all. There is one fate for the righteous and for the wicked; for the good, for the clean, and for the unclean; for the man who offers a sacrifice and for the one who does not sacrifice. As the good man is, so is the sinner; as the swearer is, so is the one who is afraid to swear. This is an evil in all that is done under the sun, that there is one fate for all men (Eccles. 9:2–3).

Death awaits us all. You can count on it. As Euripides, a Greek poet, once said, "Death is the debt we all must pay." This theme is repeated over and over again throughout Scripture:

> "By the sweat of your face you shall eat bread, till you return to the ground, because from it you were taken; for you are dust, and to dust you shall return" (Gen. 3:19).

> What man can live and not see death? Can he deliver his soul from the power of Sheol? (Ps. 89:48).

The soul who sins will die (Ezek. 18:4).

Therefore, just as through one man sin entered into the world, and death through sin, and so death spread to all men, . . . (Rom. 5:12).

Yet you do not know what your life will be like tomorrow. You are just a vapor that appears for a little while and then vanishes away (James 4:14).

And I saw a great white throne and Him who sat upon it, . . . And I saw the dead, the great and the small, standing before the throne, . . . and the dead were judged . . . (Rev. 20:11–12).

It's like the little nursery song that children sing:

> Ring around the roses,
> Pocket full of posies;
> Ashes, ashes, we all fall down.

Did you know that was a song whose origin goes all the way back to the days of the Black Plague? It was first heard by an old man pushing a cart stacked high with corpses. Many people erroneously thought that the plague came from polluted air and that walking in the garden among fresh flowers was a way to breathe cleaner air. Well-meaning medical doctors filled their pockets with petals from flowers and brought them into the hospital rooms which were full of people who couldn't get up and walk around the roses and posies outside. These physicians would sprinkle the petals onto the patient, hoping somehow the fragrance would clean their lungs of pollution. Others blew ashes into the faces of plague victims, hoping to cause a sneeze, again to clear the lungs. But they all, nevertheless, "fell down."

Now the song makes a lot more sense, "Ring around the roses, a pocket of posies; ashes, ashes [as if to sound like a sneeze], we all fall down." Try all we like, death looms large on everyone's horizon. Ultimately, we all fall down.

In one of the classics written midway through the nineteenth century—Herman Melville's famous book *Moby Dick*—it is encouraging to read the following words regarding the book of Ecclesiastes:

The mortal man who hath more of joy than sorrow in him cannot be true. And the same with books. The truest of all men was the man of sorrows; and the truest of all books, Ecclesiastes, the fine-hammered steel of woe.

When we give attention to Solomon's journal, we are reading the "fine-hammered steel" of a man telling us the truth, not the least of which is the absolute certainty of death.

If you think the first two realities were tough enough to handle, get a load of this third one!—evil and insanity fill the human heart.

Evil and Insanity Reside in the Human Heart

> . . . the hearts of the sons of men are full of evil, and insanity is in their hearts throughout their lives. Afterwards they go to the dead (Eccles. 9:3).

We've heard about the doctrine of depravity all our lives, but not much about the doctrine of insanity, right? Honestly, have you ever seen this in Scripture before? Lurking in the human heart is a permanent mixture of evil and insanity. It's enough to make shivers run up one's spine. Old Testament scholar Walter Kaiser renders insanity "every conceivable madness." What an awful mixture—meanness and madness!

Think about our day. How else can we explain the moral insanity? The sexual insanity? The homicidal insanity? The rationalization—the *insane* rationalization? The materialistic madness? The intellectual madness? The judicial madness of our times? It's absolutely insane!

Every once in a while, children come up with unbelievable and "crazy" comments about life. When they do, we laugh—and we should, because they are so innocent. I laughed at the little elementary school child who took a test on human anatomy and failed it. She was the only one in the class who failed that particular examination. This is how her test read:

> The human body is composed of three parts: the branium, the borax, and the abominable cavity. The branium contains the brain. The borax contains the lungs, the liver, and the living things. The abominable cavity contains the bowels, of which there are five: *a, e, i, o,* and *u.*

I love that answer. Sounds just like something a kid would come up with, doesn't it? That's an *acceptable* "madness." It's simply childlike innocence.

But that's not what Solomon has in mind here. He's talking about the insane actions and answers we adults come up with—which make nobody laugh! They are the answers we hear today in response to hard questions, like: "Why did you walk away from your family?" Or, "How can you continue to live like that, knowing that it's wrong and that Scripture stands against such things?" It's the actions of those who attempt to keep up the maddening pace of a workaholic world. It's insane.

You see, within the human heart there is a private polluted pool, a reservoir of insanity. You can drink from it. You can swim in it. You can be polluted by it. It's your own private pool and everybody has one. Like the prodigal who ran wild, acted out his insanity, and finally came to his senses before he went back home. Remember the story in Luke 15? Don't miss the part that says, "He came to himself." In other words, he returned to sanity.

How else can we explain the rebellion of our age? How else can we explain the response of a person who stares back over the counselor's desk and says to the professional, "Look, I know it's wrong, but forget about convincing me—I'm going for it." What better explanation can we give than this one Solomon offers: "The hearts of the sons of men are full of evil, and insanity is in their hearts through their lives."

There's a fourth reality, and like the other three, it will help immensely as we try to cope with the world in which we live. It's the reality of hope.

There Is Hope for the Living

> For whoever is joined with the living, there is hope; surely a live dog is better than a dead lion. For the living know they will die; but the dead do not know anything, nor have they any longer a reward, for their memory is forgotten. Indeed their love, their hate, and their zeal have already perished, and they will no longer have a share in all that is done under the sun (Eccles. 9:4–6).

I'm so glad we have finally arrived at something positive and affirming—hope for the living. There is nothing quite as encouraging as hope. When Solomon says that whoever is joined with the living will find hope, it turns the tide. It brings light into an otherwise dark chamber. Next he quotes an Arabic proverb familiar to him but not to us: ". . . a live dog is better than a dead lion." In our day, it doesn't have the ring of truth that it had then. Today, our pets are pampered. They are treated like little luxuries. They are fluffed up, pedigreed, and respected like human beings—some are treated *better* than we treat humans. They sleep on our beds. Some of them actually eat at our tables.

But in those days, dogs were diseased mongrels that ran in packs through city streets. People feared them. Nevertheless, Solomon says that a live dog is better than the king of the jungle who's dead. Can you guess why? It's easy—because the king of the jungle, if he's dead, has no hope. As long as there's life, there's a dream, there's the anticipation of a new plan, there's love, there's purpose. In one word, along with life comes the presence of *hope.*

Look at the journal writer's next statement: "For the living know they will die. . . ." We can get ready for it. There's the hope of getting ready, the hope of preparation ". . . but the dead do not know anything, nor have they any longer a reward, for their memory is forgotten."

I remember well the cold February of 1971. We lived in Texas then, just a few miles away from my parents. One day my dad called me on the phone and simply said, "Son, your mother is gone." I said, "Uh . . . what do you mean, Dad? Do you mean she's dead?" He said, "Yes, . . . I think she's dead." And he said, "Sis is on her way. Can you come?" "Certainly," I said. I hurriedly got into my car and raced to their little apartment. When I walked in, I looked at my mother's lifeless body on the sofa. Quite frankly, it was a corpse that had no longer any hope on this earth. She was gone. We called the physician. He told us the life signs to look for. We checked— none were present. Although we contacted the paramedics, she was declared dead soon after their arrival. Since that experience, Solomon's comment in verse 6 makes a lot of sense to me. If I may personalize it by applying it to my mother, it could read like this:

> . . . her love, her hate, her zeal had already perished, and she will no longer have a share in all that is done under the sun (Christmastime, New Year festivities, Thanksgiving delights, celebrations at Easter, the birth of grandchildren and great grandchildren—all that perished for my mom, under the sun).

Great Counsel on How to Live 365 Days a Year

The point is clear: If we are alive, we have hope. Now, since that is true, how are we to respond to these inevitable and inescapable realities? Enough of gloom! Away with despair and all those depressing philosophies! The next section of Solomon's journal addresses the other side, and it's wonderfully bright. In fact, I find the words that follow contagiously enthusiastic. I think they offer a superb credo, a great way to live.

> Go then, eat your bread in happiness, and drink your wine with a cheerful heart; for God has already approved your works. Let your clothes be white all the time; and let not oil be lacking on your head. Enjoy life with the woman whom you love all the days of our fleeting life which He has given to you under the sun; for this is your reward in life, and in your toil in which you have labored under the sun. Whatever your hand finds to do, verily, do it with all your might; for there is no activity or planning or wisdom in Sheol where you are going (9:7–10).

See how verse 7 begins? "Go then." In other words, Solomon is saying, "I don't want you to just sit there and sigh as you read over my earlier remarks. I don't want you to groan and say, 'Ahhh, I suppose that's life?'" No. He wants us to read on—go on. Get on with it! Or, as I suggested in my chapter title (which I have borrowed from my friend Dr. Ken Gangel) "Have a blast while you last!"

Live Happily Wherever You Are

Since there's hope for the living, Solomon completes the thought with ". . . eat your bread in happiness, drink your wine with a cheerful heart; for God has already approved your works."

Not many people would give us that advice today. This is one of the first glimmers of the new covenant back in the Old Testament, and it's wonderful. Life is not a sentence leveled against us. We are not designed to pine away under a ton of guilt. God is not angry with us. He is satisfied, contented, and at peace.

A couple of years ago I was away ministering to a large group of single adults in Keystone, Colorado. During one of the discussion periods, I was asked, "Chuck, when you pray, what is your image of God? What visual mental picture do you have in your mind of God?" Great question! I had never been asked that before. As best I can remember I answered, "I think of a smiling, open-armed Friend who is saying things like, 'I accept you. Come on in. Tell me what's on your heart. I love you. I'm listening. I've got time. Let's talk.' "

But you know, after I answered that question and returned to my room that evening to think about it further, it occurred to me I hadn't always had such a pleasant mental picture of God. I remember growing up with a picture of God like an old man with a long beard and a big frown. He had this club with a big railroad spike driven through it—and He was looking at me—*to get me!* What a heretical concept of the God of heaven! A lot of folks still think like that.

But this says we're approved. God "has already approved your works." Why? Because we are in Christ. We are no longer distant foes, we're intimate friends.

What a wonderful hope for believers! We don't have to live under guilt! We don't have to worry each morning about whether or not God is going to club us into eternity! We don't have to live in fear, wondering if we're in the family or not in the family. We're there. And we're approved. Isn't that great news? No wonder we can eat and drink with happiness and cheer. He's already approved us. You and I are to live happily wherever we are. So, live it up!

I can just hear someone say, "That's what I want! I've been just waiting for the green light—free and easy hedonism, here I come!" Wait a minute. Hold on long enough to read what follows.

> Let your clothes be white all the time, and let not oil be lacking on your head (v. 8).

We have to dress in white? Some dear souls take that literally, suggesting we wear white all the time. That's not the point, anymore than we are expected to let oil keep running down our head. This is one of many symbolic statements in Scripture. White is usually a symbol of purity—a beautiful symbol of righteousness. And oil? It is commonly a symbol of the Spirit of God.

Walk in Purity and in the Power of the Spirit

The idea, then, is to live a pure and godly life, walking in righteousness and letting the power of the Spirit flow through us. Because

God's grace frees us from the guilt of sin, we can be plugged into His liberating power. We are free! Now *that* is the way to walk. And I'll tell you, it is a marvelous way to live. Talk about having a blast!

Solomon's counsel continues:

> Enjoy life with the woman whom you love all the days of your fleeting life. . . .

Husbands, the target of your love is the woman God gave you; enjoy her immensely! And wives, "Enjoy life with the [man] whom you love all the days of your fleeting life which He has given to you under the sun." Isn't that great counsel? You have a wife? Live it up! You have a husband? Live it up! *Go for it!* Have a blast in that marriage of yours!

Walt Kaiser writes:

> Celibacy or abstinence is not a holier state than matrimony, for the point [the writer] is making is the same as that of the writer of the book of Hebrews. Marriage is honorable; and the marriage bed undefiled.[2]

So, to the festive delights of verses 7 and 8, Solomon adds the gratifications, comforts, and delights of enjoying life with your wife whom you love. The literal translation of the Hebrew text reads: "See life with the wife you love." The expression "to see" was used in a more comprehensive manner than we use it today in the West. It was used of those who were in the midst of experiencing the full range of human emotions and passions. So what Solomon is saying here is that God would have us thoroughly enjoy life with our mates.

Far too many married couples stop having fun. They stop laughing with their partners. They stop romancing. But Solomon encourages us to do *all* the above . . . "all the days of [our] fleeting life."

Throw Yourself Fully into . . . Whatever

> Whatever your hand finds to do, verily do it with all your might.

I see no restrictions here. I don't see any limitations. A lot of people simply can't seem to take this for what it really says. The main thing they "throw themselves into" is the bed at night, totally exhausted. But this is talking about our hands, our hearts, our whole lives! This is saying, "Throw yourself fully into all of life. Don't hold back. Don't save your strength. Don't put off living until you retire. Have a blast—do it now!"

> . . . for there's no activity or planning or wisdom in Sheol where you are going (v. 10).

If you are waiting to live it up when you're six feet under, pal, you're in for a major disappointment! The time to live is *now*. And the way to do it is to pull out all the stops and play full volume!

> Don't be bashful.
>   Bite in.
> Pick it up with your fingers and
>   let the juice that may
>   run down your chin.
>
> Life is ready and ripe
>   NOW
>   whenever you are.
>
> You don't need a knife or fork
> or spoon or napkin or tablecloth
>
> For there is no core
>   or stem
>   or rind
>   or pit
>   or seed
>   or skin
>   to throw away.[3]

Now *that's* the way to handle life. There's a contagious enthusiasm in the way we're to live. When we do life becomes exciting, infectiously happy. It's made up of eating good food and drinking good drink and enjoying a wife or husband. Believe it or not, this is life lived on the ragged edge!

There are so many grim prophets of doom in God's family who, even though they hear of this sunshine, can't get beyond the clouds. They seem afraid of having a blast—almost as if such a life is suspect. No wonder more people aren't interested in our Christianity!

WHERE DO I GO FROM HERE?

So how are we supposed to live, now that we've been exposed to this new way of life? If we take away materialism, epicureanism, humanism, and fatalism, what's left? If we follow Solomon's advice and God's plan, the options are simple. We're to live life to its fullest:

- *free of guilt*
- *contagiously happy*
- *committed to God and our marriage*
- *thoroughly involved*

As we just read, whatever your hand finds to do, whether it's a hobby or a thrill or a challenge or a pastime or work or ministry or home or travel or just plain play, get it all together there. Like the pace-setting missionary Jim Elliot once said, "Wherever you are, be all there. Live to the hilt every situation you believe to be the will of God."

Even on the mission field He wants us to have a ball! In the power of the Spirit, with all the strength and might that we've got, we're to give it every bit. Even if we should die young, we're to give it all we've got while there's breath in our lungs.

My sister, Luci Swindoll, in her first book *Wide My World, Narrow My Bed* (an extremely fine statement on the single life) describes a humorous vignette out of our past, back when we were just a couple of kids. Our family would go down to a bay cottage every summer in South Texas. Our grandfather owned a little cabin down below Palacios at Carancahua Bay. Our older brother didn't like to fish much, but Sis and I loved it. Actually, we preferred just to mess around and have a ball. During the hot afternoons we'd go out on a rickety old pier, and invariably, it seemed that summer after summer, we'd find sitting on the end of that pier an old guy who took his fishing seriously. His last name was Kutasch, and he was a very unusual person.

Down below was a muddy bay full of gunk and old tires, catfish and alligator gar, and very few other fish! But there sat Kutasch, primed and ready to snag a whale! Here's how Luci tells the story.

"That Kutasch fella is an 'odd duck,'" my father used to say. We assumed by this that Daddy must have known more about him than we. Our only exposure to him was on the pier, but those experiences, in and of themselves, were certainly peculiar enough to earn him the label "odd." Mr. Kutasch always sat some distance away from us but in plain view. From where we sat we could, amazingly enough, watch him, his cork, our lines, and each other, all at the same time. Eventually, however, we realized the most important item to watch, by far, was his cork. With the slightest bobble of it, Kutasch would jerk that line out of the water so fast that had a fish been on it, the hook would have ripped out the side of its mouth . . . and, had it survived, it would certainly have gotten away.

During all our summers of fishing with Kutasch, never once did we see him catch a single living sea animal which made its habitat in Carancahua Bay. But it wasn't because he didn't try. The voracity with which he entered into that sport spoke of his enthusiasm. This thin, flailing, beast-of-a-fishing-line of his, with its untamed hook on the end, became a menace to the waterfront. When he engaged in this characteristic maneuver prompted by almost every cork wobble, all living creatures for blocks around hit the deck. The line wrapped itself around loose pier boards, the boathouse, crab nets, drying fish heads, buckets, camp stools, towels, and on one occasion, my nose!

We simply couldn't understand it. Here was a man who gave his all to the game of fishing, totally committed to catching whatever had caused the cork to bob, but not once being rewarded for his effort. We wondered why he never gave up. But he was always there—and consistently with the same behavior.

In time, we labeled this unusual custom of his, "givin' it the Kutasch." And when things got boring on our end of the pier, there was no activity in the water, or we simply wanted to demonstrate that we were still in the fight, one of us would say to the other to "give it the Kutasch," just to liven things up. That signified: "Watch out, you fish; I'm still here and I'm ready for you. In fact, I'm out to get all you've got!"

Even now, many, many years later, when Chuck and I face a new venture, a difficult challenge, or one of us is uncertain of the outcome of an undertaking, our words of encouragement to the other might very well be, "Give it the Kutasch." We are saying, in effect, "Go for broke! Don't hold back. You may not know what's out there, but whatever it is, give it your all." It says, "Watch out world . . . here comes enthusiasm!"[4]

Luci's words provide just another way of communicating Solomon's counsel.

You're married? "Give it the Kutasch!" Get at it with all your might. You have a challenge in front of you? Go for it—free of guilt, contagiously happy, committed to God, thoroughly involved. You're single? The same applies. "Give it the Kutasch!" You've got a future that's unsure? Step confidently into it full bore, knowing that God will not leave you in the lurch! You've had an unexpected surprise? You have a move in front of you? You have a situation that's uncertain, unsure? Go after it! "Give it the Kutasch!"

One final reminder: Before you can build that kind of contagious enthusiasm, you need to blast all the other stuff out of the way—those anchors and weights and tons of needless baggage. People who "give it the Kutasch" refuse to hold back.

C'mon, join me. Let's have a blast while we last!

18

AN OBJECTIVE VIEW
OF THE RAT RACE

Journal Entry

Again I looked throughout the earth
and saw that the swiftest person does not
always win the race, not the strongest man
the battle, and that wise men are often
poor, and skillful men are not necessarily
famous; but it is all by chance, by happening to be at the right place at the right
time. A man never knows when he is going
to run into bad luck. . . .

Here is another thing that has made a
deep impression on me. . . . There was a
small city with only a few people living in it,
and a great king came with his army and
besieged it.

There was in the city a wise man, very
poor, and he knew what to do to save the
city, and so it was rescued. But afterwards
no one thought any more about him.

Then I realized that though wisdom is better . . .
if the wise man is poor, he will be despised . . .

*T*he previous chapter was certainly not designed to leave the impression that a laugh a day will drive all troubles away. No way! The world we live in is demanding, cold, expensive, and unresponsive. A glib pep talk won't cut it, will it? Furthermore, we're busy people. We don't have much time to sit around and enjoy a lot of fun and games leisure. The fast lane doesn't lend itself to an easy-going lifestyle. The pace gets pretty wild at times, doesn't it? And you and I aren't getting any younger, either.

Do you ever get the feeling that life is a violin solo and you're wearing mittens? I sure do. Maybe it's because I became a grandfather before I turned fifty. There are occasions when life seems like a race track and I'm driving a tank! Such experiences prompt us to locate the squirrel cage, jump on, and try to make up for lost time. On those occasions we start to give attention to the urgent as we ignore the important. We begin to run around in circles, putting out fires. Such is life in the rat race. Surely that is not the way God planned for us to live.

Various Ways to View Life

It occurred to me recently that there are several different ways to view life. Although each is popular, each has its own set of problems.

Optimism

By looking through rose-colored glasses, we can convince ourselves that we live on Fantasy Island, existing under cloudless skies and surrounded by oceans of love, affirmation, and support. Dreams are big here—so are expectations. There's only one problem (and it's a beast!)—*lack of reality*. There's certainly nothing wrong with optimism. But if it is allowed to run unchecked, we soon become disillusioned and terribly disappointed. Our smile fades into a sneer.

Pessimism

As we have already seen in Solomon's writings, it is easy to turn life into a grim existence. If something bad can happen, the pessimist is convinced it will. To all tight-lipped souls waiting for the other shoe to fall, the light at the end of the tunnel is the headlamp of an oncoming train. The problem here is an obvious *lack of joy*. Anyone who has spent much time around pessimists knows what I'm talking about. It takes increased effort to hold on to the joy in your own life when you're in the company of someone who has a complete lack of it in his or hers.

Suspicion

Suspicion is a deeper trench than pessimism. It often borders near the neurotic. It says, "Everyone is out to get you. You can't believe anyone anymore. The world is full of liars, cheaters, crooks, and perverts—watch out." Paranoia and defensiveness fuel the fire of these people. Their major problem? *Lack of trust*. To them, only fools rely on someone else.

Fatalism

As indicated in the preceding chapter, the fatalist says we may as well accept our lot, nothing can be done to change it. "Just bite your lip and endure to the end." Or better, "If you can check out of responsibility, do it! Stay uninvolved." What's the problem here? *Lack of hope*—the lifeline gets severed. And existence becomes a marathon of misery.

Isn't it interesting how all four of those views of life turn attention back to ourselves? The optimist lives in his own fantasy. The pessimist lives in a colorless, humorless, dark existence marked by fear and dread. The person who is suspicious trusts no one. He builds big alarm systems around himself. He lives a secret life, a protective, untouchable, inaccessible, invulnerable life, because if he lets the truth be known, someone will take advantage. The fatalist turns life into a long, sad sigh. Death is coming. Death is sure. That's the only thing that's absolutely certain.

What we need is an objective view of this rat race! And that is precisely why I'm so grateful for the ancient journal which Solomon wrote and God preserved. It won't allow me to dream my life away. Neither will it let me become a victim of pessimism. And it doesn't give me the okay to become a suspicious or fatalistic person. Again and again it says, "Live realistically. Face life as it *is*, not as you *think* it is or as you *wish* it were. *This* is life! Face it. Come to terms with reality. And, whenever possible, to the best of your ability (with God's help), enjoy it." It even grants us the right to squeeze every enjoyment out of life. Here's a paraphrase of verse 10 of chapter 9:

> Whatever your hand finds to do, do it with gusto! Because if you're waiting for the grave, there'll be no activity, no planning, and no wisdom there.

Don't wait until later. Live now. Even though we are stuck here "under the sun," let's have at it!

Some "Under-the-Sun" Counsel

Wait a minute. If we buy into that suggestion, then the rat race is on, isn't it? Acknowledging that as a possible implication, the writer doesn't finish his thoughts until he gives us the other side of the coin.

> I realized another thing, that in this world fast runners do not always win the races, and the brave do not always win the battles. Wise men do not always earn a living, intelligent men do not always get rich, and capable men do not always rise to high positions. Bad luck happens to everyone. You never know when your time is coming. Like birds suddenly caught in a trap, like fish caught in a net, we are trapped at some evil moment when we least expect it (Eccles. 9:11–12, TEV).

Whenever I scope out the scene here in southern California where I live (which is usually spent literally "under the sun"), I observe a large number of people who are pursuing the so-called successful life. They would say the way to make it in this world—the way to succeed—is to increase speed, get stronger, be competitive, think more cleverly, plan longer, and have a visionary strategy—hire people with the skills that are needed and life will be successful. The race is on. Get up earlier. Go to bed later. Make work a top priority. Don't get sentimental about stuff like children, marriage, home, and the family. All that will have to wait. Raising kids can come later. And religion? Leave that for the over-the-hill gang and preachers. Don't get too involved in it because, after all, the race to success is for the swift, the strong, and the clever.

See how easy it is to get sucked in and be seduced? It all sounds so logical, so appealing. But there is another side to be considered. Look again at verse 11:

> I again saw under the sun that the race is not to the swift, and the battle is not to the warriors, and neither is bread to the wise, nor wealth to the discerning, nor favor to men of ability; . . .

I checked the Hebrew text and found five negative references and each of the five is pushed to the first part of its phrase for the sake of emphasis. I suppose it could be rendered:

> . . . *not* to the swift is the race; *not* to the strong warrior is the winning of the battle; *not* to the clever is the getting of bread; *not* to the sharp is true wealth; *not* to the skillful comes favor and power.

In other words: Success is not what you think! The maddening rat race is for empty-headed rats—not intelligent, clear-thinking people. Folks who want to honor God refuse to be trapped in a squirrel cage.

Professionals, students, and everyone else need to heed Solomon's words. The philosophy of our day will attempt to suck us in and convince us that if we're going to make it, we've got to run faster. That is to say, we've got to be stronger and more competitive and more clever, and even more manipulative. Otherwise, we won't be successful. Don't you believe it!

Why would Solomon be so emphatic as he denies the age-old ideas regarding getting ahead? Why doesn't success—true success—accompany those who are the most competitive and the most aggressive? Read what Solomon says next: " . . . for time and chance overtake them all." We're back to another "mystery," aren't we? That which appears to have the most speed, the greatest power, and the strongest influence hangs on the thin threads of time and chance.

Once again we're talking about the sovereign hand of God. Even though we may not read a lot about God's sovereignty in the daily news, it is at work. In the final analysis His "time" and His plan (called "chance" by Solomon) win out. The hand of God has a way of bringing about contrasting results rather than expected and logical results.

Jim Thorpe, an American-born Indian, was the most incredible athlete of his day. In fact, the king of Sweden awarded him several gold medals. As the recipient of Olympic medals, he was acclaimed "the greatest athlete of all time"—until it was discovered he had played baseball for five dollars a season. For this man, literally, the race didn't go to the swift. His Olympic medals were taken away. And not until recently were they returned to the Thorpe family.

When distinguished men and women looked for those who deserved to be honored with the coveted Nobel Peace Prize, they bypassed dozens of the bright and brilliant of our day as they stepped into the ranks of the poverty-stricken, disease-infested streets of Calcutta. They selected an unassuming woman named Mother Teresa and awarded her the prize. Again, the race is not always to the swift, the wealthy, the influential.

While Hollywood was promoting its sensual and secular productions at the Academy of Motion Picture Awards several years ago, who can ever forget the film of the year? It was a simple, straight-shooting film from Great Britain that told the story of a young Scottish runner who loved Jesus Christ more than the schedule of the Olympic games. Who would've ever guessed that *Chariots of Fire* would win the top award as best film of the year?

No, the race is not always to the swift. The strong are not always the strongest. Those most clever and competitive aren't always the wealthiest. Look at Solomon's next statement.

> Moreover, man does not know his time: like fish caught in a treacherous net, and birds trapped in a snare, so the sons of men are ensnared at an evil time when it suddenly falls on them (v. 12).

We may think we're powerful, but we're "like fish caught in a treacherous net." Or "like birds trapped in a snare." The writer is drawing an analogy—". . . so the sons of men are ensnared at an evil time when it suddenly falls on them." Here's the same verse translated in another version:

> You never know when your time is coming. Like birds suddenly caught in a trap, like fish caught in a net, we are trapped at some evil moment when we least expect it (TEV).

Everything is moving in a certain direction. It's predictable. It's planned. Success is coming. It's right around the corner—maybe not this year—but, for sure, the next. Momentum is increasing. Everything has been done just right and soon all the pieces will fall together. But *suddenly* (and this is the key word) God has a way of bringing all of our plans to an abrupt halt.

The long sighs of my wife awoke me early one Friday morning. Our sleep is seldom disturbed, but she had had a rare nightmare. I held her in my arms there in bed as she told me her terrible nightmare:

"Behind us," she said, "was a mudslide and our house was beginning to slide. I couldn't stop it. So I . . . I got the children all together and put them into the car and started racing around the house, picking up a lot of things and stuffing them into the car—things that would be lasting and important in light of what was happening. Then I looked out of the car window and there was a skyscraper—out of nowhere! It had slid off its foundation and was beginning to topple over on us. So I started the car; but as I hurried out the driveway I looked next door and saw the neighbors' sofa out in the front yard. The mother was on the sofa and the daughter was wringing her hands and screaming, 'Cynthia, Cynthia, Mother's dead!' But I couldn't stop the car.

"I thought, *What am I going to do?* But then as I started to turn to race out of our cul-de-sac there was a fast-moving wind— the swiftest wind I've ever encountered—and it was blowing like mad. It seemed like all of Fullerton was blowing away. So I turned around and drove back into the driveway. Seized with panic, I walked into our house. The wind had already swept through the living room and *everything* had been blown away. I thought, *Of all the significant things we have, nothing is more valuable than our kids and they are all in the car.* So I ran back to our car, slammed the door, held onto the steering wheel and said, 'Children, this is the end of the world.' And suddenly, I awoke."

For the next hour we talked. It was a great conversation—one of the best conversations we had all year. Do you know why? Because both of us evaluated our lives from the end-of-the-world viewpoint. It was so different. The squirrel cage had ground to a halt. The rat race had ended. The "end of time" has a way of wiping away the fog of incidentals. It was a time we treasure to this day. What clear perspective we gain when we look at life from that vantage point! Solomon is now prompted to address this whole issue by telling a parable.

> Also this I came to see as wisdom under the sun, and it impressed me. There was a small city with few men in it and a great king came to it, surrounded it, and constructed large siegeworks against it (vv. 13–14).

Picture the scene. It's a quiet little hamlet. There is a wall around the town, but it offers little protection. And suddenly the marching army of a king can be heard in the distance. The people inside the village are threatened. They know that their future is short—the end is coming. And this king comes to the wall and begins to build a mound of dirt up against it so that this siegework against the wall will allow his army to scale the wall and invade the village. The insignificant unprotected village is nothing more than a clod under the boot of this strong ruler and his army. Death is sure. And suddenly within the village there is a poor wise man who speaks.

> But there was found in it a poor wise man and he delivered the city by his wisdom. Yet no one remembered that poor man (v. 15).

I appreciate the words of one writer. He says, "This parable is not a moral tale to show what people should do. It is a cautionary tale to show what they are like." The parable is a mirror showing us ourselves. We don't want to miss the lesson woven through the fabric of the parable.

Perhaps Solomon had been told that story by his father David. It's also recorded in 2 Samuel 20. It's the kind of story that King David would have never forgotten—the kind he would have passed on to his son.

The historical account from 2 Samuel begins with a man—a worthless man—who had made life miserable for the king and his followers. He had fled to a little village and was hiding there, making havoc against the nation. So King David told Joab to go and to surround the city and kill the man, and if necessary, annihilate those people who happen to get in his way. When the marching army reaches the wall of the city, there is a woman living within the wall who knows that doom is sure. She seeks an audience with Joab and talks with him about what is really the concern of the king. Joab tells her that there is this man in the city and they want his life. The woman, very quietly and wisely, goes and tells the people of the city. She says, "Here's the plan. If we cut off his head and throw it over the wall, the king will go away." That's exactly what they do! They find the man, kill him, cut off the man's head, and toss it over the wall. Joab and his men see the head, and since that's all they wanted, they back off. Mission accomplished.

The historical account from David's life may sound similar to Solomon's parable but Solomon's story is more than a simple account of a city under siege. It's a scene that communicates the importance of wisdom. I don't believe it's farfetched to suggest that the city in the parable represents a life under pressure—people like you and me in any generation, living our lives, realizing a very loud and powerful enemy is present whose desire is twofold: initially to seduce us and ultimately to destroy us.

Some "Above-the-Sun" Wisdom

Let's take the time to consider four or five statements of wisdom that come from this parable. It's like they bubble up from the bottom of a deep well of wisdom. We've already seen one: *Human ability cannot guarantee genuine success.* We saw that in verses 11 and 12— the race is not to the swift; the battle is not to the warrior; human ability cannot guarantee genuine success. But the approaching enemy won't tell us that! You see, the enemy's desire is to convince us that human ability *is* what's needed to protect the city. Elsewhere Solomon says, "The horse is prepared against the day of battle, but safety is of the Lord." We can build a wall as high as we wish, but if we listen long enough to the shouting of the enemy, the walls will cave in.

Can you hear the shouts? "Place all your attention on human ability. Give up those sentimental things like eternal priorities and lifelong commitments and a relationship with Christ. Buy into the system!" It seems all right. But human ability cannot guarantee genuine success.

Solomon gives us another statement of wisdom in verse 16: "So I said, 'Wisdom is better than strength.'" *Strength is more impressive yet less effective than wisdom.* Isn't it true? If we stand strength alongside wisdom, strength will get the public's vote practically every time. We're impressed with it. It is intimidating. It fits our times. How is strength more impressive? It's always going faster, getting stronger, getting smarter, more clever, more competitive, more skillful. "Ah! That's the way to succeed!" says strength. But in verse 16 are the words from the wise yet poor man (whom you'll recall is not remembered). His words, nevertheless, live on—"Wisdom is better than strength."

But there's a third piece of counsel given as verse 16 continues:

> . . . But the wisdom of the poor man is despised and his words are not heeded.

Wise counsel is never popular, rarely obeyed, and seldom remembered. Solomon tells us that "the wisdom of the poor man is despised." Wise, godly counsel is not popular. It's rarely obeyed. It's usually forgotten. No one remembered the poor man. "His words are not heeded."

Do you see what this is about? This isn't a simple little story about a village. This is a parable offering insight about life. And the poor man is not some big-time professional counselor who is talking with us. It's the inner heart, the conscience, the spirit within us. It's that which pulsates with Scripture—that which is in touch with the timeless sage called the Spirit of God. It is the inner man that quietly waits to be obeyed.

The fourth statement of wisdom is found in verse 17: *Human rulers will always outshout wise counselors, and fools prefer the former.*

> The words of the wise heard in quietness are better than the shouting of a ruler among fools.

Wise counselors will give accurate yet quiet counsel, but fools will prefer to hear the advice of loud rulers.

You may be struggling with integrity in your business. You may be wrestling with doing what is right. You may be struggling with ethics. The advancing enemy on the outside says, "I'll give you a plan that will work! Listen to me! Ignore all that other stuff—you know, that biblical stuff—it won't work in this day and age. The race is for the swift. It's for the strong. I'll even give you a plan where you can rationalize around wrong. You can bend it so that you won't even have a guilty conscience. I'll provide you with new ways to think . . . to reason . . . to rationalize. Just let me over the wall." He shouts loudly and convincingly. You may even have a few friends encouraging you, who say, "It's okay, relax. You're too uptight."

You may be doing battle in the realm of sexual morality. There are far more books and advisors "shouting" at you to go right ahead; "restraint is not only puritanical, it's downright unhealthy. Whoever heard of absolute abstinence from sexual activity in the 1980s?"

Your marriage may be in conflict. If you are listening to the advice of the "ruler," you'll find ample encouragement to walk away, to give it up, simply to say, "We failed." But deep within, the poor wise man is whispering, "No, don't do that." The enemy is always louder and more convincing than the quiet wise man. But if you're not a fool, you'll listen to the wise.

> Wisdom is better than weapons of war, but one sinner destroys much good (v. 18).

Here's the fifth piece of advice: *Constructive words of wisdom are no match for destructive weapons of war.* In the rat race, it is our tendency to choose the path of least resistance and to find so-called authorities who help us rationalize wrong, who offer us other definitions of and alternatives to truth. I have often used the term *accommodating theology* to describe such rationalization.

Some people are selling their souls to a secular therapist. They are listening more to the well-educated psychologist than they have ever listened to the Lord or paid attention to His Word. And as they take their cues from their counselor, they are being seduced by today's psychology.

Now I realize that there are professional, competent counselors who are deeply committed to Scripture, who love the Lord and practice their profession with great care as they, with God, help people put their lives together. I thank God for every one of them, but they are so rare. How we need godly, wise, biblically committed psychologists to help the hurting find healing! For the most part, however, the enemy shouts loudly and offers humanistic logic and superficial happiness, rather than sound biblical truth. And those who are charmed by his ways are in perilous territory!

Read the following words by Dr. William Kirk Kilpatrick from the book entitled *Psychological Seduction:*

> In C. S. Lewis' classic book *The Screwtape Letters,* Screwtape instructs Wormwood to keep his man confused. "Keep his mind off the plain antithesis between True and False"; and keep him "in a

state of mind I call 'Christianity and.' You know—Christianity and the Crisis; Christianity and the New Psychology. Christianity and the New Order. . . ."

. . . Lewis was more prophetic than he could have guessed. What was only a minor confusion in 1941 has turned into mass confusion. It is difficult to say any longer where psychology leaves off and Christianity begins.

For non-Christians, popular psychology has an equally seductive influence. Many seem to turn to it as a substitute for traditional faiths. They may even think of it as a more evolved form of religion—a more efficient and compassionate way of doing good than Christianity. Psychology levels the hills of anxiety and makes the crooked way straight. It is the rod and staff that comforts them.

The appeal psychology has for both Christians and non-Christians is a complex one. But it is difficult to make sense of it at all unless you understand that it is basically a religious appeal. For the truth is, psychology bears a surface resemblance to Christianity.

Not doctrinal Christianity, of course. Most psychologists are hostile to that. And naturally enough, so are non-Christians. Nevertheless, there is a certain Christian tone to what psychology says and does: echoes of loving your neighbor as yourself, the promise of being made whole, avoidance of judging others. Those ideas are appealing to most people, no matter what their faith.

But like most counterfeits, popular psychology does not deliver on its promises. Instead, it leads both Christians and non-Christians away from duty or proper conduct. It is a seduction in the true sense of the word. . . .

True Christianity does not mix well with psychology. When you try to mix them, you often end up with a watered-down Christianity instead of a Christianized psychology. But the process is subtle and rarely noticed.[1]

That author is associate professor of educational psychology at Boston College, a graduate of Holy Cross who holds degrees from Harvard University and Purdue University. The man is not a wild-eyed, fanatical, fundamentalistic preacher who you might think just tumbled off the turnip truck. He is an educated faculty member in the field of psychology who, with credibility, addresses the situation *as it is.*

The enemy forces are at the wall and our "village" is being threatened. If we are Christians, there is a quiet voice deep within our spirits. It is the voice of the Spirit of God, prompting us to turn to God's Book as our unerring guide. But He won't shout. He won't use force. He won't even threaten. He speaks softly and waits patiently to be heard and obeyed.

Our rat-race problems are reaching epidemic proportions. Marriages are crumbling, morals are being compromised, minds are being bent and twisted against Scripture by people who "talk" Christianity but deliver only secular psychology. And although exceptions do exist, they are rare. As a word of caution, before you submit yourself to the counsel of a professional for an extended period of time, be absolutely certain that person is listening first and foremost to the living God. First, find out if he or she cares about biblical principles being carried out in your life. If this is not a priority, then *do not submit yourself.* To do so would lead to hurt, and the impact of that hurt initially would bring pain to the lives of your immediate family and ultimately to the larger family of God.

In the rat race called living on the ragged edge, it is easy to be seduced. Listen to God, even if His counsel is painful. Even if you find few people who agree with you, if God says it, do it. Not until you do will you find relief and recovery. Only then can you truly come to terms with reality.

19

BE SENSIBLE!

Journal Entry

Dead flies will cause even a bottle of
perfume to stink! Yes, a small mistake
can outweigh much wisdom and honor.
A wise man's heart leads him to do right,
and a fool's heart leads him to do evil. . . .

If the boss is angry with you, don't
quit! A quiet spirit will quiet his bad
temper.

There is another evil I have seen as I
have watched the world go by, a sad
situation concerning kings and rulers: For
I have seen foolish men given great
authority, and rich men not given their
rightful place of dignity! I have even seen
servants riding, while princes walk like
servants!

Dig a well—and fall into it! Demolish
an old wall—and be bitten by a snake!
When working in a quarry, stones will
fall and crush you!

It is possible to live our entire lives from the wrong perspective. Believing that we are right, we can be wrong. Thinking we are hitting the target, we can be missing the mark by miles.

This was reinforced in my mind when I read a rather amazing story that comes out of American Indian lore. An Indian brave found an egg that had been laid by an eagle. Not being able to return the egg to an eagle's nest, the next best thing to do was to put it in the nest of a prairie chicken. The result was predictable. The hen sat on this eagle's egg, along with her own eggs, knowing nothing of the addition. By and by the little eaglet was hatched alongside the prairie chickens.

The story continues . . .

> All his life, the changeling eagle, thinking he was a prairie chicken, did what the prairie chickens did. He scratched in the dirt for seeds and insects to eat. He clucked and cackled. And he flew in a brief thrashing of wings and flurry of feathers no more than a few feet off the ground. After all, that's how prairie chickens were supposed to fly.
>
> Years passed. And the changeling eagle grew very old. One day, he saw a magnificent bird far above him in the cloudless sky. Hanging with graceful majesty on the powerful wind currents, it soared with scarcely a beat of its strong golden wings.
>
> "What a beautiful bird!" said the . . . eagle to his neighbor. "What is it?"
>
> "That's an eagle—the chief of the birds," the neighbor clucked. "But don't give it a second thought. You could never be like him."
>
> So the changeling eagle never gave it another thought. And it died thinking it was a prairie chicken.[1]

What a tragedy! Built to soar into the heavens, made to be the chief of the fowls of the air, this eagle settled for the life of a prairie chicken, grubbing worms and scratching around in the dirt and thrashing about as he flies just a few feet above the earth.

In a world full of fools who settle for mediocrity, who are satisfied with the ho-hum status quo, it is easy for people who ought to be eagles to live like prairie chickens. How easy to opt for a wrong way of life, thinking all the while that, because everybody's doing it, it must be the way to go. In the same way, it is easy for the child of

God to live like a child of the world—to live his or her entire life "under the sun," never above it—riveted to the humanistic horizontal.

For the longest time in his journal on ragged-edge living, the ancient King Solomon has been talking about prairie-chicken lifestyle—life that's lived strictly "under the sun." And he hasn't hedged on the truth. It is a life of endless and meaningless futility. To use the word he uses most often, it is a life of "emptiness." It doesn't satisfy. It lacks substance and significance. It doesn't lead to anything of lasting value. It's not that there is a lack of activity, noise, and involvements— it's just an everpresent, boring, monotonous cycle of "nothingness." Finally, everything within our eagle heart either screams out against the prairie chicken existence—or, worse, we sigh and think, "What's the use? That's all I can expect."

Remember Solomon's earlier comment?

> Everything that happens was already determined long ago, and we all know that a man cannot argue with someone who is stronger than he. The longer you argue, the more useless it is, and you are no better off. How can anyone know what is best for a man in this short, useless life of his—a life that passes like a shadow? How can anyone know what will happen in the world after he dies? (Eccles. 6:10–12, TEV).

There's an aching, lingering sigh when we finish reading those words, isn't there? We sense a similar feeling when we read a little later:

> It seems so unfair, that one fate comes to all. That is why men are not more careful to be good, but instead choose their own mad course, for they have no hope—there is nothing but death ahead anyway (Eccles. 9:3, TLB).

If sighs could have been recorded, I think we'd find a few in that statement. Many people with this kind of lifestyle believe the most logical solution is suicide. "Get it over with and get it over with fast!" Many more choose that option than most of us realize.

Statistics show that approximately twenty-eight thousand Americans take their own lives each year, and the number is on the increase. That's an accepted estimate, yet it may be only the tip of the iceberg. Some authorities think the number could be as much as 50 percent higher.

According to an article entitled "Suicide in America" which appeared in the January 1984 issue of *Reader's Digest:*

- Suicide now ranks *eighth* among major causes of death.

- Among adolescents, it has increased 300 percent since 1960. More and more, authorities are realizing that a basic reason for working with the youth of our day is to try to help them find a reason to live. [If you don't believe that, you haven't worked with youth lately.]

- Our murder rate is high . . . yet more people kill *themselves* than kill others.

- Psychiatrist Paul Walters, director of Stanford University Cowell Health Service, believes suicide is more often the result of a thought disorder than of depression. "For me, the key word is *emptiness.*"

- One authority states: "It boils down to finding what a person has to live for."

That sounds a lot like old Solomon's words, or what I call "prairie chicken lifestyle." It's a life of living under the sun, grubbing worms, scratching in the dirt, thrashing about trying to make meaning out of one's frustrated existence. It's seeing this bird flying above and wanting to soar, yet being told, "Ah, don't bother, you're just a prairie chicken." Something tragic happens when the eagle inside us is convinced that it's nothing but a prairie chicken—we never learn to soar.

AN INTERLUDE IN SOLOMON'S STORY

As we pick up the journal story we've been following for quite some time, we find ourselves coming upon an interlude—sort of a transition. Another body of truth is about to be introduced. It's like the opening of the curtain for the beginning of the play . . . "act 3, scene 1." As the curtain opens, we're on the edge of our seats anticipating what shape this play will take and what meaning the plot will have. This section may be one of the most difficult to understand. When you read it, you'll see what I mean.

Dead flies make a perfumer's oil stink, so a little foolishness is weightier than wisdom and honor. A wise man's heart directs him toward the right, but the foolish man's heart directs him toward the left. Even when the fool walks along the road his sense is lacking, and he demonstrates to everyone that he is a fool. If the ruler's temper rises against you, do not abandon your position, because composure allays great offenses.

There is an evil I have seen under the sun, like an error which goes forth from the ruler—folly is set in many exalted places while rich men sit in humble places. I have seen slaves riding on horses and princes walking like slaves on the land.

He who digs a pit may fall into it, and a serpent may bite him who breaks through a wall. He who quarries stones may be hurt by them, and he who splits logs may be endangered by them. If the axe is dull and he does not sharpen its edge, then he must exert more strength. Wisdom has the advantage of giving success. If the serpent bites before being charmed, there is no profit for the charmer (Eccles. 10:1–11, NASB).

See what I mean? Though it may seem simple with these earthy maxims and proverbs that hang loosely together, they appear to lack order and progression of thought. As best as I'm able to decipher this section, Solomon has several contrasts in mind, each one being an illustration of the contrast between wisdom and folly. Remember, now, this is wisdom literature. There are some truths God presents in Scripture that must *not* be forced into a tight and rigid mold. Rather, they must be treated as beautiful works of art. This is music. This is great poetry. This is to be read in the normal sense of the word, but it is to be seen as symbolic language, referring to something far more significant than flies in a jug of perfume! Solomon's underlying concern is not with flies and ointment. Those are merely symbols in a chapter on wisdom. If I may repeat the word picture from the story told earlier in this chapter, it is the beauty of an eagle soaring over a world of drab and uncreative prairie chickens!

A CONTRAST: WISDOM AND FOLLY

There seem to be three examples of this contrast in Solomon's mind: advantages vs. disadvantages, humility and patience vs. popularity and partiality, and inevitable risks vs. inexcusable stupidity.

Advantages vs. Disadvantages

To begin with, there's this elegant vase of costly perfume with flies in it. If the dead insects are left there long enough, the entire jar gets a pungent odor. Again, it's not referring simply to perfumer's oil and actual dead flies. On the contrary—he seems to have in mind a life of folly. Even a little bit of folly, if it remains in a life of dignity and honor, will cast a dark shadow over all the honor of what once characterized that life. Ultimately, one's reputation that has been built over the years loses its value. Finally, if the wrong isn't cleared up, it's ruined—it "stinks," as Solomon describes it.

Illustration: Watergate. The folly of this episode shook a nation and cast a shadow across the man who held the highest office in the land. Another illustration: Chappaquidick. What a cloud it has cast over the life of a famous senator! Because of tiny little disease-carrying flies, the entire bottle of perfume is affected. Meaning? The life of an otherwise respected man in our country is now questioned. Folly can easily ruin a reputation.

Folly is a term we don't use that often, but it is a term used rather frequently in Scripture. It suggests a lack of good sense, lack of foresight, failing to realize the consequences of a stupid act *before* it occurs. Scripture calls that "folly" or "foolishness." And it can happen in our day just as it happened in Solomon's day.

But today, be sensible! If we hope to depart from the ranks of worm-grubbing prairie chickens and soar as eagles like a Christian is designed to soar, we must come to terms with reality. We must embrace wisdom rather than folly!

Very heavy weights (like people's respect and confidence) are hung on the thin wire of reputation. And that's what Solomon communicates in the opening lines of this section.

When I first read the next statement, I thought: "What a great slogan for the Republican party!" I have never heard it used by any politician, but it fits:

> A wise man's heart directs him toward the right, but the foolish man's heart directs him toward the left.

You understand, this has nothing to do with politics. But if you like to use statements from the Bible that seem to uphold your position (even though totally out of context) then here's a classic opportunity!

"Right," however, is yet another symbol. It represents that which is worthy of our effort and pursuit. "A wise man goes in the direction of that which is worth his time and effort. A foolish person (to continue the symbolism) goes toward the left." That's the thought.

Scripture is replete with occasions depicting the right hand as where God is. The Lord Jesus is said to be seated on the right hand of the throne of God. Psalm 16:8 says that the Lord "is at my right hand." Psalm 121:5 adds that "the Lord is your shade on your right hand." It's a picture of protection and power and the very presence of God on the right hand. A wise person goes God's way. A fool doesn't. A fool plays in the left zone. A fool is encouraged by the excitement and the adventure of wrong. He or she traffics in that territory. It's as simple as left and right. Observe that deep within there is the *heart*. "A wise man's heart . . . a foolish man's heart." This isn't referring to a shallow, off the top of one's head, seldom-made mistake. No, there is a deep-seated, heartfelt *pursuit* in that direction. You'd think fools would learn!

Fools don't learn, because fools don't listen. To tell a fool to "be sensible" is to waste one's breath. Fools are notorious for their stupidity. "You can identify a fool just by the way he walks down the street!" (v. 3, TLB). There's nothing hidden. When someone is a fool, people know it. Solomon wrote a great deal about fools in another book, the Proverbs. Let me point out just a few:

> Let a man meet a bear robbed of her cubs, rather than a fool in his folly (Prov. 17:12).

Anyone who has ever worked with, gone to school with, or just "hung around" with a fool knows it's safer to run with a mother bear that's been robbed of her cubs than to mess around with a fool. Fools don't think of consequences. They act out of impulse without even caring what will happen. It's vicious. It's violent to be in close companionship with "a fool in his folly."

Here's another proverb that will leave you nodding in agreement.

> A fool does not delight in understanding, but only in revealing his own mind (Prov. 18:2).

Today, we would say they "run off at the mouth." Have you ever done a Bible study with a group of fools? I call it SYI: "Share Your

Ignorance!" Fools come, sit, talk, say nothing (though they fill the evening with words), and then leave. Or maybe just one in the group feels the need to dominate the group with empty talk—he or she just has to give an opinion or throw out an idea. Most of the time it makes little sense and has no significance. Such a setting makes this next proverb meaningful:

> A fool's lips bring strife [I like the next phrase], and his mouth calls for blows (Prov. 18:6).

This isn't just great poetry. This isn't just wisdom literature. This is "lifestyle, learn-a-lesson-quick, folks" kind of counsel. There are times that we will be strongly tempted to punch a fool in the kisser, but it would be a waste of our time! In other words, be sensible! Don't waste energy on a fool.

The first section focuses on the individual. This next part moves into the social life. We leave dead flies and ointment, fools, and folly; and we move into the realm of touching other lives. This is where tragedy strikes. If a fool lived alone, it would be bad enough; but the fact is he or she relates to a world. And those ripples that are created by that life are frequently disastrous.

Humility and Patience vs. Popularity and Partiality

> If the ruler's temper rises against you, do not abandon your position, because composure allays great offenses.
> There is an evil I have seen under the sun, like an error which goes forth from the ruler—folly is set in many exalted places while rich men sit in humble places. I have seen slaves riding on horses and princes walking like slaves on the land (Eccles. 10:4–7).

Right away, we are presented with another familiar situation. It's a hot-headed boss. If you've ever worked for one, you will nod with understanding. But here Solomon tells us how to live wisely with an unwise boss. "If the ruler's temper rises against you do not abandon your position. . . ." That could mean, "Don't change your style. Fight back with the same kind of temper." But it probably means, "Don't quit your job in a fit of anger." We might paraphrase it this way:

> If your ruler becomes angry with you, do not hand in your resignation; serious wrongs may be pardoned if you keep calm (TEV).

There are occasions when even an offended employee will suddenly realize that a quiet spirit is the best way to handle this situation. And a soft spirit will quiet a bad temper. That's precisely what *The Living Bible* says: "A quiet spirit will quiet his bad temper."

The nature of the prairie chicken is to scream back and squawk and cluck in the same angry tone as the wild-eyed boss. But if we want to live like eagles, we don't respond like that. With wisdom we respond under quiet control and our composure disarms his offense. Be sensible! Even with a hot-headed boss, we can soar like eagles.

There is yet another evil addressed here that has to do with a ruler. Probably not the boss of a company, but someone in authority— perhaps a politician. It is undoubtedly someone who is responsible for the many people under his authority. Look at Solomon's words:

> There is an evil I have seen under the sun, like an error which goes forth from the ruler—folly is set in many exalted places while rich men sit in humble places. I have seen slaves riding on horses and princes walking like slaves on the land (vv. 5–7).

Let's understand where he's coming from and forget the fact that some are rich and some are poor. Understand that the one who has the ability, the discernment, the wherewithal to handle authority and make intelligent decisions is, of all things, treated like a slave. And the one who really cannot take a responsible position is on horseback and in control of the situation. It's the picture of a helter-skelter, topsy-turvy world. It's the unhappy condition that prevails when incompetent people are in authority and place their friends in authority who are equally incompetent. And the incompetent who are in authority lord it over the ones who really ought to be in charge. What a sad state of affairs! Solomon said, "I've seen this evil."

It's what we might call, for lack of better terms, "political inequity." Unfortunately, fools are not limited to places of low esteem. Sometimes they become governors and senators, congressmen, and even presidents! Sometimes they become mayors and civic leaders, or principals of schools and pastors of churches. They can even be the ones who own the business and call the shots when, in fact, there are some under their authority who are far better qualified to lead. Yet they are not being given a chance to do so. The better qualified, the more competent, are kept down and put down and mismanaged.

I appreciate the words of fellow author Dr. Kenneth Gangel. Referring to Solomon as Qoheleth, he writes insightfully:

[Much of] politics is irrational, capricious and subject to human error. Qoheleth harbors no illusions about the equitable status of politics. He is looking back on a life of dealing with this thing. He lived with it, fought against it, and tried to give some sensible answer to nonsensical things going on all around him.

It is not our province here to be critical of our government, but certainly we see things every day, in our own country and around the world, which make us wonder whether there is a great deal more of foolishness than wisdom in every human government.

Maybe God just wants us to see how foolish we are, and how useless it is to trust in the vanities of mankind under the sun. Perhaps He indeed waits for us to confess how futile it is for man to even try to govern himself, much less do anything that has any eternal value.[2]

One wonders at times who the victim really is, or where the authority really rests! Maybe God wants us to see just how foolish we can be when left to our own ways.

What a timely book is Scripture! It's a book of wisdom. It's a book that doesn't give us fuzzy terms and make us wonder where we stand. It calls some wise and it calls others fools. It shoots straight. We hesitate to do that today as we soften honesty with diplomacy. Scripture never does that. Open your eyes, eagle, and call it what it is! Be sensible!

Inevitable Risks vs. Inexcusable Stupidity

As we arrive at the last part of this section, we happen upon some very unusual—almost funny—statements. I don't mean that disparagingly; it's just that they appear a little "scary," especially if you're a literalist:

He who digs a pit may fall into it, and a serpent may bite him who breaks through a wall. He who quarries stones may be hurt by them, and he who splits logs may be endangered by them. If the axe is dull and he does not sharpen its edge, then he must exert more strength. Wisdom has the advantage of giving success. If the serpent bites before being charmed, there is no profit for the charmer (vv. 8–11).

Try to take that literally! What in the world do these statements mean? Frankly, if we fail to see the symbolism here, we'll find ourselves woefully confused. So with that in mind, let's realize that what we have here are several dangerous situations. Fools don't see these dangers, by the way. For the sake of clarification, I will list them.

Situation	Danger
1. Digging pits	1. Falling into the pit
2. Breaking through a wall	2. Being bitten by a snake
3. Quarrying stones	3. Being hurt by falling stones
4. Splitting logs	4. Endangering oneself
5. Chopping wood	5. Overexertion due to a dull axe

It may appear elementary—even obvious. That's because it is! There's no way anyone could convince me that this brilliant writer, Solomon, is just writing about pits and stones, axes and logs. There's more here than being snake bit and chopping wood with a dull axe. This man is still talking about living on the ragged edge of life. He is hoping to interest his reader in operating his or her life with wisdom. That's why he adds, "Wisdom has the advantage of giving success."

The fool habitually "digs a pit" for someone else to fall into and then invariably gets hurt more than the victim. It's called "setting someone up." Fools not only do that, they turn right around and do it again, like laying a trap for someone to make them look bad or to injure them or embarrass them—yet in the final analysis, *they* are the ones who are hurt. Initially, it looks like they're going to win. But wisdom teaches that ultimately they are the ones who lose. Wisdom also teaches that when we try to break through some wall of obstruction so as to get something from someone—like taking advantage of them or using them—we can get "bitten" in the process. God is saying, "Be sensible! Don't do that."

Wisdom also teaches us about the quarrying of stones—like removing something of value, digging it out so that we can use it for ourselves at someone else's expense, and in the process we ourselves get hurt. Today, we call it "poetic justice." But fools can't understand this. They continue to live their entire, empty lives taking advantage of people—using and abusing them—either not knowing or, worse, not caring that they themselves are the losers in the process. How stupid can one get? Solomon's hope is to awaken us to the advantages of wisdom.

Wisdom: Two Marvelous Advantages

Solomon said, "Wisdom has the advantage of giving success." Thus, the first advantage is: *Wisdom prepares the way for success.* I don't know of a hotter subject today than success. Magazine articles, books, seminars, and sermons promote it. But success is seldom linked with wisdom. Chances are good that if we would pick up last Sunday's paper and read it through, we'd come across twenty or more references to success, yet find nothing added regarding wisdom. In today's hype about success, wisdom is conspicuous by its absence. Outside of biblical literature and biblically based books, we hardly even come across the word. But this says, in effect, "You want to soar like an eagle? You want to be truly successful? Don't miss the path of wisdom."

It may not give us great popularity and wealth and it may not mean that we will be the most respected in our fields or that we will have the most significant voice in the company, but ultimately, as God gauges it, we will be successful. Wisdom will give us discernment, perception, insight, intuition, and especially the ability to sense danger ahead of time, which brings us to the second advantage: *Wisdom thinks ahead, before the fact.*

> If the serpent bites before being charmed, there is no profit for the charmer.

That's not too tough to figure out. In certain sections of the Eastern world there have always been snake charmers. I could imagine a snake charmer getting ready to play his flute for the snake. And while he's talking to this would-be customer who's about to shell out a few shekels to watch it happen, the snake crawls out of the basket and bites the stranger on the leg. It's very doubtful that he's going to keep paying his money to watch the charmer bring the snake back out of the basket once he's been bitten by the snake.

That's another way of saying, "Think ahead." The damage is already done and charming won't create a different context. In a more relevant setting, wisdom says, "Don't think about seeking counsel after you're in the ditch. Seek counsel *before* you fall." Now there's a way to diffuse the snake. Snakes need not bite us. We may need the wisdom of a friend or an associate to help us know how to handle the would-be attack of the snake.

And how do we get all this wisdom into our "prairie-chicken" heads? According to James 1:5 we must pray for it:

> But if any of you lacks wisdom, let him ask of God, who gives to all men generously and without reproach, and it will be given to him.

God promises to give wisdom to us in abundance. It is essential, however, that we *ask* God for it.

GAINING WISDOM . . . ACCORDING TO PROVERBS

But praying is just one part of the process in gaining wisdom. Let's balance this promise from the New Testament with a few verses from the Old Testament. Getting wisdom is the result of mutual effort. It's a matter of working together with God in pulling off a wise lifestyle. God doesn't deliver wisdom at our door like the morning paper. Wisdom doesn't come in a neat package, like a carton of cool milk that's sitting there waiting to be opened. It's the result of a cooperative effort. To verify this, read the following very carefully:

> My son, if you will receive my sayings, and treasure my commandments within you, make your ear attentive to wisdom, incline your heart to understanding; for if you cry for discernment, lift your voice for understanding; if you seek her as silver, and search for her as for hidden treasures; then you will discern the fear of the Lord, and discover the knowledge of God (Prov. 2:1–5).

Each "if" in that paragraph represents another condition—our part in the process. These are *conditions* involved in gaining wisdom. And the "then" statement gives the result of meeting those conditions. "Then you will discern the fear of the Lord, and discover the knowledge of God."

The result of receiving and treasuring God's Word, of making our ears attentive and inclining our hearts is discovering the knowledge of God. It is discerning what it means to fear the Lord. Wisdom provides such perspective.

I'd call that "eagle talk." There's not a prairie chicken in the world that operates from the perspective of God's knowledge. But we've been digging. We've been listening. We've been sensitive to His

Book. We've been learning from His truths. We haven't been sidelined by all the seductions of our times. We haven't even been driven by our emotions! We hear that God has spoken in His Word and we're attentive to what He has said and we won't let Him go until He gives us insight into how to put it into practice and handle a given situation. That's smart—smart as an eagle. It's straight talk from God, with a promise to boot!

> For the Lord gives wisdom; from His mouth come knowledge and understanding (Prov. 2:6).

Here's God's promise. We've seen the conditions—"if. . . ." We've seen the results—"then. . . ." Next comes the promise— "for. . . ." The promise is direct: God will give us wisdom.

> He stores up sound wisdom for the upright; He is a shield to those who walk in integrity, guarding the paths of justice, and He preserves the way of His godly ones. Then you will discern righteousness and justice and equity and every good course (Prov. 2:7–9).

If we walk in integrity, we will not stumble. What a great thought! If we decide that we will live honestly—which means, for example, conducting an honest business—we will not stumble into dishonesty. We will model honesty. God promises He will honor that. He will protect us. That means that ultimately we win over the ungodly. We gain because we're living in the realm of honesty and they're not. He stores up sound wisdom for us. With it, He gives us a shield of protection as we walk in integrity.

Wisdom doesn't come easily. It may start with prayer, but there's so much more. To get wisdom, we must roll up our sleeves. Digging for silver is hard work. It's like trying to find hidden treasure; it's very expensive and it takes rugged labor. God will do His part if we'll only do ours. It's a mutual process.

> A pastor once made an investment in a large piece of ranch real estate which he hoped to enjoy during his years of retirement. While he was still an active pastor, he would take one day off each week to go out to his land and work. But what a job! What he had bought, he soon realized, was several acres of weeds, gopher holes, and run-down buildings. It was anything but attractive, but the pastor knew it had potential and he stuck with it.

Every week he'd go to his ranch, crank up his small tractor, and plow through the weeds with a vengeance. Then he'd spend time doing repairs on the buildings. He'd mix cement, cut lumber, replace broken windows, and work on the plumbing. It was hard work, but after several months the place began to take shape. And every time the pastor put his hand to some task, he would swell with pride. He knew his labor was finally paying off.

When the project was completed, the pastor received a neighborly visit from a farmer who lived a few miles down the road. Farmer Brown took a long look at the preacher and cast a longer eye over the revitalized property. Then he nodded his approval and said, "Well, preacher, it looks like you and God really did some work here."

The pastor, wiping the sweat from his face, answered, "It's interesting you should say that, Mr. Brown. But I've got to tell you—you should have seen this place when God had it all to Himself!"[3]

We all want to hit the mark, to live the rest of our lives on target. But we know by now that we cannot do it apart from the wisdom of God. It takes wisdom to shake off the prairie chicken mentality and reprogram ourselves to return to an eagle lifestyle—the thing we were made for in the first place.

It's not just going to happen. But God is ready to do His part whenever we're ready to do ours. Just in case you're tempted to stay where you are and grub worms with all the other prairie chickens, be sensible! Check out the consequences described in the next chapter.

20

A FOOL'S PORTRAIT

Journal Entry

It is pleasant to listen to wise words,
but a fool's speech brings him to ruin. Since
he begins with a foolish premise, his
conclusion is sheer madness. A fool knows
all about that future and tells everyone in
detail! But who can really know what is
going to happen? A fool is so upset by a
little work that he has no strength for the
simplest matter.

Woe to the land whose king is a child
and whose leaders are already drunk in
the morning. Happy the land whose king
is a nobleman, and whose leaders work
hard before they feast and drink, and
then only to strengthen themselves for the
tasks ahead! Laziness lets the roof leak,
and soon the rafters begin to rot. . . . Never
curse the king, not even in your thoughts;
nor the rich man, either; for a little bird
will tell them what you've said.

*I*n a day of soft diplomacy, straight-talk reality is rare. It seems that most statements are now couched in diplomatic terms so as not to offend anyone. Words with sharp edges are rounded off and shaped so as to fit more easily into the minds of the hearer. In many circles, for example, it is no longer appropriate to use the word *wrong* or the word *sin*. And in some social places it is inappropriate to use the word *dead*. For that matter, even certain diseases such as cancer are considered too sensitive to call by name. They're too harsh, too realistic. T. S. Eliot was correct when he said that we humans cannot bear very much reality.[1]

Even many of the photographs which appear in sophisticated magazines are now air-brushed so that we don't see any of the blemishes on the models. Every celebrity these days appears to have the skin of a newborn baby. At least that's what the pictures indicate.

That reminds me of the true story that comes out of jolly old England back in the seventeenth century. When faced with the prospect of having his portrait painted, Lord Protector Oliver Cromwell became somewhat impatient with the artist's approach. Finally, he stared into the man's eyes and said, "When you paint me, you paint me warts and all."

Not many entertainers, politicians, or other celebrities among the famous would ever make that statement. On the contrary, "Cover up the blemishes, take away the warts, no birthmarks. I don't want people to see me as I am, but as I wish I were." Vanity dies a hard death. Someone has said, "We are not what we are, we are not even what we think we are. We are what we think other people think we are."

I suppose it's this lack of hard and tough-minded reality in our day that keeps drawing us back to the Bible. There is no other book that tells it more like it is. It helps us come to terms with reality, painful though it may be to face. It yields diplomacy for the sake of truth. It calls a spade a spade. If it's wrong, the Bible says, "It's wrong." If it's irresponsible, the Bible doesn't excuse it. If it's adultery, difficult though it may be to face, adultery it is. If it's greed, Scripture doesn't look the other way.

I read somewhere years ago that we should read only those books that "bite and sting us." The author went on to say something like this: "If a book we are reading does not rouse us with a blow to the head, then why read it?" We get a lot of "blows to the head" when we read the Bible. And I don't know of any more realistic piece of writing than Solomon's journal. It continually rips off our masks. Page after page the man goes right for the jugular and exposes our excuses. It blows holes through our rationalizations as it paints life exactly as it is, warts and all.

And that is especially true when it comes to the subject of the fool. We had a brief introduction to this particular individual in the previous chapter. But now we are going to analyze and evaluate this person Scripture calls a fool. That's why I entitled this chapter "A Fool's Portrait" even though we don't use that word much today. Forget subtle diplomacy. God tells it straight—no obscure symbolisms, no mumbo jumbo—just straight talk.

It occurred to me recently that I like straight talk from three people in particular. From my CPA, I don't want generalities. I want to know exactly how things are, precisely how things stack up. When it comes to finances, nobody wants the picture air-brushed. From my car mechanic, I don't want a lot of mechanical gobbledygook. I want to know the bottom-line facts: This is the problem, this is what it will cost, and this is how long it will take. And from my surgeon, I don't want a "hit and miss" technique when he digs around inside my body. I want him to know *exactly* what he's going for. I want him to be a good student of anatomy and extremely accurate in his interpretation of X-rays. When the surgery is over, I want him to tell me precisely what he discovered. My physician and I get along a lot better when he doesn't talk in generalities. I want him to talk straight in the same way God talks straight about this particular person called a fool.

THE PERSON INSIDE THE FOOL

Let's begin by going to the core of the issue. It will help if we scope out a few introductory thoughts from Psalms and Proverbs. Both of these ancient books say quite a bit about fools. Neither one skates over the surface, concerned only with externals—they dig deeply and show us the person on the *inside*.

The Language in the Fool's Heart

Psalm 14, for example, presents the fool, "warts and all."

> The fool has said in his heart, "There is no God." They are corrupt, they have committed abominable deeds; there is no one who does good (v. 1).

Occasionally, we may toss around the word *fool*. We might be thinking of someone who is merely mischievous, a prankster, a practical joker. But that's not the fool painted on the pages of the Scriptures. When the fool is mentioned in Scripture, he is one who says to himself down in his heart, "There really is no God to worry about. There is no divine accountability. All this business about His high standard, His holy character, His desire for me to glorify Him, . . . well, I'm not so sure. In fact, I sincerely doubt that there is a God anything like that. I'm really free to live as my own god."

So we're not surprised to find that the fool lives a life of corruption. As we just read in verse 1, the fool commits "abominable deeds." One who says there is no God invariably lives lower than the standard of God—and doesn't take God's Word all that seriously.

The Bent of the Fool's Will

That language in the heart that says there is no God is there because of a certain bent in the will of the fool. Two of these willful bents in the fool are found in Proverbs 14:

> The wisdom of the prudent is to understand his way, but the folly of fools is deceit (v. 8).

Fools traffic in deceit. To put it bluntly, you can count on a fool to lie to you. Fools are deceivers. Lying is a habit in their lives. A fool, because he tells himself, "There is no God," lies, with no guilty conscience, to himself and to other people. That's part of the lifestyle of a fool—deceiving people.

> Fools mock at sin, but among the upright there is good will (v. 9).

Fools mock at sin. When it comes to wrong, the fool makes light of it. Sometimes it comes out in profanity. Sometimes it comes out in dirty jokes. At other times it is expressed in verbal garbage. But whatever it is, the fool feels a sneering cynicism when it comes to the wrong of sin. The Bible calls that "mocking" sin. It's another lifestyle of the fool.

Before we consider the next entry in Solomon's journal, let's take a look at one more proverb; and, I'll tell you right now, it isn't any prettier than the first two.

> Doing wickedness is like sport to a fool; and so is wisdom to a man of understanding (Prov. 10:23).

The fool treats wickedness like it is a sport. There's a parallel verse in Proverbs 15:21 that reads:

> Folly is joy to him who lacks sense, but a man of understanding walks straight.

The practice of wickedness brings the fool personal pleasure. It's his favorite indoor sport. Rather than grieving or causing him any sense of sorrow, the fool finds delight in wickedness. It's a sport to do wrong. It's fun. But before you get the idea that the fool is simply a "fun guy," glance at the words of Proverbs 19:3:

> The foolishness of man subverts his way, and his heart rages against the Lord.

The fool is not only characterized by deception, mockery, and the "sport" of wickedness, his entire inner person "rages against the Lord." I call that a serious thing to deal with. I don't know if you have ever dealt with someone like that, but I certainly have; and it is one beast of a task!

Perhaps it will relieve you of a great deal of anxiety to know that no amount of arguing, persuading, pleading, threatening, or even throwing profanity back at the fool will change him or her. Bargaining won't work either. Logic will break down. Tears will not be effective. Strong discipline won't even work once the fool gets old enough. Proverbs often says that the rod on the back of the fool seems to be more a waste than a help. The fool must learn in a very, very stern and severe manner—usually over a lengthy period of time— not to be foolish.

Following a worship service in our church in Fullerton, California, a young man walked up to me. A man from our church had his arm around his shoulders. They had struck up a friendship. The young man who came to speak briefly with me had just been released from prison. He said, "You know, Chuck, I really wish I had heard and heeded what you said about the fool eight years ago." The man spoke quietly and with great control. His head was down; he was tearful, a broken man—obviously repentant. Prison had done its work—it had broken him. Before me stood a man who was once a rebellious fool, a strong-willed deceiver and liar. But he had paid an awful price regarding his folly. Fools don't break easily.

So much for the inner person who lives in the heart of the fool. Let's examine the fool's portrait by looking at a few of the externals.

The External Actions of a Fool

Words from the mouth of a wise man are gracious, while the lips of a fool consume him; the beginning of his talking is folly, and the end of it is wicked madness. Yet the fool multiplies words. No man knows what will happen, and who can tell him what will come after him? The toil of a fool so wearies him that he does not even know how to go to a city. Woe to you, O land, whose king is a lad and whose princes feast in the morning. Blessed are you, O land, whose king is of nobility and whose princes eat at the appropriate time—for strength, and not for drunkenness. Through indolence the rafters sag, and through slackness the house leaks. Men prepare a meal for enjoyment, and wine makes life merry, and money is the answer to everything. Furthermore, in your bedchamber do not curse a king, and in your sleeping rooms do not curse a rich man, for a bird of the heavens will carry the sound, and the winged creature will make the matter known (Eccles. 10:12–20).

A close look at this journal entry reveals at least four ways a fool demonstrates his or her folly.

Mouth and Words

Words from the mouth of a wise man are gracious, while the lips of a fool consume him; the beginning of his talking is folly, and the end of it is wicked madness. Yet the fool multiplies words.

Pretty blunt, isn't it? But it's the absolute truth. Notice that "the lips of a fool *consume* him." The word *consume* means "to swallow up." An old reliable German commentator named Leupold offers this translation: "The lips of a fool bring about his own undoing."[2]

Who is it that suffers the most consequences in the life of a fool? The fool himself. He may make others miserable, but he's the one who is "consumed." The fool is the one who winds up in prison. The fool is the one who suffers the ultimate brunt of his actions. His own lips consume him. He utters words that lead to his own suffering and sometimes demise.

As Solomon continues to write, he takes us through a progress (maybe a better word is *regress*) notoriously familiar to fools. The fool begins his talking on the wrong basis—he's talking folly to start with; and the end of it, well, it is madness, borderline *insanity*. Have you ever tried to work with and give counsel to a fool? Don't waste your time. I know. I've wasted many an hour doing so.

Rather than hearing counsel, the fool dominates the conversation. He starts talking on the wrong basis, so you can imagine what the end of his talk will be. And you would think that the person would stop and realize how far off base he or she really is. But remember what was written? The fool just multiplies words. Words, words, words, and more words! Sometimes, you entertain the strongest urge to punch him right in the mouth! I read somewhere that a sharp tongue invites a split lip.

And the beat goes on. Words, words, more words! Like the fellow who endured a nagging wife.

"Talk, talk, talk, talk," he said to his friend. "That's all my wife ever does is talk, talk, talk."

The friend responded by asking, "Well, what does she talk about?"

"I don't know, she don't ever say."

Even though we may joke about the talk of women, in my years of dealing with the public, I've seen a lot more *men* fools than women fools. I've heard more rationalization and empty talk from husbands than from wives—though I've certainly seen both. The fool's tongue evidences tell tale signs that cannot be hidden or ignored.

Future and Predictability

> . . . No man knows what will happen, and who can tell him what will come after him?

Does this sound familiar? If you have teenagers in your home, I'll bet you've used some similar lines: "Honey, if you keep acting like that, there's no telling where you're gonna wind up." Or, "How many times do you have to learn the same lesson? Do you know that if you keep doing that, such and such might very well happen. I mean, who knows where you'll be in two years, to say nothing of the end of your life?"

It's hard enough when your teenager is a fool, but it is downright *tragic* when the fool is your husband or your wife, and you're trying to find meaning out of a maze of madness. You feel as though you're on a gyroscope, spinning, leaning, wondering how long you can go on. And such family instability affects everyone—especially the children. Christian psychologist James Dobson writes:

> . . . the most vulnerable victims of family instability are the children who are too young to understand what has happened to their parents.
>
> That tragic impact on the next generation was graphically illustrated to me in a recent conversation with a sixth-grade teacher in an upper middle-class California city. She was shocked to see the results of a creative writing task assigned to her students. They were asked to complete a sentence that began with the words "I wish." The teacher expected the boys and girls to express wishes for bicycles, dogs, television sets, and trips to Hawaii. Instead, *twenty* of the thirty children made reference in their responses to their own disintegrating families. A few of their actual sentences were as follows:
>
> "I wish my parents wouldn't fight and I wish my father would come back."
>
> "I wish my mother didn't have a boyfriend."
>
> "I wish I could get straight A's so my father would love me."
>
> "I wish I had one mom and one dad so the kids wouldn't make fun of me. I have three moms and three dads and they botch up my life."
>
> "I wish I had an M-1 rifle so I could shoot those who make fun of me."[3]

"The beginning of the talk is folly, and the end of it is wicked madness." The future of a fool is unpredictable. In some cases, the future is a terrible accident. Sometimes, as I mentioned earlier, it's prison. Sometimes it's death.

Confusion and Stupidity

There's no diplomacy in this passage—nothing but straight talk. Fools don't hear diplomacy. If they hear anything at all, they hear blunt, straight talk, the kind that would offend other people.

> The toil of a fool so wearies him that he does not even know how to go to a city.

The fool exhausts himself by his inefficient and unproductive lifestyle. He gets so confused, he doesn't even know how to go to a city. Put a fool on an elevator and he'll get lost. Put a fool on an airplane, and he can't find the way out. I mean, the most obvious thing in the world, from here to there, and the fool won't walk it. He'll get lost en route, even if it requires a straight line. If Solomon were writing today, perhaps he would put it this way: "The person is out to lunch."

Don't misunderstand, it doesn't mean they're intellectually defective. Fools can be very bright. I've met fools with impressive graduate degrees. I have seen fools with extremely high IQs. Folly has nothing to do with IQ. But it has everything to do with stupidity! His talk is empty prattle. To quote Shakespeare's Macbeth: "A tale told by an idiot, full of sound and fury, signifying nothing."

The fool can be someone you know, child or adult. The fool can even be someone you love—son or daughter, father or mother, a close friend. And as a member of a local church body, the fool is the heartbreak of the pastor—a major cause of difficulty and dissension. Author Derek Kidner writes:

> The picture begins to emerge of a man who makes things needlessly difficult for himself and for others by his stupidity. And we may need reminding that in the last analysis, this is the thing that could make fools of us all. To be ever learning—never arriving—as 2 Timothy 3:7 portrays some people, is to be a trifler who contrives to get lost on even the straightest way to the city. That is folly without even the excuse of ignorance.[4]

Solomon then pauses for a few moments and steps back long enough for us to see the big picture. Notice the change in pronoun in the interlude of verses 16 and 17:

> Woe to you, O land, whose king is a lad and whose princes feast in the morning. Blessed are you, O land, whose king is of nobility and whose princes eat at the appropriate time—for strength, and not for drunkenness.

It's like he's saying, "You, reader, *you* have something to learn in this." It's gracious of him not to link the reader with the fool. I doubt that a fool would read the words anyway. But for all of us who read it, there is a statement of woe and a statement of blessing. Look closer:

> Woe to you, O land, whose king is a lad and whose princes feast in the morning.

We're back momentarily to poetic symbolism. The prince who is actually the ruler is an *immature* ruler. He's like a child, merely a lad on the throne of an entire kingdom. "Woe to you, O land, when you find yourself governed by a fool on the throne."

That makes me think of Germany in the thirties and early forties. That country had a fool who finally manipulated his way to the "throne" of power and almost led them to their demise as a nation. Cuba in the sixties saw a fool take the "throne" of that country. And Uganda in the seventies watched as a fool took the "throne" and led its country to virtual ruin. Adolph Hitler and Fidel Castro and Idi Amin are but illustrations of a lad on the throne of a country. To paraphrase Solomon: "Woe to you, country, if you find yourself ruled by such immaturity, by such rash and ruthless fools."

There is a brief section in the prophecy of Isaiah that describes the people of Israel as going through a time of national depression. While doing so, the prophet mentions a perfect example of the "woe" in Solomon's record.

> For behold, the Lord God of hosts is going to remove from Jerusalem and Judah both supply and support, the whole supply of bread, and the whole supply of water; the mighty man and the warrior [so the land will have no defense], the judge and the prophet [no one will be telling the truth anymore], the diviner and the elder [there'll be no representative for God in your midst], the captain of fifty and the honorable man, the counselor and the expert artisan, and the skillful enchanter. And I will make mere lads their princes and capricious children will rule over them, and the people [woe to them] will be oppressed, each one by another, and each one by his neighbor; the youth will storm against the elder, and the inferior against the honorable (Isa. 3:1–5).

The tragedy of this is that it is now history. Isaiah said, "It's coming." But the people foolishly closed their ears and said, "It won't come. Leave us alone. We're moving in the right direction." And when it came, precisely what Isaiah predicted occurred. Immaturity ruled the throne—the rashness of a child having a temper tantrum. And the land fell under the "woe" of the prophet.

While there is "woe" in having fools in leadership, there's blessing for the land that has maturity. That's Solomon's point here.

> Blessed are you, O land, whose king is of nobility and whose princes eat at the appropriate time—for strength, and not for drunkenness.

I like the way that reads. The earlier king ate in the morning. He ate all day. "Don't worry about anything! Bring on the food! Let's have a feast—this is terrific! Look at all those people who have to answer to us!" There's an immature foolishness about that kind of thinking.

Then suddenly, without any transition, Solomon returns to the characteristics of a fool.

Procrastination and Poor Judgment

Fools make all kinds of promises, but they don't follow through.

> Through indolence the rafters sag, and through slackness the house leaks. Men prepare a meal for enjoyment, and wine makes life merry, and money is the answer to everything.

Up above there are sagging rafters and a leaky roof. The house has been neglected because of procrastination. Even the courtroom of the king lacks fine appointments and disciplined servants because within the king's life there is an endless routine of nothing but food, amusement, plenty of booze, and stupid comments about money. In this case, the fools are saying to themselves, "Money is the answer to everything." There's wasted time; there's a loss of priorities; there's a careless lifestyle; there's a lack of discipline toward unfinished tasks. Even though there are so many things to take care of, irresponsibility and verbosity abound.

A WARNING: CRITICISM AND CONFIDENTIALITY

Our tendency is to think, "What we need to do is just talk about how bad the fool is, and even if we're living under the rule of a fool, let's just talk about it and our conditions will improve!" On the contrary—it could make matters worse. Notice verse 20:

> Furthermore, in your bedchamber do not curse a king [not one like this], in your sleeping rooms don't curse a rich man, for a bird of the heavens will carry the sound, and the winged creature will make the matter known.

Interestingly, the saying "a little bird told me," came from this Scripture. If you think it's hard to deal with or live with a fool, wait until the fool finds out you've been talking about him! Wait until your face is the bull's-eye on his dart board. Wait until you're the object of his or her wrath. It is hell on earth! Count on it, the fool will retaliate and will come at you with both barrels blazing! Let's accept Solomon's warning. Fools can be dangerous to your health. Confidentiality is sometimes a matter of survival.

A FEW TIPS ON DEALING WITH A FOOL

So much for analysis. It's time for application. For the sake of space, I will limit my comments here to a major heartache—being married to a fool. Some people may be living with a marriage partner who has turned out to be totally different from the person they thought they married. And now they realize they've got a fool on their hands. Well-meaning friends and spiritual leaders may give all kinds of advice or teaching on how they're to be supporting and encouraging and strengthening and loving and affirming in their marriage relationship. But nothing works.

Allow me to give my solution. It may win me no popularity contests, but I will tell the truth, as I believe it to be, with three statements regarding the fool in a marriage.

First, if there is continued folly, isolation is the most effective treatment. I wouldn't dare make that statement without biblical support, because there are too many voices saying something else these days. But according to Proverbs, if there is continued folly, the most effective treatment to employ is isolation.

> Leave the presence of a fool, or you will not discern words of knowledge (Prov. 14:7).

Isn't that interesting? Our thinking will break down if we stay in the presence of and try to do verbal battle with a fool. If we try to outsmart a fool, outtrick a fool, outfight a fool, or outtalk a fool, we will lose! We will lose clear thinking. We will begin to lack true knowledge. We will lose the discernment of understanding. "Leave the presence of a fool" is a command worth taking literally.

Of course each situation must be considered independently. Great effort must be expended in prayer and counsel, and reconciliation attempts have to be tried in every conceivable manner. But when all these fail and the foolish lifestyle is still evident, reason will no longer work.

Now our tendency as Christians is to extend encouragement and affirmation forever—to go more than the mile, to go the second, to go the fifth mile, all of which is commendable. And so we come up with statements like, "Well, we ought to stay near." But the Bible says, "Isolate them." "Well, we ought to reason and talk with them. We ought to use kind and thoughtful words so they'll understand." Look again at the Proverbs.

> Excellent speech is not fitting for a fool; much less are lying lips to a prince (17:7).
> Do not speak in the hearing of a fool, he will despise the wisdom of your words (23:9).

I have long since stopped giving priceless pearls of wisdom to swine-like ears. It doesn't work. It's a waste. Some say, "Well, we ought to honor them, regardless. After all, didn't I step into this marriage with a partnership in mind?" Honorable treatment *is* appropriate— for as long as one can remain sane and safe. But there's a limit! There comes a time when honor doesn't fit a fool. Those are not my words. I'm quoting from the Scriptures.

> Like snow in summer and like rain in harvest, so honor is not fitting for a fool (Prov. 26:1).
> Like one who binds a stone in a sling, so is he who gives honor to a fool (v. 8).

There comes a time when we no longer honor a fool. We no longer take all of the sharp edges off so that life becomes comfortable for the fool—we allow the sharp edges to stay.

I don't suggest divorce, but rather a time of separation—a time when the fool is forced to face the consequences of his or her folly. Isolation is not pleasant! It's hard to live in the street. It's hard not to have your mate with you at holiday seasons. It's hard not to have the comfort and affirmation of children with their little arms around your neck on lonely nights. But it's the price the fool pays for living a fool's life. Isolation is painful, but there are extreme cases where it is necessary!

Verse 10 of Proverbs 26 says those who even hire fools are in for a lot of trouble:

> Like an archer who wounds everyone [that's a scary thought!], so is he who hires a fool or who hires those who pass by.

I hope I am still seen as a man of compassion and one who encourages others to be compassionate. But first and foremost we must be people of the truth. Although I don't advocate divorce, I believe there may be a time when separation in a marriage is essential for survival and for the children to be able to gain their equilibrium with at least one sane parent. To give a foolish father or mother all the benefits of home and all the joys of happiness and all of the affirmation and honor of a home *no matter what kind of godless life he or she is living* doesn't even make practical sense, to say nothing of biblical sense.

We must be careful about buying into a particular kind of teaching without biblical foundations. We can't let our hearts run away with our heads. I've met some fools who have been forced to live in the street. It's remarkable how broken they can become. It's encouraging how God can get their attention. It's amazing how much more committed they can be to a marriage when they have had to learn the horror of loneliness and have been forced to face the terror of having no place to live. I have seen God use isolation to bring people to their knees.

That brings me to my second statement regarding the fool in marriage: *If there is true repentance and brokenness, restoration is appropriate.* When there is repentance, the groundwork is laid for restoration. That's where it's going to be hard, quite candidly. Maybe a look at Psalm 107 will help.

> Oh give thanks to the Lord, for He is good; for His lovingkindness is everlasting. Let the redeemed of the Lord say so, whom He has redeemed from the hand of the adversary (vv. 1–2).

There were those who dwelt in darkness and in the shadow of death, prisoners in misery and chains, because they had rebelled against the words of God, and spurned the counsel of the Most High. Therefore [What did God do? Did He affirm them? No way.] He humbled their heart with labor; they stumbled and there was none to help (vv. 10–12).

When they are diminished and bowed down through oppression, misery, and sorrow, He pours contempt upon princes, and makes them wander in a pathless waste (vv. 39–40).

I call that severe treatment. God doesn't rush to their rescue and say, "Oh, I know it must hurt to suffer the consequences of a fool. Let me relieve you." God says, in effect, "You forfeit the right to those blessings if you live against Me."

Now, in that condition, they break. They repent. They turn. Look at verses 17 and 18 of Psalm 107:

Fools, because of their rebellious way, and because of their iniquities, were afflicted. Their soul abhorred all kinds of food; and they drew near to the gates of death.

They waited until conditions became extremely serious. *Then* they cried. They cried out to the Lord in their trouble; and He saved them in their distress. They were lonely, broken, empty, wasted, had no surrounding affection, no warmth—*then* they cried out to God in their condition and He trumpeted the angels to their assistance. He called in the support of affection and affirmation and encouragement. But *not until* they came to an end of themselves. There are times, my friend, when love must be tough. But when there is brokenness and true repentance, restoration is appropriate.

Now we come to statement number three: *When there is restoration from folly, let there be proclamation.* That's the redeemed of the Lord "saying so." When? When there is restoration from folly, the redeemed then proclaim the story!

Let them give thanks to the Lord for His lovingkindness, and for His wonders to the sons of men! Let them also offer sacrifices of thanksgiving, and tell of His works with joyful singing (Ps. 107:21–22).

The church needs to hear the testimony of former fools more often—in waters of baptism, in adult fellowship classes, even on occasion in Sunday worship gatherings. A proclamation is in order when fools repent and are restored. Such restoration needs to be made public!

Whether a fool happens to be a parent, a child, or even a friend, forgiveness is an integral part of the process of restoration. In his hard-hitting book, *Love Must Be Tough*, Dr. James Dobson writes:

> The toughness I have recommended in response to irresponsibility can be destructive and vicious unless it is characterized by genuine love and compassion. Our purpose must never be to hurt or punish the other person, even when retribution is deserved by him or her. Vengeance is the exclusive prerogative of the Lord (Rom. 12:19). Furthermore, resentment is a dangerous emotion. It can be a malignancy that consumes the spirit and warps the mind, leaving us bitter and disappointed with life. I'll say it again: no matter how badly we have been mistreated or how selfish our partners have seemed, we are called upon to release them from accountability. That is the meaning of true forgiveness.[5]

Even fools can come to an end of their godless folly. When they do—when repentance is obvious and authentic—*forgiveness* is the most Christian, the most magnificent response. I close with the wise words of psychologist Archibald Hart, "Forgiveness is surrendering my right to hurt you for hurting me."

21

BE BULLISH!

Journal Entry

Give generously, for your gifts will return to you later. Divide your gifts among many, for in the days ahead you yourself may need much help.

When the clouds are heavy, the rains come down; when a tree falls, whether south or north, the die is cast, for there it lies. If you wait for perfect conditions, you will never get anything done. God's ways are as mysterious as the pathway of the wind, and as the manner in which a human spirit is infused into the little body of a baby while it is yet in its mother's womb. Keep on sowing your seed, for you never know which will grow—perhaps it all will.

*W*hat are you doing to keep the cutting edge of your life razor sharp? Perhaps another way to ask that is for what are you waiting? Or for whom are you waiting? How many burglars of joy do you allow to break through the doors and windows of your life to rob you of the fun, the challenge of living life to the fullest? My friend Tim Hansel, who models a joyful lifestyle, once wrote:

> The habit of always putting off an experience until you can afford it, or until the time is right, or until you know how to do it is one of the greatest burglars of joy. Be deliberate, but once you've made up your mind—jump in.[1]

When is the last time you "jumped in" to anything? Honestly now, can you remember the last time you broke with routine and did something unusual? There's a sign along the Alaskan Highway that reads:

CHOOSE YOUR RUT CAREFULLY. YOU'LL
BE IN IT FOR THE NEXT 200 MILES

Every time I think about that sign, I shudder a little, fearing it might become the credo of my life. As I recently reached the half-century mark, I determined anew that I would continue doing everything in my power to stay out of ruts. How tragic to settle for a drab, predictable life when the options for color and creativity are so available!

To live on the dull edge is really to become a slave to life, which reminds me of the following lines out of Alex Haley's *Roots:*

> Through his sorrow, Kunta was surprised to hear that the old gardener had been called "Josephus." He wondered what the gardener's true name had been—the name of his African forefathers—and to what tribe they had belonged. He wondered if the gardener himself had known. Most likely he had died as he had lived—without ever learning who he really was.[2]

Is that happening to us? Are we allowing someone or something to enslave us, so that we will live our lives and ultimately pass from time to eternity without ever discovering who we are? Some do. That's not living; that's existing.

The older I get, the less inviting that becomes. But there's always the temptation to sigh and slip into a rocker. In fact, we'll get counsel from people who think they're helping us by saying something like, "Take it easy. Don't exert yourself."

A physician friend of mine here in Fullerton was treating a woman in her mid-80s who was in fairly good condition. She either walked very fast or jogged every day. He became quite concerned about her, even though her health was good, and he warned her about exerting herself. She heeded his advice and ceased most of her activity. Several months later he sat in the funeral parlor, attending her memorial service. He later said to me, "You know, Chuck, I could cut my tongue out for ever having told her to be careful, to stop exerting herself. I doubt that I will ever give such advice again . . . especially to older people who are enjoying life as much as she was."

In one of the chapters of a great book called *The Complete Book of Running*, these challenging words appear:

> After the Boston Marathon a year or two ago I went to a party given by some participants in their hotel suite. . . . Eventually I fell into conversation with a white-haired man named Norman Bright. Bright was nearly sixty-five years old, yet had run the race that day in an astonishing 2:59:59 and had finished in 615th place, thereby defeating two-thirds of the field. Many of the younger runners at the party, exhausted by the race and feeling creaky, were sitting down or lay sprawled on the rug, but Bright stood and talked animatedly. He was planning to go abroad soon for some races in Europe, he told me, and was looking forward to the change of scenery. Opening an orange knapsack he had stowed in a corner of the room, he began showing me the maps, brochures and entry blanks he had gathered in preparation for his trip. He was as enthusiastic as a teenager.
>
> Norman Bright is unusual, chiefly because he is an American. In this country we have some odd ideas about how older people, even those barely into their forties, ought to behave. They should like Lawrence Welk, not Bob Dylan; it is more seemly if they eat porridge, not pizza; and they ought to be dozing in a Barca-Lounger rather than working up a sweat on the road from Hopkinton to Boston. Europeans have few such preconceptions. In West Germany the Deutscher Sportbund has formed more than 40,000 athletic clubs, many of them with programs for elderly people. In Italy some 4,000 senior citizens were among the 33,000 participants in a recent Stramilano, the fifteen-mile race held each spring in Milan, and 150 Italians over sixty entered a forty-three-mile ski race, . . . several thousand Frenchmen over sixty

meet weekly for physical training. And . . . the Soviet Union . . . sponsors cross-country runs and ski meets. In the winter it adds ice swims that are said to be good for the nerves, metabolism, and will power.

All this is in contrast to what is expected of older people in the United States. "Our attitude is one of overprotection," [says Dr. Theodore G. Klumpp, a New York cardiologist].[3]

What are we protecting? We can't just "take it easy." We have to exert ourselves. We need to be bullish!

There's another piece of counsel we often hear: "Hold on to what you've got. Things are gonna get worse and people will rip you off." As a result, pessimism, paranoia, and fear dog our steps as we get older. Think of how many older people live lives of fear these days because of that doomsday advice. Think of those who are reaching the retirement years of life who have long since stopped living a carefree life. "Watch this. Be careful of that. Don't forget the danger of. . . ." Rules, rules, rules. They make us shake and shrivel. That reminds me of the words of Robert Persig in his book *Zen and the Art of Motorcycle Maintenance.* He refers to hundreds of "itsy-bitsy rules for itsy-bitsy people." Why reduce ourselves to "itsy-bitsy people" when God has made it possible for us to be cutting-edge people?

GOD'S UNCOMMON COUNSEL

The last two major sections of Solomon's ancient journal could be summed up in three commands:

- Be bold!
- Be joyful!
- Be godly!

They fit together into a lifestyle that is extremely contagious and rare. And there's no age limit. It's for the young, the middle-aged, and the older person alike. Solomon's personal remarks, as he nears the end of his journey, are full of refreshing hope. We are told to stretch, to reach, to take the challenge, to be downright bullish.

Give generously, for your gifts will return to you later. Divide your gifts among many, for in the days ahead you yourself may need much help. When the clouds are heavy, the rains come down; when a tree falls, whether south or north, the die is cast, for there it lies. If you wait for perfect conditions, you will never get anything done. God's ways are as mysterious as the pathway of the wind, and as the manner in which a human spirit is infused into the little body of a baby while it is yet in its mother's womb. Keep on sowing your seed, for you never know which will grow—perhaps it all will (Eccles. 11:1–6, TLB).

God gives our generation four commands in this passage, and each command is in strong contrast to advice we hear today.

Instead of protecting, release yourself! This first piece of advice we find implied in Solomon's opening comment: "Give generously" or as the New American Standard Bible says, "Cast your bread on the surface of the waters." Today, we might say, "Don't put the bread in the deep freeze—it'll dry out. Don't store it in the pantry or seal it in a baggie—it'll mold. Don't hoard it, thinking that it needs to be protected—release it!" And we are told to release it "on the surface of the waters." That means we are to let go of it— push it away from ourselves. I am told that this is actually an ancient Arabic proverb that reads:

> Do good. Cast your bread into the water.
> You will be repaid someday.

Perhaps Solomon heard his father David quote that proverb to him when he was just a little boy. Maybe young Solomon was raised on that and other proverbs. David Hubbard says:

> Ours may be the first generation in civilized times that has not raised its young on proverbs. From the beginning of recorded history . . . concise sayings which describe the benefit of good conduct or the harm of bad have been used to teach children how to behave.[4]

What an insightful comment! I was caught short when I read Dr. Hubbard's words because I can't remember ever having instructed my children in this proverb. I hope I've modeled it, but I don't believe I've ever sat down and said, "Son, let's think about casting your bread on the waters. Let's talk about how you can release yourself so that in return good will come." Have you done so?

The command has a promise, by the way: ". . . you will find it after many days." When bread is cast on the waters, that is, when a life is released to others, there is something remarkable about God's faithfulness in bringing back any number of benefits and blessings.

After speaking on this very subject several months ago, a woman stopped me and said, "As you were speaking about releasing yourself, I was thinking about how it affected my life in the area of personal vulnerability." She continued, "I heard you back a few years ago address the importance of forgiveness. My husband had left me. And the longer I sat and listened to you, the more convinced I became that I needed to come to terms with the offense. I didn't want to live the rest of my life in resentment and bitterness. I needed to forgive this man. And I needed to tell *him* 'All is forgiven.' " (It was not a manipulative statement. Her husband had made no inroads to come back, and there seemed to be no hope for such. She was simply "casting her bread on the waters.")

With tears she described what transpired. "I decided I would go over to his office, so early the following week I drove over there. I got out and walked through the reception area and right into his office. He looked up rather startled. I spoke quietly yet confidently and told him that I forgave him. I told him that the Lord had given me a peace in my life and that I held nothing, absolutely *nothing*, against him any longer . . . nor could I if I hoped to find any sense of victory in my life." Many, many months later, the man came back home. When she released herself, when she cast her bread, she "found it after many days."

I am not saying that works 100 percent of the time. But I *am* saying that when our ways please the Lord, "He makes even his enemies to be at peace with him" (Prov. 16:7). Releasing ourselves is God's way. He honors that kind of unguarded vulnerability. It's like tearing down the bars. It's like letting down the bridge across the moat. I sometimes refer to it as duplicating the keys to one's life and passing them around to people who have felt locked out. It's letting ourselves free. In Solomon's terms, it's casting bread on the surface of the waters. But how exactly do we do that?

Rather than hoarding, give and invest. This is the second piece of advice. In other words be bullish as you release yourself. Be bullish in the investment of yourself and the giving of yourself. "Divide your portion to seven or even to eight." In today's terms "diversify!" Let the benchmark of your life be generosity—bold, unselfish, broad-based generosity.

Henry Ford once said, "Success is not rare. It is common. Very few miss a measure of it. It is not a matter of luck or of contesting, for certainly no success can come from preventing the success of another. It is a matter of adjusting one's efforts to overcome obstacles and one's abilities to give the service needed by others. There is no other possible success. Most people think of it in terms of getting; success, however, begins in terms of giving."[5]

Are you successful? If you are a giver, the answer is yes. And you don't give in just one area—you give generously, you give liberally, you give in a variety of ways. It's "casting the bread on the waters." When we do that we can't determine the currents beneath the surface or the wind factor. It isn't just giving to our families or just giving to the person who is personally attracted to us or to whom we are attracted. It's giving broadly. It's expanding the bookends of our lives so that we gain a vision of the limitless field in front of us. How unlike the philosophy many of us were raised with! I can state it in thirteen rather abrupt words. It hangs like a motto in many a mind:

> Get all you can,
> Can all you get,
> Then sit on the can!

No thanks. Folks who live like that discover little of what ragged-edge living is all about. Old Testament scholar Walter Kaiser writes:

> "Be liberal and generous to as *many* as you can and *then some,*" is the way we would say it. So, make as many friends as you can, for you never know when you yourself may need assistance. Instead of becoming miserly just because you fear that the future may hold some evil reversal of your fortunes, leaving you in poverty and want, you should all the more distribute to as many as possible so that you can have the blessing of receiving in the event of such reverses.[6]

This does not mean we will be free from calamity or misfortune. On the contrary, look at the follow-up comment in Solomon's journal entry: ". . . you do not know what misfortune may occur on the earth." We have no idea what calamity, need, or unfortunate event may occur. Nevertheless, we give. We leave the results with our God. Take a quick glance at a couple of proverbs Solomon wrote:

> He who is gracious to a poor man lends to the Lord,
> and He will repay him for his good deed (Prov. 19:17).

The Lord says, in effect, "I will take the responsibility of repaying you. Since you are actually lending to Me and you are using him as the object of your giving, remember it is I who will repay the good deed." God has a great memory. Trust Him not to forget that promise.

> He who shuts his ear to the cry of the poor will also cry himself and not be answered (Prov. 21:13).

Going on David Hubbard's suggestion, here is a great proverb to pass along to our children, to talk about around the kitchen table, to discuss before bedtime. "If you shut your ear to the poor, someday you'll cry all alone." How our young need to be encouraged to reach out, to care, to demonstrate the compassion of the Good Samaritan!

Now, again, back to Solomon's journal. There's no guarantee that bad things won't happen, even if we try with all our might to keep them from happening. That reminds me of a humorous story I heard about a man on the streets of Belfast. Obviously, he was afraid, as many are in Belfast today. He hoped to get home safely without being attacked. Suddenly, a dark figure jumped out of the shadows and grabbed him around the neck. He stuck the point of a knife against his throat and asked, in a gruff voice, "Catholic or Protestant?" Seized with panic the man reasoned to himself, "If I say Catholic and he's a Protestant—*whoosh!* If I say Protestant and he's a Catholic, I'm a goner!" Then he thought of a way out. He said, "I'm a *Jew!*" The assailant chuckled, "Ha! I'm the luckiest Arab terrorist in Belfast!"

Sometimes, no matter how hard we try, we lose. Misfortune will occur. Solomon warns: "You do not know what misfortune may occur on the earth." We're disillusioned if we think we'll live our lives without such assailants. They'll come out of the shadows. They will come in the form of bad news or the loss of a job or a divorce or a bad report on our X-rays. They will come from one of our children or from one of our parents or both. But that's part of living on the ragged edge—it's par for the course! And we're disillusioned if we think that by dividing our portion to seven or eight, we'll guard ourselves from such difficulties and pitfalls. We won't. But the good news is, even though those difficulties occur, we will find benefit after many days. The Lord God promises us that. So we should be bullish in our generosity.

In place of drifting, pursue! Before we deal with this third piece of advice, let's track where Solomon's coming from:

> If the clouds are full, they pour out rain upon the earth; and whether a tree falls toward the south or toward the north, wherever the tree falls, there it lies. He who watches the wind will not sow and he who looks at the clouds will not reap (Eccles. 11:3–4).

He is probably describing people who spend their lives observing the obvious and noting the inevitable. Instead of occupying ourselves with the obvious, we should *pursue!* There are certain things we cannot change. We cannot change the weather, taxes, bills, final scores of ball games, people's responses, the passing of time, or the inevitability of death. We can worry about them all we like, but we can't change them! Folks who focus only on the inevitable—the clouds, rain, falling trees, and blowing wind—come dangerously close to that sign on the Alaskan Highway. How much better to steer clear of all ruts! Look at the following comments from J. Oswald Sanders:

> Four major poets who lived to be over eighty years of age did more work in the last decade of their lives than they did between ages twenty and thirty. William Gladstone took up a new language when he was seventy, and at eighty-three he became the Prime Minister of Great Britain—for the fourth time. At eighty-three! Alfred Lord Tennyson wrote *Crossing the Bar* when he was eighty. John Wesley was eighty-eight and still preaching daily with eminent success, eloquent power, and undiminished popularity. At eighty-eight! Every day! Michaelangelo painted his world-famous *The Last Judgment* when he was sixty-six.

> The late Canon C. H. Nash, who founded the Melbourne Bible Institute and trained a thousand young men and women for Christian service, retired from his principalship at the age of seventy. At eighty, he received assurance from the Lord that a further fruitful ministry of ten years lay ahead of him. This assurance was abundantly fulfilled. During those years he was uniquely blessed in a ministry of Bible teaching to key groups of clergy and laymen—probably the most fruitful years of his life. When he was nearly ninety, the author found him completing the reading of volume six of Toynbee's monumental history as a mental exercise. . . .

Mr. Benjamin Ririe retired as a missionary of the China Inland Mission when he reached the age of seventy. When he was eighty he decided to learn New Testament Greek. . . . [Greek! When I tackled Greek, I was in my twenties and had my hands full!]

. . . [Mr. Ririe] became proficient in reading the Greek New Testament [in his eighties!]. At ninety, he attended a refresher course in New Testament Greek in a . . . seminary. When he was a hundred years old, he was present at a meeting at which the author was speaking. In his pocket was a small well-worn Greek lexicon which he used to brush up on his Greek while traveling by public transport![7]

What are we doing standing around watching the wind? Why do we worry about where the tree falls? Who really cares whether the clouds bring rain or whether the day will be sunny? Who really cares whether it's hot or cold, and in the long run, what does it matter? Like these men, we should be bullish in our pursuit of life—pursuing the things that we can change, the things that offer a challenge and leaving the rest in the hand of the One who has no trouble with such details. And may I make one special request? If you really want to be different, please don't do it for the money! Greedy givers are a dime a dozen. Generous, authentic servants—ah, rare indeed!

A war correspondent was watching a humble, compassionate nun swab the blood and pus out of a young soldier's leg. Gangrene had set in. The correspondent was repulsed by the sight. He almost gagged as he turned and mumbled under his breath, "I wouldn't do that for a million bucks." Overhearing his remarks she looked up and responded, "Neither would I . . . neither would I."

Cast your bread on the waters. Divide your portion to seven or eight and *don't keep track.* Throw away the clipboard. Don't wait for letters of thanks. Don't anticipate being done in bronze for all the world to see. Don't expect to get rich or have your name in lights. Don't expect to be reciprocated either—just go for it! Instead of drifting along like a lazy cloud, doing the predictable, be bullish. Pursue this thing called life!

As an alternative to doubting, trust! This fourth piece of advice encourages us to courageously trust the living God. Just as we do not know the path of the wind, and just as we do not know how bones are formed in the tiny fetus, that little unborn child in the womb of the mother (we trust God to form the bones as He is pleased), just as we do not know any of that, we are to so trust Him in everything—courageously! See how Solomon entered this in his journal?

Just as you do not know the path of the wind and how bones are formed in the womb of the pregnant woman, so you do not know the activity of God who makes all things. Sow your seed in the morning, and do not be idle in the evening, for you do not know whether morning or evening sowing will succeed, or whether both of them alike will be good (vv. 5–6).

"Sow in the morning and don't be idle in the evening." That means that in the evening of your life, don't look for a place to hide out. As you sowed in the morning, press on in the evening. Don't look for a "Do Not Disturb" sign to hang on the door knob of your life. Resist saying, "Leave me alone; I'm retired; I've paid my dues."

The only way we can do this—the only way we can come to terms with reality—is by trusting God, *regardless*. No ifs, ands, buts, or howevers. If I am a farmer and God allows a flood to come and wash away my crops or God chooses to give me the beautiful seasonal rains and a bumper crop, I trust Him and I give Him praise. If I am in industry or some profession and someone throws me a curve and God allows my whole world to be reversed, I trust Him and I give Him praise. I take life as it occurs. I don't waste time in the pit of doubt. Nor do I worry over crop failures and strikeouts.

We can't wait for conditions to be perfect. Nor can we wait for things to be free of all risks—absolutely free, absolutely safe. Instead of protecting ourselves, we have to release ourselves. Instead of hoarding, we are to give and invest. Instead of drifting, we are to pursue life. Instead of doubting, we are to courageously trust. We have to be bullish!

God's ways are as mysterious as the pathway of the wind, and as the manner in which a human spirit is infused into the little body of a baby while it is yet in its mother's womb. Keep on sowing your seed, for you never know which will grow—perhaps it all will (vv. 5–6, TLB).

Less than two years after Cynthia and I had married, I joined the Marine Corps. The recruiting officer promised me that I would never have to go overseas—and I was foolish enough to believe him. You guessed it. I ended up eight thousand miles from home. And since Marines are not allowed to take their families overseas, Cynthia lived with her folks while I lived in the Orient—another culture, another people, another language, another *world!* My comfort zone, my plans, my preferences had been invaded and interrupted.

At first I felt offended—my rights had been assaulted! Little did I realize that it was my chance to "sow in the morning." It wasn't long, however, before it began to dawn on me.

Before I dropped the seabag off my shoulder on Okinawa, I realized I was facing the challenge of my sheltered life. I was told that the outfit that I was to become a part of was shot through with venereal disease. The lifestyle on the island was somewhere between morally loose and absolutely debauched. I was a married man. I was also a Christian. I wanted to have an impact. I wanted to be different. And frankly, I was scared.

I had no special powers—I was just like every other guy in my outfit. But I had, thank God, Jesus Christ. I remember thinking this prayer as I dropped that bag on the cement floor, *Lord, keep me pure. Give me ways to make Christ known. Let me declare it on the front end of this tour of duty so that I won't have to live in the shame of a bad memory, hoping these guys never find out later on that I'm a Christian.* I had no idea that someday I'd be in ministry, no idea whatsoever. I simply wanted to "sow in the morning," not knowing when harvest would come.

I had a bunk mate named Eddie. I spoke to Eddie about Christ early on. He wasn't interested, and he made it clear to me: "I don't want that stuff rammed down my throat, okay? You live your life; I'll live mine. Got it?" So I honored Eddie's request. Little did I realize how much he was watching me. I got involved in a Scripture memory program, got involved in a prayer ministry, got involved in street meetings and a discipleship program, all thanks to an organization called The Navigators. And a good friend of mine, Bob Newkirk, began to build into my life. He helped me know how to live for Christ (to this day I thank God for that man).

I wanted so much to reach Eddie, but I was at a loss to know how. One day it occurred to me, "Well, he doesn't want me to witness to him, but maybe he'll help me review my verses. He's got a lot of time on his hands." So I said, "Eddie, tell you what, I'm going over these verses from the Bible and I wonder if you'd just help me review them." He said, "Yeah, but don't lay your trip on me, okay? Don't lay your thing on me. I'll help you with the words, but I ain't interested in being some kind of monk!" I smiled and agreed with the plan. So we went over those verses month after month after month after month! Dear guy. He listened. He corrected me. He even encouraged me. But he never once responded. There was not even a glimmer of interest on Eddie's part. No way! Not until over twenty-five years later.

My phone rang.

"Charlie?" (They called me Charlie back in the old days.)

"Yeah, who's this?"

"This is Eddie, your old bunk buddy in Okinawa."

"Eddie! How are ya?"

"Uh, hey, listen man. I've been saved. My wife, too. Thanks for living for Christ!" (I was speechless!)

"You know, remember when you used to lay those verses on me?"

"Yeah, I remember."

"Charlie, . . . it worked!"

Remember the old gospel song?

> Sowing in the morning,
> Sowing seeds of kindness;
> Sowing in the noontime,
> And the dewy eve. . . .

Back in 1958 I was sowing. The seeds were planted. In 1984 God brought in the sheaves. What would have happened had I submerged and given in to my doubts when God sent me overseas? What if I had not trusted Him? What if I had failed to be bullish in my pursuit of life?

For Those Who Dare to Be Bullish

Allow me to wrap up this chapter with several direct words of challenge. The first has to do with getting started.

Start activating your life today *and never quit.* Find someone to invest in. Give yourself to some local church. Locate a school to which you can give time and energy. Pour your life into some young person or some peer, perhaps someone in your neighborhood or someone in need. Locate a series of people that you can become a part of and activate your life. Volunteer yourself for service. Get involved in the mainstream. Refuse to let your life collect dust. Remember that rut on the Alaskan Highway and reject anything similar! Start today. If you don't start today, chances are good you never will. Don't wait for the weather to change. Don't wait for the kids to grow up. Don't wait for your husband to come back or your wife to return. Don't wait until you have spare time or more money or stronger health or a better job or a bigger house. Don't wait for conditions to be perfect. Be bullish about this, starting today. And never quit.

Remember that wisdom must accompany action. When we read about "living life to its fullest" we tend to become supermotivated. And we want to put on roller skates and dash out into life half cocked. We are tempted to give away the store or maybe hang glide over the Royal Gorge or try flying through the air space above the Bermuda Triangle. That may be zealous, but that's not wise. That's not God's counsel. Start today, but start with wisdom. Ask God how you can unlock just one window of your life. Ask him how you can expand just one wing of your building to make room for others—how you could invest a slice of your wealth in something other than that which will return to you. Remember, wisdom needs to accompany action.

Watch out for enemy attacks during a lull in the action. Enemy attacks will come. As you set out to live a bullish life for Jesus Christ, you will find that there will be periods of time that aren't very exciting. There will be times of low tide and little production. I don't know why. I don't know how to explain it. We all have them, and they're hard to endure. But during those lulls in the action, be careful of enemy attacks. The enemy will say things like: "It's not worth it. You're a fool. Give it up. People will rip you off. Go back to the way you were. Don't waste your time. Christ? Christ answering your life's need? No . . . don't believe that!" Even though a few people will try to point out all the dangers, press on. Never forget this: Bullish living is threatening only to people who refuse to live it.

May I return to my opening questions? Perhaps you're better equipped now to answer them:

- What are you doing to keep the cutting edge of your life razor sharp?

- What are you waiting for?

- For whom are you waiting?

- How many burglars of joy do you allow to break through the doors and windows of your life to rob you of the fun and challenge of living life to the fullest?

Wait no longer. Live now! Bite right in!

In a short story by Hermann Hesse, these searching, penetrating words appear:

> Life passes like a flash of lightning
> Whose blaze barely lasts long enough to see.
> While the earth and the sky stand still forever
> How swiftly changing time flies across man's face.
> O you who sit over your full cup and do not drink,
> Tell me, for whom are you still waiting?[8]

22

ENJOYING LIFE NOW, NOT LATER

Journal Entry

It is a wonderful thing to be alive! If a person lives to be very old, let him rejoice in every day of life, but let him also remember that eternity is far longer, and that everything down here is futile in comparison.

Young man, it's wonderful to be young! Enjoy every minute of it! Do all you want to; take in everything, but realize that you must account to God for everything you do. So banish grief and pain, but remember that youth, with a whole life before it, can make serious mistakes. Don't let the excitement of being young cause you to forget about your Creator.

*I*t was a great moment in my adult life when I realized that life was meant to be enjoyed rather than simply endured. I cannot recall when that thought became a conscious reality to me. It certainly did not transpire overnight, like a sudden sunburst on the horizon of my awareness. But during an extended period of time, perhaps over a period of several years, I became convinced of it. The process of discovery seems vague to me now, though I distinctly remember being slowly freed up from former self-imposed restrictions. This resulted in giving myself permission to relax, to be who I am—regardless. I distinctly remember entertaining the thought that since I am the kind of person who really enjoys life, why should I try to hide it?

Because I am a minister, most of what I do and who I am cannot be hidden from the public eye. And if you know much about ministry, you are aware of the unrealistic expectations, the preconceived notions, and the traditional opinions which people often have of the one who does most of his speaking from a pulpit and spends most of his time with church folks. But I determined not to let that pressure turn me into someone I am not. After all, if there is anybody who ought to represent authenticity, if there is any realm of work that should model a relaxed and refreshing lifestyle, where one truly enjoys rather than endures life, seems to me it ought to be the one in ministry.

One of my favorite mentors used to say, "It's okay for us to be fundamentalists at heart, just so we don't start looking like one!" Far too many of my colleagues in ministry have begun to *look* like they're in ministry! Stooped shoulders, long faces, that tired-blood, underpaid, overextended, I'm-bearing-such-a-heavy-burden look—like the weight of the entire world must rest upon their shoulders.

I heard recently about a lady waiting in line at the grocery checkout counter. She noticed a well-dressed gentleman standing behind her who seemed especially dignified looking. She asked, "Do you happen to be a minister?" He replied, rather sharply, "No, I'm not . . . I've just been sick lately." I call that rather revealing.

Logan Pearsall Smith, in his work *Afterthoughts*, said:

> There are two things to aim at in life: first, to get what you want; and, after that, to enjoy it. Only the wisest of mankind achieve the second.

Without taking the time to pick at his first aim in life, I'd like to probe the second. Since, in Smith's opinion, "only the wisest" seem to accomplish the enjoyment factor, allow me to ask: Do *you?* Are you enjoying life now, or have you put all that on "hold"? For most people, life has become a grim marathon of misery, an endurance test full of frowns, whines, groans, and sighs. And perhaps that explains why so many who were once close to them have a tendency to drift away. Can you think of anyone who would rather spend a lot of time with those who have stopped enjoying life? They'd probably rather invest their hours in a pet, an animal that can't even talk, than in someone who resembles a depressing, dark rain cloud.

In his work *Leaves of Grass,* poet Walt Whitman confessed that was true of him:

> I think I could turn and live with animals, they are so
>   placid and self-contained.
> I stand and look at them long and long.
> They do not sweat and whine about their condition.
> They do not lie awake in the dark and weep for their
>   sins,
> They do not make me sick discussing their duty to God,
> Not one is dissatisfied, not one is demented with the
>   mania of owning things,
> Not one kneels to another, nor to his kind that lived
>   thousands of years ago,
> Not one is respectable or unhappy over the whole earth.

Maybe that explains the little bumper sticker, "Have you hugged your horse today?" That used to make me smile; now I understand. Sometimes it's easier to hug a horse than it is to stay close to another person. When you get next to a horse, it never says, "Man, have I had a rotten day!" Or, "I'm depressed today." So if we don't want to drive others away with our groans and moans, we need to learn how to enjoy life.

WHAT ARE WE WAITING FOR?

If you were to walk down the streets of the city or the town where you live and ask the people you meet, "What are you waiting for to enjoy life?" I think you would get one of three different answers, and each one finds its origin in the world's system in which we live.

Under-the-Sun Answers

Here's the first that comes to my mind: *"I'm waiting until I have the things I've always wanted. When that happens, then I'll be happy."* That directly connects happiness with material possessions. How very many people really think, "When I have those *things*, then I'll laugh at life and I'll smile back at God." This cuts cross-grain with Jesus' words:

> "Beware, and be on your guard against every form of greed; for not even when one has an abundance does his life consist of his possessions" (Luke 12:15).

In other words, even if we could have all the things we've ever wanted, we still wouldn't have what life is all about. The implication is even stronger: It's a waste to connect happiness with the things that don't comprise life. John Gardner, author of *Self-Renewal*, writes these biting, but true words:

> If happiness could be found in having material things, and in being able to indulge yourself in things that you consider pleasurable, then we, in America, would be deliriously happy. We would be telling one another frequently of our unparalleled bliss, rather than trading tranquilizer prescriptions.[1]

Compare America's prosperity with any other country. We are, of all people in all the world, the most blessed, yet we are among the saddest, the most dissatisfied. Even though we have more than any other country, our happiness on a scale of one to ten is somewhere between a two and a four.

Another answer people would give when asked "What are you waiting for to be happy?" is *"I'm waiting for a person who will fulfill my life."* Frequently, this answer comes from someone who is unhappily single. "I'm waiting until I meet my future marriage partner." Or from the couple who is anxious to start a family, "We are waiting until we have our first baby." And how about the unhappily employed? "I'm waiting for the boss to change. I'm waiting for there to be a change at the top." Or the unhappily married: "I'm waiting for things to change at home; then I'll be happy." Many would say they're waiting for a friend to pull up close and relieve their loneliness.

None of that holds water. Scripture frequently reminds us how foolish it is to trust in "the arm of flesh" to bring us hope and happiness. Psalm 41 gives us an account of David's confession regarding his rather miserable situation. And it had to do with people—maybe people with whom he had cultivated a friendship over the years who had now turned against him.

> All who hate me whisper together against me; against me they devise my hurt, saying, "A wicked thing is poured out upon him, that when he lies down, he will not rise up again." Even my close friend, in whom I trusted, who ate my bread, has lifted up his heel against me (vv. 7–9).

We can't depend on people for our happiness. Like David, we may invest much time and emotion in cultivating a close friendship, only to be let down with disappointments and heartaches. No, if you're counting on a human being to bring you happiness in life, you're in for a lifetime of waiting.

There is a third possible answer. *"I'm waiting until I have achieved my goals and realized my dreams."* How many have dreams and high hopes that are on the horizon and then think, "I'll be so happy when I accomplish my plans." Regardless of what it may be—owning a business, making a million dollars, fulfilling that educational dream, completing a desire to go around the world, or sailing a vessel from this continent to another—whatever or however great the dream may be, and as much as it may keep us plugging, chances are extremely good that it will never bring satisfaction. The realization of our dreams will never make us smile contentedly down deep inside.

At the risk of sounding simplistic, I find the following statement one of the most sensible, reasonable, and achievable answers I've ever heard:

> Dear brothers, is your life full of difficulties and temptations? Then be happy. For when the way is rough, your patience has a chance to grow. So let it grow, and don't try to squirm out of your problems. For when your patience is finally in full bloom, then you will be ready for anything, strong in character, full and complete (James 1:2–4, TLB).

Isn't that a great way to live? I'm not waiting until "someday" when I can find the pinnacle or the plateau of happiness, but I'm finding it in the climb. I'm discovering it in the struggle. I'm learning that it's in the difficult times that I really can have a lot of happiness. I don't need things or people or vast accomplishments if I have the living God as the nucleus of my life. Struggles, in fact, can become some of life's best experiences.

As I plunked myself down in the barber's chair recently, I noticed that the television in his shop was tuned to the "Donahue" show. I'm not a big fan of daytime television, but it was either look at that or count shampoo bottles and hairspray cans, so "Donahue" won out.

He had a panel of women on his program who had once been married to famous celebrities, but they were now divorced from those men whose names are household words in America. I found it fascinating how several of the panelists responded when they talked about their lives, now so different since divorce had interrupted their world. They didn't agree on everything, but there was one thing on which they were unanimous. "You know, once we had it made financially, our problems really multiplied. The best part of our married years were the struggling years."

Now these were ladies who had been surrounded by fans most of their married lives. They had plenty of money and lots of things— big and little toys. They lacked nothing that money could buy. Yet, looking back from the viewpoint of that materialistic plateau, they admitted: "The absolutely happiest days of our lives were those simple days, the tough, lean days. We didn't realize it then, but we certainly do now."

When we struggle, we pull together. We are never more together than during the days of physical hardship, financial stress, and unfulfilled dreams.

Above-the-Sun Answers

This is going to sound terribly familiar, but maybe repetition will help reinforce the truth. Happiness is for today. Joy is available now. We are not to put it on hold. Happiness isn't something that will secretly open up to us when we turn fifty-five, or when we reach some goal or find the right marriage partner. Happiness is for *now*. It is inseparably linked to the living Lord.

A catechism in the Presbyterian Church begins with the question, "What is the chief end of man?" The answer to that question is familiar to many: "The chief end of man is to love God and enjoy

Him forever." Not just serve Him, not just obey Him, not just sacrifice to Him, not simply commit ourselves to Him, but *enjoy* Him—"laugh through life with Him." Smile in His presence. So much more is included in enjoying Him forever than most would ever believe. I don't know if the Scottish Presbyterian divines back in the seventeenth century derived their answer from Solomon's journal, but they certainly *could* have! The wise monarch, as we shall see, realized the value of enjoying life to the fullest. Let's take a look at what he has to say about it.

WHAT DOES SOLOMON SAY ABOUT ENJOYING LIFE?

The first thing I notice is that *we are given permission to enjoy life.* He says:

> The light is pleasant, and it is good for the eyes to see the sun (Eccles. 11:7).

Now remember that this is picturesque, symbolic Hebrew. It is inspired poetry, not meant to be taken literally. The reader is expected to feel the romance, the rhythmic beauty, and the color of the wise man's counsel.

Frequently through the Scriptures, references to light and sunshine are used to describe the warmth of God's love. "The Lord is my light and my salvation. Whom shall I fear?" asked the psalmist. When we are enveloped in the warmth of our Father's love, we fear no one. It gives us a sense of warm security to be under His wings, surrounded by His care. That's the idea.

The light of God's everpresent, always-comforting love is pleasant. And it's good for our eyes to focus on the warmth and protection of the hand of God wrapped around our lives and to know that He is pleased with us and that He gives us permission to enjoy ourselves. When we focus on Him, He lifts the gloom and takes the stinging pain of depression out of life.

Solomon continues in verse 8:

> Indeed, if a man should live many years, let him rejoice in them all . . . (v. 8).

I love that! Happiness is to pervade all the years of our life. We don't have to wait until we reach some magical age when we are allowed to crack open the door and slip silently into the realm of happiness. It's there for us to enjoy *throughout* our days.

I was saddened to read the words of the British historian Arnold Toynbee on his eightieth birthday. He said, "I'm glad I'm growing old in England. Americans are dedicated to the new and superefficient. It must be depressing to be old in the United States." Well, my answer to Dr. Toynbee is if a person feels the need to compete or to join ranks with those who must come out first or be superefficient, it *would* be depressing to grow old here (or anywhere else, for that matter). But I need not be depressed to grow old in the United States. Solomon is saying that life has the capacity to be enjoyable, even if we should live many years. Our goal is to rejoice in them all.

By the way, growing old happily is the theme of the major section in the latter part of Solomon's journal, which we'll be looking at in the next chapter. He talks about old age and how to make the most of it.

But for now, the second thing I see Solomon saying about enjoying life is that *all the traditional limitations are removed.* Let's look at some of those supposed limitations. Many would say to be happy you must be young. That's a traditional thought. But if I read this correctly, it is saying that if you should live many years, there is happiness to be claimed, right now! Tradition also says, "Well, if you're young, then life is full of painful adjustments and difficulties along the way." This implies, "Don't plan on finding happiness until you can get out on your own." But right now you're struggling through "getting in touch with yourself." So you might as well learn how to endure it. Being a teenager is tough.

Hold on! I want to announce to teens today—what great years you are living! I'd even include the junior high years! Junior high students often don't know it. And who can imagine having more fun than in those senior high years! I look back on my wild and crazy senior high school years and I'm thankful for two things. First, I lived through them; and second, most of you don't know anything about them.

Whenever I go back and visit my high school, I'm gripped by nostalgia. Those were some of the very best years of my life. Every time I hear the song "The Way We Were," I recall how much fun, how active, energetic, and fulfilling my high school years really were. Sure there were some adjustments. I'm afraid I didn't realize it then, however. George Bernard Shaw, with a twinkle in his eye, once said, "Youth is such a wonderful thing. It's a shame to waste it on young people."

During my youngest son's eighth-grade year in junior high school, he and his class went to Washington, D.C. for almost two weeks. Prior to his trip, the two of us spent most of one day shopping for his clothes. What a day to remember! If you haven't shopped with a thirteen-year-old, you haven't lived. Full of energy, full of ideas, snappy little comments, short attention span, going for jokes, lots of fun, and in the meantime, putting dad to the test all along the way. There's nothing wrong with that. Frankly, I gave him a run for his money! "Rejoice, young man, in your youth." I'm so tired of older people saying to younger people, "You should get serious about life." Why? What's the big deal about getting serious about life? I've often been tempted to retort, "And look like you? Is that what you want?"

> Rejoice, young man, during your childhood, and let your heart be pleasant during the days of young manhood (v. 9).

Get at it! Have a ball! Enjoy! Before you know it, you'll be an adult! The line out of *Fiddler on the Roof* is so true, "Sunrise, sunset; sunrise, sunset; swiftly fly the years." And then come those midlife years. Ah, those middle-aged years! I like the way Robert Raines expresses it:

> Middle-agers are beautiful!
>   Aren't we, Lord?
> I feel for us
>   Too radical for our parents
>   Too reactionary for our kids
> Supposedly in the prime of life
>   Like prime rib
>   Everybody eating off me
>   Devouring me
>   Nobody thanking me
>   Appreciating me
>   But still hanging in there
>   Communicating with my parents
>   In touch with my kids
> And getting more in touch
>   with myself

> And that's all good
>> Thanks for making it good, Lord,
> and
>> could You make it a little better?[2]

That's what Solomon's comment is all about.

There's a tradition that says, "Have your fun now, because later it's a beast." But I don't read that in the stuff God writes about youth. I read incredible optimism in Scripture.

> Rejoice young man, during your childhood [have a great childhood], and let your heart be pleasant during the days of young manhood [enjoy your youth!]. And follow the impulses of your heart and the desires of your eyes.

We don't hear enough of that from pulpits, do we?

One of the "in" things nowadays among teenagers is toilet papering houses. Well, I was washing my daughter's car one day and decided I would clean out her trunk. When I popped open the lid, I discovered multiple rolls of toilet paper all over the trunk of the car—fifteen, maybe twenty rolls! I wanted to know what in the world she'd been up to. She then informed me that one of the fun things she and her cheerleading squad do is "TP" all the football team's homes! And the guys reciprocate (believe me, we've had our share!). And you know what? There's not a thing in the world wrong with that. Which one would you rather have on your front lawn—beer cans or toilet paper? When they "TP" us and then water down the lawn, sometimes I wonder! I mean, they did our front yard so thoroughly that every tree looked like a work of art. It looked like it had snowed. Then they sprinkled confetti and sawdust and finally the water, that "final touch" on their Renoir. In the middle of the night they came, silent as Santa Claus. I'll tell you, our four have thoroughly enjoyed their teenage years. So have their mom and dad!

Don't let the prime of life turn you into a cynic. If you're getting middle-aged, why become negative? Why all of a sudden get grim or practice frowning in front of a mirror? Why not enjoy life for as long as it lasts?

And before I get so carried away about having fun, let me mention the third thing Solomon says about enjoying life: *God inserts just enough warnings to keep us obedient.*

> Indeed, if a man should live many years, let him rejoice in them all, and let him remember [however] the days of darkness [or he'll be disillusioned], for they shall be many (v. 8).

As we instruct our children on how to live, let's be sure that they have a lot of fun when it's the years for having fun. But let's be sure that we do our very best to guard them from disillusionment. Balanced counsel spoken at the right time helps. "Honey, there are a lot of tough days in front of you." "Son, I want you to know that your life may be wrapped up in being on the ball team, having fun at school, swimming and beaching it in the summer, but there is also some rough water ahead of you." That's what I mean by balanced counsel. A few warnings need to be inserted.

Here is a warning that says, "Don't let those great days throw you. Remember this, there are a lot of things that will come to be futility." I think the emphasis should be placed on the *things*. Much of the stuff related to things will lead to futility. In other words: "Son (daughter), if you begin to be preoccupied with the *things* in life and you allow yourself to focus mainly on things, those things will ultimately leave you empty. They will demand of you more than they give you. And if you allow them to become little idols in your life, you will wind up serving them. Let me warn you ahead of time."

There's another warning here, did you notice?

> Rejoice, young man, during your childhood, and let your heart be pleasant during the days of young manhood. And follow the impulses of your heart and the desires of your eyes. Yet know that God will bring you to judgment for all these things (v. 9).

He's saying to the youth, "Relax and have fun in your childhood and have a super time in your youth. And follow those impulses (there will be many of them) and the desires of your eyes (and there will be many of *them* too). Enjoy your childhood and your adolescent years. Yet, don't forget—there'll be a day of accountability." Some may be tempted to think that the warning takes all the joy out of the whole statement.

But in that warning I see a great deal of God's compassion. He's concerned that we not go wild with our liberty. Do you have any idea what insane lives we would live if there were no anchor on the tether? Do you realize how maddening we would conduct ourselves—

even as youths—if we forgot that there is a God to whom we shall someday answer?

I have scarcely seen an exception. When I've dealt with people who have pursued a maddening drive for happiness, I've found that they mentally canceled out accountability to God somewhere along the way. But that kind of liberty is bad for us. But remember this, son. Remember this, daughter. Remember this, middle-aged career woman, entrepreneur, executive, professional person: God will bring us into account for all these things.

Again, I see a God of compassion leaning out of heaven and saying to His people, "So [I plead with you], remove vexation from your heart . . ." (v. 10). We need to know what that word means before we can appreciate Solomon's point. We don't use the word *vexation* that often today. The original Hebrew term is a combination of two ideas—anger and resentment. And when you place anger alongside resentment, then blend them together, you get rebellion.

Rebellion, by the way, has no age limit. The youth don't have a corner on rebellion. Neither do the older folks who feel ripped off in life. This mixture of anger and resentment is what Solomon has in mind when he refers to vexation. And God says, "Now let me warn you in your pursuit of happiness in life, you need to put aside a rebellious spirit."

Frankly, some people need help doing that. By that I mean they need professional help in knowing how to put aside the rebellious spirit. Rebellion is often so ingrained that they are unable on their own to remove the roots that made them that way—the way they were raised, the habits that they have cultivated, and even their mentality. This leaves them virtually helpless. That is why I suggest they need assistance in getting out of that horrible trap of rebellion.

While we are told to "Go for it!" we are also warned to "put away pain from your body." I doubt that Solomon is writing in symbolic language. Why not take this comment literally? It makes a lot of sense if we understand it to mean: "Get rid of the things that bring the body pain." For example, take a straight look at what alcohol does to your body. Take an honest look at what drugs will do to your body. Look at the effects of tobacco on your body. Face it straight on and realize the pain that your body will be forced to endure if you participate in those harmful activities. You'll suffer serious consequences if you make that a part of your lifestyle. And heed this warning: Put it away. Keep a lid on your sexual drive or the wrong uses of your leisure time. Those things can bring pain to your body. Your liberty must include some limitations!

We can see just by looking around us how harmful activities affect lives. One such example is well known by baseball fans. He's a young man I've watched and admired as a superb relief pitcher. But his battle with drugs forced him to forfeit the right to play on his team for a full year until he could get a handle on the drugs that numbed his body.

This excellent athlete, not even thirty years old, says of himself, "I'm addicted." And his words drip with heartache. He has a devoted wife and a little baby, yet this man is struggling to get back on his feet. It occurred to me recently that he is giving a message to all the youth and adults of our day who think the answer is in cocaine, alcohol, or some other chemical. I call that a modern-day example of one who would agree, "Put away the pain from your body!"

And Solomon tells us why: "Because childhood and the prime of life are fleeting." You have only one childhood. You have only one adolescence. You have only one prime of life and it is fleeting past and so soon gone. What you're doing with your life now is the memory you'll have through all your tomorrows.

It is even possible to try to pack too much into our days. We can become victims of the fast lane, trying too many things, pushing ourselves too fast, too far.

A very clever writer who writes a lot of amusing stories for children (with hidden messages to adults) is Judith Viorst. She's written a little book called *How Did I Get to Be 40 & Other Atrocities,* and in it she includes a poem called "Self-Improvement Program." It's terrific.

After a recitation of many new activities and involvements that she's participated in—needlepoint, guitar lessons, advanced Chinese cooking, primal-scream therapy, and a half dozen other things, she sighs as she concludes:

> And I'm working all day and I'm working all night
> To be good-looking, healthy, and wise.
> And adored.
> And contented.
> And brave.
> And well-read.
> And a marvelous hostess,

Fantastic in bed,
And bilingual,
Athletic,
Artistic . . .
Won't someone please stop me?[3]

God says, "Slow down!" It would do us all a lot of good to take a deep look at our shallow life spinning rapidly in a self-centered orbit. Why do we think that's going to give us happiness? The "prime of life" is fleeting ever so rapidly.

A Long-Awaited Insight

As we approach the finale of Solomon's ragged-edge journey, we are finally introduced to the One who can give life meaning.

Remember also your Creator in the days of your youth, before the evil days come and the years draw near when you will say, "I have no delight in them" (12:1).

At long last, Solomon says it! I've wanted to tell him to "remember the Creator in the days of his youth," ever since chapter 1 (Doesn't that sound like an evangelical pastor?). "Solomon, you should remember your Creator in the days of your youth. That's why you're so miserable in chapters 1 and 3 and 4 and 6 and 7 and 9 and 10!" But now he sees it on his own. And he openly admits it. In the final analysis, it's best if a person makes such a discovery on his own.

The truth is that it takes a while for some folks to see it. Some people need room to find out the hard things on their own. You and I can yell and scream, preach and stick tracts under their noses, give them phone calls, write notes, send them Bibles with underlined verses, and tell them to read so-and-so's book or to listen to some sermon on a cassette—but *they're not going to do it.* They are not ready. They are like Solomon—it will take time. They cannot be told what to do with any measure of success. They need to find out on their own.

Finally, at long last, the day comes when they bow before the King and they say, "Oh, my God! I see it all so clearly . . . Lord, I need You." When that happens—and not until—things like perception, reality, and understanding fall into place. They get their "heads together," as we often say. And it isn't long before they get their theological ducks in a row too. Prayer returns. God comes into clearer focus. Lo and behold . . . they remember their Creator.

Solomon finally does that. "Remember your Creator in the days of your youth." Isn't that great? But he doesn't say "remember" meaning, "Don't forget Him." It's not like a reminder you write with lipstick on the mirror of your bathroom, "Remember God today." It is not that kind of remembrance. In fact, this Hebrew word translated "remember" is used somewhat frequently in the Old Testament in a most insightful manner. It is used in 1 Samuel for Hannah when she was without a baby. She really wanted a baby, and she prayed for a baby. And Scripture says, "The Lord remembered Hannah." God acted on her behalf and caused her to conceive. It's the same term. It means "to act decisively on behalf of someone."

"Remember your Creator when you are young" means to act decisively on behalf of the living God. This means that we realize *He is the one essential ingredient we need for a truly happy lifestyle.* It means that we listen to what He says and act accordingly. It means we will not follow the dictates of our own heart, but that we will follow the dictates of His truth. It means we will make an intelligent, serious, independent study of what Scripture says about how to walk in obedience. We will see what the Old Testament stories have to say about how to live life, and we will not forget the counsel of Solomon in his journal, Ecclesiastes. We will remember our Creator. And having taken a serious account of what God has said about life early on, we will act decisively on His behalf—while we are young.

WHAT HINDERS THE PURSUIT OF HAPPINESS?

Quite candidly, as we wrap up our thoughts in this chapter, I can think of only two things that could hinder one's pursuit of happiness. Neither one is that complicated. What stands as a barrier, blocking our way to joy? First, *self-appointed excuses keep us from claiming daily joy.* "If so and so were only different." As we saw earlier, that's a lame excuse. "If I hadn't had the background I've got," another excuse. "If I just had a little more money." "If we could just live somewhere else." "If I just had my degree and all of that behind me." "If only I hadn't married this person" . . . or "If my wife would only come back" or "If my husband would return." Those are nothing but self-appointed excuses. "If my church were different." "If we only had another pastor." "If my kids would just obey." "If my son would grow up, I'd be happy." There are dozens more—all excuses that keep us from enjoying each day God gives us. They act as parasites, sucking the enjoyment out of life.

The second thing that hinders one's pursuit of happiness is *a self-styled independence that keeps us from remembering our Creator.* Does this sound familiar? "I'll make it on my own, thank you. I've got my own head. I've put things together pretty well. I've made it this far on my own. Nobody's fed me. I've paid for my own meals, gotten my own education. I pulled myself up by my own boot straps and I'll make it. I've gotten the professional help I needed from the therapist, and I paid for that by myself, too. I know where I'm going and I'm going to get there." They are popular words in our day—the sounds of independence.

As I mentioned at the beginning of the chapter, we get what we want in life. It is easy for that to lead to a self-styled independence. Yet we're really not independent, are we? The very fact that our heart has an electronic pulse that beats on its own is a gift from God's grace. The day it stops is the day we die. How can we say we're independent of God?

One of my favorite devotional writers was Englishman J. B. Phillips. He was one of the first to write a paraphrase of the New Testament, which, in my opinion, is still one of the best.

He also wrote books. One of my favorites is a little book entitled, simply, *Good News.* I blew the dust off it just recently and found an interesting statement about being happy.

> "Blessed" in the authorized version is very nearly the equivalent of our modern word "happy." So that Jesus, in effect, gives us a recipe for happiness in the Beatitudes. So as to make the revolutionary character of His recipe more apparent, I will quote first a little version of my own, of what most non-Christian people think.
>
> They think: "Happy are the pushers, for they get on in the world. Happy are the hard-boiled, for they never let life hurt them. Happy are they who complain, for they get their own way in the end. Happy are the blasé, for they never worry over their sins. Happy are the slave drivers, for they get results. Happy are the knowledgeable men of the world, for they know their way around. Happy are the troublemakers, for they make people take notice of them."

But Jesus said, "How happy are the humble-minded, for the kingdom of heaven is theirs. How happy are those who know what sorrow means, for they will be given courage and comfort. Happy are those who claim nothing, for the whole earth will belong to them. Happy are those who are hungry and thirsty for goodness, for they will be satisfied. Happy are the merciful, for they will have mercy shown to them. Happy are the utterly sincere, for they will see God. Happy are those who make peace, for they will be known as sons of God.[4]

To be totally honest about it, happiness is really not that complicated. I'm convinced with all my heart (and I find that it works for me) that if my relationship with the living Lord is in place by faith in Jesus Christ, if I take His perspective and look at my life as it unfolds in the valleys as well as on the mountains—it's amazing!— happiness accompanies me.

But when I roll up my sleeves and take on life (including God) with a grim determination that says, "I'm going to get what I want," I find that I sometimes get it, but happiness is never a by-product. Never. In fact, those are some of the darkest days of my life. Happiness eludes me—just as it does everyone else. The only way we can enjoy life is to find God's gift of happiness in Jesus Christ.

23

GRAY HAIRS, FEWER TEETH, YET A BIG SMILE

Journal Entry

Honor him in your youth before the evil years come—when you'll no longer enjoy living. It will be too late then to try to remember him, when the sun and light and moon and stars are dim to your old eyes, and there is no silver lining left among your clouds. For there will come a time when your limbs will tremble with age, and your strong legs will become weak, and your teeth will be too few to do their work, and there will be blindness, too. . . . And you will waken at dawn with the first note of the birds; but you yourself will be deaf and tuneless, with quavering voice. You will be afraid of heights and of falling—a white-haired, withered old man, dragging himself along; without sexual desire, standing at death's door, and nearing his everlasting home as the mourners go along the streets.

Yes, remember your Creator now. . . . .

When I mentioned to my family the title I had chosen for this chapter, they wanted to know if it was going to be an autobiographical chapter. Humph! As Rodney Dangerfield would say, "I don't get no respect."

The fact is that all of us are getting older. There is no getting around it. Each new dawn and each golden sunset—even each chime on the grandfather clock—are constant reminders that we are growing older. Not only that, more of us than ever are living longer. As a result the aged are asking new questions seldom asked in previous generations.

Grandmothers are no longer asking, "Shall I sit back and enjoy my grandchildren?" On the contrary, today's grandmother is asking, "Shall I pursue that graduate degree?" Grandfathers are also different from what they used to be. Instead of asking, "Now that I'm into my seventies, shall I retire to Leisure Village?" they are wondering, "Now that I'm into my seventies, why not move into the White House?"

The late George Gallup, in his final volume *America Wants to Know,* compiled over six hundred pages of facts regarding our nation. As we might expect, he dedicated the concluding pages of this massive volume to what he calls "longevity"—more popularly called "the graying of America." In that section Gallup writes:

> For many people, the age of "old" is arriving later than ever before. Take the case of the last three generations of a hypothetical American family. When the grandfather was born in 1900, he could have expected to outlive (barely) his mid-life crisis; the average lifespan at the turn of the century was only forty-seven years. For the father, born in 1940, the odds were against surviving to enjoy retirement; the average lifespan that year ended at about age sixty-three. Yet his son, born in 1980, can look forward to almost a decade of life after sixty-five, for the average lifespan today stretches to more than seventy-three years.[1]

You see, we're not only growing older, we really are living longer. Not that many years ago, the elderly formed a very small percentage of American population. For example, in the year 1900 only four percent of America was sixty-five years of age and older. Today it's ten percent. By the year 2000, that same category will comprise twelve percent—clearly three times that of one hundred years earlier.

346

In fact, I was interested to read in Gallup's book that there are today in America approximately twelve thousand people over the age of one hundred. I had no idea there were that many Americans who had passed the century mark.

The popular idea is that because we are living longer, we therefore live a more resourceful and meaningful life, and more people are happier. But sadly, such is not the case.

This was brought home to me late last year as my wife Cynthia and I were waiting to see a physician. Sitting in the doctor's waiting room that day was a woman in a wheelchair. She was not that old, but her hands and fingers were twisted by some awful disease—maybe arthritis—and I noticed that she was reading a book. She could bearly turn the pages. The title intrigued me: *I Don't Want to Live Like This Anymore.*

It's sad to say, but some people don't have that much to be happy about. Maybe you live with older people. Maybe you are helping your parents in the twilight years of their lives. If you are, I commend you. My sister and I assisted our aging father as we watched him die slowly and sadly. And it left an indelible impression upon both our lives, as well as the lives of our family members.

We discovered that among the people he spent his later years with, though they were few in number, there were some traditional feelings that seemed to bubble to the surface. I am able to identify about four of them as they relate not only to his peers, but to others in this day and time.

TRADITIONAL FEELINGS AMONG THE AGED

The number one common feeling among the aged is the feeling of *uselessness*, of being a bother. The elderly often think, "I am in the way. I am over the hill." Such thoughts are extremely common among those who were once very resourceful people—people whose opinions were once considered important, who were looked upon for leadership and direction in their generation, but no longer. It is the feeling that when one gets into his or her seventies or eighties, "Who really needs what I have to offer?"

Then there's the feeling of *guilt* that says, "I have totally fouled up my life. I blew it. If I could only live my life over, how differently I would rear my children!" Or, "I would pursue a line of work in which I could have been a greater success." Or, "I would handle my money differently." Or, "I would take more vacations and enjoy my leisure more." Or perhaps, "I would become more responsible." Guilt keeps saying to the older gentleman, "I'm not the man I could have been." It's like the sentiment expressed by the anonymous poet who wrote these words:

> Across the fields of yesterday
> He sometimes comes to me
> The little lad just back from play
> The boy I used to be
>
> He smiles at me so wistfully
> When once he's crept within
> It is as though he had hoped to see
> The man I might have been.[2]

The guilt seems to drip off the poet's pen. "If only . . . if only."

The combination of *bitterness and resentment* is another feeling that is commonly found among the older people of our day. It says, "I have been given a raw deal." And it's frequently targeted toward certain people. "If I had married another person." Or, "If my children were only more thoughtful." There is also a lot of *self-pity* wrapped up in this kind of response to life. "If . . . if only I could have had it easier in life. It's been so hard. I've had it so rough." I know of few people more pathetic and more difficult to be around than those who have lost the battle with self-pity.

Finally, there's the feeling of *fear* that says, "I am so afraid." The aged face many fears—fears of heights, of bankruptcy, of ill health, of dying, of being left alone, of losing one's mind, and dozens more. Fear is the unseen guest in many a home occupied by the aged.

Sometimes it's helpful for us to put ourselves into the shoes of an older person and look at life through their eyes. In our fast-paced, electronic age of computerized banking and grocery store checkstands that no longer require the familiar cash register, it's easy to become intimidated and confused . . . not to mention busy intersections and fast-moving traffic. Growing older is not fun for those who find themselves unable to keep up. It can be threatening to grow older in a world that's moving faster than ever, surrounded by people who just don't have much patience, who don't seem to care.

But wait. It seems to me that the One who gives us life and allows us to prolong our years on this earth, the One who holds the patent on aging ought to have a say in all this. Surely He offers some assistance. Indeed He does! And I am of the opinion that when He talks about aging, we ought to listen.

DIVINE PERSPECTIVE WORTH CONSIDERING

We have come to the final moments of Solomon's journey. And at long last the man has come to realize the importance of listening to and walking with his Creator. The sneering cynicism we found earlier in his journal is now conspicuous by its absence. He doesn't hesitate to write in bold, easy-to-read script, "Before all of that aging transpires, you remember your Creator—do so in the days of your youth!"

Can't you see ol' Granddad Solomon leaning over, stroking his beard, and looking patiently into the eyes of his grandson? "Now listen, young man, and don't you forget what I'm saying to you." Interestingly, he's not speaking to a grandson, he's speaking to all people down through the centuries of time, and that includes you and me.

As I mentioned in chapter 22, the ancient Hebrew term translated *remember* means "to act decisively on behalf of someone." Solomon is saying, "Act decisively on behalf of God while you are young."

Derek Kidner writes:

> To remember Him is no perfunctory or purely mental act: it is to drop our pretense of self-sufficiency and to commit ourselves to Him.[3]

Great idea! I suggest that we do just that. Let's begin to release whatever pretense of self-sufficiency we may have and say, "Living God, I commit myself to You. You created me, so You know what is best for me. I willingly adapt my life to Your plan. I am ready to go Your way!" *That* is acting decisively on His behalf.

But the flesh will answer back, "Aw what's the rush? Why not wait until you have sown a few wild oats? Why not wait thirty or forty years until you've had a pile of fun doing things your own way and *then* turn to God? I mean, you get the best of both worlds that way."

Solomon doesn't waste time answering that kind of reasoning.

"Remember Him . . . *before* the evil days come." Let that sink in. You see, it isn't just "fun and games" days; Solomon calls them "evil" days. Any investment in evil pays a dreadful dividend—consequences, scars, bad habits. It affects us mentally and emotionally. It brings anchors of heartache that we are forced to drag into today. It slows down our maturing process and dulls us spiritually. "No," says Solomon emphatically. "No! I tried that route and it's an empty journey!"

The Spirit of God is so gracious as He prompts Solomon to give us counsel before the fact. While we're young it is so easy to think we'll be young forever. Our bodies play tricks on us, trying to convince us we'll always be young. But, as I said at the beginning of this chapter, we are not only getting older, we are living longer. So we would be wise to heed some sound advice.

A Fresh Look at Physical Aging

Frankly, I don't know of a more eloquent allegory in all the Old Testament regarding aging than these words from Solomon's pen:

> Remember also your Creator in the days of your youth, before the evil days come and the years draw near when you will say, "I have no delight in them"; before the sun, the light, the moon, and the stars are darkened, and clouds return after the rain; in the day that the watchmen of the house tremble, and mighty men stoop, the grinding ones stand idle because they are few, and those who look through windows grow dim; and the doors on the street are shut as the sound of the grinding mill is low, and one will arise at the sound of the bird, and all the daughters of song will sing softly. Furthermore, men are afraid of a high place and of terrors on the road; the almond tree blossoms, the grasshopper drags himself along, and the caperberry is ineffective. For man goes to his eternal home while mourners go about in the street. Remember Him before the silver cord is broken and the golden bowl is crushed, the pitcher by the well is shattered and the wheel at the cistern is crushed (Eccles. 12:1–6).

To begin with, Solomon writes of mental aging. He then addresses the process of deterioration that occurs in our bodies. By the time we reach the end of his list, we realize the value of his great counsel to remember our Creator. As the old adage goes, "An ounce of prevention is worth a pound of cure." Let's not wait until we are white-haired to respond!

Mental Dullness and Depression

What's the rush? Well, old Father Time is moving on. He's taking over. There will be a time when "the sun, the light, the moon, and the stars are darkened." This seems to be a picture of old age, mental dullness, and depression. " . . . when the clouds return after the rain." The picture is a vivid one.

Here in southern California it is absolutely beautiful after a hard rain—the pollution is washed completely out of the sky. We love the clear, crisp view of snowcapped mountains when we can see them at a distance. But in the scene Solomon is painting, the rain ends, yet the sky does not appear. On the contrary, another heavy cloud comes, and then another. It's a picture of gloom. The symbolism he uses is that of a house that is deteriorating. Literally, it's falling apart. The cloudy weather represents the aged mind as it begins to get dull. Senility steals so much of the joy of living.

To be very candid about this, I confess that one of the things I fear the most is the losing of my memory. I draw upon my memory in my work every week, almost every day of my life. There are times when my very efficient secretary, Helen Peters, will ask me, "Where was that quote found?" And, almost without hestitation I'll say, as I point to my bookshelves, "It's in that book . . . on the right-hand side of the page about halfway down between pages 150 and 160. It's that red book right there on the shelf." And she'll pull it off my shelf, turn to page 152 and halfway down the right-hand side of the page . . . lo, and behold, there it is. I smile; she smiles. I feel a little smug, *until* I come across statements like this one in Solomon's journal.

I fear the day when she says to me, "Where's that quote found?" And I say, "What quote?" And she'll say, "Well, you said so and so." And I'll answer, "I never used that quote!" I fear not being able to reach over and pull out the book I need and locate the statement I'm looking for. I rely on my memory all the time. But there will come a day when the clouds will form in my head. I rather suspect I'll get a little depressed over my mental dullness when my memory starts to fail.

Physical Ailments and Limitations

Also accompanying those advancing years are bodily ailments and limitations. Look at verse 3:

In the day that the watchmen of the house tremble, and mighty men stoop, the grinding ones stand idle because they are few, and those who look through windows grow dim.

Continuing to use a house as the basis of the allegory, Solomon now mentions the trembling "watchmen"—the shaking of the head and the trembling of the voice and hands.

When I first came to the church I serve here in Fullerton (fourteen years ago), I immediately cultivated a number of close friends who were, by that time, approaching their later years in life—great people, such fine leaders; nevertheless they were aging. But I remember, their voices were still strong and their leadership skills were still keen. As the Bible would say, their bodies were still "mighty in battle." Well, just the other day one of those men handed me a piece of paper that he wanted me to read and I noticed how his hand shook when he handed the paper to me. Back when we first met his hands did not tremble. Now they do. It's part of the aging process—the watchmen of the house begin to tremble.

Who could ever forget the Academy Award–winning performances of Katherine Hepburn and Henry Fonda in *On Golden Pond*? What a never-to-be-forgotten example of old age as it captures the mind and turns it into a negative and vile thing! What a performance, what a reminder to all of us on how *not* to grow older! Henry Fonda's portrayal of old Norm Thayer may have won him an Academy Award, but more than that, it gave movie goers a great deal of insight into what can happen when aging runs its course.

Our bodily "house" is built on two strong pillars—our legs. They are referred to here as "mighty men." But if you read on you see that ultimately even the mighty men stoop. How true that is!

You and I who used to jump and leap and run with virtually no energy drain now must think twice before we dart off hurriedly in some direction. Like it or not, our "mighty men" are like the old gray mare—they "ain't what they used to be!"

I remember when I was a young buck in junior high school, walking to school through the woods with a couple of my buddies. A tree had fallen across a wide ravine following a storm. The old pine had been tall, but it wasn't that big around. I remember being dared by my buddies to walk across that narrow tree bridge. Without hesitation, I took off! When I got in the middle I threw my little lunch sack up over my head and caught it behind my back. I was dancing around out there in sneakers, acting like a nut.

How could I do that? My "mighty men" were strong and healthy. I was agile and young. But now? I almost have a coronary when I think about walking across that tree! I would *never* do that today. You and I would look at the fallen tree and we would think, "What wonderful timber that is," and we would keep on walking through the woods. We don't go out on trees that have fallen across canyons—we just *talk* about them! We become poets, instead of people of a dare. Why? Our "mighty men" are stooping.

And in addition to shaking legs, weak knees, and trembling hands and voice, "The grinding ones stand idle." You don't need a course in Hebrew to interpret that one! Obviously, Solomon is referring to our teeth. Dentists would say, "There is inadequate occlusion." We would say, "The uppers don't meet the lowers." It takes longer to eat, because we've got those chunks of food that have to be lined up with seven remaining teeth that don't fit together! The older we get, the more we have to "gum" our food!

I never will forget a particular trip I made to a grocery store. It was back in the days when our four children were very small, two still in diapers. I was at the baby-food section, piling those jars in my cart. Nearby was an older gentleman very carefully picking and choosing "strained this" and "mashed that." I thought, *My! That's great! Ol' granddad's buying it for the grandkids!* I smiled and said something like, "Boy, I bet it's great having those grandkids around the house!" He frowned, "This ain't for the grandkids, sonny, this is for *me!*" When old age arrives, the "grinding ones" become idle because they are few—you go back to strained food.

It just occurred to me that the older we get, the longer it takes us to get ready for bed. More and more stuff has to come out and be taken off. We look different after a night's sleep too.

Moving right along, ". . . and those who look through windows grow dim." It doesn't take a biblical scholar to figure that one out, either. What looks through windows? What grows dim with age? Of course, our eyes. As we get older, our focus is not as crisp, so our lenses get thicker. And then we have to wear glasses so thick and heavy, they make permanent indentations on the bridge of the nose!

My opthalmologist told me during my last visit that I should go into trifocals. I mean, the next step for me is a big dog and a white cane! When I speak in public and the spotlights are too bright, I'm afraid my pupils will start to smoke! We're talking mega-thick lenses!

Cataracts are another problem for aged eyes, bringing with them the fear of blindness. And it isn't just a fear. It's reality. Look at those who traffic into the opthalmologist's office. You'll see many of them in their sixties and seventies—their "windows" growing dim.

Why are we to remember Him when we're young? Obviously, when we are youthful we've got all of our physical faculties in place, but there will come a day "when the doors on the street are shut as the sound of the grinding mill is low." That's a reference to our hearing. We don't hear like we once did. One of our most frequently used expressions is "How's . . . how's that again?" Or, "What'd you say?"

As we grow older, those very special sounds we once enjoyed— delicate sounds in music, for example—we now miss. And Solomon goes even further. He adds, "One will arise at the sound of the bird." The slightest noise terminates our sleep. We used to be able to sleep through a locomotive roaring by outside the window. No longer. Now all it takes is the peck, peck, peck of a woodpecker and we can't get back to sleep.

I find it the next thing to impossible to convince today's teenager that that's really going to happen to them. They think it will happen only to great-grandmothers and "ancient" grandfathers, but "it's never gonna happen to me." Solomon's words, however, eventually impact all of us. That's the whole point. The wonderful thing about the Bible is that it's predictions and warnings are not only absolutely reliable, they are timeless. Like no other book, it tells us the truth and nothing but the truth ahead of time. And all the way through, it implies, "Believe it." In this case, remember Him now, because there will come a day when we'll have to face the inescapable factors of mental slowness and physical infirmity. It is the way God planned it. So? So come to terms with reality *now*.

I like the way he continues, "All the daughters of song will sing softly." Perhaps he means that we'll be unable to sing as we once could sing. The old pipes that once were clear and on key are no longer in that condition.

I read recently in *Time* magazine about the retirement of several big names in the opera. Leontyne Price, Beverly Sills, Marian Anderson, and others are finally forced to face the music—they can no longer handle the demands of such vocal disciplines that the opera requires. All the daughters will ultimately sing softly, even the respected and seasoned professionals.

Men are afraid of high places and terrors on the road, Solomon goes on to say. There's another one—acrophobia—"fear of heights."

It is not uncommon for the aged to shudder at the thought of being up high. Furthermore, their awareness of danger seems terribly acute. There aren't many who say "goodbye" to a grandmother without being told six to eight times about the dangers that are on the streets. And they'll name them one by one. (Fathers do that too, I must confess.)

I have to be careful when my teenaged daughter gets in her car, drops it in reverse, and gets ready to back out of the driveway for school. I have to guard against a mini-lecture on the possible perils. I just say, "Drive carefully!" Yet I'm really holding back ten or twelve specific fears that I've got. We all do that. Solomon's point is right on: The older we get, the more overprotective we become because we are increasingly preoccupied with possible dangers.

Look at the next one: ". . . the almond tree blossoms." Have you ever seen an orchard of almond trees in full bloom? That's a common sight out here in the San Joaquin Valley. It's beautiful—a silver gray appearance. Solomon is painting a word picture of graying hair.

I recently returned to my alma mater, Dallas Theological Seminary, and had a chance to minister to some of the men who had graduated with me back in the class of '63. It was interesting how so many of us had grayed. From the ceiling looking down, I'm sure we resembled almond trees. I recently received a letter from a couple Cynthia and I have known for over two decades. Since we haven't been together for many, many years, the woman was describing how much more "mature" her husband looks now. When she got to his hair, she mentioned that he refers to himself as the silver fox—but she thinks it's more appropriate to call him the gray wolf!

And ". . . the grasshopper drags himself along." It just takes longer to get where we're going. We're gonna get there, but it will take a little longer. What Solomon has in mind here is slow movement.

Furthermore, ". . . and the caperberry is ineffective." It's the idea of being unable to bear fruit, the inability to procreate. We become sexually impotent. Encouragingly, this one appears at the end of the list. Impotence is one of the last plagues of growing older. That is relieving, huh, guys?

In verse 6 Solomon suddenly returns to his opening command: "Remember Him . . ." Remember Him when? Before "the silver cord is broken . . . the golden bowl is crushed." I think he's referring to a stroke, that terrible moment when that little clot makes its way into the "golden bowl" and lodges up there in the brain. And all of a sudden we're not able to reach to that radio knob or television switch and turn it on and off. We want to. We know our head wants it to happen, but we can't move that part of our body anymore. Why? "The golden bowl is crushed."

Then—the ultimate: ". . . the pitcher by the well is shattered." Obviously, that signifies the heart. It's the tragic scene of heart failure. And the whole circulatory system becomes shattered as "the wheel at the cistern is crushed." Isn't that an eloquent way to put it? Eloquent or not, it's reality.

If the journal stopped right here, it would leave us with a very grim picture. If all we could look forward to in life were gray hairs and fewer teeth, then I'd call that a bleak future. But there is more, much more. There *is* something to smile about. What is it? Again, it is "remembering the Creator." That puts a smile on the face of the aging. When His perspective is inserted, it is like a ray of light hitting a prism and suddenly beautiful colors shine through. It's fabulous! It's amazing what He does with guilt and self-pity and feelings of uselessness and fear. His prism of color and beauty just dances all around life. And death? Why, all it does is open a new door.

Life ends as a majestic commencement into what existence is all about. Death simply allows us entrance. What I'm really saying is this: We are not ready to live until we are ready to die.

LIFE'S FINAL FACTOR

> Then the dust will return to the earth as it was, and the spirit will return to God who gave it (v. 7).

You will never read about this in *Time* or *Newsweek*. You won't read about it in tomorrow morning's newspaper or see this presented on the television news tonight, but take it from God, it will happen. You may live a bit longer, then you will die. After death, what? "The spirit *will* return to God who gave it." And if you are ready, you will see a smile like you've never seen in your earthly life. It will be on the face of your Savior. You'll hear Him say, "Come into My kingdom." And you'll hear sounds you never heard on earth, all because you turned your life over to God in your youth. You "acted decisively on His behalf." It's beautiful! Not even the aging process will cancel out His plan to make you into a new person, fitted for eternity.

But what if you don't? Read on: "Vanity of vanities . . . all is vanity!" Talk about disappointment and misery! At the end of life, all you'll have to claim is a feeling of futility. That reminds me of a little piece once written by one who spent too long at the fair.

> I wanted the music to play on forever—
>   Have I stayed too long at the fair?
> I wanted the clown to be constantly clever—
>   Have I stayed too long at the fair?
> I bought me blue ribbons to tie up my hair,
>   But I couldn't find anybody to care.
> The merry-go-round is beginning to slow now,
>   Have I stayed too long at the fair?
> I wanted to live in a carnival city, with
>   laughter and love everywhere.
> I wanted my friends to be thrilling and witty,
>   I wanted somebody to care.
> I found my blue ribbons all shiny and new,
>   But now I've discovered them no longer blue.
> The merry-go-round is beginning to taunt me—
>   Have I stayed too long at the fair?
> There is nothing to win and no one to want me—
>   Have I stayed too long at the fair?[4]

Yes. "Yes!" is the answer. I've met many a person who did that. I've even buried a few folks who "stayed too long at the fair." And I know of nothing more empty, more tragic.

Life isn't simply a great big bowl of cherries, and don't let anyone try to convince you it is. Life is a challenge. Life is tough. And only the power of Jesus Christ can give you the resiliency to handle it. Life is sickness and terminal illness. Life is brokenness—broken hearts, broken marriages, broken relationships. Life is not enough food and not enough hope. Life is discouragement and depression, times of bewilderment and uncertainty. Life is deterioration, disappointment, and ragged-edge reality. I honestly cannot imagine how anyone copes with that ragged edge apart from a relationship with Jesus Christ.

PRACTICAL ADVICE BETWEEN THE LINES

You know what's woven between the lines of Solomon's comments? Three very practical and useful statements.

First: *I must face the fact that I'm not getting any younger.* It's foolish to dress up like a high school cheerleader if I'm sixty-five or seventy. Varicose veins don't go well with saddle oxfords and mini-skirts. No, aging is a reality of life. People who try to dodge or deny the fact that they are getting older are kidding themselves.

Second: *God has designed me to be empty without Him.* God has designed you and me to experience a vacuum without Him. Like those familiar words from Augustine: "Thou hast made us for Thyself and our heart is restless till it rests in Thee." He planned us to be restless without Him. All the way through this journal we have been reminded that God has made life boring on purpose. Why? So that we would discover that beauty and color and the songs of joy come only from following His directives, not from human counsel. God made us to be empty without Him.

Third: *Now is the time to prepare for eternity.* Preparing for retirement is commendable. In fact, these days it's quite wise. But have you prepared for life beyond retirement? That's more than wise— that's essential. If you have, you can smile at whatever life throws at you. You have the hope of looking into the Savior's face and hearing Him say, "Welcome home!"

I love the story Charles Allen tells of a little boy named John Todd, born in 1800 up in Rutland, Vermont. Shortly after John's birth, the Todd family moved to the little village of Killingsworth. And by the time little John was six both of his parents had died. I'll let Dr. Allen tell the rest of the story.

> The children in the home had to be parceled out among the relatives, and a kindhearted aunt who lived in North Killingsworth agreed to take John and give him a home. With her he lived until some fifteen years later when he went away to study for the ministry. When he was in middle life, his aunt fell desperately ill and realized that death could not be far off. In great distress she wrote her nephew a pitiful letter—what would death be like? Would it mean the end of everything or would there be, beyond death, a chance to continue living, growing, loving? Here is the letter John Todd sent in reply:
>
> "It is now thirty-five years since I, a little boy of six, was left quite alone in the world. You sent me word you would give me a home and be a kind mother to me. I have never forgotten the day when I made the long journey of ten miles to your house in North Killingsworth. I can still recall my disappointment when, instead of coming for me yourself, you sent your colored man, Caesar, to fetch me. I well

remember my tears and my anxiety as, perched high on your horse and clinging tight to Caesar, I rode off to my new home. Night fell before we finished the journey and as it grew dark, I became lonely and afraid.

" 'Do you think she'll go to bed before I get there?' I asked Caesar anxiously. 'Oh no,' he said reassuringly. 'She'll sure stay up for you. When we get out of these here woods you'll see her candle shining in the window.' Presently we did ride out in the clearing and there, sure enough, was your candle. I remember you were waiting at the door, that you put your arms close about me and that you lifted me—a tired and bewildered little boy—down from the horse. You had a big fire burning on the hearth, a hot supper waiting for me on the stove. After supper, you took me to my new room, you heard me say my prayers and then you sat beside me until I fell asleep.

"You probably realize why I am recalling all this to your memory. Some day soon, God will send for you, to take you to a new home. Don't fear the summons—the strange journey—or the dark messenger of death. God can be trusted to do as much for you as you were kind enough to do for me so many years ago. At the end of the road you will find love and a welcome waiting, and you will be safe in God's care. I shall watch you and pray for you until you are out of sight, and then wait for the day when I shall make the journey myself and find you waiting at the end of the road to greet me."[5]

In other words, John Todd was saying, "Don't worry, Auntie, you are expected. I know for sure, because I saw God standing in your doorway a long, long time ago."

Likewise you and I do not have a thing to fear simply because we are growing older. If our faith is firmly fixed in the Savior, we can count on Him to be waiting at the end of the road to greet us. In fact, He'll be waiting up for us. Our room is all ready. The light is on. We are expected. He will welcome us home.

24

WRAPPING UP A
RAGGED-EDGE JOURNEY

Journal Entry

But then, because the Preacher was wise,
he went on teaching the people all he
knew; and he collected proverbs and
classified them. For the Preacher was not
only a wise man, but a good teacher; he
not only taught what he knew to the
people, but taught them in an interesting
manner. The wise man's words are like
goads that spur to action. They nail down
important truths. Students are wise who
master what their teachers tell them.

But, my son, he warned: there is no
end of opinions ready to be expressed.
Studying them can go on forever, and
become very exhausting!

Here is my final conclusion: fear
God and obey his commandments, for
this is the entire duty of man. For God
will judge us for everything we do, including
every hidden thing, good or bad.

*W*hen some people struggle with life's mysteries, few seem to care; but when others struggle, shock waves are felt halfway around the world. We are not too surprised, for example, to find a philosopher wrestling with life's complexities. The same applies to a scientist who ends most of his sentences with question marks rather than exclamation points. Neither does it surprise us when a brilliant physician or an attorney with an independent spirit struggles with disbelief or questions those things that have been traditional values throughout life. Their profession allows room for a lot of philosophical "wobble."

It seems as though it is okay for science and cynicism to walk hand in hand. Intellectualism and pessimism fit together. Doctoral dissertations aren't supposed to answer all the questions. They're supposed to ask them and leave fellow intellectuals to struggle with the issues on their own.

Those who land with both feet on hard-and-fast answers in life are criticized for committing intellectual suicide. It makes things appear too simplistic, we're told. It's sophisticated to speak of how complex issues really are. The brighter the student, the more he or she is supposed to frown and question rather than smile and rest easy. Those who make their living as instructors or professors in institutions of higher learning are paid to think, to resist the standard answers. And for them few truths remain sacred.

This was brought home to me recently when I realized that some long-time professors can virtually get away with murder in their ivy-covered halls of learning, even if they question the very textbooks from which they teach. All this reminds me of the true account told by an orthopedic surgeon in Miami who mentioned the experience one of his colleagues had in medical school. The young medical student went up to the teacher following the lecture and said, "I have been reading my text and I have been listening to your class lectures. There are various points at which your lectures disagree with the textbook assigned for the class." To which the professor replied, "Really? Bring me your book and show me where there is disagreement."

When the student did that, pointing here and there to several contradictions, the professor calmly yet deliberately ripped the pages from the book, wadded them up, and tossed them aside saying, "There . . . *now* it agrees with me."

Granted, that may be unusual. And it is certainly unorthodox! But

I doubt that many students would fail to show up for class the next day just because the teacher ripped the pages out of the text. Professors, like philosophers and scientists, are expected to probe and to question. They're paid to be cynical and humanistic, fatalistic and pessimistic.

But not preachers. When a preacher rebels, there's a scandal in the parsonage. When a minister questions the text, churches split. It can even make the headlines. It's news when a well-known preacher questions the things he once embraced. If he tears a page from his text, all of heaven rumbles above him.

There is an unwritten yet renowned law regarding ministers which says, "Thou shalt not doubt, struggle, or rebel. And if thou dost, thou art dust." It comes with the territory. And therein lies the mystery of Solomon's journey and journal. That is why we have the toughest time accepting and interpreting his words with any sense of calm resolve.

This isn't a philosopher meandering through a mental jungle of doubts. He is not some wild-eyed scientist or unbelieving, cynical physician. This is a preacher. Some have suggested that the book of Ecclesiastes is indeed the most notorious "testimony" that's ever been written. The man of the cloth has the audacity to declare, "It's all empty. Life isn't worth living! There's nothing to it."

However, when we probe into the life of the writer, we see that this is no ancient Elmer Gantry. We haven't been reading the words of an eighth century B.C. Bishop Pike kicking over the traces. This is Solomon who learned his theology at his father's knee. This is the greater-than-David man of wisdom. This is the distinguished speaker of the house, the soft-spoken diplomat, the personification of international peace—Israel's monarch *par excellence.* No wonder fire and smoke keep curling off the pages of his journal! The man's been a stalwart of the faith, but no longer. He's now soft on immorality and cynical of orthodox theology. How dare a man of his stature and heritage record a public documentation of his notorious drift!

I don't think it would have attracted anywhere near the same press if Solomon had been some philosopher of that era. But because he was a preacher (by his own admission) people were shocked, especially since he wrote his doubts for all to read. Ministers learn how and with whom to share their doubts. There are not many who can handle it when clergymen dump a few of their struggles on them.

I was going through a low-tide time in my life back in 1971 when my mother died. Nine years later, as my dad was dying, I again struggled with several issues. It seemed appropriate that I preach at both of their funerals—which added pain to an already broken heart. Even though I did my best to preach as well as I could at my father's memorial service, I was struggling rather fiercely within.

My sister Luci was there, of course, for both those occasions. Luci knows me probably as well as anyone aside from my own wife and children, so she had the freedom to ask me a few rather probing questions. "Do you believe all those things you said today? Is everything *that* fastened down?" I answered, "Uh, no, in all honesty, I can't say that I haven't been wrestling with a few doubts recently. Some things aren't all that clear to me." I'm pleased to say that she never told on me. She's told on me about other things, when we were kids, but she didn't tell on me about that one. She calmly allowed me to go through that period of doubting. There have been times of doubt since then, and they will probably come again.

For me, that could be scandalous. I'm suppose to believe everything that I say. And what makes it even harder, I'm supposed to *live* it—neither of which is true 100 percent of the time. I wish it were, but it's not. But unlike Solomon, I haven't made a public announcement of all my struggles. Through his journal, he's kept nothing from us.

The Preacher: His Theme and His Thesis

Without hesitation, Solomon has told it all. What he has lacked in pristine morality he has made up for in absolute honesty. Some may criticize his theology and lifestyle, but we have to admire his vulnerability. All the way through this book, I've referred to his work as a journal, but if we view the writer as a preacher in this final chapter, perhaps we should consider this entry more like a sermon. And since a sermon has a theme, we need to remind ourselves of his. He has stated it over and over again.

Can you remember it? After telling us that his are "the words of the preacher" (Eccles. 1:1), he states his theme: "Vanity of vanities! All is vanity" (v. 2). In other words, "Life is an empty study in futility."

I did a careful study in the Hebrew text and found that the term *vanity* appears in his sermon no less than thirty times. In all but two of the chapters he reiterates his thesis. It's the same monotonous theme repeated so often that we grow weary of reading it.

Following his shocking introduction, for example, Solomon rephrases his thesis in the form of a question:

> What advantage does man have in all his work which he does under the sun? (1:3).

It's as though he were saying, "I have begun to question everything—all the things I was taught by my father, all the things I was taught by my mother, and all the other things I picked up through my Jewish roots—and I have begun to search for answers. In doing so, I have found more questions and fewer answers, and I wonder if there's anything at all to life."

Solomon includes in his journal a *Playboy* lifestyle, a philosophical lifestyle—the life of a rebel, a skeptic, and a cynic. That's why it is so shocking when people realize that a preacher wrote this book.

Robert Short is correct:

> The author of the book of Job was a consummate dramatist. The psalmist was a lyrical poet. The author of Jonah knew how to tell a fascinating short story. The author of Genesis and Exodus was a historical novelist who could recount powerful sagas of epic proportions. But Ecclesiastes? Ah . . . the preacher was also no mean poet, but fundamentally he was an artist of another sort. He was a photographer.[1]

The word *photograph* literally means "written with light." Think of Solomon as having a camera hung around his neck throughout his desperate journey. And with this imaginary camera he takes snapshots of life—mainly in the dark shadows of the valley. Click—there is death in all of its ugly, colorless reality. Click—more shots of cynicism, doubt, despair, gloom, depression. Click, click—the endlessness of work and the futility of investments. He reveals it all as he takes one snapshot after another. None of them is in color. All of them are in stark black and white. The sun gives him the natural light he needs, his pen provides the film, developed in the darkroom of humanistic philosophies. And once he has developed and framed his prints, he affixes the same statement to each frame: "Emptiness, emptiness, emptiness. It's *all* empty." It's a grievous assignment this thing called "life." And Solomon spends one chapter after another telling us about it. He wrote it like a journal, but perhaps it is more like a sermon.

The sermon of Solomon begins with the words "Vanity of vanities!" And it ends with similar words. Good sermons are like taking a round trip in an airplane. You take off well and you land smoothly. It's exhilarating to take off, but it's a great relief to come back home, having the trip behind you. The same runway begins and ends the journey. In this case, the airstrip is named Vanity. Interestingly, in the closing section Solomon gives kind of a wrap-up of his journal and reveals some autobiographical information that we don't find anywhere else.

Looking at the structure of his closing comments, we find that they fall neatly into two sections. The first section is personal as Solomon writes mainly about himself. The second section is practical as he writes about God. The former section is horizontal; the latter, vertical.

A Closing Confession of Solomon

" 'Vanity of vanities,' says the Preacher, 'all is vanity!' " In brief, the man is confessing that his lengthy and soul-searching pursuits have come to an end. It means that he has not found any of his under-the-sun discoveries to be satisfying. Only the truth wins out. Winston Churchill, referring to our tendency toward independence, once said: "Man will occasionally stumble over the truth, but most of the time he will pick himself up and continue on." Solomon has done that. Again and again, with wearisome regularity, he has stumbled over the truth. Yet in his preoccupation, he has confessed to the emptiness of it all. "Vanity of vanities . . . nothing but vanity!"

E. Stanley Jones tells of a cruise he was on and of watching a rather corpulent couple who lived from one meal to the next. They were retired on plenty—and nothing. He writes:

> They were angry with the table stewards for not giving them super-service. They seemed to be afraid they might starve between courses. Their physical appetites seemed the one thing that mattered to them. I never saw them reading a book or paper. They sat between meals and stared out, apparently waiting for the next meal. One night I saw them sitting thus and staring blankly, when a bright idea flashed

across the dull brain of the man. He went to the mantelpiece and picked up the vases, and looked into them, and then returned to his wife with the news: "They're empty!" I came very near laughing. He was right: "They're empty!" But it wasn't merely the vases! The souls and brains of both of them were empty. They had much in their purses, but nothing in their persons; and that was their punishment. They had security with boredom—no adventure. They had expanding girths and narrowing horizons.[2]

Like so many Americans with similar girths and horizons, the miserable pair was living from one meal to the next, from one experience to the next, finally uttering in the dark despair of a Saturday night after the fact, "It's all empty." I am convinced that it is this emphasis that makes Solomon's book so relevant. We hardly need anyone to make many comments for clarification. Life without the Lord is a pathetic, hollow drag. If we expect to find happiness in life, we must get *above* the sun. And that is precisely what Solomon does as he turns the final page of his journal. Unless we connect with the living God through faith in Jesus Christ, life is reduced to an empty existence.

Solomon, having repeated his theme yet again, now moves into a brief autobiographical section which is quite personal. In this unusual section, the preacher analyzes his craft. It is a rare body of information of special interest to anyone whose responsibilities include the communication of God's truth. Candidly, I have often based my pulpit style on these very words. I have also used this section from Solomon's journal as my text when speaking to fellow ministers on the subject of preaching.

> In addition to being a wise man, the Preacher also taught the people knowledge; and he pondered, searched out and arranged many proverbs. The Preacher sought to find delightful words and to write words of truth correctly (vv. 9–10).

Solomon's opening remark should never be forgotten: the preacher, first and foremost, is to be a wise man. His primary task is to teach the people knowledge. In doing so he is to do certain things—"ponder," "search out," and "arrange." When he mentions *"ponder,"* he uses the term that means he weighs the words carefully. He sifts through their implications. (The root term means "to sift.") He feels them. He compares them. He debates with himself over them. He wrestles and sweats over them.

John R. W. Stott has referred to this as worrying over and wrestling with the biblical text as a dog would wrestle with a bone. Great word picture! Have you ever watched a dog with a bone? They'll get every little bit of the gristle down in the knuckles of the bones. As dogs worry over a bone, so it is with a good preacher. He works on words. His craft is words. He searches diligently. He tries to find just the right terms. I am often haunted by the words of one of my mentors who warned his students against "the slimy ooze of indefiniteness." Generalities lack a solid punch. They put people to sleep. Good communicators find just the right words, which requires a careful search. And such research is often exhausting.

It is not so crucial if the communicator stays on the road, traveling from group to group, from congregation to congregation. A person like that needs only a dozen or so talks and then can preach them all over the country. But when one sticks with the same congregation year in and year out, that's a whole different issue. The fun-and-games "cutesy" stuff won't cut it. They have heard all his stories and can tell when the material is fresh. They want to be nourished with solid meat. That requires pondering, searching out, and arranging the material.

Solomon suggests that in his search for truth, he attempted to find just the right words. And did he ever! "A time to be born, and a time to die. A time to mourn, and a time to dance." Who will ever forget those words?

If you could read the way Solomon originally wrote about pursuing the right words, you would find he expressed each one of these Hebrew terms in a stem that intensifies each one. We would say they are underscored, as he emphasizes each one. He says that the preacher pondered *diligently* and searched *deeply*. He arranged *carefully*. That's the idea.

If you hear good sermons from your minister week after week, it isn't because he's creatively shooting from the hip. Count on it, it is because he's doing his homework. More specifically, hard work is taking place in his study: searching, digging, meditating, reading, arranging thoughts, thinking it through, getting at it, refusing to surrender to sloth. In a word, diligence.

Why go to all that trouble? Solomon says the reason is that the preacher is seeking to find delightful words. The term *delightful* means "winsome, easy to grasp, readily applied." I don't know why, but when many hear someone who is confusing, they think he is deep.

(Since when is complexity and lack of clarity profound?) On the other hand, when some hear a person who is practical, they tend to think of him as simplistic and shallow.

Sometimes the most profound communicators are those who can make the complex simple. Ask the advertisers who are responsible for the commercials that display a complicated product. They use gifted communicators who simplify the complicated. These creative communicators and techniques cause something complicated to seem like a piece of cake. Now *that* is profound—profound simplicity. Wise Solomon says, in effect, "I searched for words that would win a hearing, terms that clarify and grab the reader's attention. I wanted those words I chose to rivet themselves into a mind that is cluttered with a lot of other things, so that my journal wouldn't just pass by unnoticed." He certainly succeeded.

Bible scholar J. B. Phillips once said:

> If words are to enter men's hearts and bear fruit, they must be the right words shaped cunningly to pass men's defenses and explode silently and effectually within their minds.

You ask, "Why should those who communicate the truth worry over that?" Well, let's ask that of your attorney. Why does he worry over just the right words he wants to use in a courtroom? The answer is obvious. If an attorney is successful, he or she is a student of terms and timing, worrying very carefully over each word—as only an attorney can worry—each term, each implication, each subtle innuendo. Preachers can learn a lot by observing such masters of their craft. Whether it's a jury or a congregation, words are vehicles that carry the freight. They are exceedingly significant.

George Butterick has said, "If only the preacher would remember that dullness is failure. . . ." I don't know of a worse sin to commit in public than being boring. Nothing magical happens, because a Bible separates a speaker from an audience. If a speaker is dull without a Bible, he or she will be dull *with* a Bible. I could not be in greater agreement with Philip Yancey's convictions regarding the need for creativity as it relates to writing:

> . . . we Christian authors must confess to having bored plenty of people. So far the evangelical reading public has been tolerant, buying millions of books of uneven quality each year. But a saturation point

is inevitable. If Christian writing is not only to maintain interest in the forgiving Christian audience, but also to arouse interest in the skeptical world beyond the Christian subculture, then it must grow up.

If we need models of how to do it well, we need only look as far as the Bible. Only ten percent of the Bible's material, the epistles, is presented in a thought-organized format. The rest contains rollicking love stories, drama, history, poetry, and parables. There, humanity is presented as realistically as in any literature.

Why else do the paired books of Samuel, Kings, and Chronicles exist, if not to give a detailed context to the environment in which angry prophets were to deliver their messages? Can we imagine a more skillful weaving of nature and supernature than the great nature psalms, the theological high drama of Job, and the homespun parables of Jesus? What literary characters demonstrate a more subtle mixture of good and evil than David, or Jeremiah, or Jacob? And, from the despair of Ecclesiastes to the conversion narratives of Acts, is any wavelength on the spectrum of faith and doubt left unexpressed on the Bible's pages?

C. S. Lewis once likened his role as a Christian writer to an adjective humbly striving to point others to the Noun of truth. For people to believe that Noun, we Christian writers must improve our adjectives.[3]

Sir Francis Bacon said, "Reading maketh a full man; speaking a ready man, writing an exact man." What an exacting craft is writing! It requires thinking through exactly what one wants to say, then selecting exactly the right way it should be said. Those who are most successful on their feet are usually the ones who have disciplined themselves with pen and paper.

I think Solomon quite probably traveled with a note pad. In that way he could invest the time necessary to put color into his journal—the inimitable style that is altogether his. Obviously, Solomon took the time to shape and arrange his thoughts into a precise fashion. That is why the things he writes stick with us!

See how he puts it? "Words are like goads. . . ." Now, it's probable that some of you have never seen a goad. I hadn't seen a goad until I traveled overseas and witnessed goads being used by Oriental farmers. I watched these men in their rice fields prodding heavy, powerful oxen along with this long stake that had an iron point—jabbing it against the hind quarters of that tough-skinned beast, saying words in Japanese that probably were best kept in Japanese. The farmer pushed this creature along with a goad. It's something that prods into action or increases speed. Words are like that. And you don't just "share your heart" when you communicate. Solomon didn't gush out a lot of afterthoughts from the top of his head. No! He framed his words so that when they reached the recipient's brain—BOOM!—they exploded. And they captured the attention of the rebel, the wanderer, the intellectual, those with small minds along with the eggheads. All of us who have read this journal felt the "goad" pushing at us.

Solomon's style and word pictures penetrate the fog of preoccupation. They awaken us to the significance of his message.

Skeptic David Hume was seen walking in the snow long before daybreak one frigid morning. He, along with many others, was making his way to a little chapel where George Whitefield was preaching. Someone who knew the skeptic said to him, "Mr. Hume, I didn't know you believed this message!" He responded, "I don't, but that man in the chapel does, and I can't stay away." There's something about words that goad even the skeptic. He can't silence the words because they are prodding at him, pushing at him, exploding silently in his mind.

Solomon doesn't stop with "goads." He goes on to say they are like "well-driven nails." I love that. His descriptive words have reference to a tent stake. It's the idea of a sharpened spike. And if you have ever put up a tent, especially if you have ever attempted to do it in a wind storm, you hardly need this explained. A well-driven stake keeps the tent in place. It secures it to the ground.

Many years ago my family and I spent several nights in a campground. One particular evening the velocity of the wind increased and a great deal of rain fell. The next morning brought quite a sight. We were surrounded by four or five tents that had washed onto our site. The stakes had been yanked up and the wind just billowed them right on over to our area. We happened to have been sleeping in a little tent camper up off the ground, so we didn't go anywhere. But those that weren't secured into place were at the mercy of the elements.

Words are like tent spikes, riveting thoughts into the mind. When we're all alone, for example, when there is nobody around and we turn off the light and let our head sink into the pillow, there are certain words that haunt us. They keep us awake. "The Word of God is alive and active, sharper than a two-edged sword." God's Word slices us up and down, penetrating right to the nucleus of our lives. And we are unveiled before the God of heaven. Naked and exposed, we are forced to come to terms with reality. *His* words are like that. You see the way this reads? These "goads," these "well-driven nails" are "given by one Shepherd."

Now, there are other words that aren't. And that's the reason he closes with words addressed to his son. Solomon has held off counseling his son until now. And what he says will make every student in school today sigh with agreement. Even faculty members have been known to say "Amen" after reading this next statement:

> But beyond this, my son, be warned: the writing of many books is endless, and excessive devotion to books is wearying to the body (12:12).

One of these days I'm going to work up the courage to bring that as a commencement address, when I'm asked to speak to a graduating body of seniors. Sheer exhaustion is reflected on their faces. Faculties tell me that April and May are the hardest months of the year in which to teach. All the pizzazz is over. The excitement of a sports program has petered out. All of the delight of new life on campus has waned. The balloons and banners are no longer flying. Now it's "depression city" and students and faculty alike try their best just to make it to the end of the year. Solomon has a splendid description for such a scene: "excessive devotion to books." It's not only true on a school campus, by the way, it's equally true in life. Alvin Tofler in *The Third Wave* states:

> The computer-operated microprinters available today on our planet can turn out 20,000 lines of verbiage every minute—which is 200 times faster than anyone on earth can read.[4]

I find that downright hilarious. Why in the world do we need equipment that turns out printed material two hundred times faster than anyone can read it? It sounds like the copying machine near my office. I don't know this for sure, but I wonder if there are little imps inside the machine that keep saying, "Print this. Print that. Send copies to everybody. Print this. Print that. Make four copies of each!" We get stacks of paper! Have you ever noticed that where you work?

I've got a simple plan: Just throw them all away and chances are good you'll never miss a thing. We are in a day of information, paper, copy, words, books—more than we can ever read (that's why he says what he does) and most of which will not do a thing for us eternally. Yet we keep punching out words. It is indeed "wearying to the body."

If you bought and read every book published just in the United States in 1982, you would have had to read 125 books a day, spending by the end of the year $1,057,658, and you would have had to add to your library 45,704 volumes. When you stop and think about it, you'll realize that's an old statistic. By the time this book is published, who knows how many *more* thousands could be added?

LET'S CONSIDER THE CONCLUSION

The thing I love about Solomon's conclusion is there isn't a ruffle of drums, a loud blast of the horns, and screaming clarinets with a crescendo of passionate emotion. There's just a simple statement. And Solomon doesn't try to be fancy about it either. When the conclusion has been heard, when it's all been said, it literally reads, "Fear God and keep His commandments, because this applies to every person." Isn't that great? I love the anti-climactic ending to this incredible journal. We've been with him through every conceivable emotion, but now he finishes the entire work by saying that there are two things we need to pay attention to—two "musts." First, we must *take God seriously.* Hold Him in highest regard. Respect and revere Him. Second, we must *do what He says.* Obey Him. You'd think Solomon slammed his journal shut and said, "Now, I'm going fishing. Got it done. Got it said." But that's not all. He knows his readers would ask why. Why should I revere God? Why should I obey His truth? His last statement explains his reason.

> Because God will bring every act to judgment, everything which is hidden, whether it is good or evil (v. 14).

You may say, "I don't believe that." To be just as candid with you, let me respond by answering, "I don't care!" In the final analysis, what's more important—what you prefer to believe or what God actually says? This is what God says and He's never once lied to mankind. If He says that He will bring every act to judgment (even though I don't know how He will do it), I know He will. I don't know His method and frankly, that doesn't bother me. What ought to bother us is that He will do it! We're so technically oriented that we want to know the process before we'll believe the fact.

Somehow in God's own timing and in God's own way, He will cause there to be a replay of our lives. In the final analysis, we'll do business with Him. Count on it. It makes a lot of sense to me that the One who made us has every right to hold us accountable. And the idea of bringing "every act to judgment," even the things we might consider "hidden," doesn't seem at all preposterous.

Dr. Wilbur Penfield, director of the Montreal Neurological Institute, said in a report to the Smithsonian Institute:

> Your brain contains a permanent record of your past that is like a single continuous strip of moving film, complete with sound track. The film library records your whole waking life from childhood on. You can live again those scenes from your past, one at a time, when a surgeon places a gentle electrical current and applies it to a certain point on the temporal cortex of your brain. As you relive the scenes from your past, you feel exactly the same emotions you did during the original experience.

Think of that! Could it be that the human race will be confronted with this irrefutable record at the judgment of God? Indeed!

Why does Solomon close with that? Because we cannot live the life of an irresponsible playboy and get away with it. We aren't free to run wild and wink in God's direction, thinking that, no matter what, the big Teddy Bear in the sky will yawn, pat us on the head, and say, "Everything is going to be just fine." No, it doesn't work like that. Our ragged-edge journey is headed for a sudden stop. And all alone, standing face to face with God in that epochal moment, we will give an account of the life we have lived. Sobering, serious thought!

Do you want to know how to handle your life in light of such a day of reckoning? Would you like to know the secret? The password? I'll give it to you in one word—Christ. He alone is the way, the truth, the life. Without "the way," there is no going. Without "the truth," there is no knowing. Without "the life," there is no living.

Remember Him in your youth, before the evil days come and you are forced to say, "I have no pleasure in all those memories." Remember Him now. If you are young with most of your life stretching out before you, remember Him, believe in Him. Act decisively on His behalf. Even if you're not young, remember Him. Jesus Christ—the One who will give you life, and life more abundant, is available. He is the only One who has the ability to wash away your sins and give you a whole new perspective. This conclusion to Solomon's journal can be your introduction to joy and forgiveness, hope and peace.

Christ graciously waits for you to come to Him today. Be like the honest young woman who said to me as I completed teaching this book, "When I saw the whole thing, Chuck, I realized it's time to remember my Creator, to believe in Him now. He is ultimate reality." Come to terms with reality, my friend. Only through Him can you and I ever hope to endure life's ragged edge.

Allow me to pray, please.

Solomon's journal has actually been straight talk from You, dear Father. Through each page we have been living on the ragged edge, seeing life as it really is. There haven't been many dreams and fantasies—no pillow talk. This has been tough stuff. Thank You for the diligence we've been able to apply as we have given our concentrated attention to Solomon's journey—which has really been our journey. Thank You for telling us the truth. Thank You especially for moving us out of "carnival city" and the stupidity of a life lived for oneself, to the real world of faith and purity and authentic godliness.

We believe in You. We believe in Your Son. We believe in Your Word. And today, as if for the first time in our lives, we place ourselves in Your care and at Your disposal. May this day mark the beginning of a new lifestyle, one that is committed to obeying the truth—nothing more, nothing less, nothing else.

In the strong name of Jesus our Lord, Amen.

CONCLUSION

Many of us are old enough to remember the first line of the lyrics to a piece of music made popular during the big-band era: "The song has ended, but the melody lingers on." It comes to my mind as we bid farewell to Solomon, turning the final page in his journal. His story has ended, but the message certainly lingers on. Does it ever!

With Israel's ancient monarch as our guide, we have journeyed the extremities of experience and we have plumbed the depths of despair. Nothing has been restrained. The man has recorded his escapades, admitted his doubts, attempted to find fulfillment in various philosophies, and stopped at nothing to gain some sense of satisfaction—all to no avail. Lasting pleasure eluded him. Not until he returned to square one, coming to terms with reality, did he derive any measure of contentment.

In the final analysis he was forced to confess that there is no lasting happiness without a relationship with the living God. Trying to find purpose and meaning under the sun apart from Him is a tragic and depressing study in futility. Despair stalks the steps of those who deny this fact. But to those who accept it and respond to it, God brings joy, encouragement, and the one ingredient we want most, inner peace—authentic and lasting *shalom*. Interestingly, it is not until the end of the journey, after all the dust has settled, that Solomon returns to the most basic of all truths. That is often the case.

This reminds me of a conversation someone had with the late theologian Dr. Karl Barth. The aging scholar had just completed an enviable and extensive trip around the world. He had lectured among the learned, engaged in further research on several continents, preached in great cathedrals, and witnessed sights that defied description. There had been ample time to walk along the shorelines of several majestic oceans, to meditate in picturesque mountain scenes, to meet with numerous people of bright minds and impressive credentials. It had been the trip of a lifetime, a fitting climax to the man's own achievements and contributions. Upon returning to his homeland, he was asked to state the single most profound thought he had considered during his travels. With a faint smile, the old gentleman responded:

> Jesus loves me, this I know;
> For the Bible tells me so.

And so it was with Solomon. Having completed his global pursuit of peace, after living on the ragged edge of existence for who knows how long, the old king finally came full circle. He must have heaved a sigh of relief as he stated his crowning observation in the simplest of terms: "Remember your Creator in the days of your youth . . . fear Him . . . obey Him . . . because some day you will stand before Him."

I stated in my introduction that this is a volume for folks "in the trenches." Now you see why. I told you that it is for those whose lives are fixed on planet Earth, "down there in the dirt of responsibility, where the grit of reality and the grind of accountability hold their feet to the fire." Now you know what I meant.

The journey has been jungle warfare—head-to-head combat in the murky swamp of disillusionment, doubt, and depression. Rather than an easygoing outing up the lazy river, it's been one of those snakes-and-alligators survival trips that has allowed us no place to hide. Solomon's words, phrases, and conclusions have slashed deep gashes across our thin skin and punched holes in our easy answers as he has wrestled with issues we'd much rather skirt.

But that is life. And that brings a healthy and necessary kind of pressure upon us. It forces from us the decisions required to move us off the wastelands of empty clichés. It is only when we have learned how to survive in the harsh arena of reality that we change from mediocrity to greatness, from passive surrender to victorious excellence.

So thank you, Solomon, for recording the whole truth. Thank you for admitting the struggles and for not deceiving us into thinking that the lifelong journey from earth to heaven is merely a hot-air balloon ride full of ecstasy, free of friction, and protected from pain. Thank you for helping us come to terms with reality, for teaching us profound lessons in a simple, straightforward manner. Most of all, thank you for the quiet confidence that comes from knowing that "the Bible tells us so."

Your story has ended, but the message lingers on. May we never ever forget it.

NOTES

Chapter 1. Journal of a Desperate Journey

1. William Least Heat Moon, *Blue Highways: A Journey into America* (Boston: Little, Brown and Company, 1982), 5.
2. From *Straight Talk to Men and Their Wives* by Dr. James C. Dobson, copyright © 1980; used by permission of Word Books, Publisher, Waco, TX.

Chapter 2. Chasing the Wind

1. Excerpt from *Jesus Rediscovered* (p. 11) by Malcolm Muggeridge. Copyright © 1969 by Malcolm Muggeridge. Reprinted by permission of Doubleday & Co., Inc.
2. David Allan Hubbard, *Beyond Futility* (Grand Rapids, MI: William B. Eerdmans Publishing Company, 1976), 13–14. Used by permission.
3. Hugh Prather, *Notes to Myself* (New York: Bantam Books, Inc., 1976).
4. Richard Eder, a book review of *Lost in the Cosmos: The Last Self-Help Book* by Walker Percy, *Los Angeles Times*, 5 June 1983.

Chapter 3. Eat, Drink, . . . and Be *What?*

1. Billy Graham, *World Aflame* (Garden City, NY: Doubleday & Co., Inc., 1965), 25.
2. H. C. Leupold, *Exposition of Ecclesiastes* (Grand Rapids, MI: Baker Book House, 1952), 59.
3. Pitirim Sorokin, *The American Sex Revolution* (Boston: Porter Sargent Publisher, 1956), 17–19.
4. Leupold, *Exposition of Ecclesiastes*, 60.
5. Hubbard, *Beyond Futility*, 33–35.
6. E. A. Robinson, "Richard Cory" (1897).

Chapter 4. More Miles of Bad Road

1. Ralph Barton. Quoted by Denis Alexander in *Beyond Science* as published by Lion Publishing. Copyright 1972, p. 123.
2. Hubbard, *Beyond Futility*, 39–40.
3. *Los Angeles Times*, 10 June 1983. Copyright 1983, *Los Angeles Times*. Reprinted by permission.

4. Derek Kidner, *The Message of Ecclesiastes* (Downers Grove, IL: Inter-Varsity Press, 1976), 34. Formerly titled *A Time to Mourn and A Time to Dance.*

5. From *Newsweek* magazine, September 25, 1972. Copyright 1972, by Newsweek, Inc. All Rights Reserved. Reprinted by Permission.

6. Used by permission.

Chapter 5.   Do You Know What Time It Is?

1. Isaac Watts, "O God, Our Help."

2. William James, *Quote Unquote*, Lloyd Cory, ed. (Wheaton, IL: Victor Books, 1977), 181.

3. C. S. Lewis, *The Problem of Pain* (London: Collins Publishers, 1962), 93.

4. Malcolm Muggeridge, *A Twentieth Century Testimony* (Nashville: Thomas Nelson, Inc., Publishers, 1978), 18.

5. From *Spiritual Leadership* by J. Oswald Sanders, copyright © 1967, 1980, Moody Press. Moody Bible Institute of Chicago. Used by permission.

6. From "Sunrise, Sunset" (Jerry Bock, Sheldon Harnick). Copyright © 1964 Alley Music Corp. and Trio Music Co. Inc. All rights administered by Hudson Bay Music Inc. Used by permission. All rights reserved.

7. *Los Angeles Times*, 9 November 1984. Copyright 1983, *Los Angeles Times.* Reprinted by permission.

8. Reprinted by permission of *The Wall Street Journal*, © Dow Jones & Company, Inc., 1983. All Rights Reserved.

9. Ibid.

10. Ibid.

11. "In His Time," by Diane Ball, copyright © 1978 Maranatha! Music. As recorded by the Maranatha! Singers on *Praise 4.* All rights reserved. International copyright secured. Used by permission only.

12. From "God's Trombones," by James Weldon Johnson. Copyright 1927 by the Viking Press Inc. Copyright renewed 1955 by Grace Nail Johnson. Reprinted by permission of Viking Penguin Inc.

Chapter 7.   Confessions of a Cynic

1. Tom Sullivan, quoted in a speech given to the Million Dollar Round Table 1983 Annual Meeting.

2. Charles W. Colson, *Loving God* (Grand Rapids, MI: Zondervan Publishing House, 1983), 241–43.

Chapter 9.   One Plus One Equals Survival

1. Charles R. Swindoll, *Dropping Your Guard: The Value of Open Relationships* (Waco, TX: Word Books, 1983).

2. Dinah Maria Mulock Craik, "Friendship."

3. David W. Smith, *The Friendless American Male* (Ventura, CA: Regal Books, 1983), 96.

4. "Bridge over Troubled Waters." Copyright © 1969 Paul Simon. Used by permission.

Chapter 10. What Every Worshiper Should Remember

1. Thomas J. Peters and Robert H. Waterman, Jr., *In Search of Excellence* (New York: Harper & Row, Publishers, 1982), 13.

2. Anne Ortlund, *Up with Worship* (Ventura, CA: Regal Books, 1975).

3. Kidner, *The Message of Ecclesiastes*, 53.

4. John White, *The Fight: A Practical Handbook to Christian Living* (Downers Grove, IL: InterVarsity Press, 1978), 32.

5. Hubbard, *Beyond Futility*, 70–71.

Chapter 11. Straight Talk to the Money-Mad

1. G. Frederick Owen, *Abraham to Middle East Crisis* (Grand Rapids, MI: William B. Eerdmans Publishing Company, 1957), 56.

2. Kidner, *The Message of Ecclesiastes*, 54.

3. William McDonald, *Chasing the Wind*, Moody Press, copyright 1975, 47.

4. Reprinted by permission from *The Friendship Factor*, pages 20–21, by Alan Loy McGinnis, copyright Augsburg Publishing House.

Chapter 12. The Few Years of a Futile Life

1. Reprinted by permission of Schocken Books, Inc. from *When Bad Things Happen to Good People* by Harold S. Kushner. Copyright © 1981 by Harold S. Kushner.

2. Ibid., 148.

3. Ibid.

4. Robert Louis Stevenson, *Virginibus Puerisque, III: An Apology for Idlers*.

5. From *Blessed Is the Ordinary* by Gerhard E. Frost. Copyright © 1980 Gerhard E. Frost. Published by Winston Press, 430 Oak Grove, Minneapolis, MN 55403. All rights reserved. Used with permission.

6. Lewis, *The Problem of Pain*.

Chapter 13. Wise Words for Busy People

1. From *Witness to Power* by John D. Ehrlichman. Copyright © 1982 by John D. Ehrlichman. Reprinted by permission of Simon & Schuster, Inc.

2. From "Sunrise, Sunset" (Jerry Bock, Sheldon Harnick). Copyright © 1964 Alley Music Corp. and Trio Music Co. Inc. All rights administered by Hudson Bay Music Inc. Used by permission. All rights reserved.

3. Lewis, *The Problem of Pain*, 40.

4. Ibid., 47–48.

5. Philip Yancey, *Where Is God When It Hurts?* (Grand Rapids, MI: Zondervan Publishing House, 1978), 179–83.

Chapter 14.   Putting Wisdom to Work

1. Sanders, *Spiritual Leadership,* 145–46.

2. Helmut Thielecke, *Encounter with Spurgeon* (Philadelphia: Fortress Press, 1963). Quoted by J. Oswald Sanders in *Spiritual Leadership,* p. 46.

3. *The Reaper,* July 1942, 96.

4. Ray C. Stedman, "Whoever Said Life Was Fair?" *Discovery Papers,* 31 October 1982 (Palo Alto, CA: Peninsula Bible Church Discovery Publishing, 1982), 3.

Chapter 15.   The Qualities of a Good Boss

1. Helmut Thielecke, *Encounter with Spurgeon,* 26.

2. Samuel P. Carey, *William Carey* (London: Carey Press, 1934, reprinted 1942), 256.

3. Clarence W. Hall. *Samuel Logan Brengle: A Portrait of a Prophet* (New York: Salvation Army, Inc., 1933), 275.

4. Colson, *Loving God,* 27–28.

Chapter 16.   Mysteries That Defy Explanation

1. A. W. Tozer, *The Knowledge of the Holy* (New York: Harper and Brothers Publishers, © 1961), 66.

2. Kushner, *When Bad Things Happen to Good People,* 6, 7, 26.

3. From *Tell Me Again, Lord, I Forget* by Ruth Harms Calkin. Published by Tyndale House Publishers, Inc., © 1974 by Ruth Harms Calkin. Used by permission.

4. *Five Smooth Stones for Pastoral Work* by Eugene H. Peterson. Copyright John Knox Press 1980. Used by permission.

5. Copyright 1971 by Manna Music, Inc., 2111 Kenmere Ave., Burbank, CA 91504. International copyright secured. All rights reserved. Used by permission.

Chapter 17.   Have a Blast While You Last!

1. "She's Got to Be a Saint" by Joe Paulini and Mike DiNapoli. Copyright © 1970 Galleon Music, Inc. International copyright secured. All rights reserved. Used by permission.

2. Walter Kaiser, *Ecclesiastes: Total Life* (Chicago: Moody Press, 1979), 99–100.

3. Used by permission. *When I Relax I Feel Guilty* by Tim Hansel. Copyright © 1979 David C. Cook Publishing Co., Elgin, IL 60120.

4. From the book *Wide My World, Narrow My Bed: Living and Loving*

the Single Life by Luci Swindoll, copyright 1982 by Multnomah Press, Portland, OR 97266. Used by permission.

Chapter 18. An Objective View of the Rat Race

1. Dr. William Kirk Kilpatrick, *Psychological Seduction* (Nashville: Thomas Nelson Publishers, 1983), 14–15.

Chapter 19. Be Sensible!

1. Anecdote retold from *What a Day This Can Be*, John Catoir, ed., Director of the Christophers (New York: The Christophers).

2. Kenneth O. Gangel, *Thus Spake Qoheleth* (Camp Hill, PA: Christian Publications, Inc., 1978), 129.

3. Taken from *The Pursuit of Excellence* by Ted W. Engstrom. Copyright © 1982 by The Zondervan Corporation. Used by permission.

Chapter 20. A Fool's Portrait

1. T. S. Eliot, "Burnt Norton" in *Four Quartets* (New York: Harcourt Brace Jovanovich).

2. Leupold, *Exposition of Ecclesiastes*, 246.

3. From *Love Must Be Tough* (p. 13) by Dr. James C. Dobson, copyright © 1983; used by permission of Word Books, Publisher, Waco, TX.

4. Kidner, *The Message of Ecclesiastes*, 93.

5. Dobson, *Love Must Be Tough*, 206.

Chapter 21. Be Bullish!

1. Hansel, *When I Relax I Feel Guilty*, 95.

2. Alex Haley, *Roots* (Garden City, NY: Doubleday & Co., Inc., 1976), 357.

3. From *The Complete Book of Running* by James F. Fixx, Copyright © 1977 Random House, Inc.

4. Hubbard, *Beyond Futility*, 109.

5. Gangel, *Thus Spake Qoheleth*, 138.

6. Kaiser, *Ecclesiastes: Total Life*, 114.

7. J. Oswald Sanders, *Robust in Faith* (Chicago: Moody Press, 1965), 87–88.

8. From *Klingsor's Last Summer* by Hermann Hesse. Copyright © 1970 by Farrar, Straus & Giroux, Inc. Reprinted by permission.

Chapter 22. Enjoying Life Now, Not Later

1. John Gardner, *Self-Renewal* (New York: W. W. Norton & Co., 1981). Quoted by Tim Hansel in *When I Relax I Feel Guilty*, 109.

2. Robert A. Raines, "Middle Agers Are Beautiful!" *Lord, Could You Make It a Little Better?* (Waco, TX: Word Books, Publishers, 1976). Used by permission.

3. Judith Viorst, *How Did I Get to Be 40 & Other Atrocities* (New York: Simon and Schuster, 1978), 45.

4. From *Good News: Thoughts on God and Man* by J. B. Phillips. Copyright © J. B. Phillips 1963. Used by permission of Macmillan Publishing Company and Collins Publishers.

Chapter 23.   Gray Hairs, Fewer Teeth, Yet a Big Smile

1. George Gallup, *America Wants to Know* (New York: A. & W. Publishers, 1983), 596.

2. Dobson, *Straight Talk to Men and Their Wives*, 182.

3. Kidner, *The Message of Ecclesiastes*, 100.

4. Billy Barnes, "I Stayed Too Long at the Fair." Copyright 1957, Tylerson Music Co. Used by permission.

5. Charles L. Allen, *You Are Never Alone* (Old Tappan, NJ: Fleming H. Revell Company, 1978), 77–78.

Chapter 24.   Wrapping Up a Ragged-Edge Journey

1. Robert L. Short, *A Time to Be Born, a Time to Die* (New York: Harper & Row, Publishers, 1973), 3.

2. E. Stanley Jones, *Growing Spiritually* (Nashville, TN: Abingdon, 1953), 4.

3. From "Pitfalls of Christian Writing" by Philip Yancey, *Open Windows*, copyright © 1982. Used by permission of Good News Publishers/Crossways Books, Westchester, IL 60153.

4. Alvin Tofler, *The Third Wave* (New York: Bantam Books, Inc., 1980).

LIVING
ABOVE THE
LEVEL OF
MEDIOCRITY

I know of no one who better models the
message of this book than my wife Cynthia
and those who work on her leadership
team at *Insight for Living*.

With admirable virtue, contagious
enthusiasm, and tireless effort,
each one represents an unconditional
commitment to excellence.

Because *mediocre* is not even a word in
their vocabulary, they have become
a pacesetting group of innovative
thinkers and creative leaders,
encouraging others to live above
the level of mediocrity.

It is with great delight that
I dedicate this volume to those
eagles who soar high . . .
and love every
minute of it.

CONTENTS

AIM SO HIGH
YOU'LL NEVER BE BORED!

The greatest waste of our natural resources is the number of people who never achieve their potential. Get out of that slow lane. Shift into that fast lane. If you think you can't, you won't. If you think you can, there's a good chance you will. Even making the effort will make you feel like a new person. Reputations are made by searching for things that can't be done and doing them. Aim low: boring. Aim high: soaring.

INTRODUCTION
WHO'S CALLING YOUR CADENCE?

... it is a wretched taste to be gratified with mediocrity when the excellent lies before us.

—Isaac D'Israeli, 1834

Soaring. That's what this book is about. Not grubbing for worms or scratching for bugs like a pen full of chickens, but soaring like a powerful eagle ... living above the level of mediocrity, refusing to let the majority shape your standard. Being different on purpose. Aiming high. Soaring isn't something that comes naturally, you understand, nor is it easy. But it can happen, believe me.

Thirty years ago I was a raw recruit in boot camp. Even back then the Marine Corps was "looking for a few good men," so I decided to give it my best shot. What a decision! I'm still a little amazed I lived to tell the story.

The strange world I stepped into was full of bewildering, shocking, and unpredictable activities. The schedule was busy and demanding, one designed to turn undisciplined young civilians into determined fighting men (an objective I heard repeated numerous times during those weeks of basic training). Time and again—especially when our enthusiasm began to flag—we were reminded that the difficulty of the training was *imperative*. Like it or not, we were soft. And in order for us to overcome the odds we were sure to face in battle, we must be prepared. The rigors of warfare would blow us away unless our minds and bodies were tough enough to withstand the demands made upon us.

Looking back, I realize that one of the reasons (no doubt, the major reason) my buddies and I survived was this: We learned to respect our "final voice of authority"—namely, the drill instructor. You will understand how I mean it when I say that for those weeks in boot camp . . . he was "God." Without question, we did precisely what he said to do. Without hesitation, we went precisely where he pointed. We jumped at his command. We marched to his cadence . . . no questions asked.

Matter of fact, we learned to distinguish his voice from the many others on the drill field. Hard as it may be for you to believe, we could follow his directions without difficulty on a field full of a dozen or more other DIs, each one barking out commands and verbal orders. It took time, but within a few weeks each company of young Marines knew the master's voice. When another shouted his instructions, we deliberately ignored the order. But when ours gave the order, we moved instantly. It took weeks to develop that kind of discipline; but finally, after endless hours of constant, painful repetition, it all fell into place.

Three decades have passed since those unforgettable days in boot camp. But some of the lessons learned back then are still with me—lessons like listening to the right voice, like ignoring the movements of the majority, and like being disciplined enough to filter the essential from the incidental. The ramifications of this kind of discipline have been life-changing. They include, for example, committing myself to excellence while many are comfortable with the mediocre, aiming high though most seem to prefer the boredom of aiming low, and marching to the distinct beat of another drummer while surrounded by a cacophony of persuasive sounds pleading for me to join their ranks. Remember Henry David Thoreau's immortal words?

> If a man does not keep pace with his companions, perhaps it is because he hears a different drummer. Let him step to the music which he hears, however, measured or far away.

One of Thoreau's contemporaries, James Russell Lowell, put it another way. He placed great value on aiming high:

> Life is a leaf of paper white
> Whereon each one of us may write
> His word or two, and then comes night.
>
> Greatly begin! though thou have time
> But for a line, be that sublime—
> Not failure, but low aim, is crime.

Long enough has mediocrity called our cadence! Long enough have we taken our cues from those who ask, "Why be different?" or reason, "Let's do just enough to get by." Long enough have we settled for less than our best and convinced ourselves that quality and integrity and authenticity are negotiables. Call me a dreamer, but I'm convinced that achieving one's full potential is still a goal worth striving for—that excellence is still worth pursuing even if most yawn and a few sneer. And, yes, even if I should fail occasionally while reaching. Failure, remember, is not the crime.

Somehow I feel I'm not alone. While there may not be millions out there who think like this, there are some. You are probably among them or you wouldn't have picked up this book in the first place. If I'm talking your language, then stay with me. There's a lot more to be said!

Before doing so, I must express my gratitude to Ernie Owen and Kip Jordan of Word Books. Their mutual encouragement has spurred me on! Beverly Phillips, my editor at Word, deserves high praise for her tireless efforts as she has assisted me through the painstaking process of making my thoughts more readable. I'm also grateful to Michael Standlee for his creative design of both book jacket and division pages. The splendid drawings of eagles throughout the book were done by Dennis Hill, who went far beyond the call of duty in both his careful research and vivid artistry. And, again, I am indebted to Helen Peters, my faithful and diligent secretary, whose own commitment to excellence has never once wavered. Were it not for her remarkable ability to interpret my handwritten sheets, I'm afraid these pages would represent the very thing I stand against—*mediocrity*. I am especially grateful for her assistance with my footnotes—the bane of any author who is not a perfectionist. I could name many others— mentors, friends, colleagues, and family members—whose words and lives have contributed immensely to this volume. I consider myself enriched to have been surrounded by such models of excellence.

And so, my fellow eagle, we're off! And by the time we have completed this flight, we shall be more committed than ever to a life of excellence. We'll be so encouraged that it's doubtful we can ever be satisfied living anywhere near the level of mediocrity again. But then why should we? That's where life gets dull, drab, predictable, and tiring. Or perhaps the most descriptive word is *boring*, a direct result of low aim. Let's lift our sights and aim so high that we start doing the thing God made us for: soaring.

Chuck Swindoll
Fullerton, California

Part One

Confronting Mediocrity Takes Thinking Clearly

*The mountains are fountains of
men as well as of rivers, of
glaciers, of fertile soil. The great
poets, philosophers, prophets, able
men whose thought and deeds have
moved the world, have come down
from the mountains—
mountain-dwellers who have
grown strong there with the forest
trees in Nature's workshops.*

John Muir
1938

1

IT STARTS
IN YOUR MIND

Soaring never just happens. It is the result of strong mental effort—thinking clearly, courageously, confidently. No one ever oozed his way out of mediocrity like a lazy slug. Everyone I know who models a high level of excellence has won the battle of the mind and taken the right thoughts captive. The risks notwithstanding, these individuals have chosen to fill the role of an active pen flowing with ink rather than a passive blotter that only sits and soaks up what others do; they've decided to get personally involved with life rather than sit back, frown, and watch life dwindle to a trickle and ultimately stagnate.

In 1947 San Francisco's Potrero Hill was not only a poor South City neighborhood, it was a real ghetto. That year was the year Oren was born. Rickets, a poverty-related disease actually caused by malnutrition, was Oren's major problem. His vitamin-mineral deficient diet caused his bones to soften. His legs began to bow under the weight of his growing body.

Even though the family was too poor to afford braces, Oren's mom refused to sit back, sigh, and resign herself to the inevitable. Being an eagle type, she rolled up her sleeves and took charge. She rigged up a homemade contraption in hopes of correcting her son's pigeon-toed, bowlegged condition. How? By reversing his shoes! Right shoe, left foot; left shoe, right foot; plus an improvised metal bar across the shoe tops to keep his feet pointing straight. It didn't work perfectly, but it was good enough to keep the boy on his feet and ultimately able to play with his buddies.

By the time he was about six years of age, his bones had hardened, his legs were still slightly bowed, his calves were unusually thin, and his head was disproportionately large. Nicknames from other kids followed him around: "Pencil-legs," "Waterhead"; but he refused to let all that hold him back. He compensated by acting tough. Street gangs on Potrero Hill were common: the Gladiators, Sheiks, Roman Gents, Persian Warriors. By age thirteen Oren had fought and won his way to being president of the Gladiators. For all the fighting, he was arrested only three times; that was the crowning achievement of his early youth.

What ultimately happened to Oren? How in the world does a kid with two malformed legs, an oversize head, a juvenile arrest record, and his whole identity connected with a ghetto, *ever* soar? Believe me, he did!

His legs are still a little bowed from the rickets. His head still seems a little large. He still remembers the embarrassment of being bailed out of the slammer at midnight by his mother . . . still recalls those cruel nicknames and each member of the infamous Gladiators. But Oren doesn't have to act tough anymore. He is tough, tough enough to be secure and gentle. Like his brave mother, he's learned to soar.

Those who don't know his background could easily think he got all the breaks. As they look at him today and see this fine and refined gentleman, they would assume he's always been wealthy. He lives in the exclusive Brentwood district of Los Angeles, drives a luxurious car, and has his elegant office (furnished against tones of brown and rust with wood and suede) in an elite bank building. He is now a busy executive with his own production company. He personally handles most of his own financial affairs and business negotiations. He has contracts with the media and various entertainment firms and agencies. In today's terms, Oren has it made. I wouldn't be surprised if he didn't have a statue of an eagle somewhere in his office. What a guy!

But don't think for a minute that he isn't thankful. His memory of the past only heightens his gratitude for all he now enjoys. The home in Brentwood. The many successful careers, including football. That plush office with his name on the door belongs to Orenthal James Simpson. Yes, none other than "the Juice," O. J. Simpson.

The world is full of folks, however, who would quickly give up. They sit back with folded arms, deep frowns, and skeptical stares. Their determination, unlike that of O. J.'s mom, is shortlived. Their favorite words are *"Why try? . . . Give up . . . We can't do that . . . Nobody ever does those things."* And they miss out on most of the action, to say nothing of all the fun! They've got the rules memorized, and their minds are closed to new and creative possibilities. Like rats in a sewer pipe, their whole focus is limited to a tight radius of don'ts, won'ts, can'ts, and quits.

But periodically we bump into a few refreshing souls, who have decided that they aren't going to live in the swamp of the status quo, or run scared of being different, even though others will always say, "It can't be done." Those who aim high are strong-willed eagle types who refuse to be bothered by the negativism and skepticism of the majority. They never even use the words "Let's just quit!" They are the same ones who believe that mediocrity must be confronted. And that confrontation must first take place in the *mind*—the seed plot of endless and limitless possibilities.

WE BECOME WHAT WE THINK

I'm sure it comes as no surprise to most of us that we act out precisely what we take in. In other words, we become what we think. Long before that familiar line found its way into Psychology 101 and hyped-up sales meetings, the Bible included it in one of its ancient scrolls; it just said it in a little different way: "For as he thinks within himself, so he is" (Prov. 23:7).

The secret of living a life of excellence is merely a matter of thinking thoughts of excellence. Really, it's a matter of programming our minds with the kind of information that will set us free. Free to be all God meant us to be. Free to soar! It will take awhile, and it may be painful—but what a metamorphosis!

Sid was an ugly caterpillar with orange eyes. He spent his life groveling and squirming in the dirt on God's earth. One day Sid got a terrific idea. He crawled up the stem of a bush, made his way to a branch, and secreted a translucent fluid onto that branch. He made a kind of button out of the fluid, turned himself around, and attached his posterior anatomy to that button. Then he shaped himself into a "J," curled up, and proceeded to build a house around himself. There was a lot of activity for a while, but before long Sid was entirely covered up and you couldn't see him anymore.

Everything became very, very still. You might have concluded that nothing at all was happening. But, as a matter of fact, plenty was happening. Metamorphosis was taking place.

One day Sid began to raise the window shades of his house. He let you look in and see a variety of colors. On another day an eruption took place. Sid's house shook violently. That little cocoon jerked and shook until a large, beautiful wing protruded from one of the windows. Sid stretched it out in all its glory. He continued his work until another gorgeous wing emerged from a window on the other side of the house.

At this stage of Sid's life you might have wanted to help. But you didn't, for if you tried to pull the rest of Sid's house off you would maim him for the rest of his life. So you let Sid convulse and wriggle his way to freedom without any outside intervention.

Eventually Sid got his house off his back, ventured out onto the branch, stretched, and spread his beautiful wings. He was nothing like the old worm he used to be. And do you know what? Sid didn't crawl back down the bush and start groveling and squirming in the dirt again. No indeed! Instead, he took off with a new kind of power—flight power. Now, instead of swallowing dust, Sid flies from flower to flower, enjoying the sweet nectar in God's wonderful creation.[1]

Perhaps you read those words with a sigh: "Well, that may be the way it is for a caterpillar named Sid, but somehow I just don't qualify; flight power *sounds* stimulating, but I'm made for mediocrity, swallowing dust not sniffing flowers."

Hogwash! With that kind of attitude, you've managed to think your way *out* of the very things you long to enjoy. You have become what you've been thinking. No wonder your metamorphosis is on hold!

THE MIND: TARGET OF THE ENEMY

Let me get to the heart of the issue. Since the mind holds the secrets of soaring, the enemy of our souls has made the human mind the bull's-eye of his target. His most insidious and strategic moves are made upon the mind. By affecting the way we think, he is able to keep our lives on a mediocre level.

There are a couple of extremely significant sections in the New Testament that address Satan's scheming nature. Let's look first at Ephesians 6:10–11.

> Finally, be strong in the Lord, and in the strength of His might. Put on the full armor of God, that you may be able to stand firm against the schemes of the devil.

Notice those four final words: "schemes of the devil." The Greek term translated "schemes" is *METHODIA,* from which we get our English word *method.* The Amplified Bible captures the correct idea by rendering it "strategies of the devil." He has a well-thought-through strategy, time-honored and effective—a plan that works like a charm. To understand it we need to remember that the battle is not in the visible realm. "For our struggle is not against flesh and blood . . ." (Eph. 6:12). The struggle (that's a good word for it, isn't it?) is not a flesh-and-blood struggle. It's not tangible; it's mental—it's simply not in the realm of something we can see, touch, or hear.

Remember that as we look next at a similar statement made in another part of the New Testament:

> But whom you forgive anything, I forgive also; for indeed what I have forgiven, if I have forgiven anything, I did it for your sakes in the presence of Christ, in order that no advantage be taken of us by Satan; for we are not ignorant of his schemes (2 Cor. 2:10–11).

Obviously, the larger subject here is forgiveness. Those people in ancient Corinth were being chided because they had half-forgiven a fellow in their church. By failing to forgive fully, they provided Satan with an "advantage," an opportunity to infiltrate and demoralize them. Note that the writer Paul adds a most insightful comment: ". . . we are not ignorant of his schemes." Earlier, the Greek word translated "schemes" was the root word for "method." But here the Greek term comes from a root word meaning "the mind." May I suggest a loose paraphrase? "Our desire is that the enemy not get a grip on us by twisting our thoughts, for we are not unaware of his mind-oriented strategy." Satan plays mind games with us, and unless we're clued in, he will win! Maybe Paul was not ignorant of the Devil's mind-oriented strategy, but most people I meet are. Frankly, for years I was too. Not until I became aware of the things I'm about to share with you in this chapter did I even begin to realize what it meant to soar.

Travel with me a little bit further in this same letter to the Corinthians:

> And even if our gospel is veiled, it is veiled to those who are perishing, in whose case the god of this world has blinded the minds of the unbelieving, that they might not see the light of the gospel of the glory of Christ, who is the image of God (2 Cor. 4:3–4).

Once again we find the enemy (called here "the god of this world") working in his favorite territory, the mind. Those who live in unbelief do so because he has "blinded the minds of the unbelieving." Many—in fact, most—live their lives in spiritual blindness. It's as if a thick, dark veil were draped across their thinking to keep them from seeing the light. Only the power of Christ can penetrate that veil and bring light and hope and happiness. Paul describes this so vividly a couple of verses later:

> For God, who said, "Light shall shine out of darkness," is the One who has shone in our hearts to give the light of the knowledge of the glory of God in the face of Christ (2 Cor. 4:6).

Thankfully, there are those who turn from darkness to light. But don't think for a moment that the enemy relinquishes his long-held territory without a fight, a fight that endures throughout life! Before you challenge that, take a good look at these words:

> For though we walk in the flesh, we do not war according to the flesh, for the weapons of our warfare are not of the flesh, but divinely powerful for the destruction of fortresses. We are destroying speculations and every lofty thing raised up against the knowledge of God, and we are taking every thought captive to the obedience of Christ (2 Cor. 10:3-5).

What descriptive language! Clearly, the scenes of battle are woven through those lines. You can almost smell smoke and hear the reports of massive weapons, except for one problem—it isn't a "war according to the flesh." As we learned earlier, it's a mind-oriented struggle, a "warfare . . . not of the flesh." It all takes place in the invisible, intangible realm of the mind.

THE BATTLE: AN INSIDIOUS STRATEGY

Even though Paul uses military words and ideas that suggest physical combat, it is imperative that we keep the right perspective. Everything being described in 2 Corinthians 10:3-5 occurs in the mind. What we find here is the strategy used against us to keep us ineffective and defeated—in other words, *mediocre*.

In ancient days cities were built within thick, massive walls. The wall provided a formidable barrier that protected the city, holding the enemy at bay. Before any alien force could expect to conquer a city, it first had to overcome that protective shield. Towers were even erected in strategic places within the wall. In times of battle, seasoned men with an understanding of military warfare would position themselves in these stations that towered above the surrounding wall. From these vantage points, they would be able to see the location of the advancing troops and shout their commands in hopes of counteracting the enemy attack.

In order for the enemy to take the city, three objectives had to be accomplished. First, the wall had to be scaled or penetrated. Second, the towers had to be invaded. Third, the men of military strategy had to be captured. (After capturing—or killing—the military leaders, conquering the inhabitants was no big deal.) Such was the strategy of first-century battles. In 2 Corinthians 10, we have this very principle illustrated—not in a city, but in a mind.

Don't forget what we discovered earlier: Our minds were originally enemy-held territories. For years we were blinded by the power of the enemy. The mind was his "base of operations" until the light shone within. At that time, the veil was lifted and we were no longer blinded. It was a supernatural event in which new life was given, and the enemy was relieved of his command.

But I am increasingly more convinced that Satan doesn't want to give up his territory. He is a defeated foe who knows his future. But he fights to the last degree to maintain the hold he has had on us. His "stronghold" reveals itself in our humanistic, horizontal nature—in the habits we established back then, and the whole lifestyle we lived under enemy command. This is one of the reasons that those who become Christians later in life have such tremendous battles in the realm of the mind. The intensity of the warfare can hardly be exaggerated!

The verses we've been looking at describe the battle in detail. Remember the reference to "the destruction of fortresses" and "destroying speculations"? Let that represent the wall around the mind. Perhaps the speculations represent the reasonings, the thought patterns, the traditional habits of thinking built in by the enemy for many, many years. In order for the truth of God to win, those speculations that encompassed our mind have to be penetrated. How does that happen? The Lord brings a divinely powerful weapon, the Holy Spirit, with His magnificent armory of truths from Scripture, His remarkable filling, and His dynamic empowering.

Once the Lord breaks through the wall-like fortress and speculations, He encounters those "lofty things." Remember the verse ". . . destroying . . . every lofty thing raised up against the knowledge of God . . ."?

Let's call these "lofty things" the mental blocks we've erected against spiritual viewpoints. You and I are prompted to go back to carnal habits when under pressure, when under attack, when undergoing a test, when doing without, when persecuted, when maligned, criticized, or done wrong. Our tendency is to rely on those traditional "lofty things"—those established thoughts that were passed on to us by our parents, our friends, and our colleagues. Such mental blocks are natural and humanistic to the core.

I am indebted to Roger von Oech for his insights regarding what he calls "mental locks." In his creative book *A Whack on the Side of the Head* (you owe it to yourself to read it!), he lists no less than ten statements that hold us back, keeping us from soaring into new, innovative realms. If you are like me, you will smile by the time you get to the end of the list; we've heard them and said them so much they are cast in mental concrete!

1. "The Right Answer."
2. "That's Not Logical."
3. "Follow The Rules."
4. "Be Practical."
5. "Avoid Ambiguity."
6. "To Err Is Wrong."
7. "Play Is Frivolous."
8. "That's Not My Area."
9. "Don't Be Foolish."
10. "I'm Not Creative."[2]

God is interested in our breaking free from such locks. He realizes each "lofty thing" has dug in its heels and must be dislodged. As we often say, "Old habits are hard to break." For too many years, we have convinced ourselves that *we lack this* or *we cannot do that . . . we should not risk . . . we are sure to fail . . . we ought to accept the status quo as our standard.* But these programmed "lofty things" <u>must</u> be conquered! We occasionally need "a whack on the side of the head"!

And what is God's ultimate goal? Just as we read in 2 Corinthians 10:5—to take "every thought captive." When He invades those lofty areas, His plan is to transform the old thoughts that defeat us into new thoughts that encourage us. He has to repattern our whole way of thinking. And He is engaged in doing that continually because old habits are so hard to break. Can you see now why those reactions you've had for dozens of years are still problem areas? Finally, you have some insight on your battle with lust, or envy, or pride, or jealousy, or extreme perfectionism, or a negative, critical spirit. And, more importantly, now you realize that there is hope beyond such mediocre mindsets. God's offer is nothing short of phenomenal! Remember it? It is "taking every thought captive to the obedience of Christ." Or, as one paraphrase reads;

> It is true that we live in the world, but we do not fight from worldly motives. The weapons we use in our fight are not the world's weapons but God's powerful weapons, which we use to destroy strongholds. We destroy false arguments; we pull down every proud obstacle that is raised against the knowledge of God; we take every thought captive and make it obey Christ (2 Cor. 10:3-5, TEV)

Conquering Mediocrity: A Mental Metamorphosis

The essential question isn't difficult to state: *How?* How can I, a person who has absorbed so many years of mediocre thinking, change? How can I, like Sid the caterpillar, move from squirming in the dirt to enjoying the sweet nectar in God's creation? As in Sid's case, a radical metamorphosis must occur. It is a process that will be difficult, demanding, and lengthy—but, oh, how sweet the results! If you are really serious about conquering mediocrity (which, remember, starts in the mind), then I have three words to offer—memorize, personalize, and analyze.

Memorize. In order for old defeating thoughts to be invaded, conquered, and replaced by new, victorious ones, a process of reconstruction must transpire. The best place I know to begin this process of mental cleansing is with the all-important discipline of memorizing Scripture. I realize it doesn't sound very sophisticated or intellectual, but God's Book is full of powerful ammunition! And dislodging negative and demoralizing thoughts requires aggressive action. I sometimes refer to it as a mental assault.

Where to begin? How about setting up a strong strategy of assault with several victorious promises? For example:

> But thanks be to God, who gives us the victory through our Lord Jesus Christ. Therefore, my beloved brethren, be steadfast, immovable, always abounding in the work of the Lord, knowing that your toil is not in vain in the Lord (1 Cor. 15:57-58).

> The horse is prepared for the day of battle, but victory belongs to the Lord (Prov. 21:31).

> But thanks be to God, who always leads us in His triumph in Christ, and manifests through us the sweet aroma of the knowledge of Him in every place (2 Cor. 2:14).

> I can do all things through Him who strengthens me (Phil. 4:13).

> For whatever is born of God overcomes the world; and this is the victory that has overcome the world—our faith (1 John 5:4).

> Yet those who wait for the Lord will gain new strength; they will mount up with wings like eagles, they will run and not get tired, they will walk and not become weary (Isa. 40:31).

> How can a young man keep his way pure? By keeping it according to Thy word. With all my heart I have sought Thee; do not let me wander from Thy commandments. Thy word I have treasured in my heart, that I may not sin against Thee (Ps. 119:9-11).

I can also think of a few scriptures that I repeat to myself when I get a little weak-kneed in the daily battle:

> But Moses said to the people, "Do not fear! Stand by and see the salvation of the Lord which He will accomplish for you today; for the Egyptians whom you have seen today, you will never see them again forever. The Lord will fight for you while you keep silent" (Exod. 14:13-14).

> Be on the alert, stand firm in the faith, act like men, be strong (1 Cor. 16:13).

> "Ask, and it shall be given to you; seek, and you shall find; knock, and it shall be opened to you. For every one who asks receives, and he who seeks finds, and to him who knocks it shall be opened" (Matt. 7:7-8).

Thy words were found and I ate them, and Thy words became for me a joy and the delight of my heart (Jer. 15:16).

Therefore, take up the full armor of God, that you may be able to resist in the evil day, and having done everything, to stand firm. Stand firm therefore, having girded your loins with truth, and having put on the breastplate of righteousness (Eph. 6:13-14).

But He gives a greater grace. Therefore it says, "God is opposed to the proud, but gives grace to the humble" (James 4:6-7).

"Do not fear, for I am with you; do not anxiously look about you, for I am your God. I will strengthen you, surely I will help you, surely I will uphold you with My righteous right hand" (Isa. 41:10).

"These things I have spoken to you, that in Me you may have peace. In the world you have tribulation, but take courage; I have overcome the world" (John 16:33).

No need for me to list more. The possibilities are virtually endless. All you have to do is get hold of a Bible, read it thoughtfully, and when you come across a statement that addresses some issue you're struggling with or some area of need in your life, write it down and spend part of your day tucking it away in the folds of your mind. You'll be amazed at the strength it will give you.

Personalize. Here's where the excitement intensifies. As you begin the process of replacing old, negative thoughts with new and encouraging ones, put yourself into the pages of the Bible. Use *I, me, my, mine* as you come across meaningful statements. To show you what I mean, let's go back again to 2 Corinthians 10:3-5:

For though [I] walk in the flesh, [I] do not war according to the flesh [then I meditate on that thought], for the weapons of [my] warfare are not of the flesh, but divinely powerful for the destruction of fortresses. [I am] destroying speculations and every lofty thing raised up against the knowledge of God, and [I am] taking every thought captive to the obedience of Christ.

Get the idea? That's called personalizing Scripture. Here is another example. First, let's look at how the words appear in the New American Standard Bible:

Be anxious for nothing, but in everything by prayer and supplication with thanksgiving let your requests be made known to God. And the peace of God, which surpasses all comprehension, shall guard your hearts and your minds in Christ Jesus.

Finally, brethren, whatever is true, whatever is honorable, whatever is right, whatever is pure, whatever is lovely, whatever is of good repute, if there is any excellence and if anything worthy of praise, let your mind dwell on these things (Phil. 4:6–8).

I suggest you personalize them like this:

[I should not be anxious about anything], but in everything by prayer and supplication with thanksgiving, [I need to] let [my] requests be made known to God. And the peace of God, which [passes] all [my] comprehension, shall guard [my heart and mind] in Christ Jesus.

Finally, [put your name here], whatever is true, whatever is honorable, whatever is right, whatever is pure, whatever is lovely, whatever is of good repute, if there is any excellence and if anything worthy of praise, [I should let my] mind dwell on these things.

Got the picture? Believe me, if you keep this up, it won't be long before the old "fortresses" will be scaled, the "lofty things" will be invaded, and your thoughts will begin to be transformed.

Analyze. Instead of continuing to tell yourself you are little more than a helpless victim, take charge! As soon as you catch yourself responding negatively or defensively, think—analyze the situation. If you are a student, do a little analysis of your situation at school. If you're in business, working in an office where the turkeys outnumber the eagles (that's usually true!), analyze the circumstances with the understanding that you and they will never be "in step," marching to the same cadence. Then ask yourself a few tough questions. "Why am I getting so hot and bothered by this?" Or "Is there something I'm afraid of?" Or, maybe, "Am I reacting negatively because I have a reason or simply because I've formed some bad habits?" Yes, those are thought questions, but without such analysis, we tend to become like those around us or get even worse. Breaking longstanding mental habits is neither easy nor quick, but those who don't can erode into cranky and crotchety folks who wind up alone and miserable.

Maybe the challenge to memorize, personalize, and analyze seems too simplistic to you. Perhaps you expected something else. You really expected some high-powered "secret" to success.

No, I have no quick 'n' easy secret, no overnight-success pill you can take. Perhaps the best single-word picture is *visualize*. Those who break through the "mediocrity barrier" mentally visualize being on a higher plane. Then once they "see it," they begin to believe it and behave like it! People who soar are those who refuse to sit back, sigh, and wish things would change. They neither complain of their lot nor passively dream of some distant ship coming in. Rather, they visualize in their minds that they are not quitters; they will not allow life's circumstances to push them down and hold them under.

The next time you find yourself tempted to succumb to life's hard knocks, take a mental journey back to an office in Brentwood and remember it is occupied by that bowlegged eagle who soared all the way from a pathetic ghetto in Potrero Hill to the National Football League Hall of Fame . . . and far beyond.

2

IT INVOLVES
ANOTHER KINGDOM

Ours is the YUPPIE generation. Yes, YUPPIE—young urban professionals.

What a difference between the hippies of the 1960s and the yuppies of the 1980s! They not only look different, but they ask different questions. Today's upwardly mobile young adult isn't burning draft cards and questioning the establishment. Instead, he's asking, "What's in it for me? How much will I make? What are the benefits, the perks you can promise? How rapidly will I be promoted?" The implications in their questions are bold and brazen: "What's so bad about greed?" And, "Why not look out for number one?" Their three-piece suits are neatly pressed, and their professional intensity reflects strong determination. They not only look trim and proper, they even smell good.

How different from the hippies! Those who bothered to attend classrooms back then wore cut-offs and often no shirt at all, sometimes no shoes. One of the last things they cared about was their appearance. And least important to them was prosperity and success. How times change!

Early in the 1980s *Fortune* magazine published an article that left nobody in doubt regarding today's young entrepreneur. Even the title was revealing—"On a Fast Track to the Good Life." The article gave research findings on the attitudes and the values of twenty-five-year-olds who were taking their places in the current business world. The purpose of the research was to give readers an idea of what to expect from young adults during the next decade. Talk about an accurate crystal ball!

One astute thinker has analyzed the results in six observations:

1. These young people believe that a successful life means financial independence and that the best way to gain financial independence is to be at the top of a major corporation.

2. They believe in themselves. They believe that they have the abilities and capacities to be the best. There is no "humble talk" among them.

3. They believe in the corporate world. They are sure that the corporations they would lead are the most worthwhile institutions in the world.

4. They view as "a drag on success" any relationship that slows their ascent of the corporate ladder. Marriage is an acceptable option only if it does not interfere with their aspirations for success. Having children, for most of them, is something to which they will have to give a great deal of thought.

5. Loyalty is not high on their list of values. Unlike "The Organization Man," described by William Whyte, Jr., in his book of the same name during the '50s, the young Turks of this new breed have their resumés ever at hand. They are ready to move from one company to another and believe that loyalty to one company could lead to staying in a system that might not maximize upward mobility.

6. They are convinced that they are more creative and imaginative than those who now hold top corporate positions, and they believe that there is not much they can learn from these older types before they take their places.[1]

In a hard-hitting book entitled *Money, Sex, and Power*, author Richard Foster exposes the soft underbelly of today's yuppie philosophy. He goes to the heart of the issue when he writes:

> The demon in money is greed. Nothing can destroy human beings like the passion to possess. . . .
> The demon in sex is lust. True sexuality leads to humanness, but lust leads to depersonalization. Lust captivates rather than emancipates. . . .
> The demon in power is pride. True power has as its aim to set people free, whereas pride is determined to dominate.[2]

Then, toward the end of his book, as he returns to the subject of power, Foster concludes:

> Power destroys relationships. Lifelong friends can turn into mortal enemies the moment the vice-presidency of the company is at stake. Climb, push, shove is the language of power. Nothing cuts us off from each other like power. . . . Power's ability to destroy human relationships is written across the face of humanity.[3]

What does all of this have to do with living above the level of mediocrity? Everything, really. To live on that level requires thinking clearly, thinking beyond today. Frankly, it requires dealing with selfishness and putting the axe to the roots of greed. If we hope to demonstrate the level of excellence modeled by Jesus Christ, then we'll have to come to terms with which kingdom we are going to serve: the eternal kingdom our Lord represented and told us to seek (Matt. 6:33) or the temporal kingdom of today, whose philosophy could best be described in a different version of an old hymn:

> I'll have my own way, Lord, I'll have my own way,
> I'll be the potter, You be the clay;
> I'll mold You and make You after my will,
> While You are waiting, yielded and still.

In a world like ours, it's terribly, terribly difficult to think through the maze, especially since a number of religious groups have climbed on the yuppie bandwagon. They tell us, "If you want anything bad enough, you just claim it and God will give it to you. He's a good God, and He's certainly a prosperous God. He owns the cattle on every hill. He'll sell some and make it possible for you to enjoy whatever you really want in life." Sounds so appealing, so right. But when we examine it closely we find that it is light-years removed from everything Jesus taught and modeled. The kingdom He represented and urged His followers to embrace was a kingdom altogether different from the me-ism world of today.

LET'S UNDERSTAND WHAT "KINGDOM" MEANS

Before we press on in our pursuit of overcoming mediocrity, let's pause long enough to understand what I'm referring to when I mention the *kingdom*. It's one of those terms we like to use but seldom define. Part of our problem is that it is a tough thing to analyze.

For example, while the kingdom is full of righteousness, peace, and joy, it isn't a physical, tangible thing. It isn't something we can touch or see. "For the kingdom of God is not eating and drinking, but righteousness and peace and joy in the Holy Spirit" (Rom. 14:17).

Furthermore, this kingdom isn't verbal, something we can actually hear with our ears, even though it is powerful. "For the kingdom of God does not consist in words, but in power" (1 Cor. 4:20).

If that isn't mysterious enough, I should add that while it is unshakable, it isn't visible either!

> Therefore, since we receive a kingdom which cannot be shaken, let us show gratitude, by which we may offer to God an acceptable service with reverence and awe (Heb. 12:28).

How about that! We're supposed to seek something we cannot see, feel, or hear. And we're expected to embrace something that is intangible, inaudible, and invisible.

Enough tongue-twisting. Generally speaking, *God's kingdom is a synonym for God's rule.* Those who choose to live in His kingdom (though still very much alive on Planet Earth) choose to live under His authority.

Maybe a supersimple outline of the Bible will help us understand the definition of God's kingdom even better. But first let me warn you—it's so basic you'll probably sneer!

I.   God creates the heavens and earth and all things in them, including mankind. That's Genesis 1 and 2.

II. Mankind, alone, rebels against God's authority. That's covered in Genesis 3.

III. God moves through history to reestablish His authority over all creation. That's Genesis 4 through Revelation 22.

How's that for a quick summary?

If you're wondering where you and I fit into this oversimplified outline, take a look at category three. For centuries God has been at work reestablishing His rulership. Jesus' words in Matthew 6 describe the problem:

> "No one can serve two masters; for either he will hate the one and love the other, or he will hold to one and despise the other. You cannot serve God and mammon. . . .
> "For all these things the Gentiles eagerly seek; for your heavenly Father knows that you need all these things. But seek first His kingdom and His righteousness; and all these things shall be added to you" (vv. 24, 32–33).

All this leads me to some helpful news, some bad news, and some good news! The kingdom is the invisible realm where God rules as supreme authority. That's *helpful news*. The *bad news* is that we, by nature, don't want Him to rule over us; we much prefer to please ourselves. We'd much rather serve mammon (the word means "money") than the Master. Illustration: the yuppie lifestyle, materialism. More bad news is this: Most people do serve mammon. Just look around. Who's in charge, God or mammon? What's happening? The mediocre majority have bought into a mammon lifestyle.

Now, the *good news*. We don't have to live that way. God has given us an avenue of escape. It's called a birth from above. Jesus spoke of it when He met with a Jewish leader late one night.

> Among the Pharisees there was a man named Nicodemus, a ruler of the Jews, who visited Jesus by night and said to Him, "Rabbi, we know that You are a teacher who has come from God; for no one can work the signs You work unless God is with him."
> Jesus answered him, "Truly I assure you, unless a person is born from above, he cannot see the kingdom of God." Nicodemus said to Him, "How can a man be born when he is old? Can he enter his mother's womb a second time to be born?" Jesus replied, "Truly I assure you, unless one's birth is through water and the Spirit, he cannot enter the kingdom of God. What is born of the flesh is flesh, and what is born of the Spirit is spirit" (John 3:1–6, MLB).

Nicodemus struggled back then just as we do today. To put it bluntly, we don't want anybody other than ourselves ruling over us! Much like those people in a story Jesus once told, "We do not want this man to reign over us!" (Luke 19:14). Not until we experience a spiritual rebirth will we submit to God's rule.

So when I write of God's kingdom, I'm referring to His rightful authority over our lives. Only then can we experience true excellence.

OUR MAJOR STRUGGLE WITH GOD'S KINGDOM

God's kingdom authority isn't easily accepted in our yuppie generation. We've got too much pride to submit without a fight. As I mentioned at the beginning of this chapter, we like being in charge. We want our way. We push for the top spot—the place of glory. In doing so, we opt for a lifestyle that has no room for submission. That's nothing new.

In ancient days there lived a king whose middle name could have been Pride. He strutted his stuff all over Babylon. His surroundings were impressive and his lifestyle was opulent. But King Nebuchadnez-zar had a dream which troubled him. To make matters worse, he could find no one in his vast kingdom who could interpret that dream. No one, that is, until he heard about a Jewish prophet named Daniel. Once the two men stood face to face, things started to pop. Daniel not only told him the reality of the dream, he also leveled the monarch with a prophecy concerning his future:

> "It is you, O king; for you have become great and grown strong, and your majesty has become great and reached to the sky and your dominion to the end of the earth.
>
> "This is the interpretation, O king, and this is the decree of the Most High, which has come upon my lord the king: that you be driven away from mankind, and your dwelling place be with the beasts of the field, and you be given grass to eat like cattle and be drenched with the dew of heaven; and seven periods of time will pass over you, until you recognize that the Most High is ruler over the realm of mankind, and bestows it on whomever He wishes.
>
> "Therefore, O king, may my advice be pleasing to you: break away now from your sins by doing righteousness, and from your iniquities by showing mercy to the poor, in case there may be a prolonging of your prosperity" (Dan. 4:22, 24-25, 27).

The prophet's counsel was tough but true. In effect, he told Nebu-chadnezzar to release his grip on his possessions, to empty himself of all that stubborn self-will—in essence to recognize God's rightful authority over his life. Do you think that proud king would do such a thing? Well, ultimately, yes, but not before he went nuts. Read the next episode of this true story very thoughtfully.

> All this happened to Nebuchadnezzar the king. Twelve months later he was walking on the roof of the royal palace of Babylon. The king reflected and said, "Is this not Babylon the great, which I myself have built as a royal residence by the might of my power and for the glory of my majesty?" While the word was in the king's mouth, a voice came from heaven, saying, "King Nebuchadnezzar, to you it is declared: sovereignty has been removed from you, and you will be driven away from mankind, and your dwelling place will be with the beasts of the field. You will be given grass to eat like cattle, and seven periods of time

will pass over you, until you recognize that the Most High is ruler over the realm of mankind, and bestows it on whomever He wishes." Immediately the word concerning Nebuchadnezzar was fulfilled; and he was driven away from mankind and began eating grass like cattle, and his body was drenched with the dew of heaven, until his hair had grown like eagles' feathers and his nails like birds' claws (Dan.4:28–33).

Nebuchadnezzar remained in that tragic condition for an undetermined period of time. When he finally saw the light, the struggle ended. The once-proud king did a 180-degree turnaround.

"But at the end of that period I, Nebuchadnezzar, raised my eyes toward heaven, and my reason returned to me, and I blessed the Most High and praised and honored Him who lives forever;

> For His dominion is an everlasting dominion,
> And His kingdom endures from generation
>   to generation.
> And all the inhabitants of the earth are
>   accounted as nothing,
> But He does according to His will in the host
>   of heaven
> And among the inhabitants of earth;
> And no one can ward off His hand
> Or say to Him, 'What hast Thou done?'

"At that time my reason returned to me. And my majesty and splendor were restored to me for the glory of my kingdom, and my counselors and my nobles began seeking me out; so I was reestablished in my sovereignty, and surpassing greatness was added to me. Now I Nebuchadnezzar praise, exalt, and honor the King of heaven, for all His works are true and His ways just, and He is able to humble those who walk in pride" (Dan. 4:34–37).

Look again at those concluding words of Nebuchadnezzar's testimony. Pay close attention to his comments about God's dominion, God's kingdom, God's authority, God's works, God's ways. What a change! Here was a broken man who finally surrendered. Only then was he able to fulfill his God-appointed role and reach his full potential on the earth.

The same is true today. People who live proud, unbroken lives may become great, gain popularity, and accomplish incredible feats, but all that power and pride stand against the qualities that God considers great.

It is extremely difficult to have these thoughts embraced in our world of high-powered hype. This is the day when people consider it the greatest thrill in life to have their picture in a magazine or to appear in films or on television. Malcolm Muggeridge made an insightful comment in his penetrating work *Christ in the Media* (Wm. B. Eerdmans, 1977). He said if Jesus were to return to earth today and endure a similar wilderness experience with Satan throwing those three temptations at Him, the adversary would surely add a fourth: to appear on national television.[4]

What a cunning, driving force is Ambition, twin sister of Pride. Those who pursue true excellence, those who soar, are people who've come to terms with pride.

OBSERVATIONS AND APPLICATIONS

Okay, okay, I can hear your thoughts. You're wondering what all this kingdom stuff has to do with living above the level of mediocrity. You're thinking you missed a couple of pages in the transition, right? Well, you didn't. What I have wanted to communicate in this chapter is that a life which soars is one that doesn't get caught in the trap of the temporal. People of excellence are those who see through the clutching greed of our times—people who have declared their undivided allegiance to Christ's message, a message that (like the restored king of Babylon) praises and exalts and honors the King of heaven, knowing He is able to humble those who walk in pride. Such a commitment represents authentic excellence, leaving no excuse for mediocrity. People who soar, that is, soar like God intended, are people who have humbled themselves to Christ's sovereign authority. They are citizens of His invisible kingdom.

Jesus spoke often of God's kingdom to those who wished to follow Him. In fact, right up to the end He had kingdom authority on His mind. Before His ascension back to the Father, He met with His own. And the topic of discussion? The kingdom.

> To these He also presented Himself alive, after His suffering, by many convincing proofs, appearing to them over a period of forty days, and speaking of the things concerning the kingdom of God (Acts 1:3).

What a revelation! Did you realize that's what Christ talked about between His resurrection and His ascension? It wasn't a lengthy class on theoretical prophecy, not at all. It was practical, relevant teaching about how to live under His authority and for His glory—how to live a life above the mediocre level (that level where you push and shove to get your own way). No doubt, He passed along some insightful techniques, some truths his followers could apply when tempted to live like the majority.

Did these early disciples learn their lesson well? Let's find out by working our way through the balance of the Book of Acts, which traces the history of these followers of Jesus from His ascension to the last half of the first century. In each one of the following vignettes, we'll find something extremely significant about life that is lived above the level of mediocrity, "kingdom living" in action.

Our First Stop-off: Acts 8:12–13

> But when they believed Philip preaching the good news about the kingdom of God and the name of Jesus Christ, they were being baptized, men and women alike. And even Simon himself believed; and after being baptized, he continued on with Philip; and as he observed signs and great miracles taking place, he was constantly amazed (Acts 8:12–13).

Interesting. "Even Simon himself believed. . . ." Who's Simon? The previous three verses tell us.

> Now there was a certain man named Simon, who formerly was practicing magic in the city, and astonishing the people of Samaria, claiming to be someone great; and they all, from smallest to greatest, were giving attention to him, saying, "This man is what is called the Great Power of God." And they were giving him attention because he had for a long time astonished them with his magic arts (vv. 9–11).

Simon was a magician whose reputation had won him the title "the Great Power of God." Talk about a man people today would turn out to see . . . all the television networks would be after this guy! Yet, upon hearing Philip's message, "the good news about the kingdom of God," Simon accepted it, no questions asked. Believing the good news is both simple and quick. Fleshing it out is a different matter. Simon would soon find that out.

Then they began laying their hands on them, and they were receiving the Holy Spirit. Now when Simon saw that the Spirit was bestowed through the laying on of the apostles' hands, he offered them money, saying, "Give this authority to me as well, so that everyone on whom I lay my hands may receive the Holy Spirit" (vv. 17–19).

Why, of course! That's exactly the way yuppies would respond. "This kind of power is worth whatever it costs. . . . I want to buy fifty shares!" So Simon offered them money. "I would love to get into that act. I'll market it. Gimme some of that Holy Spirit power!"

Look at Peter. There are times when he really distinguishes himself, and this is one of those wonderful moments:

. . . "May your silver perish with you, because you thought you could obtain the gift of God with money! You have no part or portion in this matter, for your heart is not right before God. Therefore repent of this wickedness of yours, and pray the Lord that if possible, the intention of your heart may be forgiven you. For I see that you are in the gall of bitterness and in the bondage of iniquity" (vv. 20–23).

Now that's what I'd call a rebuke! No doubt about it, Peter had gotten this guy's attention. I mean, here's Simon, "Okay, okay." But it wasn't a surly kind of okay. Look at his response.

But Simon answered and said, "Pray to the Lord for me yourselves, so that nothing of what you have said may come upon me" (v. 24).

There was someone honest enough to say, "Simon, you're off base. That has nothing to do with the kingdom of God. That's mediocre pizzazz. That's hype. That's carnal merchandising. You're out of line, Simon." And when Simon realized his fault, he acknowledged it.

The observation that we need to remember from this incident is *kingdom authority diminishes the significance of all other powers.* The accompanying application is equally important:

WHEN FACING THE TEMPTATION TO MAKE A NAME FOR YOURSELF, CALL ON KINGDOM POWER.

If you are greatly gifted, you may be able to do marvelous things that would cause the public to be swept up in your skills and in your abilities. In the process of your growing, you will find great temptation to make a name for yourself, to make a big splash, to gain attention, to get the glory, to strut around, to increase your fees, to demand your rights, and to expect kid-glove treatment. You're in authority now! People are talking about you! But instead, remember Simon. Realize, as well, the ministry of small things.

> In experiences of hiddenness we learn that the ministry of small things is a necessary prerequisite to the ministry of power. . . .
> The ministry of small things is among the most important ministries we are given. In some ways it is more important than the ministry of power. . . .
> Small things are the genuinely big things in the kingdom of God. It is here we truly face the issues of obedience and discipleship. It is not hard to be a model disciple amid camera lights and press releases. But in the small corners of life, in those areas of service that will never be newsworthy or gain us any recognition, we must hammer out the meaning of obedience.[5]

Ruth Harms Calkin does a masterful job on this same subject in her poem "I Wonder":

> You know, Lord, how I serve You
> with great emotional fervor in the limelight.
> You know how eagerly I speak for You at a Women's Club.
> You know my genuine enthusiasm at a Bible study.
> But how would I react, I wonder,
> if You pointed to a basin of water
> and asked me to wash the calloused feet
> of a bent and wrinkled old woman
> day after day, month after month,
> in a room where nobody saw and nobody knew?[6]

Still enamored by the lights, Simon continued to look for ways to promote himself, until he learned about kingdom authority. So whenever you're faced with the temptation to claim glory for yourself, call on kingdom power.

Our Second Stop-off: Acts 14:21-22

As we jump ahead, we move from Samaria to the little city of Lystra. Lystra means nothing to most people on the street, but to Bible students it means the place where Paul was a victim of stoning. Literally, he was left for dead. Yet, he came out from under those rocks more determined than ever. It took him awhile, but he brushed himself off, gathered his senses, and pressed on to present the gospel to that area of the world where God had called him. Watch what happened.

> And after they had preached the gospel to that city and had made many disciples, they returned to Lystra. . . . (Acts 14:21).

Can you believe it? The very place he was stoned. That's like going back to the job where you were fired. That's like returning to a friendship that the other person has cut off. But they returned to Lystra anyway:

> . . . strengthening the souls of the disciples, encouraging them to continue in the faith, and saying, "Through many tribulations we must enter the kingdom of God" (Acts 14:22).

Once again, allow me to present our yuppie point of view. First of all, yuppies hate the thought of suffering. "I don't wanna suffer, because I want gratification. I don't simply want gratification, I want *instant* gratification. I don't want to wait if I can get it now. And if I can get it now, I want more rather than less." And yet Paul says that through many tribulations we must enter the kingdom of God. It's a rigorous statement and, without question, an unpopular one.

Now the observation is clear: *Kingdom living involves many tribulations.* I think of a related truth found in 2 Timothy 3:12 which says: "And indeed, all who desire to live godly in Christ Jesus will be persecuted." But the accompanying application reveals a source of strength:

WHEN GOING THROUGH TIMES OF TESTING, COUNT ON KINGDOM ENDURANCE.

Now if you're in life only for yourself, you'll have no endurance. On that precarious top of the ladder, you'll always have to maintain your balance by maneuvering and manipulating, lying, deceiving, and scheming. But if you're committed to kingdom-related excellence, when you go through times of testing, you can count on kingdom endurance to get you through.

British theologian John R. W. Stott writes on this unpopular subject of suffering in his book *Christian Counter Culture*:

> Few men of this century have understood better the inevitability of suffering than Dietrich Bonhoeffer. He seems never to have wavered in his Christian antagonism to the Nazi regime, although it meant for him imprisonment, the threat of torture, danger to his own family and finally death. He was executed by the direct order of Heinrich Himmler in April 1945 in the Flossenburg concentration camp, only a few days before it was liberated. It was the fulfillment of what he had always believed and taught: "Suffering, then, is the badge of true discipleship. The disciple is not above his master. Following Christ means *passio passiva* suffering because we have to suffer. That is why Luther reckoned suffering among the marks of the true Church, and one of the memoranda drawn up in preparation for the Augsburg Confession similarly defines the Church as the community of those 'who are persecuted and martyred for the gospel's sake' . . . Discipleship means allegiance to the suffering Christ, and it is therefore not at all surprising that Christians should be called upon to suffer."[7]

God has great lessons to teach us when we go through painful times. I love the words of the country preacher who said: "When the Lawd sends us tribulation, He 'spects us to tribulate!"

Our Third Stop-off: Acts 19:8

> And he entered the synagogue and continued speaking out boldly for three months, reasoning and persuading them about the kingdom of God (Acts 19:8).

The scene changes from Lystra to Corinth. Paul, once he won a hearing in the synagogue, spoke openly for three months, "persuading" those who attended. About what? "The kingdom of God." I'm sure he must have started with the basics, saying "You will not find yourself better off because you believe, that is, more prosperous, more popular, more successful, or in greater demand. You will find that some of this message is going to cut deeply into your life."

I know that must have been hard for the Corinthians to hear because Paul uses the words *speaking out boldly, reasoning,* and *persuading.* The words *speaking out boldly* mean "to declare, as if making a proclamation." You can be sure that caught their attention.

The next word (*reasoning*) carries with it the idea of "dialoguing." In fact, it's from the Greek term *dialegomai* from which we get the word *dialogue*. It includes the thought of "pondering" and "disputing." One scholar renders it "debating." So Paul threw out to them thoughts of the kingdom, and then he entertained their disputes. Perhaps this same dialogue continued for three months as Paul tried to *persuade* them. The word *persuading* means "to prevail upon so as to bring about a change." Today we would call it "selling them." And the result? "Some were becoming *hardened*." See that word *hardened*? Interesting. It means "to dry." And it conveys the idea of being austere, stern, even severe. "They dried up" is the idea. Some were drying up with that message.

They were hardened and disobedient. Remember the line out of Jesus' story, "We will not have that man rule over us"? That's what these people were thinking in their hearts.

> But when some were becoming hardened and disobedient, speaking evil of the Way before the multitude, he withdrew from them and took away the disciples, reasoning daily in the school of Tyrannus (Acts 19:9).

The observation is clear: *Kingdom emphasis thins the ranks*. The accompanying application:

WHEN WONDERING WHY MOST PREFER MEDIOCRITY, REALIZE THE KINGDOM SEPARATES.

I think when the kingdom presses itself into a life, an individual fully embraces it or simply cannot tolerate it. So rather than facing it and releasing the pride, many—maybe most—will run. We should not be surprised to find the majority opting for a mediocre lifestyle, even some who once played roles as religious leaders. Kingdom truth does its own pruning. As Jesus Himself taught, we *cannot* serve two masters at the same time.

Our Fourth Stop-off: Acts 20

Here, we find Paul in the little coastal town of Miletus. He calls for the elders of the church at Ephesus, and then delivers his swan song. In verses 18-35, he pours out his soul to his friends from Ephesus, not knowing what would happen to him in Jerusalem. Note what he says to them in verses 20 and 27:

> ". . . I did not shrink from declaring to you anything that was profitable, and teaching you publicly and from house to house.
> "For I did not shrink from declaring to you the whole purpose of God."

The observation is obvious: *Kingdom truth is central to the whole purpose of God.* What I want you to notice by my quoting those two verses is that it's easy to shrink from the message. It's easy for me to shrink from preaching it. When tempted to do so, I need to remember 2 Timothy 4:2:

> . . . preach the word; be ready in season and out of season; reprove, rebuke, exhort, with great patience and instruction.

Why? The passage goes on to say:

> For the time will come when they will not endure sound doctrine; but wanting to have their ears tickled, they will accumulate for themselves teachers in accordance to their own desires (v. 3).

I ask you, is that relevant for today? Is it possible for you to find a teacher who'll tell you what you want to hear? Sure is. In fact, you don't have to look very far or very long; you'll find someone who will tell you how great you are, how wonderful things are, and how prosperous you can become.

So the accompanying application is obvious:

WHEN COMING TO TERMS
WITH THE WHOLE PURPOSE OF GOD,
REMEMBER KINGDOM COMMITMENT.

If you say that you're the kind of Christian who wants to embrace excellence, who really wants the whole purpose of God, then you dare not leave out *kingdom commitment.* That means your motives must be investigated. For example, every time you make plans to acquire a sizable possession—a car, an expensive boat, a house, and such like— you must deal with it before God and ask: Is this His will? Would this honor Him? Would this glorify Him? Before you hang onto something for a long, long time, you have to ask yourself: Is this worth hanging onto? It may be, but the question should still be asked. Is this the kind of thing that honors His kingdom? . . . that helps me seek His righteousness? This type of self-examination is the outworking of "the whole purpose of God."

When I became convinced of the importance of quality Christians becoming actively involved in "another kingdom," I spoke on the subject at the church I serve as senior pastor in Fullerton, California. Many of the things I've emphasized in this chapter, I openly declared from the pulpit that day. Sitting in the congregation was a man who listened very carefully and came to terms with his relationship with the Lord. Later, he wrote me this letter.

> I have attended the Fullerton Church for about two months. I've reached a pivotal point in my 40-year life. . . . I married at 18, had three sons by age 21 and spent years in drug and alcohol abuse. At age 25 I gave my life to the Lord but slipped back a couple of times.
>
> A year ago I had a beautiful 23-foot sailboat, a beautiful car, a beautiful van, a beautiful home, etc. At that time I was with a new company and my boss said he would get health insurance but lied about that and other things.
>
> Last February my wife had a brain aneurysm and almost died, but with prayer and surgery she lived. I lost everything but my family.
>
> I drive an old car about to break down. I am broke financially and my new boss emotionally destroys me, but I need the job. I said it with my mouth that the Lord giveth and the Lord taketh, blessed is the Lord, but my heart was still bitter. In your message I could relate very much with King Nebuchadnezzar, and you ended with a story that hit me so hard. I walked to my car with tears streaming down my cheeks and a pain in my throat. I came home and my wife and I cried and talked and prayed. At that time I gave it all to our Lord.
>
> I know I will struggle in my life, but I see everything differently now. I am undereducated, but very talented. I will work as unto the Lord. I need a church home for me and my family and believe I have found where we belong.[8]

Am I suggesting that you take a vow of poverty? No, not that. My message is not that you go hungry and give up all nice things. I just say you give up control of them. I'm not saying that because you're a Christian now, every day of your life is supposed to be grim, and you're supposed to carry yourself around like a prophet of doom, wearing only black and looking somber. I'm simply suggesting that those who live—I mean really soar—above the grubby, greedy level of mediocrity, have learned how to live from the perspective of another kingdom. They've learned to give all they have to the Lord God and to trust Him to give back all that they need.

Legend has it that a man was lost in the desert, just dying for a drink of water. He stumbled upon an old shack—a ramshackled, windowless, roofless, weatherbeaten old shack. He looked about this place and found a little shade from the heat of the desert sun. As he glanced around he saw a pump about fifteen feet away—an old, rusty water pump. He stumbled over to it, grabbed the handle, and began to pump up and down, up and down. Nothing came out.

Disappointed, he staggered back. He noticed off to the side an old jug. He looked at it, wiped away the dirt and dust, and read a message that said, "You have to prime the pump with all the water in this jug, my friend. P.S.: Be sure you fill the jug again before you leave."

He popped the cork out of the jug and sure enough, there was water. It was almost full of water! Suddenly, he was faced with a decision. If he drank the water, he could live. Ah, but if he poured all the water in the old rusty pump, maybe it would yield fresh, cool water from down deep in the well, all the water he wanted.

He studied the possibility of both options. What should he do, pour it into the old pump and take a chance on fresh, cool water or drink what was in the old jug and ignore its message? Should he waste all the water on the hopes of those flimsy instructions written, no telling how long ago?

Reluctantly he poured all the water into the pump. Then he grabbed the handle and began to pump . . . squeak, squeak, squeak. Still nothing came out! Squeak, squeak, squeak. A little bit began to dribble out, then a small stream, and finally it gushed! To his relief fresh, cool water poured out of the rusty pump. Eagerly, he filled the jug and drank from it. He filled it another time and once again drank its refreshing contents.

Then he filled the jug for the next traveler. He filled it to the top, popped the cork back on, and added this little note: "Believe me, it really works. You have to give it *all* away before you can get *anything* back."

People who risk living like that really soar.

3

IT COSTS
YOUR COMMITMENT

*E*ven though we're not very far along in this book, you have already noticed several references I have made to soaring. Obviously, my favorite analogy to illustrate that word picture is an eagle.

For thousands of years the eagle has been respected for its grandeur. There is something inspiring about its impressive grace in flight, its great wingspan, its powerful claws. It glides effortlessly at breathtaking altitudes, seemingly unaffected by the turbulent winds that whip across and between mountain crevices. Eagles do not travel in flocks nor do they conduct themselves irresponsibly. Strong of heart and solitary, they represent qualities we admire.

The eagle mates for life and returns to the same nest each year, making necessary repairs and additions. He takes an active role in providing for his family, protecting it from approaching dangers, and teaching little eaglets to fly. Responsibility, liberty, beauty, stability, and a dozen other admirable traits seem woven into the eagle's makeup, and such qualities cause me to agree with Solomon that "the way of an eagle in the sky" is nothing short of "wonderful" (Prov. 30:18–19).

Perhaps because eagle sightings are so rare, we don't easily forget those times when we've seen one soaring. I love the outdoors, and through the years, I've spent time fishing and hunting. During those outings, I've enjoyed many of the indescribable beauties of nature and encountered its harsh realities as well. But in spite of the numerous occasions I have been on streams and lakes, in the wilderness, and high up in the mountains, only twice have I spotted a bald eagle in flight—once while my sons and I were fishing for salmon and hunting caribou in Alaska and once while we were fishing for walleye and northern pike in central Canada. I can recall both moments to this day. All alone, the majestic bird seemed buoyed by the strong wind currents beneath its massive wings, soaring to its destination apparently without the slightest concern for us down below. While enraptured with the sight, each time I envisioned some day writing a book that would use the eagle as an illustration of living above the level of mediocrity—an illustration of the importance of being so committed to a standard of excellence that nothing deters us from our flight plan.

We may not be very far along in this study of excellence, but no doubt you are already aware of the fact that an eaglelike lifestyle doesn't come cheap. Being different is costly, especially when most are satisfied to blend in with the majority. There aren't many magnets on earth stronger than peer pressure. Even though all of us have only a few years to spend on this little planet in space, rare are the ones who decide to ignore the "average" and fight against the pull of the mediocre magnet. Face it—it's tough! As a familiar motto goes, "It's hard to soar like an eagle when I'm surrounded by so many turkeys!"

A Psalm That Sets Us Free

Tucked away neatly in the heart of the Hebrews' ancient hymnal is a simple prayer I often repeat to myself. It comes on the heels of several references to the brevity of life. I'm thinking of Psalm 90:

- Our years are "like yesterday" (v. 4).
- Life is "as a watch in the night" (v. 4).
- Our days are swept away "like a flood" (v. 5).
- Looking back over our lives, time seems almost "like grass," flourishing in the morning and fading by dusk (vv. 5–6).
- We finish our journey "like a sigh" (v. 9).

No one has done a better job paraphrasing the opening lines of this grand old hymn than Ken Taylor. Read his words slowly and thoughtfully:

Lord, through all the generations you have been our home! Before the mountains were created, before the earth was formed, you are God without beginning or end.

You speak, and man turns back to dust. A thousand years are but as yesterday to you! They are like a single hour! We glide along the tides of time as swiftly as a racing river, and vanish as quickly as a dream. we are like grass that is green in the morning but mowed down and withered before the evening shadows fall. We die beneath your anger; we are overwhelmed by your wrath. You spread out our sins before you—our secret sins—and see them all. No wonder the years are long and heavy here beneath your wrath. All our days are filled with sighing.

Seventy years are given us! And some may even live to eighty. But even the best of these years are often emptiness and pain; soon they disappear, and we are gone (Ps. 90. 1–10, TLB).

Yes, "we glide along the tides of time as swiftly as a racing river" for seventy, maybe eighty years; then it's curtains! What is it we need so desperately to live differently? The psalmist tells us in the simple prayer that follows these vivid verses:

Teach us to number our days and recognize how few they are; help us to spend them as we should (v. 12, TLB).

That's it! Gripped by the inescapable reality of life's brevity and death's inevitability, the man prays for all of us ("Teach us") and asks for wisdom for the balance of our days on earth ("help us to spend them as we should").

May I press the point? He doesn't ask "help us to spend them like the majority" but *"as we should"*—uniquely, fully, triumphantly. Not like a pen full of turkeys preoccupied only with life's mediocre demands, but like an independent-thinking, strong-minded eagle who lives a cut above, soaring freely across the trackless paths of incredible heights. If that's your prayer, be ready to pay a price.

In 1776 Thomas Paine, American Revolution patriot and writer, wrote about the price of freedom:

What we obtain too cheap, we esteem too lightly; 'tis dearness only that gives everything its value. Heaven knows how to put a proper price upon its goods; and it would be strange indeed, if so celestial an article as *Freedom* should not be highly rated.[1]

I sometimes think that those of us who choose to live like soaring eagles need to sign a mental declaration of independence. Let's put our name on the line, pledging ourselves with firm resolve, much like those brave men did on July 4, 1776, in Philadelphia when they signed the Declaration of Independence.

Did you know that of the fifty-six courageous men who signed that original document in Philadelphia, many did not survive the war that followed? Five were captured by the British and tortured before they died. Nine others died in the Revolutionary War, either from its hardships or its bullets. Twelve had their homes sacked, looted, burned, or occupied by the enemy. Two lost their sons in battle. One had two sons captured. Yes, the price of freedom was high indeed for those men. But deciding to be free, to think and live independently, to soar above the masses is always a costly decision.

As we discovered in the previous chapter, people who consecrate themselves to such a lifestyle must actually think in terms of another kingdom. And we learned that this kind of thinking thins the ranks—literally!

A MESSAGE THAT THINS THE RANKS

Some folks have the mistaken idea that Jesus deliberately tried to draw big crowds. It's true that large gatherings frequently followed Him during His three-plus years of earthly ministry, but never once did He attempt to generate a big audience. On the contrary, more than once He deliberately addressed certain issues that quickly diminished the number of onlookers. On one occasion, for instance, He pressed His points so stringently that many listeners walked away:

> Many therefore of His disciples, when they heard this said, "This is a difficult statement; who can listen to it?" . . .
> As a result of this many of His disciples withdrew, and were not walking with Him any more (John 6:60, 66).

On another occasion, Jesus did a similar thing. Both times it was *commitment* that thinned the ranks. Let's take a closer look at what happened in that second encounter Jesus had with the growing crowds. Dr. Luke sets the stage: "Now great multitudes were going along with Him . . ." (Luke 14:25).

A groundswell of curiosity had created quite an interest among the public regarding Jesus. His popularity had pulled people from villages all around. Many had come merely to gawk, to see a few miracles, and nothing more. Realizing that anything of a sensational nature could easily increase the frenzy of the crowd—something He loathed—Jesus found Himself unable to overlook the situation for one more minute:

He turned and said to them, "If anyone comes to Me, and does not hate his own father and mother and wife and children and brothers and sisters, yes, and even his own life, he cannot be My disciple. Whoever does not carry his own cross and come after Me cannot be My disciple. For which one of you, when he wants to build a tower, does not first sit down and calculate the cost, to see if he has enough to complete it? Otherwise, when he has laid a foundation, and is not able to finish, all who observe it begin to ridicule him, saying, 'This man began to build and was not able to finish.' Or what king, when he sets out to meet another king in battle, will not first sit down and take counsel whether he is strong enough with ten thousand men to encounter the one coming against him with twenty thousand? Or else, while the other is still far away, he sends a delegation and asks terms of peace. So therefore, no one of you can be My disciple who does not give up all his own possessions" (Luke 14:25-33).

Here was a "great multitude" merely "going along" for the ride—a gigantic crowd of mediocre tirekickers, who were spectators, nothing more. It was a situation which prompted Jesus to look them squarely in the eye and confront their lack of commitment. Who wouldn't be stabbed awake by His thrice-repeated "You cannot be My disciple"? We're talking straight talk here! Jesus touches three nerves as He addresses the cost of commitment—*personal relationships, personal goals and desires*, and *personal possessions*.

Personal Relationships

"If anyone comes to Me, and does not hate his own father and mother and wife and children and brothers and sisters, yes, and even his own life, he cannot be My disciple" (v. 26).

When Jesus mentions that we're to "hate" father and mother, wife, children, and sister or brother, He doesn't suggest that we're to treat them maliciously and be ugly toward them. What He is doing is emphasizing the very real possibility of *competition in our loyalty* between Himself and those we love so dearly. Top-flight, uncompromising commitment to Christ mixed with the quality of life He expects of His followers leaves no room for competition. Outsiders who don't understand a Christian's commitment to put Christ first might observe such devotion to the Lord and misjudge it as hatred toward other relationships. It isn't hatred, but rather a matter of priorities—deciding who or what comes first. I discuss priorities in much greater detail in chapter 7.

Personal Goals and Desires

> "Whoever does not carry his own cross and come after Me cannot be My disciple" (v. 27).

Here the penetration of Jesus' words goes a level deeper as He refers to surrendering our personal goals and desires to His authority. Negatively speaking, it means saying a firm *no* to what you and I want and *yes* to what God wants. Already we can understand why many decided not to hang around any longer.

In the first century if anyone was seen "carrying his own cross," it was clear to everyone that he was on his way to die. Jesus uses that word picture to describe dying to our own personal pursuits and, instead, following Him fully. Such self-denial is rare in our day, as rare as a soaring eagle.

Denying oneself is not to be equated with losing one's uniqueness or becoming of no value. There have been great people in each generation who modeled self-denial as they made significant contributions to humankind. One such man was General Robert E. Lee, commander-in-chief of the Confederate troops during the Civil War. Few eagles soared higher during these darkest days of our nation's history than General Lee. In fact, none of his biographers have overlooked his trait of self-denial when describing the qualities of that Southern gentleman. Douglas Southall Freeman, in fact, concludes his lengthy volume, *Lee*, with these moving words that illustrate the extent of the General's humility:

> Of humility and submission was born a spirit of self-denial that prepared him for the hardships of the war and, still more, for the dark destitution that followed it. This self-denial was, in some sense, the spiritual counterpart of the social self-control his mother had inculcated in his boyhood days, and it grew in power throughout his life. His own misfortunes typified the fate of the Confederacy and of its adherents. Through it all, his spirit of self-denial met every demand upon it, and even after he went to Washington College and had an income on which he could live easily, he continued to deny himself as an example to his people. Had his life been epitomized in one sentence of the Book

he read so often, it would have been in the words, "If any man will come after me, let him deny himself, and take up his cross daily, and follow me." And if one, only one, of all the myriad incidents of his stirring life had to be selected to typify his message, as a man, to the young Americans who stood in hushed awe that rainy October morning as their parents wept at the passing of the Southern Arthur, who would hesitate in selecting that incident? It occurred in Northern Virginia, probably on his last visit there. A young mother brought her baby to him to be blessed. He took the infant in his arms and looked at it and then at her and slowly said, "Teach him he must deny himself."[2]

That's good advice for anyone who wants to soar.

Personal Possessions

> "So therefore, no one of you can be My disciple who does not give up all his own possessions" (v. 33).

Here again we see the accommodating language used so often by our Lord. He employs dramatic terms to communicate the intensity of His point. In today's vernacular, committed individuals live with shallow tent pegs. They may own things, but nothing owns them. They have come to terms with merchandise that has a price tag and opted for commitment to values that are priceless.

We're back to some of the things I was getting at in chapter 2, aren't we? It is this precise principle (the principle of shallow tent pegs) that disqualifies full-fledged yuppies from being highflying eagles. They are hanging on to too much stuff!

Now take a look at a few related scriptures. Each of these is so relevant, so self-explanatory, that additional comment from me would be superfluous. Simply read and think about how each applies to you.

> And He said to them, "Beware, and be on your guard against every form of greed; for not even when one has an abundance does his life consist of his possessions" (Luke 12:15).

> "Sell your possessions and give to charity; make yourselves purses which do not wear out, an unfailing treasure in heaven, where no thief comes near, nor moth destroys. For where your treasure is, there will your heart be also" (Luke 12:33–34).

> "He must increase, but I must decrease" (John 3:30).

But godliness actually is a means of great gain, when accompanied by contentment. . . .

Instruct those who are rich in this present world not to be conceited or to fix their hope on the uncertainty of riches, but on God, who richly supplies us with all things to enjoy. Instruct them to do good, to be rich in good works, to be generous and ready to share, storing up for themselves the treasure of a good foundation for the future, so that they may take hold of that which is life indeed" (1 Tim. 6:6, 17–19).

Eagles that soar up where the air is pure and thin aren't weighed down by a lot of excess baggage. For them, materialism is a menace, a terminal disease. If we want to soar like eagles we must free ourselves from the fetters of materialism.

AN EXPLANATION THAT MAKES SENSE

Sandwiched between those last two points Jesus made is some more helpful information. Read what He says carefully and see if you don't agree.

"For which one of you, when he wants to build a tower, does not first sit down and calculate the cost, to see if he has enough to complete it? Otherwise, when he has laid a foundation, and is not able to finish, all who observe it begin to ridicule him, saying, 'This man began to build and was not able to finish.' Or what king, when he sets out to meet another king in battle, will not first sit down and take counsel whether he is strong enough with ten thousand men to encounter the one coming against him with twenty thousand? Or else, while the other is still far away, he sends a delegation and asks terms of peace" (Luke 14:28–32).

These two stories explain why Christ spoke in such stringent terms to the crowd. The first has to do with *building* and the second, with *fighting*. In each case, Jesus emphasizes the importance of quality. In building a tower that will last, quality builders are essential. And they cost a lot. In fighting a battle, quality soldiers (not the quantity of them, please notice) are all-important. They, too, are costly.

For years I taught that *we* are to "count the cost." It seemed so plausible. But suddenly one day, it dawned on me that Jesus never once told His followers to count the cost. No—*He's* the One who has already done that. He is the "king" (v. 31) who has already determined what it will take to encounter and triumph over life's enemies. And what *will* it take? A few strong, quality-minded champions whose commitment is solid as stone. And the cost will be great.

TOUGH QUESTIONS ONLY YOU CAN ANSWER

I've not pulled any punches in this chapter. But you have hung in there with me, and I commend you. These haven't been easy pages to write, but they are expressions I felt it necessary to make. Instead of wrapping up these thoughts in a traditional manner, I think it would be of greater benefit to ask a few pointed questions. So here they are. Don't hurry through them. Chew on each one, pondering your answer before going on to the next. Since confronting mediocrity takes thinking clearly, be painfully honest with yourself. There is no better time than now to make up your mind about these issues.

- Since life is so brief, what are the things you need to deal with that will enable you to soar during your remaining years? Be specific.

- Has peer pressure paralyzed you? Is that the reason you've not made your own "declaration of independence"? How can you overcome this paralysis?

- Where are you in the Luke 14 account? Among the few close followers or the many spectators? Why?

- Do you have any personal relationships that hinder your commitment to Christ-honoring excellence?

- What about your own goals and desires? Is self-denial your strong suit . . . or your downfall? Are you willing to surrender to Him?

- Does materialism have you in its grip?

- Isn't it about time for you to enlist as a full-fledged, committed follower of Christ? What's holding you back?

- If our country were overtaken by an enemy force that denied us the privilege of living openly for Christ, how would you react? Would your commitment be firm enough to keep you true?

Stories from the underground church in Russia never fail to jolt us awake. I came across another one just this past week. A house church in a city of the Soviet Union received one copy of the Gospel by Luke, the only scripture most of these Christians had ever seen. They tore it into small sections and distributed them among the body of believers. Their plan was to memorize the portion they had been given, then on the next Lord's Day they would meet and redistribute the scriptural sections.

On Sunday these believers arrived inconspicuously in small groups throughout the day so as not to arouse the suspicion of KGB informers. By dusk they were all safely inside, windows closed and doors locked. They began by singing a hymn quietly but with deep emotion. Suddenly, the door was pushed open and in walked two soldiers with loaded automatic weapons at the ready. One shouted, "All right—everybody line up against the wall. If you wish to renounce your commitment to Jesus Christ, leave now!"

Two or three quickly left, then another. After a few more seconds, two more.

"This is your last chance. Either turn against your faith in Christ," he ordered, "or stay and suffer the consequences."

Another left. Finally, two more in embarrassed silence with their faces covered slipped out into the night. No one else moved. Parents with small children trembling beside them looked down reassuringly. They fully expected to be gunned down or, at best, to be imprisoned.

After a few moments of complete silence, the other soldier closed the door, looked back at those who stood against the wall and said, "Keep your hands up—but this time in praise to our Lord Jesus Christ, brothers and sisters. We, too, are Christians. We were sent to another house church several weeks ago to arrest a group of believers—"

The other soldier interrupted, ". . . but, instead, *we were converted!* We have learned by experience, however, that unless people are willing to die for their faith, they cannot be fully trusted."[3]

In segments of the world where Bibles are plentiful and churches are protected, faith can run awfully shallow. Commitment can stay rather lukewarm. Eagles can learn to fly dangerously low. "What we obtain too cheap, we esteem too lightly."

4

IT CALLS FOR
EXTRAVAGANT LOVE

Please do not touch. That brief imperative is seldom ever found scrawled out in a bold manner; instead it's usually neatly printed in elegant places, stating the obvious. Because there are always a few fools who are anxious to rush in where angels would not dare, those four words appear as a warning so people won't try to handle priceless things in a careless manner. The untouchable may be something as small as a fine china cup or as large as a one-of-a-kind classic car. Instead of handling such things, we are encouraged merely to enjoy them from a distance. Look, but keep your hands off.

Many years ago a group of tourists was making its way through the house where the great German composer Ludwig van Beethoven spent his last years. As they arrived at that special conservatory where the man had spent so many hours at the piano, the guide paused and spoke quietly, "And here is the master's instrument." A well-meaning but thoughtless woman in the back of the group pushed her way up front, sat down at the bench, and immediately began to play one of Beethoven's great sonatas as she said, "I suppose a lot of people love to play this piano." The guide placed his hand on hers to stop her as he answered, "Well, Ignace Paderewski was here last summer. Several in the group wanted him to play. But he responded, 'Oh, no . . . I am not worthy to play the same keyboard as the great Beethoven.'"

There are certain scenes in Scripture that seem too sacred, too priceless to touch. Some are majestic psalms of praise; others are intimate prayers and scenes of tragic grief. But I especially feel a sense of reverence when I come to the passages that record the last week of Jesus' life. It's almost as if a small sign should appear before all who enter this section: "Please do not touch." There is something sacred about a place where someone has died, certainly someone as valuable and significant as Jesus. I never arrive at the record of His final hours without a heightened sense of respect. Instead of plunging in without regard for his dignity, like the tourist at Beethoven's piano, I find myself hesitant.

It is almost as though the Holy Spirit has guided us here, then put His hand on ours and said, "Here is where He spent His final days. Here is what He did. Here is the way He died. Just be quiet and experience it. Take time to feel the emotion, to grasp the significance of these words."

In the first three chapters of this book, we traveled rather rapidly from one scene to the next. We found that the mind is of utmost importance, a veritable battleground of mental warfare. We even went a step further and found that there is a choice of kingdoms, which forces us to get off the fence if we hope to confront and conquer mediocrity. In the chapter that followed, we discovered that such a decision is costly. Commitment is essential if we hope to soar like an independent, keen-thinking eagle.

Now it's time to change the pace. Let's slow down and stroll quietly through a scene that will add some needed perspective. Before we get so intensely independent and start operating as if excellence means isolation, let's linger at a place where love was so extravagant it was shocking.

Setting the Scene

Let me see if I can set the scene in such a way that you can appreciate it as it was meant to be appreciated. I'll try to handle it with great care.

> Now the feast of the Passover and Unleavened Bread was two days off; and the chief priests and the scribes were seeking how to seize Him by stealth, and kill Him; for they were saying, "Not during the festival, lest there be a riot of the people" (Mark 14:1-2).

If there were calendars hanging in Jewish kitchens in the first century, for sure, Passover would have been circled in red. What Thanksgiving is to America, Passover was to the ancient Jews, and, oh, so much more. It was a time of hearty celebration, the singing of great Jewish songs, the acting out of a drama dripping with emotion. It was a time in which signal fires were lighted around the city of Jerusalem. Trumpets blared and banners waved as the festivities continued. The festive spirit was contagious. People poured into Jerusalem from Galilee and Peraea and regions beyond. Like a vast family reunion, thousands upon thousands filled the streets for days as they relived their historic deliverance from bondage in Egypt. Ordinary business ceased as everyone in Jerusalem observed the holiday.

But even though a festive spirit was in the air, this year not everyone waved banners and sang songs. A few religious officials in high places were planning an execution. These men were putting the final touches on a plot that would lead to Jesus' death. They're identified as ". . . chief priests and scribes [who] were seeking how to seize Him by stealth." That word *stealth* means "a trick, a surprise tactic." (Who would've ever expected a kiss from one of the disciples? "That's perfect—just perfect.") Today we would say, "A conspiracy was being fine-tuned."

While the city was preoccupied with celebrating, singing, and laughing, those priests and scribes, alone and quiet, were frowning. Within a matter of hours Jesus would be nailed to a cross. Why would they want to kill Him? What was it that drove these men to such extreme rage?

The late British commentator, G. Campbell Morgan, clearly explains:

> . . . He had rebuked their ideals through the whole course of His public ministry. Ideals are always closely related to conduct; consequently the whole tenor of His teaching had been to rebuke their conduct.
>
> During the latter days of His ministry He had rebuked their failures as shepherds of the people. . . . Their hatred of Jesus was consequently of One Who had revealed their failure.[1]

Can't you just hear their whispered murmurings? "Why, the *audacity* to tell us that we are failures!"

The problem was, of course, that more and more people believed Jesus. According to a comment recorded in John 12, "Many of the Jews were . . . believing in Jesus" (v. 11). So the chief priests and scribes had a problem. I can almost hear them plotting, "We want to kill Him, but not during the festival, lest there be a riot. He has a lot of followers. People are believing in this fool, this liar, this troublemaker." And they probably thumped their fingers on the desk and stroked their beards as they waited for just the right moment to strike.

Suddenly, we are lifted from that scene in Jerusalem and transported a few miles away to a modest home in Bethany, where more than a dozen people are reclining around a table, relaxing and enjoying themselves.

> And while He was in Bethany at the home of Simon the leper . . . (Mark 14:3).

The residence is identified as the home of Simon the leper. Obviously, no one would eat with a leper unless the leper had been healed (or, to use the biblical word, "cleansed"), and that is exactly what had happened to Simon. What an irony! Simon owed his entire life to the One who had cleansed him from leprosy—the same One others were planning to kill. Another guest also owed his life to Jesus. That guest was Lazarus—a man recently raised from the dead by Jesus.

What stories Simon and Lazarus could tell! Wouldn't you love to have been invited to that dinner with Lazarus? You could hear him tell how it was three to four days beyond death. Think of it! You could even ask Simon, "How was it as a leper? How is it now?" And in addition to these two, Jesus would be there. And with Jesus, most of the twelve disciples. And with a group that large, you need to have someone serving. Guess who? Right—that called for Martha. She was there serving. Martha was always serving!

The dinner must have been great, and the conversation even greater. Maybe there was some laughter, maybe not. Whatever, they must have had a memorable time. Don't you love places and times like that? Everyone relaxed. Everybody knowing each other—everyone at ease.

But someone was conspicuous by her absence. She has appeared only twice in Scripture in a significant way. Once (Luke 10) she was sitting at the feet of Jesus listening while her sister Martha was serving. And the other time she was falling on her face before our Lord (John 11) after her brother died. Mary was not one of the more prominent characters, not until this moving, almost-sacred scene we're about to witness. Here, she distinguishes herself as a woman who was unafraid of others' opinions and committed to excellence.

Extravagant Devotion—Extreme Reaction

Now you have to understand that things are quite different today in America from what they were in those days in Jerusalem. Back then, a Jewish woman never reclined at a table full of men. And she certainly never let her hair down in public. She would prepare the meal and serve it to the men, but then she would back away to eat in another room, like the kitchen, much like the custom in Arabia to this day. I mention that so you will be properly prepared for the shock of what occurred. Hang on!

> And while He was in Bethany at the home of Simon the leper, and reclining at table, there came a woman with an alabaster vial of costly perfume of pure nard; and she broke the vial and poured it over His head (Mark 14:3).

Genuine nard was made from dried leaves of a rare Himalayan plant. And the particular vase Mary used, if it were like others used in that day to hold expensive contents, was itself a thing of beauty. Commonly, such vases were capable of holding not less than a Roman pound, *twelve full ounces*, of this costly perfume.

Allow me to interrupt the narrative long enough to acquaint you with the cost of certain fragrances today. One authority I spoke to recently informed me that Jean Patou 1000 is perhaps the finest. It sells for $110 a quarter-ounce. The next, in the opinion of this person, is Pheromone, which goes for a cool $150 a half-ounce!

But Mary's vase most likely contained twenty-four times that amount. This woman had a perfume so expensive that if you were to weigh its significance in dollars and cents you could have fed hundreds of families an entire meal. Over a year's wage was contained in that little vase. We're talking superextravagant, top-notch quality stuff!

And without hesitation, Mary broke the vase and poured its entire contents over Jesus' head. (In John's account, we read that she also took her hair and wiped Jesus' feet with this magnificent perfume.) Imagine the fragrance which swept across that room when Mary broke open the vase, and poured its contents down across Jesus' head. Then to the amazement of everyone except Jesus, she poured the last of the perfume across His feet, pulled down her hair, and then wiped His feet with her hair.

> Mary therefore took a pound of very costly, genuine spikenard ointment, and anointed the feet of Jesus, and wiped His feet with her hair; and the house was filled with the fragrance of the ointment (John 12:3).

What an explosive act . . . what extravagance! How *could* she?

> The delicious fragrance ran down over His shining hair and thick beard. It enfolded His body with its delightful aroma. Even His tunic and flowing undergarment were drenched with its enduring pungency. Wherever He moved during the ensuing forty-eight hours, the perfume would go with Him: Into the Passover: into the Garden of Gethsemane: into the high priest's home: into Herod's hall: into Pilate's praetorium: into the crude hands of those who cast lots for His clothing at the foot of the cross.
>
> The special rite of perfuming the head and body was a rare ritual reserved only for royalty. It was the most lofty honor that could be bestowed by a common person. Jesus recognized this and so did those around Him. It was a significant moment of momentous meaning.[2]

That helpful insight reminds us that Mary's devotion lingered; it wasn't just for that moment, then quickly forgotten. Since His garments weren't changed, the aroma went with Him everywhere He went until shortly before His death. Even those who later gambled for His garments must have recognized the lingering fragrance. Don't forget, Mary had poured it all over Him. Talk about excellence . . . talk about extravagant love . . . *I love it!*

But not everyone loved it. The magnificence of the moment was marred by the murmur of some small-minded men. Those who watched this act were men who made their bed under the stars and ate figs they picked from trees and fish they caught in the sea. I mean, those guys calculated life by the bits and pieces. And their logical minds, their two-dimensional figuring simply couldn't put this together. They absolutely couldn't believe Mary had broken the whole thing! She didn't just dip her finger in the vase and wipe a little here and there, she broke it and poured it all out. They were indignant. How could she do such a thing? They were in shock. You think I'm imagining that? Read for yourself:

> But some were indignantly remarking to one another, "For what purpose has this perfume been wasted?" (Mark 14:4).

Now wait a minute. Before we get too sophisticated about all this, remember we're observing a scene that happened in the first century. Folks like us have had nineteen centuries to think about it. Extravagant deeds such as this were considered appropriate and even heroic a few hundred years later. One would wonder how many great cathedrals were raised against the wishes of the public, how many fine pieces of art were built in spite of the sneering crowd who calculated by exacting weights and measures. This kind of expense never makes sense at the moment, especially to those of an extremely practical mindset. And if you figure everything on the basis of bare essentials, any expression of art is considered extravagant!

So these men shouted that the perfume had been wasted. "How could she? Do you realize what could have been done with this amount?" They've already got it figured out.

> "For this perfume might have been sold for over three hundred denarii, and the money given to the poor." And they were scolding her (Mark 14:5).

There will always be a breakdown in the logic of extreme devotion if the basis of comparison is the poor. Furthermore, there will never be an understanding by those who confine themselves to operating in that tight, rigid radius. You miss that, you miss it all. People to this day operate with that mentality. Function still gets more votes than devotion. Practicality will always win over beauty. "Lighten up on the music so we can serve more food . . . no need for sculpture or fine paintings or lovely structures so long as the poor are present. If black-and-white is cheaper, color is wasteful . . . if a little electronic organ will do the job, a pipe organ is extravagant!" On and on the argument goes.

We shouldn't be too surprised to read that these men "scolded" Mary. We're not told what they said, but you can certainly imagine—especially if you are an eagle who has soared in the heights of "extravagance" on occasion.

JUSTIFICATION AND DEFENSE

Jesus not only defends Mary's action, He justifies the woman on the basis of purity of motive and urgency of the hour. Don't miss that.

Jesus said, "Let her alone." (In today's terms, "Shut up, men. Be quiet.")

> . . . why do you bother her? She has done a good deed to Me. For the poor you always have with you, and whenever you wish, you can do them good; but you do not always have Me. She has done what she could; she has anointed My body beforehand for the burial (Mark 14:6–8).

Jesus' death and burial were two of the last things His disciples wanted to think about that day. I can just hear them saying, "This evening meal is a delightful time of celebration together; don't talk about death, talk about life."

But Mary had her focus right. She wasn't enamored by the celebration of the season; she had not forgotten that her Lord's days were numbered. "You don't know when it will happen, men. . . . She's simply giving Me everything she owns. She's broken the vase in honor of My death." It was an "early embalming." How that changed the perspective!

I hope you didn't overlook Jesus' comment, "The poor you always have with you." There has to be some kind of implication in that statement. You and I know, for sure, that it is not, in any sense of the word, a put-down of the poor. We know Jesus better than that. No one has been a more significant instrument for helping the poor than Jesus of Nazareth. No one has demonstrated a greater heart of compassion. Then what could He mean by that comment? He's looking at Mary's act in light of its overall perspective. He sees His death as imminent. He sees her devotion as properly extravagant. And so He says, in effect, "It's all right. Don't criticize or try to stop her. For this moment [allow Me], *forget* the poor! Her 'extravagance,' in this case, is absolutely appropriate. In fact, commendable!"

Jesus accepts Mary's act of praise which she gave for all the right motives. Her commitment of sincere devotion may seem to us to be an overreaction, but He did not consider it so. Not at all.

> "And truly I say to you, wherever the gospel is preached in the whole world, that also which this woman has done shall be spoken of in memory of her" (Mark 14:9).

This follow-up statement by Jesus is one of those often forgotten lines. It tells us that He planned for this whole incident to have a perpetual impact. Unfortunately, this woman's act of devotion has not always been given the prominence it deserves. The truth is that Mary is seldom, if ever, remembered. And when she is mentioned, it is almost with the wave of a hand, "Merely a gush of fanaticism, irresponsible extravagance, little more." Yet Jesus considered her deed worthy of being mentioned throughout time, around the world. How greatly we need the memory of Mary, and yet how seldom we hear of it! She is one of those misunderstood people who chose to live above the level of mediocrity—one who truly soared like the eagles, a model of elegant excellence.

LASTING MEMORIAL—LINGERING LESSONS

As I said in the beginning of this chapter, this episode at Simon's home is one of those accounts that needs to be handled with care. In some ways it is so sacred an event that I hesitate to touch it. But since it contains such important lessons for those who want to soar through life, living above mediocrity, I will risk returning to the story and reflecting on it from the viewpoint of excellence.

In a nutshell, I believe this event has been preserved to teach one major message: *There are certain times when extravagance is appropriate.* I will go further. In our day of emphasis on high-tech calculations and finely tuned budgets with persistent reminders of cost, restraint, and propriety (that is, never being "guilty" of doing anything outside the bounds of the ordinary), *anything* beyond the basics can be misconstrued as excessive. If you buy into that ever-present Spartan philosophy, then everything you build will be functional, ordinary, and basic. Everything you purchase will be at the lowest cost. Everything you do will be average.

We used to laugh at a comment one of the American astronauts made years ago, but the laughter has hushed since the *Challenger* tragedy. The way the story goes, someone stuck his head inside the nose capsule before the team of astronauts had launched and asked, "Well, how does it feel?" With a grin, one of them replied, "It really makes you think twice in here when you realize everything in this whole project was constructed according to the lowest bid!" Many— dare I say, most—conduct their entire lives "according to the lowest bid." This is never more obvious than in the evangelical community today. Let anything appear the least bit expensive and you can expect a critical response.

Not only is abundance suspected as being inappropriately extravagant, it is openly criticized. The majority will never understand. They will always make the ordinary their standard. I challenge that! On the basis of this magnificent story, I feel there are times when "extravagant" gifts are not only appropriate, they are occasionally essential! So are "extravagant" purchases and "extravagant" expressions of love, especially if we are determined to live above the level of mediocrity. "Extravagant" memorials need to be erected. "Extravagant" art needs to be appreciated. Yes, even "extravagant" displays of our devotion to the living Lord. I believe there are times when God, as it were, shouts with a smile, "Break a vase!"

Think back. Do you know what God did when He built that magnificent tabernacle in the wilderness? He broke a vase. Of all things, He instructed those wilderness wanderers to construct a fabulous, albeit temporary, place of worship—a tabernacle. And they followed His design to the nth degree. Lots of gold. Beautiful tapestry. Lovely wood craftsmanship. Impressive creativity. And throughout those years in the wilderness God's glory resided in that so-called "extravagant" worship center.

As the years passed, God's people settled down in a land they could call their own. By and by, their king, Solomon—a man of peace—heard God's voice again: "Break a vase, Solomon!" And the result? An incredible temple, which became one of the ageless "wonders of the world." Study the details for yourself. You won't believe its beauty. You talk about extravagance! You talk about quality and creative craftsmanship! So perfectly shaped and polished were those stones that comprised the walls in that awesome building, not a sound was heard as each stone was slipped into place by the stonemasons. And what about those veils, the colorful curtains, the ornate windows, the elegant steps, the mercy seat! Gold—some of it solid, much of it beaten, other sections overlaid—it was everywhere! God broke a vase. Yes, it was an exception all right, but it was also a call to excellence—a call to live above the level of mediocrity. Likewise, there are times today when extravagance is appropriate, especially if we are to soar like an eagle.

Paul himself said, "I have learned how to be abased and how to abound." So we see that occasionally God broke a vase in Paul's journeys, too. There were times He let Paul stay in the penthouse. Some of us would have great difficulty staying in a penthouse. Our reasoning might go something like this: "It just isn't right. It's too extravagant. But I'dsure like to try it a time or two." (Just now I can picture a wife saying to her husband, "Honey, listen to something Swindoll wrote . . . and listen closely.")

Have you ever taken a close look at the "new Jerusalem" in Revelation? Ever done an intelligent study of the heavenly city where God has designed for His people to spend eternity? We're talking *wall-to-wall broken vases!* If that thought makes you nervous, you'll be nervous throughout eternity.

I'm told that Harry Ironside, a fine pastor and conference speaker of yesteryear, once checked into a hotel where a church had made reservations for him. Without a word, one of the bell-boys led the pastor to the designated accommodations and unlocked the door. One look and Ironside realized he was in the penthouse. It was like nothing he had ever seen. At first he just stood in the doorway staring in disbelief at the plush furnishings—among them a silver service sitting on a carved table and lots of highly polished brass. On further investigation he discovered multiple rooms, including several bathrooms with thick, luxurious towels and marble finishings. Immediately, Pastor Ironside went to the phone and called the desk attendant downstairs, "I think there's been a mistake," he said.

The receptionist asked, "Are you Harry A. Ironside?"

"Yes."

"Are you ministering at such and such a church tomorrow?"

"Yes."

"Well, I have a note here that I don't understand, but it says, 'If Dr. Ironside calls you and has any concerns, just say, "We want you to learn how to *abound*, Dr. Ironside."'"

Before you get your hopes up, remember, that's not what we can expect . . . nor should we. Like the account of Mary's anointing Jesus, such rare moments need to be handled with care, not flaunted. Vases were not broken over the Savior every day. He didn't smell of luxurious perfume throughout His life. But how perfectly fitting it was at this moment.

Now for a few pointed questions:

- Must all the places where God is represented look mediocre?
- Must all the furnishings be of lowest quality or just moderate?
- Must every semblance of art be omitted?

- Must we live all our lives under constant restraint and self-imposed guilt, for fear of being told that we are overlooking the poor?

- Must *everything* be just "adequate"? Why not occasionally use something of the highest quality?

Let me give you a new thought: *If you can explain it, it may not be extravagant enough!* Did you notice that Mary never once said a word here or in any other passage of Scripture explaining herself? She never said one word, not even when they rebuked her. How could she even begin to explain such extravagance? A better question: Why should she? Even if she tried, they were the type who would never have understood. So Mary simply did what her heart told her to do—without explanation.

It takes pure motive and a strong inner confidence to be that secure. Such extravagant love cannot be explained nor can it be justified to calculating, rigid, narrow minds. And because the majority will always be driven by what is practical, the majority will never understand.

There's an old theatrical expression actors sometimes use in jest when a person is about to go out on the stage: "Hey, break a leg." I've got a new one for quality-minded, high-flying eagles. When we greet one another: "Hey, break a vase!" When's the last time you broke a vase? When's the last time you did it and you were so secure you didn't even feel the need to explain it, though you were questioned and criticized? Believe me, those who soar will understand. Those who don't, I repeat, won't.

One who understands writes:

> In Mary we see the gaiety of abandoned praise. With glorious imprudence she broke the container and with loving care used the whole contents. She was liberated out of herself in a dramatic devotion. Her unimpaired impulses moved her to give a great gift. The serendipity of love had a free agent. It was not smothered with caution and prejudice. She was lifted out of arithmetic calculation to abandoned compassion.
>
> She did not allow reserve to keep her from the moment which would never come again. . . . There is a time . . . when people should be careful, but there is also a time when they ought not to be cautious. There is something to be said for careful saving of our resources in order to make possible a great moment of unrestrained thanksgiving. . . . The

Christian is not a tight-fisted, clenched-teeth, grim-faced person. Rather, he is one who loves and laughs and gives himself to Christ lavishly. In Mary we are challenged by extravagant love. . . . "A certain excessiveness is an important ingredient of greatness."[3]

Do you at times act upon that impulse to abandon restraint? Do you ever have the courage to risk an extravagant expression of love? Then you're on your way to living above the level of mediocrity. Extravagance is an exception, I remind you, but there are times when it is appropriate.

Not long ago one of my staff members told me he had made a decision that was most unusual for him. He had decided he would take his wife to Hawaii. And they were going to take the trip without the kids. They had wanted to go for years, but were never able to afford it. When they sold their home, they had made a little extra, so he decided to splurge. I distinctly remember grabbing him by the shoulders and saying, "Good for you. That's great! It's about time you soared like an eagle." He smiled, "You sound like my wife."

I know of a school that has raised a memorial to a couple of very significant people in their history. The school decided to place a lovely (and I might add, expensive) set of chimes in the center of the campus in honor of this husband-wife team, alumni who have contributed so much to the life of that school. I openly applaud the school for the "extravagance" of that memorial. It fits. It's beautiful. It's right! When the president of that fine institution risked that decision, he "broke a vase!" What a refreshing, delightful thing to do!

I don't know how many times I have enjoyed reading Anne Ortlund's insightful words on this very subject. She approaches this story from a slightly different angle, but because her thoughts fit so beautifully, I draw this chapter and the first section of my book to a close with her comments.

A while back, Ray preached on Mark 14:3. "Here came Mary, . . . with her alabaster vase of nard to the dinner where Jesus was. She broke the bottle and poured it on Him."

An alabaster vase—milky white, veined, smooth, precious.

And pure nard inside! Gone forever. According to John 12:3, the whole house became filled with the fragrance.

Some story.

Christians file into church on a Sunday morning. One by one by one they march in—like separate alabaster vases.

Contained.

Self-sufficient.

Encased.

Individually complete.

Contents undisclosed.

No perfume emitting at all.

Their vases aren't bad looking. In fact, some of them are the Beautiful People, and they become Vase-Conscious: conscious of their own vase and of one another's. They're aware of clothes, of personalities, of position in this world—of exteriors.

So before and after church (maybe during) they're apt to talk Vase talk.

Mary broke her vase.

Broke it?! How shocking. How controversial. Was everybody doing it? Was it a vase-breaking party? No, she just did it all by herself. What happened then? The obvious: all the contents were forever released. She could never hug her precious nard to herself again.

Many bodies who file into church, no doubt, do so because they have Jesus inside of them. Jesus!—precious, exciting, life giving. But most of them keep Him shut up, contained, enclosed all their lives. And the air is full of NOTHING. They come to church and sit—these long rows of cold, beautiful, alabaster vases! Then the cold, beautiful, alabaster vases get up and march out again, silently—or maybe talking their cold alabaster talk—to repeat the ritual week after week, year after year.

Unless they just get too bored and quit.

The need for Christians everywhere (nobody is exempt) is to be broken. The vase has to be smashed! Christians have to let the life out! It will fill the room with sweetness. And the congregation will all be broken shards, mingling together for the first time.

Of course it's awkward and scary to be broken! Of course it's easier to keep up that cold alabaster front.

It was costly for Mary too.[4]

You talk about something too beautiful for words, something so valuable, it's priceless. It is a living vase, broken before others. But don't worry, the "do not touch" sign no longer applies. When the vase is broken, its contents fill a room. And interestingly, it says to everyone, "Please *do* touch."

For some of you, the broken vase is long overdue. I'm talking about an extravagant gift to the work of Christ, the kind Mary gave. And what was that? Herself. For some of you it would be the first time ever that you gave yourself to anyone. Christ invites you to give yourself to Him, completely, extravagantly—a living vase broken before others. Do it now and discover what soaring is all about—become a Christian.

Part Two

Overcoming Mediocrity Means Living Differently

*Death and sorrow will be the
companions of our journey;
hardship our garment; constancy
and valor our only shield. We must
be united, we must be undaunted,
we must be inflexible.*

*Sir Winston Churchill
1940*

5

VISION: SEEING BEYOND
THE MAJORITY

*F*or four chapters we have underscored the fact that confronting mediocrity takes thinking clearly. Everything we deal with in life begins in the mind, so we began there. We discovered the intensity of the battle that rages in our minds. We also learned that those who confront mediocrity must do so through the perspective of another kingdom, ruled not by ourselves but by our Lord Himself—a surrender which costs dearly. It costs our commitment. And when that commitment expresses itself (as in Mary's case in the days of Jesus), it is revealed periodically in expressions of extravagant love.

Having come to terms with the importance of thinking clearly, we are ready to tackle the second challenge: *living differently*. Whoever clears away the mental fog is no longer satisfied drifting along with the masses. *Vision* replaces mental resistance. *Determination* marches in, overstepping laziness and indifference. And it's then that we begin to realize the value of *priorities*, a step which dictates the need for personal *accountability*. I will define each of these four terms a little later. But for now, consider them as one domino bumping the next. Each one of these stages precedes the next, forming a unit that spells out the basics of living differently—with excellence—in a world of sameness, boredom, and futility.

Throughout this book I continue to refer to our "world." That may throw you a curve, since I'm usually not referring to the planet we live on when I use the term. By "world" I mean the invisible yet surrounding atmosphere in which we live that "erodes faith, dissipates hope, and corrupts love," as Eugene Peterson puts it.[1] It may be a system of thought that includes human intelligence, persuasive winsomeness, clever and appealing logic, competition, creativity, and resourcefulness, but it lacks the essential ingredients that enable us to soar like an eagle.

The most treacherous part of all is the way we become brainwashed by the system, thus blocked from reaching our full potential. The end result is predictable: internal anxiety and external mediocrity.

Three Indisputable Facts about the World System

Let's go a little deeper into an understanding of the world system. To give ourselves a point of reference, let's look again at Jesus' words. Pay close attention to His repeated remarks about being anxious.

> "No one can serve two masters; for either he will hate the one and love the other, or he will hold to one and despise the other. You cannot serve God and mammon. For this reason I say to you, do not be anxious for your life, as to what you shall eat, or what you shall drink; nor for your body, as to what you shall put on. Is not life more than food, and the body than clothing? Look at the birds of the air, that they do not sow, neither do they reap, nor gather into barns, and yet your heavenly Father feeds them. Are you not worth much more than they? And which of you by being anxious can add a single cubit to his life's span? And why are you anxious about clothing? Observe how the lilies of the field grow; they do not toil nor do they spin, yet I say to you that even Solomon in all his glory did not clothe himself like one of these. But if God so arrays the grass of the field, which is alive today and tomorrow is thrown into the furnace, will He not much more do so for you, O men of little faith? Do not be anxious then, saying, 'What shall we eat?' or 'What shall we drink?' or 'With what shall we clothe ourselves?' For all these things the Gentiles eagerly seek; for your heavenly Father knows that you need all these things. But seek first His kingdom and His righteousness; and all these things shall be added to you. Therefore do not be anxious for tomorrow; for tomorrow will care for itself. Each day has enough trouble of its own" (Matt. 6:24–34).

I never read those familiar words without becoming aware of the difference between the way people *naturally* live (full of worry and anxiety) and the way our Lord planned for us to live (free of all that excess baggage). Then why? Why do we opt for a lifestyle that is the very antithesis of what He designed for us? Because the "system" sucks us in! We yield to a lesser lifestyle because "all those things the Gentiles eagerly seek" (v. 32) occupy our attention and ultimately dominate our lives. As I see it, there are three interrelated factors.

1. <u>We live in a negative, hostile world.</u> Face it, my friend, the system that surrounds us focuses on the negatives: what is wrong, not what is right; what is missing, not what is present; what is ugly, not what is beautiful; what is destructive, not what is constructive; what cannot be done, not what can be done; what hurts, not what helps; what we lack, not what we have. You question that? Pick up your local newspaper and read it through. See if the majority of the news doesn't concern itself (and the reader) with the negatives. It's contagious!

This negative mindset leads to incredible feelings of anxiety. Surround most people with enough negatives and I can guarantee the result: fear, resentment, and anger. Negative information plus hostile thinking equals anxiety. And yet Jesus said again and again, "Don't be anxious." The world system, I repeat, works directly against the life God planned for His people. The realization of this led Isaac Watts, over 250 years ago, to write:

> Are there no foes for me to face?
> Must I not stem the flood?
> Is this vile world a friend to grace
> To help me on to God?[2]

2. <u>We are engulfed in mediocrity and cynicism</u> (a direct result of living in a negative world). Without the motivation of divinely empowered insight and enthusiasm, people tend toward the "average," doing just enough to get by. Thus, the fallout from the system is mediocrity. The majority dictates the rules, and excitement is replaced with a shrug of the shoulders. Excellence is not only lost in the shuffle, whenever it rears its head, it is considered a threat.

3. <u>Most choose not to live differently.</u> Those who take their cues from the system blend into the drab backdrop of the majority. Words like "Just go with the flow" and "Don't make waves" and "Who cares?" begin to gain a hearing.

Stop and think. In a world where all that cynicism is present, what is absent? Courage! That strong muscle of character that gives a nation its pride and gives a home its purpose and gives a person the will to excel is gone. I'm certainly not the first to point out the danger of a lack of courage. Aleksandr Solzhenitsyn's speeches frequently include such warnings:

> Must one point out that from ancient times a decline in courage has been considered the beginning of the end?[3]

What, then, does it take to live differently? In chapters 5–8 I will be concentrating on four specifics: vision, determination, priorities, and accountability. When I think of *vision*, I have in mind the ability to see above and beyond the majority. Again I am reminded of the eagle, which has eight times as many visual cells per cubic centimeter than does a human. This translates into rather astounding abilities. For example, flying at 600 feet elevation, an eagle can spot an object the size of a dime moving through six-inch grass. The same creature can see three-inch fish jumping in a lake five miles away. Eaglelike people can envision what most would miss.

By *determination*, I think of inner fortitude, strength of character—being disciplined to remain consistent, strong, and diligent regardless of the odds or the demands. Again, the eagle represents this trait. Bald eagles are adamant in the defense of their territory and their young. The strength in the eagle's claws is nothing short of phenomenal—sufficient to grasp and break large bones in a man's forearm. Eagle types possess tenacity.

The other two are virtually self-explanatory. *Priorities* have to do with choosing first things first—doing essential things in the order of importance, bypassing the incidentals. And *accountability* relates to answering the hard questions, being closely in touch with a few individuals rather than living like an isolated Lone Ranger. Eaglelike folks may be rare, but they possess an incredible loyalty when they do link up.

For the remainder of this chapter, let's concentrate on the value of vision.

TWO COURAGEOUS MEN
WHO DISAGREED WITH THE MAJORITY

The best way I know to stimulate you toward a renewed commitment to excellence is to return to Scripture for an inspired account. The one I have in mind is tucked away in the fourth book of the Old Testament, the Book of Numbers, chapter 13.

Some Background

Five things should be remembered in order for us to be brought up to speed here in Numbers 13.

First, there has been an exodus. The Israelites have been set free from Egyptian bondage. Pharaoh has let the people go. They have departed from Egypt with all their belongings and with all their family members.

Second, under Moses' leadership God's chosen people have arrived at the edge of the Promised Land. According to the last verse of chapter 12, "the people . . . camped in the wilderness of Paran," right at the edge of Canaan (the Promised Land). In the exodus God showed Himself strong. He displayed His miraculous power when the Israelites went through the Red Sea and when He directed them safely across the wilderness to the land of Canaan. When they arrived at the border, the Israelites could see smoke rising from the cities in the misty distance. Perhaps from that vantage point they could even see some of the walls that surrounded the larger cities. I'm sure their hearts beat faster as they expressed their relief and excitement: "Finally . . . we made it!"

Third, the new territory was theirs to claim. God promised it to them.

> "Send out for yourself men so that they may spy out the land of Canaan, which I am going to give to the sons of Israel; you shall send a man from each of their fathers' tribes, every one a leader among them" (v. 2).

God clearly promised His people the land. "You'll have to invade it and fight, but I promise you that victory is *guaranteed*." Nobody on this earth ever had a better deal in battle than those people!

When General Dwight Eisenhower and his brain trust were about to lead our troops through the Normandy Invasion back in World War II, they were filled with anxiety brought on by uncertainty. And anxiety increased when the weather worsened. "Shall we proceed? Shall we wait? Shall we abort the mission entirely?" We can hardly imagine the churning uneasiness. And even though Eisenhower had this massive assault ready to move into operation, he wasn't sure that the troops could make a safe landing, to say nothing of what they might encounter from the enemy forces. Finally, with anxious uncertainty, the general signaled thumbs up.

The Israelites faced nothing like that. They had the sure promise of God. "You will have the land." No troops ever had greater reason to fight with assurance.

Fourth, God commanded Moses to spy out the land. In order to plan an intelligent battle strategy, he was to send in a few selected scouts to spy out the land. So Moses cooperated. Remember this: Not once were the spies asked to give their opinion about whether they could take the land. No need for that since God had already promised. Instead they were told precisely what to do.

> So Moses sent them from the wilderness of Paran at the command of the Lord, all of them men who were heads of the sons of Israel. These then were their names: from the tribe of Reuben, Shammua the son of Zaccur; from the tribe of Simeon, Shaphat the son of Hori; from the tribe of Judah, Caleb the son of Jephunneh; from the tribe of Issachar, Igal the son of Joseph; from the tribe of Ephraim, Hoshea the son of Nun; from the tribe of Benjamin, Palti the son of Raphu; from the tribe of Zebulun, Gaddiel the son of Sodi; from the tribe of Joseph, from the tribe of Manasseh, Gaddi the son of Susi; from the tribe of Dan, Ammiel the son of Gemalli; from the tribe of Asher, Sethur the son of Michael; from the tribe of Naphtali, Nahbi the son of Vophsi; from the tribe of Gad, Geuel the son of Machi. These are the names of the men whom Moses sent to spy out the land; but Moses called Hoshea the son of Nun, Joshua (vv. 3–16).

Back in those days each one of those names was familiar. They were like twelve famous mayors in America today, or twelve of our more prominent governors or senators. They were famous men among the Israelites. I emphasize that point because I don't want you to think for a moment that some of those men were over-the-hill-type guys, lacking good sense. All twelve were leader types, but only two soared above the restrictive mindset so common in the system.

Fifth, their assignment was clear. Painfully, explicitly clear.

> When Moses sent them to spy out the land of Canaan, he said to them, "Go up there into the Negev; then go up into the hill country. And see what the land is like, and whether the people who live in it are strong or weak, whether they are few or many. And how is the land in which they live, is it good or bad? And how are the cities in which they live, are they like open camps or with fortifications? And how is the land, is it fat or lean? Are there trees in it or not? Make an effort then to get some of the fruit of the land . . ." (vv. 17–20).

End of assignment. Once they found out those things, mission accomplished! Never once does Moses say, "And when you return, advise us on whether we ought to invade the land." No, that wasn't their mandate. They were told to scope out the land, to do a quick, secret reconnaissance, and to come back with a report about what they had observed.

The spies left and stayed gone for forty days.

> So they went up and spied out the land from the wilderness of Zin as far as Rehob, at Lebo-hamath. When they had gone up into the Negev, they came to Hebron where Ahiman, Sheshai and Talmai, the descendants of Anak were. (Now Hebron was built seven years before Zoan in Egypt.)
>
> Then they came to the valley of Eshcol and from there cut down a branch with a single cluster of grapes; and they carried it on a pole between two men, with some of the pomegranates and the figs. That place was called the valley of Eshcol, because of the cluster which the sons of Israel cut down from there.
>
> When they returned from spying out the land, at the end of forty days, they proceeded to come to Moses and Aaron and to all the congregation of the sons of Israel in the wilderness of Paran, at Kadesh; and they brought back word to them and to all the congregation and showed them the fruit of the land. Thus they told him, and said, "We went in to the land where you sent us; and it certainly does flow with milk and honey, and this is its fruit" (vv. 21–27).

While these twelve men were in the land of Canaan, they took samples of the fruit and brought them back. Once they returned to the Israelite camp, they displayed the grapes and showed them the fruit of the land.

And all the people gathered around and listened as the report was given. So far so good. Beautiful fruit. Delicious. Impressive report. I'm sure there were a few oohs and aahs.

Negative Report

But while everyone was getting excited, ten of the spies went on:

> "Nevertheless, the people who live in the land are strong, and the cities are fortified and very large; and moreover, we saw the descendants of Anak there. Amalek is living in the land of the Negev and the Hittites and the Jebusites and the Amorites are living in the hill country, and the Canaanites are living by the sea and by the side of the Jordan."

... "We are not able to go up against the people, for they are too strong for us" (vv. 28–29, 31).

I find myself wanting to shout back, "Hey, wait a minute! Who asked you? Nobody wants to know if we're able to go up or not. That wasn't your assignment, men. God has already promised us that it is our land. We just want to know what the land is like."

Notice that these ten men went far beyond their assignment.

> So they gave out to the sons of Israel a bad report of the land which they had spied out, saying, "The land through which we have gone, in spying it out, is a land that devours its inhabitants; and all the people whom we saw in it are men of great size. There also we saw the Nephilim (the sons of Anak are part of the Nephilim); and we became like grass-hoppers in our own sight, and so we were in their sight" (vv. 32–33).

"Wow! You people cannot believe the size of those giants!" Today I suppose we would say, "They looked like professional athletes!"

Ever been at courtside at a professional basketball game? If you have, then you know what it is like to be around people who make you feel like a grasshopper. I distinctly recall standing alongside the Los Angeles Lakers center, Kareem Abdul-Jabbar. We're talking, "Chuck, the grasshopper."

I have spoken at several professional football pre-game chapel services. And invariably, I feel as if I am surrounded by giants! One time, most of the men were sitting on one side of the room. I asked if some would mind moving to the other side, since the room was beginning to sink on that side. When they began to move about, I definitely felt like an insect. I just hoped one of them wouldn't step on me as they lumbered out the door after the service. That's bound to be how those spies felt back in Moses' day.

Now what kind of impact did this narrow vision have on the people? Just in case you wonder if negativism and restrictive vision are contagious, keep reading:

> Then all the congregation lifted up their voices and cried, and the people wept that night. And all the sons of Israel grumbled against Moses and Aaron; and the whole congregation said to them, "Would that we had died in the land of Egypt! Or would that we had died in this wilderness!" (Num. 14:1–2).

You say, "How could they ever say such a thing? God *promised* they would have the land!" Because negativism is infectious. Because lack of vision from the world system engulfs us. Human reasoning overrules faith! Natural thinking says you can't whip people that big. You can't win if you invade that land. I mean, look at how many there are! Count them: There are the Jebusites and the Hittites and the Amorites and the Canaanites—probably even "the termites." *Everybody* in the land is against this wandering band of Hebrews! And add to that list the sons of Anak, the giants! Can't you just hear those Israelites, "We've got to face the giants!" When you think like that, it's retreat city!

> So they said to one another, "Let us appoint a leader and return to Egypt" (v. 4).

There's always some guy who has a creative idea like "Let's retreat! Let's go back. Too formidable!" You wonder what impact it had on Moses and Aaron?

> Then Moses and Aaron fell on their faces in the presence of all the assembly of the congregation of the sons of Israel (v. 5).

When the majority lack vision, their short-sightedness tends to take a severe toll on those trying to lead.

Positive Report . . . Unlimited Vision

Now the good news is that those ten spies were not the only ones who gave a report. I have purposely left out two courageous men until now. One is named *Caleb*.

> Then Caleb quieted the people before Moses, and said, "We should by all means go up and take possession of it, for we shall surely overcome it" (13:30).

The other is named *Joshua*.

> And Joshua the son of Nun and Caleb the son of Jephunneh, of those who had spied out the land, tore their clothes (14:6).

Both men ripped their garments when they saw Moses and Aaron on their faces and said, "Wait a minute! There's another side to all this. In fact, there is an issue at stake. It's time for us to be courageous. Let's start seeing this challenge through eyes of faith!"

> And they spoke to all the congregation of the sons of Israel, saying, "The land which we passed through to spy out is an exceedingly good land. If the Lord is pleased with us, then He will bring us into this land, and give it to us—a land which flows with milk and honey. Only do not rebel against the Lord; and do not fear the people of the land, for they shall be our prey. Their protection has been removed from them, and the Lord is with us; do not fear them" (vv. 7–9).

I love those courageous words. They always remind me of the opening lines of Psalm 27:

> The Lord is my light and my salvation;
> Whom shall I fear?
> The Lord is the defense of my life;
> Whom shall I dread?
> When evildoers came upon me to devour my flesh,
> My adversaries and my enemies, they stumbled and fell.
> Though a host encamp against me,
> My heart will not fear;
> Though war arise against me,
> In spite of this I shall be confident (vv. 1–3).

With vision there is no room to be frightened. No reason for intimidation. It's time to march forward! Let's be confident and positive! And after a Caleb-Joshua speech, people are ready to applaud and say, "Good job. Let's go!" Right?

Wrong—look for yourself. "But all the congregation said to stone them with stones" (Num. 14:10). Which tells you what people think of positive thinking. Here are two men God smiled upon. Two men Solzhenitsyn would have been proud of. Two men you and I admire, men of rare vision. But the majority said, "They're out to lunch. They're wrong. We can't possibly stand against such obstacles." This kind of majority attitude reminds me of a quote by Arnold Toynbee that goes something like this: "It is doubtful if the majority has *ever* been right." Those words always make me smile.

One Quality Essential for Uniqueness

Now, we are not studying ancient history. We're thinking about living today. My interest isn't in writing a book that traces the Hebrews from Paran into Canaan. I'm far more interested in helping people like us to cope with and conquer today's obstacles. And they are nonetheless formidable. If you told a group of people that giants stand against you, without hesitation most folks would say, "Give up now, surrender, quit." Enter: anxiety. Exit: peace. But since when do people of faith conduct their lives on the basis of sight?

Did you observe something conspicuously absent from that story? The first thing that goes when you imbibe the system is courageous vision. Vision—the one essential ingredient for being an original in a day of copies gets lost, overwhelmed by the odds. Too bad! We start focusing on the trouble. We start numbering the people. We start measuring their height and weighing them in. Then we start comparing the odds. The result is predictable: We become intimidated and wind up *defeated.*

What is your Canaan? What is your challenge? Which giants make you feel like a grasshopper when you face them? What does your future resemble when you measure it on the basis of facts and figures? You'd like not to surrender, right? You'd like to be courageous, wouldn't you? There is a way through, but you'll need one essential quality—vision.

Vision is the ability to see God's presence, to perceive God's power, to focus on God's plan in spite of the obstacles.

I sometimes like to spell out things in A-B-C fashion. So let's close this chapter with an "alphabet" of vision—A-B-C-D-E.

A.   *Attitude.* When you have vision it affects your attitude. Your attitude is optimistic rather than pessimistic. Your attitude stays positive rather than negative. Not foolishly positive, as though in fantasy, for you are reading God into your circumstances. So when a situation comes that cuts your feet out from under you, you don't throw up your arms and panic. You don't give up. Instead, you say, "Lord, this is Your moment. This is where You take charge. You're in this." Caleb and Joshua came back, having seen the same obstacles the other ten spies saw, but they had a different attitude. Remember their words? "We are well able to handle it." So are you, my friend.

B. *Belief.* This is nothing more than having a strong belief in the power of God; having confidence in others around you who are in similar battles with you; and, yes, having confidence in yourself, by the grace of God. Refusing to give in to temptation, cynicism, and doubt. Not allowing yourself to become a jaded individual. Belief in oneself is terribly important.

> People need an atmosphere in which they can specialize, hone their skills, and discover their distinctiveness. The biographies of the great are sprinkled with accounts of how some teacher or some kindly employer looked closely enough to see a spark no one else saw and for periods, at least, believed in their ability to perfect that gift when no one else did. The Taft family . . . was evidently good at pushing their children to cut their own swath and to find a specialty of which to be proud. When Martha Taft was in elementary school in Cincinnati she was asked to introduce herself. She said, "My name is Martha Bowers Taft. My great-grandfather was President of the United States. My grandfather was United States senator. My daddy is ambassador to Ireland. And I am a Brownie."[4]

C. *Capacity.* What I have in mind here is a willingness to be stretched. When God has you look at your Canaan with all its formidable foes, He says, in effect, "You must be willing to be stretched. You have to allow your capacity to be invaded by My power."

I like what William James wrote:

> Everyone knows on any given day that there are energies slumbering in him which the incitements of that day do not call forth. . . . Compared with what we ought to be, we are only half awake. Our fires are damped, our drafts are checked. We are making use of only a small part of our possible mental and physical resources. . . . Stating the thing broadly, the human individual thus lives far within his limits; he possesses powers of various sorts he habitually fails to use.[5]

Isn't that the truth! Alleged "impossibilities" are opportunities for our capacities to be stretched.

D. *Determination.* I'm going to save most of my comments on this until the next chapter. Suffice it to say, determination is hanging tough when the going gets rough. I have no magic wand to wave over your future and say, "All of a sudden everything is going to fall into place." Vision requires determination, a constant focus on God who is watching and smiling.

E. *Enthusiasm*. Great word, *enthusiasm*. Its Greek origin is *éntheos*, "God in." It is the ability to see God in a situation, which makes the event exciting. And, by the way, do you know that He *is* watching? Do you realize that? Something happens to our vision that is almost magical when we become convinced that God our heavenly Father is involved in our activities and is applauding them.

Bob Richards, the Olympic pole vaulter of years ago, loved to tell the story of the goof-off who played around with football. He was somewhere between the bench and off the team. If there was mischief to be done, this kid was doing it. Everything was casual, no big deal. And he added very little to the team. He practiced, but he wasn't committed. He had a uniform and would show up to play, but never with enthusiasm.

He liked to hear the cheers, but not to charge the line. He liked to wear the suit, but not to practice. He did not like to put himself out. One day the players were doing fifty laps, and this showpiece was doing his usual five. The coach came over and said, "Hey kid, here is a telegram for you." The kid said, "Read it for me, Coach." He was so lazy he did not even like to read. The coach opened it up and read, "Dear son, your father is dead. Come home immediately." The coach swallowed hard. He said, "Take the rest of the week off." He didn't care if he took the rest of the year off.

Well, funny thing, game time came on Friday and here came the teams rushing out on the field, and lo and behold, the last kid out was the goof-off. No sooner did the gun sound than the kid said, "Coach, can I play today? Can I play?" The coach thought, "Kid, you're not playing today. This is homecoming. This is the big game. We need every real guy we have, and you are not one of them." Every time the coach turned around, the kid badgered him: "Coach, please let me play. Coach, I have got to play."

The first quarter ended with the score lopsided against the coach and his team. At half time, they were still further behind. The second half started, and things got progressively worse. The coach, mumbling to himself, began writing out his resignation, and up came the kid. "Coach, Coach, let me play, please!" The coach looked at the scoreboard. "All right," he said, "get in there, kid. You can't hurt anything now."

No sooner did the kid hit the field than his team exploded. He ran, blocked, and tackled like a star. The electricity leaped to the team. The score evened up. In the closing seconds of the game, this kid intercepted a pass and ran all the way for the winning touchdown!

The stands broke loose. The kid was everybody's hero. Such cheering you never heard. Finally the excitement subsided and the coach got over to the kid and said, "I never saw anything like that. What in the world happened to you out there?" He said, "Coach, you know my dad died last week." "Yes," he said, "I read you the telegram." "Well, Coach," he said, "my dad was blind. And today was the first day he ever saw me play."[6]

Today may be the first day you realized that your heavenly Father is watching you in life. He really is not absent, unconcerned, blind, or dead. He is alive. He is watching. He cares. That can make all the difference in the world.

Even in a world that is negative and hostile. Even in a world where the majority says, "We can't," you can. Trust God today. With eyes of faith, get back in the game. Play it with great enthusiasm. It's time to start soaring ... which is another way of saying it's time to live differently, which starts with seeing beyond the majority.

The word is *vision*.

6

DETERMINATION:
DECIDING TO HANG TOUGH

A disclaimer is probably in order. I would feel a little better if I could set the record straight, lest anyone have an expectation that is unrealistic. The disclaimer? There is no rabbit's foot hidden on some page in this book, so don't look for one.

In a volume that emphasizes the things I have been writing about, it would be easy for some to think that I know a magical secret, some hocus-pocus, cure-all miracle thought that is guaranteed to result in soaring. Sorry, I have no such offer. Living above the level of mediocrity is not going to happen by our taking a pill or repeating a mantra or learning and applying a quick-fix formula. The quality of life I have in mind is definitely possible, but it is definitely *not* a utopia softly and easily entered through the gates of Fantasyland.

When Jesus tells us to *"seek* first the kingdom of God," the very word *seek* implies a strong-minded pursuit. J. B. Phillips paraphrases the idea with "set your heart on." The Amplified Bible says, "Aim at and strive after." The Greek text of Matthew's Gospel states a continual command: "Keep on continually seeking. . . ." The thought is determination, which I define as "deciding to hang tough, *regardless."*

There is a well-known local coach in Fullerton, California, whose thirty-five-plus years in athletics have been eminently successful. Hal Sherbeck grew up in big-sky country and became a winning coach at Missoula High School. This led to a coaching career at the University of Montana, where he distinguished himself with an enviable win-loss record. Ultimately, Hal came to our city where he has been coaching at Fullerton Community College faithfully for many years. His incredible career in Southern California speaks for itself. When he was interviewed by the *Los Angeles Times*, the sportswriter wanted to know his secret. What was it that made him so successful? Without hesitation Coach Sherbeck said that his credo could best be stated in words written by an anonymous author. Ever since he was a boy growing up in Big Sandy, Montana, he has lived by these words:

> Press on.
> Nothing in the world
> Can take the place of persistence.
> Talent will not;
> Nothing is more common
> Than unsuccessful men
> With talent.
> Genius will not;
> Unrewarded genius
> Is almost a proverb.
> Education will not;
> The world is full of
> Educated derelicts.
> Persistence and determination
> Alone are important.[1]

Coach Sherbeck had no quick and easy formula for success; he lives by his strong commitment to persistence and determination.

Don't misunderstand. I have in mind being determined to accomplish what is right. I realize that criminal types could just as easily take this credo and commit themselves to a life of crime or some other irresponsible pursuit. But when the objective is good and the motive is pure, there is nothing more valuable in the pathway leading to genuine success than persistence and determination. Following one's dream requires these disciplines.

Almost every week I come in contact with people who have been misled, thinking that success depends solely upon talent or brilliance or education. But the list doesn't end there. For some it's getting the breaks, pulling the right strings, having the right personality, being in the right place at the right time, knowing the right people, playing their cards right, or (I smile every time I hear this) waiting for their ship to come in. Motivational speaker Charlie "Tremendous" Jones says it best: "A lot of people are waiting for their ship to come in even though they never sent one out!"

No, the thing that makes for greatness is determination, persisting in the right direction over the long haul, following your dream, staying at the task. Just as there is no such thing as instant failure, neither is there automatic or instant success. But success is the direct result of a process that is long, arduous, and often unappreciated by others. It also includes a willingness to sacrifice. But it pays off if you stay at the task. In our world of instant everything, these thoughts are not very popular. That's why I emphasized the word *seek* at the beginning of this chapter. If we really want to soar like an eagle, we must keep on continually pursuing—we must keep on seeking.

DEFINING THE KEY TERMS

In the previous chapter our thoughts centered on *vision*. In this chapter the focus is on *determination* and *following one's dream*. Because these three terms are significant in the lives of people who set their hearts on living differently, we need to define each one a little more specifically.

Vision

Vision is the ability to see above and beyond the majority. Vision is perception—reading the presence and power of God into one's circumstances. I sometimes think of vision as looking at life through the lens of God's eyes, seeing situations as He sees them. Too often we see things not as they are, but as *we* are. Think about that. Vision has to do with looking at life with a divine perspective, reading the scene with God in clear focus.

Whoever wants to live differently in "the system" must correct his or her vision. And, trust me, this kind of vision correction won't come naturally. How can I say that? Let me show you a couple of scriptures that verify the fact that vision is not a natural trait.

The first verse I want to look at is 1 Samuel 16:7. Samuel thinks he has found the Lord's anointed. The former king (Saul) has failed. So God sends Samuel to find a new king. He comes to the home of Jesse where the oldest son, Eliab, is marched in front of Samuel. The old man is so impressed with Eliab's size and his handsome physique that he immediately thinks this must be the man! But the Lord stops Samuel short and tells him Eliab's *not* the one.

But the Lord said to Samuel, "Do not look at his appearance or at the height of his stature, because I have rejected him; for God sees not as man sees, for man looks at the outward appearance, but the Lord looks at the heart."

You see, it is our natural tendency to focus on the external, to be overly impressed with that which is seen. Wouldn't it be wonderful to develop the ability to look at a heart? Wouldn't it be great to be free of the limitations of strictly physical sight so that we could read hidden character traits? Frankly, I think those who are physically blind often see more than those of us who are sighted. They often perceive much more than we can in the tone of a voice or in the sound of approaching footsteps or in the grip of a handshake. But we who have sight usually lack this insightful depth perception; we lack the kind of vision that can detect the deeper things, the unspoken, the character, the hidden condition of the unspoken. And although God is able (and willing) to give us such vision, it isn't something we're born with.

The second scripture I want to consider is a similar thought written by the prophet Isaiah.

"For My thoughts are not your thoughts, neither are your ways My ways," declares the Lord. "For as the heavens are higher than the earth, so are My ways higher than your ways, and My thoughts than your thoughts" (Isa. 55:8–9).

Once again we are made aware of the difference between natural sight and supernatural vision. When we look at life with vision, we perceive events and circumstances with God's thoughts. And because His thoughts are higher and more profound than mere horizontal thinking, they have a way of softening the blows of calamity and giving us hope through tragedy and loss. It also enables us to handle times of prosperity and popularity with wisdom.

Following a worship service in the church I serve as senior pastor, I met a couple from Mexico City who had endured that awful earthquake back in 1986. They spoke quietly and even reverently of what they had learned through it. There was something unique about their handshake and embrace as well as a gracious compassion in their voices. They had lost family members. They had been brought back to the very basics of what life is all about. They had seen God's ways; they had sensed His presence. In that tumultuous event they had come to terms with some of the trappings that had become superficial hang-ups for the majority. Clearly, so many things were now much different to them—much different. What was it that pervaded their lives? Vision.

Determination

This is a major step beyond vision. It involves applying the discipline to remain consistent regardless of the obstacles or the odds. I often think of it as faith in the long haul.

One man writes:

> Many people fail in life because they believe in the adage: If you don't succeed, try something else. But success eludes those who follow such advice. Virtually everyone has had dreams at one time or another, specially in youth. The dreams that have come true did so because people stuck to their ambitions. They refused to be discouraged. They never let disappointment get the upper hand. Challenges only spurred them on to greater effort.[2]

I'll be frank with you. I know of no more valuable technique in the pursuit of successful living than sheer, dogged determination. Nothing works in ministry better than persistence—persistence in godliness, determination to stay diligent in study, persistence in commitment to the priorities of ministry, determination in working with people. I often remind myself of those familiar words in 2 Timothy 4:1, "Preach the word; be ready in season and out of season." That's a nice way of saying, "Hang tough! Do it when it comes naturally and when it is hard to come by. Do it when you're up, do it when you're down. Do it when you feel like it, do it when you don't feel like it. Do it when it's hot, do it when it's cold. Keep on doing it. Don't give up."

I once heard W. A. Criswell, long-time beloved pastor of the famous First Baptist Church in Dallas, Texas, tell a story about an evangelist who loved to hunt. As best I recall, the man bought two pups that were topnotch bird dogs, two setters, I believe. He kept them in his large backyard, where he trained them. One morning, an ornery little vicious-looking bulldog came shuffling and snorting down the alley. He crawled under the fence into the backyard where the setters spent their days. It was easy to see he meant business. The evangelist's first impulse was to take his setters and lock them in the basement so they wouldn't tear up that little bulldog. But he decided he would just let the creature learn a lesson he would never forget. Naturally, they got into a scuffle in the backyard, and those two setters and that bulldog went round and round and round! There were growls and yipes as bulldog hair flew everywhere. The little critter finally had enough, so he squeezed under the fence and took off. All the rest of that day he whined and licked his sores. Interestingly, the next day at about the same time, here came that same ornery little bulldog . . . back under the fence and after those setters. Once again those two bird dogs beat the stuffing out of that bowlegged animal and would have chewed him up if he hadn't retreated down the alley. Would you believe, the very next day he was back! Same time, same station, same results. Once again after the bulldog had had all he could take, he crawled back under the fence and found his way home to lick his wounds.

"Well," the evangelist said, "I had to leave for a revival meeting. I was gone several weeks. And when I came back, I asked my wife what had happened. She said, 'Honey, you just won't believe what has happened. Every day, at the same time every morning, that little bulldog came back in the backyard and fought with our two setters. He never missed a day! And I want you to know it has come to the point that when our setters simply hear that bulldog snorting down the alley and spot him squeezing under the fence, they immediately start whining and run down into our basement. That little, old bulldog struts around our backyard now just like he owns it.'"

That is persistence and determination. Staying at it. Hanging tough with dogged discipline. When you get whipped or when you win, the secret is staying at it.

Dream

There is another dimension to hanging tough we dare not miss. It is the thing that keeps you going with vision, the reason behind the determination. I call it a dream. I don't mean those things we experience at night while we're asleep. When the prophet Joel writes of dreaming dreams and seeing visions, he doesn't have in mind some nocturnal images stemming from the subconscious. No, by dream, I mean a God-given idea, plan, agenda, or goal that leads to God-honoring results. People who soar like eagles, people who live above the drag of the mediocre, are people of dreams. They have God-given drive because they have received God-given dreams.

Most of us don't dream enough. If someone were to ask you, "What are your dreams for this year? What are your hopes, your agenda? What are you trusting God for?" could you give a specific answer? I don't have in mind just occupational objectives or goals for your family, although there's nothing wrong with those. But what about the kind of dreaming that results in character building, the kind that cultivates God's righteousness and God's rulership in your life?

Here are a few more ideas about dreams. Dreams are specific, not general. Dreams are personal, not public. God doesn't give anyone else my dreams on a public computer screen for others to read. He gives them to me personally. They're intimate images and ideas. Dreams can easily appear to others as extreme and illogical. If you share your dreams with the crowd, they'll probably laugh at you because you can't make logical sense out of them. Dreams are often accompanied by a strong desire to fulfill them. And they are always outside the realm of the expected. Sometimes they're downright shocking. They cause people to suck in their breath, to stand staring at you with their mouth open. A common response when you share a dream is, "You've gotta be kidding! Are you serious?"

One more thought on dreams: This is the stuff of which leaders are made. If you don't dream, your leadership is seriously limited. I have a close friend who leads an organization that is admired and appreciated by many. He sets aside one day every month to do nothing but pray and dream. I am not surprised that his organization is considered a pacesetter.

This isn't mental voodoo, but simply thinking outside the realm of the seen. It becomes a natural part of one's life. I love the way Henry David Thoreau once put it:

> If one advances confidently in the direction of his dreams, and endeavors to live the life which he has imagined, he will meet with a success unexpected in common hours.

Mental dreams assist us in determining our flight plan as eagles who soar. The wonderful added benefit is that we "meet with a success unexpected" in a most natural manner—no manipulation, no big-time hype, not even the need for pushing our own selves or promoting our own image.

TWO DREAMERS WITH DETERMINATION

In the previous chapter we met two men who were men of vision: Caleb and Joshua. Let's go back to their story now and travel even further with them.

You will remember that Caleb and Joshua were among the twelve spies who went into the Promised Land on a reconnaissance mission. Forty days later the group returned with a divided opinion. Unlike the majority who panicked, these two brought back a good report. Ten said, "No way!" But these two disagreed. "We are well able. By all means, we should go up and possess the land." Now don't forget, Joshua and Caleb were surrounded by a majority of peers who were convinced the Israelite army could not do it. They were also facing a huge congregation of Hebrews who agreed, "It's impossible. Let's go back to Egypt." Yet in the midst of all those negative voices, these two men calmly stood their ground, "We can do it."

Now, I ask you, how can intelligent men look at the same scene so differently? The answer is not difficult: two have vision, determination, and dreams; the other ten do not. It's that simple. That story is an illustration of life. We spend our years facing the very same dichotomy. To make things even more complicated, those who don't have vision or determination, and refuse to dream the impossible, are *always* in the majority. Therefore, they will always take the vote. They will always outshout and outnumber those who walk by faith and not by sight, those who are seeking the kingdom of God and His righteousness. Those who choose to live by sight will always outnumber those who live by faith.

Ten saw the problem; two saw the solution. Ten saw the obstacles; two saw the answers. Ten were impressed with the size of the men; two were impressed with the size of their God. Ten focused on what could not be accomplished; two focused on what could easily be accomplished by the power of God. Again, the persistence demonstrated by Caleb and Joshua is nothing short of remarkable. Neither was more intelligent than the other ten, nor more talented. They simply possessed bulldog determination.

Napoleon Hill, who studied the lives of many successful people, stated, "I had the happy privilege of analyzing both Mr. Edison and Mr. Ford, year by year, over a long period of years, and therefore the opportunity to study them at close range, so I speak from actual knowledge when I say that I found no quality save persistence, in either of them, that even remotely suggested the major source of their stupendous achievements."[3]

Do you recall these words from the heart of Caleb's and Joshua's speech?

> "If the Lord is pleased with us, then He will bring us into this land, and give it to us—a land which flows with milk and honey. Only do not rebel against the Lord; and do not fear the people of the land, for they shall be our prey . . ." (Num. 14:8-9).

These men are reminding the Hebrews that the Egyptians had already been killed at the Red Sea and that the people they are about to confront in Canaan have no protection either. It's been removed from them. ". . . Their protection has been removed from them, and the Lord is with us; do not fear them" (Num. 14:9).

Talk about courage! Caleb and Joshua had the audacity to stand alone and challenge the people to trust God. And God honored their courage. I didn't mention it earlier, but something amazing occurred before tragedy struck.

> But all the congregation said to stone them with stones. Then the glory of the Lord appeared in the tent of meeting to all the sons of Israel (Num. 14:10).

Whoa! It's time to seal the lips, to be quiet and listen. Somehow the shining brilliance of God's presence broke on that camp, and God spoke audibly.

> And the Lord said to Moses, "How long will this people spurn Me? And how long will they not believe in Me, despite all the signs which I have performed in their midst? I will smite them with pestilence and dispossess them, and I will make you into a nation greater and mightier than they." But Moses said to the Lord, "Then the Egyptians will hear of it, for by Thy strength Thou didst bring up this people from their midst, and they will tell it to the inhabitants of this land. They have heard that Thou, O Lord, art in the midst of this people, for Thou, O Lord, art seen eye to eye, while Thy cloud stands over them; and Thou dost go before them in a pillar of cloud by day and in a pillar of fire by night. Now if Thou dost slay this people as one man, then the nations

who have heard of Thy fame will say, 'Because the Lord could not bring this people into the land which He promised them by oath, therefore He slaughtered them in the wilderness.' But now, I pray, let the power of the Lord be great, just as Thou hast declared, 'The Lord is slow to anger and abundant in lovingkindness, forgiving iniquity and transgression; but He will by no means clear the guilty, visiting the iniquity of the fathers on the children to the third and the fourth generations.' Pardon, I pray, the iniquity of this people according to the greatness of Thy lovingkindness, just as Thou also hast forgiven this people, from Egypt even until now" (Num. 14:11-19).

"Lord, what will we say to the Egyptians? That's the reason they let the people go, in the first place . . . because You're their God. And if You annihilate everyone, then the Egyptians will have the last laugh. You'll be a mockery to them."

Great speech, Moses. And was it effective! Observe the impact:

So the Lord said, "I have pardoned them according to your word; but indeed, as I live, all the earth will be filled with the glory of the Lord. Surely all the men who have seen My glory and My signs, which I performed in Egypt and in the wilderness, yet have put Me to the test these ten times and have not listened to My voice, shall by no means see the land which I swore to their fathers, nor shall any of those who spurned Me see it. But My servant Caleb, because he has had a different spirit and has followed Me fully, I will bring into the land which he entered, and his descendants shall take possession of it" (Num. 14:20-24).

Don't miss that! Caleb had "a different spirit." Was he some kind of superman? Or genius? No, we never read such a thing here or elsewhere. He was simply a man with vision who dreamed great dreams and stuck by them. No wonder he soared!

And as a result, God protected him and Joshua from death in the wilderness.

" 'Surely you shall not come into the land in which I swore to settle you, except Caleb the son of Jephunneh and Joshua the son of Nun. Your children, however, whom you said would become a prey—I will bring them in, and they shall know the land which you have rejected. But as for you, your corpses shall fall in this wilderness. And your sons shall be shepherds for forty years in the wilderness, and they shall suffer for your unfaithfulness, until your corpses lie in the wilderness. According to the number of days which you spied out the land, forty days, for every day you shall bear your guilt a year, even forty years, and you shall know My opposition. I the Lord have spoken, surely this I will do to all this evil congregation who are gathered together against Me. In this wilderness they shall be destroyed, and there they shall die'" (Num. 14:30-35).

I call that a serious judgment. God took all the people who had been a part of the original group that had voted to stone the leaders, and He said, "You'll die in the wilderness. It'll take forty years of wandering." Can you imagine the disappointment? They were right on the edge of the land of promise, yet they retreated and wandered, virtually in a circle, for the next forty years while the old generation of negative thinkers died off. Their corpses literally littered that region. And every tombstone was a reminder that God means what He says.

Why weren't Caleb and Joshua numbered among the doomed? They had a different spirit. There was something about those two men that marked them as distinct.

Did Caleb End Well?

Caleb and Joshua began well, but the real question is, Did those two eagles keep on soaring? We find our answer in the Book of Joshua. We'll see if Caleb ended well (Joshua 14) and then we'll look briefly at Joshua's ending (Joshua 24).

By now the old generation has died off. Those who lived on invaded the land and fought their way to victory. Just as He had promised, God gave them the land. And now they're about to parcel it out to the tribes of the nation. When Caleb's turn comes, he stands tall and delivers one of the greatest speeches recorded in all the Bible:

> "I was forty years old when Moses the servant of the Lord sent me from Kadesh-barnea to spy out the land, and I brought word back to him as it was in my heart. Nevertheless my brethren who went up with me made the heart of the people melt with fear; but I followed the Lord my God fully. And now behold, the Lord has let me live, just as He spoke, these forty-five years, from the time that the Lord spoke this word to Moses, when Israel walked in the wilderness; and now behold, I am eighty-five years old today. I am still as strong today as I was in the day Moses sent me; as my strength was then, so my strength is now, for war

and for going out and coming in. Now then, give me this hill country about which the Lord spoke on that day, for you heard on that day that Anakim were there, with great fortified cities; perhaps the Lord will be with me, and I shall drive them out as the Lord has spoken" (Josh. 14:7-12).

I love it! Caleb, though eighty-five years old, did not say, "Give me this rocking chair." No, not Caleb. He said, "Give me that mountain—up there where those giants live!" He is *still* unafraid of the giants. The last thing we see of Caleb is his trudging up that mountain at eighty-five years old, rolling up his sleeves to take on the giants. Don't you love people like that—people who live above mediocrity? The majority thinks they are half nuts, but that's okay. Since when do we worry about the majority opinion? By now we understand the reason Caleb could do it, don't we? He had a dream. He had vision. He had determination. And age had nothing whatever to do with it.

Some time ago the United Technologies Corporation published in the *Wall Street Journal* a full-page message entitled, "It's What You Do, Not When You Do It." The message contained a listing of many eaglelike people who soared at various ages in their lives.

IT'S WHAT YOU DO—NOT WHEN YOU DO IT

Ted Williams, at age 42. slammed a home run in his last official time at bat.

Mickey Mantle, age 20, hit 23 home runs his first full year in the major leagues.

Golda Meir was 71 when she became Prime Minister of Israel.

William Pit II was 24 when he became Prime Minister of Great Britain.

George Bernard Shaw was 94 when one of his plays was first produced.

Mozart was just seven when his first composition was published.

Now, how about this? *Benjamin Franklin* was a newspaper columnist at 16 and a framer of the United States Constitution when he was 81.

You're never too young or too old if you've got talent. Let's recognize that age has little to do with ability.[4]

You remember that the next time you're tempted to use age as an excuse, okay? You keep telling yourself that age has NOTHING to do with dreams and determination and vision.

Did Joshua End Well?

So much for Caleb. What about his sidekick? Did Joshua end as well as Caleb? Was his determination still intact? Like Caleb, he, too, delivered a great speech. After reviewing God's hand on their lives as a nation, Joshua warns the people to:

> "Be very firm, then, to keep and do all that is written in the book of the law of Moses, so that you may not turn aside from it to the right hand or to the left, in order that you may not associate with these nations, these which remain among you, or mention the name of their gods, or make anyone swear by them, or serve them, or bow down to them (Josh. 23:6-7).

His point? Drive out the enemy! How about that! Here is an older man telling a younger generation, "Finish the job. Stay at it . . . get it done." Finally, Joshua refers to his own family.

> "Now, therefore, fear the Lord and serve Him in sincerity and truth; and put away the gods which your fathers served beyond the River and in Egypt, and serve the Lord. And if it is disagreeable in your sight to serve the Lord, choose for yourselves today whom you will serve: whether the gods which your fathers served which were beyond the River, or the gods of the Amorites in whose land you are living; but as for me and my house, we will serve the Lord" (Josh. 24:14-15).

Yes, there is no doubt in anyone's mind that Joshua finished well. He is as strong in his convictions as he was in his earlier life. But he isn't "cranky." Since there is no way you can force righteousness out of anyone, Joshua chose rather to model it, to communicate it. He realized that a pursuit of godliness is something you have to leave with the will of each individual to make his or her own choice. Far too many of us have tried to force people into righteousness! I remember when I wasn't the least bit interested in spiritual things, and my mother (for all the right reasons) dragged me from one church to another. And each time I couldn't wait to get seated so I could go to sleep. I wanted to prove to her that I wasn't interested in the stuff she was interested in. Thankfully, over a period of time, my interest in eternal things began to change. My whole perspective on the Lord was altered, and then you couldn't keep me away from the things of God. But, you see, I couldn't be forced. I had to make a choice. Joshua states that fact beautifully. But in doing so he leaves no doubt in anyone's mind where he stood personally.

OBSBRVATIONS WORTH REMEMBERING

Three significant observations stand out as we come to the end of this account. First: <u>Age has little to do with achievement and nothing to do with commitment.</u>

Both Joshua and Caleb were young men when they stood alone before their peers. Yet when they grew older they were still standing strong. Both men persisted in their convictions regardless of the passing years. Both men remained true even when they grew old. The ranks of humanity are full of those who *start* well. With determination and persistence, we can also end well. These days in my life I look for people who are finishing well. I love to meet folks in their sixties, seventies, and eighties who are still visionaries, who are still dreaming, still excited about going on with their life, still positive about the future—men and women who are useful in their spheres of influence.

That brings us to the second observation: <u>A godly walk is basic to a positive life.</u> Joshua and Caleb kept repeating their full and firm commitment to the Lord their God. I believe that's a major reason they stayed so positive. Without a proper divine perspective, it is easy for negativism and cynicism to creep in. So if you want to maintain a positive, fulfilling life, you have to keep the Lord in the nucleus of your motivation.

Now for the third observation: <u>Convictions are a matter of choice, not force.</u> Parents of growing, learning children keep this in mind. Remember there is nothing like the magnet of a model. You can shout and scream. You can discipline and punish and threaten. But there's nothing those kids will remember like the model you leave them. That will be cemented in their memory. You just live it, keep living it, and persist in your walk. That alone will be a magnet that will draw them. They will want to know, especially as they reach the older years, how you do it. If they don't know by then, that's your moment to tell them. That's your time. Our kids have a way of signaling when they're ready to be taught—even when they reach adulthood.

APPLICATIONS WORTH DUPLICATING

Let me suggest four "nevers." That may seem a little strange since my emphasis has been so positive, but I think each "never" will be more easily remembered.

- Never use age as an excuse.
- Never take your cues from the crowd.
- Never think your choices obligate anyone else. (If you do, you'll become a self-appointed martyr.)
- Never quit because someone disagrees with you.

If you're so insecure that you must have everybody agreeing with you before you can go on, you are in for an extremely uncertain future. Leadership will elude you, I fear. May our Lord give you fresh courage to stand firm even when others disagree.

Several years ago I met a gentleman who served on one of Walt Disney's original advisory boards. What amazing stories he told! Those early days were tough; but that remarkable, creative visionary refused to give up. I especially appreciated the man's sharing with me how Disney responded to disagreement. He said that Walt would occasionally present some unbelievable, extensive dream he was entertaining. Almost without exception, the members of his board would gulp, blink, and stare back at him in disbelief, resisting even the thought of such a thing. But unless *every member resisted the idea*, Disney usually didn't pursue it. Yes, you read that correctly. The challenge wasn't big enough to merit his time and creative energy unless they were unanimously in disagreement! (I suppose when you're a Disney, you're free to press on when the board says "shut 'er down!") Is it any wonder that Disneyland and Disney World are now realities?

THE WORLD NEEDS MEN . . . [and I might add *women*]

who cannot be bought;
whose word is their bond;
who put character above wealth;
who possess opinions and a will;
who are larger than their vocations;
who do not hesitate to take chances;
who will not lose their individuality in a crowd;
who will be as honest in small things as in great things;
who will make no compromise with wrong; .
whose ambitions are not confined to their own selfish desires;
who will not say they do it "because everybody else does it";
who are true to their friends through good report and evil report,
 in adversity as well as in prosperity;
who do not believe that shrewdness, cunning, and
 hardheadedness are the best qualities for winning success;
who are not ashamed or afraid to stand for the truth when it is
 unpopular;
who can say "no" with emphasis, although all the rest of the
 world says "yes."[5]

Once you've decided to live differently, let God be your guide and hang tough—follow your dreams with determination. Before you know it you'll be soaring like an eagle.

7

PRIORITIES: DETERMINING
WHAT COMES FIRST

*L*ife is a lot like a coin; you can spend it any way you wish, but you can spend it only once. Choosing one thing over all the rest throughout life is a difficult thing to do. This is especially true when the choices are so many and the possibilities are so close.

At Christmastime I was given the book *A Sense of History* by one of my close friends. Knowing my love for history, he selected one of those volumes you need to read slowly with a lot of thinking time to muse things over. Interestingly, the first thirty-seven pages form a section entitled, "I Wish I'd Been There." Numerous historians, scholars, authors, and editors were asked to choose the one event in American history they would most like to have witnessed. Each was asked to respond to the same intriguing question: "What is the one scene or incident in American history you would most like to have witnessed— and why?"

I found myself glued to those thirty-seven pages, fascinated by the answers. Here is a sampling:

- One historian said he would like to have been among that small company of sailors in the moonlit predawn moment, October 12, 1492, when a lookout aboard a small vessel hailed the sand cliffs of an island never before seen by the eyes of Europeans.

- Another commented he would like to have had an extra long life, enabling him to sit on a pier between A.D. 1200 and 1500 to see who *besides Columbus and Sebastian Cabot* showed up.

- Another said he would like to have been with Lewis and Clark in November of 1805 when they first glimpsed the object of their labors, the Pacific Ocean. He wished he could have looked over the shoulder of William Clark as he scribbled in his log book, "Ocean in view—oh, the joy!"

- A rather interesting selection came from one who wished he could have witnessed that intimate, nostalgic moment when Abraham Lincoln, the President-elect, said farewell to his neighbors in Springfield.

- A history professor at Yale selected for his fantasy the opportunity to look inside the mind of Col. Robert E. Lee on the occasion when Lee was being offered the command of the *Union* forces in 1861.

- Another moved ahead in history to the Emancipation Proclamation. He didn't choose to be by President Lincoln's side, but rather in a little community in South Carolina where a number of people had gathered, including a large number of slaves, to hear the report of that decision that black people were now free. He wished he could have seen the flag as it waved in the sky and could have heard the spontaneous singing of the slaves who were at that moment free. First, a strong, male voice, rather cracked and elderly, began to sing . . . into which two women's voices instantly blended, singing as if by an impulse that could not be repressed, "My country 'tis of thee, sweet land of liberty, of thee I sing."

- Another wanted to be by Franklin Delano Roosevelt's side on December 7, 1941, when he received the news of the Japanese attack. He said he would like to have seen the one who brought the Pearl Harbor dispatch and then to find out whom Roosevelt contacted first . . . and to have known when he first began his "Day of Infamy" speech.

- One said, there was a time when he would like to have been a fly on the wall of the bunker watching the last days and hours of the Third Reich. "But no longer. For the last decade I have yielded entirely to the wish that I could have been there in the White House on that day when Richard Nixon decided to resign his Presidency and knelt with my old friend Henry Kissinger to pray."[1]

What makes the opening section of that history book so interesting is that it is all based on priorities. These scholarly historians were asked to point out one plant from the vast field of history that covers hundreds of years; out of an entire meadow, they were asked to choose one flower they would like to have seen bloom—the one moment in time they would like to have experienced.

OUR TOP PRIORITY

The task those historians had is somewhat like that of those who wish to live above the level of mediocrity. We are forced to choose on the basis of first things first. We will never fly like an eagle until we are willing to determine who and what comes first. Life places before us hundreds of possibilities Some are bad. Many are good. A few, the best. But each of us must decide, "What is my choice? What is my reason for living?" In other words, "What priority takes first place in my life?"

To be completely truthful with you, however, we aren't left with numerous possibilities. Jesus Himself gave us the top priority. We have looked at it several times already.

"But seek first His kingdom and His righteousness; and all these things shall be added to you" (Matt. 6:33).

He said, in effect, "This is your priority; this comes first." He even uses the words "But seek *first*," meaning above and beyond everything else, pursue this *first*.

Before going any further, let's take a closer look at this command. The Greek word translated "seek" means "to search, to strive for, to desire strongly." The action is continuous—"keep on striving for, keep on searching after, keep on desiring." Today, we would say, "Go for this *first*. . . ."

Now look even closer and notice the objectives: The kingdom of God and the righteousness of God. Frankly, we don't even have to pray about our top priority. We just have to know what it is, then do it. If I am to seek first in my life God's kingdom and God's righteousness, then whatever else I do ought to relate to that goal: where I work, with whom I spend my time, the one I marry, or the decision to remain single. Every decision I make ought to be filtered through the

Matthew 6:33 filter: where I put my money, where and how I spend my time, what I buy, what I sell, what I give away. That means a two-pronged question needs to be asked each time: Is it for His kingdom? Does it relate to His righteousness?

A Reminder of Unseen Values

God's kingdom and His righteousness are unseen, you understand. We will never find His kingdom in tangible form on this earth in our lifetime. We will never hear the sounds of His kingdom or see Him ruling or hear the gavel in the hands of the Lord Jesus coming down in a court room where He sits as Judge. No, as we learned earlier, for the present time His kingdom is invisible, it is inaudible, it is eternal. So those of us who wish to soar above mediocrity have a commitment to His kingdom that forces us to press the whole of life through the filter of something invisible, inaudible, and eternal.

This filter (Matthew 6:33) helps me to conduct myself in terms of this top priority. Should I do this? Is it for God's kingdom? Is it for His righteousness? Should I respond this way? Will my decision uphold His righteousness? Believe me, that can get pretty exacting. Priorities are always tough things to determine. Furthermore, there are times we *think* we are on target, but we're not. If our hearts are right, God will graciously yet firmly overrule even the things we ask Him for.

Our lives can turn out like the unknown Confederate soldier who admitted:

> I asked God for strength that I might achieve.
> I was made weak that I might learn humbly to obey.
>
> I asked God for health that I might do greater things.
> I was given infirmity that I might do better things.
>
> I asked for riches that I might be happy.
> I was given poverty that I might be wise.
>
> I asked for power that I might have the praise of men.
> I was given weakness that I might feel the need of God.
>
> I asked for all things that I might enjoy life.
> I was given life that I might enjoy all things.
>
> I got nothing that I asked for—
> but everything I had hoped for. . . .

Almost despite myself, my unspoken prayers were answered.
I am among all men most richly blessed.[2]

As I ponder Jesus' command, I notice that it begins with a contrast, "*But* seek first," the implication being that others are *not* seeking those things. But who are they? The preceding verse identifies them for us. They're called the Gentiles.

In fact, look at what that verse says:

"For all these things the Gentiles eagerly seek; for your heavenly Father knows that you need all these things" (Matt. 6:32).

To identify "these things" we need to go all the way back to verse 24:

"No one can serve two masters; for either he will hate the one and love the other. or he will hold to one and despise the other. You cannot serve God and mammon."

This helps us understand that "the Gentiles" are those who are trying to serve two masters. But Jesus makes no bones about it—"You cannot possibly serve both God and money." Be careful, now. He isn't saying it is impossible to soar and make money. The key word is *serve*. We cannot be a servant of both. Living out the kingdom life means that everything must remain before the throne and under the authority of the ruler. Everything must be held loosely.

I'll never forget a conversation I had with the late Corrie ten Boom. She said to me, in her broken English, "Chuck, I've learned that we must hold everything loosely, because when I grip it tightly, it hurts when the Father pries my fingers loose and takes it from me!" Things of significant value are the unseen things, aren't they? But that is easy to forget.

I have a friend who, in mid-career, was called into the ministry. In fact, God ultimately led him overseas. At that point he found it necessary to move all his family and as many of their possessions as possible beyond these shores, all the way to the island of Okinawa. He told me, "We packed everything we could in barrels and shipped them on ahead. And then we put all of our possessions that were a part of our trip into our station wagon. We packed that car all the way to the top of the windows."

While driving to the place where they would meet the ship that would take them to the Orient, they stopped for a rest and a bite to eat. While they were inside the restaurant, a thief broke into their station wagon and took *everything* except the car. Nice of him to leave the car, wasn't it? "The only thing we had," he said, "were the articles of clothing on our backs. Our hearts sank to the bottom!" When asked about it later, he said, "Well, I had to face the fact that I was holding real tight to the things in that car. And the Lord simply turned my hands over and gave them a slap . . . and out came everything that was in that car. And it all became a part of the Father's possession."

What tangibles are you holding onto? What are you gripping tightly? Have they become your security? Are you a slave to some image? Some name you're trying to live up to? Some job? Some possession? Some person? Some goal or objective? (Nothing wrong with having goals and objectives; but something is wrong when they have you in their grip.) Now let me give you a tip. If you cannot let it go, it's a priority to you. It is impossible to be a slave to things or people and at the same time be a faithful servant of God.

Now before we let this idea of "letting go" appear too stark, look again at the wonderful promise in verse 33. The latter half of it says, "all these things shall be added to you." How interesting! Remember verse 32—"these things the Gentiles eagerly seek"? Well, now Jesus is saying "these things shall be added unto you." Those who seek them are off target. But those who seek Him are provided with whatever they need. When you think all that through, it just depends on where your priorities are. Isn't that a relief? Once you have given them to the Lord, who knows, He may turn right around and let you enjoy an abundance. Or He may keep them from you at a safe distance and just every once in a while let you enjoy a few. But they'll all be added to you from His hand rather than from your own. God never runs out of ways to bring this into perspective.

You may be able to identify with the man who wrote these words:

> I am 42 years old. I work for a large corporation. But I'm no longer moving "up."
>
> I know that working for a large corporation is not exactly *au courant*, but my father owned a small retail store, and after 30 years of his standing behind the counter, neither of us saw the magic of doing "your own thing."

But a big corporation—something plucked right off the Fortune 500; a company with interlocking, multinational profit centers; with well-defined vertical and horizontal reporting relationships—that was just what the doctor ordered, and that was exactly what I got.

Going in, I knew there would be a price to pay. Too much structure can be confining. But for me, the organizational chart was like a children's playground—a place to climb, swing and scramble all the way to the top.

And that was where I was headed. After all, isn't that what it's all about?

Year by year, level by level, I made my way up; and if I wasn't laughing all the way, only rarely did I doubt choosing the corporate life.

Never being one for team sports, never having served in the Army, I enjoyed the camaraderie that comes from being "one of the boys."

I also enjoyed the competition.

Whatever the reason . . . I was immediately perceived to be "a star." And though my corporation was too conservative to have a "fast track," I did burn a few cinders as a steady procession of blue memos charted my upward progress. Over the years I gained titles, windows, salary and perks. These incentives fueled a fire that was burning very bright indeed. I knew in my bones that I would someday reach the top. Some men might stumble. Others might even fall by the wayside. But not me; never me.

Or so I believed, right up to the day, right up to the instant, when I learned the fire was out, the star was extinguished, the climb was over. . . .

. . . I could expect the average salary increases due the average employee. But there would be no more leapfrog advancements. No more seductive little perks. No more blue memos.

I was no longer climbing. I had plateaued out. . . .[3]

No doubt, this man felt the same sense of loss that my missionary friend experienced when he said, "The Lord simply turned my hands over . . . gave them a good slap . . . and out came everything!"

Now I wouldn't wish that jolt on anyone, but it happens to many. If some corporate position is the god of your life, then something terrible occurs within when it is no longer a future possibility. If your career, however, is simply a part of God's plan and you keep it in proper perspective, you can handle a demotion just as well as you can handle a promotion. It all depends on who's first and what's first.

Who's on First?

In searching out what it takes to live differently in our world, we have considered vision, determination, and now priorities. But as I address priorities, I feel the pinch a little tighter, don't you? So it goes for those who are determined to live their lives above the mediocre level. Breaking the magnet which draws things ahead of God is a lengthy and sometimes painful process. There is a line found in the Jewish Talmud that puts it well: "Man is born with his hands clenched; he dies with them wide open. Entering life, he desires to grasp everything; leaving the world, all he possessed has slipped away."

A few words from Colossians 1 never fail to encourage me when things begin to slip away. Since life is like a coin and it can be spent only once, these words are good reminders of the one deserving of our investment. They begin with a reference to God the Father:

> For He delivered us from the domain of darkness, and transferred us to the kingdom of His beloved Son, in whom we have redemption, the forgiveness of sins (vv. 13–14).

That is a wonderful statement of God's eternal rescue. He delivered us from darkness to light. And He transferred us, notice, to a new kingdom—the unseen kingdom—where there are values worth investing in, where we live beyond the entrapment of things and people and events and human ideas. It is called "the kingdom of His beloved Son [Jesus Christ]." He has transferred us to a new realm of existence where we are enveloped in the Son's perfect righteousness and forgiveness.

And what a statement follows!

> And He is the image of the invisible God, the first-born of all creation. For in Him all things were created, both in the heavens and on earth, visible and invisible, whether thrones or dominions or rulers or authorities—all things have been created through Him and for Him (vv. 15–16).

Everything created was through Christ and His power, and furthermore, it was created for His honor. That includes everyday things today. You have a good job? It's to be enjoyed for Him. You have a nice salary? It's to be enjoyed and invested for Him. You have good health? It is for Him. You have a family? The family members are for Him. You're planning a move? It's to be for Him. You're thinking about a career change? It needs to be for Him. That is true because He's the ruler of our kingdom. He is Lord. And that's not simply the title of a chorus Christians sing; it's a statement of faith. He has the right to take charge of our decisions so that He might be honored through them. Every day I live I must address that. Again, it is a matter of priorities.

> And He is before all things, and in Him all things hold together (v. 17).

Isn't this a wonderful section of Scripture? In all these things, Christ is the center. He is in things, He's through things, He's holding things together. He's the glue that makes stuff stick together. He put the stars in space, and their movement is exactly according to His sovereign chronometer, precisely as He arranged it. And everything out there hangs in space exactly as He set it up. His problem is not with planets in space, however. His wrestling match is with people on earth who have been put here but want to go their own way. Note the next verse:

> He is also head of the body, the church; and He is the beginning, the first-born from the dead; so that He Himself might come to have first place in everything (v. 18).

Take your time with those final four words. Read them aloud. Think them through. You're dating a young man. You think you're falling in love with this man. Does Christ have *first place* in that relationship? Or have you decided that a moral compromise really feels better? Maybe you have chosen not to maintain such a strict standard of purity as before. If you've made that priority decision, then face it—Christ really isn't in first place in that romance.

Are you struggling right now between a decision that requires doing what is exactly right and losing closeness with an individual or giving in a little and keeping that friendship? You know the rest of the story. If Christ is going to have top priority, it must be according to the standard of His righteousness. There has to be credibility in what we do or it doesn't fall into the category of seeking His kingdom and His righteousness, does it? Why am I coming on so strong? Because He is to have *first place* in everything. Those who are really committed to excellence give Him top priority.

A RESPONSE OF INCREDIBLE RELEVANCE

On one occasion Jesus was having a meal with a group of people. When the other guests began picking out places of honor at the table, Jesus told them a story about humility. And to the host he said:

> "... when you give a reception, invite the poor, the crippled, the lame, the blind and you will be blessed, since they do not have the means to repay you. ..."
>
> And when one of those who were reclining at table with Him heard this, he said to Him, "Blessed is everyone who shall eat bread in the kingdom of God!" (Luke 14:15).

How interesting! Someone else says this to Jesus. The light finally dawned. He's gotten the message! "Lord, I've heard what You have said and it's clear that the one who is really fulfilled, deeply satisfied, genuinely joyful, is the one who enjoys Your food, who takes Your provisions, and lives in light of them while he's on this earth. I believe that, Lord. Count me in!" That's the general idea.

Jesus heard his response and told another story that illustrates everything I have been trying to say in this chapter.

> But He said to him, "A certain man was giving a big dinner, and he invited many; and at the dinner hour he sent his slave to say to those who had been invited, 'Come; for everything is ready now'" (Luke 14:16–17).

"Ding-a-ling-a-ling-a-ling, supper is ready! Come on in, the meal is served." But wait. This isn't a literal meal He's talking about. This is a parable, remember? He is talking about a spiritual meal—that which satisfies one's life in the kingdom realm. He's saying, "I've served a meal, and it will satisfy you. Come and eat." You'd think everybody would have jumped up and joined in. Not so.

> "But they all alike began to make excuses. The first one said to him, 'I have bought a piece of land and I need to go out and look at it; please consider me excused'" (Luke 14:18).

I would say this man's decision is amazingly relevant. Here is a guy who has made an investment. Like many, he has bought a piece of land. If you've ever bought a piece of land, you know there's nothing quite as encouraging as walking across the dirt. You want to sort of dig your toes in it and walk rather hard and wriggle your toes, and face it—you feel like Nebuchadnezzar. "It's mine! . . . My land! My piece of property! I own this! I've invested in this!" You see, he was preoccupied with his purchase. He planned to accept the master's invitation, but he thought he would come later. "Right now I want to look over my investment. Please consider me excused. My purchase comes first."

Jon Johnston pulled no punches when he wrote:

> Self-denial is the perennial challenge of humanity. A rampant selfishness is omnipresent in every generation, and the church of the eighties is not immune to me-ism. In fact, many declare our Zion has opted for a double dose. Clergy and parishioner alike calculate every move to maximize personal benefit. . . .
>
> Today, our bonfires of selfishness are fueled by the gasoline of affluence. . . .
>
> Today's self-centered churchgoer asks the same question of God, coupled with another one: "What will you do for me soon?" God is pictured as the dispenser (and withholder) of life's prizes—a television game-show host.
>
> . . . We conclude that such things as good health, fortune, and success are sure indicators of his approval for our lives. This is the Protestant ethic gone to seed. . . .[4]

But let's get back to Jesus' story and see how others responded to the dinner invitation.

> "And another one said, 'I have bought five yoke of oxen, and I am going to try them out; please consider me excused'" (Luke 14:19).

Most of us don't buy oxen today. Nor do we try out oxen. We buy a lot of other things, though. Whatever we buy, we love to try out. We like to take care of it. We like to shine it. We like to look at it. If the truth could be told, deep down inside we tend to make a little shrine out of it, because we worked so hard for it and it means so much. This guest is doing that. He's saying, "I've got this possession and I . . . I want to try it out. Please consider me excused."

I am especially intrigued at the third person's excuse. Look at what this guy has to say:

> "And another one said, 'I have married a wife, and for that reason I cannot come'" (Luke 14:20).

Now there's a creative excuse! "Lord, come on. Gimme a break. At least wait till after the honeymoon. You know, give me a little time. I'll be there later, I promise; but right now there is a relationship that keeps me from coming to Your meal."

Not one of these things is wrong in and of itself. There is nothing wrong with land. Nothing wrong with oxen. Nothing wrong with marriage. So what's wrong then? Well, as good as they are, they prevented these three individuals from being satisfied with the priority of eating a kingdom meal. They took first place, that's all. But that's EVERYTHING . . . really, that's EVERYTHING! And that is precisely Jesus' point.

You wonder how the Lord felt?

> "And the slave came back and reported this to his master. Then the head of the household became angry and said to his slave, 'Go out at once into the streets and lanes of the city and bring in here the poor and crippled and blind and lame'" (Luke 14:21).

If you look at this strictly through first-century eyes, you know Jesus is referring to Jews and Gentiles. "I've given this message to My own people; My own people have rejected it. I came to My own people and My own people did not receive Me. Open it up to the Gentiles. Let the cripples in. Let the lame in. Let the people who get it by grace take advantage of it. It's for all of them." But the application is broader than that.

You see, kingdom life doesn't have to be enjoyed only by those in good health. Sometimes the cripples have things in clearer perspective, sometimes the lame, sometimes the sick, sometimes the blind.

> "And the slave said, 'Master, what you commanded has been done, and still there is room'" (Luke 14:22).

"We still have a lot of room in this place, Master. There are a lot of plates full of food that won't be eaten, still a lot of room in this kingdom."

Look at the next command:

> "And the master said to the slave, 'Go out into the highways and along the hedges, and compel them to come in, that my house may be filled. For I tell you, none of those men who were invited shall taste of my dinner'" (Luke 14:23–24).

William Barclay writes,

> It's possible to be a follower of Jesus without being a disciple; to be a camp-follower without being a soldier of the king; to be a hanger-on in some great work without pulling one's weight. Once someone was talking to a great scholar about a younger man. He said, "So and so tells me that he was one of your students." The teacher answered devastatingly, "He may have attended my lectures, but he was not one of my students." There is a world of difference between attending lectures and being a student. It is one of the supreme handicaps of the Church that in the Church there are so many distant followers of Jesus and so few real disciples.[5]

I think the ranks were thinned. I think He purposely said, "I don't want a big crowd following Me if it means that all these people want to do is feed their bellies and watch miracles and listen to My stories and passively respond to lectures. I want those who give me top priority."

If I stated to you in one succinct sentence the message of this chapter, it would be: Our choice of priorities determines at which level we soar. Stated another way: Whatever is in first place, if it isn't Christ alone, it is in the wrong place. Life is a lot like a coin; you can spend it any way you wish, but you can spend it only once. What are you spending it on?

No need to linger any longer. The point has been made. This final question puts the ball squarely in your court: What is really first in your life?

8

ACCOUNTABILITY: ANSWERING THE HARD QUESTIONS

We need heroes. I mean *genuine* heroes, authentic men and women who are admired for their achievements, noble qualities, and courage. Such people aren't afraid to be different. They risk. They stand a cut above. Yet they are real human beings with flaws and failures like anyone else. But these soaring eagles inspire us to do better. We feel warm inside when we think about this rare breed of humanity. The kind we can look up to without the slightest suspicion of deception or hypocrisy. The kind who model excellence when no one is looking or for that matter when half the world *is* looking.

When Aleksandr Solzhenitsyn concluded his Nobel lecture on literature, he closed by quoting a Russian proverb: "One word of truth outweighs the whole world." By changing only two words I think that proverb would say what I believe about heroes: "One person of truth impacts the whole world."

I'm concerned that we seem to be running shy of folks like that. Certainly, there are some, but not nearly as many, it seems, as when I was a small boy. Back then I distinctly recall looking up to numerous people in various segments of society—politics, athletics, education, science, the military, music, religion, aviation—all of whom not only stood tall during their heyday, but they *finished* well. Society mourned their passing. This was no childhood fantasy, you understand; these were not make-believe matinee idols. I can still remember my dad being just as impressed as I was with certain folks—maybe more so. Some of our father-son conversations are still logged in my memory bank. And because he was inspired, so was I.

Perhaps that explains why author Bruce Larson's moving words grabbed my attention. I could easily identify with his experience as a little lad many years ago.

When I was a small boy, I attended church every Sunday at a big Gothic Presbyterian bastion in Chicago. The preaching was powerful and the music was great. But for me, the most awesome moment in the morning service was the offertory, when twelve solemn, frock-coated ushers marched in lock-step down the main aisle to receive the brass plates for collecting the offering. These men, so serious about their business of serving the Lord in this magnificent house of worship, were the business and professional leaders of Chicago.

One of the twelve ushers was a man named Frank Loesch. He was not a very imposing-looking man, but in Chicago he was a living legend, for he was the man who had stood up to Al Capone. In the prohibition years, Capone's rule was absolute. The local and state police and even the Federal Bureau of Investigation were afraid to oppose him. But singlehandedly, Frank Loesch, as a Christian layman and without any government support, organized the Chicago Crime Commission, a group of citizens who were determined to take Mr. Capone to court and put him away. During the months that the Crime Commission met, Frank Loesch's life was in constant danger. There were threats on the lives of his family and friends. But he never wavered. Ultimately he won the case against Capone and was the instrument for removing this blight from the city of Chicago. Frank Loesch had risked his life to live out his faith.

Each Sunday at this point of the service, my father, a Chicago businessman himself, never failed to poke me and silently point to Frank Loesch with pride. Sometime I'd catch a tear in my father's eye. For my dad and for all of us this was and is what authentic living is all about.[1]

I love that story. Written between the lines are strong, spine-tingling feelings of respect, the right kind of pride, and an inner compulsion to be all that one ought to be. Wonderful feelings! Essential, in fact, if we hope to soar high, far above mediocrity's drag.

Tell me, who needs to walk by for you to poke your son, daughter, or friend and whisper, "Now, that's a person worth following. Pattern your life after him (or her) and you'll never be sorry"? If you can think of some, I would call them your heroes. Not too many, are there?

You may be surprised to know that for any number of other people, *you* are the person others point to. It may be in the place where you work, and no one has even told you. It may happen in your neighborhood, and no neighbor has been brave enough to encourage you by saying, "You're the one everybody watches. You're very unique. We all respect you." It may be in your profession where you are admired by colleagues and peers. If you knew how many felt that way, I'm convinced you would be all the more careful with the way you practice your profession or the way you conduct your business.

I am certain of this—if you *are* one of those people, then you're not like the majority. You're living differently, and I commend you for it. We are learning in these chapters that it takes unusual people to make a difference in our world. Mediocre people impact no one, at least not for good. But one person of truth can impact the whole world.

For several chapters I have been writing about being that person. If I were asked to make a list of what is involved in such a person's life, I would include at least four qualities.

Essential Characteristics That Make an Impact

First, people who live differently are people of *vision*. Vision is the ability to see above and beyond the majority, to be unenamored by statistics, unintimidated by the odds, unmoved by obstacles like so-called impossibilities, restrictions, and difficulties. They are people like Frank Loesch who don't hold back even though their lives are threatened, who don't churn through life, worried over whether a few glass panes in their home will be broken or whether their children may suffer a little because their dad or mother is different. They have vision.

Second, people who impact others model *determination*. Determination is nothing more than deciding to stay at it, even though it's tough. Determination is hanging in there, not giving up, not lessening one's convictions when the road gets long or rough. I cannot think of a hero who failed to have determination.

Third, those who soar above mediocrity are people of *priorities*. They think in terms of who and what are first in the home, at work, in possessions, and in relationships as well. People who have priorities keep that in perspective. They work hard, but work doesn't become their god; it is a responsibility not a shrine. It is a way by which money is earned. And with the money they buy possessions; but again, their priorities determine which possessions they hang onto and why.

Now, there is a fourth essential characteristic when it comes to living differently, and I warn you; it is the least popular of the four. After vision and determination and priorities, I should also mention *accountability.* People who really make an impact model this rare quality as well as the first three I have named.

What do I mean by accountability? In the simplest terms, it is answering the hard questions. Accountability includes opening one's life to a few carefully selected, trusted, loyal confidants who speak the truth—who have the right to examine, to question, to appraise, and to give counsel.

Not much has been said or written about accountability. Practically every time I've spoken on the subject, I've had people say afterwards, "I never hear this addressed. I don't read much about it. In fact, I have seldom even used the word!" Because this concept has not been hammered out openly and often, the term itself seems strange. It can also be misused, since it is so easily misunderstood.

I do not have in mind some legalistic tribunal where victims are ripped apart with little concern for their feelings. There is too much of that going on already! Such savagery helps no one. It doesn't build up others nor encourage them to do better. And because many fear that accountability means only criticism, they resent even the mention of the word. I realize it is possible to clip people's wings so severely they will never soar. But trust me, that's the farthest thought from my mind when I write of accountability.

FOUR QUALITIES IN ACCOUNTABILITY

People who are accountable usually have four qualities:

- *Vulnerability*—capable of being wounded, shown to be wrong, even admitting it before being confronted.
- *Teachability*—a willingness to learn, being quick to hear and respond to reproof, being open to counsel.
- *Availability*—accessible, touchable, able to be interrupted.
- *Honesty*—committed to the truth regardless of how much it hurts, a willingness to admit the truth no matter how difficult or humiliating the admission may be. Hating all that is phony or false.

That's a tough list! As I look back over those four qualities, I am more than ever aware of why accountability is resisted by the majority. Those with fragile egos can't handle it. And prima donna types won't tolerate it. They have a greater desire to look good and make a stunning impression than anything else. I mean, "the very idea of someone probing into my life!"

Again, don't misunderstand. I'm not suggesting for a moment that accountability gives the general public carte blanche access to any and all areas of one's private life. If you will glance back a few lines you will notice I referred to "a few carefully selected, trusted, loyal confidants." They are the ones who have earned the right to come alongside and, when it seems appropriate and necessary, ask the hard questions. The purpose of the relationship is not to make someone squirm or to pull rank and devastate an individual; no, not at all. Rather, it is to be a helpful sounding board, to guard someone from potential peril, to identify the possibility of a "blind spot," to serve in an advisory capacity, bringing perspective and wisdom where such may be lacking.

In our society where privacy is a reward of promotion and a life of virtual secrecy is the prerogative of most leaders, a lack of account- ability is considered the norm. This is true despite the fact that *un*accountability is both unwise and unbiblical, not to mention downright perilous! My hope is to arouse a greater awareness among all eagle-type folks that too much independence can be dangerous to our health as well as detrimental to the organization or ministry we represent. Therefore, I sincerely plead with you to hear me out before you turn me off.

SCRIPTURAL ANALYSIS OF ACCOUNTABILITY

If there is anything to this idea of accountability, then we certainly should be able to find it supported in the Bible. Trust me, there is plenty there! Let's uncover some of it.

Biblical Principles

I find three major principles in support of accountability.
1. *Accountability to God is inescapable and inevitable.*

> "The good man out of his good treasure brings forth what is good; and the evil man out of his evil treasure brings forth what is evil. And I say to you, that every careless word that men shall speak, they shall render account for it in the day of judgment" (Matt. 12:35–36).

No one knows precisely how that "accounting" will transpire. Many have guessed, some have assumed, but no one knows the details of the process. We are simply told that there will be a day when we will give an account of ourselves before our God. It is inescapable, and it is inevitable.

> But you, why do you judge your brother? Or you again, why do you regard your brother with contempt? For we shall all stand before the judgment seat of God. For it is written, "AS I LIVE, SAYS THE LORD, EVERY KNEE SHALL BOW TO ME, AND EVERY TONGUE SHALL GIVE PRAISE TO GOD." So then each one of us shall give account of himself to God (Rom. 14:10-12).

I call that straight and to the point. What else can be said? God's Book teaches that a future, individualized accountability to God is both inescapable and inevitable. This brings us to another principle.

2. *Accountability to spiritual leaders is commanded by God and is profitable to us.* Most folks have no argument with being accountable to God. He is our Father; He is perfect. He has every right to hear about our lives. He is able to judge us without preconceived ideas or prejudices. But the rub occurs when we think about giving an account to *anyone* on earth. This is especially true among those who are independent-minded, self-made men and women and certainly those who have been burned by spiritual leaders in the past.

> Be on the alert, stand firm in the faith, act like men, be strong. Let all that you do be done in love. Now I urge you, brethren (you know the household of Stephanas, that they were the first fruits of Achaia, and that they have devoted themselves for ministry to the saints), that you also be in subjection to such men and to everyone who helps in the work and labors. And I rejoice over the coming of Stephanas and Fortunatus and Achaicus; because they have supplied what was lacking on your part (1 Cor. 16:13-16).

What an interesting series of thoughts! I am tempted to linger here a little longer, but I won't. He mentions men by name who were leaders—Stephanas, Fortunatus, and Achaicus. These three gentlemen had contact with Paul. They brought a good report from Corinth to Paul regarding a number of the Corinthians. They also brought some difficult news regarding other things. Paul says, in effect, "I plead with you to submit yourself to these spiritual leaders." Why? Interestingly, that question is answered quite well in another section of the New Testament.

> Obey your leaders, and submit to them; for they keep watch over your souls, as those who will give an account. Let them do this with joy and not with grief, for this would be unprofitable for you (Heb. 13:17).

Why be accountable? Because spiritual leaders have been given, among other responsibilities, the difficult assignment of keeping "watch over your souls." And not only that, but we are told it is profitable for us to be accountable to them.

Let me try to spell that out so no one misunderstands. There are times when the minister of a church or perhaps an elected official in the church may find it necessary to pull up alongside and ask questions regarding your life. When this happens, it isn't idle or needless probing. And it certainly isn't for the purpose of gossip. This individual has your good at heart because he or she is accountable to God for your life. According to what we read in Hebrews 13, you are to answer the questions graciously, and listen to the counsel gratefully. That is precisely what accountability means; answering the hard questions.

I have been a pastor for some twenty-five years and have encountered the full spectrum of responses from people when it has been my duty to carry out this hard job. There have been times when I have had to get close to an individual and ask hard questions or reprove an individual (always in private, of course) for something that is hurting the testimony of the church. On the one hand, I have had people grateful for the reproof and even *thank* me for it and later tell me how much it has helped them. And even though it was difficult for both of us, even though it hurt, they knew it helped in the long run. People who really want to soar above mediocrity appreciate periodic reproof—and say so!

On the other hand (though I made every effort to handle the situation in a sensitive manner), I have had others resent my remarks and become so offended that I could hardly finish my conversation before they literally walked away. I have even had a few argue with me. Some have said to me later that it was none of my business or I was harsh or too strong a leader, or if I had known them better, I wouldn't have even mentioned the matter.

Allow me this one further comment. Not one of us is an island. We need one another. Sometimes we need to hear another's reproof. Believe me, if you think it is tough to *hear* such reproof, try giving it! Few assignments are more difficult for a spiritual leader. If one has the courage to call you into account and does it in the right way, with the right motive, be humble enough to accept the confrontation. Understand that it was terribly difficult to work up the courage to say anything in the first place. And know that that person has the good of the church at heart, not some private vendetta. In the long run, your commitment to excellence will be enhanced, and you will be able to fly higher.

3. *Accountability to one another is helpful and healthy.* This process is not limited to spiritual leaders, however. We need it on a personal level as well.

Take the time to digest the following scriptures. Read each word. Linger long enough to absorb the truth. And try hard not to be defensive.

> Let love be without hypocrisy. Abhor what is evil; cling to what is good. Be devoted to one another in brotherly love; give preference to one another in honor; not lagging behind in diligence, fervent in spirit, serving the Lord; rejoicing in hope, persevering in tribulation, devoted to prayer, contributing to the needs of the saints, practicing hospitality. Bless those who persecute you; bless and curse not. Rejoice with those who rejoice, and weep with those who weep. Be of the same mind toward one another; do not be haughty in mind, but associate with the lowly. Do not be wise in your own estimation (Rom. 12:9-16).

> Now we who are strong ought to bear the weaknesses of those without strength and not just please ourselves. Let each of us please his neighbor for his good, to his edification. . . .

> And concerning you, my brethren, I myself also am convinced that you yourselves are full of goodness, filled with all knowledge, and able also to admonish one another (Rom. 15:1-2, 14).

> If we live by the Spirit, let us also walk by the Spirit. Let us not become boastful, challenging one another, envying one another.

> Brethren, even if a man is caught in any trespass, you who are spiritual, restore such a one in a spirit of gentleness; looking to yourselves, lest you too be tempted. Bear one another's burdens, and thus fulfill the law of Christ (Gal. 5:25-6:2).

So far everything is theoretical and safe, because I haven't gotten painfully specific. But now I want to risk getting *that* specific. Please know that I write these things with your good in mind. And that is my sole motive. All of us go through stressful times. If we have no one near during an extended period of high-level stress, chances are good we may lose our perspective. If the stress gets great enough, we could crack. The solution? We need to be accountable!

Now let's go a step further. Say you are a high-powered person with a great deal of responsibility and authority. Left to yourself, you could begin to abuse this power without even realizing it. You will be a better steward of your responsibility if there is someone who knows you well enough to tell you the truth. Solution? You need to be accountable!

Perhaps you have begun to make a lot of money, more than ever in your life. Thanks to this burst of prosperity, there are unseen, beneath-the-surface, mines in the harbor of your future. If you have no one who will give you counsel on how to handle yourself or your money, you will likely blow it if you try to handle it alone. Solution? You need to be accountable!

If you are a husband or a wife, accountability needs to be built into that relationship. Marriages that flourish have this safeguard built in. But if there is a breakdown in accountability, it is only a matter of time before there will be a breakdown in the marriage relationship.

There also has to be accountability in a home between children and parents. Without it there is poor communication—ultimately anarchy, which leads to delinquency. I repeat, there must be accountability! We have it with our teachers at school, our bosses at work, our coaches on the team, the bank that holds the mortgage on our home, and the cop on the corner. Strangely, somehow we don't feel the need to cultivate it on a personal level. The home is an ideal place to learn how to be accountable.

I have a theory that might help explain why there is so little voluntary accountability among adults. In the process of growing up and leaving home, we step away from possibly one of the healthiest situations we've ever had, especially if the home was a balanced, stable one. The healthy relationship we step away from includes the accountability we developed with our parents. About the time we reach eighteen or twenty, we move into a dormitory or join the military or move into our own apartment or we marry and establish our own home with our mate. Often at that point, the relationship of accountability that had been consistently in motion for so long suddenly stops. And an unhealthy independence gets set in concrete. Too much privacy replaces previous days of openness. We adopt a lifestyle that includes too much time strictly on our own. Before long, we're living like isolated islands. No one feels the freedom to step in, not even parents, lest they appear to be meddling. And unless we invite a few close friends to come alongside, most will continue leaving us alone.

Moms and dads don't want to say much. They see things, but they are hesitant to comment. Young adults on their own don't want to ask for much advice, lest it appear as if they are still dependent. A chasm, a void of communication, is created. After all, one of the perks of being on one's own is privacy, right? One of the prerogatives of leadership is independence, right? But the hidden part of the equation is seldom addressed. Too much privacy is unhealthy. Too many hours of independence easily leads to a fall—ethically or morally, financially or spiritually. Stop and think. Those you know who have slipped spiritually or fallen into extra-marital affairs or gotten caught in some financial fiasco were not accountable on a regular basis to anyone, were they? Without the safety net of checks and balances, a fall can be not only far but fatal.

I have formed the habit of asking about accountability when stories of someone's spiritual defection or moral fall comes to my attention. Without fail, I ask something like, "Was _____ accountable to anyone on a regular basis? Did he (or she) meet with one, two, or three folks for the purpose of giving and receiving counsel, prayer, and planning?" Without exception—*hear me, now*—without a single exception, the answer has been the same: *NO!* There is no safe place to be in a world system like ours, where anyone can find immunity from the dangers of too much privacy.

Frankly, the ministry is more perilous than most other vocations. Why? The answer isn't that complicated. There are few roles in life where one is granted greater independence, more privacy, and higher respect. Without personal, regular accountability—not forced but invited—few are strong enough to handle the battles alone. To me, that fact best explains the epidemic in the 1970s and 1980s of moral defection and marital failures among those in vocational Christian service. It is one thing to soar high and alone as an eagle, above the level of mediocrity. But it is another thing entirely, to be so alone that we encounter winds we cannot handle. At such times, flying with a few fellow eagles is essential.

HISTORICAL EXAMPLES FROM BIBLICAL DAYS

Not long ago I went on a quick safari through both Old and New Testaments looking for examples of strong-minded, eagle-like people who lived busy, responsible lives, but took the time to cultivate an accountable relationship with at least one (often more than one) other person. Here is what I found.

Lot was accountable to his Uncle Abraham. When that relationship ceased, Lot sank into the mire at Sodom (Gen. 13, 19).

While he was in the home of Potiphar, *Joseph was accountable to Potiphar.* And even when Potiphar's wife repeatedly made those seductive advances toward Joseph, which Joseph refused, he remained accountable to Potiphar (Gen. 39).

When Saul became Israel's first king, he got in a hurry for Samuel the prophet to arrive so an offering could be made. When Samuel was late, Saul got antsy and ran ahead and gathered together the offering, and offered it. He disobeyed, for kings had no business doing that. When Samuel finally did arrive, if you can believe it, he—a prophet —rebuked the king of Israel! And Saul took it on the chin without an argument. Why? Because *Saul the king was accountable to Samuel the prophet* (1 Sam. 13).

When David fell with Bathsheba and the entire nation was scandalized because of his adultery, Nathan the prophet stood before the king of the nation and said to David, "You are the man." King David didn't fight him or try to have him killed. Instead, David confessed, "I have sinned." Why? Because *David was accountable to Nathan the prophet* (2 Sam. 12).

When Nehemiah became convinced he should go to Jerusalem and lead the project of building the wall around the city, he first had to get a green light from Artaxerxes. He refused to leave without it. Even though God had spoken to him and was leading him on that future mission, *Nehemiah was accountable to the king* for whom he worked as a cupbearer (Neh. 1–2).

When Daniel lived as a man of God through several generations of kings, *Daniel made himself accountable to each king*—some great, some not so great. On one occasion his colleagues called the officials of the land and made accusations against Daniel. With search warrants they personally moved in and checked on him. They left no stone unturned! But even after a thorough search, they couldn't find a solitary thing against him. He was clean! But Daniel didn't fight them.

The fact is, when he found out about it later, he was very much at ease. There was nothing to hide. *Daniel lived accountable to his peers* (Dan. 1–6). Accountability has a way of keeping one's private life squeaky clean.

Let's now move into the New Testament. When Jesus came to this earth, one of the things that marked his life was submission to the Father's will. John tells us on more than one occasion that Jesus always did the things that pleased the Father. *The Son of God was accountable to His heavenly Father.*

When Christ selected twelve men to work with Him, men to whom He would pass the torch of the work of ministry, there is no question that *the disciples were accountable to Jesus.* Ultimately, *they became accountable to one another.*

When John Mark went on a journey with Paul and Barnabas, *John Mark was accountable to those older men.* In fact, the two older men traveled together for the same reason. *Paul and Barnabas, in turn, were accountable to the church at Antioch,* as were Paul and Silas later on. *Timothy was accountable to Paul,* his father in the faith.

Onesimus the slave was accountable to Philemon. And Paul, when writing the letter to Philemon, said, in effect, "He is willing to come back. Please accept him. Onesimus is accountable to you."

When John the apostle wrote the little letter of Third John, he mentioned Diotrephes. He said, "When I come, I will set the record straight." Why? *Diotrephes was accountable to John as an elder.* A major battle John had with that man was his unwillingness to be accountable to anyone.

I have just hit the high points like a rock skipping across a lake. But that's sufficient for you to get the picture. The Bible is *full* of examples of accountability. Again and again, people in biblical days benefited from others' presence, counsel, warnings, and encouragement.

Today, we, too, need others to hold us accountable. Sometimes an objective opinion will reveal a blind spot. Sometimes a straight-from-the-shoulder piece of advice will preserve a friend from a fall. Other times a strong reproof will get the wayward back on track. On another occasion, we may simply need a sounding board to help keep us on target. One man hails the benefits of accountability like this:

> . . . Behavioral sciences in recent years have expounded the simple truth that "behavior that is observed changes." People who are account-

able by their own choice to a group of friends, to a therapy group, to a psychiatrist or a pastoral counselor, to a study group or prayer group, are people who are serious about changing their behavior, and they are finding that change is possible.

Studies done in factories have proven that both quality and quantity of work increase when the employees know that they are being observed. If only God knows what I am doing, since I know He won't tell, I tend to make all kinds of excuses for myself. But if I must report to another or a group of others, I begin to monitor my behavior. If someone is keeping an eye on me, my behavior improves.[2]

An unaccountable leader is dancing too close to the edge of risk. Unaccountable radio personalities and/or television evangelists live with too much authority and too much privacy. They need others! An unaccountable counselor has too much responsibility and needs too much self-control to handle everything alone. An unaccountable physician can easily stumble. An unaccountable banker, CPA, or attorney can fall as well. Unaccountable entrepreneurs are especially vulnerable. It's simply too great a chance to take without someone or a small group of confidential, objective friends alongside who have your good at heart, those whom you have invited into your private world.

Sometimes blind spots result in notorious disasters. Jonestown is a classic example of an unaccountable leader who went wild with authority. He simply went too far too fast—he was too isolated. No one, finally, was allowed to be honest with Jim Jones.

Some of you are probably wondering about me. You need to know that I am definitely, willingly, and regularly accountable to a carefully chosen, small group of men. Not all of them are part of the church I serve. They are men of wisdom and integrity. They love me too much not to tell me the truth. Just recently Cynthia and I both spent several hours with these trusted, objective, honest men as they hammered away at particular facets of our lives. It was painful at times, but, oh, so beneficial!

Are you accountable to someone outside your family? Someone who can ask you straight questions, hard questions, and make honest observations? Do you spend some time with this person on a regular basis, looking at each other's life? Are you committed to mutual encouragement? Do you think together? Pray together? Play together? I hope so.

PRACTICAL ADVANTAGES OF PERSONAL APPRAISAL

Chances are good that someone will read this chapter and misunderstand me. "Sounds like a torture chamber you're suggesting, Chuck. Who needs to face a gestapo group every other week?" Hold it. Just in case my words have given you that false impression, allow me to set the record straight. To be sure, accountability can degenerate into a dreadful, threatening scene if it is handled the wrong way or if you have the wrong people involved. (By the way, some people would love to make the world accountable to them. They are the frowning ones who wear hair shirts and feel "called of God" to be your personal Nathan who will point out all your wrongs. They have the unique "gift of criticism." They'll be happy to exercise it on your behalf— *often!* My advice? Avoid those folks like the plague! They hurt much more than they help.) That's not what I have in mind.

I'm talking about people who love you too much to let you play in dangerous traffic. They also love you too much to let you start believing in your own stuff. When they spot conceit rearing its head, they say so. But they also love you too much to let you be too hard on yourself. Like Jonathan with David, they are messengers of great encouragement. That's the bright side, and it needs to be emphasized. Soaring eagles need wind beneath their wings!

I can think of at least three practical advantages of accountability— all based on statements found in the ancient Books of Proverbs and Psalms.

First advantage: *When we are regularly accountable, we're less likely to stumble into a trap.* Other eyes, more perceptive and objective than ours, can see traps that we may fail to detect.

> Through presumption comes nothing but strife,
> But with those who receive counsel is wisdom. . . .
> The teaching of the wise is a fountain of life,
> To turn aside from the snares of death. . . .
> Poverty and shame will come to him who neglects discipline,
> But he who regards reproof will be honored. . . .
> He who walks with wise men will be wise,
> But the companion of fools will suffer harm (Prov. 13:10, 14, 18, 20).

The last statement is not a verse written to teenagers in high school, though it certainly would apply. I clearly remember my high school years, don't you? Many of us ran around with others who were tougher than we, so we could cover up our own feelings of inadequacy. My mother kept saying to me, "Charles, every time you run with the wrong crowd, you do wrong. When you are with the right crowd, you do right." That was objective, accurate counsel that I didn't want to hear, but she said it often enough to drill truth into my head. Her counsel is still true. If I were to run with the wrong crowd, I would be tempted to do wrong.

And it doesn't stop when we turn twenty. It goes on into adult years as well. If you choose a wrong set of co-workers, you'll practice wrong things in your business. If you choose a wrong set of friends, you'll practice wrong things in your social life. Run with those who do drugs, and you'll wind up doing the same.

But—the flip side—those who walk with the wise learn from them. You need someone who will say, I'm not sure how healthy that is. I'm glad you asked me. Let's talk about it." And that person will help point out the traps you could fall into if you kept tracking in that direction. A couple more statements on this same advantage:

> He whose ear listens to the life-giving reproof will dwell among the wise. He who neglects discipline despises himself, but he who listens to reproof acquires understanding. The fear of the Lord is the instruction for wisdom, and before honor comes humility (Prov. 15:31–33).

I like the way Solomon calls this counsel "life-giving reproof." That's exactly what it is!

Now for the second advantage of accountability: *When we are regularly accountable, we are more likely to see the whole picture.* When we have a sounding board, an accountable partner or group who traffics in truth, we're more likely to see the whole picture. I notice that my life tends to get quite narrow if my world is reduced to my own perspective—just a restricted, tight radius. But with the counsel of a friend, my world expands. I become more aware; I gain depth and I discover innuendo and I find another vista or dimension I would have missed all alone with my two-by-four mind. "Iron sharpens iron, so one man sharpens another" (Prov. 27:17).

Let me expand on that refining process a little. One woman sharpens another; one homemaker sharpens another; one dentist sharpens another (no pun intended); one attorney sharpens another;

one physician sharpens another; one businessman sharpens another; one salesman sharpens another; one minister sharpens another. Why? Because the world in which one person lives is too limited and restricted. When rubbing shoulders with another, we gain a panoramic view, which allows us to see the whole picture, "As in water face reflects face, so the heart of man reflects man" (Prov. 27:19).

That's so picturesque! People provide a clear reflection of what is in the heart. A mirror goes only skin deep. The counsel of a friend reflects what is down inside.

Plato, in his *Apology*, wrote, "The life which is unexamined is not worth living." If you are not reflecting on your life, I have news for you: It isn't long before you'll accept mediocrity. Are you doing what you did last year and perhaps the year before that? If so, you're becoming less effective. We need the discipline of self-examination in order to achieve excellence.

The third advantage of accountability; *When we are regularly accountable, we are not likely to get away with sinful and unwise actions.* "Faithful are the wounds of a friend, but deceitful are the kisses of an enemy" (Prov. 27:6).

I've thought a lot about that proverb. Not only because I have been wounded (in the right way) by counselors who had my good at heart, but because I have been curious about how it works in any life. I did an analysis of verse 6 and found that the original Hebrew text reads something like this:

> Trustworthy are the bruises caused by the wounding of one who loves you, but deceitful are the kisses of one who hates you.

Among other things, that limits those who wound us to those who love us. This tells me that not everyone has a right to climb into our life and come down on us with a rebuke. No, that is a privilege and responsibility of someone with whom we have established a love relationship. A love relationship, based on time spent together and a deep knowledge of each other, provides the oil rebukes need in order for them to be accepted. There are times when it is necessary for us to be bruised by a friend's straight talk.

I can't remember where I first read the following words but I will never forget them: "Apart from blunt truth, our lives sink decadently amid the perfume of hints and suggestions."

AN HONEST EVALUATION OF OURSELVES

It is possible to read a chapter like this and never take it personally. Some read it and think, "I have to get my husband to read this!" Or, "It's too bad my pastor hasn't read this chapter. Maybe I can loan him the book—and underline certain statements in chapter 8!" Bad idea. Instead of wishing someone else were reading this, let's play like it's just the two of us. I have the privilege of writing about something that is very, very personal to you—*your* life, *your* private world. To make it palatable, allow me to ask you a few questions. I would like you simply to answer them "Yes" or "No." They are hard questions, I warn you. And you may be embarrassed if someone saw your answers, perhaps, because you wouldn't be able to explain them fully. So just think your answer, okay? Take your time, however. Don't answer too quickly.

Question 1. <u>Can you name one or more people outside your family to whom you have made yourself regularly accountable?</u> And before you answer, this is what I mean. That person has quick and easy access to your life. He (or she) is free to ask you things like "What's going on?" and "Why?" This person wouldn't hesitate to probe if he were concerned about something you were doing that seemed unwise or hurtful. This friend usually knows your whereabouts and can regularly vouch for your motives. He or she has your private phone number. He isn't afraid to interrupt you. There's a well-developed love connection between you. You've helped cultivate it. Do you have at least one person like that, preferably two or three?

If your answer is "No," rather than just stopping here with a deep sigh, thinking, *I'm out of luck,* take this as a challenge. Say to yourself, "I need to search for someone, a person that I know will take that kind of time with me. And I'm going to invite that person to begin a friendship. We're going to have a meal or two together, and we're going to get to know each other, and I'm going to see if perhaps this is the one to whom I should open my life." I plead with you, don't put it off.

Question 2. <u>Are you aware of the dangers of unaccountability?</u> Again, before you answer, I'm talking about dangers like unattractive blind spots, unhealthy relationships, unchecked habits, unspoken motives that will never be known without such a friend. Are you aware of where these dangers will lead if unaccountability continues? Be honest now. Ponder the consequences of an unaccountable life.

Maybe you have to admit that you've been far too proud, lived much too secretly. When I decided to let down my guard a number of

years ago, I wrote out this simple prayer to God. It helped break down
my resistance to the counsel of others.

> Lord, I am willing
> To receive what You give
> To lack what You withhold
> To relinquish what You take
> To suffer what You inflict
> To be what You require.
> And, Lord, if others are to be
> Your messengers to me,
> I am willing to hear and heed
> What they have to say. Amen.

Question 3. <u>When was the last time you gave an account for the
"private areas" of your life to someone outside your family?</u> Like your
finances, sizable purchases, or your pattern for giving? Does anyone
know how much (or how little) you give? Does anyone give you
counsel on what seems wise and what seems a bit irresponsible in the
use of your money? Has someone ever talked to you about sacrificing
in the realm of finances? They won't without your invitation.

How about occupational diligence? Does anyone know how much
or how little time you really spend at the office? Is anybody aware of
the attitude you have there, so that he or she is able to help you see its
impact on the lives of others? Maybe someone needs to say you're
working *too many* hours. Does someone have a right to that secret
world of yours?

How about a schedule of activities? Have you had anyone pull up
to you recently and say, "You know you're just too busy. You're away
from home too many hours. Why do you say yes so often?" You may
be approaching "burnout" without realizing it.

How about addressing your lust? Does anybody know how much
you struggle with pornography? Anyone know what you check out at
the video stores, or which magazines you linger over? How about a
level of entertainment that you've decided you can get away with
because nobody knows? Those aren't petty questions; they're hard
ones.

I warned you I'd be writing straight talk. I care about your remaining strong and eaglelike. I care about your soaring. I care if you've
begun to slump and settle for mediocrity. And I think you care too. I
think you really *want* to impact others. Remember my paraphrase of

Solzhenitsyn's statement? "One person of truth impacts the whole world."

Recently I read about a woman who, on the advice of her doctor, had gone to see a pastor to talk about joining the church. She had recently had a facelift and when her doctor dismissed her, he gave her this advice:

> "My dear, I have done an extraordinary job on your face, as you can see in the mirror. I have charged you a great deal of money and you were happy to pay it. But I want to give you some free advice. Find a group of people who love God and who will love you enough to help you deal with all the negative emotions inside of you. If you don't, you'll be back in my office in a very short time with your face in far worse shape than before."[3]

Wise counsel!

Those heroes who soar high above the level of mediocrity possess vision, apply determination, and maintain priorities. But how is it they keep from danger and do not suffer a fall from those heights? By now you know the secret. Accountability—they don't avoid the hard questions.

Part Three

Combating Mediocrity Requires Fighting Fiercely

*Enemy-occupied territory—that
is what the world is. Christianity is
the story of how the rightful King
has landed in disguise, and is
calling us all to take part in a great
campaign of sabotage.*

C. S. Lewis
1952

9

WINNING THE BATTLE
OVER GREED

*I*n our nation of fast foods and quick fixes, the great hope of Americans is overnight change. Many are too impatient to wait for anything and too lazy to work long and hard to make it happen. We want what we want when we want it, and the sooner the better—which explains our constant pursuit of hurry-up formulas. Everything from diet fads promising rapid weight loss to immediate financial success through clever schemes captures our fancy and gets our vote. The famous showman P. T. Barnum knew what he was talking about, didn't he? Promise instant anything and some sucker will bite. Everybody, it seems, expects instant transformation.

All this reminds me of a funny story I heard recently. A fellow was raised in the back hills of West Virginia—I mean, so far out in the sticks, never in his life had he even seen a big city, to say nothing of modern inventions and neon lights. He married a gal just like himself and they spent all their married years in the backwoods. They had one son, whom they creatively named Junior. Around the time Junior reached his sixteenth birthday, his dad began to realize it wouldn't be too many years before their son would become a man and would strike out on his own. It troubled him that his boy could reach manhood and wind up getting a job in the city, not prepared to face the real world. He felt responsible and decided to do something about it.

He and his wife started saving for a trip the three of them would take to the city. About three years later the big day arrived. They tossed their belongings in the ol' pickup and started the long journey over winding, rough roads to the city. Their plan was to spend several days at a swanky hotel and take in all the sights. As they approached the outskirts of the metropolis, Papa began to get a little jumpy: "Mama, when we pull up at th' hotel, you stay in th' truck while

519

Junior an' I go in an' look around. We'll come back and git ya, okay?"
She agreed.

Flashing neon lights and uniformed doormen greeted them as they
pulled up. Mama stayed put as Papa and Junior walked wide-eyed
toward the lobby. Neither could believe his eyes! When they stepped
on a mat, the doors opened automatically. Inside, they stood like
statues, staring at the first chandelier either of them had ever seen. It
hung from a ceiling three stories high. Off to the left was an enormous
waterfall, rippling over inlaid stones and rocks. "Junior, look!" Papa
was pointing toward a long mall where busy shoppers were going in
and out of beautiful stores. "Papa, looka there!" Down below was an
iceskating rink—*inside.*

While both stood silent, watching one breathtaking sight after
another, they kept hearing a clicking sound behind them. Finally,
Papa turned around and saw this amazing little room with doors that
slid open from the center. "What in the world?" People would walk
up, push a button and wait. Lights would flicker above the doors and
then, "click," the doors would slide open from the middle. Some
people would walk out of the little room and others would walk inside
and turn around as, "click," the doors slid shut. By now, dad and son
stood *totally* transfixed.

At that moment a wrinkled old lady shuffled up to the doors all by
herself. She pushed the button and waited only a few seconds. "Click,"
the doors opened with a swish and she hobbled into the little room.
No one else stepped in with her, so "click," the doors slid shut. Not
more than twenty seconds later the doors opened again—and there
stood this fabulously attractive blonde, a young woman in her
twenties—high heels, shapely body, beautiful face—a real knockout!
As she stepped out, smiled, and turned to walk away, Papa nudged his
boy and mumbled, "Hey, Junior . . . *go git Mama!*"

Seems like everybody these days is looking for a room like what
Papa thought he had found. Just push the right button, wait momentarily for the door of opportunity to slide open, then "click," magic! In
only a matter of seconds we are instantly transformed. Whom are we
kidding? That makes a pretty good joke, but when it comes to reality,
nothing could be further from the truth. This is especially true when it
comes to the cultivation of character. Honestly, I know of nothing that
takes longer, is harder work, or requires greater effort than breaking
the old habits that hold us in the grip of mediocrity. No eagle
instantly or automatically soars!

This constant struggle to cultivate and maintain good character explains why I think of this third section of the book as a combat zone—a series of four chapters that portray the scene of a fierce fight. There are four major enemies that must be identified, attacked, and conquered if we hope to achieve and maintain excellence: *greed, traditionalism, apathetic indifference,* and *joyless selfishness.* And we shall take them in that order. But keep in mind that each one of these opponents of excellence dies a slow and painful death. About the time we think we've got 'em whipped, they're back on their feet and coming at us from another angle.

Greed under the Scope

Let's take a brief yet close look at greed. Practically speaking, greed is an inordinate desire for more, an excessive, unsatisfied hunger to possess. Like an untamed beast, greed grasps, claws, reaches, clutches, and clings—stubbornly refusing to surrender. The word *enough* is not in this beast's vocabulary. Akin to envy and jealousy, greed is nevertheless distinct. Envy wants to have what someone else possesses. Jealousy wants to possess what it already has. But greed is different. Greed is forever discontented and therefore insatiably craving, longing, wanting, striving for more, more, more.

Perhaps there is nothing more tragic to behold than a greedy person—a person who is never fully at rest, always in pursuit of something else, something more, something beyond. The bondage this creates serves as an anchor so huge and heavy, no set of wings, no matter how massive, can lift its victim to soar.

Four Faces of Greed

The first and most common face greed wears is the green mask of money, money, money! <u>Greed is an excessive motivation to have more money.</u> It is a face we see all around us. Most people I meet in the workplace want more money for what they are doing. Before challenging that, stop and think of those you work around. Most are woefully discontented with their salary. And by the way, you don't have to be rich to be greedy. I know more people who haven't enough money who are greedy than I know who have more than they need. Most often, greed appears as a gnawing, ruthless hunger to get more, to earn more, and even to hoard more money.

Second, greed often wears the face of things, material possessions. Greed is an excessive determination to own more things. Again, think before you reject that thought. We never quite have enough furniture. Or the right furniture. Have you noticed? We never have the right carpet or just the drapes we'd like to have. And then there's the woodwork like we've always dreamed of having. Or the car we've always wanted to own. Whether it's little trinkets we happen to collect or some big thing like a home or an RV or a boat—it's always something. It's that driving desire to own more things. To say it straight, greed is raw, unchecked materialism.

Third, greed can wear the face of fame. Greed is also an excessive desire to become more famous, to make a name for oneself. Some are so determined to be stars, to be in lights, they'd stop at nothing to have people quote them or to be seen in celebrity circles. Thankfully, not all who are famous fall into the greedy category. It's wonderful to meet people who are stars and don't know it.

While my family and I were at a Dodgers game last summer, I saw some little fellows waiting for autographs from some of the players in the Los Angeles Dodgers' organization. It was terrific to watch some of those fine athletes—big, strong, and muscular—drop down on one knee and pull a little boy over closer and say, "Sure, I'll sign that," and then write his name on the kid's baseball. Each boy walked away with a new hero added to his list. Approachable professional athletes, politicians, and teachers who take time for young people can make an enormous impression for good!

I remember when I lived in Boston, our older son was just a little bit too young to go to the games. On one occasion I spoke at the Red Sox' pregame chapel. Afterwards I was given a baseball signed by every player who came to the chapel service as a thank-you gesture. They told me to take it home and give it to Curt. They thought he would like that. So did I! Written all over the ball were these famous names. I was careful not to smear the autographs as I took this baseball home to Curt. I rushed into the house and yelled, "Curt, look, this is a new baseball from the Red Sox!" The little guy held it, frowned, and said, "Gee, Daddy, somebody *wrote all over it!*" My little guy was just a couple of years too young to realize what a treasure it was to have a baseball signed by celebrities.

Isn't it great to find famous men and women who are still accessible? They're still real, still vulnerable, still able to put their arms around a little kid, still able to take time for their family, for people. Greed for fame doesn't have to happen.

Fourth, greed can wear the face of control. Such <u>greed is an excessive need to gain more control</u>—to gain mastery over something or someone, to always be in charge, to call all the shots, to become the top dog, the king of the hill. The great goal in many people's lives is to manipulate their way to the top of whichever success ladder they choose to climb.

At the risk of sounding terribly simplistic in my analysis, greed can be traced back in Scripture to that day our original parents, Adam and Eve, fell in the garden. When they turned their attention from the living God back to themselves, greed entered and polluted the human bloodstream. It has contaminated human nature ever since. In order for our greed to be controlled, a fight is inevitable. It is a battle for you, and it is a battle for me—a bloodless yet relentless warfare.

Our Lord realized what a hold material things can have on humanity. In no less than seventeen of His thirty-seven parables, Jesus dealt with property and the responsibility for using it wisely. One of those stories seems significant enough for us to examine.

GREED EXPOSED AND DENOUNCED

What we find in Luke 12:13–34 is one of the clearest and most forthright discourses on greed that you'll find anywhere in all of literature. It's not difficult at all to understand. But be forewarned: It will take us the rest of our lifetime to obey!

Let me summarize the Luke 12 account in a simple manner. It seems to fall neatly into four parts. In verses 13–14, there's a dialogue. In verse 15, Jesus gives a brief principle. Then in verses 16–21, there's a story that He tells about a greedy man who made his living as a successful farmer. Then in verses 22–34 we shall find a series of truths.

The Dialogue

> And someone in the crowd said to Him, "Teacher, tell my brother to divide the family inheritance with me." But He said to him, "Man, who appointed Me a judge or arbiter over you?" (vv. 13–14).

Out of the crowd emerges a man who boldly tells Jesus what to do. Interestingly, he neither asks a question nor makes a request. The man doesn't graciously say "Please." There isn't even a "Sir." He has the audacity to instruct Jesus on what to do. Realizing how complicated and counterproductive such family squabbles can be, Jesus refrained. He never got involved in issues that weren't related to the big-picture purpose of His goal on earth. I have always respected that about Christ.

By the way, there's a great lesson to be learned here in bowing out of other people's business. People who want to rope us into the petty details of their lives will toss issues in our direction that we have no right to get involved in. When little would be gained from running that rabbit trail, we must have the foresight and discipline to say, "I'm not qualified to address that. I'm really not the one you ought to talk to." It is comforting to remember that Jesus didn't attempt to meet *every* person's need or become entangled in *every* person's affairs. He was selective. Those needs He did meet were directly related to His big-picture mission. No wonder He, like none other who ever lived on this vast globe, maintained a high-level commitment to excellence. He never lost sight of His priorities.

But apparently Jesus heard in the tone of the man's voice, or realized from the issue that was raised (a family inheritance), that this was a perfect place to address the bigger issue of greed. After all, that is what prompted the man's opening statement to Jesus, when he asked Jesus to take sides. Instead, He stated a principle for all to follow.

The Principle

> And He said to them, "Beware, and be on your guard against every form of greed; for not even when one has an abundance does his life consist of his possessions" (Luke 12:15).

Don't miss the pronouns. In verse 14, "He said to *him*." But in verse 15, "He said to *them*." Jesus answers the man in verse 14, but then He turns to the crowd and speaks to *them* about a broader subject. In doing so, He declares a warning: "Watch out—be on guard!" About what? "Be on your guard against every form of greed." Jesus employs the word *form*. Earlier I used the word *face*. Greed has many faces, but Jesus' word is better. "Every FORM of greed, whether money or things or fame or control, in whatever form it may appear, watch out."

The Greeks had a curious word they used when referring to *greed*. The word used in verse 15 means "a thirst for having more." To illustrate, it's probably fanciful yet fairly descriptive to think of a fellow who is thirsty taking a drink of *salt* water, which only makes him thirstier. His thirst causes him to drink even more, which ultimately results in making him terribly sick. And if he continues to drink he could die. That's the whole point of greed. You'll want more and more of something that really isn't good for you. And in the getting of it, you'll suffer the painful consequences. That is why Jesus warns, "Beware. Be on your guard. This thing is like a cancer—an insatiable leech that will suck the life right out of you." Enough will never be enough, which explains the reason our Lord adds: ". . . for not even when one has an abundance does his life consist of his possessions." Life does not—*cannot*—revolve around things if one hopes to achieve true excellence. The battle with greed must be won if we hope to soar.

The Parable

> And He told them a parable, saying, "The land of a certain rich man was very productive. And he began reasoning to himself, saying, 'What shall I do, since I have no place to store my crops?' And he said, 'This is what I will do: I will tear down my barns and build larger ones, and there I will store all my grain and my goods. And I will say to my soul, "Soul, you have many goods laid up for many years to come; take your ease, eat, drink and be merry."' But God said to him, 'You fool! This very night your soul is required of you; and now who will own what you have prepared?' So is the man who lays up treasure for himself, and is not rich toward God" (Luke 12:16–21).

Before we call down wholesale condemnation upon this farmer, let's be sure we understand that the man is not wrong because he is successful and prosperous. There isn't a word here or anywhere else in Scripture against well-earned or well-deserved success or financial prosperity. This man is clearly a success; he has worked long and hard. Furthermore, he's not wrong because he is lazy. Neither do we find one word here about the man's being dishonest. He hasn't earned a dishonest living. On the contrary, he's apparently been very diligent and careful as a farmer. He's planted and he has harvested. In previous days he prepared the soil and faithfully rotated the crops. It seems that he's done everything correctly. And so what he sees as he looks outside the windows of his farmhouse is a bumper crop. It must have been beautiful to behold. There's nothing wrong with a bumper crop—or with any of the things that brought him to prosperity. Then, what is wrong?

I find three glaring, tragic failures about this man.

First: He didn't really know himself. It never entered his mind that he might not live for many years to come; he talked to his soul as if he were immortal. He also never stopped to consider that his abundance would never, ever satisfy his soul down deep inside. He was so preoccupied with the temporal that he didn't bother to give eternal thoughts the time of day. Such horizontal thinking is the epitome of a mediocre lifestyle.

Are you ready for a shocking thought? Some of you reading these words right now may very well be dead in a year. Some of you won't be alive in five years. We simply don't have many years. And it seems that so many people are dying younger these days. We haven't yet eradicated heart disease, cancer, or the AIDS virus.

The farmer in Jesus' story didn't really understand himself because he didn't stop to think that his abundance in crops would not bring ultimate satisfaction. Remember what he said? "Take your ease, eat, drink, and be merry." Those are words of false satisfaction. Elsewhere, Scripture calls it presumption. He's thinking that by getting more, there'll be a sense of satisfaction in his soul.

I was speaking to a businessman at breakfast just this past week who has finally come to terms with his business. With a burst of emotion he said to me, "Chuck, that business was my god! I was anxious, preoccupied, seldom at home, and nursing an ulcer. I thought my work would bring me the satisfaction I needed. But I have finally come to see that it won't. At last I am operating my life with an eternal dimension in mind. I have put the Lord in a perspective I've never had Him in before, and I've never been happier." There was contentment written all over that man's face. He had come to know himself—realistically, spiritually, deeply. That's what the farmer in Jesus' parable missed. He didn't realize that he wouldn't live forever and never even stopped to think about it.

Second: He didn't really care about other people. His remarks are thoroughly, completely, unashamedly full of himself. He is occupying the throne of his own life. In the English version of my Bible, I count six "I's" and five "my's." Never once do we find "they," "them," "their"—no, not even once. Why? Because he doesn't care about "they," "them," and "their." He cares only about "I," "me," and "my." Greed personified.

William Barclay writes:

> It was said of a self-centered young lady, "Edith lived in a little world, bounded on the north, south, east, and west by Edith."[1]

Have you ever spent much time around people like that? Sure you have. It's all around us! As I said earlier, it's in our bloodstream. From our earliest years we bear the marks of greed.

To date, Cynthia and I have three darling (and amazingly intelligent!) grandchildren. We love it! And we're looking forward to having *more* of them. I joked with our two married kids, "Keep having 'em. They are just great. Bring 'em over when they're clean and cute and smell great. Take 'em home when they don't." It's wonderful! But there is something funny about these adorable little people. They're all born with their granddaddy's problem—*selfishness*. They all grab and grasp. They all want, take, keep. "Mine! Mine! Mine!" Funny, no one had to teach them that word. It's built into their nature. A stubborn desire for more is like a massive muscle flexing inside each one of them. Already their parents (and grandparents) are having to do battle with their vigorous greed. Winning the battle over greed is a lifetime assignment.

Third: <u>The man didn't really make room for God.</u> He lived his entire life in the tight radius of himself, just as if there were no God. Imagine the shock when the death angel said to him, "You fool! Tonight is curtains! It's over, man—it's all over. Then to whom are you going to leave all these things? Who will have the right to these things that you've prepared?"

There once lived a French artist who read this story Jesus told. Afterwards, he produced a masterful representation of it on canvas. Maybe you've seen it or read about it. It's one of the few paintings painted *on both sides* of the canvas. On one side there is this rather portly farmer sitting at his desk. In front of him are several bags bulging with money. Through the window behind him you can see crops glistening in the evening sun; they're starting to lean over, heavy with grain, with corn. Nothing but dark green fields as far as the eye can see. And sitting on a long shelf above the farmer's head are more bags of money. He has the marks of abundance all around him, sort of like a Silas Marner sitting alone at the desk. He's got that faraway look in his eye like, "What will I do with it now?"

The painter read the story again with a sigh. He frowned at what he had painted. Dissatisfied, he flipped the canvas over and began the same picture on the other side. Same man, same desk, same window and bumper crops, same little bags of money, same shelf above the man's head. But this time he painted everything covered with a thin layer of dust. And something else has been added, too. The death angel is standing near with his hand on the man's shoulder and his lips are pursed as if to be saying, "Fool."

A Series of Truths

On the basis of that story, Jesus presents what appears to be a mini Sermon on the Mount. And in some ways it is. Notice what comes next: "He said to His disciples. . . ." (See the difference? In verse 14 He spoke to the man, and in verse 15 He addressed the crowd. But finally He gets alone with His twelve and talks with His closest friends—the disciples.)

> And He said to His disciples, "For this reason I say to you, do not be anxious for your life, as to what you shall eat; nor for your body, as to what you shall put on. For life is more than food, and the body than clothing. Consider the ravens, for they neither sow nor reap; and they have no storeroom nor barn; and yet God feeds them; how much more valuable you are than the birds! And which of you by being anxious can add a single cubit to his life's span? If then you cannot do even a very little thing, why are you anxious about other matters? Consider the lilies, how they grow; they neither toil nor spin; but I tell you, even Solomon in all his glory did not clothe himself like one of these. But if God so arrays the grass in the field, which is alive today and tomorrow is thrown into the furnace, how much more will He clothe you, O men of little faith! And do not seek what you shall eat, and what you shall drink, and do not keep worrying. For all these things the nations of the world eagerly seek; but your Father knows that you need these things. But seek for His kingdom, and these things shall be added to you. Do not be afraid, little flock, for your Father has chosen gladly to give you the kingdom. Sell your possessions and give to charity; make yourselves purses which do not wear out, an unfailing treasure in heaven, where no thief comes near, nor moth destroys. For where your treasure is, there will your heart be also" (Luke 12:22–34).

As I study Jesus' magnificent talk, four major truths emerge. The first comes from several negative commands like: "Don't be anxious" and "Don't seek what to eat or wear." He's saying, "Don't be preoccupied. Don't let your life revolve around your wardrobe or your coiffure." Don't have your life revolve around things that are going to burn up and be gone in a matter of time. And again, "Don't be afraid."

Here's what I learn from all these negative commands. *Those who lose the battle with greed are characterized by anxiety and a pursuit of the temporal.* I'll not elaborate on that, but it deserves some meditation. Read it again to make sure you've let it sink in.

I also notice several positive commands in Jesus' speech: "Consider the ravens" and "Consider the lilies." Also, "Seek His kingdom." (Of course, you remember that one since we've mentioned it numerous times in earlier chapters.) These positives lead me to a second major truth: *Those who win the battle over greed realize their value in God's sight and simply trust Him.*

When we arrive at Jesus' powerful conclusion (vv. 33-34), a third truth emerges: *Overcoming greed requires deliberate and assertive action.* "Sell! Give! Make!" Those are demanding imperatives. Take your time, and study what Jesus said about each one of them. It isn't simply a stimulating idea from one of today's theologians. It isn't some slogan from the headquarters of some denomination. This is *Jesus'* teaching. And He was teaching His first converts, His early disciples. "Make deliberate and assertive decisions, men, regarding greed. Don't allow it in your life. And as soon as you see it coming, kick it out." That's the underlying idea.

There's nothing in the world wrong with making a nice living. Nor is there anything wrong with being eminently wealthy if you earn and handle it correctly. But there's something drastically wrong when you keep it all to yourself! God gave it to you so you could, in turn, give it back to Him, to others—yes, in *abundance.* The only reason I can imagine for God's allowing anyone to make more than one needs is to be able to *give* more. We certainly can't take it with us, that's for sure.

I have a close friend in the ministry who traveled across the country for a week of meetings. The only problem was, his baggage didn't make it. As I recall, the bags went on to Berlin! He really needed a couple of suits. So he went down to the local thrift shop and was pleased to find a row of suits. When he told the guy, "I'd like to get a couple of suits," the salesman smiled and said, "Good, we've got several. But you need to know they came from the local mortuary. They've all been cleaned and pressed, but they were used on stiffs. Not a thing wrong with 'em; I just didn't want that to bother you." My friend said, "No, that's fine. That's okay." So he hurriedly tried some on and bought a couple for about twenty-five bucks apiece. Great deal!

When he got back to his room, he began to get dressed for the evening's meeting. As he put one on, to his surprise there were no pockets. Both sides were all sewed up! Though surprised, he thought, *Why of course! Stiffs don't carry stuff with 'em when they depart!* The suits looked as if they had pockets, but they were just flaps on the coat. My friend told me later, "I spent all week trying to stick my hands in my pockets. Wound up having to hang my keys on my belt!" The minister was reminded all week long that life is temporal. And he probably preached all the better for that thought!

Finally, a fourth truth comes from Jesus' words ". . . where your treasure is, there your heart will be." *Personal valuables—real valuables—are sealed in our hearts.*

Combating mediocrity requires fighting fiercely. Don't ever forget it! The greed of our lives won't be conquered without a fight. Greed and brokenness cannot coexist. When Jesus, our Lord, finally surrendered to the Cross, totally broken before the Father, He turned it all over to Him. He said, "If it is at all possible not to allow this to happen, let the cup pass from Me—take it from Me; nevertheless, Your will be done, not Mine." That is the maximum statement of brokenness. Put yourself in His place. Dare to say the same prayer He uttered. "If it's Your will, Lord, that I have any of this, then fine. But if it's Your will that it all be taken away, take it all—even my life— because I'd rather be broken on earth and rich in heaven than have my way down here and be poor up there."

These thoughts remind me of one of the most helpful poems I ever committed to memory:

TREASURES

One by one God took them from me,
All the things I valued most,
Till I was empty-handed;
Every glittering toy was lost.

And I walked earth's highway, grieving,
In my rags and poverty,
Till I heard His voice inviting,
"Lift your empty hands to Me!"

So I turned my hands toward heaven,
And He filled them with a store
Of His own transcendent riches
Till they could contain no more.

And at last I comprehended
With my stupid mind and dull,
That God could not pour His riches
Into hands already full![2]

—Martha Snell Nicholson

10

SLAYING THE DRAGON
OF TRADITIONALISM

*F*or years I have appreciated J. B. Phillips' paraphrase of a line from Paul's letter to the Romans. Even though the thought originally appeared in the apostle's mind and flowed from his century-one pen, it is as relevant as any counsel we could hear today: "Don't let the world around you squeeze you into its own mold" (Rom. 12:2, *Phillips*).

Great advice! Whoever decides to soar in the clear, clean heights, well above the level of mediocrity, must first fight through the flatland fog which hangs heavy over the swamp of sameness. It isn't uncommon for eagles to fight for survival. American poet and artist e. e. cummings, realizing this same truth about humans, wrote:

> . . . to be nobody but yourself in a world which is doing its best, night and day, to make you everybody else, means to fight the hardest battle which any human being can fight; and never stop fighting.[1]

That's why I said earlier that I think of this third section of the book as a combat zone, where fierce fighting takes place. Because I haven't the time to address all the opponents of excellence, I am forced to limit the four chapters in Part Three to four of the toughest enemies we can encounter.

In chapter 9 we squared off with *greed*. We weren't two pages into the subject before we realized what a choking grip greed can get on us. I wrote some suggestions on how to win the battle over greed in hopes of helping you not to "let the world around you squeeze you into its own mold." In this chapter we face a second foe, no less aggressive than greed in principle but far more subtle in appearance—*traditionalism*.

IDENTIFYING THE DRAGON

Let's be careful to identify the right opponent. It isn't tradition per se; it's traditionalism. I'm not trying to be petty, only accurate. The right kind of traditions give us deep roots—a solid network of reliable truth in a day when everything seems up for grabs. Among such traditions are those strong statements and principles that tie us to the mast of truth when storms of uncertainty create frightening waves of change driven by winds of doubt. In my book *Growing Deep in the Christian Life*, I address many of those essentials: believing in the authority of holy Scripture, knowing and loving God, bowing to the Lordship of Jesus Christ, committing ourselves to others, and becoming people of genuine encouragement. Such traditions (there are others, of course) are valuable absolutes that keep us from feeling awash in a world of relativism and uncertainty.

In case you haven't noticed, we are specifically commanded to cling to the traditions of faith: "stand firm and hold to the traditions which you were taught" (2 Thess. 2:15). Even though many—the majority, in fact—will elect to walk a contrary path, "not according to the tradition" which Scripture clearly asserts, we are instructed to stay on target (2 Thess. 3:6).

Understand now, I'm thinking of the big picture, where truth is at stake, not tiny scenes of lesser importance, where mere taste and custom are a matter of preference. Some insist, for example, that all Protestants must conduct themselves according to the tradition of the Reformers, "just because the Reformers did it that way." While I appreciate those great men, I disagree. John Calvin wore a hat in church. That's enough for some to say, "Everybody should do the same." But before every man and woman planning to worship next Sunday runs out and buys a hat, something needs to be said as to *why* Calvin wore a hat. Actually there are two reasons: "because the church had (a) drafts and (b) pigeons."[2]

There is a great deal of difference between tradition and traditiona*lism*. Jaroslav Pelikan puts his finger on the crux of the issue: "Tradition is the living faith of those now dead; traditionalism is the dead faith of those still living."[3]

By traditionalism, I have in mind mainly an attitude that resists change, adaptation, or alteration. It is holding fast to a custom or behavior that is being blindly and forcefully maintained. It is being suspicious of the new, the up-to-date, the different. It is finding one's security, even identity, in the familiar and therefore opposing whatever threatens that. And if you'll allow me one more, it is substituting a legalistic system for the freedom and freshness of the Spirit—being more concerned about keeping rigid, manmade rules than being flexible, open to creativity and innovation.

By now you've guessed where I stand. Clearly, my position is on the side of openness, allowing room for the untried, the unpredictable, the unexpected—all the while holding fast to the truth. When this philosophy is embraced, eagle eggs are laid, eagles are hatched, and eagles are given room to fly. When traditionalism rules the roost, you can expect nothing but parrots—low-flying creatures that stay on a perch and mimic only what they are told to say. Believe me, there are plenty of people around who feel it is their calling to tell others what to do and what to say. They are self-appointed wing-clippers who frown on new ways and put down high flight. To use J. B. Phillips' words again, they work hard to "squeeze you into their mold."

A New Venture

When my wife and I decided to link arms and venture into a radio program, we had zero experience. Neither of us had a background in reaching the public via the media, nor did we know much of anything about the complicated intricacies of a nonprofit corporation. To quote an attorney of ours, we didn't start at scratch, we started *"below* scratch"! Thankfully, there were a few close and competent friends who helped us slide out of the boat into the ocean without hurting ourselves, but since that time we have taught ourselves to swim through the swift currents of this particular extension of our lives. The result? An innovative, one-of-a-kind radio outreach named "Insight for Living" that doesn't pattern itself after any other program on the air. Why should it? Duplications are a drag. I'm not suggesting that ours is the only effective radio ministry. Of course not! But it *is* unique, from start to finish.

The systems we use, we designed. The techniques we employ, we devised. My style is my own—in no way do I attempt to be like or sound like or compete with any other person or broadcast. Why should I? I'm *me*—and I'm an eagle. To be like someone else is to become a parrot. No, thanks. The fund-raising letters are strictly mine—I write every word of them. The philosophy behind them is ours, not some professional organization that provides a script for us to follow. Our mailings are dreamed up, designed, and produced within our own organization by people we have employed—people who possess incredibly innovative, creative skills. How we appreciate them and love them!

We're not the biggest (never worry over size) but we are determined to remain a pacesetting organization. We're certainly not the richest (never worry over finances) but we do employ vast vision while maintaining a close watch over our expenditures, always refusing to cut quality for the sake of quantity. Yes, always. Our policies are of the highest standard of integrity—that, we *do* worry over. And every thing we promote, produce, proclaim, and provide has one identifying mark: EXCELLENCE. Whether it's a cruise we sponsor or a brochure we design, a conference we participate in or a study guide we make available to our listeners, excellence is our middle name.

And why not? We represent the King of kings. If I may put this in today's terms, He is a class act—absolute tops. Lord, in fact! We're the ones who ought to cause the world to turn its head, not the other way around. Eagles don't have any business scratching around like a cage of parrots or a pen full of turkeys. Let me put it straight: Long enough have evangelicals been the ugly ducklings of Christendom!

Do we get criticism? Of course! Can't let that worry us, though. There will always be those who think we should do this or should not do that. Because we have always refused to consult the party line and get in step with what the so-called "experts" suggest, we are often told, "This won't work, you'll see," or "You should do that, instead," or "You can't. . . . You're being unrealistic." But it's amazing! Most (I'm resisting saying *all*) of the things we were told could not be done *are* now being done. We're doing them, by the grace of God. The things we were told would never fly, not only flew—they soared!

Cynthia and I are neither brilliant nor worldly wise, but we do learn fast and we stay flexible, always open to innovative ideas. Mainly, there is too much eagle in either one of us to be satisfied with the dull, standard operating procedures established by the lowest common denominator of human opinion. If a fresh idea, never tried before, makes sense, we'll give it a whirl! If it fails, we learned. If it works, we get all the more excited.

I will be quick to add that we openly acknowledge God's gracious faithfulness and forgiveness as we have grown and groaned together— and we are equally grateful for a carefully selected board of directors.

They know how to direct and respond to these two eagles without clipping our wings. We are accountable to them but not intimidated by them. Not one, by the way, is bound by traditionalism. They would not be on our board if they were. Why? Because traditionalism is a vicious dragon that must be slain if we hope to move into the twenty-first century with excellence, enthusiasm, momentum, and relevance. Traditionalism breeds parrots; it must not be tolerated. If you're fighting it, good for you! Don't stop. That old dragon is bad about squeezing the very life out of its victims, so never stop fighting. It's a matter of survival.

FIRST-CENTURY TRADITIONALISM

In Jesus' day the dragon of traditionalism reared its ugly head in a different way from what it does today. In the first century traditionalism was synonymous with Pharisaism. The Pharisees embraced it, promoted it, and modeled it. Whenever Christ encountered them, He encountered *it!* When others were cheering Him, the Pharisees were frowning Him down. A classic case in point? That time He was confronted by the sourpuss group while He was having dinner with a roomful of sinners. Maybe you don't know the background. Allow me:

A fellow named Matthew (called Levi by Dr. Luke) was invited to leave his profession as a tax-gatherer and become a disciple—a close follower of Jesus. He did. In fact, he threw a party at his place in honor of the Master. I suppose we could call it a farewell celebration as Levi left his career.

Naturally, the place was packed with guys Levi had run around with for years—fellow tax men and other cronies, none of them religious but all of them his friends and colleagues. Here's the way Dr. Luke describes the scene:

> And after that He went out, and noticed a tax-gatherer named Levi, sitting in the tax office, and He said to him, "Follow Me." And he left everything behind, and rose up and began to follow Him. And Levi gave a big reception for Him in his house; and there was a great crowd of tax-gatherers and other people who were reclining at table with them (Luke 5:27–29).

I'm smiling as I think about those guys at that meal. Can't you just imagine? Lots of clinking of dishes, loud talking, periodic uproars of laughter, different ones standing up and offering a toast, an all-around fun time. And nobody enjoyed it more than Jesus! (Too bad we don't have a few pictures painted of Jesus at this table.) These were *real* men. No phony-baloney stuffed shirts, no let's-try-to-impress-the-guy-in-the-white-robe clowns. Just upfront sinner types who knew Levi and came to have a good time.

There was plenty of food and lots of wine. Maybe even a first-century "roast" where Levi took it on the chin. There was a lot of telling and sharing and listening to stories. They were having a whale of a good time together, just plain fun—except, of course, for the Pharisees. I can just imagine their standing outside, looking in the window, staring and not smiling. The tax-gatherers and other friends, along with Jesus and His disciples, were reclining at the table together. But when the religious hotshots heard the noise, they began taking verbal shots at Jesus and His men.

> And the Pharisees and their scribes began grumbling at His disciples, saying, "Why do you eat and drink with the tax-gatherers and sinners?" (Luke 5:30).

You see, the main problem was that the disciples of Jesus were mixing with and enjoying themselves among the sinner types. The Pharisees believed (and taught!) that they should remain separate from these types. They should not associate with sinners, and they should *absolutely* not be having fun together. I mean, the very idea! By the way, did you notice that Luke first refers to "tax-gatherers and other people" (v. 29)? But note the difference when he quotes the Pharisees. The phrase changes to "tax-gatherers and *sinners*" (v. 30).

"How could You, Jesus—You, of all people—how *could* You sit down at a meal and enjoy eating and drinking with these tax-gatherers and sinners? Ugh! I mean, what will people say? What about Your testimony?"

The disciples are speechless, probably because they are scared spitless. They don't know what to say. Most Jews back then were paralyzed in their thoughts when Pharisees confronted them; but never Jesus. Completely unintimidated by the presence of Pharisees, He gave them a straight answer. I love that about Him. Jesus looks right into their eyes and says: ". . . It is not those who are well who need a physician, but those who are sick" (v. 31). It was another way of saying, "Knock it off!" (Swindoll paraphrase). But it sounds better to say, "What these people need is healing. Since I'm a healer, since that's what I'm about, then I don't want to run around with people who think they don't need healing. These people are sick. They make no bones about it; they don't hide it. They need help. That's why I'm here."

If that isn't enough to slam them to the mat, read on: "I have not come to call righteous men but sinners to repentance" (v. 32). Stab . . . twist. I think if I had been at the table I would have said (in Aramaic, of course), "All right, Jesus, go for it!" I probably would have whistled and applauded, too! Jesus was right on target when He answered, "I've not come to call people who think they are righteous, but people who *know* they are sick. That's My ministry, plain and simple. They need Me and are open. You don't think you need Me, so you're closed!"

Well, if you think the Pharisees left Him alone after that, you don't understand the nature of the dragon, traditionalism. All that meant to them was that the coin had been flipped and it was time to kick off. The violent game was on, and the Pharisees answer Jesus with:

> . . . "The disciples of John often fast and offer prayers; the disciples of the Pharisees also do the same; but Yours eat and drink" (v. 33).

That is supposed to be a sarcastic put-down. "You may have time for this jesting, but not us! This is serious business. We're into fasting. You and Your people are in there eating and drinking with those nasty sinners and having fun. Don't You know that life is much too serious for all this?"

Look at the answer.

> And Jesus said to them, "You cannot make the attendants of the bridegroom fast while the bridegroom is with them, can you?" (v. 34).

What a superb rebuttal! Back then, as long as the bridegroom was around, it was nonstop eating and drinking, laughing and having fun—constant rejoicing. But when the bridegroom left, it got sad because everyone had to go back to work. A lot of serious stuff also began to happen. And Jesus (referring to Himself) said, in effect, "The bridegroom is among His friends. This is not the time to fast and look somber and sad and act as if we're mad at the world. There will be a time for that later."

"But the days will come; and when the bridegroom is taken away from them, then they will fast in those days" (v. 35).

"At that time, the time I go to the cross and die, you won't hear any laughing. You won't hear the clinking of goblets. There will be no feasting then because everything will be serious. I'll be gone."

The Pharisees were strangely silent. They stared, struggling to grasp His meaning. Apparently, they were unable to piece it together so Jesus tells them a brief story. If I live to be one hundred years old, I will never cease to be amazed at what a marvelous communicator He really was. Nobody ever slept when Jesus was speaking. His talks were always brief and to the point—a rare skill among preachers! Furthermore, He referred to things that anybody could understand. He was never interested in impressing His audience with some profound, ultra-deep statement—even though He could have easily wowed them and caused them to leave His presence, saying, "What was that all about?" "I don't know, but it was deep, man. Nobody understood it." That may be our style but it certainly wasn't Jesus' style. His words penetrated with deadly accuracy. When He got through talking, listeners were yanking big darts out of their bodies. He was forever stabbing them awake with the truth. Notice His approach in verse 36. He does it in a simple, disarming way. He does it with comments having to do with old and new garments, with old and new wine.

... "No one tears a piece from a new garment and puts it on an old garment; otherwise he will both tear the new, and the piece from the new will not match the old" (v. 36).

Anyone who has had new clothing shrink would understand. Even today, if you take an old garment and cover a tear with a new patch, you know it is going to shrink. Ultimately, it may tear away. That's what verse 36 is all about. Well, not altogether. He is using clothing as His subject, but He has something deeper in mind (would you believe, traditionalism?). You see, these Pharisees were committed to the old. They majored in *ancient* history, and they swore by the Law. They were set in concrete into the precepts and statutes of the Law. They could quote those words exactly as they appeared on the ancient scroll of the Torah. To make matters worse, they added over six hundred additional rules (really!) so everybody would understand how *they* interpreted the way everyone should live. And they were rigid about it!

You see, they are the "old garment." Jesus' point: You can't match something new with something old. It will tear away.

He drives His point home by speaking of wine:

> "And no one puts new wine into old wineskins; otherwise the new wine will burst the skins, and it will be spilled out, and the skins will be ruined" (v. 37).

In fact, when Matthew tells the story, he adds, "Neither will be preserved. You'll lose both skin and wine." I don't know much about wine, but I do know if you take fresh wine and pour it into an old, worn-and-brittle wineskin bag that is no longer supple, you're in for a leaky surprise. It won't be long, thanks to fermentation, before the wine's change will cause the bag to bulge and stretch. Finally, it will rip just like an old used balloon. It won't hold it.

Just as Jesus wasn't talking about literal old and new fabrics, neither is He now talking about literal wine and wineskins. This is a parable, remember—a story that uses the literal and familiar to teach the spiritual and unfamiliar. Jesus' audience understood that these words were missiles carrying a massive payload.

Sometimes, even today, we'll use words that everyone understands should not be taken literally. I carry my family around in my wallet. If you ask, I'll show you my family. "No," you say, "you don't actually carry your family around in your wallet." You're right, I really don't. I carry a *picture* of them. But I pull it out and say, "Here's my family." But, there again, the words I use can't be taken literally. You understand that it is just a picture of my family. Jesus' story is simply a picture of something far more significant. He presses His point home:

"But new wine must be put into fresh wineskins" (v. 38). Hmmmm. All of a sudden, the picture is coming into clear focus, which makes the Pharisees terribly nervous.

You know why? Because Jesus says, in effect, "You like the old."

> "And no one, after drinking old wine wishes for new; for he says, 'The old is good enough'" (v. 39).

The old Judaic-traditionalism skin could not contain the new wine of the revolutionary gospel Christ was offering. It split the skin. There they stood, representing all those manmade regulations, observing this revolutionary, risky message about liberty, grace, freedom, forgiveness, deliverance from the Law, compassion, and hope. (How new can you get?) But their wineskin couldn't contain it. They were so entrenched and inflexible, the new wine dripped through. Finally, it burst the bag completely. Exposed, they were forced to see that their attempt to squeeze Jesus into their mold had backfired. The old simply could not contain the new.

Oh, but how they loved their own traditions! They preferred them to the Truth of God, believe it or not. Matthew's account includes a rebuke from Jesus to the Pharisees about how they were holding their traditions so tightly that they were resisting God's revelation. His rebuke? "You invalidated the word of God for the sake of your traditions" (Matt. 15:6). Isn't that an indictment? In effect, He is saying, "You are so defensive of your hardened, old wineskin bag, you totally reject the new wine I'm offering you." No eagle ever soared higher or was hated more. Let's face it—truth that sets people free is the greatest threat to traditionalism.

TWENTIETH-CENTURY NEW-WINE TRUTHS

So much for first-century wines and wineskins. Our interest, as I have said before, is not simply to discover and develop truth from ancient times. It is to see how relevant that truth is for *our* times.

A couple of very significant things seem to jump out at me when I think about Jesus' parable. Here's the first one: *God is a God of freshness and change.* That's the wine. In January of every new year, God puts together twelve months of wine. Twelve fresh vats are placed in storage (the contents unknown to us). Each vat will run out in a month. This new wine is vital. It is sparkling, fresh, and ready to fill new skins. God is a God of freshness and change. But wait, before I leave that thought, let me make something very clear: "God Himself isn't changing, nor is His Son. He is the same yesterday and today, yes and forever" (Heb. 13:8). Isn't that a great thought? God is no different this year than He was last year or a decade ago. Nor will He change one hundred years from now. But even though He is the same, His working is different. It stays fresh. His ways and methods are forever fresh, unpredictably new.

I find that thought woven throughout the Scriptures. The Old Testament speaks of a new song, a new heart, a new spirit, a new covenant, and new things that God is doing. In the New Testament we're called "new creatures." Through Him "all things become new." We're told that we have been given a "new birth." We are instructed to live by a "new commandment." We are people with "a new self," living in "a new man." We are even looking forward to a "new heaven and new earth." The last reference to *new* in the entire Bible is very near the end, in Revelation 21:5 where our Lord says He's "making all things new."

I need to warn you, if you like things to stay the same, you're going to be terribly uncomfortable in heaven. Everything is going to be new. God is a God of freshness and change. He flexes His methods. He alters His way so much, it's as if you've never seen it before. You can't imagine what it may be like next time. How does this personally apply? My answer is found in the first verse of Ephesians, chapter 5:

> Therefore be imitators of God, as beloved children; and walk in love, just as Christ also loved you, and gave Himself up for us, an offering and a sacrifice to God as a fragrant aroma.

God says we are to be "imitators" of Him which really means we are to "mimic." Since God is a God of freshness and change, so we should be. If we are to fulfill this command "to be mimics of God, as His beloved children," then I suggest that we stay fresh—that we remain open, innovative, willing to change.

It's been my observation that every generation tends to be more strict and rigid than the last. We tend to tighten the lid tighter on traditionalism. Even though our God of freshness and change has given us all those vats of new wine to use, we'll not let it go; we'll find ways to conserve it, to protect it, to maintain it—to save it for a "rainy day."

Remember the manna God gave His people to eat in the wilderness? One of the first things they had to forget about doing was saving it. They wanted to hold onto more of it. Why? Because they were afraid they were going to run out of food. They were afraid fresh manna wouldn't be delivered tomorrow morning. The only time they had to worry about that was on Friday because when Saturday came, there wouldn't be a delivery. But God even took care of that! On Friday they were to gather a two-day supply that would stay fresh and not spoil. So they had nothing to worry about, everything to enjoy. But still there was that tendency to hoard.

Do you remember the bronze serpent Moses held up in the wilderness when the people were being bitten by snakes and dying? God provided that bronze serpent for their healing. But did you know they dragged that serpent around in the wilderness, as well as in Canaan, for generations? Perhaps you didn't realize that. Well, here's the passage that tells it all.

> He removed the high places and broke down the sacred pillars and cut down the Asherah. He also broke in pieces the bronze serpent that Moses had made, for until those days the sons of Israel burned incense to it; and it was called Nehushtan (2 Kings 18:4).

There they were, still hanging onto that old bronze snake they'd been dragging around all those years. What was it now? It was just Nehushtan—meaning, "a piece of brass." What were they supposed to have done? Get rid of it! Instead, they were *worshiping* it. If we are going to "mimic God," we must stay fresh and open. Dump the Nehushtans! Otherwise, we won't stay flexible, creative. Those who resist mediocrity are models of innovation.

Now for the second significant fact I see from Luke, chapter 5: *New wineskins are essential, not optional.* Every age knows the temptation to try to restrict God's dealings. The majority of people in this world are maintainers. Once we get things set, we don't like them changed.

Let me give you a couple of illustrations. Sometime after beginning my pastorate in California, I looked closely at the order of service and decided we had done the "Doxology" at the beginning of the service long enough! So I put it at the *end* of the service. A number of people asked, "How can we sing it at the end? I mean, I'm not sure it will *work* at the end." (That made me smile, I confess.) It worked. In fact, only on rare occasions now do we even sing it. But when we do, it is more meaningful than ever!

But the one that really threw the congregation a curve was when we had the audacity to put the announcements at the *beginning* of the worship service. Can you believe I actually took them out of the sacred central part of the worship service (though I have never heard a worshipful announcement in my entire life)? Announcements can become a sacred cow. No, they're just wineskin. We continually look at the worship service and think of fresh skin in which to pour fresh wine. We try new things all the time. It's wonderful! Some still get a little nervous at times. I love that look on their faces. It says, "Does Chuck know this is going on?" when actually I was in on the planning, all along. I mean, you name it—it's new skin—it's just a bag. But what it holds is significant. It's the innovation of it all that keeps it fresh, vital, creative, new. Let me go further.

There was a time when aviation in missions was unheard of. Then along came a man like Jim Truxton (who is a part of our congregation, by the way). And he and a few committed people said, "There's no reason there couldn't be an arm of missions that becomes a flight service for people living out in the bush. We'll fly people and supplies in and out." Enter the birth of Missionary Aviation Fellowship. Unheard of, but it worked! And now they are using helicopters. Of course!

One of my mentors at Dallas Theological Seminary tells me about the time when the first chalk talk was used in his church many years ago. Many frowned and muttered, "They use that in the secular world, don't they? We don't believe in chalk talk in the church. Next thing you know, somebody will use a flannel-graph board." How liberal can you get? Hey, that stuff is wineskin; that's *all* it is. Now it's films and television and computers and other yet-to-be discovered inventions. It is new styles of music. It is new methods that assault the mindset of the old lifestyle. It still makes many uncomfortable because it's threatening. But it has nothing to do with the wine. If it does, there is something wrong with it. It is only the skin. The wine stays fresh because it is from God. But the skins? That's where we need to flex.

We must guard against wrapping the Christianity of the 1980s and 1990s in the garb of the 1960s! If we're not careful, we'll become so committed to "the way we were" we'll dull the cutting edge of relevance and leave this generation in the dust. I repeat: NEW WINESKINS ARE ESSENTIAL. Organizations don't change; people change. Churches don't flex; people flex. There is no flex in walls or wood. No flex in the stone or structure. It is in us. We're the skin. If we hope to soar into the 1990s, we *must* come to terms with rigidity. The dragon of traditionalism *must* be slain!

TWO PENETRATING QUESTIONS

Here are a couple of probing questions: First, *is the wine still fresh?* Or are you living on wine from yesteryear? Are you tapping into that fresh wine that is still bubbling, still sparkling, still exciting? Or do you have to go back to early 1970—or September of 1977? "Great time back then, great progress! God did great things." But what about today? People need to know how Jesus Christ addresses today's issues in today's world. He wants to know how fresh the wine is. You may be thinking, "That sounds pretty radical, Chuck. I don't know. I've gone along with you for nine chapters, but, man, this one is getting pretty loose." For you, especially, I bring this reminder: "And the threshing floors will be full of grain, and the vats will overflow with the new wine and oil" (Joel 2:24).

Joel, the prophet, is looking far into the future. Imagine this: He's got his sights trained as far away as the 1980s and 1990s. "There will be an overflow of new wine," he says. But that isn't all.

> "Then I will make up to you for the years that the swarming locust has eaten, the creeping locust, the stripping locust, and the gnawing locust, my great army which I sent among you" (Joel 2:25).

What does God call the locust? "My great army which I sent among you." It's as if He is saying, by way of application, "I will discover that mentality, that traditionalism, that old enemy of freshness, and I'll say to the locust, 'Sic 'em.' They'll come in and eat away. They'll gnaw away. They are My army."

But did you notice what the Lord promises? He promises to make up to you for the years the locust has eaten, once the pests have been removed:

> "And you shall have plenty to eat and be satisfied, and praise the name of the Lord your God, Who has dealt wondrously with you; then My people will never be put to shame. Thus you will know that I am in the midst of Israel, and that I am the Lord your God and there is no other; and My people will never be put to shame.
>
> "And it will come about after this that I will pour out My Spirit on all mankind; and your sons and daughters will prophesy, your old men will dream dreams, your young men will see visions" (Joel 2:26–28).

What a promise for the future—and for *today!* Through his scriptural binoculars, the prophet is seeing the future. How are the dreams coming along? How about the visions? Any fresh, creative ideas? We must have new thoughts and dreams for these new times.

In 1984 *Esquire* magazine released a special issue entitled "Golden Anniversary Collector's Issue," which included an anthology of fifty different men and women who are called "American originals." And when you read through the smaller print, you see that the magazine's subtitle, "Man at His Best," is correct. I spent the better part of a week several years ago leafing through it, reading various authors' works and studying more about these great personalities, most of whom are instantly recognizable.

Except for a very brief reference to a theologian, only one well-known Christian appeared in the anthology. Of the fifty who made a difference in the last fifty years, only a couple of Christians appear. I realize *Esquire* is not a Christian publication. I also know they are not looking into our ranks that closely. And, of course, some who were named could have been Christians. But honestly, *where* are all the Christians? Which high-flying eagles will make any difference during the next fifty years? Do you want a challenge? Plan now to make a difference. Do you know what I noticed about each person named in that special issue of *Esquire?* Each one is an eagle—there's not a parrot in the whole group. Eagles make things happen; they are the ones, as I said in an earlier chapter, who challenge our world to "break a vase!" In this chapter I come with another plea: Make a difference!

There's a second question on my mind: *Is the wineskin still flexible?* Now what do I mean by flexible? All right, let's start with the word *mobile.* Are you ready to move? I know, I know, you just got your stuff together. You finally got that last payment out of the way. You finally got settled down. Don't bet on it. This year a whole bunch of people will be on the move. And you may be one of them.

Here's another word: *change.* Are you open to change in your whole career? Are you willing to risk? Are you flexible enough to innovate? Are you willing to tolerate the sheer possibility of making a massive change in your direction for life? People who make a difference have supple wineskins. They can be stretched, pulled, pushed, and changed, "Lord, is it South America? Great! Or Indonesia? I'll do it. I'll move or change my profession. *Fine!* Are You leading me into a new venture? I'll do it. Count me in!" That's the spirit! It may mean moving across the street. It may mean moving across the States. It may mean moving across the seas. How flexible are you? It may not involve a move at all, only a willingness.

Read these words very carefully. They are dragon-slaying words!

. . . Today's followers of Christ must learn the full significance of the pattern of the children of Israel in the desert, who went or stopped when the cloud moved or stayed. They must learn to wait upon the Lord, to be sensitive to his leadings and to depend less and less on the arm of flesh. . . .

In many ways, we Christians today are reliving the New Testament age. These are days of rapid church growth, and yet also of uncertainty, apostasy, threatening persecution and, above all, the expectation of the return of Christ. This was the situation of the early church. First-generation Christians thought Christ would come back. He didn't. . . .

The church seems impotent before the ecological crisis, for example, or in the face of mindless technology or the worldwide web of political power and intrigue. But the weapons of our warfare are spiritual, not carnal. Using the world's weapons, the church does not stand a chance. But when the church uses God's weapons (Eph. 6:14-17), it is the world which becomes weak.

These are not days for the church to turn inward, curl up in a corner and passively await the end. The world has yet to see what the Spirit can do.[4]

Stop letting the world around you squeeze you into its own mold. Out with the dragon of traditionalism! This is a new year, a new generation, a new era.

11

REMOVING THE BLAHS
FROM TODAY

Monotony and mediocrity mesh like teeth in gears. One spawns the other, leaving us yawning, bored, and adrift. In referring to monotony, I do not have in mind a lack of activity as much as a lack of purpose. We can be busy yet bored, involved yet indifferent. Life becomes tediously repetitious, dull, humdrum, pedestrian. In a word, *blah*.

Who would ever expect such a thing to be an enemy? Seems too mild, too passive to even mention. Not so! It is one of the deadliest darts in the Devil's quiver. Once it strikes, the poison spreads rapidly, leaving us listless, careless, and disillusioned. Our vision gets blurred and our shoulders start to stoop. We become putty in the enemy's hand. That explains why C. S. Lewis wrote:

> The safest road to Hell is the gradual one—the gentle slope, soft underfoot, without sudden turnings, without milestones, without signposts (*The Screwtape Letters*, letter 12).

> The long, dull, monotonous years of middle-aged prosperity or middle-aged adversity are excellent campaigning weather [for the Devil] (*The Screwtape Letters*, letter 28).[1]

Why, certainly! In our world of four-day work weeks, lengthy vacations, and extended periods of leisure, more and more wonder what to do with their time. That's one kind of *blah*. Far more subtle, however, is the tedious sameness that accompanies routine of any kind. Even a routine that results in good pay and great popularity.

Look into the faces of entertainers *off* the stage. Talk to physicians *out* of the office and hospital corridors. Those in the political arena are equally susceptible. Both John Dean (in his book *Blind Ambition*) and Chuck Colson (in *Born Again*) confessed that boredom accompanied their lives in the busyness of all their high-profile activities. Strangely, on the heels of Richard Nixon's landslide victory, Colson admitted that he should have been exhilarated, but he felt empty. Athletes often feel the same. Ministers aren't immune, either. Cartoonist Ralph Barton, although successful and in demand, took his own life, leaving a note nearby that included these words, "I am fed up with inventing devices to fill up twenty-four hours of the day."

None of these people were standing around collecting dust. They were skilled, competent, responsible individuals, but monotony siphoned the joy and motivation from their tank. Assignments lacked meaning. Work lacked purpose. Boredom held them back, like an iron anchor that had slipped out of the boat and snagged and dragged on the bottom. Show me an individual who once soared, whose life was characterized by enthusiasm and excellence, but who no longer reaches those heights, and I'll show you a person who has probably become a victim of the *blahs*.

A *blah* attack may sound harmless, but it can leave us in an emotional heap, seriously questioning if life is worth it. Yes, those "long, dull, monotonous years of middle-aged prosperity or . . . adversity" are enough to bring even the strongest eagle down with a thud.

A section on fighting fiercely would certainly be incomplete if we failed to address the *blahs* of monotony and indifference. It is essential that we be engaged in a winning battle against this enemy if we hope to achieve excellence. The two cannot coexist. Surely, if this sneaky opponent of excellence is that powerful, there ought to be some insights and techniques that help us fight it out in the trenches. Indeed there are! In fact, I have often used the same ones I want to mention in this chapter and have found them effective. Believe it or not, they find their source in a prayer written by Moses many centuries ago.

A Prayer with a Punch

Psalm 90 is the only psalm specifically attributed to Moses. He may have written others, but we know for sure he wrote this one. Remember Moses? Most think of him as a man of action, an aggressive leader, point man in the exodus, outspoken giver of the Law. But it is easy to overlook the repetitious, monotonous routine he endured. Between ages forty and eighty, Moses led his father-in-law's flock of sheep in the desert. Following the exodus, he led the Hebrews another forty years as they wandered across and around the wilderness. I'd say he knew about the *blahs*. Same terrain, same scenes, same route, same ornery people, same negative outlook, same complaints, same miserable weather, same *everything!* The prayer he wrote could have been his means of maintaining sanity! Moses addresses his Lord specifically (vv. 1, 2, 13, 17) and spells out His personal involvement in everyday affairs.

Breaking the Spell

Frequently, our problem with boredom begins when we fall under monotony's "spell." In this quasi-hypnotic state, we get sucked into a bland, "who cares?" mentality. Mediocrity and passive cynicism await those who let themselves get trapped. How to cope? We must direct our attention (as Moses does) to (a) the right object that we might gain and (b) the right perspective.

> Lord, Thou hast been our dwelling place in all generations. Before the mountains were born, or Thou didst give birth to the earth and the world, even from everlasting to everlasting, Thou art God (Ps. 90:1-2).

As this ancient shepherd-leader did, we too must begin by crying out to our God: "Lord!" What a relief to be able to call on Him! In doing so, it helps to rehearse before Him our real place of residence. It isn't here on this measly piece of real estate called Earth. It is with Him. Did you get that? "Lord—*You* are my home . . . my habitation . . . my hiding place."

Moses goes even further, in the opposite order of creation. Originally, God made this world, the mountains, dry land, and finally mankind. Moses turns it around:

World ◄——Mountains ◄——Dry Land ◄——Man

If we take our minds as far back as possible, we arrive at the vanishing point of the past—infinity. Moses is saying: "God, even at the vanishing point of the past and the future—the most distant place we can imagine—You are there!"

We can't fathom such a journey. We can only imagine it. But when we go as far back as possible in our minds (the vanishing point of the past) and step off, there is God. And when we project ourselves to the vanishing point of the future, the misty infinity of tomorrow, again there is our God.

What he is saying is this: As I go from the vanishing point of yesterday to the vanishing point of tomorrow and find that God is present, then there is not a place in the entire scope of my everyday existence where God is not there. And to make it even more personal, as Francis Schaeffer put it, "He is there and He is not silent." There is purpose, there is meaning in the presence of God. Even in the things that we may consider to be pointless, insignificant, trivial.

I find it amusing to read certain critics who say that Moses groveled in a sort of ignorant theology. Frankly, I find from this psalm that he possessed a rather sophisticated theology. The man who wrote the creation story had a pretty good grasp of what it was all about. And this psalm reveals that, to him, God was in it all, even when he led those stubborn woolies across the backside of the desert. Even when he led those wayward people through the wilderness. To make it much more personal—even during *your* drab and seemingly meaningless assignments of life, He is there! He cares! He knows! Thoughts like that help us soar, don't they?

And don't miss the right perspective: "From everlasting to everlasting, Thou art *God*." From my yesterday to my tomorrow—God. From the little involvements to the big ones—God. From the beginning of school to the end of school—God. From the assignments that will never really make the headlines (which seems to me mere busy work) all the way to those things that gain international attention—God. From my children's earliest years to our last year together—God! You are in it, Lord. You're there! Yes, even when everything goes wrong.

Verdi's opera "La Traviata" was a failure when it was first performed. Even though the singers chosen for the leading roles were the best of the day, everything went wrong. The tenor had a cold and sang in a hoarse, almost inaudible voice. The soprano who played the part of the delicate, sickly heroine was one of the stoutest ladies on or off stage, and very healthy and loud.

At the beginning of the Third Act when the doctor declares that consumption has wasted away the "frail, young lady" and she cannot live more than a few hours, the audience was thrown into a spasm of laughter, a state very different from that necessary to appreciate the tragic moment!

Who doesn't have days like that when everything goes wrong, when we become overwhelmingly conscious of our frailty and imperfection? At those times it is good to remember this is not our world. The earth is the Lord's. "You cannot stir a flower without troubling a star." And so the sooner we learn to walk closely with God, who is in charge and who does not change, the happier we will be.[2]

We entertain the feeling on those "bad" days that we deserve better, almost as though we own our lives. When, in fact, it is in the menial assignments of life that God reminds us, "No, I own your life. You are Mine. I have purpose in this that seems to you so purposeless." Try this. The very next time you feel those clammy, cold fingers of the *blahs* reaching around you, remember, "From yesterday until tomorrow, You, O Lord, are there, You care!" It will help you mount up with wings as an eagle. I know. I have put it to the test numerous times.

Probing the Soul

So much for breaking the spell. Probing the soul takes up where that leaves off. As I probe my soul during times of such wrestlings, almost without exception, I find three thoughts washing around in my head. First, I think: Life is so short. We really don't have many years. And to spend them doing dumb stuff seems like such a waste. If that isn't depressing enough, you come across the words of some clown who writes that most of those who fill the pages of *Who's Who* were or are under thirty years of age! You had every intention of being there too, but you are now fifty-six and, would you believe, fast approaching sixty! You feel more like you belong in *Why Me?* You're still doing the assignments that will never make the headlines. Is life really short? Yes.

> Thou dost turn man back into dust, and dost say, "Return, O children of men." For a thousand years in Thy sight are like yesterday when it passes by, or as a watch in the night. Thou hast swept them away like a flood, they fall asleep . . . (Ps. 90:3–5).

Talk about vivid word pictures! Life moves so rapidly it is as if we have been swept through time like a *flood*. Quickly passing as a three-hour *watch* in the night, like *yesterday!* And then we fall asleep and die.

> ... In the morning they are like grass which sprouts anew. In the
> morning it flourishes, and sprouts anew; towards evening it fades, and
> withers away (Ps. 90:5-6).

Another reminder of the brevity of life. "Toward evening it fades, and
withers away" like *grass*.

Those thoughts have a way of haunting a person who really wants
his life to amount to more than just a tiny period printed on the page
of time, don't they? We want to offer at least a sentence. But what I see
growing out of these lines in Moses' prayer is that it is God who
controls our marks in this world. He sets the limit. In fact, He's the
One who says, "Return, O children of men." And without hesitation,
they return. What seems all-important can change almost overnight.
When the Controller says, "Return," it's amazing how quickly that
return can occur.

I was intrigued several years ago when reading about some ghost
towns littered across the plains of Nevada. The writer pointed out that
there was every indication between the middle and the end of the 1800s
that these towns would flourish forever. There were people by the
thousands. There was gold in abundance. There were new buildings,
vast plans, a spirit of excitement. There was wild and wooly entertainment at every corner—houses and hotels, brothels and taverns, mines
and money. The Gold Rush looked as if it would last forever. But
suddenly, everything screeched to a halt. Almost overnight those bustl-
ing, loud population centers became vacant dust collectors. The sound
of the cash register ceased. Today, except for a handful of eccentric
desert dwellers, the stores and streets are empty. Those windswept ghost
towns are now silent, hollow shells along forgotten sandy roads. Whatever happened to the boomtowns of Nevada? May I suggest a very
simple answer? The Lord said, "Return, O cities of Nevada."

The Kennedy family also comes to mind when I think of this kind
of dramatic change. I vividly remember the upward swing and enormous popularity of the whole Kennedy clan as they came on the
scene in the 1960s. It was meteoric. It looked as though we would have
Kennedys in leadership for two or three decades! And what happened?
In the briefest period of time, a few rapid-fire events changed everything: John was murdered—assassinated; Robert was assassinated; and
Ted was stigmatized—a scandal and a fractured marriage dogging his
heels. What really happened? No one can fully explain, but it seems
as if God said to a family that looked like it would continue in

leadership forever, "Return, O Kennedy family." Sovereignly, He puts up one and sets down another.

Why do I mention those two examples? Because they perfectly describe life. What often looks as if it is here to stay and make a perpetual impact can be frighteningly temporary. When God says, "That's it; that's curtains," it's only a matter of time. It is the perspective in all of this that holds us together. Our God is in complete control. He lets nothing out of His grip. He starts one and stops another. He pushes one ahead and holds another back.

Look again at Moses' prayer. He brings up a second thought that plagues me when the *blahs* come: <u>My sins are so obvious.</u> Do you ever feel like that in the midst of this routine called life and time? Sure you do. Moses did, too.

> For we have been consumed by Thine anger, and by Thy wrath we have been dismayed. Thou hast placed our iniquities before Thee, our secret sins in the light of Thy presence. For all our days have declined in Thy fury; we have finished our years like a sigh (Ps. 90:7–9).

Remember the secret sin that haunted Moses—the murder of that Egyptian? I wonder how many rocks he walked around in the desert only to hear that same skeleton rattle. I cannot imagine how many days he must have finished with "a sigh." Couldn't hide it, couldn't dodge it, couldn't deny it. "My sins are so obvious, Lord. How can I put it all together? I am weary of feeling the stinging reminder of Your wrath!" Immediately on the heels of those feelings, Moses writes:

> As for the days of our life, they contain seventy years, or if due to strength, eighty years, yet their pride is but labor and sorrow; for soon it is gone and we fly away (v. 10).

These are the words of a man who feels cornered by an attack of the *blahs*. Few in the Christian family bother to address the everpresent feeling that says down deep inside, "My sins are so obvious." At the end of a week, that thought hangs in our head. And even at the beginning of the next week, we face another seven days, only to be reminded how obvious our sin is.

That is bad enough, but when Moses tosses in God's "wrath," it is sufficient to make the strongest saint throw in the towel. One notable Bible teacher explains all this in these words:

Surely this phrase "the wrath of God" is greatly misunderstood. Many think, invariably, of some sort of peeved deity, a kind of cosmic, terrible-tempered Mr. Bang, who indulges in violent uncontrolled displays of temper when human beings do not do what they ought to do. But such a concept only reveals the limitations of our understanding. The Bible never deals with the wrath of God that way. According to the Scriptures, the wrath of God is God's moral integrity. When man refuses to yield himself to God, he creates certain conditions, not only for himself but for others as well, which God has ordained for harm. It is God who makes evil result in sorrow, heartache, injustice, and despair. It is God's way of saying to man, "Now look, you must face the truth. You were made for Me. If you decide that you don't want Me, then you will have to bear the consequences." The absence of God is destructive to human life. That absence is God's wrath. And God cannot withhold it. In His moral integrity, He insists that these things should occur as a result of our disobedience. He sets man's sin and His wrath in the same frame.[3]

I think what he's saying is that our Lord is not some tyrannical God who stomps across heaven like the giant in *Jack and the Beanstalk,* swinging a club and waiting to give us a smashing blow to the head. No. Rather, it is as if He says to us, "You're Mine and I want you to walk in step with Me. I've arranged a plan so that walking with Me will result in a righteous lifestyle. If you make a decision *not* to walk with Me, I've also arranged consequences that will happen and you must live with them."

Yes, life is short. Yes, our sins are obvious; no one can deny that. And if those thoughts aren't hard enough to handle, there's a third feeling: <u>My days are so empty.</u> Listen to Moses' grand desire:

So teach us to number our days, that we may present to Thee a heart of wisdom (Ps. 90:12).

Now Moses isn't suggesting that we keep a calendar, obviously. Nor does He mean we need to remember when our birthday is or simply how old we are. It is much deeper than that.

Look at the word *teach*—"teach us." The word means "cause to know." And the word *number* means "to reckon" or "assign" or "appoint" something. One lexicon suggests the phrase "that we may present to Thee" could be rendered "that we may gain." All these observations lead me to this paraphrase of verse 12:

"So cause us to know how to assign significance to our days so that we may gain the ability to see life as You see it."

To say that in the form of a prayer: "Lord, in the daily, monotonous assignments of life, cause me to learn how to view each day as You look at it."

Think of the person who is in sales. He faces the competitive battle of a monthly quota. He fights that tough assignment (talk about boring!) to keep himself clothed and his family fed. How does verse 12 apply? "Lord, show me, in the struggle to meet my quota, how to see all this as You see it." How about the teacher? "Show me, as a teacher who faces the same routine in classes week after week, year after year, the ultimate investment I am making in these lives." Or what about those in vocational Christian service? "Lord, cause me to see that when I carry out my call to ministry, there are dimensions of meaning far beyond what I am able to understand or see." And the home-maker? "Help me, Lord, to see the value of my role as a mother with three, four, five kiddos." Or, "Show me as one who has no children, your plan for me." Or perhaps, "In our home without the children any longer—now only a couple drawn back together—teach us the wisdom of taking life a day at a time. Cause us to learn how to make these days *significant* days. Help us to keep on soaring!"

Bringing the Song

After breaking the spell and probing the soul, the psalmist introduces us to a very special song, "Do return, O Lord; how long will it be? And be sorry for Thy servants" (Ps. 90: 13). The idea is for God to have pity upon them. The song continues: "O satisfy us in the morning with Thy lovingkindness, that we may sing for joy and be glad all our days" (v. 14). It sounds to me as if Moses has broken through the *blahs*. I don't know about you, but with me it often happens in the morning. The night before may have seemed dark and dreary. Those night hours are often the backwash of boredom. By morning, however—usually early, when there's sort of a fresh breath of air, the smog is gone, and the day is cool—it is amazing how God brings something fresh. Psalm 30:5 also describes this feeling of renewal.

For His anger is but for a moment, His favor is for a lifetime; weeping may last for the night, but a shout of joy comes in the morning.

The Living Bible puts it like this: "Weeping may go on all night, but in the morning there is joy."

Ruth Calkin describes God's faithfulness in the very middle of our "aching exhaustion":

IN THE MORNING

Today, Lord,
I have an unshakable conviction
A positive, resolute assurance
That what You have spoken
Is inalterably true.

But today, Lord,
My sick body feels stronger
And the stomping pain quietly subsides
Tomorrow . . .

And then tomorrow
If I must struggle again
With aching exhaustion
With twisting pain
Until I am breathless
Until I am utterly spent
Until fear eclipses the last vestige of hope
Then Lord—
Then grant me the enabling grace
To believe without feeling
To know without seeing
To clasp Your invisible hand
And wait with invincible trust
For the morning.[4]

Want a little extra advice without extra charge? (I have learned this lesson the hard way.) If you are facing a tough assignment and it's possible to wait until the morning to deal with it, then wait. This is especially true if the decision that you must make will affect other lives and could hurt them if you handle things wrongly. Just hold off and sleep on it. If you must spend a restless night turning and tossing with your decision, so be it. That struggle may last "all night long." Somehow a freshness of thought, even new joy, bursts into bloom the next morning. I cannot explain it, but a new gladness comes.

After the satisfaction that comes from fresh joy in the morning, there is restoration: "Make us glad according to the days Thou hast afflicted us, and the years we have seen evil" (Ps. 90:15).

The phrase "according to the days Thou hast afflicted us" seemed troubling to me when I first read it. Then I noticed that the marginal reference in my New American Standard Bible suggests "Make us glad *as many days* as Thou hast afflicted us." Now I understand. "Lord, when You bring satisfaction to what seemed to me to be a monotonous life, that satisfaction is in proportion to the days that once seemed meaningless." *The Living Bible* says, "Give us gladness in proportion to our former misery." God has a way of balancing out the good with the bad.

Finally, after all that, there is motivation:

> Let Thy work appear to Thy servants, and Thy majesty to their children (v. 16),

and confirmation:

> And let the favor of the Lord our God be upon us; and do confirm for us the work of our hands; yes, confirm the work of our hands (v. 17).

Confirm means "to give meaning, to make permanent." It is this idea: "Cause me to see it as significant." Instead of my thinking of these days as just about as futile as emptying wastebaskets, help me to see the significance of them in light of Your plan. When God confirms the work of our hands, He helps us see the value of the routine, the importance of what we once considered mundane, humdrum—the same ol' thing.

Hang in There! It Is Worth It

After having lunch with a couple of friends at the Orange County Medical Center several years ago, I was surprised to see a deep impression in the grass right next to the sidewalk. Strangely, it was the outline of a human body. I stopped, frowned, and studied the impression. The grass was still pressed down flat. I could detect where the head had been. It had gone through the sod so deeply that the dirt could be seen. I was stunned, my stomach turned. My companions stood silently beside me as I stared down. Finally, I asked, "What is that?"

"See that window way up there on the fifth floor?" One friend pointed up as the other spoke. "A woman jumped from that window early this morning. This is where she landed."

I confess that immediately I imagined an aged person who could see no end to the tunnel of pain—someone who probably thought, *It's no use . . . my life is finished.* Staring down again, I asked, "Was it an older person?"

"Oh, no," he responded. "Matter of fact . . . a mother of five. She was still in her thirties—a rather attractive young woman."

"Five kids? In her thirties? What in the world drove her to this? How could it be?" I'll never forget my friend's answer.

"Those who were around her a lot got to know her. On a number of occasions, they had heard her say, 'Life just doesn't have any more meaning. I'm empty. All I face is a lifetime of more demands, endless chores, no relief'"

What did she lack? She lacked the "confirmation of the work of her hands," as Moses put it. She lacked any sense of permanence or significance in the monotonous assignments of life.

For sure, one of the toughest assignments in all of life is staying by the stuff at home, handling the endless, thankless tasks of parenting—and seeing meaning and purpose in it day after demanding day. Dealing with the constant demands of children and teenagers is extremely difficult, but oh, so important! If that is your lot, hang in there, my eagle friend! Those eaglets may be overly demanding today, but someday you will look back with a smile and say, "It really *was* worth it all!"

Some time back we had a young medical intern in our church who set all kinds of academic records. I distinctly remember talking with him one Sunday morning. I started the conversation, "Well, my young doctor friend, how are you doing?"

He lit up: "Really great!"

"That's good," I smiled. "I'm glad to hear it."

He went on, "This is the first weekend I've had off in I forget how many weeks." He continued, "You know, Chuck, something bothers me. I'm surrounded by a large number of Jews in my training. I wonder at times what meaning there is in all of this—if I should really move in and openly declare where I stand. Actually, they *know* where I stand. But it's almost as though we live in that quiet world of two bubbles. They know where I stand, and I know where they are. We do things together and watch each other, but we're not building many bridges. I feel as if I should be moving in."

I pressed him, "You're sure they know that you're committed to Jesus Christ and Him only?"

"Yes, there is no question about it."

"Then they know where you are. God is working, even though you may not be able to see it. Believe me, they are watching!"

I then told him about a doctor friend of mine whose practice is with a medical group on the East Coast. This friend is virtually surrounded by non-Christians—not only his patients, but those other physicians in the group. He often struggled with the day-by-day *blahs*, wondering, *Is any of this making an impact?* But one day he discovered otherwise. Here's the story he told me:

"One of the guys in the group owns his own airplane and flies regularly. He also has a lot of other things going on outside of his own marriage. Other women, other affairs. I've never condemned him, but he knows where I stand. I thought he wasn't even hearing what I was saying, just enduring the monotonous routine of practicing medicine (even that gets monotonous, seeing one patient after another, after another, after another). I thought the guys in the group had just written me off. But the other day as I was packing my things, planning to move, the playboy physician said to me right out of the blue, 'Before you move, I want to talk to you. My life is *100 percent empty*. You told me once that any time I wanted to, I could come and talk to you. I've been watching your life, day after day. I've watched almost every move you make. That's why I'm here. You've got something I don't have. What is it?'" You can guess the outcome. One doctor led the other to an understanding of Christ. And the playboy physician decided to put his faith and trust in the Great Physician.

In the monotonous assignments of daily living, God can take something that seems routine and dull and use it as a platform on which to do His significant work. Remember this: Those who achieve excellence are faithful in the tedious, monotonous details of life. It is there amidst the *blahs* of boredom that we rise above the level of mediocrity and soar. One final warning before I wrap up this chapter: Watch out for those long, dull middle-aged years of prosperity and adversity. They kill more eagles than all the other years combined.

12

BECOMING A MODEL
OF JOYFUL GENEROSITY

I promised myself when I started this book that I would not let it degenerate into a grim-faced, morbid monster. That's a tough promise to keep, especially in a section dealing with enemies like greed, traditionalism, and indifference. Maybe it is time to look up and stretch, to remind ourselves that fighting may be a part of life—but it isn't *all* of life. Some don't want us to believe that. A you-better-get-with-it doomsday face is fast becoming the identifying mark of the Christian. And that's too bad—tragic, in fact.

I am genuinely concerned that joy is being replaced with a host of pathetic substitutes, none of them nearly as important. Don't think the world overlooks this fact, either. A man was standing behind a woman at the check-out counter of a local grocery store. He was well-dressed and his facial expression was quite stern. The woman glanced back at him a time or two as she finished unloading her basket. Finally, unable to restrain herself any longer, she asked the serious-looking gentleman, "Excuse me, but do you happen to be a minister?"

"No, I'm not," he replied. "I've just been sick for a couple of weeks."

There seems to be more of everything these days than joy. There's certainly more Bible study than joy. There is more prayer than joy—more church attendance, more evangelism, more activity, even more discernment than joy. And those of us who are leaders in religious service are often a major cause.

Some Christians look like they've been baptized in lemon juice. Many have such long faces they could eat corn out of a Coke bottle! There are some exceptions, but therein lies the problem. Why are the joyful ones the exceptions?

If I read the Book correctly, joy is the runner-up virtue. If the "fruit of the spirit" is listed in the order of importance, love gets the blue ribbon, joy the red, right? If God awarded us medals, as they do in the Olympics, love would win the gold, joy the silver, and peace the bronze. I call that second-place finisher significant! Where are all the silver-medal eagles? We need more!

Check out the average ministerial staff or, for that matter, the faces at a pastor's conference. Believe me, I have. Listen for frequent laughter. Look for joyful spirits. You'd think the morticians had landed! You'll probably find a fair amount of love, lots of compassion, a good deal of purity, patience, hope, and gentleness. And all that is marvelous. But where's the joy? Why have we relegated joy to the nonessentials, for that matter, to the suspicious? What's wrong with a well-developed sense of humor? It really concerns me that congregations seldom enjoy real laughter, those delightful lighthearted times when the nervous system gets flushed out, cleansed by joy. I find it amazing that the only ones on this planet who have every right to smile at the future and enjoy life seldom do. Why, you'd think we have been hired to carry the weight of the world on our shoulders!

I know, I know—"life is serious business." If I hear that one more time, I think I'll gag. I fully realize that too much humor can become offensive. I recognize that it can be taken to such an extreme that it is inappropriate. But doesn't it seem we have a long way to go before we are guilty of *that* problem? The final result of a joyless existence is sad—a superhigh-level intensity, borderline neurotic anxiety, an absence of just plain fun in one's work, a lack of relaxation, and the tendency to take ourselves much too seriously. We need to lighten up! Yes, spirituality and fun do go well together.

Scripture speaks directly to this issue, you know—especially the Proverbs.

> A joyful heart makes a cheerful face, but when the heart is sad, the spirit is broken (Prov. 15:13).

Amazing how that proverb goes right to the heart of the problem (no pun intended). We're not talking about a person's face here as much as we are about the heart. Internal joy goes public. We can't hide it. The face takes its cue from an inside signal. "All the days of the afflicted are bad, but a cheerful heart has a continual feast" (v. 15).

Isn't that a delightful way to put it? A cheerful heart serves the rest of the body (and others) a "continual feast." And what a sumptuous banquet! A well-developed sense of humor reveals a well-balanced personality. Maladjusted people show a far greater tendency to miss the point in a funny remark. They take jokes personally. They take things that are meant to be enjoyable much too seriously. The ability to get a laugh out of everyday situations is a safety valve. It rids us of tensions and worries which could otherwise damage our health. You think I'm exaggerating the benefits? If so, maybe you've forgotten another proverb: "A joyful heart is good medicine, but a broken spirit dries up the bones" (Prov. 17:22).

Isn't that eloquent? Look even more closely. Literally, it says, "A joyful heart causes healing." What is it that brings healing to the emotions, healing to the soul? A joyful heart. And when the heart is right, a joyful countenance accompanies it.

I mentioned our radio program, "Insight for Living," earlier in this section of my book. When I decided to go on radio, I specifically chose not to alter my style of communication. It is my nature and approach to enjoy a good laugh on occasion—to tell a joke—to find a little humor rather regularly. That is my style in life, so I figured, why not continue it in my teaching? It would be inauthentic for us to edit out all the fun and joy. So we decided to leave it in. I cannot tell you how many times I have heard from listeners who write in and say, "Chuck, don't stop laughing!" Some have gone even further: "You can stop teaching, but don't stop laughing. You're the only laughter we hear over the radio." Several have even admitted, "Yours is the only laughter I hear in our home."

I think it was Erma Bombeck who said, "We sing 'Make a joyful noise unto the Lord' while our faces reflect the sadness of one who has just buried a rich aunt who left everything to her pregnant hamster." I've laughed with Erma for years. She's the one who says that God understands even her shallow prayers that implore, "Lord, if You can't make me thin, then make my friends look *fat!*"

If I may press the point, eagles who soar, who pursue excellence, who are determined to live high above the level of mediocrity must remember the value of joy. Yes, there are times of great grief and sadness. No, life isn't a big bowl of cherries. But in complete candor, I cannot grasp how anyone can justify a continual long face. Surely, God never intended such! And it isn't just a matter of personality. Or simply a matter of temperament. It's mostly a matter of the heart and often a matter of habit. We need to be ever alert to joylessness—an enemy that will break and enter, robbing us of one of life's most prized possessions.

Joylessness is never a more evident enemy than when the subject of giving surfaces. But if I read God's Book correctly, He takes no delight in a grim giver, but rather in a cheerful one. He loves it when hilarity and generosity meet at the offering plate! When they do, I have this sneaking suspicion that He smiles broadly. To the surprise of many, the Bible frequently connects a laughing heart with a giving hand. So I think it might be best to approach this subject of joy from the viewpoint of being generous as well. First, I want us to see the statement in the New Testament that gives us the overriding principle in a few words, and then I'd like us to observe several examples or models of joyful generosity.

A STATEMENT WORTH PONDERING

Two letters in the New Testament were written to the church at Corinth. Both were from the same man, Paul, who spent a little over a year and a half getting that particular church established. The Corinthian church was loaded with potential. It had numerous spiritual gifts and fine teachers. It had money and influence. It was a place you and I would have wanted to attend had we lived in first-century Corinth. It was winsome and exciting. Probably the best description is *contagious.* But it also had some people who reverted to carnality. These people had made great promises to God regarding their commitment, but only a few months later they'd grown cold and backed off. They needed to be reminded of what they had promised God. That is part of the reason Paul wrote them—actually, the major reason he wrote them the second letter.

You see, many miles removed from Corinth was another church, much older, and struggling financially. I'm referring to the mother church in Jerusalem. That church, though older, was now economically strapped. Their need for assistance was acute. So Paul was involved in raising funds for the Jerusalem church, a project which brought him to the region of Macedonia, just north of Corinth.

Even though the Macedonian Christians were also in an economically depressed area, Paul appealed to them, urging them to respond to the needs in Jerusalem. They gave generously—abundantly, in fact. A year earlier the Corinthians also had promised to give to this need. When word reached Paul that the Corinthians had long since set aside this project and had failed in their efforts to raise the funds that they promised to give, he decided to write them to remind them of their previous commitment.

> For it is superfluous for me to write to you about this ministry to the saints; for I know your readiness, of which I boast about you to the Macedonians, namely, that Achaia has been prepared since last year, and your zeal has stirred up most of them. But I have sent the brethren, that our boasting about you may not be made empty in this case, that, as I was saying, you may be prepared (2 Cor. 9:1–3).

In other words, Paul is saying that if he were to bring some Macedonian Christians with him to Corinth and have them pick up the measly Corinthian offering to take back to Jerusalem, he would be red-faced. Why? Because it was the Corinthian example (Paul had mentioned them to those in Macedonia) that prompted the Macedonians to give over and above their ability. So he writes to spur them on. Drawing on an age-old agricultural analogy, he begins:

> Now this I say, he who sows sparingly shall also reap sparingly; and he who sows bountifully shall also reap bountifully (2 Cor. 9:6).

In effect, Paul is saying, "There is a basic principle I taught you while I was with you in Corinth. If you plant only a little bit of seed, you'll get a meager harvest. But if you plant a lot of seed, you'll harvest an abundance. Which makes better sense?" He goes further: "Let each one do just as he has purposed in his heart; not grudgingly or under compulsion; . . ." (2 Cor. 9:7). The word *grudgingly* means "reluctantly," the idea of holding onto something because you don't want to part with it.

If you have little children or if you have been around little ones, then you've seen the same scene dozens of times. The child gets a toy. He's the older of the two. Let's say he's got this special little truck he loves to play with. He plays with it so much he virtually wears all the paint off the little thing. One day he leaves it sitting on the toy box. Nobody is touching it. Along comes little sister who toddles up to the table and reaches her tiny hand over to pick up the truck, only to have it snatched away by young King Kong, as he yells, "That's *my* truck!" He doesn't want to part with something he considers that important. When his mother makes him let her play with it, he "grudgingly" does so. It means reluctantly giving up something because it represents so much.

In the 2 Corinthians passage, we are also instructed not to give under compulsion. That means "feeling forced because of what someone may say or think." You see, compulsion results in even greater reluctance. When we are compelled to do something, we are all the more reluctant to give it up.

To return to my truck story, when Mom looks down and says, "Let her play with it," it's doubtful that he would ever say, "Why, of course! Here, Sis, I'm sorry I was selfish." You're smiling. Older kids *never* say that! Instead, you hear, "That's mine! That's mine!" And you have to pull his grip loose to wrench that little truck out of his hand. He doesn't want to give it up. Strangely, our compulsion makes him grip it even tighter.

Those are the word pictures implied here regarding giving. I find it almost amusing that the standard approach in fund-raising today is causing people to feel forced, compelling them to give. If God means what He says (doesn't He always?), then there's got to be another way. To the shock of most people, the other way is JOY! Generosity prompted by joy.

I've built to the climax that appears at the end of verse 7: ". . . for God loves a cheerful giver."

In the ancient days when the Greek text was written, interesting things occurred in the formation of words in a phrase or sentence. When words were placed out of order at the beginning of a sentence, it was usually for the purpose of emphasis. Guess what appears first in this last sentence: *cheerful*, not *giver*. Not even God. No, the word *cheerful* is the first major word to appear in the text. "For the cheerful one, who is a giver, God prizes." If I may return to my earlier example, "It's the *cheerful* giver who gets the silver medal; it's the *cheerful* giver who gets the red ribbon."

Hover for a moment over the key word, *cheerful*. In Greek it is the term *hilaros*, from which we get our word *hilarious*. It is such an unusual word it appears nowhere else in all the New Testament. Several times it surfaces in the Old Testament Greek version of the Bible (the Septuagint), but never any other place in all the New Testament. Literally, the sentence reads, "For the hilarious giver God prizes." Do you know why He prizes the hilarious giver? Because the hilarious giver gives so generously. He has no special possession or gift or skill or amount of money that he grips tightly. No, when the heart is full of cheer, it is amazing how it causes the pockets to turn inside out.

Unlike the mediocre majority, those who soar are full of joy that expresses itself in greathearted generosity.

At our church in Fullerton, California, the First Evangelical Free Church, we needed about eight thousand dollars for a group of high schoolers to go to Paraguay one summer. The teens had raised most of their support, but they came up eight thousand dollars short. We presented the need, and in less than twenty-four hours *more* than eight thousand dollars was given. Because we're rich? No. Because I begged? No. You know better than that! Compulsion backfires, remember. Simply because cheerful hearts created a spirit of such generosity, the momentum accomplished the goal.

But wait, let me quickly state that I'm not limiting these thoughts to money. I'm talking about being joyfully generous with our time and talents, too. I also have in mind compassion, possessions, and skills. Such joyful generosity is beautifully illustrated in other places of Scripture.

Examples Worth Remembering

In the Old Testament

Way back in the Book of Exodus, we find a classic example of joyful generosity. The people of God are now out of Egypt and on their trek across the wilderness en route to Canaan. Smack dab in the middle of no-man's land, God gives them an architectural plan for a portable worship center. Look:

> Then the Lord spoke to Moses, saying, "Tell the sons of Israel to raise a contribution for Me; from every man whose heart moves him you shall raise My contribution. And this is the contribution which you are to raise from them: gold, silver and bronze, blue, purple and scarlet material, fine linen, goat hair, rams' skins dyed red, porpoise skins, acacia wood, oil for lighting, spices for the anointing oil and for the fragrant incense, onyx stones and setting stones, for the ephod and for the breastpiece (Exod. 25:1–7).

Wait. Hold on, here. I ask you, couldn't Bill Cosby do a number on these verses? "I want you to raise a contribution. I want you to get porpoise skins and acacia wood and oil for lighting and rams' skins dyed red. And I want something to go on a breastplate. And I want onyx stones and setting stones." Give me a break! What is that all about? What are they going to do? I would love to see Cosby do a take-off on those words!

Why do all this? Read on;

"And let them construct a sanctuary for Me . . ." (v. 8). Are you ready? It was a fund-raising drive for a building, right from the Bible! Some of you, I'm sure, are ready to slam the book shut. You've heard enough! But hang with me. The plot thickens and the response becomes so joyful that the scene gets downright contagious. These people were told to construct a first-class portable building, a tabernacle, which they were to carry across the wilderness. It would be a structure for worship in which God Himself would dwell. His *Shechinah* (a bright, blinding light) would dwell in its most sacred center, the "holy of holies." Actually, He had never resided in a place on earth before. So we can be sure this structure would be built exactly as He specified.

> "According to all that I am going to show you, as the pattern of the tabernacle and the pattern of all its furniture, just so you shall construct it" (v. 9).

And beginning at verse 10 of Exodus, chapter 25, all the way through to chapter 35, God presents the specifications, the inspired drawings to Moses. In these plans God tells the Israelites everything they are to make and how they are to make it. It was an ingenious plan, brilliantly thought through and beautifully designed.

You can probably guess what followed. Earlier Moses was there by himself. But now he brings the people in, because that is where the funds will come from. In chapters 35 and 36, Moses assembles all the congregation and breaks the news to them.

> And Moses spoke to all the congregation of the sons of Israel, saying, "This is the thing which the Lord has commanded, saying, 'Take from among you a contribution to the Lord; whoever is of a willing heart, let him bring it as the Lord's contribution: gold, silver, and bronze, and blue, purple and scarlet material, fine linen, goats' hair, and rams' skins dyed red, and porpoise skins, and acacia wood, and oil for lighting, and spices for the anointing oil, and for the fragrant incense, and onyx stones and setting stones, for the ephod and for the breastpiece (Exod. 35:4-9).

Go back and underscore a phrase you may have passed over: "whoever is of a willing heart." In essence, Moses is saying, "We want no one to give grudgingly or under compulsion to participate, only *willing hearts*." (Sound vaguely familiar?) And then what? ". . . let him bring it as the Lord's contribution."

Moses goes even further.

> "'And let every skillful man among you come, and make all that the Lord has commanded: the tabernacle, its tent and its covering, its hooks and its boards, its bars, its pillars, and its sockets; the ark and its poles, the mercy seat, and the curtain of the screen; the table and its poles, and all its utensils, and the bread of the Presence; the lampstand also for the light and its utensils and its lamps and the oil for the light; and the altar of incense and its poles, and the anointing oil and the fragrant incense, and the screen for the doorway at the entrance of the tabernacle; the altar of burnt offering with its bronze grating, its poles, and all its utensils, the basin and its stand; the hangings of the court, its pillars and its sockets, and the screen for the gate of the court; the pegs of the tabernacle and the pegs of the court and their cords; the woven garments, for ministering in the holy place, the holy garments for Aaron the priest, and the garments of his sons, to minister as priests'" (vv. 10–19).

By now, I really believe the people's mouths must have dropped open and their hearts began to beat faster. "Ah, are we going to have a great place of worship! God is going to dwell among us. This is my chance to use my skill, my talents, my treasure, my craft, to assist in providing a place where God's people will meet for worship. What a privilege . . . what an opportunity!"

Now read very carefully, paying close attention to the comments related to their "hearts" and their "spirits."

> Then all the congregation of the sons of Israel departed from Moses' presence. And everyone whose heart stirred him and everyone whose spirit moved him came and brought the Lord's contribution for the work of the tent of meeting and for all its service and for the holy garments (vv. 20–21).

What could these nomads possibly give? They're in the wilderness. They're living in tents. Well, they had some valuables they had taken with them when they left Egypt. And not one of them held tightly to those possessions.

Then all whose hearts moved them, both men and women, came and brought brooches and earrings and signet rings and bracelets, all articles of gold; so did every man who presented an offering of gold to the Lord. And every man, who had in his possession blue and purple and scarlet material and fine linen and goats' hair and rams' skins dyed red and porpoise skins, brought them. Everyone who could make a contribution of silver and bronze brought the Lord's contribution; and every man, who had in his possession acacia wood for any work of the service, brought it. And all the skilled women spun with their hands, and brought what they had spun, in blue and purple and scarlet material and in fine linen. And all the women whose heart stirred with a skill spun the goats' hair. And the rulers brought the onyx stones and the stones for setting for the ephod and for the breastpiece; and the spice and the oil for the light and for the anointing oil and for the fragrant incense. The Israelites, all the men and women, whose heart moved them to bring material for all the work, which the Lord had commanded through Moses to be done, brought a freewill offering to the Lord (vv. 22–29).

·I love that scene! By the hundreds, by the thousands, by the tens of thousands they came with their offerings, bringing them before their Lord in the wilderness. Skilled men stood ready with saw and hammer and chisel. Skilled ladies stood by with their needle, thread, and fabric to do the fine embroidery and needlepoint that would be a part of the veil (the curtain that would divide the holy place from the holiest of all) and the other beautiful tapestries and curtains. The tabernacle was a beautiful, skillful work of art, masterfully engineered. There would be those who worked in gold, silver, and fine gems who would finish the precious metals and the jewels just as God directed through the skill He had given them. God really "broke a vase" when He designed this baby! It must have been something to behold.

Now this is where the story gets really exciting. You are going to meet a couple of men you've probably never heard of before. That is the way it often is with skilled craftsmen, in this case, the construction superintendents.

Then Moses called Bezalel and Oholiab and every skillful person in whom the Lord had put skill, everyone whose heart stirred him, to come to the work to perform it (Exod. 36:2).

There is no guilt. There is no external compulsion, no manipulation whatsoever. Rather, with joyful hearts moved and stirred, they came eagerly to work on this project.

> And they received from Moses all the contributions which the sons of Israel had brought to perform the work in the construction of the sanctuary. And they still continued bringing to him freewill offerings every morning (v. 3).

Morning after morning God continued to stir the hearts of people. As a result they brought bracelets and brooches, jewels and earrings, along with pieces of gold and bronze and silver. True joy had invaded the camp. There were miles of smiles. God Himself must have smiled back at such joyful generosity.

> And all the skillful men who were performing all the work of the sanctuary came, each from the work which he was performing, and they said to Moses, "The people are bringing much more than enough for the construction work which the Lord commanded us to perform." So Moses issued a command, and a proclamation was circulated throughout the camp, saying, "Let neither man nor woman any longer perform work for the contributions of the sanctuary." Thus the people were restrained from bringing any more. For the material they had was sufficient and more than enough for all the work, to perform it (vv. 4–7).

That's right. I'm not kidding, Moses had to issue a command: "No more offerings. Please don't give any more!" How would that come across on a Sunday morning at your church? "Folks, we're not going to take an offering today because you people have unloaded the truck on us for the last two Sundays, so we're going to pass it up today! Do not give any more!" Don't get your hopes up! But the truth is this: When there is such a spirit of hilarity, when genuine joy overflows, people do have to be *stopped* from giving! Because our ability so outstrips the need, we can't keep handling all the funds that would pour into the treasury. What a wonderful change of scenery: "The people were restrained from bringing any more."

Can you imagine the joy? The camp of Israel was never happier. You could have heard singing among the carpenters working with wood, singing among the jewelers, singing among the ladies who worked with their fabrics and their design and other pieces of art. What a place to be! What an absolutely irresistible magnet in the wilderness! But "Operation Tabernacle" is just one scene. The tent of worship was built and God met with the people. They praised His name and found cleansing and forgiveness in that tabernacle for years, really for centuries.

Now here is another scene. Tragically, the Hebrews later forgot God and were swept away into captivity in Babylon. They finally left Babylon, faltering in their steps, stumbling back to Jerusalem to rebuild the city which had been destroyed by the heathen. They returned to their beloved Zion. Nehemiah led one of the groups back, and he wasn't there long before he realized the wall around the city had to be rebuilt or the people would be plundered by enemies. Finally, after surveying the need, he came before the people and presented a challenge in hopes of raising their support and getting them involved:

> Then I said to them, "You see the bad situation we are in, that Jerusalem is desolate and its gates burned by fire. Come, let us rebuild the wall of Jerusalem that we may no longer be a reproach" (Neh. 2:17).

By the way, we must not hurry over the intrinsic motivation Nehemiah used in that speech. He appealed to their heart when he said, "Can you imagine what people all over the region are saying about our God? They're saying, 'You're telling me that your God is great? Look at the awful place you live in. This place is the pits!'" As the people began to imagine such thoughts, they were motivated from within to respond. When they considered the need, their patriotic pride pushed them into action. Winston Churchill, a master of intrinsic motivation, constantly rallied the people of the British Isles by reminding them of the importance of upholding their British heritage. He linked them with the pride of their fortune.

Well, that was Nehemiah's approach: "How good it would be to have a wall that stands tall and strong around this city, men and women, one that represents the strong name of our God, so that when the enemy looks over at us and sees us dwelling in peace in Zion, they will say, 'My, their God is the One to revere!'"

Who knows? Sir Winston Churchill may have learned how to do it from Nehemiah. Remember the Prime Minister's words?

> I have not become the King's First Minister in order to preside over the liquidation of the British Empire (Speech at the Lord Mayor's Day Luncheon, London [Nov. 10, 1942]).
>
> I have nothing to offer but blood, toil, tears, and sweat (First statement as Prime Minister, House of Commons [May 13, 1940]).
>
> Never give in, never give in, never, never, never, never—in nothing, great or small, large or petty—never give in except to convictions of honor and good sense (Address at Harrow School [Oct. 29, 1941]).[1]

Hitler laughed at Great Britain. But Churchill and the Britons had the last laugh. May I repeat? He appealed to the intrinsic motivation of the people of Great Britain. That is what Nehemiah does here.

> And I told them how the hand of my God had been favorable to me, and also about the king's words which he had spoken to me. Then they said, "Let us arise and build." So they put their hands to the good work (Neh. 2:18).

What do you see in that statement? I see cheer. I see motivation. I don't hear any grumbling. And I don't find anybody feeling under pressure. Everyone says, "Let's do it. It's only right. Let's go for it! Lead us, Nehemiah, and we will do it." And that is exactly what happens. They put their hands to the work.

> So we built the wall and the whole wall was joined together to half its height, for the people had a mind to work (Neh. 4:6).

The word translated "mind" in this verse is literally, "heart." It is like the line out of the popular song of yesteryear, "You gotta have heart." When eagles soar, they "gotta have heart." When we keep pursuing a standard of excellence, surrounded by mediocrity, we "gotta have heart."

And those Hebrews definitely had heart! They stayed at it against incredible odds until they finished the task.

> So the wall was completed on the twenty-fifth of the month Elul, in fifty-two days. And it came about when all our enemies heard of it, and all the nations surrounding us saw it, they lost their confidence; for they recognized that this work had been accomplished with the help of our God (Neh. 6:15-16).

Isn't that great? Those on the outside couldn't deny the incredible feat these Hebrews had accomplished. As they walked by the completed wall, they looked at it with a whole different perspective, wondering, *What kind of God do they serve?*

You have to realize that for the longest time these enemies had been badgering the people of Israel—taunting, tempting, and insulting them, trying their best to shut down "Project Rebuild." Really, their scheme was to rob them of their joy—the fuel of morale. But that wall kept going up against all odds until finally the enemy stuffed his hands in his pockets and said, "I can't believe it. They got that thing built." The Hebrew's success in rebuilding the wall reminds me of the verse, "He who sows bountifully shall also reap bountifully" (2 Cor. 9:6).

In the New Testament

When we arrive at the New Testament, one of the first things we encounter is a set of gifts brought by some wise men to the King. We are less than two full chapters into the New Testament before we come across a few men, called magi, who have come to visit the baby Jesus.

> And when they saw the star, they rejoiced exceedingly with great joy. And they came into the house and saw the Child with Mary His mother; and they fell down and worshiped Him; and opening their treasures they presented to Him gifts of gold and frankincense and myrrh (Matt. 2:10-11).

What characterized the attitude of these visitors? Joy. Exceedingly great joy. And what was the result? Great generosity. They gave gold, frankincense, and myrrh to this little Child. Oh, I know all sorts of symbolic things have been said, but if you'll allow me the simplicity of literalism, they brought what they had. And they lavished upon Him sheer extravagance—they worshiped as they gave expensive gifts. Why? Because they had cheerful hearts.

I could go on. Rather obscure men like Epaphroditus and Onesiphorus gave themselves to Paul, as did Dr. Luke. The church at Philippi, out of great joy, gave more than once to Paul, over and above his needs, so that he could say from their example, "I have learned to abound." What joy Paul modeled! In fact, have you thought lately about our ultimate home in heaven? Take a quick glimpse now:

> And I saw the holy city, new Jerusalem, coming down out of heaven from God, made ready as a bride adorned for her husband. And I heard a loud voice from the throne, saying, "Behold, the tabernacle of God is among men, and He shall dwell among them, and they shall be His people, and God Himself shall be among them, and He shall wipe away every tear from their eyes; and there shall no longer be any death; there shall no longer be any mourning, or crying, or pain; the first things have passed away" (Rev. 21:2–4).

What will be the eternal sound of heaven? No tears, pain, or sorrow. Sounds like laughter and joy to me! Count on it—heaven will be the first place where joy will be in the majority.

JOYFUL GENEROSITY CAN BE OURS TODAY

We've spent sufficient time on biblical examples. Let's think about how we can bring some much-needed joy back into our lives today. I have four suggestions in mind.

1. <u>Reflect on God's gifts to you.</u> In case you need a little help, read through Psalm 103:

> Bless the Lord, O my soul; and all that is within me, bless His holy name. Bless the Lord, O my soul, and forget none of His benefits; who pardons all your iniquities; who heals all your diseases; who redeems your life from the pit; who crowns you with lovingkindness and compassion; who satisfies your years with good things, so that your youth is renewed like the eagle. The Lord performs righteous deeds, and judgments for all who are oppressed (Ps. 103:1–6).

The psalmist lists several benefits to prod our thinking. As we reflect on God's gifts to us, it's helpful to be specific.

Do you have eyesight? It's a gift. Do you have a good mind? It's a gift. How about dexterity in your fingers? Or special skills that allow you to work in your occupation? Do you have leadership abilities that cause others to follow? A good education? Do you have the ability to sell? These are all gifts. Has He given you a family? Has He given you sufficient clothes? How about a nice, warm, soft bed at night or a comfortable place to live in the hot summer? Why, some even have more than one home! These are all gifts from God's hand. Reflect on His numerous gifts to you. It will increase your joy. And a smile will soon replace that frown.

2. Remind yourself of God's promises regarding generosity. God promises if you sow bountifully, you will reap bountifully. If you give in abundance, a tabernacle can be erected. If you work hard with one another, a wall can be built. So give! Give abundantly! Even extravagant giving is honored by God. I've never known anyone who went bad because he or she was *too* generous. Remind yourself of His promises regarding generosity and start releasing! My good friend, Ron Blue, has helped Cynthia and me more than any other person when it comes to generosity. By his example and professional financial assistance, he has challenged us and shown us ways to increase our charitable contributions to incredible proportions. I strongly recommend your reading *Master Your Money* by Ron Blue.[2] Don't be afraid of outgiving God. It is absolutely impossible to do that. He will keep every one of His promises related to generosity. Try Him!

3. Examine your heart (this is going to be the tough one). I don't want you to examine your tax records from last year. That will merely speak to your mind. I want you to talk to your heart. I don't want you to examine your neighbor or some other person, because you will be better than your neighbor or whichever individual you choose. Don't even compare yourself with the way you used to give, because you probably are doing better than you used to do. I challenge you to *examine your heart.*

Here are some questions for you to ask yourself:

- Do I really believe there is a need?
- Am I responding out of pressure or because I really care?
- Is my gift an appropriate expression of my income or is it more of a last-minute, unplanned get-it-over-with act?
- Have I prayed, or is this impulsive giving?
- Is joy prompting me? Am I genuinely thrilled about what God is doing in my life as well as through my giving?
- Does generosity characterize my life?

4. Glorify God by being extremely generous. I think a unique way to look at it is to scare yourself a little. Remember when you didn't

have much and you gave more than you should have given, at least for logic's sake? You scared yourself a little, didn't you? Wasn't that fun? Wasn't that absolutely delightful? And the good news is you made it. You didn't starve. Chances are good you are still rather well fed. And sufficiently clothed. But are you joyful? Honestly now, has the enemy, Joyless Living, taken charge of you? If so, I can guarantee that you have become less generous. How about cultivating extreme generosity? Talk about being a rare species of eagle!

I find it interesting that most people picture their heavenly Father as frowning and wringing His hands or sort of pulling His beard when His Son left heaven. I don't think so. I wonder if there wasn't a smile in heaven. Even when our Lord faced the cross and thought of dying in agony, what spurred Him on was "the joy that was set before Him." And can you imagine the shout of joy from heaven when the resurrection occurred? "Raised from the dead! That's My Son!" How about when the Father welcomed Him back to the throne! I would imagine the greatest joy possible surrounded that reunion. And speaking of the greatest—

God	the greatest Giver
so loved	the greatest motive
the world	the greatest need
that He gave	the greatest act
His only Son	the greatest gift
that whosoever	the greatest invitation
believes in Him	the greatest opportunity
should not perish	the greatest deliverance
but have eternal life	the greatest joy

Do you want to know the endless source of joy? Jesus Christ. Through Him alone we receive salvation—an act of love, fulfilled with joy, resulting in peace. Thanks be to God for His indescribable Gift. All that He is and all that He provides is enough to make me laugh out loud!

We've spent enough time in the combat zone. While here, we have taken on four of the more prominent enemies of soaring: greed, traditionalism, indifference, and joylessness. These opponents of excellence, as we have learned, will not surrender easily. On the contrary, they are so entrenched, they require strong and consistent bombardment. But the good news is this: *They can be overcome!* May God give us strength to face each one without fear.

Part Four

Resisting Mediocrity Includes Standing Courageously

*Must one point out that from
ancient times a decline in courage
has been considered the first
symptom of the end?*

Aleksandr I. Solzhenitsyn
1978

13

STANDING ALONE
WHEN OUTNUMBERED

One of the great American myths is that we are all a bunch of rugged individualists. We would like to think that, but it simply is not true. There are some exceptions, of course, but for the majority it is not that way at all.

Deep within, we imagine ourselves as a mixture of Patrick Henry, Davy Crockett, John Wayne, and the prophet Daniel! But the truth of the matter is that most of us would do anything to keep from being different. We'd much rather blend into the woodwork. One of our greatest fears is being ostracized, rejected by "the group." Ridicule is a pain too great for most to bear.

There are other fears—fear of being made to look foolish, fear of standing out in a crowd, fear of being talked about and misunderstood. Rather than rugged individualists, we are more like Gulliver of old, tied down and immobilized by tiny strands of fear, real or imagined. The result is both predictable and tragic: loss of courage.

> We can see these symptoms . . . throughout society, but the most visible one is loss of courage. People stand by and watch a fellow citizen being beaten or stabbed and they do not interfere. They are afraid. Our political leaders watch Communism gobble up other nations and they do nothing. They are afraid. People complain in private about the state of affairs but will not speak out in public. They are afraid. . . .[1]

Because this is true, I have decided to combine the final four chapters of my book under one major heading: Courage. Living above the level of mediocrity includes standing courageously. In the final analysis, whoever decides to soar will be forced to face and come to terms with the great temptation to conform. This is obvious since those who don't want to soar will ridicule those who do. Eagles will always be outnumbered. Standing alone when outnumbered and opposed can be an uncomfortable, threatening experience.

Over thirty years ago I worked as a machinist in a shop where the vast majority were members of the local union. It didn't take me long to realize that the maintenance of a mediocre standard was one of the unwritten laws of that shop. Pressure was applied to anyone who worked unusually hard or produced more than the lower-than-average quota. Why? It made all the others look bad, and there was no way they would tolerate such a thing! Mild suggestions, if unheeded, would be followed by gentle nudges. Then, if still unheeded, the nudges would be followed by direct confrontation. If *that* was ignored, there were stronger measures taken to maintain the level of mediocrity. They would have no part of excellence. Conform or else! We had our moments, to say the least.

Such pressure is not uncommon in numerous slices of life. The hard-charging high achiever at school is usually viewed with suspicion, not respect. Instead of others in the class picking up the pace and trying their best to do better, they would rather put down the student out front and make him or her look foolish. The same can be true on a sales team or for that matter in a residential neighborhood. People don't want anyone to soar, especially if they prefer to slump! Chances are good that you feel the same pressure I'm illustrating. If not, color yourself fortunate. Few are the places today where eagle types pursuing excellence are admired and encouraged to reach greater heights. Because this is so common, I feel we need to seriously consider what is involved in standing courageously.

A BRIEF ANALYSIS OF CONFORMITY

Earlier I mentioned the significance of certain lines from chapter 12 of the Letter to the Romans. I'd like us to return to that thought and spend a few more minutes on the overall setting in which that line occurs.

> I urge you therefore, brethren, by the mercies of God, to present your bodies a living and holy sacrifice, acceptable to God, which is your spiritual service of worship. And do not be conformed to this world, but be transformed by the renewing of your mind, that you may prove what

the will of God is, that which is good and acceptable and perfect (Rom. 12:1–2).

Allow me to mention six observations from those two verses:

1. <u>This truth is mainly for the Christian.</u> "I urge you, *brethren....*" If I haven't made this clear before, I need to say it straight now. Apart from a personal and vital faith in Jesus Christ, it is impossible to wage a winning effort against the system called "the world." Trying to soar on one's own, overcoming the powerful magnet of the majority without help from above, would be a frustrating and counterproductive effort. Only God can give us such transforming power through our faith in His Son.

2. <u>There is an urgency in this message—intense urgency, in fact.</u> Paul doesn't say, "Oh, by the way, it might be nice if..." No, he says, "I *urge* you." The writer is pressing his pen hard; he feels passionate about this. And so must we. No one ever eased effortlessly out of conformity.

3. <u>This urgency is related to a sacrifice.</u> The point being, the process of commitment is a "holy sacrifice." We never sacrifice something easily. The whole idea of sacrifice is yielding something that is important to us—releasing, giving over, letting go, surrendering. The urgency will call for sacrifice. Notice that the sacrifice is not only "holy," it is a "living" sacrifice. One of the major problems of a living sacrifice is that it keeps crawling off the altar!

4. <u>This sacrifice touches two realms: the inner person and the outer person.</u> The *inner person* is addressed in the word *present*—"I urge you... to present your bodies." This is a decision we make deep down inside ourselves. Next is the *outer person*, "your bodies"—that part of you that touches the system around you. "I urge you by the mercies of God," says Paul, "that you Christians make a deep-down, gut-level decision to present your bodies."

Listen to the words of the late Donald Barnhouse:

> There are two things involved here—our innermost self that does the presenting and our bodies that are presented. It should almost go without saying that it is useless to give our bodies if we have not, first of all, given ourselves.[2]

This matter of presenting our bodies is a very practical thing. I had to consciously come to terms with it when I went overseas in the

Marine Corps for many long months. I knew before I ever set foot in the barracks that more than likely, most of the forty-seven other guys would be just alike, especially in the moral realm. Marines have never been known for their moral virtue (you're smiling). I knew my buddies were going to be unfaithful. I knew they were going to traffic in sensual things. I knew in my heart they would buy into the world's system. While on that massive troop ship steaming across the Pacific, I can recall as clearly as if it were yesterday thinking hard about the issue of conformity. I had enough sense to say, "Lord, God, I give myself to You during these months in front of me. I don't want to come off as a self-righteous monk who stands aloof, but I do desire to walk a path that honors Your name. Therefore, Lord, I need Your strength to stand alone. I present my body to You . . . for Your glory."

I'm not talking out of theory. I know firsthand that this kind of commitment works. During those months when I was surrounded by fellow Marines with totally different moral standards from those I held, I did not yield to peer pressure. I did not conform. I remained faithful to my wife. By God's grace and power, I maintained a walk with Jesus Christ. I do not intend to sound like a goody two-shoes. I want to verify that *it works*. Therefore, I can say to you teenagers who wake up on Monday morning and know that when you go to school you're going to be surrounded by the system, *you can handle it!* You *cannot* counteract it alone, however. You're too weak and it's too appealing, too attractive. But by presenting yourself to the Lord on a day-by-day basis, almost until it is a habit, you can handle it. To do so, there must be a harmony—an agreement—in your inner and outer person.

5. The sacrifice is essentially a spiritual one. As far as God is concerned, a consistent godly life is well pleasing, acceptable to Him. As far as you are concerned, it is an act of worship. It is a "spiritual service of worship."

I need to be very candid here. If you are a "Sunday Christian," you will not stand alone when outnumbered. Anybody can soar—anyone can walk in victory while sitting in church. But the kind of "service of worship" Romans 12:1–2 is talking about affects your Monday, your Thursday, your Saturday lifestyle—your entire week, in fact, all fifty-two of them every year. So at the deepest level there is the presenting of oneself to God—at lunch time, if you please; before a date; during a date; before a trip; in the middle of a vacation. During any scene in which you find yourself, you give yourself to God. "Lord, in this body there are certain drives and many desires. In my eyes, there are interests that are not from You. In these ears of mine and in these hands and in various parts of my body there are things that are attracted, like a magnet, to the world system. Therefore, I deliberately and willingly give You my eyes, my ears, my senses, my thought processes as an act of worship. I am Yours, Lord. Please take control of each one of these areas."

All this brings me to a final observation:

6. This sacrifice leads to a practical and radical decision. Look again at the second verse: "Do not be conformed to this world (that is the practical decision), but be transformed by the renewing of your mind (that is the radical decision)." I mentioned J. B. Phillips' paraphrase of this verse in chapter 10, but it's worth repeating: "Don't let the world around you squeeze you into its own mold" (Rom. 12:2). *The Living Bible* says, "Don't copy the behavior and customs of this world." Many read that and think only of hairstyle or clothing, which could be merely a superficial application. But it seems to me, what Paul had in mind is that the whole world system is at odds with God.

We are like tiny islands of truth surrounded by a sea of paganism, but we launch our ship every day. We can't live or do business in this world without rubbing shoulders with those driven by the world's desires. God calls very few to be monks in a monastery. So we must make a *practical* decision not to be conformed while we are in the system, and at the same time, we must make a *radical* decision to give God the green light to transform our minds.

Let me clarify those thoughts. First, what does it mean to be *conformed?* The word means "to assume an outward expression that does not come from within." When I conform to something, I masquerade; I wrap myself in a mask that isn't true to what I am on the inside. Deep inside of me is the Person of Jesus Christ. When the outside of me is involved in actions that are un-Christlike, I am conforming. But when the living Christ within me is expressed on the outside, I am not conforming. I am being authentic. When He lives out His life through me, there is genuine expression, not a masquerade.

Second, what does it mean to be *transformed?* That word is different from *conformed.* The biblical term means "an outward expression that comes from within." Not only is it different, but it is the antithesis of *conform.* The Greek word underlying the term *transformed* here is the verb *metamorphoō,* from which come the English words *meta-*

morphose and *metamorphosis*. To be "transformed" is to be "metamorphosed."

When a grub becomes a butterfly, there has been a metamorphosis, a radical transformation. When a tadpole becomes a frog, there has been a transformation. When the real Christ expresses Himself through our lives, there is evidence of dramatic change. What occurs is nothing short of a striking, radical transformation. And how does it occur? Paul says, "Do this by the renewing of your mind." In my opinion, that is where the techniques begin. For there to be victorious transformation rather than defeating conformity, there must be renewing thoughts.

In order for you and me to keep ourselves from conforming, we must have a renewed mind. The primary battleground, as I wrote at the beginning of this book, is the mind—that inner part of our being where we decide who we are and where we stand. As someone once wrote, "We are not what we are. We are not even what others think we are. We are what we think others think we are." At the deepest level, even though the majority may not want to admit it, most people are conformists. That is why it is correctly termed a radical decision. Only a radically different mindset can equip folks like us to stand alone when we're outnumbered. Conformity will always be there inviting us in, appealing to our insecurities, painting a comfortable, rosy picture that says, "Aw, come on and join us. Why be so different?"

FOUR OBJECTIVES OF THE WORLD SYSTEM

The world system is committed to at least four major objectives, which I can summarize in four words: fortune, fame, power, pleasure. *First and foremost: Fortune, money.* The world system is driven by money; it feeds on materialism. I've already said a lot about this, but eagles don't soar until they realize the reality of this constant pull. *Second: Fame.* That is another word for popularity. You wrestle with it, your kids are wrestling with it, your grandkids will wrestle with it. Fame is the longing to be known, to be somebody in someone else's eyes. I'm not referring to being someone's hero, but someone's god. I'm talking about a celebrity mindset. *Third: Power.* This is having influence, maintaining control over individuals or groups or companies or whatever. It is the desire to manipulate and maneuver others to do something for one's own benefit. *Fourth: Pleasure.* At its basic level, pleasure has to do with fulfilling one's sensual desires. It's the same mindset that's behind the slogan: "If it feels good, do it." The world is ruthless and relentless as it works overtime to communicate this fortune-fame-power-pleasure syndrome.

Deposit your child into a system like that with no information, little help or technique on how to handle it, and I can almost guarantee you that in only a matter of months that youngster will think like, look like, sound like, and worst of all, *act* like the system. If your child's close friends are into profanity or immorality, chances are good your son or daughter will conform. If they are into alcohol or drugs, you can expect the same at home.

Several years ago I stumbled upon a verse of Scripture that seemed to leap off the page. Right in the middle of 1 Corinthians 15, which is a chapter on the doctrine of resurrection, is this very practical thought: "Do not be deceived 'Bad company corrupts good morals'" (v. 33). *The Living Bible* puts it this way: "Don't be fooled by those who say such things. If you listen to them you will start acting like them."

Monkey see, monkey do. When we spend enough time around those in a particular scene, our actions usually become similar. It is just the way we're made. And it is especially true if the one in the minority is insecure and unsure. If you doubt that, you are merely deceiving yourself. Wake up, eagle! Realize the overwhelming power of peer pressure on you as well as your kids. Some call it the "herd instinct." All things being equal, if you run with bad company, you will be corrupted. The good won't rub off on them. Their bad will rub off on you. It's like putting on a pair of white gloves on a muddy day and picking up that mud and mixing it around in your hands. Interestingly, the mud never gets "glovey," but the gloves get muddy. Never saw "glovey" mud in my entire life!

An Old Scene with a Modern Message

In light of what 1 Corinthians 15:33 says about the dangers of peer pressure, let's look at Deuteronomy 6:10–15. The people being addressed in this scripture are the new-generation Hebrews we discussed earlier—those who lived to see the Promised Land after wandering in the wilderness for forty years until they buried all those who had doubted Moses' leadership. Except for Caleb and Joshua, only the young Israelites survived. Now they are on the verge of invading Canaan. Just before entering it, Moses pulls them aside and gives them a few warnings. In no uncertain terms, he tells them about the perils lurking in the shadows once they take up residence in that new territory. Though Moses himself would not be going in with them, he loved them too much to simply step aside and hope for the best. He wanted them to be aware of what they would soon encounter. I suppose we could call his words "good fatherly advice." In any case, Moses' counsel would later come back to haunt the Hebrews. Read carefully his words of advice.

> "Then it shall come about when the Lord your God brings you into the land which He swore to your fathers, Abraham, Isaac and Jacob, to give you, great and splendid cities which you did not build, and houses full of all good things which you did not fill, and hewn cisterns which you did not dig, vineyards and olive trees which you did not plant, and you shall eat and be satisfied, then watch yourself, lest you forget the Lord who brought you from the land of Egypt, out of the house of slavery. You shall fear only the Lord your God; and you shall worship Him, and swear by His name. You shall not follow other gods, any of the gods of the peoples who surround you" (Deut. 6:10-14).

Today, we'd say, "You are going to be tempted to go along with the crowd, so watch it! You must continue to swear by one name—the name of the living God—even though you will be surrounded by people who don't!"

> For the Lord your God in the midst of you is a jealous God; otherwise the anger of the Lord your God will be kindled against you, and He will wipe you off the face of the earth (Deut. 6:15).

Don't think for a moment that God doesn't care about the conduct of His chosen ones. He is jealous for our love and allegiance. Look back over Moses' words. Notice his repeated reminders of what God had done for them: cities they had not built, houses full of things they had not filled, wells they had not dug, trees they had not planted. How easy it would be for them to feel indulged! And how dangerous! In light of all those things they would soon get for nothing, he warned them against the ultimate trap: forgetting the Lord their God. Between the lines, I think he was urging them to keep on standing alone:

"Don't yield to peer pressure! Maintain your distinctiveness! Be very courageous! Remember, you are unique!" Sounds a lot like the advice parents give their older teenager just before he (or she) leaves for college, doesn't it?

Four Practical Principles for Today

As I think about Moses' warnings, four principles emerge—each one leading to the next.

1. <u>Getting something for nothing can breed irresponsibility.</u> When a lot of things are suddenly laid in our laps, it is easy to pick up an attitude of "Who needs God?" Sort of a spoiled-child syndrome. Too many toys, too much luxury, all too easily acquired—a breeding ground for irresponsibility. You and I have seen it happen.

2. <u>Irresponsibility creates a careless attitude.</u> When there is an abundance of things freely unloaded, a carelessness emerges—an inability to discern the right scale of values. "What does it matter?" or "Who really cares what I do with it?" That's the reason for the warning: "Watch yourself, lest you forget the Lord."

3. <u>Carelessness leads to a loss of standards.</u> Those Hebrews would soon be surrounded by a majority of people who worship other gods. If the Hebrews became careless about their spiritual standards the most natural response would be for them to embrace the same gods of the people around them. In fact, that is exactly what they did! Carelessness creates a loss of spiritual, moral, and ethical standards. That is why Moses said, "Fear only the Lord your God; and . . . worship Him."

4. <u>A loss of standards prompts personal insecurity.</u> Think about this one, especially. That is precisely the problem of second- and third-generation Christians. Parents, you and I forged out our theology. Many of us got saved off the street. Originally, we didn't know the Lord from a lizard. Out of the blue we were brought face to face with the claims of Christ, and we surrendered to Him. Then things changed, especially for our kids. We gave birth to a generation who have fought for nothing. They've been given virtually everything on a silver platter. Our kids don't know what it is to be on the street, spiritually. They have heard the name of Jesus all their lives. In most cases, they have never had to struggle to forge a theology of their own, so they don't really care. Watch out—it won't be long before they get picky and spoiled and even careless with spiritual things. That's when real trouble starts.

Here is your son, raised by a family who cares, in a good church, surrounded by good people who love the Lord Jesus. He's got all the breaks! Then why in the world is he on drugs? What is it that turned him off, spiritually? Why isn't he an eagle like his mom and dad? Take another look at those four principles just mentioned. The syndrome sucked him in! He's part of that irresponsibility which breeds carelessness, which in turn leads to a loss of standard and ultimately results in insecurity.

How can we stop this downward spiral syndrome? Let me suggest four mind-renewing thoughts that have certainly helped me. They are brief yet powerful statements we can say to ourselves and ultimately pass on to our offspring.

First: *"I am responsible."* I said that to myself so many times in the Marine Corps that I got sick of hearing myself say it! "Swindoll, *you* are responsible." Nobody was around, no parents, no wife, nobody who knew me. I had no reputation to uphold, no fear of being "found out." And so I began to renew my thought life with, "I am responsible." To this day, I still repeat those three words in my mind. With a family it works out this way: "Son, daughter, you are responsible."

Second: *"I must not forget."* Remember Moses' counsel? Though centuries old, it is still relevant.

> ". . . watch yourself, lest you forget the Lord who brought you from the land of Egypt, out of the house of slavery" (Deut. 6:12).

You see, when you haven't been brought out of Egypt, when you haven't had to fight to survive, it is easy to forget God. Your kids and mine don't know a thing about Egypt. We do, but they don't. We must not forget the Lord our God. And neither can we afford to let them forget.

Third: *"I am accountable."* I am accountable to God whether I'm in Fullerton or Asia, at the tip of South America or at the North Pole. I am accountable to my Lord.

Fourth: *"I get my standard and security from Him."* Not from my friend, not from my business, not from my neighbors—not even from within myself. Christ is my surety. Don't be fooled by the crowd. I remember an old saying, "There's safety in numbers." Well, not always. Sometimes there's danger in numbers. Just because "everybody's doing it" doesn't mean it's either safe or right.

All this reminds me of a story I read years ago about a bright young fly who unfortunately sought safety in a crowd.

> Once a spider built a beautiful web in an old house. He kept it clean and shiny so that flies would patronize it. The minute he got a "customer" he would clean up on him so the other flies would not get suspicious.
>
> Then one day this fairly intelligent fly came buzzing by the clean spiderweb. Old man spider called out, "Come in and sit." But the fairly intelligent fly said, "No, sir. I don't see other flies in your house, and I am not going in alone!"
>
> But presently he saw on the floor below a large crowd of flies dancing around on a piece of brown paper. He was delighted! He was not afraid if lots of flies were doing it. So he came in for a landing.
>
> Just before he landed, a bee zoomed by, saying, "Don't land there, stupid! That's flypaper!" But the fairly intelligent fly shouted back, "Don't be silly. Those flies are dancing. There's a big crowd there. Everybody's doing it. That many flies can't be wrong!" Well, you know what happened. He died on the spot.
>
> Some of us want to be with the crowd so badly that we end up in a mess. What does it profit a fly (or a person) if he escapes the web only to end up in the glue?[3]

It takes courage to think alone, to resist alone, to stand alone—especially when the crowd seems so safe, so right. But remember God. Keep flying high, eagle—far above the glue that snares the crowd. Up there it doesn't just seem safe and right, it *is* safe and right.

14

STANDING TALL WHEN TESTED

A few years ago psychologist Ruth W. Berenda and her associates carried out an interesting experiment with teenagers designed to show how a person handled group pressure. The plan was simple. They brought groups of ten adolescents into a room for a test. Subsequently, each group of ten was instructed to raise their hands when the teacher pointed to the longest line on three separate charts. What one person in the group did not know was that nine of the others in the room had been instructed ahead of time to vote for the *second*-longest line.

Regardless of the instructions they heard, once they were all together in the group, the nine were not to vote for the longest line, but rather vote for the *next*-to-the-longest line. Here are the charts as they appeared before each group when the votes were taken.

CHART 1   CHART II   CHART III

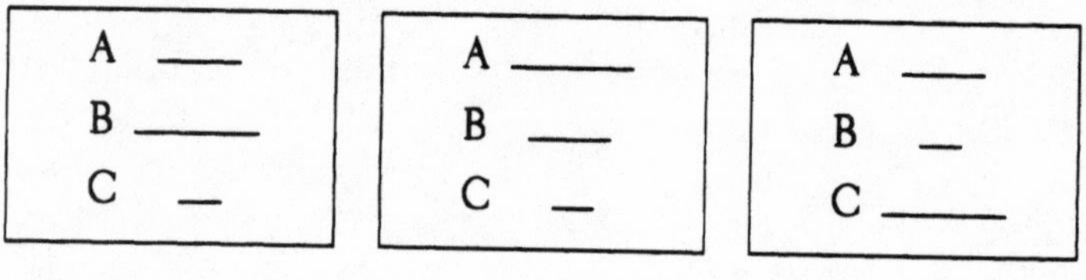

A ——   A ——   A ——
B ———   B ——   B —
C —   C —   C ———

The desire of the psychologists was to determine how one person reacted when completely surrounded by a large number of people who obviously stood against what was true.

The experiment began with nine teen-agers voting for the wrong line. The stooge would typically glance around, frown in confusion, and slip his hand up with the group. The instructions were repeated and the next card was raised. Time after time, the self-conscious stooge would sit there saying a short line is longer than a long line, simply because he lacked the courage to challenge the group. This remarkable conformity occurred in about seventy-five percent of the cases, and was true of small children and high-school students as well. Berenda concluded that, "Some people had rather be president than right," which is certainly an accurate assessment.[1]

That basic test was removed from any feeling of emotion. It was simply a logical examination to see how a person handled group pressure. My point? It is one thing for peer pressure to be determined in a classroom. Things are safe under the watchful eye of a professional psychologist. It is another thing entirely when it happens to be your child or mine (or you or me!) who is surrounded by a majority that says, "The-next-to-longest line is really the longest line." The moral and ethical implications that accompany such an experiment are frightening.

I want to make a forceful statement here, but one I believe with all my heart. *If your child is not taught how to stand alone when surrounded by those who put him to the test, he won't be able to stand tall.* He or she will go through self-doubts, then uncertainty, and finally slump into complete conformity. If our kids are not given a good deal of practical help on how to handle peer pressure, chances are good they will fail when the tests come. Let me illustrate. Let's say your son has been raised in a Christian home, has gone to school in Christian schools, has run with Christian friends, and has spent all his formative years in that rather sheltered environment. To make matters more complicated, you have said little about the "real world" and done nothing to equip him for what he is sure to face. When he goes off to college he is thrust into a school that is not Christian. He is surrounded by young adults who, for the most part, are not Christians. Almost overnight, he is introduced to an environment he hardly knew existed. That is where the rubber meets the road. That is when all theory either works or goes down the tube—when he will either stand tall and model secure courage even though outnumbered or begin to waver. The test is on! That's one of the toughest assignments for moms and dads—to get our offspring ready for life's examinations without damaging their self-esteem in the process. Somehow the eaglet must learn to fly on its own, but no responsible eagle just abandons the nest, thinking, "Sure hope the little guy makes it!"

A LITTLE MORE HISTORY, PLEASE

In chapter 13 we spent time studying the theoretical warnings in Deuteronomy. Now let's go to reality. We find it in the Book of Judges. I want to show you what happened to those Hebrews who heard the great words Moses delivered as they were about to enter the Promised Land. Waiting just around the corner were the Canaanites. Why?

> And they were for testing Israel, to find out if they would obey the commandments of the Lord, which He had commanded their fathers through Moses (Judg. 3:4).

God had warned the Hebrews that the Canaanites would be all around them: "They will be there, you'll see. I'm leaving them there for one reason: a test! And when you arrive, you'll have to drive them out. If you don't, they're going to take over. Those tough-minded people are in the conquering business. They have many gods, and none of them will lead you to the true God of heaven. On the contrary, they will try to draw you into their lifestyle. Your God, Jehovah, will take you through this time of testing, but you must stand tall as I've commanded you. Do it." So they did—at least at the beginning. But by and by, they began to compromise.

The former president of The Navigators, Lorne Sanny, made an interesting comment to me several years ago. He said, "If I could wrap up all of my father's counsel into one sentence, it would be four words, 'Get with it, son.'" That's not bad counsel, is it? That's what God said to Israel. "All right, get with it, sons. When you go into the land, take it. Stand alone. If you don't, you'll lose."

Let's go back to the first chapter of Judges and take a look at the situation when the Hebrews encountered the Canaanites. Three things characterized their lives when they moved from theory into reality.

1. <u>They were alone and uncertain.</u> The Israelites felt just like you feel when you face your first day on a new job, or when you come to the first day on the campus and you're a greenhorn freshman, or your first day in boot camp. Another example might be the way you feel when you first move out on your own and you discover you are the only one in your apartment complex who has strong moral convictions.

I once heard of a large apartment house in a metropolitan area where the residents were expected to participate in their favorite game. It came at the close of their weekly party when all the gals tossed their apartment keys out into a big pile near the swimming pool. All the guys then rushed to the pile and grabbed a key. Obviously, each guy would then spend the night with the girl whose key he had retrieved. In a case like that, either you stand alone or you don't. By the way, that kind of thing is not uncommon—and it doesn't occur just in California!

The Hebrews were alone and they were uncertain.

> Then Judah said to Simeon his brother, "Come up with me into the territory allotted me, that we may fight against the Canaanites; and I in turn will go with you into the territory allotted you" (Judg. 1:3).

Although God was with them, their leaders were dead and they really felt alone. They didn't know which direction to go. There was no manual to follow, so they decided to slug it out in teams. The Lord had simply told them, "When you get into the land, drive them out." They got into the land, but then they began to wonder, *Joshua's dead. Moses is dead. Wonder where we go from here?*

By the way, that is often the way your kiddos feel. They can't admit it in so many words, but that's how they feel. You are not there (and they don't want you there!). Yet in their hearts, they wonder, *To whom do I turn now?* They feel insecure and uncertain. And to make matters more complicated, the world *feeds* on uncertainty and aloneness. The majority preys on the unsuspecting. When in doubt, conformity is always ready to be called into action! The insecure will do anything to be a part of the group, to break that feeling of loneliness or isolation.

2. <u>Those Hebrews were inexperienced and vulnerable.</u> They had not seen firsthand God's mighty works in Egypt and the wilderness. The generation Moses and Joshua had addressed had died off.

> And all that generation also were gathered to their fathers; and there arose another generation after them who did not know the Lord, nor yet the work which He had done for Israel (Judg. 2:10).

How about that? The generation of combat troops who sat at Moses' feet and fought alongside Joshua, those veterans who had been involved in the victories that brought them into the land of Canaan were now gone from the scene. In their place there emerged the next generation. Two things were true of those new folks: they didn't know the Lord, and they didn't know what He had done in the previous years. They lacked the knowledge of what brought them there; they had no awareness of what their liberty had really cost!

Something massive is lost when a nation loses its historical and spiritual heritage. If for no other purpose, that alone is reason enough for us to be good students of history. It builds deep roots into our character to know the price others paid for what we enjoy, to be aware of the things God did on behalf of our parents and our grandparents.

We must never forget the importance of a historical and spiritual heritage in the training of our children. How does one go about such training? It's simple. Let them know what God has done in your life. And rehearse before them the significant battles of the past! Don't hesitate telling them what God did. If you fail to do that, how will they ever know?

I didn't know much about my own father's spiritual condition for the longest time. I'm honest—I'd lived with my dad for years. In fact, after my mother died, he moved in with us out here in California and stayed with us for several years. Yet, I still didn't know where he stood spiritually. Late one evening, years ago, I could wait no longer to find out.

I slipped into his room and said, "Dad, I want to talk to you about something that is very important. I want to talk to you about your relationship with the Lord. I have never heard you tell how you came to know Christ." Then I came right out and asked him, "Do you know the Lord?" That's when he first described to me what God had done in his life. Beginning with his boyhood, I journeyed with him through his spiritual pilgrimage as he reviewed his experiences at various stages of his life. Now there I was, a man more then forty years old, listening to my dad, and I was choking back tears of delight as he related his story to me. What a great time we had together that evening. I received full assurance of his salvation. What a relief! And on top of that, I gained fresh courage to soar even higher.

That's what can happen in the lives of your kids when they become acquainted with the victories you've experienced. They want to hear how you came to know the Lord. And they need to hear what God has done in your life. It brings them special delight and it gives them extra courage. And by the way, *don't leave out the failures*. Don't paint some flawless picture as though you qualify to sit for a modern-day portrait of Saint Francis of Assisi. (They know better than that!) Say to them, "when I got to that place in my life, I blew it! But let me tell you what God did in spite of that." Our kids can also learn from our failures.

What I have been illustrating here are the kinds of things that make up one's spiritual heritage. And that is precisely what those ancient Hebrews failed to relate to the next generation. They didn't do their homework. Deuteronomy 6 says, in effect, "Tell your kids." But the parents died and the kids didn't even know the Lord. Maybe they were too busy fighting battles. That can happen, can't it? No wonder the new generation was so vulnerable! They had never gone to battle. They didn't know how to handle life in the trenches. They were not hardened, made tough by enduring the rigors of war. They had never experienced opposition firsthand. So there they stood, not knowing the Lord, not knowing their history, and absolutely inexperienced in warfare.

It's a foolish, apathetic mistake to pamper and indulge our younger generation. Instead, we need to provide them with techniques for doing battle. Let's take a quick peek at Proverbs 29.

> The rod and reproof give wisdom, but a child who gets his own way brings shame to his mother (v. 15).

The marginal reference in my New American Standard Bible gives "But a child *left to himself*" as a more literal translation for "who gets his own way." Interestingly, the Hebrew text uses just the word for *left* and leaves it at that. "But a child *left* brings shame to his mother." Meaning what? Left in his room? No. It suggests "left in the same condition in which he was born." A child left without training will bring shame to his mother.

You might be engaged in spiritual activities day after day, even teaching Bible classes on a regular basis. You can be a faithful preacher, an evangelist, a Christian worker, a solid Christian business-man, and still omit the training of those little ones. And guess what? Chances are good they will grow up lacking the things that made you great. They *must* have your help.

Because those ancient Hebrews didn't have help from their parents, they didn't know how to handle hand-to-hand combat—not just physically, but especially spiritually and emotionally. In today's terms, they were spiritual wimps, ready to be picked off like sitting ducks.

Thus far we have considered two things that characterized the lives of the Hebrews as they encountered the Canaanites. They were alone and uncertain. And they were inexperienced and vulnerable. But there's a third characteristic we must not overlook.

3. They were surrounded and outnumbered.

> These nations are: the five lords of the Philistines and all the Canaanites and the Sidonians and the Hivites who lived in Mount Lebanon, from Mount Baal-hermon as far as Lebo-hamath. And they were for testing Israel, to find out if they would obey the commandments of the Lord, which He had commanded their fathers through Moses. And the sons of Israel lived among the Canaanites, the Hittites, the Amorites, the Perizzites, the Hivites, and the Jebusites (Judg. 3:3–5).

You're probably thinking, *Who in the world were all those "ites"? Why mention them?* They were the Canaanites, the various tribes poised for battle—tough-minded heathen who weren't about to give up their territory without a fight.

If you ever want an eye-opening experience, do a little study on the Canaanites. You will find, to your amazement, that pornography originated with them. You will also find that idolatry reached its most debasing level among the Canaanites. And you will find that it wasn't uncommon for the social diseases to devastate those ancient communities. One archaeologist writes this:

> New vistas of knowledge of Canaanite cults and their degrading character and debilitating effect have been opened up by the discovery of the Ras Shamra religious epic literature. . . . These cults were utterly immoral, effete, and corrupt, dangerously contaminating. . . . [2]

Those words describe the neighborhood the Hebrews moved into! Today, it would be like moving from a solid, sheltered home in Montana or Nebraska to live in downtown Los Angeles, San Francisco, New York, or Miami, surrounded by the dangerous, sleazy scenes that are so common among those sidewalk jungles. Day in, day out, day in, day out, that's where the Hebrew kids played. That's where they lived and moved and chose their circle of friends. No wonder God said, "Be distinct! Stand tall when tested by the Canaanites! If you don't, they'll ruin you."

And so, how do the Israelites react? Again, there are three reactions. *First of all, there was lack of total obedience.* In Deuteronomy 7:1–2, we read where the Lord had in essence said, "Don't let any of them live. Annihilate them." Well, they did that for a while, and they did a pretty good job of fighting. They were battling under Judah and under various tribes. But finally, when the going got tough and the battles got long, they backed off and let the enemy live.

> Now the Lord was with Judah, and they took possession of the hill country; but they could not drive out the inhabitants of the valley because they had iron chariots (Judg. 1:19).

Very interesting. I cannot help but wonder: *They could not or they would not?* You see, they came up against a tough group of Canaanites. And so their thinking probably went something like: *Hey, they're way down in the valley. What does it really matter? They won't bother anybody down there.* What a subtle inroad of limited courage! Someone once wrote, "Sow a thought, reap an act. Sow an act, reap a habit. Sow a habit, reap your character. Sow your character, reap your destiny." In the valley of the Canaanite country those Israelites sowed a thought: *Aw, let's not get so fanatical about this. A few Canaanites won't hurt. God's on our side.* So they left the door open. Notice how others followed suit. It's an incredible example of erosion. One compromise led to another, until what had begun as a tiny hole in the dike had become a deadly rupture.

> But the sons of Benjamin did not drive out the Jebusites who lived in Jerusalem; so the Jebusites have lived with the sons of Benjamin in Jerusalem to this day (Judg. 1:21).

And further . . .

> But Manasseh did not take possession of Beth-shean and its villages, or Taanach and its villages, or the inhabitants of Dor and its villages, or the inhabitants of Ibleam and its villages, or the inhabitants of Megiddo and its villages; so the Canaanites persisted in living in that land (v. 27).

Again and again (vv. 28-32), right down the line we find that God's people failed to destroy the inhabitants of the land.

Finally:

> Naphtali did not drive out the inhabitants of Beth-shemesh, or the inhabitants of Beth-anath, but lived among the Canaanites, the inhab-

itants of the land; and the inhabitants of Beth-shemesh and Beth-anath became forced labor for them (v. 33).

Did you catch that? The enemy is no longer down in the valley. Hebrews and Canaanites are now *living* together. The Hebrews started thinking, *Why sweat it? We'll just make these people serve us. We'll use them as forced labor. What harm can that do? No sense wasting all that manpower.* But the wicked and immoral ways of the conquered Canaanites eventually conquered their captors.

Got the picture? Are you seeing the analogy, my eagle friend? Standing tall when tested takes courage—constant, relentless, never-give-up courage! You can be sure that the old flesh will fight for its arousal and satisfaction. All it takes is a little rationalization—just a little. Just look the other way. Just shrug it off. Don't sweat it. And before long you have a rattlesnake in your sleeping bag.

After a few fast-moving years, that little tolerance of rebellion in your home leads to a child you can no longer handle. And by the time he reaches his teen years, he rules the place. If you compromise, you will ultimately have to pay the fiddler. The way of the transgressor is indeed hard!

What exactly happened? Three things, actually.

First, remember, *they lacked total obedience.* They rationalized around it; they mentally imagined obedience, but they acted out compromise.

Second, they suffered a loss of spiritual distinctiveness. Because they lacked total obedience, they decided to leave the Canaanites in the valley. Instead of destroying them, the Hebrews used the Canaanites as forced labor, but eventually the Israelites themselves bowed down to the Canaanite gods.

> Then the sons of Israel did evil in the sight of the Lord, and served the Baals, and they forsook the Lord, the God of their fathers, who had brought them out of the land of Egypt, and followed other gods from among the gods of the peoples who were around them, and bowed themselves down to them; thus they provoked the Lord to anger (Judg. 2:10–12).

Can you believe it? They forsook the Lord and served Baal and the Ashtaroth. Frankly, in my study of Ashtaroth, I discovered there isn't much I would be free to discuss in this book about the subject. It includes some of the most debasing, obscene things you can imagine. In fact, one writer, although apparently an unbeliever, wrote, "The author now begs freedom from more detail." You seldom come across an author who says that. He chose not to add any more descriptive explanations concerning the worship of Ashtaroth. And yet those Hebrews bowed down and served that idol. How could they? Why did they? The answer can be given in one word: *Compromise.* Through compromise their spiritual distinctiveness was eroded.

The third Israelite reaction was a looseness of marital ties.

> And they took their daughters for themselves as wives, and gave their own daughters to their sons, and served their gods (Judg. 3:6).

Never fails, does it? Let a nation drift morally and before long the same values or lack of values will move right into the home. The Israelites chose immoral friends, and before long their marital ties were loosened.

> And the sons of Israel did what was evil in the sight of the Lord, and forgot the Lord their God, and served the Baals and the Asheroth (v. 7).

Sow the wind and, for sure, you'll reap the whirlwind. Eagles may be strong birds, but when the wind velocity gets fierce enough, it takes an enormous amount of strength to survive. Only the ultrapowerful can make it through the whirlwind.

Evangelist Billy Graham, while speaking to a packed house at the Urbana '84 Student Missions Convention in Illinois, addressed the importance of Christians being people of great inner strength.

> Not long ago *Newsweek* magazine reported on what it called the new wave of mountain men. It's estimated that there are some sixty thousand serious mountain climbers in the United States. But in the upper echelon of serious climbers is a small elite group known as "hard men." For them climbing mountains and scaling sheer rock faces is a way of life. In many cases, climbing is a part of their whole commitment to life. And their ultimate experience is called free soloing: climbing with no equipment and no safety ropes.
>
> John Baker is considered by many to be the best of the hard men. He has free-soloed some of the most difficult rock faces in the United States with no safety rope and no climbing equipment of any kind. His skill has not come easily. It has been acquired through commitment, dedi-

cation and training. His wife says she can't believe his dedication. When John isn't climbing, he's often to be found in his California home hanging by his fingertips to strengthen his arms and hands.

Where are the hard men and women for Jesus? Where are those who will bring all their energies to bear for the sake of Christ? That's the kind of people it's going to take to spread the gospel around the world in these closing years of the twentieth century.[3]

Three Encouragements for Standing Tall

Before closing this chapter allow me to offer three suggestions for standing tall.

First: *Standing tall starts with the way we think*. It has to do with the *mind*. As I've said so often, being a person of inner strength is really a mental factor: excellence starts in the mind. It has to do with the way we think about God, ourselves, and others. Then it grows into the way we think about business, the way we think about dating, the way we think about marriage and the family, the way we think about the system that is designed to destroy faith and bring us down to a lower standard.

Second: *Standing tall calls for strong discipline*. This has to do with the *will*. Disciplining the eyes, the ears, the hands, the feet. Keeping moral tabs on ourselves, refusing to let down the standards. People of strength know how to turn right thinking into action—even when insistent feelings don't agree.

Third: *Standing tall limits your choice of personal friends*. This has to do with *relationships*. What appears harmless can prove to be dangerous. Perhaps this is as important as the other two factors combined. Cultivate wrong friendships and you're a goner. This is why we are warned not to be deceived regarding the danger of wrong associations. Without realizing it, we could be playing with fire. That is exactly how the ancient Hebrews met their Waterloo.

Several weeks ago, a personal friend of mine told me a true story that illustrates so vividly the reality of what I've been saying all the way through this chapter.

Two young women from Southern California spent the day doing some last-minute Christmas shopping in Tijuana, a Mexican border town several miles below San Diego. After a successful day of bargain hunting, they returned to their car. One of the ladies glanced down in the gutter and noticed something moving, sort of squirming, as if in pain. As they bent down and looked closer, the two women saw what appeared to be a dog—a tiny Chihuahua—struggling for its life. It was breathing heavily, shivering, and barely able to move. Their hearts went out to the pathetic little animal. Their compassion wouldn't let them drive off and leave it there to die.

They decided to take it home with them and do their best to nurse it back to health. Afraid of being stopped and having the little creature detected by border patrol officers, they carefully placed it on some papers among their packages in the trunk of their car. No problem. Within minutes they were back in California and only a couple of hours from home. One of the women held the sick little Chihuahua the rest of the way home.

As they pulled up in front of one gal's home, they decided she would be the one to keep the little orphan through the night and do everything she could to help it regain strength. She tried feeding it some of her food, but it wouldn't eat. She patted it, talked to it, cuddled it, and finally wrapped it in a small blanket and placed it beneath the covers on her bed to sleep beside her all through the night. She kept feeling it to make sure it was okay.

By early the next morning she could see it was not doing at all well. Before dawn she decided to take it to an emergency animal clinic nearby. Handing the weakened animal to the doctor on duty, she began to describe all the things she had done to help the tiny creature.

He quickly interrupted her and asked, "Where did you *get* this animal?"

For fear of being reprimanded for bringing an animal across the border, she told him that she was keeping it for a friend who had found it.

"I'm not letting you leave," he insisted sternly, "until you tell me where you got this thing."

She said, "We were shopping in Tijuana and found this little Chihuahua in the gutter near our car. Our hearts went out to it when . . ."

"This is no Chihuahua, young lady. What you brought home with you is a rabid Mexican river rat!"

What appeared to be harmless to these two young women proved to be extremely dangerous. The same is true of relationships—peer pressure can be downright deadly. Standing tall when testing comes (and teaching our young to do the same) reflects the way we think about God, ourselves, and others. It isn't easy. It takes strong discipline to maintain high, personal standards and to avoid undesirable friendships. But most of all it takes courage. Without courage we can forget about soaring above mediocrity.

15

STANDING FIRM
WHEN DISCOURAGED

*E*ven eagle types have down days—blue days; dark and dismal days; the kind of days my keen-thinking friend, the late Joe Bayly, once portrayed so vividly in his "Psalm in a Hotel Room."

> I'm alone Lord
> alone
> a thousand miles from home.
> There's no one here who knows my name
> except the clerk
> and he spelled it wrong
> no one to eat dinner with
> laugh at my jokes
> listen to my gripes
> be happy with me about what happened today
> and say that's great.
> No one cares.
> There's just this lousy bed
> and slush in street outside
> between the buildings.
> I feel sorry for myself
> and I've plenty of reason
> to.
> Maybe I ought to say
> I'm on top of it
> praise the Lord
> things are great
> but they're not.
> Tonight
> it's all
> gray slush.[1]

Can you remember a recent "gray slush" day? Of course you can. So can I. The laws of fairness and justice were displaced by a couple of Murphy's Laws. Your dream dissolved into a nightmare. High hopes took a hike. Good intentions got lost in a comedy of errors, only this time nobody was laughing. You didn't soar, you slumped. Instead of "pressing on the upward way," you felt like telling Bunyan to move over as you slid down into his Slough of Despond near Doubting Castle, whose owner was Giant Despair.

Discouragement is just plain *awful.*

A HOPE TRANSPLANT

One of the greatest benefits to be gleaned from the Bible is perspective. When we get discouraged, we temporarily lose our perspective. Little things become mammoth. A slight irritation, such as a pebble in a shoe, seems huge. Motivation is drained away and, worst of all, hope departs.

God's Word is tailor-made for gray-slush days. It sends a beam of light through the fog. It signals safety when we fear we'll never make it through. Such big-picture perspective gives us a hope transplant, and within a brief period of time, we have escaped the bleak and boring and we're back at soaring.

There is a magnificent thought nestled in the fifteenth chapter of Romans that promises all this. To the surprise of some folks, the promise is connected to a major reason God has preserved the Old Testament:

> For whatever was written in earlier times was written for our instruction, that through perseverance and the encouragement of the Scriptures we might have hope (Rom. 15:4).

Go back and read that again—this time much more slowly. Linger over each phrase and then we'll analyze them.

When the writer refers to that which was "written in earlier times" he had us in mind, too. All those things "were written for our instruction." *Instruction* is a broad, general word that means "teaching." Whatever passage you choose from the Old Testament—from Genesis to Malachi—those writings were preserved to teach us things today, right now! God had an ultimate goal in mind: that "we might have hope." And what is it that leads to such a goal? Two things: "perseverance" and "encouragement" from the Scriptures. Again, the goal is hope. God has not designed a life of despondency for us. He wants His people to have hope. And He says such hope comes from the teaching of the Old Testament. Through endurance and through encouragement from the Scriptures, we can gain hope

As you sit there you may say, "I don't have much endurance. Furthermore, I feel terribly discouraged." Read the next verse. It is written for everyone who feels that way.

> Now may the God who gives perseverance and encouragement grant you to be of the same mind with one another according to Christ Jesus (Rom. 15:5).

God wants to give us both perseverance and encouragement. He says, in effect, "If you will submit yourself to the teaching of Old Testament truth, I will give you perseverance (the word literally means 'endurance'—that ability to hang in there) and 'encouragement'—a lifting up of your spirits." He will replace discouragement with fresh hope. And, ultimately, what?

> That with one accord you may with one voice glorify the God and Father of our Lord Jesus Christ (Rom. 15:6).

What a priceless nugget of truth there is in these three verses! What I find here is the scriptural basis for encouragement. God offers instruction, but then it's our move. We must *accept* His instruction and *apply* it to our lives. Then, and only then, can we expect to cash in on the benefits of His instruction. So you see, application is the essential link between instruction and change.

Imagine, if you will, that you work for a company whose president found it necessary to travel out of the country and spend an extended period of time abroad. So he says to you and the other trusted employees, "Look, I'm going to leave. And while I'm gone, I want you to pay close attention to the business. You manage things while I'm away. I will write you regularly. When I do, I will instruct you in what you should do from now until I return from this trip." Everyone agrees. He leaves and stays gone for a couple of years. During that time he writes often, communicating his desires and concerns. Finally he returns. He walks up to the front door of the company and immediately discovers everything is in a mess—weeds flourishing in the flower beds, windows broken across the front of the building, the gal at the front desk dozing, loud music roaring from several offices, two or three people engaged in horseplay in the back room. Instead of making a profit, the business has suffered a great loss. Without hesitation he calls everyone together and with a frown asks, "What happened? Didn't you get my letters?" You say, "Oh, yeah, sure. We got all your letters. We've even bound them in a book. And some of us have memorized them. In fact, we have 'letter study' every Sunday. You know, those were really great letters." I think the president would then ask, "But what did you *do* about my instructions? And, no doubt, the employees would respond, "Do? Well, nothing. But we read every one!"

In the very same way, God has sent us His instruction. He has preserved every word of it in a Book, the Bible. It's all there, just as He communicated it to us. When He returns for His own, He is not going to ask us how much we memorized or how often we met for study. No, He will want to know, "What did you *do* about my instructions?" He promises us hope—relief from discouragement. Yes, it's available. And we can actually stand firm through discouraging times but only if we apply His instructions.

Hard as it may be for you to believe, you will be able to walk right through those "gray slush" days with confidence. The One who gives perseverance and encouragement will escort you through the down days, never leaving you in the lurch. Discouragement may be awful, but it is not terminal. You will soar again.

GUIDELINES FOR HANDLING DISCOURAGEMENT

From this nugget of truth in Romans 15, let's return to the Old Testament Book of Judges for a brief look at the life of a man you may have never even heard of. He was an ancient eagle type named Gideon. Before meeting him, however, it will help if we first read the key verse of the Book of Judges. It is the very last statement in the book and succinctly reveals why Judges is a record of defeat and failure.

> In those days there was no king in Israel; everyone did what was right in his own eyes (Judg. 21:25).

The first half of the verse explains the latter. There was no monarch in charge, no one to give direction or set the pace, no one to model truth or instruct the people in righteousness. The result was predictable: "Everyone did what was right in his own eyes." "Do your own thing" is not some modern motto. It began in the days of the judges. They were adrift in a sea of shifting feelings and carnal impulses. Each person did what felt good. And so, in light of that, we should not be surprised to read these words earlier in the book: "The sons of Israel did what was evil in the sight of the Lord" (Judg. 6:1). When folks are free to choose the path of least resistance, wrongdoing becomes commonplace—it's the direction most choose to go.

Historical Situation

Let's spend a few moments reconstructing the historical scene. We learned in my previous chapter that when the Israelites came into the land of Canaan, they had a chance to drive out all the enemies, as God had commanded; but they compromised. In the final analysis they failed to do that. They left some Canaanites in the valley, and that number began to grow. When word of this compromise passed to another tribe of Israel, they followed suit and also left another pocket of idolators in another part of the Promised Land. And it wasn't long before some of the heathen tribes actually outnumbered the Hebrews. Finally, the tail wagged the dog. The Israelites began to serve the Canaanites' gods. Through intermingling of lifestyle and intermarriage, it soon reached a point where it was hard to tell an Israelite from a Canaanite. By failing to stand courageously, God's chosen people lost their distinctiveness as well as their identity.

But the tragic part of the story is that the consequences of disobedience do not decrease; they intensify. Look for yourself:

> And the power of Midian prevailed against Israel. Because of Midian the sons of Israel made for themselves the dens which were in the mountains and the caves and the strongholds (Judg. 6:2).

In other words, they were forced to live like animals. They had *no homes.* Their "gray slush" days were now coming in spades. Think of the discouragement!

> For it was when Israel had sown, that the Midianites would come up with the Amalekites and the sons of the east and go against them. So

they would camp against them and destroy the produce of the earth as far as Gaza, and leave no sustenance in Israel as well as no sheep, ox, or donkey (Judg. 6:3–4).

How demoralizing! Not only were the Israelites stripped of their homes, but they had *no peace* either. When they planted crops to grow food for their families, the Midianites, along with the Amalekites, invaded. They mercilessly destroyed the crops after taking just enough produce for themselves. So the Israelites began to starve. On top of all their other troubles, now they had *no sustenance.*

> For they would come up with their livestock and their tents, they would come in like locusts for number, both they and their camels were innumerable; and they came into the land to devastate it (v. 5).

Try to imagine such a scene. If you've never planted and then lost what you planted, you don't know how discouraging that could be. I, personally, have the gift of killing whatever is green! Whatever I try to plant dies—and I mean fast! Believe it or not, I tried no less than nine different times to plant grass in our front yard. Nine times! I would lie awake at night wondering what demons were out there in the soil stealing those tiny blades of grass from us. I began to feel like an Israelite being invaded by the Midianites and the Amalekites. But we persevered to the end. Which, being translated, means that I hired a gardener. When I got *my* hands out of the soil, presto! Instant green. He tactfully asked me to look but not touch.

Now in the case of the Hebrews, the reason their crops didn't grow was clear: the enemy devastated their land! Wholesale discouragement swept over everyone: "Israel was brought very low." In fact, one translation says, "Israel was impoverished (MLB)." How true! They had no homes. They had no food. They had no belongings they could claim as their own. They were waist deep in "gray slush" discouragement. People may have talked of those days when courageous eagles once flew, but now none could be seen in the sky. So much for the historical scene.

Spiritual Analogy

Picture for a moment the barrenness and bleakness that happens in a life when compromise occurs. It doesn't come immediately. At first it's fun to run with the wrong crowd. There's some zip, a little excitement; there's a measure of thrill and pizzazz in being a part of the in-group. But inevitably the fleshly investment starts to yield its carnal dividends. And when that happens you suffer as you've never suffered before. At first, it may have seemed a little stimulating for the Hebrews to worship the demonic gods of Amalek and Midian. Finally, however, those idols vomited out tragic consequences upon Israel. So much so that Israel was forced to live in dens like wild animals, discouraged and impoverished. These sad words describe their misery: "Israel was brought very low because of Midian . . ." (Judg. 6:6).

Perhaps the words *"very low"* paint a picture of bleakness that describes you at this very moment. You have ignored God's warnings and pushed your strong convictions aside as you associated with the wrong crowd. But now you are at the end of your rope. You're discouraged. You have failed miserably. And, of all things, you're seeing your life pass in review as you read about the bleak barrenness of this ancient nation. You're thinking, *What a terrible way to live!*

All of us have spent time in that miserable camp called Reaping What Was Sown. En route, there's enough pleasure to make it seem like fun, but when it's all said and done, it's downright awful. There is no discouragement like the discouragement that comes from self-generated wrongdoing. Enduring the consequences of one's own irresponsibility creates feelings of grief and discouragement that defy description. No one ever said it better than F. B. Meyer:

> This is the bitterest of all—to know that suffering need not have been; that it has resulted from indiscretion and inconsistency; that it is the harvest of one's own sowing; that the vulture which feeds on the vitals is a nestling of one's own rearing. Ah me! This is pain! There is an inevitable Nemesis in life. The laws of the heart and home, of the soul and human life, cannot be violated with impunity. Sin may be forgiven; the fire of penalty may be changed into the fire of trial: the love of God may seem nearer and dearer than ever and yet there is the awful pressure of pain; the trembling heart; the failing of eyes and pining of soul; the harp on the willows; the refusal of the lip to sing the Lord's song.[2]

Practical Correction

That's enough about the problem. What we really need are specific suggestions that get us back on track. I find no less than five such guidelines woven through the biblical narrative concerning the Israelites and the Midianites.

1. Openly acknowledge what caused your condition.

> So Israel was brought very low because of Midian, and the sons of Israel cried to the Lord.
>
> Now it came about when the sons of Israel cried to the Lord on account of Midian, that the Lord sent a prophet to the sons of Israel, and he said to them, "Thus says the Lord, the God of Israel, 'It was I who brought you up from Egypt, and brought you out from the house of slavery. And I delivered you from the hands of the Egyptians and from the hands of all your oppressors, and dispossessed them before you and gave you their land, and I said to you, "I am the Lord your God; you shall not fear the gods of the Amorites in whose land you live. But you have not obeyed Me"'" (Judg. 6:6–10).

That's what I call *direct counsel*. But, you'll notice, it comes on the heels of the Israelites' cry for help. God never holds back when we openly acknowledge the whole truth of our condition. And doing that, by the way, is a mark of excellence. Hold nothing back! Even though it may be painful, total honesty is important. If you are discouraged because of compromise, a truthful acknowledgment of your condition is the place to begin.

Openly admit that you have failed to stand alone as a true child of God and therefore you have begun to live like a heathen Midianite. The problem is you weren't built to live that way. As we have seen throughout the pages of this book, you were meant to soar, not to slump and stumble through life. You have allowed someone else to call your cadence. You're marching out of step with your Instructor. And the Lord speaks directly: "You have not obeyed Me."

What stands out in my mind, though, is the swift and open fashion with which our God deals with wrong. Our problem is that we usually wait much too long to acknowledge our need and call for help.

I love the story that describes Peter when he stepped out of the boat onto the water. As he was walking toward the Lord on the stormy sea (what an incredible experience), he suddenly looked around and was seized with fear. Scripture says, "Beginning to sink, he cried. . . ." Did you get that? *"Beginning* to sink, he cried out." That provides a perfect reminder for what we must do when we find ourselves sinking. Don't wait to cry out. Yell "HELP!" fast.

Are you ready for some superencouraging news? When we openly acknowledge our condition before our God, He won't reject us. Nor will He put us on probation and watch us squirm. On the contrary, we'll find the Lord to be explicitly interested and compassionate, quick to forgive. I find that wonderfully inviting.

And now, back to the story. We're about to meet Gideon:

> And the angel of the Lord appeared to him and said to him, "The Lord is with you, O valiant warrior." Then Gideon said to him, "Oh my lord, if the Lord is with us, why then has all this happened to us? And where are all His miracles which our fathers told us about, saying, 'Did not the Lord bring us up from Egypt?' But now the Lord has abandoned us and given us into the hand of Midian" (vv. 12–13).

While Gideon is evaluating the situation, he is confused. So he says, "Where's the Lord in all of this?" Unlike those around him, his own personal walk with the Lord has been consistent. But he has suffered because the great majority of those around him have not lived pleasing lives before the Lord. Now he's wrestling with doubts. *How much is the Lord really with us?* he wonders. *Has He abandoned us?*

Look at the Lord's answer:

> And the Lord looked at him and said, "Go in this your strength and deliver Israel from the hand of Midian. Have I not sent you?" And he said to Him, "O Lord, how shall I deliver Israel? Behold, my family is the least in Manasseh, and I am the youngest in my father's house." But the Lord said to him, "Surely I will be with you, and you shall defeat Midian as one man" (vv. 14–16).

What confidence-building words! In effect He was saying, "You'll stand firm, Gideon, 'as one man.'" (Never doubt the impact of one strong individual.) And when Gideon was convinced that what he heard came from the Lord, he built an altar.

> Then Gideon built an altar there to the Lord and named it The Lord is Peace. To this day it is still in Ophrah of the Abiezrites (v. 24).

This provides us with the second guideline.

2. <u>Focus directly on the Lord, not on the odds against you.</u> As I sit here today writing these words about standing firm when discouraged,

I realize some will think, *Oh, you don't have any idea of the odds that are against me, Chuck. Where I work . . . where I go to school . . . in my particular profession it's filled with skeptics and cynics—I mean, you can't believe the odds against me!* I hear you, but quite frankly, my answer stands. Everything depends on where your focus is. You must discipline yourself to focus directly on the Lord, not on those odds!

At first all Gideon could see were odds. Finally, he heard the Lord's word, "Have I not sent you?" Then Gideon says, "I'm the youngest." He felt incapable. He felt as if he were not the man to do the job. And the Lord said, "Look, I'll be with you. Even though you're one man, you'll do it." And He promised him, "Peace to you, do not fear; you shall not die." How comforting!

Get this straight and never forget it: You will not stand alone when outnumbered or stand tall when tested or stand firm when discouraged if your focus remains on the odds. Your eyes must be trained on the Lord.

It's helpful for me to remember that our eyes are focused on one of four places at all times: on our *circumstance*, on *others*, on *ourself*, or on *the Lord*. If they focus on any one of the first three and not on the Lord, we will drift and ultimately fail. It's only a matter of time. It took awhile, but Gideon finally got his eyes focused on the Lord.

While speaking last week with one of the foremost authorities on eagles, I learned a fact nothing short of fascinating. An eagle's eyes are amazingly keen. It has an unbelievable ability to focus on specific objects that are vast distances away. Remember, as I mentioned in chapter 5, it's not uncommon for these phenomenal birds to spot small fish in a lake miles away.

My point is obvious: If we are hoping to develop eaglelike qualities in our commitment to excellence, we must cultivate a keen focus on the Lord, not on the odds.

The next time we find our friend Gideon, he is all alone, outnumbered, opposed—but definitely *not* discouraged.

> Then all the Midianites and the Amalekites and the sons of the east assembled themselves; and they crossed over and camped in the valley of Jezreel. So the Spirit of the Lord came upon Gideon; and he blew a trumpet, and the Abiezerites were called together to follow him. And he sent messengers throughout Manasseh, and they also were called together to follow him; and he sent messengers to Asher, Zebulun, and Naphtali, and they came up to meet them (vv. 33–35).

What's happening? Gideon is gathering a following. He stood alone. And the Lord had said, in effect, "You stand alone, I'll take care of the odds." Gideon did just that. By the use of a trumpet, he made it known on which side he stood.

3. Declare your allegiance publicly. Somehow that trumpet blast announced something significant to the people in those days. I don't fully understand how they could interpret what it meant. But they interpreted it to mean, "That man is the one to follow." God used the blowing of that trumpet to call a group to follow Him. When Gideon declared his allegiance publicly, God honored his courage. And others fell in rank behind him.

Have you made it known to others where you stand spiritually? I'm not suggesting a trumpet, but I am suggesting a clarion communication of your allegiance to Christ as Lord.

You may still be single and interested in discovering God's partner for your life. Have you compromised morally, or have you made it clear where you stand? If you have compromised, that explains why you're struggling with such feelings of discouragement. Perhaps not one person you are dating knows where you stand spiritually. If that is true, no wonder you're having such a battle in your intimate life! You have not declared your allegiance. Until you do, you will not stand strong and stable and secure. Don't be afraid to blow the trumpet of your testimony. It is amazing what occurs when you do.

A student on a college campus or a soldier in the military who declares his faith in Jesus Christ is used of God to be a leader for others to rally around. It has also been my observation that those who fail to take a stand are intimidated until they do. But as soon as a stand is taken, it is just beautiful how it disarms the enemy.

The remarkable story of Jim Vaus is such an account. On one occasion years ago, I heard Jim tell about the time he was secretly entangled with the Mickey Cohen gang. What made that rather interesting is that at the same time Jim was also employed by the Los Angeles Police Department. Fun, huh? During that time the Lord brought Jim Vaus to Himself. It occurred during the 1949 Billy Graham Crusade in Los Angeles. And the conversion was trumpeted across the pages of the newspaper, since Vaus was a fairly notorious individual.

When Jim's allegiance to Christ was declared, naturally the Mafia heard about it. The new convert was then faced with a decision. I will never forget his words, which went something like this: "I was in my home shortly after I had given my testimony at a Billy Graham Crusade. I'd turned the lights out in one room after another. Suddenly, I stopped and looked out in my driveway as two long, black limousines pulled up—very familiar cars." Knowing full well that the mission of those inside the cars was to kill him, Jim prayed, "Lord, my life is in Your hands. I trust You right now." He opened the front door and walked right out in the driveway—no doubt a surprise to the occupants of the limousines. Immediately the doors on both vehicles swung open and several men in three-piece suits stepped out. They stood in a group around Jim as he told them calmly yet directly, "I have trusted Jesus Christ and Him only as my Lord and my Savior. And I can no longer work with you." God marvelously protected him from harm and preserved his life. Jim stood alone, and he stood firm. He didn't hide his faith or deny his Lord. When he declared his allegiance at that threatening moment, God changed the gang's plan to kill him. As his heart pounded in his throat, Jim watched the men return to the limousines and drive away.

This reminds me of one of the greatest promises in all the Proverbs: "When a man's ways are pleasing to the Lord, He makes even his enemies to be at peace with him" (Prov. 16:7).

I have seen that happen in a Marine Corps barracks. I've seen it happen on a college campus. I've seen it happen in a business office. I've seen it happen in a medical group. I've seen it happen in a neighborhood. When you declare your allegiance to Him, God does something wonderful in the lives of others around you.

The story of Gideon continues with an intriguing plot. Read it carefully so that you don't miss the way God whittles down the number of people who will fight with Gideon. It's amazing!

> And the Lord said to Gideon, "The people who are with you are too many for Me to give Midian into their hands, lest Israel become boastful, saying, 'My own power has delivered me.' Now therefore come, proclaim in the hearing of the people, saying, 'Whoever is afraid and trembling, let him return and depart from Mount Gilead.'" So 22,000 people returned, but 10,000 remained (Judg. 7:2–3).

That tells you how thrilled most of the Israelites were about fighting. As soon as they had a chance, they split—22,000 of them! It also tells you how many people had begun to follow Gideon, at least

32,000. He originally had 32,000 people on his heels following him, but now it's down to 10,000. But God isn't through. He always works out a way to keep us trusting Him, doesn't He?

> Then the Lord said to Gideon, "The people are still too many; bring them down to the water and I will test them for you there. Therefore it shall be that he of whom I say to you, 'This one shall go with you,' he shall go with you; but everyone of whom I say to you, 'This one shall not go with you,' he shall not go." So he brought the people down to the water. And the Lord said to Gideon, "You shall separate everyone who laps the water with his tongue, as a dog laps, as well as everyone who kneels to drink." Now the number of those who lapped, putting their hand to their mouth, was 300 men; but all the rest of the people kneeled to drink water. And the Lord said to Gideon, "I will deliver you with the 300 men who lapped and will give the Midianites into your hands; so let all the other people go, each man to his home" (vv. 4–7).

4. Remember that God prefers to work through a remnant. God does His best work, it seems, when those who serve Him are fewer than those against Him. The twelve disciples who walked with Christ, for instance, formed a remnant. People who change a campus are invariably not the majority, but a remnant. Those on the ball team who stand firm in their testimony are fewer than those who don't. The same is true in God's world mission program. The missionaries are always fewer in number than those being reached. God prefers to work in that unusual circumstance, and that is exactly what happened in Gideon's case.

These few fighting eagle types became courageous, devoted to God, and absolutely invincible. It was only a matter of time before the Midianites fell into their hands.

> Now the Midianites and the Amalekites and all the sons of the east were lying in the valley as numerous as locusts; and their camels were without number, as numerous as the sand on the seashore. When Gideon came, behold, a man was relating a dream to his friend. And he said, "Behold, I had a dream; a loaf of barley bread was tumbling into the camp of Midian, and it came to the tent and struck it so that it fell, and turned it upside down so that the tent lay flat." And his friend answered and said, "This is nothing less than the sword of Gideon the son of Joash, a man of Israel; God has given Midian and all the camp into his hand" (vv. 12–14).

Gideon was simply listening to a fellow tell his dream, but look what happened:

> And it came about when Gideon heard the account of the dream and its interpretation, that he bowed in worship . . . (v. 15).

Suddenly Gideon realized, "God *is* working!" And at that moment, he paused to worship. He communed with his God. He "practiced the presence of God," as the old Puritans would say.

As a result of this strange strategy, God used Gideon to turn the tide. He won the battle. He led God's people to victory. Now, for the first time since many could remember, they had homes, they had crops, they had camels and horses. Finally, the Israelites had begun to walk in prosperity. Unlike before, when they had not fought for victory, the Israelites were now humble and grateful. In fact, they invited Gideon to be their leader.

> Then the men of Israel said to Gideon, "Rule over us, both you and your son, also your son's son, for you have delivered us from the hand of Midian." But Gideon said to them, "I will not rule over you, nor shall my son rule over you; the Lord shall rule over you" (Judg. 8:22–23).

5. <u>Do not accept the glory after God uses your life.</u> Our most vulnerable moment, as you may have heard before, is immediately after a great victory. With masterful restraint, Gideon models godly (and rare) humility.

It is exciting for me to imagine how some who read this chapter will put these guidelines to use. You will discover that you can declare your allegiance and you will begin to stand alone. You will give it a try. God will change the hearts of those who were once enemies. He may even give you a large following. He may use you in the lives of those in the office or on the campus or in the neighborhood as you have never been used before.

Those who appreciate your stand will say, "Wow! What a great person you are!" *Wait* a minute. *Watch* yourself at that vulnerable moment. Continually think of yourself as a mirror, reflecting the light of Jesus Christ to them, or as a servant, honoring the Master. Don't let the crowd get their eyes on you and make an idol out of you. Keep giving God the glory.

Isn't it interesting that when God uses our lives and we truly begin to soar as an eagle, it is easy to gravitate to one of two erroneous extremes? Either we embrace a false humility, failing to recognize and exercise our gifts as fully as we could; or we fall into the clutches of pride and arrogance so totally that God no longer uses us in mighty ways.

Gideon guards against the latter by saying, "Look, I won't rule over you." In fact, if you study the latter part of his life, you'll find that he continued to live in his own home and he ultimately died a very quiet death. I am truly impressed with the strength of the man's life and the humility with which he wore it. Gideon was used of God to break the people free from the grip of discouragement, but he refused to prance around like a peacock when everyone sang his praises. God is still looking for such people!

THE INFLUENCE OF JUST ONE

Periodically, I return to a single verse of Scripture from the pen of the prophet Ezekiel because it never fails to challenge me.

> "And I searched for a man among them who should build up the wall and stand in the gap before Me for the land, that I should not destroy it; but I found no one" (Ezek. 22:30).

Same God, same need, different era. Here God admits His pursuit for one person who would stand in the gap. He's not looking for a flock; just one eagle will do. Today God is still looking for Gideons. But there is one major problem: They are scarce.

You may be that one person God wants to use in your sphere of influence. And if it is discouragement that is keeping you from being totally available to Him, come to terms with whatever brought it on. Get rid of it so that God can launch you and use you greatly.

I remember an evening several years ago when my family and I did something we had never done before. It was about eight o'clock, and we were finishing supper after a very big day. I was tired and weary. And everyone else seemed fairly low, too. I said, "Okay, let's hear two things from everybody at the table tonight: your *lowest moment* in the day and your *highest moment* in the day." It was a little tough getting going, but once we did, everybody participated. From the youngest to me, the dad—all the way around the table. You know what I discovered? I discovered hurts that I had not even known were there in that one day. We listened. We cared. We wept. We comforted. We encouraged. And I discovered heights that I didn't know were there because until then we'd never given a chance for them to be shared. We took our time. We rejoiced. We even applauded! For all I know, we may have hatched a few eagle eggs. Hopefully, we all began to soar a little higher. You might want to try that same project tonight.

Yes, eagle types can have down days. Sometimes the cold, gray slush can get pretty thick. In fact, some eagles get so weighed down with discouragement that they can't get airborne again. Why? Because there is no one with whom to share their burden. Maybe this is the place for you to begin. Cultivate one friend with whom you can share your discouragement. That could free you and get you back in the air as a modern-day "Gideon eagle." The Lord knows, we can always use a few more! Not only does He know it, but He is forever on a search for one who will be courageous enough to "stand in the gap."

Are you available?

16

STANDING STRONG
WHEN TEMPTED

T hroughout these chapters I have been addressing the things that lead to excellence. I have also been exposing the things that hinder us from achieving it. From start to finish, my favorite word picture has been the eagle—soaring high and free, thousands of feet above the distractions of earth, virtually impervious to the turbulence and temperatures of its habitat. I have chosen the eagle because no other creature better exemplifies my theme: living above the level of mediocrity. Eagles represent independence, responsibility, strength, freedom, keenness of vision, rarity, and a dozen other admirable traits that we wish to emulate.

But, though strong of heart and awesome on wing, eagles are not superbirds incapable of being captured or immune to accident or disease. Like all other creatures, they have weaknesses. They can make mistakes, misjudge distances, and miscalculate dives. Falling victim to such perils can leave them with broken bones, earthbound and defenseless, soon to be devoured by much slower and less elegant yet more powerful beasts of prey.

We seldom think of eagles in such vulnerable conditions. Can you remember the last time you saw a photograph or drawing of a helpless eagle? I never have seen one. The eagle is always portrayed in graceful flight or diving for the kill, never in the claws or mouth of its captor. And for that reason, it is easy to become so convinced of the eagle's magnitude, solitude, and fortitude that we cannot imagine its ever falling prey to a mightier creature. But just remember I am using the eagle only as a symbol. To think of the eagle (really, ourselves) as invincible is to immortalize the analogy and to carry it to the point of fantasy. The pages of history are strewn with the litter of "eagle skeletons," each one a mute reminder of how the mighty have fallen.

FOUR POWERFUL PERILS

May I remind you of four of the more powerful perils that can level even the mightiest of eagle types? They are fortune, fame, power, and pleasure. Each works overtime to win a hearing, to gain a foothold, to woo us in. With relentless persistence, each message bombards the eagle's nest with missilelike pleadings for acceptance. Whether subliminal, subtle, strong, or supreme, these messages search for chinks in our armor as they appeal to our natural appetites. "Get rich!" (fortune). "Become known!" (fame). "Gain control!" (power). "Be satisfied!" (pleasure). Each of these attractive snares invites our attention, holds out a juicy carrot, makes beautiful promises; yet each is an enemy always crouching and ready to plunge. Being masters of deceit, these messages employ one favorite method throughout our lives—*temptation.* And why not? It's worked for centuries. All it takes to be effective is our nod of acceptance—it doesn't even need to be visible—and the once-strong, high-flying eagle is reduced to mediocrity, like the majority. My concern is that we stay riveted to reality. Let all who soar take heed lest they take a fatal dive!

A ONCE-MIGHTY EAGLE WHO BIT THE DUST

Rather than leaving everything in the theoretical realm, let's put a flesh-and-blood example before us. I find that it's much easier to build a case with a real person than with a nice-sounding theory that looks good on paper but allows no room for identification. The person I have in mind is a biblical character that you have probably heard of but may not have studied very closely. Just the mention of his name will tell you why I have chosen him as the example: Samson. He's the one I often think of as a he-man with a she-weakness. Few eagle types ever had the potential to fly higher or fall harder than Samson.

Favorable Circumstances

Contrary to popular opinion, the man had a godly heritage and was born into a tremendously secure, solid home.

> Now the sons of Israel again did evil in the sight of the Lord, so that the Lord gave them into the hands of the Philistines forty years. And

there was a certain man of Zorah, of the family of the Danites, whose name was Manoah; and his wife was barren and had borne no children (Judg. 13:1–2).

Samson's mother is never named in Scripture; she is simply called the wife of Manoah. Manoah and his wife were waiting before the Lord for God to answer and provide for them a child. That's exactly what happened. The long-awaited promise was finally heard.

Then the angel of the Lord appeared to the woman, and said to her, "Behold now, you are barren and have borne no children, but you shall conceive and give birth to a son" (v. 3).

Ancient Hebrew women lived with no greater stigma than barrenness. Manoah's wife was no exception. She must have been elated when God visited her and said words that brought music to her ears. Her son-to-be was in rare company. Most births were not preceded by angelic visits. But like John the Baptizer and Jesus of Nazareth, Samson's birth was divinely announced.

In addition to heralding the birth of Samson, the angel also clearly revealed the purpose for Samson's life. ". . . He shall begin to deliver Israel from the hands of the Philistines" (v. 5).

Not only were these parents thrilled to hear that they would have a baby, but they were also informed of the direction his life would take. Wouldn't that be great to know, moms and dads? We wouldn't have to wrestle with career guessing games. Right off the bat we could help our kids make the right choices in life that would prepare them for that particular God-given calling.

Let's look a little closer at what Manoah and his wife heard. They were told that their son would *"begin to deliver Israel from . . . the Philistines."* He was not to be the only deliverer; he was to *begin* to deliver his people from Philistine oppression. I take it that God had a plan, sort of a one-two punch. Samson was the "one." Someone else, later on, would be the "two." Samson would *begin* to drive the initial wedge, locally, among the Danites and then there would come another who would finish the job, nationally.

Samson was also fortunate to have been born to parents who were deeply spiritual. Look at the words in verse 8, "Then Manoah entreated the Lord. . . ." Manoah was a godly Jew surrounded by godless Jews in the tribe of Dan, most of whom had begun to live like the

Philistines. Not this man! He still sought the Lord, still waited before God in prayer. And this godly father-to-be says:

> . . . "O Lord, please let the man of God whom Thou hast sent come to us again that he may teach us what to do for the boy who is to be born" (v. 8).

In other words, "Lord, we want to hear all we can from Your angel because we want to know exactly how to direct our boy's life." What father hasn't felt that urgency at times? "Lord, reveal to me how to rear my son. Help me know the right steps to take." He realized the spiritual indifference of those around him, so he requested help in knowing God's clear direction. He also knew the impact young Samson's environment could have on him. He wanted to do all he could to train his son correctly.

> And God listened to the voice of Manoah; and the angel of God came again to the woman as she was sitting in the field, but Manoah her husband was not with her. So the woman ran quickly and told her husband, "Behold, the man who came the other day has appeared to me." Then Manoah arose and followed his wife, and when he came to the man he said to him, "Are you the man who spoke to the woman?" And he said, "I am." And Manoah said, "Now when your words come to pass, what shall be the boy's mode of life and his vocation?" (vv. 9–12).

That's just like a father, isn't it? That is the way dads think: *Now, what's going to be his vocation? I know he's going to deliver Israel, but how is he going to make a living? What will be his work? What will be his style of living?* So we find both Manoah and his wife genuinely seeking God's mind for the rearing of their son.

This is an ideal moment for me to put in a plug for godly parents. Were you raised by spiritually minded, eagle-type parents? You may have to say, "Well, *one* of them was." Or, "Well, later on in life they were." Whatever, have you ever stopped to thank them? Ever stopped to spell out specific reasons for your gratitude? Let me encourage you to do that soon. Don't wait. Your interest in soaring like an eagle is probably strong because your parents first set the pace. Though imperfect, they wanted what was best for you. Few blessings are greater than being influenced by good parents.

But there's another factor I must mention: Being godly parents is no absolute guarantee you'll have godly kids. Doing a good job of training children and teens provides no airtight promise that they're going to turn out exactly right. You and your mate might walk very close to God today. You might have begun to walk with Him soon after your child was born. You may have had the highest hopes for your child, but you're not experiencing the delight of your heart. At least, not yet. Nothing thrills us more than to know that our children are walking in the truth and nothing hurts us more than to realize they're not. There is an ache that cannot be described in the heart of a mother or father whose child deliberately departs from good training. I mention that because it is precisely what happened in Samson's life. All these favorable circumstances were not sufficient to guarantee Samson's spirituality. He had all the makings of a powerful eagle, an impressive, high-flying model of excellence, but his refusal to heed his parents' counsel and to stand strong when tempted led to a tragic downfall, as tragic as any on biblical record.

Unfavorable Characteristics

As Samson grew, his story doesn't get better, it gets worse. Little by little the boy's character was being chipped away. The erosion was silent but steady. By the way, I should point out before we get into his life any further that Samson was set apart to be a Nazarite. According to the Law of God, whoever took such a vow maintained a strict adherence to three disciplines. First, he watched his diet very closely. He neither drank alcoholic beverages nor ate certain foods. Second, he never went near the dead. Whether a cadaver or carcass, he never went near a dead animal or a dead human. Third, he never cut his hair. Since God revealed to his parents that Samson was to be a Nazarite from the womb, those three requirements applied to their son. Surely, throughout his early years, they must have drilled these disciplines into his head.

The next time we read of Samson, we find him fully grown. We're never told what happened during his childhood. But we do know that both his parents were with him through those formative years and watched with keen interest as he reached adulthood. As Samson shows up on this next scene, he may be grown physically, but he's not emotionally or spiritually mature. When the man makes his first appearance on the scriptural scene, we immediately detect a character flaw. He possesses a lustful, passionate drive that he does not attempt to restrain—neither now nor later.

> Then Samson went down to Timnah and saw a woman in Timnah, one of the daughters of the Philistines. So he came back and told his father and mother, "I saw a woman . . ." (Judg. 14:1–2).

I think it is highly significant that the first four recorded words from Samson's lips are, "I saw a woman." That is the story of his life. *He focused on the wrong objective.*

> . . . "I saw a woman in Timnah, one of the daughters of the Philistines; now therefore, get her for me as a wife." Then his father and his mother said to him, "Is there no woman among the daughters of your relatives, or among all our people, that you go to take a wife from the uncircumcised Philistines?" But Samson said to his father, "Get her for me, for she looks good to me." . . . So he went down and talked to the woman; and she looked good to Samson (vv. 2–3, 7).

Right off the bat, we see that lust becomes Samson's foremost unfavorable characteristic, something that would haunt him all his days.

Samson's focusing on the wrong objectives proved to be his downfall. First, he focused on physical appearance and little else. Second, he focused on pleasing himself and no one else. Twice we read in this account that the Philistine woman "looked good" to the young Israelite. Let me get painfully specific. As he looked at the daughter of Timnah, Samson liked the way she was built. Today he would come right out and say she had sex appeal. He liked her body. Frankly, it turned him on. There is not a word in this passage regarding her character. Why? Well, first of all, he didn't bother to notice. Second, since she was a Philistine, there was no spiritual character there to appeal to a Jew. But he could not care less. She "looked good" and that was all that mattered to him.

This is a good time to be very candid regarding the issue of physical attraction as seen through the eyes of males. There is an incredible difference between the sexual appetite of a man and the sexual appetite of a woman. Dr. James Dobson, my longtime friend and a much-respected professional psychologist heard by many of you on his radio program, "Focus on the Family," writes helpful words regarding two major differences between what excites men in contrast to what excites women.

First, men are primarily excited by *visual* stimulation. They are turned on by feminine nudity or peek-a-boo glimpses of seminudity. (Phyllis Diller said she had the first peek-a-boo dress: men would "peek" at her, and then they would "boo"!) Women, by contrast, are much less visually oriented than men. Sure, they are interested in attractive masculine bodies, but the physiological mechanism of sex is not triggered typically by what they see; women are stimulated primarily by the sense of touch. Thus, we encounter the first source of disagreement in the bedroom: he wants her to appear unclothed in a lighted room, and she wants him to caress her in the dark.

Second (and much more important), men are not very discriminating in regard to the person living within an exciting body. A man can walk down a street and be stimulated by a scantily clad female who shimmies past him, even though he knows nothing about her personality or values or mental capabilities. He is attracted by her body itself. Likewise, he can become almost as excited over a photograph of an unknown nude model as he can in a face-to-face encounter with someone he loves. In essence, the sheer biological power of sexual desire in a male is largely focused on the physical body of an attractive female. Hence, there is some validity to the complaint by women that they have been used as "sex objects" by men. This explains why female prostitutes outnumber males by a wide margin and why few women try to "rape" men. It explains why a roomful of toothless old men can get a large charge from watching a burlesque dancer "take it all off." It reflects the fact that masculine self-esteem is more motivated by a desire to "conquer" a woman than in becoming the object of her romantic love. These are not very flattering characteristics of male sexuality, but they are well documented in the professional literature. All of these factors stem from a basic difference in sexual appetites of males and females.

Women are much more discriminating in their sexual interests. They less commonly become excited by observing a good-looking charmer, or by the photograph of a hairy model; rather, their desire is usually focused on a *particular* individual whom they respect or admire. A woman is stimulated by the romantic aura which surrounds her man, and by his character and personality. She yields to the man who appeals to her emotionally as well as physically. Obviously, there are exceptions to these characteristic desires, but the fact remains; sex for men is a more physical thing; sex for women is a deeply emotional experience.[1]

Samson's opening line is a classic example of Dr. Dobson's observations. But for Samson, the *only* thing that mattered was satisfying his lust. The man was driven by one of the most natural and powerful drives in the human male. I find it interesting that the young Philistine woman is never called by name. Why? Again, all Samson saw was a body, and he wanted that body for his own sexual gratification. He focused completely on the physical and nothing more.

I can imagine a man's reading this chapter and thinking, *Does this mean that I am lustful even to consider physical beauty? Am I wrong to look at a woman's beauty and be attracted by it?* Of course not! My point here is that Samson's focus was physical attraction *only*. That four-letter word *only* is all-important when it comes to understanding why Samson yielded to the alluring charms of temptation.

Now there is a second characteristic of Samson that was also unfavorable. *He handled his leisure carelessly.* Do you remember what the angel said about the purpose of his life? He was to "begin to deliver Israel." Seems to me he is getting sidetracked. So far he has spent very little time delivering Israel. The man is mainly into pleasing himself.

You need to know that when Samson made one of his trips to visit this girl, he killed a lion. Then on a later trip, he found the remains and observed something strange: the lion's carcass had a beehive built within it. He paused long enough on his way to see his woman to eat a little honey out of the hive. By the way, that little sidetrack broke his Nazarite vow, since he had to touch the dead lion to get the honey. How careless he was! But that was only the beginning.

In customary fashion, when Samson finally arrived with his father to marry the Philistine, a number of her friends were invited to a big feast.

> Then his father went down to the woman; and Samson made a feast there, for the young men customarily did this. And it came about when they saw him that they brought thirty companions to be with him. Then Samson said to them, "Let me now propound a riddle to you; if you will indeed tell it to me within the seven days of the feast, and find it out, then I will give you thirty linen wraps and thirty changes of clothes. But if you are unable to tell me, then you shall give me thirty linen wraps and thirty changes of clothes." And they said to him, "Propound your riddle, that we may hear it." So he said to them, "Out of the eater came something to eat, and out of the strong came something sweet" . . . (Judg. 14:10–14).

Hold it! Here's a guy who should have been soaring, beginning to deliver Israel, as God had commanded. But what is he doing? Posing riddles to these ding-a-lings from Philistia!

They scratched their heads and yanked their beards for three days and couldn't come up with the answer. Well, certainly not. Who could? What in the world did it matter, anyway? What's a God-given eagle doing sitting around with the mediocre rabble making up poetry? What's he doing leisurely hanging around a Philistine camp cultivating friendships? The man was so off target it was almost humorous.

Well, the Philistines couldn't figure out the riddle, and it ticked them off. Embarrassed and perturbed, they moved in on the woman with this threat:

> . . . "Entice your husband, that he may tell us the riddle, lest we burn you and your father's house with fire. Have you invited us to impoverish us? Is this not so?" (v. 15).

Camp on that word *entice* for a moment. The original Hebrew term used in this passage literally means "to be wide open." It can also mean "to seduce, to persuade." They must have realized that Samson was open-minded, even gullible. A lustful eye isn't difficult to detect. Determined not to be narrow like his "rigid" mother and father, Samson shoved the pendulum to the opposite extreme.

So they said, in effect, "Look, toots, seduce this man or we'll burn your place down!" Great group of guys to have at your wedding, huh?

So Samson's wife turned on woman's most powerful weapon, TEARS. Did she ever!

> And Samson's wife wept before him and said, "You only hate me, and you do not love me; you have propounded a riddle to the sons of my people, and have not told it to me." And he said to her, "Behold, I have not told it to my father or mother; so should I tell you?" However she wept before him seven days . . . (vv. 16–17).

Try to imagine that scene. Seven days of "You don't love me . . . you hate me . . . ," plus sobs and tears. Seven days! That's a long, torturous time. No man can withstand seven days, day in, day out, no appetite, no kisses, just crrryyying. She nagged him and nagged him and cried in front of him until finally he would have told her anything to quiet the crying. Finally, she pressed him so hard he told her the riddle.

> And it came about on the seventh day that he told her because she pressed him so hard. She then told the riddle to the sons of her people (v. 17).

I confess I'm getting pretty impatient about now. What in the world is this Israelite eagle doing scratching around in enemy territory with a pen full of Philistine turkeys, making up riddles and spending his time with a gobbler like this? What a waste! Mediocrity on display. No wonder temptation won the first round. The man does not know how to handle his leisure.

Let's hurry on—maybe things will change, right? As much as I hate to disappoint you: The answer is *Wrong!* Let's put two verses together to emphasize a contrast:

> So he judged Israel twenty years in the days of the Philistines.
> Now Samson went to Gaza and saw a harlot there, . . . (15:20–16:1).

After twenty years of judging Israel (whether it was spectacular or spotted, we're not told), the eagle with limitless potential is right back at the same old stuff. In his leisure he's hustling an unnamed prostitute down in Gaza. And if that is not enough, he turns right around and locates yet another woman down in the valley of Sorek.

> After this it came about that he loved a woman in the valley of Sorek, whose name was Delilah (16:4).

Again, I remind you, he isn't interested in delivering Israel—he's on the prowl for another female. To Samson, leisure was synonymous with lust. It was bad enough that he fanned the flame of lust, but in addition to that, he continued to run with a bad bunch. We've learned by now that this combination inevitably spells disaster.

Now we come to Samson's third unfavorable characteristic: *He developed a close alliance with the wrong crowd.* Complete corruption was just around the corner, thanks to the bad company Samson kept. All that time spent with the Philistines was the catalyst—the major force—that caused him to fall prey to Delilah's advances.

After this it came about that he loved a woman in the valley of Sorek, whose name was Delilah. And the lords of the Philistines came up to her, and said to her, "Entice him, and see where his great strength lies and how we may overpower him that we may bind him to afflict him. Then we will each give you eleven hundred pieces of silver" (16:4-5).

Sound a little familiar? "The guy's a pushover. *Seduce* him, Delilah. Find out where his strength lies; he's a mystery to us. He can whip a thousand of us without even breaking into a sweat. Find out how come he is able to fight like that." Apparently, Samson didn't look like Arnold Schwartzenegger but just like any other Jewish male of that day. "Find out how he can be so strong and yet look like everybody else? Get at it, Delilah. Do your thing. *Entice him.*"

Running with the wrong crowd, Samson is heading straight for trouble. The man is dancing to temptation's addicting tune, so he plays right into Delilah's hands. Every time I read this story, I wonder how the man could have been so stupid.

So Delilah said to Samson, "Please tell me where your great strength is and how you may be bound to afflict you" (v. 6).

Honestly, you've got to be pretty thick to miss their plot. In so many words, Delilah says, "Samson, honey, would you tell us why you are strong? You see, we plan to trap you. And if you will simply tell us your secret, we'll just finish you off!" Playboy Samson must have thought, *Well, that'll be a lot of fun. I'll play their game.* So he gives her a few clever possibilities. For starters he says:

. . . "If they bind me with seven fresh cords that have not been dried, then I shall become weak and be like any other man" (v. 7).

So she did that—she whipped up the fresh cords and wrapped them around him and yelled, "The Philistines are upon you, Samson." Pop! He snaps all the cords and moves out. And the Philistines whine, "Aw, we've been deceived" because Samson's strength was not discovered. But don't think they're about to quit. Samson may be playing around, but they're not.

Delilah goes right back.

. . . "Behold, you have deceived me and told me lies; now please, tell me how you may be bound." And he said to her, "If they bind me tightly with new ropes which have not been used, then I shall become weak and be like any other man" (vv. 10-11).

Hey, here's the Israelite eagle who ought to be delivering Israel from the hand of the Philistines, still messing around with the mediocre mob. Ridiculous! Same song, third verse:

> Then Delilah said to Samson, "Up to now you have deceived me and told me lies; tell me how you may be bound." And he said to her, "If you weave the seven locks of my hair with the web [and fasten it with a pin, then I shall become weak and be like any other man." So while he slept, Delilah took the seven locks of his hair and wove them into the web.] And she fastened it with the pin, and said to him, "The Philistines are upon you, Samson!" But he awoke from his sleep and pulled out the pin of the loom and the web (vv. 13-14).

Notice what is happening? In the fun 'n' games of the moment the eagle gets perilously close to danger in his dive near the craggy rocks. He starts to play with his hair, the sacred secret of his life. Now you and I know that Samson's strength wasn't actually in his hair, but his hair was a *sign* of his strength. It was a *reminder* of his vow. Nevertheless, while he was playing around, he blurted out, "Well, why don't you just weave my hair into this web?" And so she did.

Samson is beginning to presume upon sacred things. And that's his fourth major flaw: *He didn't take his vow seriously.* Let's just change the word *vow* to *God*. Samson didn't take his God seriously. I wonder if he remembered something about mom and dad's setting him aside, back when he was just a child, for the Nazarite vow. Maybe he reminisced for a moment, but thought, *Aw, I can handle it; I'm bigger than that now.* So he impulsively says, "Why don't you just mess around with my hair?" And so she did. But once again Samson's strength was not diminished.

> . . . "How can you say, 'I love you,' when your heart is not with me? You have deceived me these three times and have not told me where your great strength is" (v. 15).

Can't you just picture it? "Samsey baby . . . how could you?"

Finally, Samson poured it all out; he told her *everything.* "A razor has never come on my head. . . . If I am shaved, then my strength will leave me and I shall become weak and be like any other man" (v. 17). All of a sudden, he was in so deep he couldn't back out. The old eagle miscalculated his final, fateful dive. This time he struck the ledge! How could he? Why hadn't he realized the peril of his situation? What was it that had drawn him closer, closer, closer to that ledge?

What was the secret of Samson's defeat? Simply this: He didn't choose to say NO to temptation. The following words from Dietrich Bonhoeffer provide the most plausible explanation of temptation I've ever read.

> In our members there is a slumbering inclination towards desire which is both sudden and fierce. With irresistible power desire seizes mastery over the flesh. All at once a secret, smouldering fire is kindled. The flesh burns and is in flames. It makes no difference whether it is sexual desire, or ambition, or vanity, or desire for revenge, or love of fame and power, or greed for money, or, finally, that strange desire for the beauty of the world, of nature. Joy in God is in course of being extinguished in us and we seek all our joy in the creature. At this moment God is quite unreal to us, he loses all reality, and only desire for the creature is real; the only reality is the devil. Satan does not here fill us with hatred of God, but with forgetfulness of God. And now his falsehood is added to this proof of strength. The lust thus aroused envelops the mind and will of man in deepest darkness. The power of clear discrimination and of decision are taken from us. . . .
>
> It is here that everything within me rises up against the Word of God. Powers of the body, the mind and the will, which were held in obedience under the discipline of the Word of which I believed that I was the master, make it clear to me that I am by no means master of them. "All my powers forsake me," laments the psalmist. They have all gone over to the adversary. The adversary deploys my powers against me. In this situation I can no longer act as a hero; I am a defenseless, powerless man. God himself has forsaken me. Who can conquer, who can gain the victory?[2]

Heroes, listen up! Spiritual leaders, pay attention! My fellow eagle, take heed! "[Every man] is tempted when he is carried away and enticed by his own lust" (James 1:14). The Greek word translated "enticed" means "to lure by a bait." The bait is dropped, and the fish, seeing the bait, is lured away from its safe hiding place. Likewise, we move closer to grab the bait of pleasure, and as we do so God becomes quite unreal. In fact, He's momentarily *forgotten*. The bait is real; God is not. And for that brief moment we are thinking of one thing—how pleasurable it will be to grab that morsel.

Let me mention another very practical thing about temptation. I have found that if I can stop the process fairly early, I'm safe. But if I leave my hiding place and venture toward the bait, there is a point of no return. I cannot turn around. If I go that far, I'm sunk.

That's the way it is with us, and that's the way it was with Samson. He pandered with leisure and played with the wrong crowd and messed around with the bait so much he could not turn around. At that point God had become totally unreal to him. With God blocked out, "He told her all that was in his heart." No wonder we read that he didn't even know the Spirit of God had departed from him. I think how great it would have been if Samson had suddenly stopped, dashed out of that place and into the street, and lifted up his arms and screamed, "O God, I am so weak—so near the ledge. Give me the strength I need right now. Help me to soar again!" If only the man had called for help. If only—

The Inevitable Consequences

Within a matter of seconds, "The Philistines seized him." The very first action they took against him was to gouge out both his eyes. Why, of course—his EYES, the gateway to lust! Those Philistines knew him better than he knew himself. They didn't want any further trouble in Philistia from this weak shell of a man who could not resist temptation. So they blinded the eagle; he never flew again, not like before.

J. Oswald Sanders, in his book *Robust in Faith*, titles his chapter on Samson, "The Champion Who Became a Clown."[3] The Philistines dumped Samson in a prison—". . . and bound him with bronze chains, and he was a grinder in the prison" (v. 21).

Many years ago I read something by someone who summed up the wages of temptation in six tragic words: "sin blinds, sin binds, sin grinds." That is so true—so tragically true. The Israelite champion was now reduced to nothing more than a clown in a Philistine house of horrors.

Two inevitable consequences follow in the wake of those who play the fool and yield to temptation's alluring bait. Both expose lies from the world system.

First: *We are weakened, not strengthened.* The world says that a playboy lifestyle will make you strong. Ever heard words like this? "By being exposed to temptations, by getting up close to lust, you learn you can handle those temptations." No, Samson shows us that such a lifestyle really weakens us. If we don't break away, it isn't long before the weakness becomes an addiction, leading to a tragic end.

> Radio personality Paul Harvey tells the story of how an Eskimo kills a wolf. The account is grisly, yet it offers fresh insight into the consuming, self-destructive nature of sin.
>
> "First the Eskimo coats his knife blade with animal blood and allows it to freeze. Then he adds another layer of blood, and another, until the blade is completely concealed by frozen blood.
>
> "Next, the hunter fixes his knife in the ground with the blade up. When a wolf follows his sensitive nose to the source of the scent and discovers the bait he licks it, tasting the fresh-frozen blood. He begins to lick faster, more and more vigorously, lapping the blade until the keen edge is bare. Feverishly now, harder and harder the wolf licks the blade in the Arctic night. So great becomes his craving for blood that the wolf does not notice the razor sharp sting of the naked blade on his tongue nor does he recognize the instant at which his insatiable thirst is being satisfied by his *own* warm blood. His carnivorous appetite just craves more—until the dawn finds him dead in the snow!"[4]

Second: *We become enslaved, not freed.* The system says, "Free love frees you up." Well, that's a lie. It actually puts you into bondage. Samson became a victim of the very ones he was supposed to conquer.

When I was stationed in the Orient with the Marines, I lived in a Quonset hut with forty-seven other guys. The whole unit was shot through with an illicit lifestyle. A large percentage of them had either previously had or at that time had some kind of venereal disease. Those guys could withstand anything but temptation!

One young man—I'll call him Bobby (not his real name)—lived regularly in open sin. He had come from a fairly strict home and had never known what it was like to be free of parental guidance. But once he was on his own, the guy went wild. One weekend he went into the village and shacked up with a prostitute. By the time he returned to the base, late Sunday night, he was terribly afraid he had contracted a disease. He stumbled half drunk down to the bunk where I was. He was talking with another guy and then turned and grabbed hold of me and said, "Hey, Swindoll, I want you to talk to me. I'm scared to death."

We took a walk that night down by the mess hall and then over toward the only place that was lit through the night—the chapel. The farther we walked and the longer we talked, the more he sobered up. That very night Bobby got down on his knees and openly confessed his bondage to lust. I will never forget his simple words: "I ask Jesus Christ to come into my life. How I need Him!" And I also remember his saying, "Lord, I have a habit that You've got to help me break." I'll never forget his praying that. For the next seven months we worked closely together. The battle was a long, tough one. But finally, he began to soar above and beyond his bondage. Another eagle was in the sky by means of a power other than his own—the power of Christ.

AN EAGLELIKE STRATEGY FOR FLIGHT

This chapter is plenty long already. No need to lengthen it with numerous words. So let me close with a straightforward, succinct strategy for a soaring flight.

First: *Our natural focus must be counteracted.* The natural focus for some is homosexuality, a subtle, gnawing temptation. The natural focus for others is a continuation of illicit affairs outside the marriage bond. The habit for others is some kind of hidden, more shameful sensuality.

That natural focus must be counteracted. Openly confess your weakness. Hide nothing. One of the best ways to get back in the air and soar as you once did is through consistent, systematic Scripture memory. I detailed this at length in the first chapter of this book. Scripture memory replaces sensual thoughts with spiritual thoughts.

Another essential technique is to learn how to handle the eye gate. "I made a covenant with my eyes," said Job. "I will not stare at a girl." And guys, you and I have to make that kind of covenant or we will stare. No problem with the first glance. Our problems occur with the second look, which leads to the long stare. A casual glance is no big deal. But what we need is a covenant, a vow before God, and a regular accountability before others. Develop a disciplined technique to counteract your natural focus.

Second: *Our leisure time must be guarded.* Students, you can't tolerate an aw-so-what? flippant attitude when you face the summer. Business men and women who travel, your leisure can lead to your downfall. Cultivate a plan, perhaps an exercise program, an intensive reading program, a hobby, a series of practical projects which occupy your time. Watch out for those video movies piped into your room! If necessary, keep the television off. And stay away from the magazine rack. Lust can no more be trusted than a snake. Don't mess with it!

LeRoy Eims offers superb counsel in his book *Be the Leader You Were Meant to Be:*

> Rattlesnakes are fairly common where I live. I encounter one almost every summer. It is a frightening experience to see a rattlesnake coiled, looking at you, ready to strike. He's lightning quick and accurate. I have a two-point program for rattlesnakes: shun and avoid. You don't need much insight to figure out what to do with something as dangerous as an old diamondback rattler. You don't mess around.[5]

Third: *Our close companions must be screened.* Take a good look at your circle of friends. Do an honest evaluation of those with whom you spend personal time. I can offer you a principle you can bank on: Until you clean up your companionships, you'll never clean up your life. You may want to. You may have sincere desires and the highest of ambitions, but if you plan to soar, pick your partners with great care. Remember, eagles fly with only a few other eagles—never in flocks.

Fourth: *Our vow to God must be upheld.* Just as jealously as we would guard the marriage vows, we're to guard our promises to God and our commitment to purity. May I remind you of your primary vow?

> I urge you therefore, brethren, by the mercies of God, to present your bodies a living and holy sacrifice, acceptable to God, which is your spiritual service of worship. And do not be conformed to this world, but be transformed by the renewing of your mind, that you may prove what the will of God is, that which is good and acceptable and perfect (Rom. 12:1–2).

When we personalize those words, we understand them to contain the warning, "Don't let the world around you squeeze you into its mold." Need a place to start? Start with these words. Read them before the Lord and say something like this: "Father, this is where I want to start. Before facing any kind of temptation today, I want to declare my allegiance to You. Give me strength to stand all alone, to stand strong in Your power. Renew my mind. This is my vow, and I take it seriously before You."

Isn't it time you got serious about soaring? You know it is! I don't care if you've begun a hundred other times, don't let anyone try to tell you that it is useless to begin again. It is never too late to start doing what is right.

Excellence—moral, ethical, personal excellence—is worth whatever it costs. Pay the price. Start today! You are made for one great purpose—soaring! Nothing less will ever satisfy you or glorify God.

CONCLUSION
WHO'S APPRAISING
YOUR EXCELLENCE?

Badness you can get easily, in quantity: the road is smooth, and it lies close by. But in front of excellence the immortal gods have put sweat, and long and steep is the way to it, and rough at first. But when you come to the top, then it is easy, even though it is hard.

—Hesiod, 700 B.C.

When I embarked on this literary journey many moons ago, I entertained one major concern: "Can I communicate the importance of excellence without leaving the impression that it is a synonym of success?" I mean success as the world uses the word. In my opinion we have more than enough books on that subject already. Motivational material, sales techniques, and self-help success-oriented volumes are all about us. Some are helpful, others little more than hype. But all too little is written about a commitment to excellence—true excellence, the kind of excellence that conveys superior quality, attention to significant detail, care about that which really matters.

Excellence is a difficult concept to communicate because it can easily be misread as neurotic perfectionism or snooty sophistication. But it is neither. On the contrary, it is the stuff of which greatness is made. It is the difference between just getting by and soaring—that which sets apart the significant from the superficial, the lasting from the temporary. Those who pursue it do so because of what pulsates within them, not because of what others think or say or do. Authentic excellence is not a performance. It is there whether anyone ever notices or tries to find out.

When the Statue of Liberty received her much-needed facelift back in 1985–86, she was examined with a fine-tooth comb. The craftsmen and artists who did the repairs had ample opportunity to study the original workmanship. They were impressed—perhaps a better word is *amazed*—with the design of her sculptor, the noted Frenchman, Frederic Bartholdi, and his crew who applied their artistic skills over one hundred years ago. Nothing had been overlooked. One example is the beautiful work that was done high atop Liberty's spiked crown and head. The superb attention to detail was carried out so thoroughly, one would have thought that this section would have been viewed by everyone. But the fact is, no one would see her from above. Once she was raised to her full height, 151 feet, only a few seagulls would ever notice her coiffure. Little did those French artisans even imagine a day when helicopters would hover, giving time for the human eye to observe and enjoy such exquisite beauty. But you see, excellence characterized the design of Liberty's head whether or not anyone would ever stop to notice or admire.

Mediocrity is fast becoming the by-word of our times. Every imaginable excuse is now used to make it acceptable, hopefully preferred. Budget cuts, time deadlines, majority opinion, and hard-nosed practicality are outshouting and outrunning excellence. Those forces seem to be winning the race. Incompetence and status quo averages are held up as all we can now expect, and the tragedy is that more and more people have virtually agreed. Why worry over the small stuff? Why concern yourself with soaring when so few even glide anymore? Why bother with the genuine now that the artificial looks so real? If the public buys it, why sweat it?

To make it painfully plain, why think clearly since most folks want someone else to think for them? Why live differently in a society where it's so much easier to look the same and swim downstream? Why fight fiercely when so few seem to care? Why stand courageously if it means risking ridicule, misunderstanding, or being considered a dreamer by some and a fool by others?

Why, indeed? To quote young David just before he took on that Philistine behemoth in the Valley of Elah, "Is there not a cause?" Must we wait for someone else to establish our standard or to set our pace? Not on your life! There is too much eagle in some of us to be comfortable taking our cues from the majority. It is my firm conviction that those who impact and reshape the world are the ones committed to living above the level of mediocrity. There are still too many opportunities for excellence, too much demand for distinctiveness, to be satisfied with just getting by. As Isaac D'Israeli once wrote,

". . . it is a wretched taste to be gratified with mediocrity when the excellent lies before us."[1]

Although I never knew him, the late Albert Schweitzer seemed to be a model of remarkable excellence. Norman Cousins, having spent considerable time with Dr. Schweitzer at his little hospital at Lambaréné in French Equatorial Africa, wrote of those days long after they had passed. His recollections are well worth repeating.

> The biggest impression I had in leaving Lambaréné was of the enormous reach of a single human being. Yet such a life was not without the punishment of fatigue. Albert Schweitzer was supposed to be severe in his demands on the people who worked with him. Yet any demands he made on others were as nothing compared to the demands he made on himself. He was not concerned about the attainability of perfection; he was concerned, however, about the pursuit of perfection. He considered the desire to seek the best and work for the best as a vital part of the nature of man. When he sat down to play the piano or organ, and he was alone, he might stay with it for hours at a time. He might practice a single phrase for two hours or more. The difference between the phrase when he first played it and when he himself was satisfied with it might have been imperceptible even to a trained musical ear. But he had a stern idea of his own capacity for interpreting Bach, for example, and he felt he must stretch himself to whatever extent was necessary to achieve it. This was no mere obsession. He sought his own outermost limits as a natural part of purposeful living. . . .
>
> History is willing to overlook almost anything—errors, paradoxes, personal weaknesses or faults—if only a man will give enough of himself to others. . . .
>
> . . . If sacrifice is required, we shall have to sacrifice. If we are to lead, what we say and what we do must become more important in our own minds than what we sell or what we use. . . .[2]

As I have emphasized throughout this book, a commitment to excellence is neither popular nor easy. But it is essential. Excellence in integrity and morality as well as ethics and scholarship. Excellence in physical fitness and spiritual fervor just as much as excellence in relationships and craftsmanship. A commitment to excellence touches the externals of appearance, communication, and products just as much as the internals of attitude, vision, taste, humor, compassion, determination, and zest for life. It means not being different for difference' sake but for God's sake. After all, He is the One in whose Book we read, "if there be any excellence . . . set your mind on these things" (Phil. 4:8).

That's it in a nutshell: A setting of our minds on these things—even if no one else on earth cares or dares.

It matters not, I repeat, what others may think or say or do. We must seek our own "outermost limits"—not merely drift along with the tide or half-heartedly catch a wave and wash ashore. No, *we must soar*. Since it is the living Lord in the final analysis who appraises our excellence, it is He whom we must please and serve, honor and adore. For His eyes only we commit ourselves to living above the level of mediocrity. He deserves our very best; nothing more, nothing less, nothing else.

That alone is excellence.

NOTES

Chapter 1. It Starts in Your Mind

1. Earl D. Radmacher, *You & Your Thoughts* (Carol Stream, IL: Tyndale House Publishers Inc., 1977), 51–52.

2. Roger von Oech, *A Whack on the Side of the Head* (New York: Warner Books, Inc., 1983), 9.

Chapter 2. It Involves Another Kingdom

1. From *Who Switched the Price Tags?* (pp. 25–26) by Anthony Campolo, copyright © 1986; used by permission of Word Books, Publisher, Waco, TX.

2. Richard J. Foster, *Money, Sex & Power* (San Francisco: Harper & Row, Publishers, 1985 [© 1985 by Richard J. Foster]), 13.

3. Ibid., 176.

4. From *Christ and the Media* (p. 30) by Malcolm Muggeridge. Copyright © 1977 by Wm. B. Eerdmans Publishing Co., Grand Rapids, MI.

5. *Money, Sex & Power*, 218–219.

6. From *Tell Me Again Lord, I Forget* (p. 23) by Ruth Harms Calkin, published by Tyndale House Publishers, Inc. © 1974. Used by permission.

7. John R. W. Stott, *Christian Counter-Culture* (Downers Grove, IL: InterVarsity Press, 1978), 53.

8. Used by permission of the author.

Chapter 3. It Costs Your Commitment

1. Thomas Paine, *The American Crisis*, no. I [December 23, 1776].

2. Douglas Southall Freeman, *Lee, Abridgment in One Volume* by Richard Harwell of the four-volume *R. E. Lee* by Douglas Southall Freeman (New York: Charles Scribner's Sons, 1961), 587–588.

3. Hal Lindsey, *Combat Faith* (New York: Bantam Books, 1986), 1–2.

Chapter 4. It Calls for Extravagant Love

1. G. Campbell Morgan, *The Gospel According to Mark* (Westwood, NJ: Fleming H. Revell Company, 1957), 284.
2. From *Rabboni* (pp. 222–223) by W. Phillip Keller. Copyright © 1977 by W. Phillip Keller. Published by Fleming H. Revell Company. Used by permission.
3. From *Life Without Limits* (pp. 248–249) by Lloyd J. Ogilvie, copyright © 1975; used by permission of Word Books, Publisher, Waco, TX.
4. From *Up with Worship* (pp. 22–24) by Anne Ortlund. Copyright © 1975, Regal Books, Ventura, CA 93006. Used by permission.

Chapter 5. Vision: Seeing beyond the Majority

1. Eugene H. Petersen, *A Long Obedience in the Same Direction* (Downers Grove, IL: InterVarsity Press, 1980), 11.
2. Isaac Watts, "Am I a Soldier of the Cross?" (1709).
3. Aleksandr I. Solzhenitsyn, "A World Split Apart," commencement address delivered at Harvard University, June 8, 1978. Copyright © 1978 by Aleksandr I. Solzhenitsyn. English language translation copyright © 1979 Harper & Row, Publishers, Inc. Published in *East and West* (New York: Harper & Row, Publishers, 1980), 45.
4. Reprinted by permission from *Bringing Out the Best in People* (p. 35) by Alan Loy McGinnis, copyright © 1985 Augsburg Publishing House.
5. Ibid., 38.
6. From *Life Is Tremendous* (pp. 62–64) by Charles E. Jones. Published by Tyndale House Publishers, Inc. 1968. Used by permission.

Chapter 6. Determination: Deciding to Hang Tough

1. Author unknown.
2. Don B. Owens, Jr., *Quote Unquote*, ed. Lloyd Cory (Wheaton, IL: Victor Books, a division of SP Publications, 1977), 236.
3. From *Think and Grow Rich* (p. 164) by Napoleon Hill. Published by E. P. Dutton, Inc., 1958. Used by permission.
4. "It's What You Do, Not When You Do It" (Hartford, CT: United Technologies, 1979). Used by permission.
5. Taken from *The Making of a Christian Leader* (p. 120) by Ted W. Engstrom. Copyright © 1976 by The Zondervan Corporation. Used by permission. Ted Engstrom retells this story from *What a Day This Can Be*, ed. John Catoir (New York: The Christophers).

Chapter 7. Priorities: Determining What Comes First

1. From "I Wish I'd Been There," *A Sense of History* (New York: American Heritage Press, 1985), 1–37.

2. From *When I Relax I Feel Guilty* (p. 89) by Tim Hansel, © 1979. Used with permission by David C. Cook Publishing Co.

3. Robert Goldman, "Getting Stuck on the Way Up the Corporate Ladder," *Wall Street Journal,* January 6, 1986. Used by permission.

4. Jon Johnston, "Growing Me-ism and Materialism," *Christianity Today* (p. 16-I), January 17, 1986. Copyright © 1986 by Christianity Today, Inc., Carol Stream, IL. Used by permission.

5. William Barclay, *The Gospel of Luke, The Daily Study Bible* (p. 203). Reproduced by kind permission of The Saint Andrew Press, Edinburgh, Scotland.

Chapter 8. Accountability: Answering the Hard Questions

1. From *There's a Lot More to Health Than Not Being Sick* (p. 74) by Bruce Larson, copyright © 1981, 1984; used by permission of Word Books, Publisher, Waco, TX.

2. Ibid., 61.

3. Ibid., 67–68.

Chapter 9. Winning the Battle over Greed

1. William Barclay, *The Gospel of Luke, The Daily Study Bible* (p. 168). Reproduced by kind permission of The Saint Andrew Press, Edinburgh, Scotland.

2. Martha Snell Nicholson, "Treasures," *Ivory Palaces* (Chicago: Moody Press, 1949).

Chapter 10. Slaying the Dragon of Traditionalism

1. e. e. cummings, in a letter written in 1955, as cited in *You Bring the Confetti* by Luci Swindoll (Waco, TX: Word Books, 1986), 35–36.

2. Robert M. Brown, *Quote Unquote,* ed. Lloyd Cory (Wheaton, IL: Victor Books, a division of SP Publications, 1977), 341.

3. Jaroslav Pelikan, *The Vindication of Tradition* (New Haven, CT: Yale University Press, 1984), 65.

4. From *The Problem of Wine Skins* (pp. 189–190) by Howard A. Snyder. Copyright 1975. Used by permission of InterVarsity Press, Downers Grove, IL.

Chapter 11. Removing the Blahs from Today

1. C. S. Lewis, *The Screwtape Letters* (London: Geoffrey Bles, 1942), 65, 143.

2. From *No One's Perfect* (pp. 21–22) by Betty Carlson, copyright © 1976. Used by permission of Good News Publishers/Crossway Books, Westchester, IL 60153.

3. Unpublished sermon by Dr. Ray Stedman, pastor of Peninsula Bible Church, Palo Alto, CA. Used by permission.

4. From *Tell Me Again, Lord, I Forget* (p. 83) by Ruth Harms Calkin. Published by Tyndale House Publishers. Inc. © 1974. Used by permission.

Chapter 12. Becoming a Model of Joyful Generosity

1. Sir Winston Churchill, as cited in *Familiar Quotations* (New York: Little, Brown and Company, 1955), 746, 743, 745.

2. Ron Blue, *Master Your Money* (Nashville, TN: Thomas Nelson Publishers, 1986).

Chapter 13. Standing Alone When Outnumbered

1. Taken from *Rebirth of America* (p. 77). Copyright © 1986 by The Arthur S. DeMoss Foundation, Saint David's Center, Saint David, PA 19087. Edited by Robert Flood. All rights reserved. Used by permission.

2. Donald Grey Barnhouse, *Romans, Vol IX, God's Discipline* (Grand Rapids, MI: Wm. B. Eerdmans Publishing Co., 1964), 8.

3. From *The Log*, published by The Navigators, Colorado Springs, CO (date unknown).

Chapter 14. Standing Tall When Tested

1. From *Hide or Seek* (pp. 126–127, revised edition) by James Dobson, copyright © 1974, 1979 by Fleming H. Revell Company, Old Tappan, NJ. Used by permission.

2. Merrill F. Unger, *Unger's Bible Dictionary* (Chicago: Moody Press, 1966), 172.

3. Billy Graham, *Faithful Witness, Urbana '84* (Downers Grove, IL: InterVarsity Press, 1985), 139.

Chapter 15. Standing Firm When Discouraged

1. From *Psalms of My Life* (p. 29) by Josephy Bayly. Published by Tyndale House Publishers, Inc. © 1969. Used by permission.

2. F. B. Meyer, *Christ in Isaiah* (Grand Rapids, MI: Zondervan Publishing House, 1950), 9–10.

Chapter 16. Standing Strong When Tempted

1. From *What Wives Wish Their Husbands Knew about Women* (pp. 114–116) by James Dobson. Published by Tyndale House Publishers, Inc., Copyright © 1975. Used by permission.

2. Dietrich Bonhoeffer, *Temptation* (London: SCM Press, 1955), 33–34.

3. J. Oswald Sanders, *Robust in Faith* (Chicago: Moody Press, 1965), 102.

4. Chris T. Zwingelberg, "Sin's Peril," *Leadership* 8 (Winter 1987): 41. Used by permission.

5. LeRoy Eims, *Be the Leader You Were Meant to Be* (Wheaton, IL: Victor Books, a division of SP Publications, 1975), 105.

Conclusion. Who's Appraising Your Excellence?

1. Isaac D'Israeli, *Curiosities of Literature* [1834] "On Quotation," as cited in *Familiar Quotations*, ed. John Bartlett (Boston: Little, Brown and Company, 1980), 417.

2. Norman Cousins, *Albert Schweitzer's Mission* (New York: W. W. Norton & Company, 1985), 135, 138, 140. Used by permission.